Understanding and Troubleshooting Your PC

Gary B. Shelly
Thomas J. Cashman
Jean Andrews
Lisa Strite Jedlicka

COURSE TECHNOLOGY
25 THOMSON PLACE
BOSTON MA 02210

Australia • Canada • Denmark • Japan • Mexico • New Zealand • Philippines • Puerto Rico • Singapore
South Africa • Spain • United Kingdom • United States

Understanding and Troubleshooting Your PC

Gary B. Shelly
Thomas J. Cashman
Jean Andrews
Lisa Strite Jedlicka

Executive Director:
Cheryl Costantini

Senior Acquisitions Editor:
Dana Merk

Senior Editor:
Alexandra Arnold

Product Manager:
Reed Cotter

Editorial Assistant:
Selena Coppock

Marketing Manager:
Brian Berkeley

Print Buyer:
Laura Burns

Associate Production Manager:
Christine Freitas

Designer:
Betty Hopkins

Development Editor:
Deb Kaufmann

Copy Editor:
Gary Michael

Proofreader:
Nancy Lamm

Cover Art:
Nancy Goulet

Compositor:
GEX Publishing Services

Printer:
Banta Menasha

COPYRIGHT © 2004 Course Technology, a division of Thomson Learning, Inc. Thomson Learning™ is a trademark used herein under license.

Printed in the United States of America

1 2 3 4 5 6 7 8 9 10
BM 08 07 06 05 04

For more information, contact Course Technology
25 Thomson Place
Boston, Massachusetts 02210

Or find us on the World Wide Web at:
www.course.com

ALL RIGHTS RESERVED. No part of this work covered by the copyright hereon may be reproduced or used in any form or by any means — graphic, electronic, or mechanical, including photocopying, recording, taping, Web distribution, or information storage and retrieval systems — without the written permission of the publisher.

For permission to use material from this text or product, submit a request online at **www.thomsonrights.com**

Any additional questions about permissions can be submitted by e-mail to **thomsonrights@thomson.com**

Course Technology, the Course Technology logo, the Shelly Cashman Series® and **Custom Edition**® are registered trademarks used under license. All other names used herein are for identification purposes only and are trademarks of their respective owners.

Course Technology reserves the right to revise this publication and make changes from time to time in its content without notice.

ISBN 0-619-20223-8

CONTENTS

Understanding and Troubleshooting Your PC

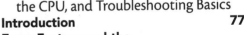

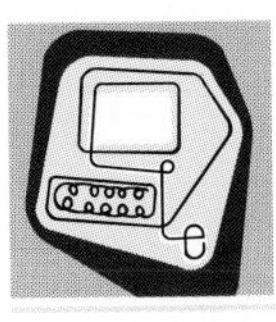

CHAPTER 1

CHAPTER 1
Introducing Hardware

CHAPTER 2

CHAPTER 2
How Hardware and Software Work Together

CHAPTER 3

CHAPTER 3
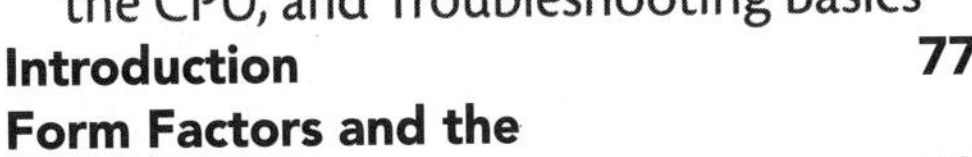

Understanding the Motherboard, the CPU, and Troubleshooting Basics

CHAPTER 3

CHAPTER 4

Managing Memory

CHAPTER 4

CHAPTER 5

Understanding, Installing, and Troubleshooting Disk Drives

CHAPTER 5

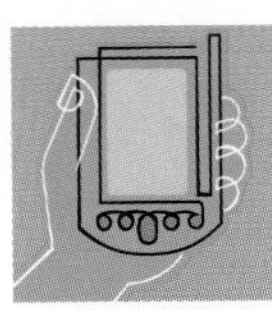

CHAPTER 6

CHAPTER 6

Supporting Input, Output, and Multimedia Devices

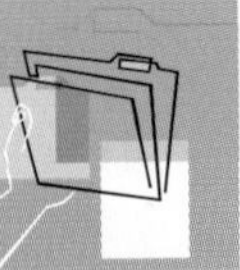

CHAPTER 7

CHAPTER 7

Supporting Printers

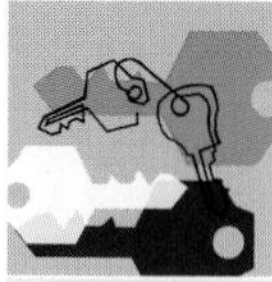

CHAPTER 8

CHAPTER 8
Installing and Using Windows XP Professional

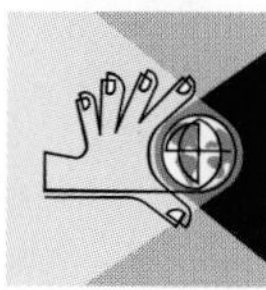

CHAPTER 9

CHAPTER 9
Managing and Supporting Windows XP

CHAPTER 10

CHAPTER 10

Connecting PCs to Networks and the Internet

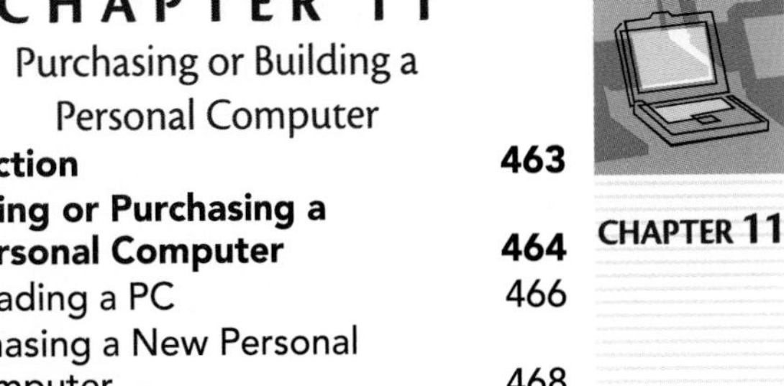

CHAPTER 11

CHAPTER 11

Purchasing or Building a Personal Computer

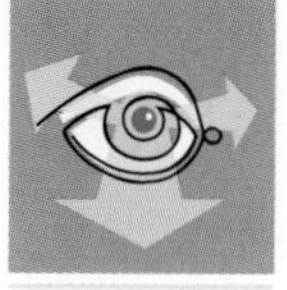
CHAPTER 12

CHAPTER 12
Maintenance and Troubleshooting Fundamentals

APPENDIX A

APPENDIX A
Error Messages and Their Meanings

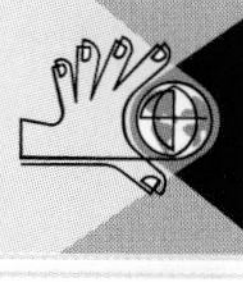
APPENDIX B

APPENDIX B
Using the Command Prompt

APPENDIX C

APPENDIX C
Number Systems and Coding Schemes

APPENDIX D

APPENDIX D

Working as a PC Technician

APPENDIX E

APPENDIX E

Introducing Linux

PREFACE

The Shelly Cashman Series® offers the finest textbooks in computer education. We are proud of the fact that our textbooks have been the most widely used books in education. We are pleased to announce the addition of *Understanding and Troubleshooting Your PC* to the series. This text continues with the innovation, quality, and reliability that you have come to expect from the Shelly Cashman Series.

In *Understanding and Troubleshooting Your PC* you will find an educationally sound, highly visual, and easy-to-follow pedagogy that engages students interest with clear, easy-to-read content and a wide range of additional features. The FAQ features provide additional information to help answer common questions, while the More About features provide detailed in-depth information on key topics to expand the student's understanding. The Your Turn features provide hands-on exercises that allow students to put concepts and skills learned in the chapter to practical, real-world use. The Quiz Yourself and Learn It Online features present a wealth of additional exercises to ensure your students have all the reinforcement they need. The chapter material is developed to ensure that students will see the importance of learning to understand, maintain, and troubleshoot personal computers.

Overview

Understanding and Troubleshooting Your PC is an introduction to personal computer hardware and software designed to help learners become comfortable and skilled with installing new hardware and software, troubleshooting hardware and software problems, and making decisions about upgrading or purchasing new hardware and operating systems. The text emphasizes the importance of understanding how to troubleshoot and maintain a personal computer as an end-user, as well as in the role of a PC technician.

Using this book, students learn about each of the major hardware and software components in a personal computer, along with step-by-step instructions on installation, maintenance, optimizing system performance, and troubleshooting. The book focuses on newer hardware and the Windows XP Professional operating system, but also recognizes the real world of PC repair, where some older technology remains in widespread use and still needs support. The Your Turn feature and assignments teach students to apply skills in a structured environment, so they gain confidence using those skills in maintenance and troubleshooting situations. Extensive end-of-chapter exercises emphasize the development of critical-thinking skills.

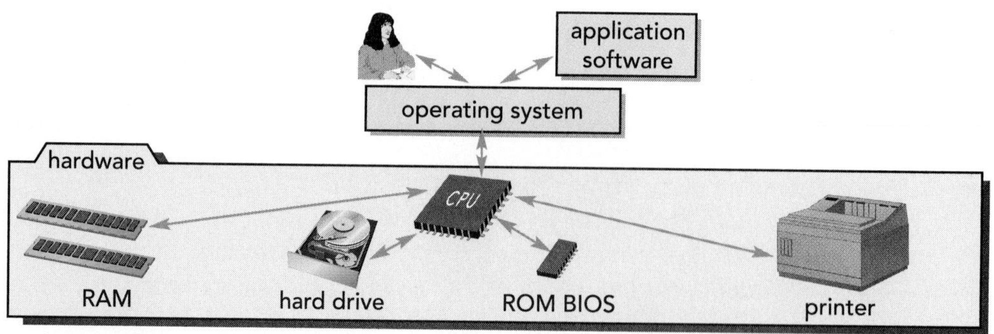

- A working PC with Windows XP Professional installed, along with the Windows XP setup CDs (can be the same or a different PC than the one above).

Your instructor likely will make this equipment available to you in a classroom or lab environment.

Safety Precautions to Protect Yourself and Your Computer When you work on a computer, it is possible to damage the computer and cause yourself harm. To protect yourself and the computer, you should take the following safety precautions as you work on a computer:

Turn off power to the computer. To protect both yourself and the equipment when working inside a computer, turn off the power, unplug the computer, and always use a ground bracelet as described below and in Chapter 1. You should never open the case on a power supply or monitor unless you are working with an expert or are qualified to do so and know exactly what you are doing. Both the power supply and the monitor can hold a dangerous level of electricity even after they are turned off and disconnected from a power source.

Protect Against ESD. Electrostatic discharge (ESD), commonly known as static electricity, is an electrical charge that can build up on the surface of insulating materials, such as clothing or plastic. ESD can cause total failure of an electronic component, or it can damage the component so it does not perform well, or works only intermittently. To protect against ESD, always ground yourself before touching electronic components, including the hard drive, motherboard, expansion cards, processors, and memory modules. Ground yourself and the computer parts, using one or more of the following static control devices or methods:

- *Ground bracelet or static strap.* A ground bracelet is an antistatic strap you wear around your wrist. The wrist strap grounds you by attaching to a grounded conductor such as the computer case or a ground mat. The bracelet also contains a resistor that prevents electricity from harming you. It should be considered essential equipment when working on a computer.
- *Ground mat.* A ground mat provides a grounded surface on which to place components with which you are working. A ground bracelet also can be connected to a ground mat, some of which come equipped with a cord to plug into a wall outlet. As you work, remember that if you lift the component off the mat, it is no longer grounded and is susceptible to ESD.
- *Static shielding bag.* A new computer component often is shipped in a static shielding bag. When working on a PC, you can lay components on these static shielding bags. The bags also can be used to store other devices that are not currently installed in a PC.

The best solution to protect against ESD is to use a ground bracelet together with a ground mat. Consider a ground bracelet to be essential equipment when working on a computer.

Follow Additional Safety Precautions. Other safety precautions that can help prevent accidents while you are working on a computer include the following:

- Make notes as you work so you can go back step-by-step to check your work later if necessary.
- When unpacking hardware or software, remove the packing tape and cellophane from the work area as soon as possible.
- Keep components away from your hair and clothing.
- Keep screws and spacers orderly and in one place, such as a cup or tray.

Objectives of This Textbook

Understanding and Troubleshooting Your PC is designed to:

- Provide a clear introduction to the hardware and software "under the hood" in a personal computer so students are comfortable addressing issues
- Explain in simple, easy-to-follow language, PC maintenance techniques to help prevent problems and optimize performance
- Provide step-by-step troubleshooting procedures to help resolve problems that occur
- Discuss how to address operating system and boot problems using tools available in the Windows XP operating system
- Present practical guidelines for upgrading or purchasing a new PC, as well as detailed, step-by-step procedures for building a PC on your own
- Stress the importance of safe computing practices and preventive maintenance, including planning for and scheduling backups
- Introduce newer technologies, such as wireless networking, multimedia, and LCD monitors
- Provide hands-on skills practice in the Your Turn and Apply Your Knowledge questions
- Allow for in-depth learning on advanced topics or older technologies by providing additional online content in the More About features

Organization of This Textbook

Understanding and Troubleshooting Your PC contains 12 chapters and 5 appendices:

Chapter 1 — Introducing Hardware provides an overview of the major personal computer hardware components used for input, output, processing, and storage, as well as components that allow communications within the computer and provide an electrical supply. This chapter also provides a look at how to protect your computer system from electrostatic discharge, EMI, and other power problems, as well as how to protect you as your work on your computer.

Chapter 2 — How Hardware and Software Work Together offers an overview of operating systems and their key functions, such as controlling hardware devices inside the computer and providing an interface for users and applications to command and use hardware. The chapter also explains how system resources help hardware and software communicate. Finally, the chapter reviews the steps in the boot process and tools you can use to examine the system, such as Device Manager and System Information.

Chapter 3 — Understanding the Motherboard, the CPU, and Troubleshooting Basics introduces form factors and computer cases, followed by a detailed review of the components on the motherboard. The chapter then explains the basic procedures for building a computer and describes how to install a motherboard. Finally, the chapter provides tips on troubleshooting a motherboard and the electrical system.

Chapter 4 — Managing Memory provides a detailed look at memory, including the different kinds of physical memory (RAM) used on the motherboard and how Windows manages memory. The chapter also explains how to upgrade memory modules and troubleshoot memory to help improve a system's performance.

Chapter 5 — Understanding, Installing, and Troubleshooting Disk Drives focuses on hard drive technology, explaining how hard drives work and organize data and how to install and troubleshoot a hard drive. This chapter also examines floppy disk drives, optical storage technologies such as CD-ROMs and DVD-ROMs, and external and removable storage. Finally, the chapter provides an introduction to managing and troubleshooting disk drives to help optimize performance.

Chapter 6 — Supporting Input, Output, and Multimedia Devices explains how to install and support input and output devices, including how to connect peripherals using ports, wireless connections, and expansion slots. The chapter covers input and output devices such as keyboards, pointing devices, and monitors, as well as multimedia devices such as digital cameras and MP3 players.

Chapter 7 — Supporting Printers focuses on various types of printers, including laser, ink-jet, and dot-matrix printers; how they work; and how to support them. After reviewing how to install a local printer or share a printer with others on a network, the chapter discusses how Windows handles print jobs. Finally, the chapter addresses how to maintain a printer and troubleshoot printer problems.

Chapter 8 — Installing and Using Windows XP Professional focuses on Windows XP Professional, including how it uses memory and how it manages hard drives using partitions and NTFS. The chapter also covers how to install and use Windows XP and how to install hardware and applications using Windows.

Chapter 9 — Managing and Supporting Windows XP provides information on supporting Windows XP Professional. The chapter introduces consoles and snap-ins used to manage Windows XP, along with security features that protect the Windows XP system, its users, and their data. You also will learn about the Windows XP registry, how to troubleshoot the Windows XP boot process, and the many Windows XP troubleshooting and maintenance tools.

Chapter 10 — Connecting PCs to Networks and the Internet discusses how PCs are connected in networks. In addition to introducing various types of networks and network topologies, the chapter reviews how networking works with Windows and how to install a network card, connect to a network, and share network resources. Finally, the chapter explains how the TCP/IP suite of networking protocols is used, how to create and troubleshoot dial-up and broadband connections to the Internet, and how to access Internet resources using a Web browser.

Chapter 11 — Purchasing a PC or Building Your Own presents guidelines for upgrading or purchasing a new PC, as well as detailed, step-by-step procedures for building a PC on your own. After discussing when it is appropriate to upgrade a PC, the chapter reviews considerations for buying a new PC, such as purchasing a brand name PC or a clone, selecting hardware, software, or a total package. Finally, the chapter provides a detailed look at the steps involved in building your own PC from components.

Chapter 12 — Troubleshooting and Maintenance Fundamentals introduces how to create a preventive maintenance plan, including planning for and scheduling backups. It also discusses safe computing practices used to protect your computer from computer viruses, Trojan horses, and worms. Finally, the chapter covers important troubleshooting tools and a methodical approach to troubleshooting that will help you isolate and resolve an issue.

Appendix A — Error Messages and Their Meanings describes common error messages and their meanings, including a detailed explanation of BIOS beep codes, numeric codes, and error messages that can be used to troubleshoot the boot process.

Appendix B — Using the Command Prompt explains how to use the Command Prompt window available in Windows XP and provides a list of the more widely used commands, along with some of their more common options.

Appendix C — Coding Schemes and Number Systems explains several types of coding schemes, including ASCII, EBCDIC, and Unicode and discusses parity. Appendix C also describes number systems used with computers, including decimal, hexadecimal, and binary.

Appendix D — The Professional PC Technician provides a practical guide to help further your career as a PC technician, addressing how to satisfy customers, keep records of support calls, provide good service in a range of situations, and ensure software copyrights are followed. It also discusses ways to pursue career opportunities by joining professional organizations and obtaining professional certification.

Appendix E — Introducing Linux provides an overview of the Linux operating system, covering strengths and limitations of Linux, the use of window managers, and the basics of Linux accounts and directory structures. Appendix E also covers basic Linux commands, together with simple examples of how some are used.

FOR THE STUDENT

The Shelly Cashman Series wants you to have a valuable learning experience that will provide you with the knowledge and skills you need to be successful. With that goal in mind, we have included many activities, games, and learning tools. We hope that you find them to be interesting, challenging, and enjoyable.

Equipment Required for Hands-On Practice Many of the exercises in this book provide an opportunity for hands-on practice. To complete the hands-on exercises, you will need the following equipment:

- A PC toolkit that includes at least a ground mat, a ground bracelet or static strap, a flat-head screwdriver, and a Philips-head screwdriver. Other tools to consider adding to your toolkit include a Torx® screwdriver, particularly size T15, insulated tweezers, a chip extractor, and a three-pronged parts retriever. Before purchasing each item separately, look for existing toolkits that include most of these tools. Your instructor may have suggestions on where to purchase a toolkit.
- A working PC that can be taken apart and reassembled. If possible, use a computer with a Pentium (or equivalent) chip.

- Do not stack boards on top of each other; you could dislodge a chip accidentally.
- When handling motherboards and expansion cards, do not touch the chips on the boards. Hold expansion cards by the edges. Do not touch any soldered components on a card, and do not touch chips or edge connectors unless it is absolutely necessary.
- Do not touch a chip with a magnetized screwdriver.
- Do not use a graphite pencil to change DIP switch settings, because graphite is a conductor of electricity, and the graphite can lodge in the switch.
- Always turn off a computer before moving it. A computer's hard drive always spins while it is on, unless it has a sleep mode. Therefore, it is important not to move, kick, or jar a computer while it is running.
- To protect disks, keep them away from magnetic fields, heat, and extreme cold. Do not open the shuttle window on a floppy disk or touch the disk's surface.
- In a classroom environment, after you have reassembled everything, have your instructor check your work before you put the cover back on and power up.

End-of-Chapter Exercises You will find the following exercises in every text chapter:

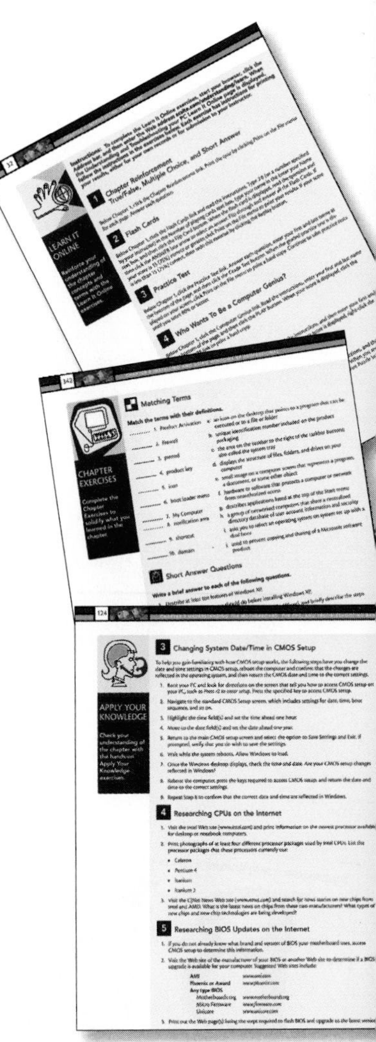

- **Learn It Online** Each chapter features a Learn It Online page comprised of six exercises. These exercises utilize the Web to offer chapter-related reinforcement activities that will help you gain confidence in understanding and troubleshooting your PC. These exercises include True/False, Multiple Choice, Short Answer, Flash Cards, Practice Test, and several learning games.
- **Chapter Exercises** In this section, you will find five Multiple Choice, Fill in the Blank, and Short Answer questions, as well as a Matching exercise. These exercises allow you to apply your knowledge of the material and will help to prepare you for tests and assessments.
- **Apply Your Knowledge** This section includes several in-depth hands-on exercises per chapter. Each exercise requires you to apply the knowledge and skills you learned in the chapter, helping to ensure you not only understand the concepts, but also can execute problem-solving and troubleshooting steps on your own.

FOR THE INSTRUCTOR

The Shelly Cashman Series is dedicated to providing you all of the tools you need to make your class a success. Information on all supplementary materials is available through your Course Technology representative or by calling one of the following telephone numbers: Colleges and Universities, 1-800-648-7450; High Schools, 1-800-824-5179; Private Career Colleges, 1-800-477-3692; Canada, 1-800-268-2222; and Corporations and Government Agencies, 1-800-340-7450.

Instructor Resources CD

The Instructor Resources CD-ROM (0-619-20223-8) for this textbook includes both teaching and testing aids. The contents of the CD are listed below:

- **Instructor's Manual** The Instructor's Manual is made up of Microsoft Word files. The Instructor's Manual includes detailed lecture notes with page number references, teacher's notes, classroom activities, discussion topics, and projects to assign.

- **Course Syllabus** Sample syllabi are included, and can be customized easily customized for your course.
- **PowerPoint Presentations** PowerPoint Presentations is a multimedia lecture presentation system that provides PowerPoint slides for each chapter. Presentations are based on the chapters' objectives. Use this presentation system to present well organized lectures that are both interesting and knowledge based. PowerPoint Presentation provides consistent coverage at schools that use multiple lecturers in their programming courses.
- **Figure Files** Illustrations for every figure in the textbook are available in electronic form. Use this ancillary to present a slide show in lecture or to print transparencies for use in lecture with an overhead projector. If you have a personal computer and LCD device, this ancillary can be an effective tool for presenting lectures.
- **Solutions to Exercises** Solutions are included for all end-of-chapter exercises, as well as the Chapter Reinforcement activities.
- **Test Bank & Test Engine** The test bank includes 110 questions for every chapter (25 multiple-choice, 50 true/false, and 35 fill-in-the-blank) with page number references and, when appropriate, figure references. A printable version of the test bank also is included. The test bank comes with a copy of the test engine, ExamView. ExamView is a state-of-the-art test builder that is easy to use. ExamView enables you quickly to create printed tests, Internet tests, and computer (LAN-based) tests. You can enter your own test questions or use the test bank that accompanies ExamView.
- **Additional Activities for Students** These additional activities consist of Chapter Reinforcement Exercises, which are true/false, multiple choice, and short answer questions that help students gain confidence in the material learned.

Online Content

Course Technology knows what it takes to develop and deliver an online course that will keep you and your students engaged from start to finish. That is why we provide you with all the tools you need to teach an interactive, informative class. From ready-to-use online content to our own content delivery platform, tools from Course Technology make teaching online easier than ever.

- **MyCourse 2.1** A flexible, easy-to-use course management tool, MyCourse 2.1 allows you to personalize your course home page, schedule your course activities and assignments, post messages, administer tests, and file the results in a grade book. You also can add your own content, select from a pool of test bank questions, or create questions yourself. MyCourse 2.1 is hosted by Thomson Learning, allowing you hassle-free maintenance and student access at all times. For more information, visit *www.course.com/onlinecontent*
- **Blackboard and WebCT Online Content** Course Technology offers you options for online content. For those who want online testing, we provide a Blackboard test bank and a WebCT test bank, available for download in the Instructor Resources section on course.com. For more information, visit *www.course.com/onlinecontent*

CHAPTER 1

Introducing Hardware

Introduction

Like millions of other computer users, you probably use your computer for a wide range of tasks. Each day, you turn on your computer, start a software program, and then use that software to explore the Internet, write a term paper, play games, build spreadsheets, or send e-mail to friends around the world. You can use all these applications without knowing exactly how your computer works. As you continue to use your computer, however, you may want to understand more about what is happening inside it. This book focuses on all aspects of PC hardware and software. It is designed to help you better understand how your computer works, so that you can install new hardware and software, troubleshoot hardware and software problems, and make decisions about upgrading or purchasing new hardware and operating systems.

This chapter introduces you to many of the basic components of your computer. You will learn more about these components and how they work together in later chapters. This chapter also provides a look at how to protect your computer system, including how to safeguard your computer from power problems.

OBJECTIVES

In this chapter, you will learn:

1. That a computer requires both hardware and software to work
2. About the different hardware components that are inside and connected to a computer
3. About basic ways to protect yourself and your computer system as you work on a computer

Up for Discussion

For the last six months, you have been working as a customer service representative for Sunrise Computers, a local computer store. A major part of your responsibilities is to help train new employees so that they are comfortable answering customer questions. Today, Ann Bartoski, a recent graduate from the local college, started her new job as a salesperson for Sunrise Computers. She spent the morning working with a salesperson on the sales floor to learn more about the sales process. Your manager has asked you to spend the afternoon helping her to handle more technical questions that customers might have. Ann has some familiarity with computers, but she admitted to you that, although she used computers at school to write papers, send e-mail, and create presentations for class, she never learned much about what happens inside a computer to make it work. She's hoping that you can help her better understand more about the components of a computer, as well as how they function together. She also noted that, while she was working with the salesperson this morning, many customers were expressing concern about the upcoming hurricane season and wondering how to protect their computer against power surges caused by storms and blackouts. As you head to the training room, you begin to explain more about the hardware components inside a computer. You also agree to set aside time to review how she can help customers protect their computers against power surges and other electrical problems.

Questions:

- What are the key components of a computer?
- How can you learn more about the hardware in a computer system?
- How can you protect your computer against electrical problems?

Hardware Needs Software to Work

In the world of computers, the term **hardware** refers to the computer's physical components, such as input devices, output devices, the central processing unit, memory chips, storage devices, and communications devices. The term **software**, or **program**, refers to the set of instructions that directs the hardware to accomplish a task. Hardware accepts instructions from software to complete four basic functions: input, processing, output, and storage (Figure 1-1). Hardware components also must communicate both data and instructions among themselves. This chapter introduces the hardware components of a computer system, provides an overview of how they work, and introduces the electrical system that provides power to the hardware components. Chapter 2 addresses how hardware and software work together to communicate data and instructions to all the components of a computer.

Data is processed in one of two ways: analog or digital. Humans process data that is **analog**, in the form of continuous up-and-down wave patterns of light and sound that represent data to the eyes and ears. You hear sounds when your ears pick up pressure waves created by vibrating objects. You see objects and color when light waves interact and strike your eyes.

A personal computer, by contrast, processes data that is **digital**, which means it is in one of two states: positive (on) and non-positive (off). This technology of storing and reading only two states of data is called **binary**. Computers use a **binary number system** to express the positive state as number 1 and the non-positive state as the number 0. A 1 or 0 in this system is called a **bit**, which is an abbreviation for *bi*nary digi*t*. A string of eight bits (0s and 1s) in various combinations that a computer can process as a group is a **byte**. A byte can be used to represent 256 individual characters, including letters, numbers, and so on. The combinations of 0s and 1s that represent characters are defined by patterns called a **coding scheme**. The coding scheme most widely used in personal computers is **ASCII** (**American Standard Code for Information Interchange**). In ASCII, each letter, number, or character is represented by a specific string of eight bits.

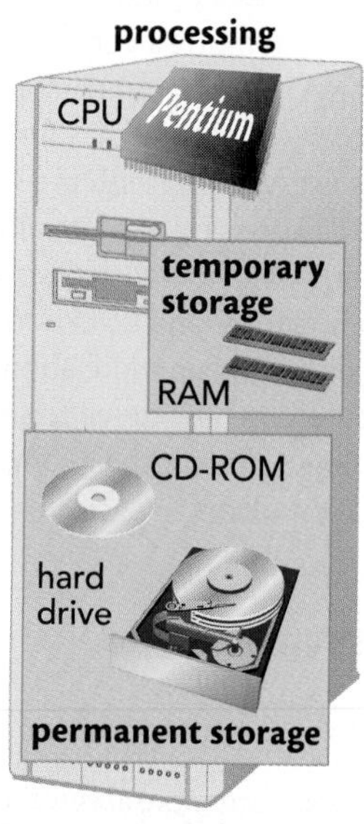

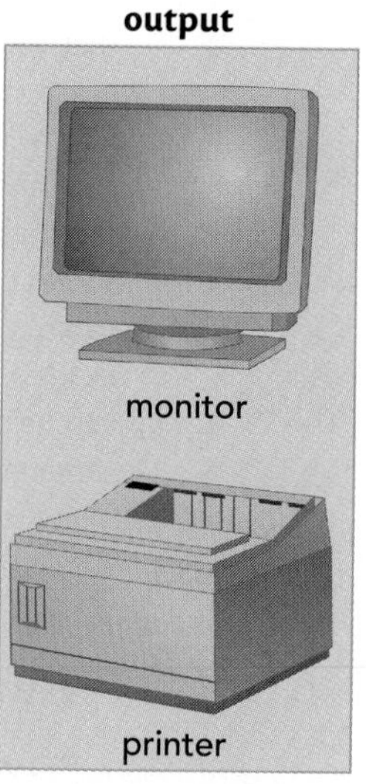

Figure 1-1 Computer activity consists of input, processing, output, and storage.

A person interacts with a computer in a way that he or she understands, inputting analog data and instructions using a keyboard, mouse, or other input device (Figure 1-2). Computer hardware and software then convert the data and instructions into the binary form that the computer understands. All letters and characters entered into a computer are converted to a binary form before being stored in the computer. For example, the number 3 is represented in ASCII as 00110011, the number 55 as 00110101, and the uppercase letter D as 01000100 (Figure 1-3).

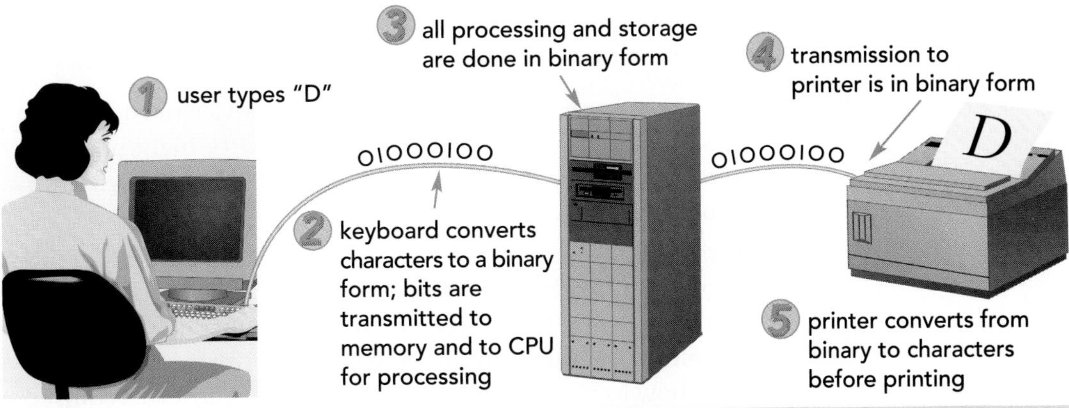
user types "D"
01000100
keyboard converts characters to a binary form; bits are transmitted to memory and to CPU for processing
all processing and storage are done in binary form
01000100
transmission to printer is in binary form
D
printer converts from binary to characters before printing

Figure 1-2 All communication, storage, and processing of data inside a computer are in binary form until presented as output to the user.

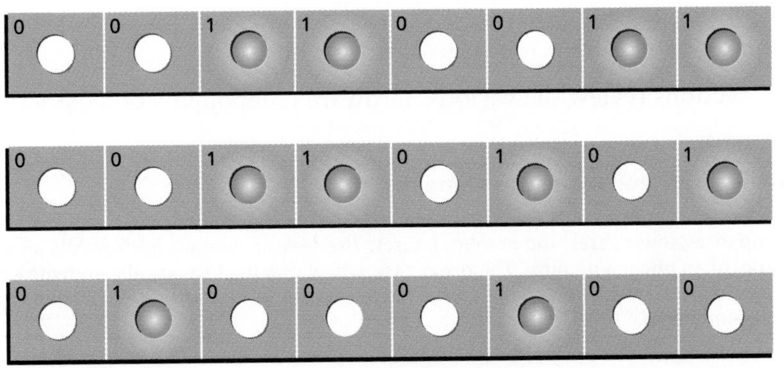
0 0 1 1 0 0 1 1
0 0 1 1 0 1 0 1
0 1 0 0 0 1 0 0

Figure 1-3 All letters and numbers are stored in a computer as a series of bits, each represented in the computer as "on" or "off."

FAQ 1-1

How are numbers above 9 represented using the ASCII coding system?

In ASCII, each letter, number, or character is represented by a specific string of eight bits. The numbers 0 through 9 are represented using 8 bits. For example, a 2 is represented in ASCII as 00110010, while a 5 is 0010101. Any number above 9 requires two bytes (16 bits) to be represented in ASCII. The number 25 thus would require a string of 8 bits for the 2 and a string of 8 bits for the 5.

More About

Number Systems and Coding Schemes

To learn more about the binary and hexadecimal number systems, as well as the ASCII and Unicode coding schemes, visit the Understanding and Troubleshooting Your PC More About Web page (**scsite.com/understanding/more**) and then click Number Systems and Coding Schemes below Chapter 1.

Personal Computer Hardware Components

This section provides an overview of the major personal computer hardware components used for input, output, processing, and storage, as well as components that allow communications within the computer and provide an electrical supply. Most input and output devices are outside the **computer case**, while most processing, storage, communication, and power supply components are contained inside the computer case.

The most important component inside the case is the **central processing unit** (**CPU**), also called the **microprocessor** or **processor**. As its name implies, the CPU is central to all processing done by the computer. The CPU reads and writes data and instructions to and from storage devices and performs calculations and other data processing.

Many other computer components also must communicate with the CPU. In fact, each hardware input, output, or storage device requires these elements to operate:

- *A method to communicate with the CPU.* Every device must have a way to send or receive data to and from the CPU. The CPU might need to control the device by passing instructions to it, or the device might need to request service from the CPU.
- *Software to instruct and control the device.* A device is useless without software to control it. Each device responds to a specific set of instructions based on its particular functions. The software must have an instruction for each possible action the device is expected to perform, and the software must know how to communicate with a device at the level required by the device. The CPU also must have access to this software in order to interact with the device.
- *Electricity to power the device.* Devices can receive power from the power supply inside the computer case, or they can have their own power supplied by a power cable connected to an electrical outlet.

The next sections review the various hardware components of a computer.

FAQ 1-2

Are all computer cases the same?

Computer cases for personal computers and notebooks fall into three major categories: desktop cases, tower cases, and notebook cases. The desktop case sits horizontally on a desktop, often under a monitor. The tower case, which usually sits vertically under the desk, is one to two feet tall. The notebook case is used for notebook computers (also referred to as laptop computers).

Outside the Computer Case: Input and Output Devices

Most input and output devices reside outside the computer case. These devices communicate with components inside the computer case through a wireless connection or through cables attached to the case at a connection called a port. A **port** is a physical connector that allows a cable from a peripheral device to be attached to the computer. A **peripheral device**, such as a keyboard, mouse, monitor, or printer, is a device that is not located directly on the motherboard but communicates with the CPU. Peripheral devices often are connected to the computer's motherboard via a port or wireless connection.

Most computer ports are located on the back of the case, as shown in Figure 1-4, but some computers have ports on the front of the case for easy access. For wireless connections, a wireless device communicates with the system using radio frequency (RF) technology or an infrared port.

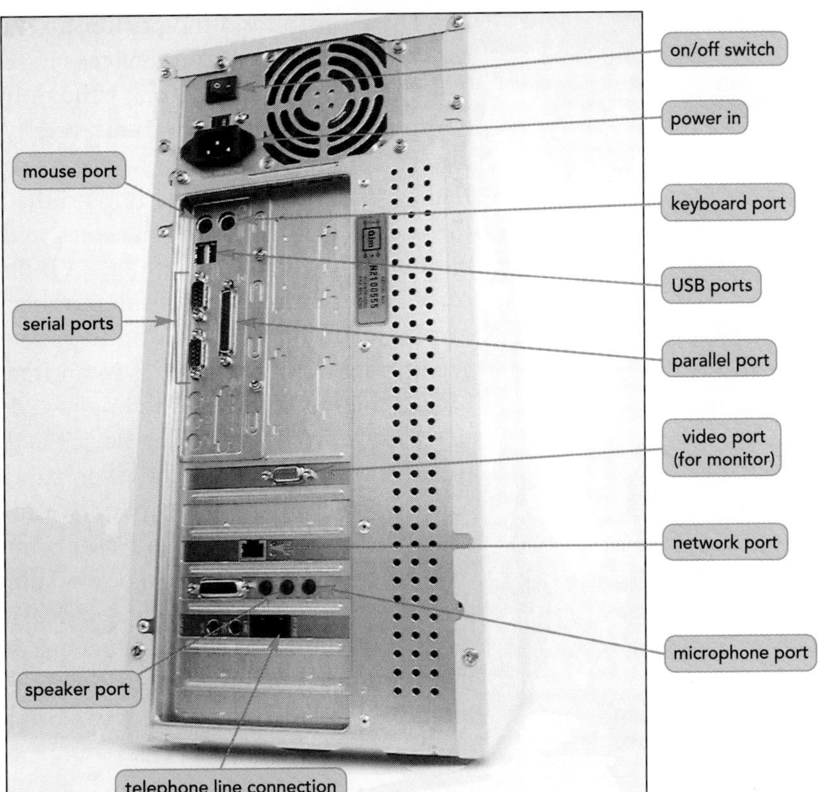

Figure 1-4 Input and output devices connect to the computer via ports usually found on the back of the computer case.

The keyboard and the mouse are the most widely used input devices. A **keyboard** is an input device that contains keys users press to enter data and send instructions to a computer (Figure 1-5 on the next page). The keyboards that are standard today are called *enhanced keyboards* and have 104 keys. Other types of keyboards include ergonomic keyboards that are curved to make them more comfortable for the hands and wrists, and wireless keyboards that rely on RF technology.

A **mouse** is a pointing input device used to move a pointer on the screen and to make selections. The bottom of a mouse houses a rotating ball or an optical sensor that tracks movement and controls the location of the pointer on the screen. The one, two, or three buttons on the top of the mouse serve different purposes for different software. For example, Windows XP uses the left mouse button to execute a command and the right mouse button to display information about the command. Some keyboards come equipped with a port to attach a mouse to the keyboard, although it is more common for the mouse port to be located directly on the computer case. Other types of mice rely on RF technology and do not use cables to connect to the computer.

More About

Wireless Devices

To learn more about wireless connections used for devices such as mice and keyboards, visit the Understanding and Troubleshooting Your PC More About Web page (**scsite.com/understanding/more**) and then click Wireless Devices below Chapter 1.

Figure 1-5 Input devices such as the keyboard and the mouse often have 6-pin connectors and cables that connect to ports on the computer case.

The monitor and the printer are the two most widely used output devices (Figure 1-6). The **monitor** visually displays the output of the computer. Hardware manufacturers typically describe a monitor by the size of its screen in inches (measured diagonally) and the monitor's resolution. **Resolution** refers to the sharpness and clearness of an image. A monitor's resolution is a function of the number of dots, or **pixels**, used for display on the screen. The greater the number of pixels in an image, the higher the resolution of the image.

A very important output device is the **printer**, which produces output on paper, often called **hard copy**. The most popular printers available today are ink-jet and laser printers. The monitor and the printer need power supplies separate from the computer with electrical power cords that connect to electrical outlets. Sometimes the computer case has an electrical outlet for the monitor's power cord, so that it can be plugged directly into the computer case.

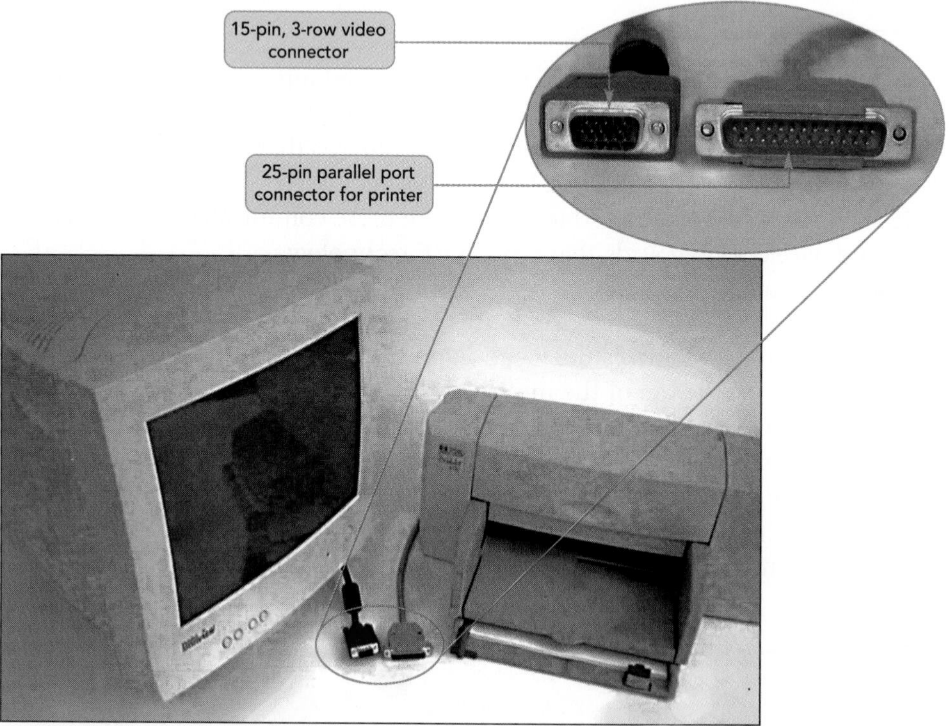

Figure 1-6 Output devices such as a monitor and printer have connectors and cables that connect to ports on the computer case.

Inside the Computer Case: Processing, Communication, Storage, and Power

All processing of data and instructions and most storage are handled by devices that are inside the computer case (Figure 1-7), including:

- a motherboard containing the CPU, memory (primary storage), and other components
- expansion cards (circuit boards) used by the CPU to communicate with devices inside and outside the case
- secondary storage devices such as a floppy drive, hard drive, CD-ROM drive, or DVD-ROM drive
- a power supply with power cords supplying electricity to all devices inside the case
- cables connecting devices to circuit boards and the motherboard

As shown in Figure 1-7, two types of cables are found inside the computer case: data cables, which connect devices to one another, and power cables or power cords, which supply power. Most often, you can distinguish between the two by the shape of the cable. Data cables tend to be flat and wide (and sometimes are called ribbon cables). Power cords tend to be round and small. Some exceptions to this rule exist, so the best way to identify a cable is to trace its source and destination.

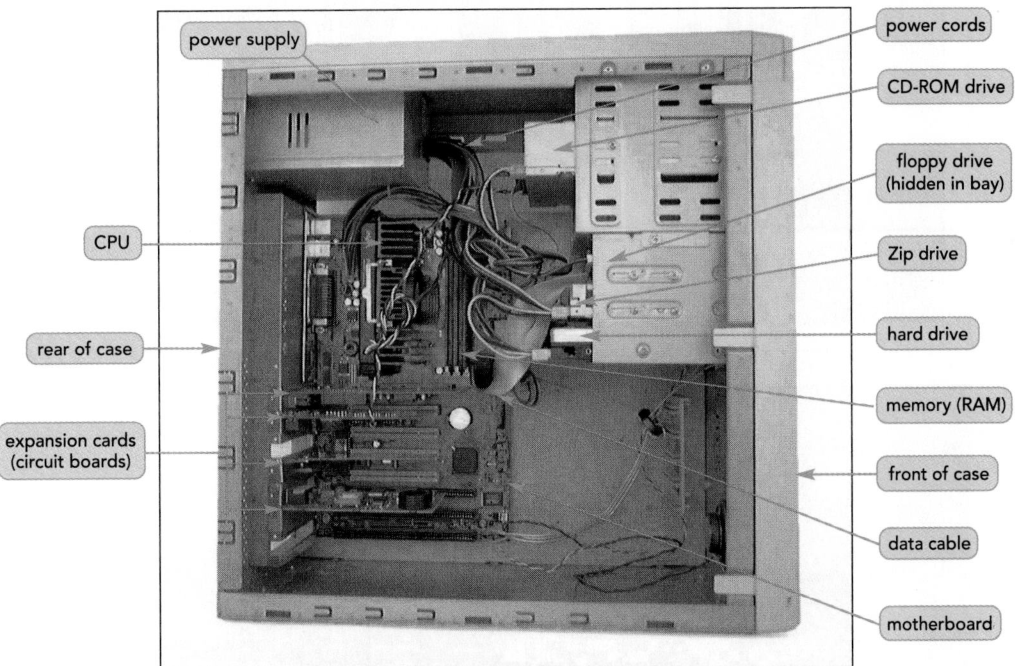

Figure 1-7 View of devices inside the computer case.

THE MOTHERBOARD When you look inside a computer case, the circuit boards are among the most visible devices. A **circuit board** is an insulated board that holds microchips, and the circuitry that connects these chips. A **microchip**, also called a **chip** or **integrated circuit** (**IC**), is a small piece of silicon or another semiconductor material that contains millions of electronic components to transmit signals and perform other functions. A CPU, for example, is a type of chip found on a circuit board.

The largest and most important circuit board in the computer is the **motherboard**, also called the **main board** or **system board** (Figure 1-8a). The motherboard contains the CPU, the component which performs most processing inside the PC. The motherboard, which is the most complex piece of equipment inside the case, is covered in more detail in this chapter and in Chapter 3. Other types of circuit boards, called **expansion cards**, are installed in long narrow **expansion slots** on the motherboard.

Because all devices must communicate with the CPU on the motherboard, all devices in a computer are installed directly on the motherboard, are indirectly linked to it by expansion cards, or are directly linked to it by a cable connected to a port on the motherboard. Some ports on the motherboard stick outside the case to accommodate external peripheral devices, such as a keyboard. Other ports provide a connection for internal peripheral devices, such as a hard disk drive.

Figure 1-8b shows the external ports supplied by this motherboard: a keyboard port, a mouse port, a serial port, a parallel port, four USB ports, a network port, a FireWire port, and sound ports. In a **serial port**, data is transferred serially, which

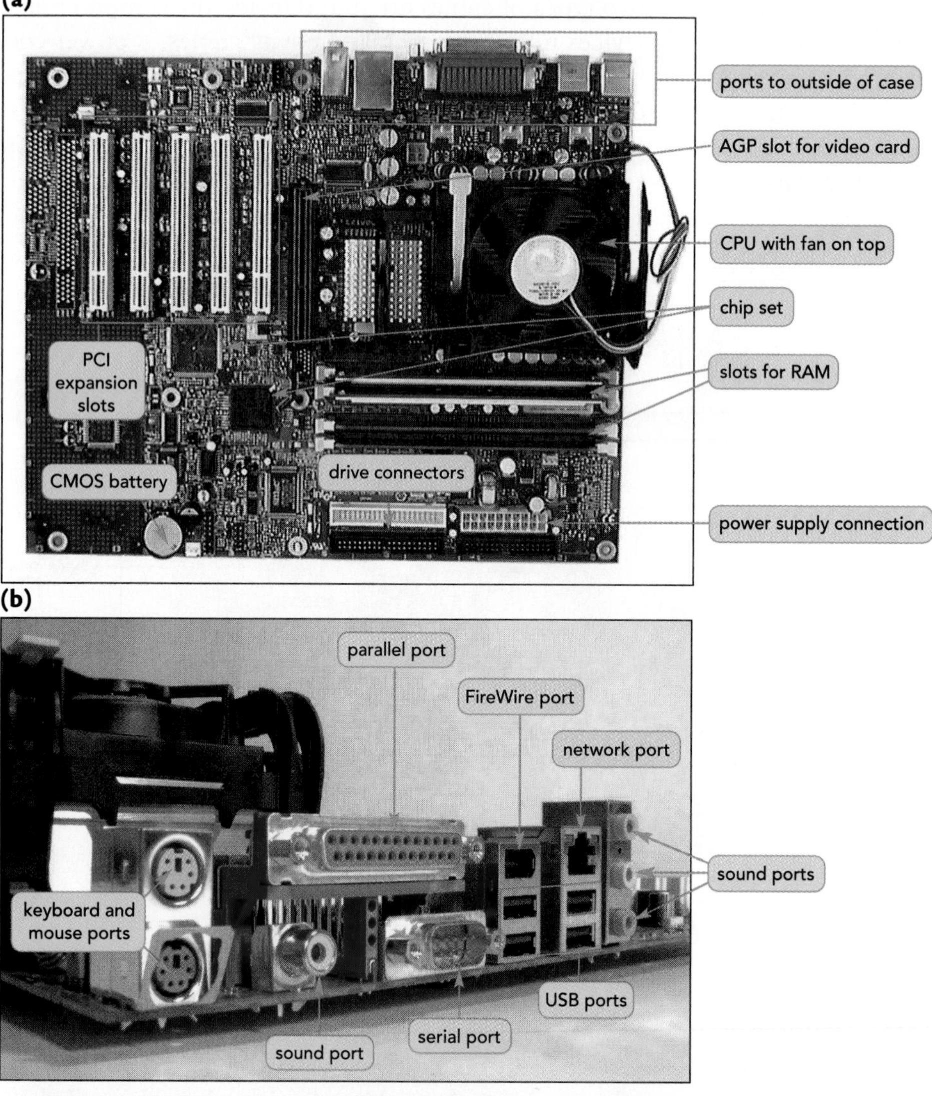

Figure 1-8 (a) The motherboard includes many important components, which are discussed later in the chapter. (b) Because all hardware devices must communicate with the CPU, the motherboard also provides numerous ports to connect a wide range of peripheral devices.

means one bit follows the next. A **parallel port** transmits data in parallel (side by side, as if in lanes) and is most often used by a printer. A **USB (universal serial bus) port** can connect to many different input and output devices such as keyboards, printers, scanners, and mice. A **FireWire port** is used for high-speed multimedia devices such as digital camcorders. A **sound port** provides an interface for devices such as headphones, speakers, or microphones.

Figure 1-9 lists several other major components that are found on all motherboards, including the CPU and chip set, memory, instructions and setup data, and communications components. The following sections discuss these components in detail.

Components on a Motherboard	
Components used primarily for processing	• Central processing unit (CPU), the computer's most important chip • Chip set that supports the CPU by controlling many motherboard activities
Components used for temporary storage	• Random access memory (RAM) to hold data and instructions as they are processed • Cache memory to speed up memory access (optional, depending on the type of CPU)
Instructions and setup (configuration) data stored on the motherboard	• ROM chip used to store instructions that control basic hardware functions • CMOS RAM chip that holds setup and configuration data
Components that allow the CPU to communicate with other devices	• Buses that use traces, or wires, on the motherboard to allow for communication between devices • Expansion slots to connect expansion cards to the motherboard • System clock to keep communication in sync • Ports to provide connections for other devices
Electrical system	• Power supply connections to provide electricity to the motherboard and expansion cards

Figure 1-9 Several major computer components are located on a motherboard.

THE CPU AND THE CHIP SET The CPU, or microprocessor, is the chip inside the computer that performs most of the actual data processing. The CPU could not do its job without the assistance of the **chip set**, a group of microchips on the motherboard that control the flow of data and instructions to and from the CPU, providing careful timing of activities, as shown in Figure 1-8a. While this book will touch on different types of computers, it focuses on IBM-compatible personal computers (PCs), which are the most widely used personal computers. IBM-compatible PCs use microprocessors and chip sets manufactured by Intel Corporation, AMD, VIA Technologies, and other manufacturers. The Macintosh family of personal computers, manufactured by Apple Computer, use a family of microprocessors manufactured by Motorola Corporation. You will learn more about the CPU and the chip set in Chapter 3.

MEMORY (PRIMARY STORAGE) As shown earlier in Figure 1-1 on page 2, a computer relies on two kinds of storage: temporary and permanent. The CPU uses temporary storage, also called **primary storage** or **memory**, to hold data and instructions temporarily while it is processing them.

More About

Primary and Secondary Storage

To learn more about primary and secondary storage, visit the Understanding and Troubleshooting Your PC More About Web page (**scsite.com/understanding/more**) and then click Primary and Secondary Storage below Chapter 1.

Primary storage is provided by chips located on the motherboard and on other circuit boards. These chips, referred to as memory or **random access memory (RAM)**, can be installed individually on the motherboard or in banks of several chips on a small board that plugs into the motherboard (Figure 1-10). Most motherboards today use boards called **DIMMs** or **dual inline memory modules**. Chapter 6 provides more detail on DIMMs, as well as other types of boards that hold memory chips, including **SIMMs** (**single inline memory modules**) and **RIMMs** (memory modules manufactured by Rambus, Inc.).

Whatever information is stored in RAM is lost when the computer is turned off, because RAM chips need a continuous supply of electrical power to hold data or software stored in them. Because it loses its contents when a computer's power is turned off, RAM is considered to be **volatile**. By contrast, another kind of memory, called **ROM** (**read-only memory**) holds its data permanently, even when the power is turned off. ROM thus is considered to be **nonvolatile**.

Figure 1-10 A SIMM, DIMM, or RIMM holds RAM and is mounted directly on a motherboard.

 Your Turn

Learning About Your Computer Hardware

What type of CPU does your computer have and how much memory is installed? You can learn more about the hardware in your computer using the System Properties window in Windows XP.

To examine the hardware in your computer, perform the following steps:

1. Click the Start button and then right-click My Computer on the Start menu.
2. Click Properties on the shortcut menu.
3. When the System Properties window is displayed, click the General tab, if necessary.

   The General tab lists basic information about the operating system installed on your computer, the CPU type and speed, and the amount of RAM (Figure 1-11).

After reviewing the information, perform the following steps to take a screen capture:

1. Press ALT+PRINT SCRN to copy a screen capture to the Windows Clipboard.
2. Click the Start button and then point to All Programs on the Start menu.
3. Point to Accessories on the All Programs submenu and then click Paint.
4. When the Paint window is displayed, click Edit on the menu bar and then click Paste.

   Windows pastes the screen capture from the Windows Clipboard to the Paint window.
5. To print a copy of the screen capture, click File on the menu bar, click Print on the File menu, and then click the Print button in the Print dialog box.
6. Click File on the menu bar and then click Save As. Click the Save in box arrow and then click 3½ Floppy (A:) (or a different location provided by your instructor) in the Save in list.
7. Type Ch01YT-System in the File name text box and then click the Save button.
8. Click the Close button on the Paint window to quit Paint.

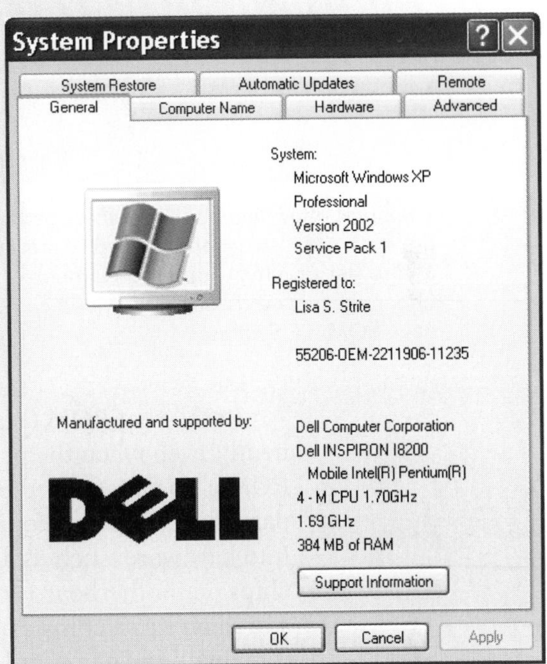

Figure 1-11

To review other hardware components on your computer, perform the following steps:

1. Click the Hardware tab and then click the Device Manager button in the Device Manager area.
2. When the Device Manager window is displayed, click the expand (+) buttons next to the categories to view the hardware components.
3. Click Action on the menu bar and then click Print. In the Report type area, click System Summary and then click the Print button.

   Windows prints a report listing information about the system, including the type of CPU, disk drives, memory, and more. Clicking All devices and system summary in the Report area will print a more detailed report, listing devices available on the system and additional information.
4. Click the Close button in the Device Manager window, then click the Close button in the System Properties window.

INSTRUCTIONS STORED ON THE MOTHERBOARD AND OTHER BOARDS In addition to RAM chips used for memory, the motherboard also includes a ROM chip to store basic data and programs used to start up the computer, relate to simple hardware devices such as a floppy disk and keyboard, and search for an operating system stored on a storage device such as a hard drive or CD. These data and programs comprise the **basic input/output system** or **BIOS** (pronounced *bye-ose* or *bye-oss*). The BIOS typically is stored on a ROM chip on the motherboard, called the **ROM BIOS chip** (Figure 1-12).

Figure 1-12 The ROM BIOS chip on the motherboard contains the data and instructions needed to start up the PC and to perform many other fundamental tasks. Other circuit boards, such as a video card, also may have ROM BIOS chips.

Storing these basic instructions on a ROM BIOS chip ensures that the BIOS will not be damaged by disk failures, making it possible for a computer to start even if the hard drive fails. The BIOS can be categorized according to its three main purposes:

- the BIOS used to manage simple devices is called **system BIOS**;
- the BIOS used to start the computer is called **startup BIOS**; and
- the BIOS used to change some settings on the motherboard is called **CMOS BIOS** or **CMOS setup**.

Recall that ROM (read-only memory) is nonvolatile and holds its data permanently, even when the power is turned off. In the past, the instructions stored by a ROM chip were etched permanently into it during fabrication. The instructions were part of the chip and could not be changed easily. (Program instructions embedded into hardware, such as a ROM chip, often are referred to as **firmware**). Today, ROM chips on motherboards can be reprogrammed. Called **flash ROM**, the software stored on these chips can be *flashed*, or updated with new software, which will remain on the chip until it is flashed again.

MOTHERBOARD CONFIGURATION SETTINGS The CMOS setup instructions are stored on the motherboard as part of the ROM BIOS chip, as previously noted, or in a separate chip called **CMOS RAM chip**, **CMOS setup chip,** or **CMOS configuration chip**. (**CMOS** stands for **complementary metal-oxide semiconductor**, a technology used to manufacture these chips.)

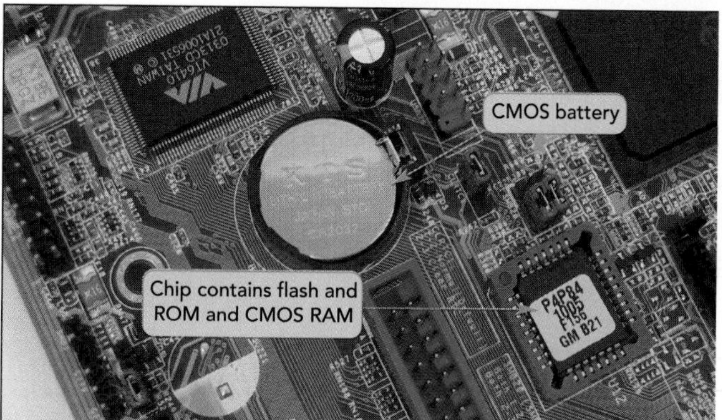

Figure 1-13 This chip contains flash ROM, which stores the BIOS, and CMOS RAM, which stores the CMOS setup instructions. The CMOS RAM is powered by the CMOS battery located near the chip.

Because older ROM chips did not use flash ROM and had to be replaced when updates were needed, the CMOS setup instructions were stored on a separate chip. On newer motherboards, the ROM BIOS and CMOS RAM are combined in a single chip (Figure 1-13).

A CMOS RAM chip contains a very small amount of memory to hold configuration or setup information about the computer. This chip stores information such as the current date and time, which hard drives and floppy drives are present, and how the serial and parallel ports are configured. When the computer is turned on, it looks to the CMOS RAM to determine what hardware it should expect to find. The CMOS RAM chip is powered by a small battery located on the motherboard or computer case, usually close to the CMOS RAM chip itself. This constant source of electricity ensures that the CMOS RAM chip still retains its data even when the computer is turned off.

FAQ 1-3

Why would I change the information stored in CMOS RAM?

CMOS setup normally does not need to be changed, except when there is a problem with hardware, a new floppy drive is installed, or a power-saving feature needs to be disabled or enabled. To change the information, you access the CMOS setup program by pressing a specific key or keys as the computer system is starting up. Different BIOSs use different keystrokes to access CMOS setup. The keystrokes are displayed on the screen during startup (for example, *Press the F1 key to enter setup*). Chapter 2 provides more detail on the steps to change CMOS setup information.

A motherboard also can retain setup or installation information using different settings of jumpers or DIP switches on the board. A **jumper** is a pair of prongs that are electrical contact points set into the computer motherboard or an adapter card. The jumper acts as a switch that closes or opens an electrical circuit. A jumper is closed if the cover is in place, connecting the two pins that make up the jumper; a jumper is open if the cover is not in place (Figure 1-14). A group of jumpers, sometimes called a jumper block, is sometimes used to tell the system at what speed the CPU is running, or to turn a power-saving feature on or off.

A **DIP (dual inline package) switch** is similar to a light switch, and is on or off depending on the direction in which the small switch is set. Many motherboards have a single bank of DIP switches (Figure 1-15 on the next page), as well as one or more jumpers. Newer motherboards, however, include most setup information in CMOS, rather than requiring you to set jumpers or DIP switches to support new devices or settings.

Figure 1-14 Setup information can be stored using jumpers. A jumper is closed if the cover is in place, connecting the two pins that make up the jumper; a jumper is open if the cover is not in place.

Figure 1-15 A motherboard may include a bank of DIP switches used to define configuration settings.

MOTHERBOARD COMPONENTS USED FOR COMMUNICATION AMONG DEVICES As shown in Figure 1-16, the surface of the motherboard has many fine lines on both the top and the bottom. These lines, sometimes called **traces**, are circuits or paths that enable data, instructions, and power to move from component to component on the motherboard. The paths used for communication and the protocols and methods used to send transmissions via these paths collectively are referred to as a bus. (A **protocol** is a set of rules and standards that any two entities use for communication.) A **bus** is an electrical channel that transfers bits internally within the circuitry of a computer, allowing all of the devices to communicate with each other. Although many different types of buses exist, as you will learn in Chapter 3, one of the more important lines is the **data bus**, which transfers actual data.

Figure 1-16 The bus includes lines (or traces) that enable data, instructions, and power to move from component to component on the board. On the bottom of the motherboard, these bus lines terminate at the CPU socket.

Data is transmitted via a data bus by placing voltage on each line of the data bus. The CPU or other devices interpret the voltage, or lack of voltage, on each line of the data bus as a binary digit (0 or 1). Figure 1-17 shows a bus that is transmitting data between the CPU and memory. The bus has 8 lines, and each of the bits in a byte are placed on a line of the data bus simultaneously. The lines with a voltage represent a 1; the lines without a voltage represent a 0. The result is the binary code 01000001, which represents the letter A.

The number of lines, or width, of a data bus is called the **data path size**. For example, the bus in Figure 1-17 has eight wires, or lines, to transmit data. It thus is considered to have a data path size of 8 and is called an 8-bit bus. Today, buses typically have wider data paths of 16, 32, 64, or 128 bits. Most buses today also use an additional bit for error checking. Adding a check bit for each byte allows the component reading the data to verify that it is the same data written to the bus.

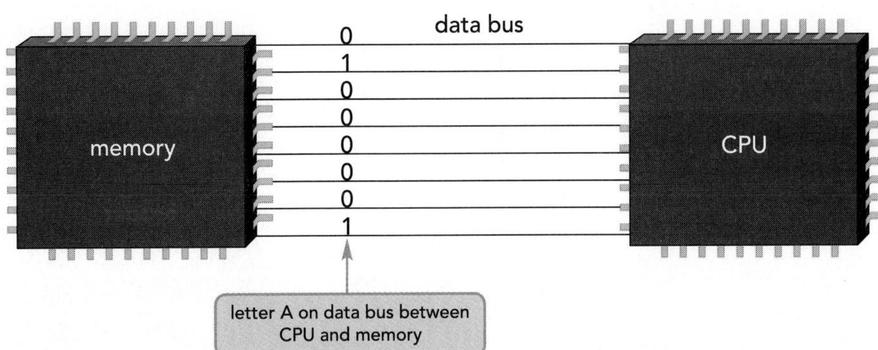

Figure 1-17 A data bus has lines that carry voltage interpreted by the CPU and other devices as bits. Remember that a computer only recognizes two states: on (1) and off (0). On a bus, these states are represented as voltage for 1 and no voltage for 0. This bus has voltage on two lines and no voltage on the other six lines, creating the binary code 01000001, to pass the letter A on the bus.

Does data actually travel down a data bus?

No. When trying to understand the concept of a data bus, it can be helpful to visualize that bits are traveling down the bus in parallel. In actuality, however, the voltage placed on each line of a data bus is not traveling down the line, but rather is all over the line. When one component at one end of the line wants to write data to another component, the two components get in sync for the write operation. Then the first component places voltage on several lines of the bus, and the other component immediately reads the voltage on these lines.

A motherboard can have more than one bus, each using a different protocol, speed, data path size, and so on. The main bus on the motherboard that communicates with the CPU, memory, and the chip set goes by several names: **system bus**, host bus, memory bus, front side bus, or external bus. On today's motherboards, the data portion of most system buses is 64 bits wide, with or without additional lines for error checking.

An important line, or trace, on the system bus is used by the **system clock**, which helps the CPU control the timing of all computer operations. The crystal on the motherboard, similar to that found in watches, generates the oscillation that produces the continuous pulses or cycles of the system clock (Figure 1-18). One line, or trace, on the motherboard carries these pulses over the motherboard to chips and other devices to ensure that all activities are performed in a synchronized fashion.

Figure 1-18 The system clock is a pulsating electrical signal. One line on the motherboard is dedicated to carrying this pulse.

The speed of the cycles of the system clock is called the **clock speed**. Clock speed is measured in **hertz (Hz)**, which is one pulse of the system clock or cycle per second. As shown in Figure 1-19, other measures used for clock speed include **megahertz (MHz)**, which is one million cycles per second; and **gigahertz (GHz)**, which is one billion cycles per second. Most motherboard buses today operate at speeds between 100 MHz and 800 MHz. In other words, data or instructions can be put on the system bus at the rate of 800 million bits every second.

Clock Speed Term	Clock Speed in Hertz (Hz)
kilohertz (kHz)	10^3 Hz or 1,000 Hz
megahertz (MHz)	10^6 Hz or 1,000,000 Hz
gigahertz (GHz)	10^9 Hz or 1,000,000,000 Hz
terahertz (THz)	10^{12} Hz or 1,000,000,000,000 Hz

Figure 1-19 Clock speed is measured in relationship to one hertz, which is a measure of frequency based on one pulse of the system clock or cycle per second.

FAQ 1-5

What types of computer tasks are timed by the system clock?

Everything in a computer is digital (binary) — that is, on and off — including the activities performed inside the computer. Instead of continuously working to perform commands or move data, the CPU, bus, and other devices work in an on and off fashion — completing an operation, stopping, completing another operation, stopping, and so on. Some devices, such as the CPU, do two or more operations on each cycle of the system clock, some do one operation for each cycle, while others complete an operation on every other beat. Regardless of the particular timing, every device works according to cycles defined by the system clock.

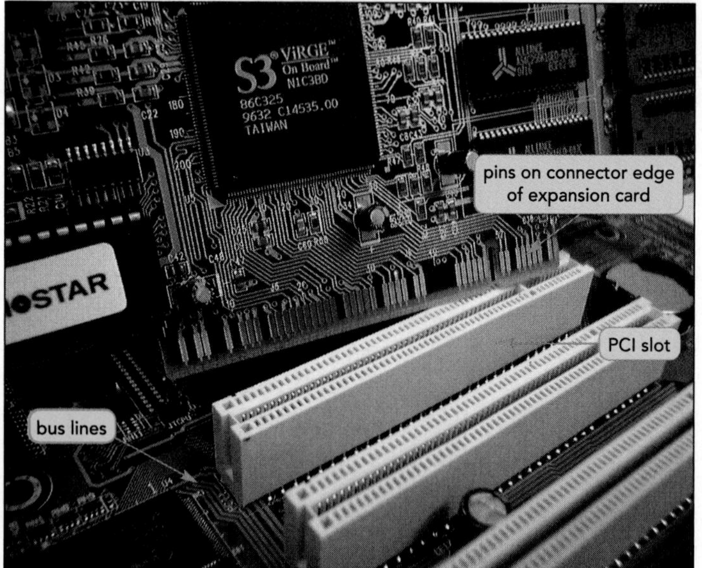

Figure 1-20 The lines of a bus on the motherboard terminate at an expansion slot, where they connect to pins that connect to lines on the expansion card inserted in the slot.

EXPANSION CARDS The lines of a bus often extend from the CPU to the expansion slots used to hold expansion cards (Figure 1-20). As you have learned, expansion cards are circuit boards designed to provide additional functionality or to provide a connection to a peripheral device. Expansion cards also are called circuit cards, adapter cards, adapter boards, interface cards, or just cards.

The size and shape of an expansion slot depends on the kind of bus it uses. Figure 1-21 shows three types of expansion slots:

- PCI (Peripheral Component Interconnect) expansion slot used for high-speed input/output device; uses a PCI bus
- *AGP (Accelerated Graphics Port)* expansion slot used for a video card; uses an AGP bus
- *ISA (Industry Standard Architecture)* expansion slot used by older and/or slower devices; uses an ISA bus

As you will learn in Chapter 3, each of the buses used for these expansion cards – the PCI bus, AGP bus, and ISA bus – connects to the system bus, which, in turn, connects to the CPU. Each bus runs at different speeds and provides different features to accommodate the expansion cards that use these different slots.

Figure 1-22 shows the motherboard and expansion cards installed in the expansion slots inside a computer case. A video card is installed in the one AGP slot, a sound card and network card are installed in two PCI slots, and a modem card is installed in an ISA slot. Figure 1-23a on the next page shows the ports for these cards, located at the rear of the computer case. The **video card** provides a port for the monitor. The **sound card** provides ports for speakers and microphones. The **network card** provides a

Figure 1-21 Expansion slots can be identified by their length, by the position of the breaks in the slots, and by the distance from the edge of the motherboard to a slot's position. PCI bus expansion slots are shorter than ISA slots and offset farther; the one AGP slot is set further from the edge of the board.

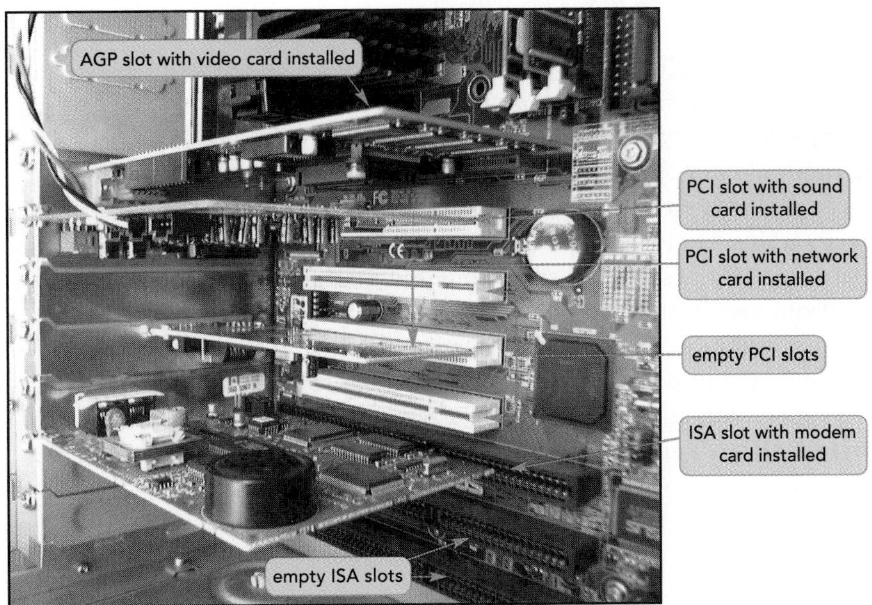

Figure 1-22 Expansion cards are installed in the expansion slots on a motherboard. In this computer, two PCI slots and two ISA slots are not used.

port designed to fit a network cable to connect the PC to a network, and the **modem card** provides one or two ports to connect to the Internet or a network via telephone lines. Often the easiest way to determine the function of a particular expansion card is to see what type of port is at the end of the card that fits against the back of the computer case (Figure 1-23b). As you examine the ports on the back of your PC, recall that, in addition to the ports provided by expansion cards, the motherboard also provides ports, as shown earlier in Figure 1-8 on page 8.

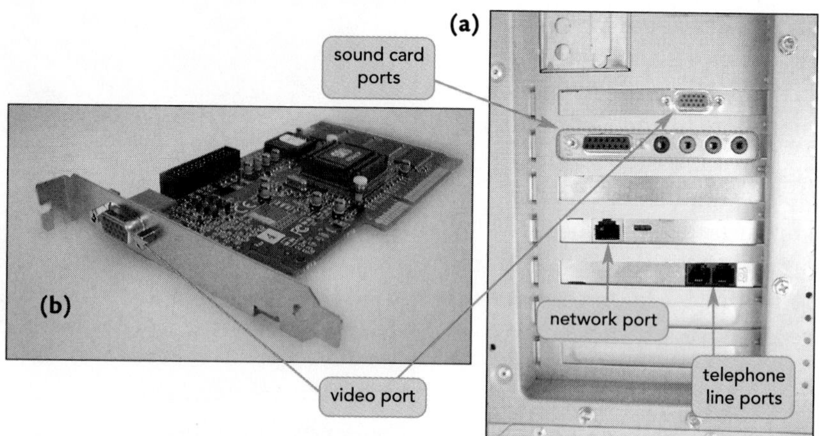

Figure 1-23 (a) Cards installed on a motherboard have ports on the end of the card, which extend to the back of the computer case and provide ports to connect peripheral devices or a network. (b) Often, the easiest way to identify a card, such as a video card, is to look at the port on the end of the card.

SECONDARY STORAGE When data and instructions are not being used and thus are not in memory (primary storage), they must be kept in permanent storage or **secondary storage**, such as a hard disk, floppy disk, CD-ROM, or DVD-ROM. Data and instructions cannot be processed by the CPU from secondary storage; they first must be copied into memory (RAM) for processing. RAM thus temporarily holds both data and instructions as the CPU processes them, while secondary storage media (medium is the singular) store data and instructions permanently.

A **storage medium** is the physical material on which a computer keeps data, instructions, and information. A key characteristic of a storage medium is its **capacity**, or the number of bytes it can hold. Figure 1-24 shows the terms used to describe capacity in terms of a **kilobyte** (**KB**), which is one thousand bytes; a **megabyte** (**MB**), which is one million bytes; and a **gigabyte** (**GB**), which is one billon bytes.

Storage Term	Approximate Number of Bytes	Exact Number of Bytes
kilobyte (KB)	1 thousand	2^{10} or 1,024
megabyte (MB)	1 million	2^{20} or 1,048,576
gigabyte (GB)	1 billion	2^{30} or 1,073,741,824
terabyte (TB)	1 trillion	2^{40} or 1,099,511,627,776
petabyte (PB)	1 quadrillion	2^{50} or 1,125,899,906,842,624
exabyte (EB)	1 quintillion	2^{60} or 1,152,921,504,606,846,976

Figure 1-24 The capacity of storage media is measured by the number of bytes it can hold.

A **storage device**, such as a hard drive, Zip drive, CD-ROM drive, DVD-ROM drive, or floppy drive, is the computer hardware that writes and/or reads data to and from storage media. **Writing** is the process of transferring data from memory to a storage medium, and **reading** is the process of transferring data from a storage medium into memory.

If my computer shuts off, will I lose my work?

If you have not saved your work, you will lose it. Remember that primary storage, or RAM, is temporary. As soon as you turn off the computer, any information in RAM is lost. You always should save your work frequently into secondary storage. When you turn off or lose power to your computer, the information in secondary storage remains intact.

A **hard drive** is a sealed case containing one or more circular platters or disks that store data, instructions, and information (Figure 1-25). A hard disk drive stores data magnetically and is a read/write storage medium, meaning it can be read from and written to any number of times.

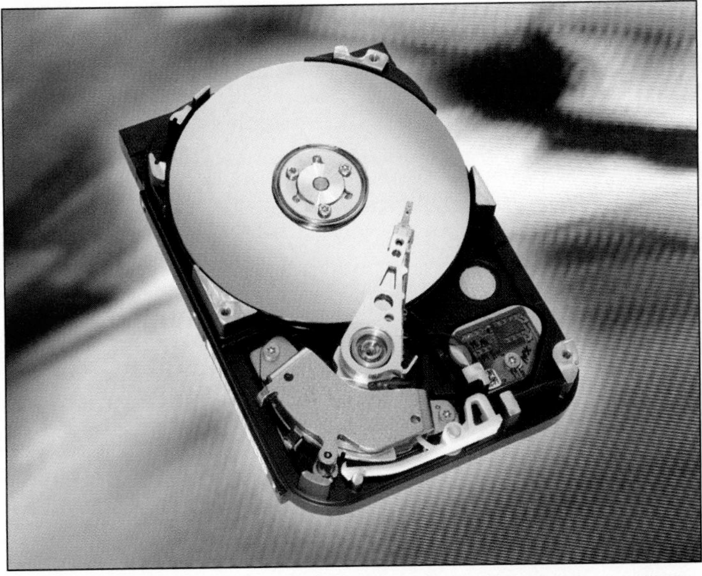

Figure 1-25 Hard drive with sealed cover removed.

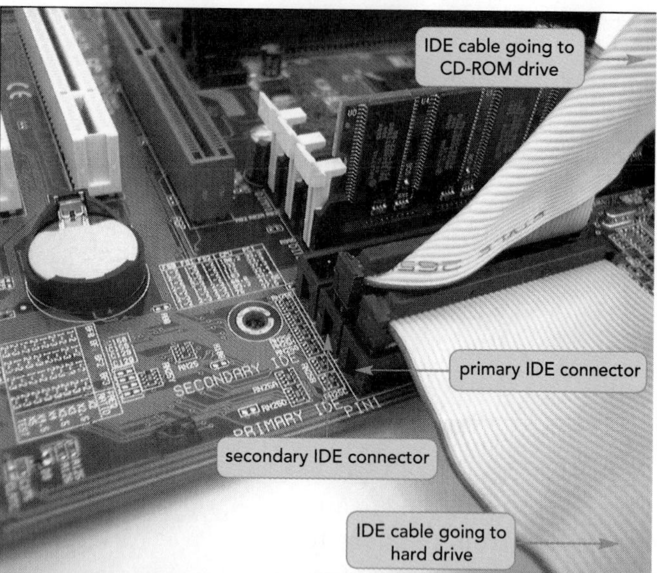

Figure 1-26 A motherboard usually has two IDE connectors, each of which connects to an IDE cable that can accommodate two devices. A hard drive usually connects to the motherboard using the primary IDE connector.

Most hard drives today use a technology called EIDE (Enhanced Integrated Drive Electronics), which originated from IDE technology. **IDE (Integrated Drive Electronics)** is a standard that defines how the motherboard communicates with secondary storage devices. A motherboard usually has two IDE connectors for data cables called IDE cables. A typical system has one hard drive connected to one IDE connector and a CD-ROM drive connected to the other (Figure 1-26).

Each IDE cable has a connection at one end for one IDE device and a connection in the middle of the cable for a second IDE device. Figure 1-27 shows the inside of a computer case with three IDE devices. The hard drive uses the primary IDE cable, while the CD-ROM drive and Zip drive share the secondary IDE cable. Other devices also can use these four IDE connections, which are controlled by the chip set.

A **Zip drive** is a device that reads from and writes to a **Zip disk**, which is a removable magnetic medium that can store from 100 MB to 750 MB of data. Zip disks, which were developed by Iomega Corporation, typically are used to transport many files or large items and to back up data and information.

A **CD-ROM (compact disc read-only memory) drive** is a drive that uses a laser beam to read data from a **CD-ROM**, which is a type of optical disc that uses laser technology to store 650 MB of data, instructions, and information. You will learn more about other types of compact discs, such as CD-RW (compact disc-rewritable), in Chapter 5.

A **DVD-ROM (digital versatile disc read-only memory) drive** uses laser technology to read data from a high capacity optical disc called a DVD-ROM. A **DVD-ROM** is the same size as a CD-ROM, but can store up to 25 times more information, from 4.7 GB to over 17 GB of data. DVDs thus frequently are used to store large video files used for movies.

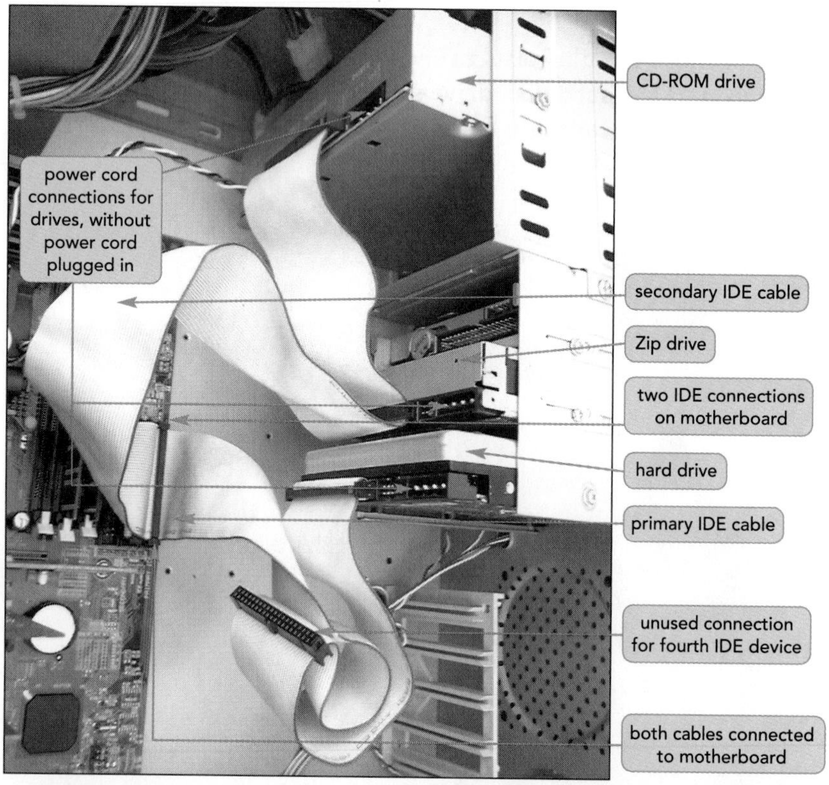

Figure 1-27 In this computer, the hard drive uses the primary IDE cable, while the CD-ROM drive and Zip drive share the secondary IDE cable. (The power cords are not connected, in order to make it easier to see the data cable connections.)

Another type of secondary storage device is a floppy drive. A **floppy drive** can read from and write to a floppy disk. A **floppy disk**, also called a **diskette**, is a portable, inexpensive storage medium that consists of a thin, circular, flexible plastic Mylar film with a magnetic coating, enclosed in a square-shaped plastic shell. Newer floppy drives read 3.5-inch disks that hold about 1.44 MB of data. Most motherboards supply a connection for a floppy drive (Figure 1-28). A floppy drive cable can accommodate two drives. The computer system considers the drive at the end of the cable as drive A. If another drive is connected to the middle of the cable, the computer system considers it drive B.

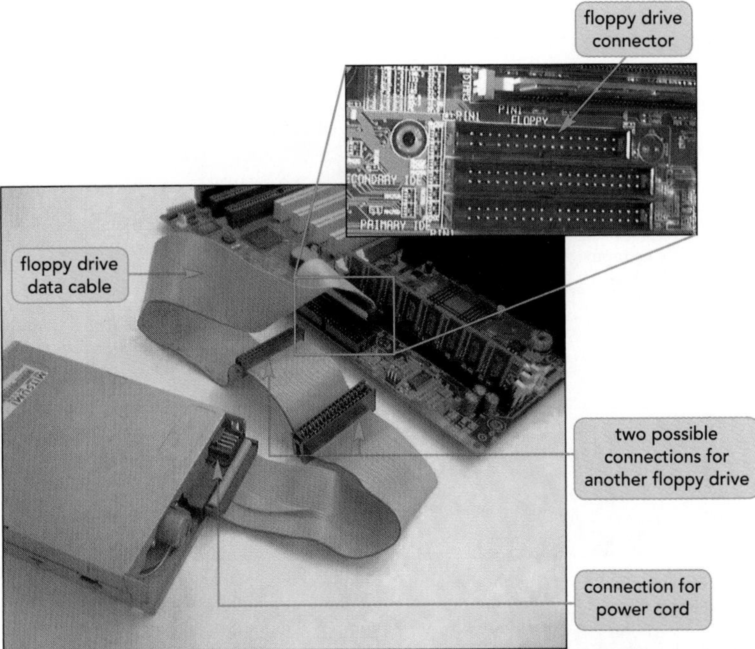

Figure 1-28 A motherboard usually provides a connection for a floppy drive cable, which can support one or two floppy drives.

FAQ 1-7

Is it possible for my computer not to have a floppy drive?

For years, floppy drives came in two sizes: 3.5 inches and 5.25 inches, based on the size of the floppy disk the drives could hold. Eventually, the older 5.25-inch disks were replaced by 3.5-inch diskettes that used more advanced technology and held more data. Today, even 3.5-inch floppy drives are not as necessary as they once were, because the industry is moving toward storage media that can hold more data, such as CDs and DVDs. Today, many newer notebook computers do not have a floppy drive, and some manufacturers offer floppy drives on desktop systems as add-on options only.

Quiz Yourself 1-1

To test your knowledge of hardware components used for processing, input, output, and storage, visit the Understanding and Troubleshooting Your PC Quiz Yourself Web page (scsite.com/understanding/quiz). Click Quiz Yourself 1 below Chapter 1.

THE ELECTRICAL SYSTEM The most important component of the computer's electrical system is the power supply, which is usually located near the rear of the case (Figure 1-29). This **power supply** does not actually generate electricity, but converts the power received from a standard power outlet and reduces it to a voltage that the computer can handle.

In addition to providing power for the computer, the power supply runs a fan directly from the electrical output voltage to help cool the inside of the computer case. Temperatures over 185 degrees Fahrenheit (85 degrees Celsius) can cause components to fail. When a computer is running, this fan and the spinning of the hard drive and CD-ROM drive are the primary noisemakers.

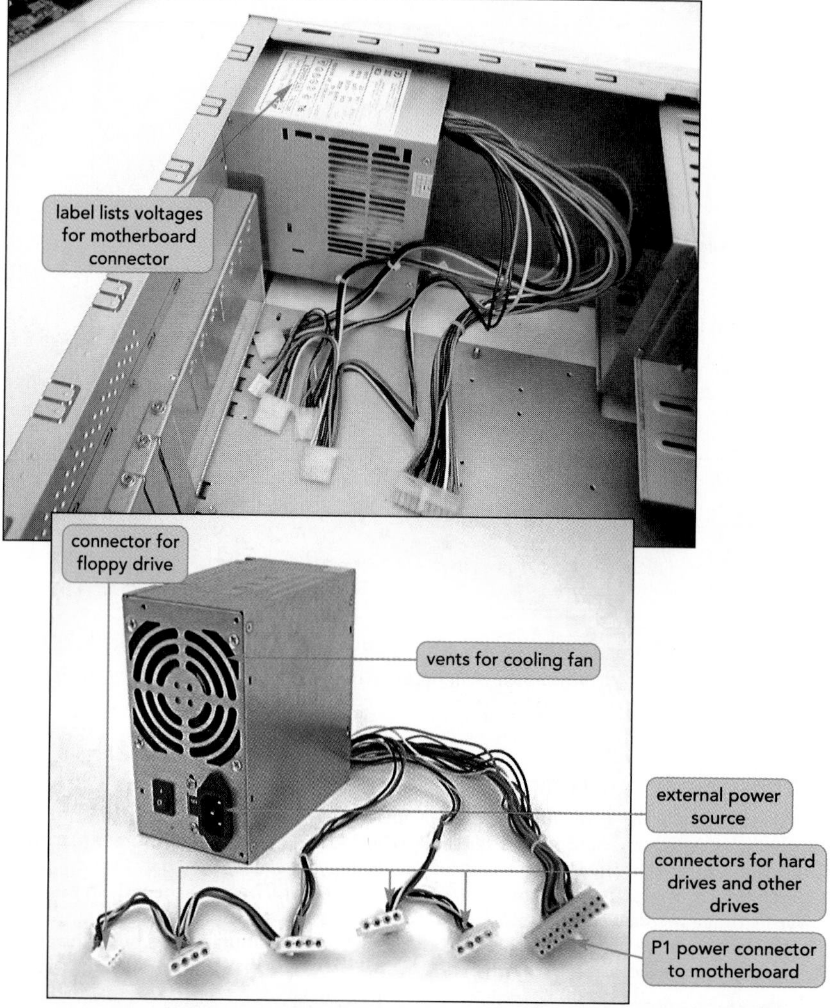

Figure 1-29 The power supply, which usually is near the rear of the computer case, does not actually generate electricity but converts and reduces it to a voltage that the computer can handle.

Every motherboard has one or two connections to receive power from the power supply (Figure 1-30). This power is used by the motherboard, the CPU, and other components that receive their power from ports and expansion slots coming off the motherboard. Secondary storage devices, such as a hard drive, receive power from a power supply. CD-ROM drives, Zip drives, and floppy drives also include connections for power cords, as shown earlier in Figure 1-27 on page 20. In addition, there might be other power connectors on the motherboard to power a small fan that cools the CPU, or to power the CPU itself.

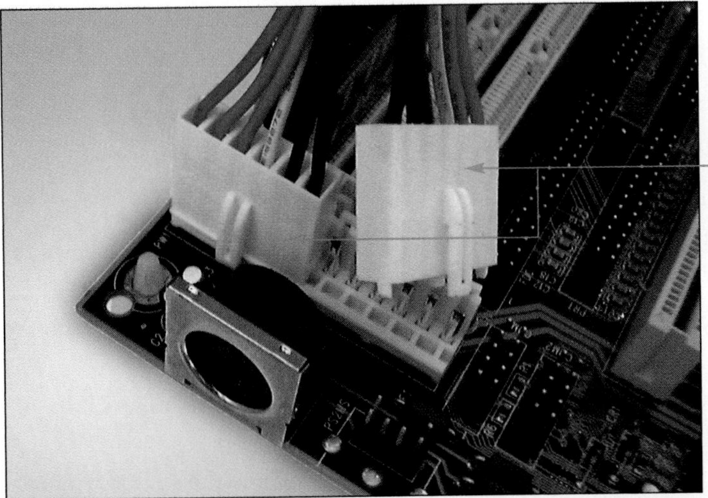

Figure 1-30 The motherboard receives its power from the power supply by way of one or two connections located near the edge of the board.

More About

The Power Supply

To learn more about the electricity coming into your computer and how it is handled by the power supply, visit the Understanding and Troubleshooting Your PC More About Web page (**scsite.com/understanding/more**) and then click Power Supplies below Chapter 1.

Quiz Yourself 1-2

To test your knowledge of motherboard components used for communication among devices and instructions stored on the motherboard and other boards, visit the Understanding and Troubleshooting Your PC Quiz Yourself Web page (**scsite.com/understanding/quiz**). Click Quiz Yourself 2 below Chapter 1.

Protecting Your Computer System

As previously discussed, the devices in your computer receive power from a power supply inside the computer case or via a power cable connected to an electrical outlet. As you work with your computer, it is important to consider ways to protect yourself and your computer system from electricity and other dangers.

Experimenting with your computer without taking basic precautions can injure you, damage the computer, or erase software or data. Following basic safety precautions, such as those listed in Figure 1-31 on the next page, can help prevent such accidents. Computers also are susceptible to changes in electrical current, as well as electrostatic discharge and electromagnetic interference. The following sections review these topics and provide an overview on how to protect your computer and yourself from electricity.

More About

Electronic Components

Understanding the basic electronic components of a PC and how they work is important. To learn more about these components, visit the Understanding and Troubleshooting Your PC More About Web page (**scsite.com/understanding/more**) and then click Electronic Components below Chapter 1.

Safety Precautions for Working on a Computer

- Make notes as you work so that you can go back step-by-step to check your work later if necessary.
- When unpacking hardware or software, remove the packing tape and cellophane from the work area as soon as possible.
- Keep components away from your hair and clothing.
- Keep screws and spacers orderly and in one place, such as a cup or tray.
- Do not stack boards on top of each other; you could dislodge a chip accidentally.
- When handling motherboards and expansion cards, do not touch the chips on the boards.
- Hold expansion cards by the edges. Do not touch any soldered components on a card, and do not touch chips or edge connectors unless it is absolutely necessary. Do not touch a chip with a magnetized screwdriver.
- Do not use a graphite pencil to change DIP switch settings, because graphite is a conductor of electricity, and the graphite can lodge in the switch.
- Always turn off a computer before moving it. A computer's hard drive always spins while it is on, unless it has a sleep mode. Therefore, it is important not to move, kick, or jar a computer while it is running.
- To protect disks, keep them away from magnetic fields, heat, and extreme cold. Do not open the shuttle window on a floppy disk or touch the disk's surface.
- To protect both you and the equipment when working inside a computer, turn off the power, unplug the computer, and always use a ground bracelet. Never touch the inside of a computer that is turned on.
- The power supply and the monitor can hold a dangerous level of electricity even after you turn them off and disconnect them from a power source. Never remove the cover or put your hands inside this equipment unless you know about the hazards of charged capacitors and have been trained to deal with them. *The power supply and monitor contain enough power to kill you, even when they are unplugged.*
- In a classroom environment, after you have reassembled everything, have your instructor check your work before you put the cover back on and power up.

Figure 1-31 Following several general safety precautions can help prevent accidents while you are working on a computer.

Protecting Against Electrostatic Discharge (ESD)

Electrostatic discharge (ESD), commonly known as **static electricity**, is an electrical charge that can build up on the surface of insulating materials, such as clothing or plastic. When two objects with dissimilar electrical charges touch, static electricity passes between them until the dissimilar charges become equal. To see how this works, turn off the lights in a room, scuff your feet on the carpet, and touch another person. If you can feel the charge in your fingers, then you discharged at least 3,000 volts of static electricity. If you hear the discharge, then you released at least 6,000 volts. If you see the discharge, then you released at least 8,000 volts of ESD. A charge of much less than 3,000 volts can damage electronic components. You can touch a chip on an expansion card or motherboard, damage the chip with ESD, and never feel, hear, or see the discharge.

ESD can cause total failure of an electronic component, or it can damage the component so that does not perform well, or works only intermittently. Computer components are designed by manufacturers to avoid ESD hazards when they are enclosed in the computer case. When you are servicing a computer or handling circuit boards, however, the components are far more susceptible to ESD. To protect the computer against ESD, always ground yourself before touching electronic components, including the hard drive, motherboard, expansion cards, processors, and memory modules. Grounding involves connecting yourself directly to the earth or other surface that maintains no electrical charge. You can ground yourself and the computer components using one or more of the following static control devices or methods:

- *Ground bracelet or static strap.* A **ground bracelet** is an antistatic strap you wear around your wrist (Figure 1-32). The wrist strap grounds you by attaching to a grounded conductor such as the computer case or a ground mat. The bracelet also contains a resistor that prevents electricity from harming you. It should be considered essential equipment when working on a computer.
- *Ground mat.* A **ground mat** provides a grounded surface on which to place components with which you are working (Figure 1-33). A ground bracelet also can be connected to a ground mat, some of which come equipped with a cord to plug into a wall outlet. As you work, remember that, if you lift the component off the mat, it is no longer grounded and is susceptible to ESD.
- *Static shielding bag.* A new computer component often is shipped in a static shielding bag (Figure 1-34 on the next page). When working on a PC, you can lay components on these static shielding bags. The bags also can be used to store other devices that are not currently installed in a PC.

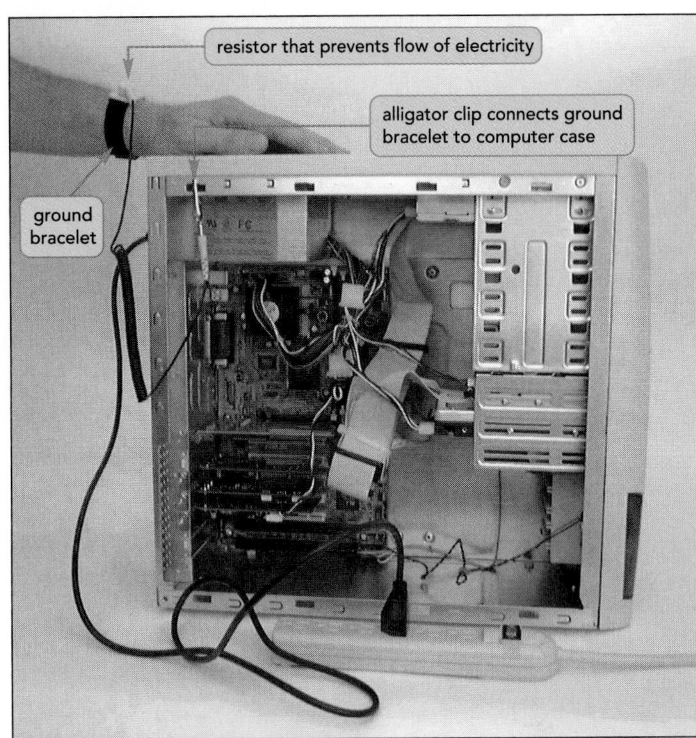

Figure 1-32 A ground bracelet, which protects computer components from ESD, can clip to the side of the computer case and eliminates ESD between you and the case.

The best way to guard against ESD is to use a ground bracelet together with a ground mat. If you are in a situation where you must work without one, however, touch the computer case or the power supply before you touch a component. When passing a chip to another person, ground yourself and then touch the other person before you pass the chip. Leave components inside their protective bags until you are ready to use them. Work on hard floors, not carpet, or use antistatic spray on the carpets. Generally, do not work on a computer if you or the computer has just come from the cold, because the potential for ESD is higher. A monitor also can damage components with ESD. Do not place or store expansion cards on top of or next to a monitor, which can discharge as much as 29,000 volts onto the screen.

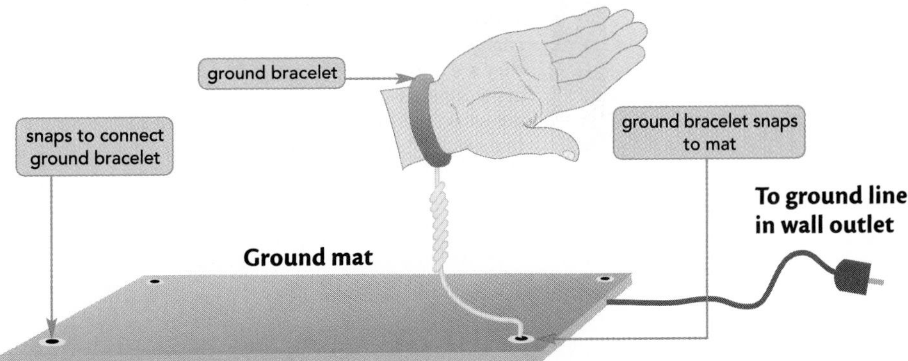

Figure 1-33 A ground bracelet can be connected to a ground mat, which is grounded by the wall outlet.

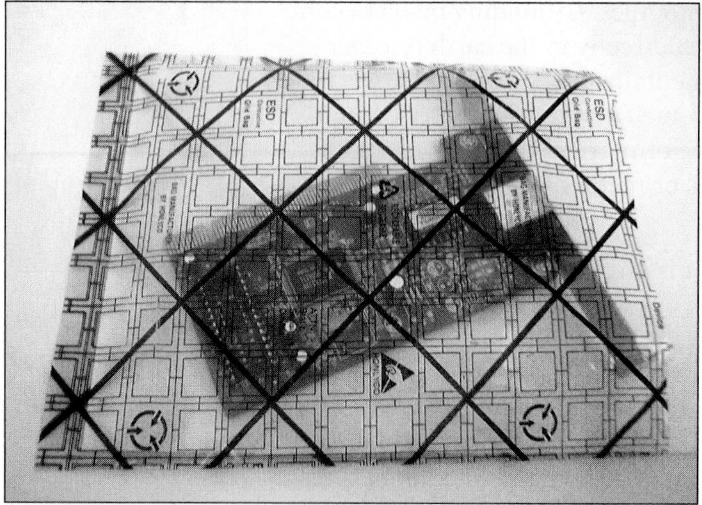

Figure 1-34 Static shielding bags help protect components from ESD.

In addition to using a ground bracelet and ground mat, you also should unplug the power cord to the PC before you work inside the case. Note that two different viewpoints exist as to whether you should unplug the computer or leave it plugged in as you work. One viewpoint says you should leave the computer plugged in (but turned off) as you work on it. With the computer plugged in, any static electricity is discharged along the ground bracelet to the computer's case and then through the power cord into the 3-pronged grounded receptacle of your electrical outlet.

The other viewpoint — the one used in this book — states that you should unplug your computer as you work on it. When you leave the computer plugged in, it is easy to turn it on by accident; forget it is plugged in and insert in an expansion card; or drop a screw on the motherboard — any of which can result in damage to the computer or a serious shock to you. Further, if you happen to touch an exposed area of the power switch inside the case when the computer is plugged in, you may get a shock. Because of these risks, this book directs you to use a ground bracelet and ground mat, as well as to unplug the power cord to the PC before you work inside the case.

FAQ 1-8

Are there times when I should *not* be grounded while working on a PC?

Yes. You do not want to be grounded when working inside a monitor or with a power supply, or with high-voltage equipment such as a laser printer. These devices maintain high electrical charges, even when the power is turned off (enough electricity to stop your heart, even when they are unplugged). You should never open the case on a power supply or monitor unless you are working with an expert or are qualified to do so and know exactly what you are doing. If you are working with a power supply or monitor, be careful not to ground yourself or wear a ground bracelet, because you would provide a path for the voltage to discharge through your body.

Protecting Against EMI (Electromagnetic Interference)

Another phenomenon that can cause electrical problems with computers is **electromagnetic interference** (**EMI**). When electricity flows, it creates an electromagnetic field in a radio frequency range. The internal circuits of personal computers generate electromagnetic fields in the radio frequency, as do many computer monitors. Unfortunately, these emissions from one device can interfere with other devices, causing EMI. EMI can lead to data loss, picture quality degradation on monitors, and other problems with your computer, or problems with radio and TV reception.

One of the reasons computers have a case is to reduce the EMI emitted to other nearby computers. Power supplies are also shielded to prevent them from emitting EMI. To help decrease EMI between computers, always install face plates in empty drive bays or slot covers over empty expansion slots. You also should avoid having computers on the same circuit as high-powered electrical equipment. If intermittent errors persist on a PC, EMI may be the cause. To solve the problem, try moving the computer to a new location a few feet away. If the problem continues, move the computer to a location that uses a different electric circuit.

How can I detect the presence of electromagnetic interference?

Using an inexpensive AM radio is one simple way to detect the presence of EMI. Turn the tuning dial down to a very low-frequency channel range, such as below 500 on the tuning dial. With the radio on, you can hear the static that EMI produces. Try putting the radio next to several electronic devices to detect the EMI they emit. If EMI poses a significant problem, you can use a line conditioner to filter the electrical noise causing the EMI.

Providing Surge Protection and Battery Backup

In addition to protecting your PC against ESD and EMI, you need to consider how the power (known as *AC* or *alternating current*) coming into a computer is regulated. Many devices are available to filter the AC input from a wall socket to a computer and its peripherals, as well as to provide backup power when the AC fails. These devices, installed between the house current and the computer, fall into three general categories: surge suppressors, power conditioners, and uninterruptible power supplies (UPSs). Each device provides protection against temporary voltage surges, called overvoltages or spikes, and temporary voltage reductions caused by brownouts. These devices are measured by the load they support in watts, volt-amperes (VA), or kilovolt-amperes (kVA), each of which is a measure of electricity. These devices also should have the UL (Underwriters Laboratory) logo to indicate that the device has passed certain safety certification standards.

SURGE SUPPRESSORS A **surge suppressor**, also called a **surge protector**, provides a row of power outlets and an on/off switch that protects equipment from overvoltages on AC power lines and telephone lines. Surge suppressors can come as power strips (note that not all power strips have surge protection), wall-mounted units that plug into AC outlets, or consoles designed to sit beneath the monitor on a desktop. Some surge suppressors also provide telephone jacks to protect modems and fax machines from power surges.

More About

Measuring Electricity

Electrical energy has properties that you can measure in various ways, including volts, amps, ohms, and watts. To learn more about these measures, visit the Understanding and Troubleshooting Your PC More About Web page (**scsite.com/understanding/more**) and then click Measuring Electricity below Chapter 1.

More About

UPS Devices

To read more about features and functions of UPS devices, as well as tips on how to purchase a UPS or other power protection device, visit the Understanding and Troubleshooting Your PC More About Web page (**scsite.com/understanding/more**) and then click UPS Devices under Chapter 1.

The most important measure of a surge suppressor is the **let-through voltage**, which is the maximum voltage the surge suppressor allows to reach your equipment. This often is listed as the UL 1449 rating. A surge suppressor rated at 330 volts lets through the least amount of electricity and provides the most protection. Also look for surge suppressors that guarantee protection against damage from lightning, and that reimburse for equipment destroyed while the surge suppressor is in use.

FAQ 1-10

Should I unplug my computer during a power outage?

Whenever a power outage occurs or you expect a lightning storm, the safest approach is to unplug all power cords to the PC, printers, monitors, and other devices. When the power returns, sudden spikes often are accompanied by another brief outage. In addition, once the fuse inside the suppressor blows, a surge suppressor no longer protects equipment from a power surge. Also, if the surge protector is not grounded using a three-prong outlet, it cannot do its job.

POWER CONDITIONERS A **power conditioner** or **line conditioner** provides protection against spikes. It also regulates, or conditions, power by providing continuous voltage during spikes or brownouts. The electricity that powers your computer is vulnerable to power surges or noise, which travel along the power line and enter your system. If this noise is allowed to pass through continually to the electronic components of your computer system, it can cause them to malfunction and ultimately to fail.

A power conditioner, which comes as a small unit, is a good investment if the power in your home, office, or other location suffers excessive spikes and brownouts. However, a device rated under 1 kVA will probably only provide corrections for brownouts, not for spikes. Power conditioners, like surge suppressors, provide no protection against a complete loss of power during a blackout.

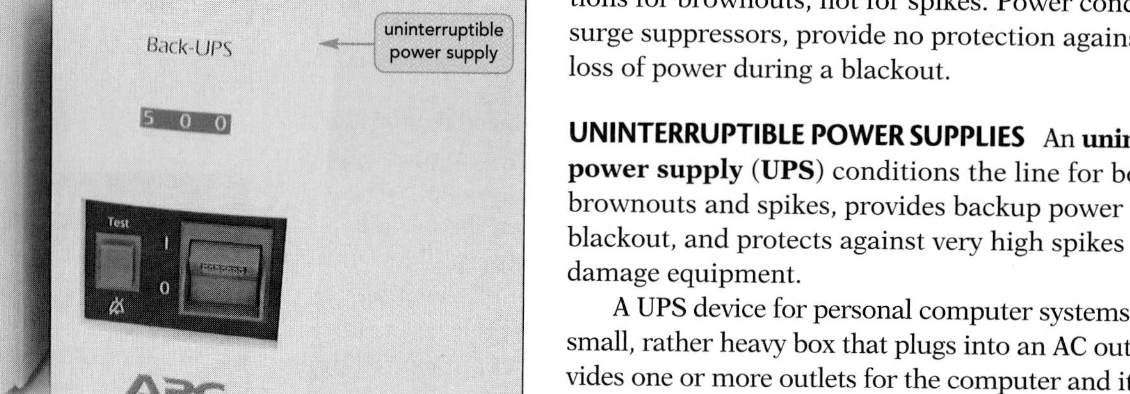

Figure 1-35 A UPS provides backup power if the power fails completely.

UNINTERRUPTIBLE POWER SUPPLIES An **uninterruptible power supply** (**UPS**) conditions the line for both brownouts and spikes, provides backup power during a blackout, and protects against very high spikes that could damage equipment.

A UPS device for personal computer systems typically is a small, rather heavy box that plugs into an AC outlet and provides one or more outlets for the computer and its peripherals (Figure 1-35). It has an on/off switch, requires no maintenance, and is very simple to install. Another type of UPS, called a **smart UPS** or **intelligent UPS**, allows you to manage the UPS using software installed on your computer.

Quiz Yourself 1-3

To test your knowledge of safety precautions to protect you and your computer, visit the Understanding and Troubleshooting Your PC Quiz Yourself Web page (scsite.com/understanding/quiz). Click Quiz Yourself 3 below Chapter 1.

High-Tech Talk

Some Like It Hot (Some Like It Neutral or Ground)

Ever wonder how power comes into your home from the power station miles away? The answer lies in a series of lines that are considered to be hot, neutral, or ground. When AC comes to your house from the power source at the power station, it travels on a hot line. The AC then completes the circuit from your house back to the power source on a neutral line, as shown in Figure 1-36. When the two lines reach your house and enter an electrical device, such as a lamp or radio, electricity flows through the device to complete the circuit between the hot line and the neutral line. The device contains resistors and other electrical components that control the flow of electricity between the hot and neutral lines. The hot source seeks and finds ground by returning to the power station on the neutral line. *Grounding* a line means that the line is connected directly to the earth, so that, in the event of a short, the electricity flows into the earth and not back to the power station.

A *short circuit*, or a *short*, occurs when uncontrolled electricity flows from the hot line to the neutral line or from the hot line to ground. Electricity naturally finds the easiest route to ground. Normally that path is through some device that controls the current flow and then back through the neutral line. If an easier path (one with less resistance) is available, the electricity follows that path. This can cause a short, a sudden increase in flow that can also create a sudden increase in temperature — enough to start a fire and injure both people and equipment. Never put yourself in a position where you are the path of least resistance between the hot line and ground!

A fuse is a component included in a circuit and designed to prevent too much current from flowing through the circuit. A fuse is commonly a wire inside a protective case, which is rated in amps. If too much current begins to flow, the wire gets hot and eventually melts, breaking the circuit and stopping the current flow. Many devices have fuses, which can be easily replaced when damaged.

To prevent the uncontrolled flow of electricity from continuing indefinitely, the neutral line to your house is grounded many times along its way and is grounded at the breaker box where the electricity enters your house. You can look at a three-prong plug and see the three lines: hot, neutral, and ground.

What does this mean for your computer? It is very important that computer components be properly grounded. You never should connect a PC to an outlet or use an extension cord that does not have the third ground plug, because the third line can prevent a short from causing extreme damage. Grounding is a simple step to take in order to keep your computer safe, which does not like it hot — and much prefers ground.

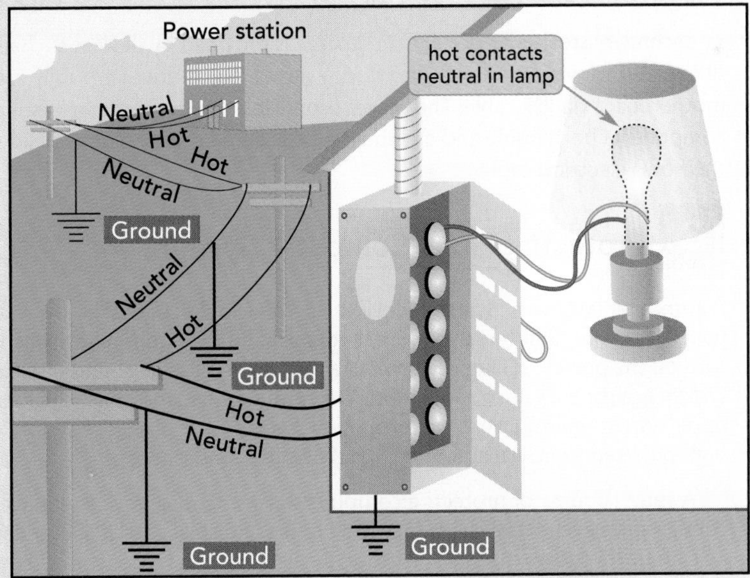

Figure 1-36 Normally hot contacts are neutral to make a closed circuit in the controlled environment of an electrical device such as a lamp. An out-of-control contact is called a short, and the flow of electricity then is diverted to the ground.

CHAPTER SUMMARY

The Chapter Summary reviews the concepts presented in this chapter.

1 Hardware Needs Software to Work

A computer requires both hardware and software to work. The four basic functions of the computer are input, output, processing, and storage of data. Data and instructions are stored in a computer in binary form, which uses only two states for data — on and off, or 1 and 0 — which are called bits. Eight bits equal one byte. Letters and other characters must be assigned a numeric value before they can be manipulated or stored in a computer.

2 Personal Computer Hardware Components

The four most common input/output devices are the printer, monitor, mouse, and keyboard. The most critical component inside the computer case is the motherboard, also called the main board or system board. It contains the most important microchip inside the case, the central processing unit (CPU). Each hardware device needs a method to communicate with the CPU, software to control it, and electricity to power it.

Devices outside the computer case connect to the motherboard through ports on the case. Common ports are serial, parallel, USB, sound, keyboard, and mouse ports. A circuit board inserted in an expansion slot on the motherboard can provide an interface between the motherboard and a peripheral device, or can itself be a peripheral. The chip set on a motherboard controls most activities on the motherboard.

Primary storage, called memory or RAM, is temporary storage the CPU uses to hold data and instructions. RAM is stored on single chips, SIMMs, DIMMs, and RIMMs. ROM BIOS holds the basic software needed to start a PC and load the operating system. Most ROM BIOS chips are flash ROM, meaning that these programs can be updated without exchanging the chip. The CMOS RAM chip on a PC's motherboard stores setup, or configuration, information. This information also can be set by means of jumpers and DIP switches.

The system clock sends continuous pulses over the bus that different components use to control the pace of activity on the motherboard. A motherboard has several buses, including the system bus, the PCI bus, the AGP bus, and the ISA bus. The frequency of activity on a motherboard is measured in megahertz (MHz) or gigahertz (GHz).

Secondary storage or permanent storage is provided by devices such as hard drives, CD-ROM drives, DVD drives, Zip drives, and floppy drives. These drives typically are connected to the motherboard via IDE cable. The power supply inside the computer case supplies electricity to components both inside and outside the case. Some components outside the case get power from their own electrical cable.

3 Protecting Your Computer System

A computer has many electrical devices, so you should take safety precautions to prevent harming yourself or your computer. To protect yourself and the equipment when working inside a computer, turn off the power, unplug the computer, and always use a ground bracelet. To protect a computer system against ESD, use a ground bracelet, ground mat, and static shielding bags. To protect a computer system against EMI, cover expansion slots, do not place the system on the same circuit as high-powered electrical equipment, and use line conditioners.

A surge suppressor protects a computer against damaging spikes in electrical voltage. Line conditioners level the AC to reduce brownouts and spikes. A UPS provides enough power to perform an orderly shutdown during a blackout. Smart UPSs can be controlled remotely using utility software.

KEY TERMS

After reading the chapter, you should know each of these Key Terms.

analog (*2*)
ASCII (American Standard Code for Information Interchange) (*2*)
binary (*2*)
binary number system (*2*)
BIOS (basic input/output system) (*12*)
bit (*2*)
bus (*14*)
byte (*2*)
capacity (*18*)
CD-ROM (*20*)
CD-ROM (compact disc read-only memory) drive (*20*)
central processing unit (CPU) (*3*)
chip (*7*)
chip set (*9*)
circuit board (*7*)
clock speed (*16*)
CMOS BIOS (*12*)
CMOS (complementary metal-oxide semiconductor) (*12*)
CMOS configuration chip (*12*)
CMOS RAM chip (*12*)
CMOS setup chip (*12*)
CMOS setup (*12*)
coding scheme (*2*)
computer case (*3*)
data bus (*14*)
data path size (*15*)
digital (*2*)
DIMM (dual inline memory module) (*10*)
DIP (dual inline package) switch (*13*)
diskette (*21*)
DVD-ROM (*20*)
DVD-ROM (digital versatile disc read-only memory) drive (*20*)
electromagnetic interference (EMI) (*27*)
electrostatic discharge (ESD) (*24*)
expansion card (*8*)
expansion slot (*8*)
FireWire port (*9*)
firmware (*12*)
flash ROM (*12*)
floppy disk (*21*)
floppy drive (*21*)
gigabyte (GB) (*18*)
gigahertz (GHz) (*16*)
ground bracelet (*25*)
ground mat (*25*)
hard copy (*6*)
hard drive (*19*)
hardware (*2*)
hertz (Hz) (*16*)
Integrated Drive Electronics (IDE) (*20*)
integrated circuit (IC) (*7*)
intelligent UPS (*28*)
jumper (*13*)
keyboard (*5*)
kilobyte (KB) (*18*)
let-through voltage (*28*)
line conditioner (*28*)
main board (*8*)
megabyte (MB) (*18*)
megahertz (MHz) (*16*)
memory (*9*)
microchip (*7*)
microprocessor (*3*)
modem card (*18*)
monitor (*6*)
motherboard (*8*)
mouse (*5*)
network card (*17*)
nonvolatile (*10*)
parallel port (*9*)
peripheral device (*4*)
pixels (*6*)
port (*4*)
power conditioner (*28*)
power supply (*22*)
primary storage (*9*)
printer (*6*)
processor (*3*)
program (*2*)
protocol (*14*)
RAM (random access memory) (*10*)
reading (*19*)
resolution (*6*)
RIMM (*10*)
ROM (read-only memory) (*10*)
ROM BIOS chip (*12*)
secondary storage (*18*)
serial port (*8*)
SIMM (single inline memory module) (*10*)
smart UPS (*28*)
software (*2*)
sound card (*17*)
sound port (*9*)
startup BIOS (*12*)
static electricity (*24*)
storage device (*19*)
storage medium (*18*)
surge protector (*27*)
surge suppressor (*27*)
system BIOS (*12*)
system board (*8*)
system bus (*15*)
system clock (*15*)
trace (*14*)
uninterruptible power supply (UPS) (*28*)
USB (universal serial bus) port (*9*)
video card (*17*)
volatile (*10*)
writing (*19*)
Zip disk (*20*)
Zip drive (*20*)

LEARN IT ONLINE

Reinforce your understanding of the chapter concepts and terms with the Learn It Online exercises.

Instructions: To complete the Learn It Online exercises, start your browser, click the Address bar, and then enter the Web address **scsite.com/understanding/learn.** When the Understanding and Troubleshooting your PC Learn It Online page is displayed, follow the instructions in the exercises below. Each exercise has instructions for printing your results, either for your own records or for submission to your instructor.

1 Chapter Reinforcement True/False, Multiple Choice, and Short Answer

Below Chapter 1, click the Chapter Reinforcement link. Print the quiz by clicking Print on the File menu for each page. Answer each question.

2 Flash Cards

Below Chapter 1, click the Flash Cards link and read the instructions. Type 20 (or a number specified by your instructor) in the Number of playing cards text box, type your name in the Enter your Name text box, and then click the Flip Card button. When the flash card is displayed, read the question and then click the ANSWER box arrow to select an answer. Flip through and answer all the Flash Cards. If your score is 15 (75%) correct or greater, click Print on the File menu to print your results. If your score is less than 15 (75%) correct, then redo this exercise by clicking the Replay button.

3 Practice Test

Below Chapter 1, click the Practice Test link. Answer each question, enter your first and last name at the bottom of the page, and then click the Grade Test button. When the graded practice test is displayed on your screen, click Print on the File menu to print a hard copy. Continue to take practice tests until you score 80% or better.

4 Who Wants To Be a Computer Genius?

Below Chapter 1, click the Computer Genius link. Read the instructions, enter your first and last name at the bottom of the page, and then click the PLAY button. When your score is displayed, click the PRINT RESULTS link to print a hard copy.

5 Wheel of Terms

Below Chapter 1, click the Wheel of Terms link. Read the instructions, and then enter your first and last name and your school name. Click the PLAY button. When your score is displayed, right-click the score and then click Print on the shortcut menu to print a hard copy.

6 Crossword Puzzle Challenge

Below Chapter 1, click the Crossword Puzzle Challenge link. Read the instructions, and then enter your first and last name. Click the SUBMIT button. Work the crossword puzzle. When you are finished, click the Submit button. When the crossword puzzle is redisplayed, click the Print Puzzle button to print a hard copy.

Multiple Choice

Select the best answer.

1. Which of these is not required by an electronic hardware device to function properly?
   a. method for the CPU to communicate with the device
   b. software to instruct and control the device
   c. flash ROM to store instructions permanently
   d. electricity to power the device
2. How many bits are in a byte?
   a. 16
   b. 8
   c. 4
   d. 2
3. Which of the following does not necessarily protect your computer from electrical spikes?
   a. surge conditioner
   b. UPS
   c. surge suppressor
   d. power conditioner
4. Which of these ports does not come directly off the motherboard to be used by external devices?
   a. serial port
   b. jumper port
   c. parallel port
   d. USB port
5. Which of these is not a way that configuration information can be stored on a motherboard?
   a. traces
   b. jumpers
   c. CMOS RAM
   d. switches

Fill in the Blank

Write the word or phrase to fill in the blank in each of the following questions.

1. Input, processing, output, and ________ are the four primary functions of hardware.
2. The computer could not do its job without the assistance of the ________, a group of microchips on the motherboard that control the flow of data and instructions to and from the CPU.
3. The motherboard also is referred to as the main board or ________.
4. A measure called ________ indicates the maximum voltage the surge suppressor allows to reach your equipment.
5. ROM BIOS chips that can be upgraded without replacing the chips are called ________.
6. ________ is a standard that defines how the motherboard communicates with secondary storage devices.
7. ________, commonly known as static electricity, is an electrical charge at rest which can build up on the surface of insulating materials.

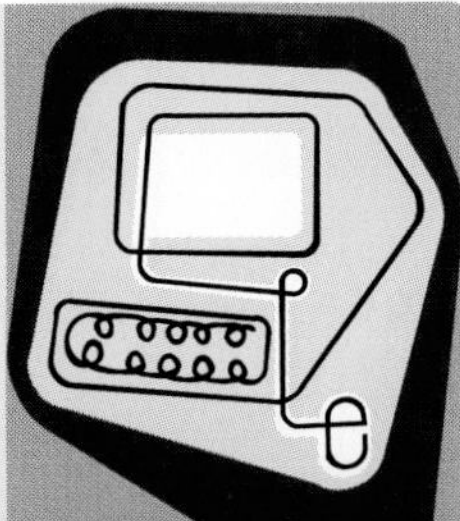

CHAPTER EXERCISES

Complete the Chapter Exercises to solidify what you learned in the chapter.

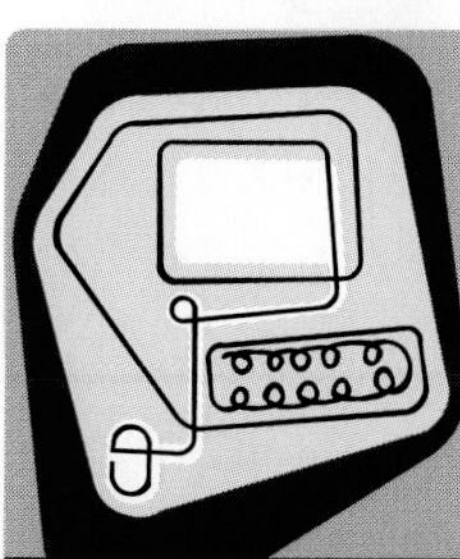

CHAPTER EXERCISES

Complete the Chapter Exercises to solidify what you learned in the chapter.

8. A ________ is an antistatic strap you wear around your wrist.
9. A ________ is a board that holds microchips and the circuitry that connects these chips.
10. Devices that the CPU communicates with that are not directly on the motherboard are called ________ devices.

Matching Terms

Match the terms with their definitions.

________	1. volatile	a.	component on the motherboard used primarily for processing
________	2. hertz (Hz)	b.	refers to temporary memory that needs a constant electrical charge to hold data
________	3. bit	c.	unit of measurement for clock speed (frequency)
________	4. motherboard	d.	a 0 or 1 used by the binary number system
________	5. UPS	e.	basic input/output system; firmware that controls much of a computer's input and output functions
________	6. BIOS	f.	provides a grounded surface on which to work
________	7. power supply	g.	provides backup power in the event that the power fails completely during a blackout.
________	8. data bus	h.	largest and most important circuit board in a computer
________	9. ground mat	i.	box inside the computer case that supplies power to the motherboard and other devices
________	10. CPU	j.	lines on the CPU used to send and receive data

Short Answer Questions

Write a brief answer to each of the following questions.

1. Based on what you have learned in this chapter, when working on a word processing document, why is it important to save your work often? Explain your answer using the two terms, primary storage and secondary storage.
2. Why do you think the trend is to store configuration information on a motherboard in CMOS setup, rather than by using jumpers or switches?
3. Why would it be difficult to install four hard drives, one CD-ROM drive, and one DVD drive in a single system?
4. What is the purpose of an expansion slot on a motherboard?
5. What are some important safety precautions to take when working on a computer system?

APPLY YOUR KNOWLEDGE

Check your understanding of the chapter with the hands-on Apply Your Knowledge exercises.

1 Identifying Motherboard Components

Being able to recognize motherboard components and to identify these components in documentation is very important. Copy the diagram in Figure 1-37 and label as many of the components on the diagram as you can, using the photograph in Figure 1-8 on page 8 and other photographs in the chapter.

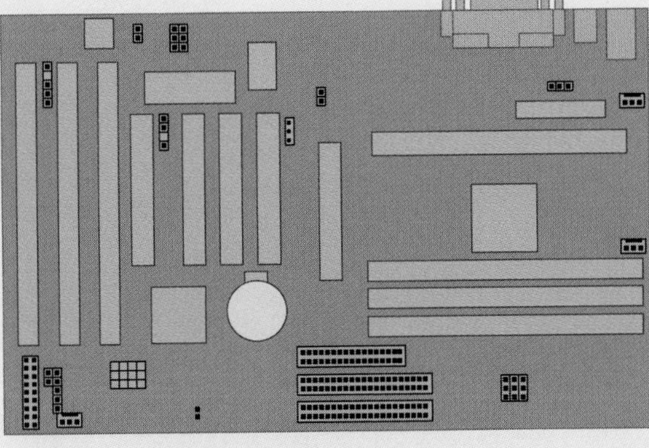

Figure 1-37

2 Identifying Ports on a Computer

Look at the back of your home or lab computer and make a diagram showing the ports. Label all the ports in the diagram and note which ones are used and which are not used.

3 Research on the Internet

The Internet is an incredibly rich source of information about computer hardware and software. Answer these questions, using the Internet as your source:

1. What is the frequency (measured in Hz) of the fastest CPU for a desktop computer that you can find advertised on the Web? Print the Web page showing the CPU and its frequency.
2. Print a Web page advertising a motherboard. What is the frequency of the system bus?
3. Print a Web page advertising computer memory. How much RAM is on one module?
4. Print the Web page for a surge suppressor. Does it provide an acceptable level of protection for your system, based on the let-through voltage?

4 Researching a UPS for Your Computer System

A UPS used with a personal computer is designed as a standby device, an inline device, or a line-interactive device (which combines features of the first two). Several variations of these three types of UPS devices are on the market at widely varying prices. Using print advertisements, visits to a local computer store, or Web sites, research and report on the features and prices of a UPS. Include the following information in your report:

- Standby UPS, inline UPS, or line interactive UPS
- Volt-amperes (VA) or wattage supported
- Length of time the power is sustained during total blackout
- Line-conditioning features
- Surge suppressor present or not present
- Number of power outlets (often listed as 5-15R output receptacles)
- Other key features
- Guarantees (for example, against power surges, lightning strikes)
- Brand name, model, vendor, and price of the device

intel
pentium 4

CHAPTER 2

How Hardware and Software Work Together

Introduction

In this chapter, you will learn about the functions of software called an operating system (OS) and how the OS controls hardware devices inside the computer. You also will learn about different OSs and how they provide an interface for users and applications to command and use hardware. Finally, the chapter reviews what happens when you first start your computer and the hardware boots up to the point where the operating system is loaded, as well as how to troubleshoot the boot process.

OBJECTIVES

In this chapter, you will learn:

1. About operating systems and their key functions
2. How system resources help hardware and software communicate
3. About the steps in the boot process
4. How to use Device Manager and System Information to examine the system

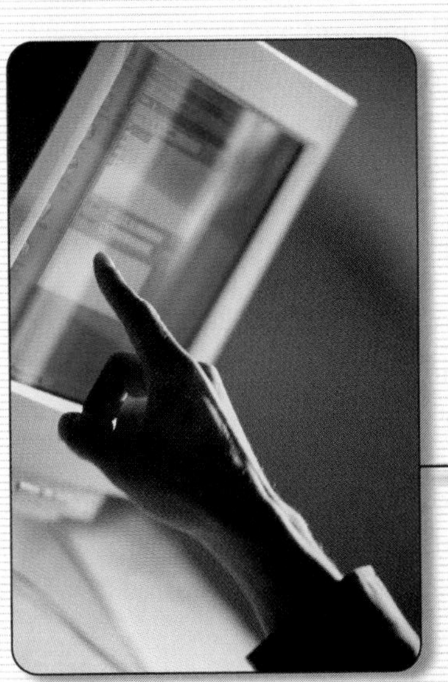

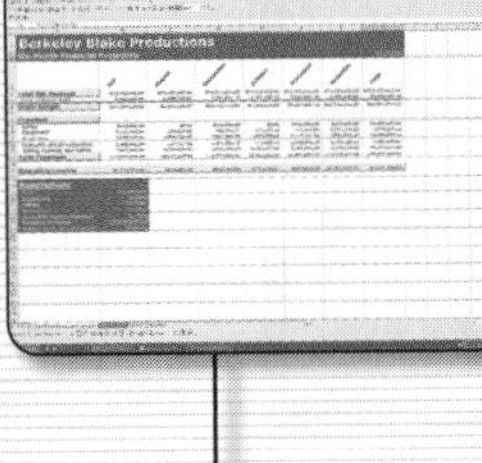

Up for Discussion

Shortly after Sunrise Computers opened on Wednesday, Scott Cormier stopped by the store to ask for your recommendations on buying a new printer. When you asked what type of printer he had in mind, he responded simply, "One that works with Windows XP." Scott then told you that he's perfectly happy with his older model DeskWriter printer. When he got a computer running Windows XP, however, he could not make the printer work with the new computer. When he couldn't determine the source of the problem, Scott called the manufacturer, who informed him that Windows XP does not have a driver to support his older model printer, nor did they intend to develop a driver for it. Scott noted that, although he doesn't fully understand what drivers are or what they do, he did clearly understand one thing: if he wanted to print using his new Windows XP machine, he needed to purchase a new printer.

After talking with him about his printing needs, you show him a few printers that have the required features and are in his price range. Scott particularly likes a new color ink-jet printer that will allow him to print a range of documents, as well as photos. Still feeling frustrated from his experience with his last printer, Scott asks you how to tell if Windows XP has built-in drivers to support the printer or if the manufacturer can provide drivers that work with Windows XP.

Questions:

- What are device drivers and what purpose do they serve?
- How can you learn more about whether Windows XP includes drivers for a hardware device and/or if a device will run under Windows XP?
- How can you obtain and install updated drivers for a device?

Introducing Operating Systems

An **operating system** (**OS**) is software that contains instructions that coordinate all the activities among computer hardware resources. An operating system provides an interface for users; stores, retrieves, and manipulates files; runs applications; and manages hardware. For example, operating systems recognize input from the keyboard, keep track of files on the hard disk, and control disk drives. In general, an operating system acts as the middleman between applications and hardware (Figure 2-1). A computer must have an operating system installed to run other programs and to allow a user to interact with the computer.

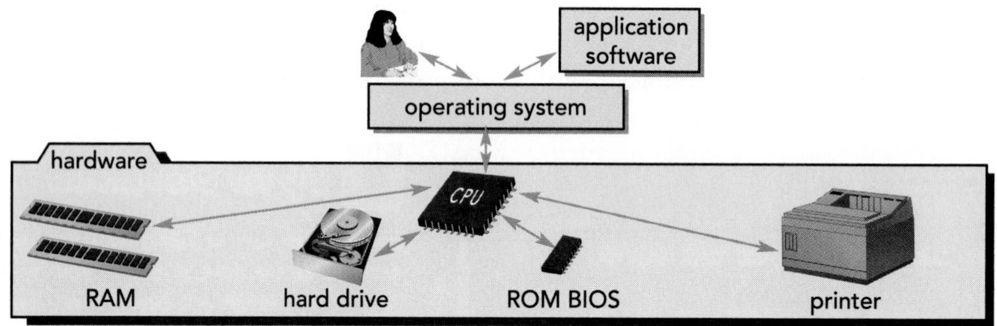

Figure 2-1 Users and applications depend on the OS to relate to all hardware components.

Operating System Components

Every operating system has two main internal components: the shell and the kernel (Figure 2-2). A **shell** is the portion of the OS that relates to the user and to applications. The shell provides a command, menu, or icon interface to the user using various interface tools such as Windows Explorer, the Control Panel, or My Computer. The **kernel**, which is the core of an operating system, is the part that loads when you first turn on your computer. The kernel stays in memory while the computer is running to help manage memory, maintain the computer clock, start applications, and assign resources such as devices, programs, data, and information.

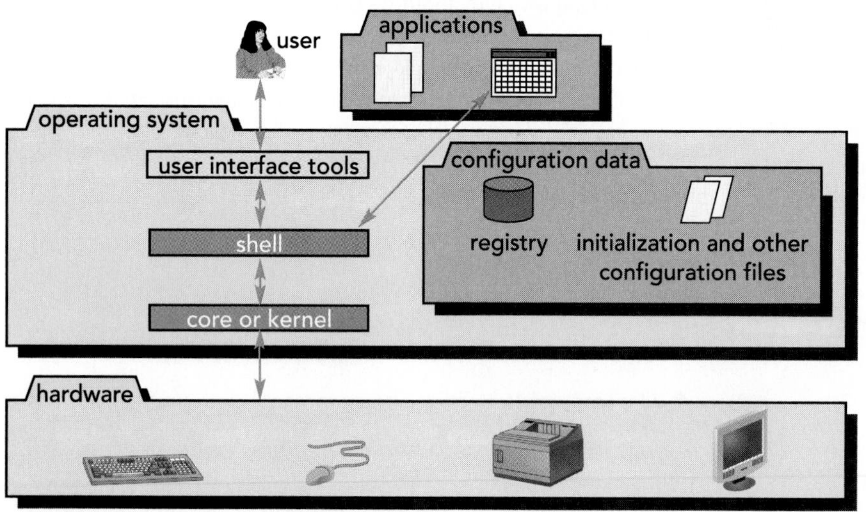

Figure 2-2 Inside an operating system, different components perform various functions.

An operating system also needs a place to keep hardware and software configuration information, user preferences, and application settings that are used when the OS is first loaded. The Windows operating system uses a database called the **registry** to store most of this configuration information. In addition, some data is kept in text files called

initialization files, which often have an .ini or .inf file extension. (See FAQ 2-3 on page 42 for more on file extensions.)

FAQ 2-1

Why is the kernel described as memory resident?

Because the kernel stays in memory while the computer is running, it is considered to be *memory resident.* Other parts of the operating system, considered to be *nonresident,* are stored in secondary storage on the hard disk until they are needed.

Types of Operating Systems

Several types of operating systems are available today, including DOS, Windows, Mac OS, Unix, Linux, and OS/2. Each operating system is designed to support different types of hardware systems and user needs.

- *DOS.* **DOS (Disk Operating System)** was the first OS used for IBM and IBM-compatible computers. DOS was used widely after it was developed in the early 1980s by Microsoft. It is used significantly less today, because it uses a command-line interface, where the user has to enter specific commands, instead of the graphical user interface of the Windows and Macintosh operating systems. Most Windows operating systems continue to support DOS (or a DOS-like user interface) to allow users to execute commands and complete specific tasks.
- *Windows.* As shown in Figure 2-3 on the next page, many versions of **Windows** operating systems have been developed by Microsoft over the past few decades. Each version was designed to provide additional features for specific users, whether for personal use or in business settings. Windows XP is the most recent version of Windows designed for end users, while Windows Server 2003 is designed to manage and maintain a network.
- *Unix.* **Unix** is a popular OS used to manage networks, to support multiple users, to handle a high volume of transactions, and to support applications used on the Internet. Unix is unique in that it is not owned by a leading computer company. Instead, it is **open source**, which means the source code for the program is made available for use or modification by any user or developer.
- *Linux.* **Linux** is a scaled-down version of Unix that was designed to provide a low-cost but efficient and secure operating system for personal computer users. Linux also is used for server applications, because it is considered to be a very efficient and fast-performing system. In its basic form, Linux is free and open source, so that users and developers can modify the code. Linux also is available in commercial versions, such as Red Hat, LindowsOS, Slackware, and others.
- *OS/2.* **OS/2**, developed by IBM and Microsoft, is less common for home desktop PCs, but is used in certain types of networks. In addition to running DOS and programs written specifically for OS/2, the operating system also runs most Windows programs.
- *Mac OS.* **Mac OS** is available only for Apple Macintosh computers. The Mac OS long has been the model for ease of use and good user interface design. Newer versions also provide features such as built-in network support and strong multimedia capabilities. Macintosh computers, often referred to as just Macs, often are used by people working with graphics applications, by students in educational settings, and by home users.

Windows Version	Description
Windows 3x	Early Windows versions, including Windows 3.1 and Windows 3.11 (collectively referred to as Windows 3x) provided a graphical interface to what was essentially still a DOS system.
Windows 9x	The Windows 9x operating systems — Windows 95, Windows 98, and Windows Me (Millennium Edition) — are true operating systems (unlike the Windows 3x operating environment). The Windows 9x OSs rely on a DOS core, while providing a user-friendly interface and advanced features such as Plug and Play, more integrated Internet capabilities, and support for hardware devices such as DVDs.
Windows NT	Windows NT comes in two versions: Windows NT Workstation for end-user computers and Windows NT Server to manage and maintain a network. Windows NT contains more advanced security features, network support, and user administration features. Windows NT was designed primarily for businesses and technical users.
Windows 2000	An upgrade of Windows NT, Windows 2000 provides additional features including greater network support and increased stability. Several versions of Windows 2000 are available: Windows 2000 Professional is popular as an OS for business use, while Windows 2000 Server, Windows 2000 Advanced Server, and Windows 2000 Datacenter Server are network operating systems.
Windows XP	Windows XP combines the strengths of Windows 2000 with the user-friendly features of Windows 98 and Windows Me — for the first time using the same code for the consumer and corporate operating systems. Windows XP provides an upgraded user interface, support for multiple users, better performance to help programs run faster, and more support for multimedia such as audio and video. Windows XP is available in five versions: Professional, Home Edition, Media Center Edition, Tablet PC Edition, and 64-Bit Edition.
Windows Server 2003	Windows Server 2003 is a network operating system with additional features for managing and maintaining a network. Windows Server 2003 provides increased security, enhanced file and print server support, support for remote access, and more. Windows Server 2003 comes in several versions including a Standard Edition, Enterprise Edition, Datacenter Edition, Web Edition, and Small Business Server 2003.

Figure 2-3 Many versions of the Windows operating systems have been developed by Microsoft over the past few decades. Each version was designed to provide additional features for specific users, including home or business users.

The Windows operating system is the operating system most widely used on today's personal computers. Although this book focuses on managing and supporting Windows XP, information about other versions of Windows are included where appropriate.

What an Operating System Does

Regardless of the specific type of operating system, the OS performs key functions such as providing a user interface, managing files and folders, running applications, and managing hardware. The following sections review each of these functions in detail.

An OS Provides a User Interface

When a PC first is turned on, the operating system is loaded. After the OS is in control, it either automatically executes a program or waits for its next instruction from a user. If you are working with the OS, you see an interface on the monitor screen. This interface can be a command-line interface, a menu-driven interface, or a graphical user interface.

COMMAND-LINE INTERFACES With a **command-line interface**, you type commands or press specific keys to enter data and commands to instruct the OS to perform operations (Figure 2-4a). When working with a command-line interface, such as DOS, the set of commands entered to provide instructions is called the command language. Network administrators and other users familiar with these commands use a command-line interface to configure devices, manage system resources, and troubleshoot network connections.

(a) command-line interface

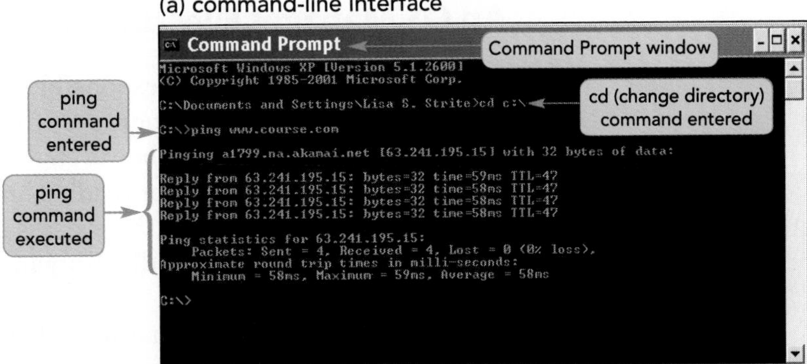

(b) graphical user interface (GUI)

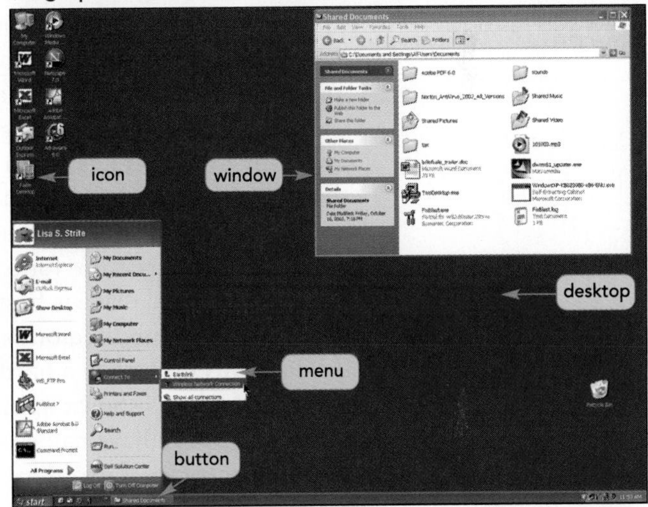

Figure 2-4 A command-line interface and a graphical user interface (GUI).

MENU-DRIVEN INTERFACES A **menu-driven interface** provides menus as a way to enter data and commands. Menu-driven interfaces are easier to learn than command-line interfaces because users do not have to learn the command language used to enter commands. Instead, they just have to select functions from a menu.

GRAPHICAL USER INTERFACES Most of today's operating systems use a graphical user interface. With a **graphical user interface** or **GUI** (pronounced *goo-ee*), you issue commands by selecting icons, buttons, windows, or other graphical objects on screen. Graphical user interfaces also incorporate menus, as shown in Figure 2-4b. When an operating system is started, the initial screen that appears with menus, commands, and icons is called the **desktop**.

FAQ 2-2

Does a graphical user interface, such as Windows XP, provide access to a command-line interface?

Windows XP provides a command-line interface in the form of the Command Prompt window. To access the Command Prompt window using Windows XP, click the Start button on the Windows taskbar, point to All Programs, point to Accessories, and then click Command Prompt. Appendix B provides additional detail on using the Command Prompt window to perform tasks.

An OS Manages Files and Folders

An operating system is responsible for storing and organizing the files on a secondary storage medium such as a CD-ROM, floppy disk, or hard disk. Before any files can be stored on a disk, however, the disk must be formatted. **Formatting** is a process of preparing a disk for reading and writing by defining how files will be organized on the disk. While the process of formatting a disk is covered in detail in Chapter 5, some aspects of a disk's organization are important to understanding how formatting works.

For example, during formatting, a hard disk can be partitioned. **Partitioning** is the process of logically dividing the hard disk into segments, which are called partitions. Partitioning allows you to organize a hard disk into partitions for different users or programs and lets you run multiple operating systems on a single computer. You also can keep the entire hard disk as one partition. After a disk partition has been formatted, it is referred to as a **volume** or **logical drive**.

The process of formatting a disk or partition places a file system on the drive. An operating system relies on an organizational method called a **file system** to use the space available on a disk to store and retrieve files and to store information about the disk's directory, or folder, structure.

The folder structure for a disk is defined during the formatting process. In general, when a hard drive is first installed and formatted, a single **directory table**, or list of files and subdirectories, is created on the drive. This directory table is called the **root directory**. On a hard drive, the root directory typically is found on drive C and labeled C:. As shown in Figure 2-5, this root directory can hold files or other directories, which can have names such as C:\Tools. These directories, called **subdirectories**, **child directories**, or **folders**, can, in turn, have other subdirectories. The hard disk thus is organized at several levels, with the operating system managing the files and folders stored on the drive at all levels (Figure 2-6).

FAQ 2-3

What is a path and how does it relate to a directory?

When you refer to the drive and directories that point to the location of the file — for example, C:\wp\data\myfile.txt — the drive and directories are called the **path**. The first part of the file before the period is called the **filename** (myfile); the part after the period is called the **file extension** (txt). The file extension identifies the file type, such as .doc for Microsoft Word document files or .xls for Microsoft Excel spreadsheet files. In Windows and DOS, the file extension always has three or fewer characters.

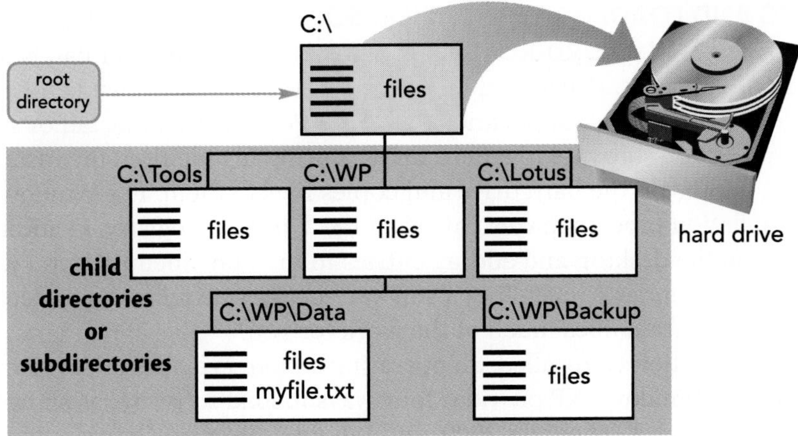

Figure 2-5 A hard drive is organized into groups of files stored in directories. The first directory is called the root directory. All directories can have child directories or subdirectories. In Windows, a directory is called a folder.

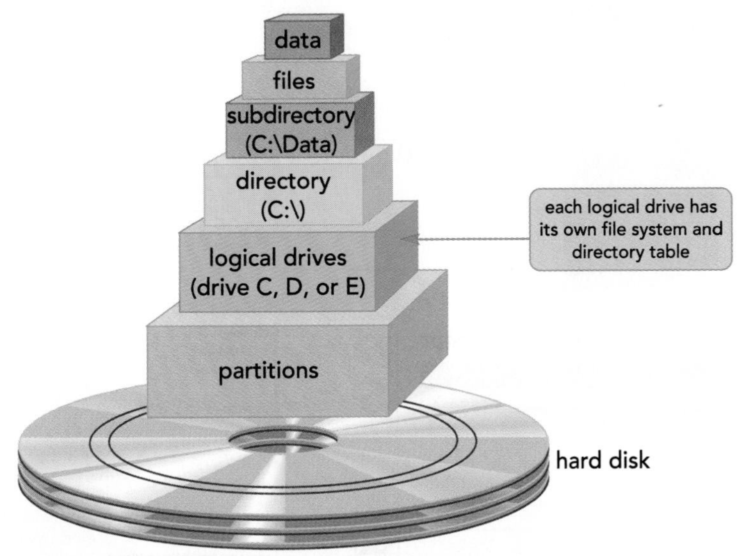

Figure 2-6 A hard drive is divided and organized at several levels.

More About

File Systems

To learn more about file systems and how data is organized on a hard disk, visit the Understanding and Troubleshooting Your PC More About Web page (**scsite.com/understanding/more**) and then click File Systems below Chapter 2.

An OS Manages Applications

An operating system is responsible for managing all other software on the PC, including installing and running applications. An application depends on an OS to provide access to hardware resources, manage its data in memory and in secondary storage, and perform many other background tasks. For example, consider a situation in which Windows XP loads and executes an application. The application cannot run or even load itself without Windows XP, much as a document cannot be edited without a word processing program. Windows XP stays available to the application for the entire time the application is running. The application passes certain functions to Windows XP, such as reading from a CD-ROM or printing.

INSTALLING AND LOADING APPLICATION SOFTWARE Application software typically is distributed on DVD-ROMs, CD-ROMs, or floppy disks or can be downloaded from the Internet. Because application software usually must be installed on a hard drive in order to run, application software comes with an install or setup program that installs the software to a hard drive. During installation, the install program creates folders on the hard drive and copies files to them. For Windows, the software installation process makes entries in the Windows registry, in addition to placing icons on the desktop and adding entries to the Start menu. As you will learn in more detail in Chapter 8, installing a software package usually is simple, because the installation program does much of the work for you.

Once an application is installed, an operating system provides a way to execute, or load, software. Windows XP provides four ways to load software, as shown in Figure 2-7. Windows NT, Windows 2000, and Windows 9x also allow you to execute software using the same four methods, following similar steps.

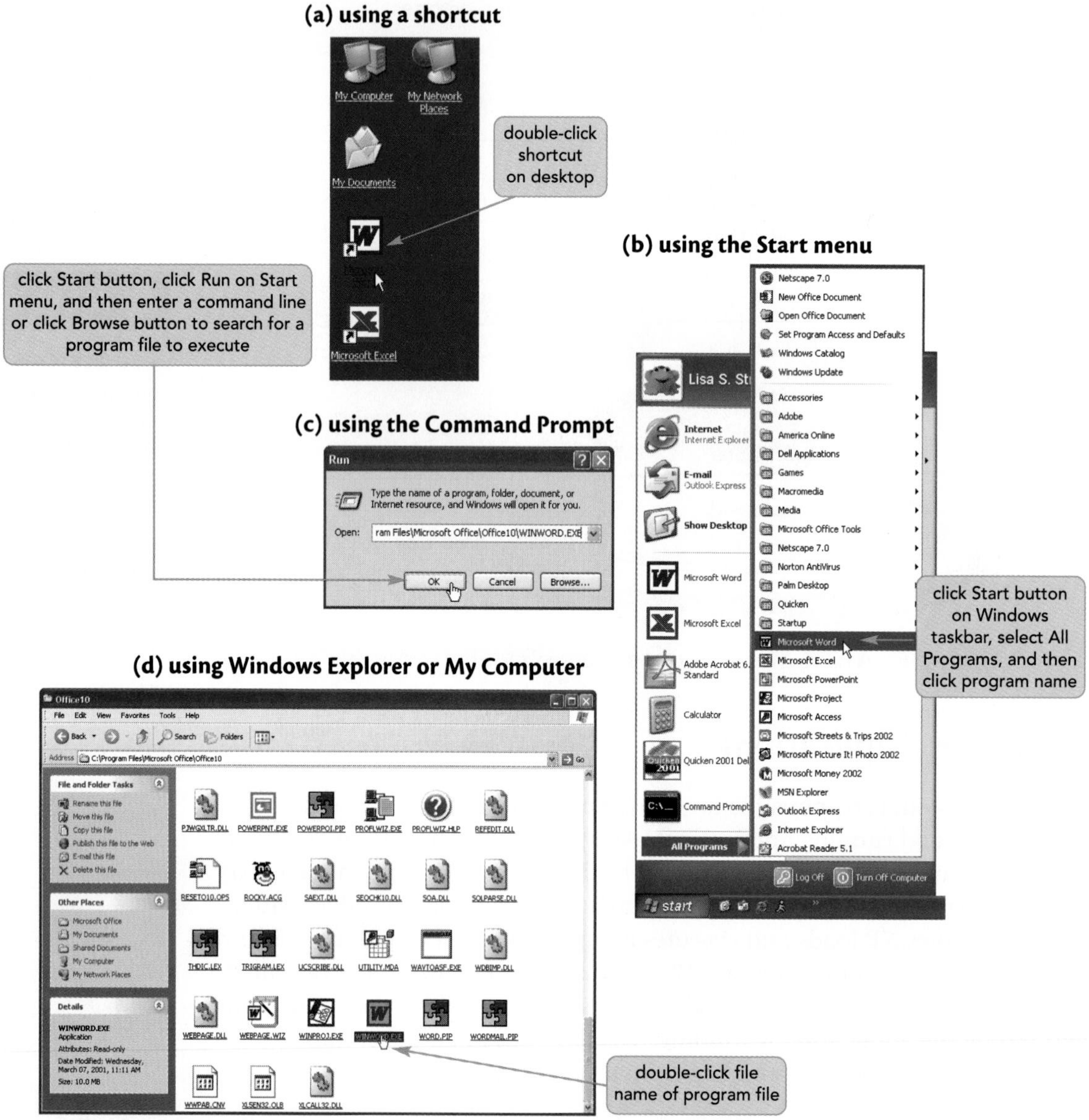

(a) using a shortcut

double-click shortcut on desktop

(b) using the Start menu

click Start button on Windows taskbar, select All Programs, and then click program name

(c) using the Command Prompt

click Start button, click Run on Start menu, and then enter a command line or click Browse button to search for a program file to execute

(d) using Windows Explorer or My Computer

double-click file name of program file

Figure 2-7 Once an application is installed, an operating system provides a way to execute, or load, software. For example, Windows XP provides four ways to execute software.

FAQ 2-4

How does a shortcut work to execute an application?

A shortcut links to the command line used to execute an application, open a file, or complete another task. To view the command line associated with a shortcut icon, right-click the shortcut icon for a program such as Outlook Express and then click Properties on the shortcut menu. The Target text box in the Properties dialog box shows the path or command line that the shortcut represents. For Outlook Express, for example, the shortcut target is *C:\Program Files\Outlook Express\MSIMN.EXE,* which shows the path to *MSIMN.exe,* the executable file used to start Outlook Express.

FAQ 2-5

Can I install the same application on my PC and my Mac?

An application written to work with one OS, such as Windows XP, does not necessarily work with another, such as the Mac OS (with some exceptions). Further, an application written for Windows 95 likely will not run under Windows XP. To take full advantage of an operating system's power and an application's power, you should buy application software written specifically for your OS.

More About

Real Mode and Protected Mode

To learn more about real mode and protected mode, visit the Understanding and Troubleshooting Your PC More About Web page (**scsite.com/understanding/more**) and then click Real Mode and Protected Mode below Chapter 2.

HANDLING MULTIPLE PROGRAMS Some operating systems only allow one program to run at a time, while others allow multiple programs to run at once. A **single tasking** operating system allows only one program to run at a time. For example, if you were working on a spreadsheet and then wanted to check your e-mail, you would have to close the spreadsheet program before starting the e-mail program. DOS, which was used on older PCs, is a single tasking operating system. Today, PDAs and other small computing devices use single tasking operating systems, while most PCs use a multitasking operating system.

A **multitasking** operating system allows you to work with two or more programs that reside in memory at the same time. With a multitasking operating system, you could leave the spreadsheet program running while you launch your e-mail program. When a computer is running multiple programs concurrently, one program is in the foreground, while the other programs are in the background. The program in the *foreground* is the one actively in use; the other programs that are running but not in use are in the *background* (Figure 2-8).

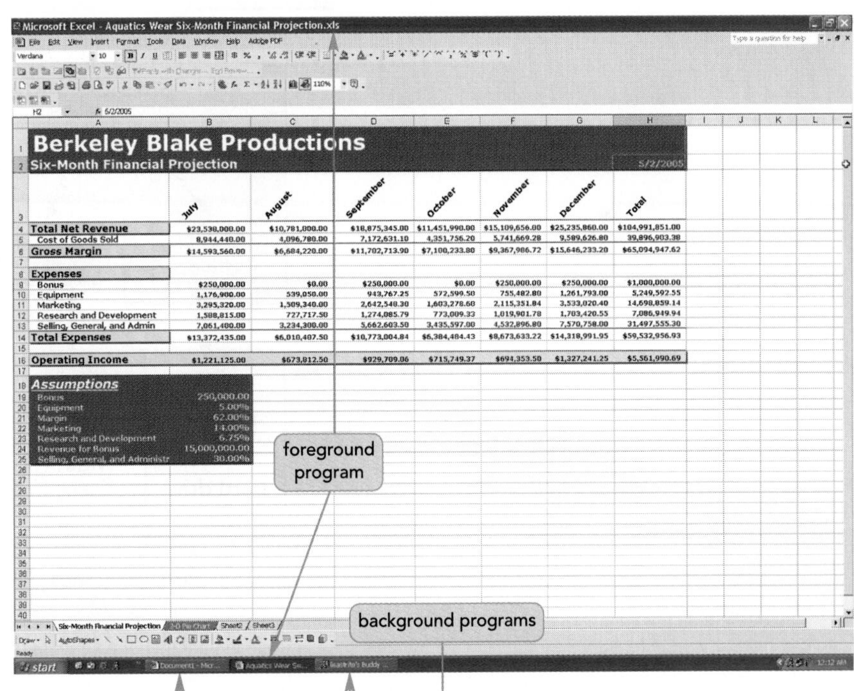

Figure 2-8 Windows XP allows you to run multiple programs at the same.

For an operating system to support multitasking, the CPU must be running in protected mode. In **protected mode**, the CPU processes 32 bits of data at one time, and more than one program can run at the same time. In **real mode**, by contrast, the CPU processes 16 bits of data at one time. In real mode, an application has complete access to all hardware resources, but in protected mode, the OS controls how an application can access hardware using preemptive multitasking. With **preemptive multitasking**, the operating system allots CPU time to an application for a specified period, and then preempts the processing to give the CPU to another application. Here lies the meaning behind the two terms, real and protected. Real mode means that the software has real access to the hardware; protected mode means that more than one program can be running, and each one is protected from other programs accessing its hardware resources.

An OS Manages Hardware

An operating system also is responsible for communicating with hardware, but the OS does not relate directly to the hardware. Rather, the OS uses device drivers or the BIOS to interface with hardware (Figure 2-9).

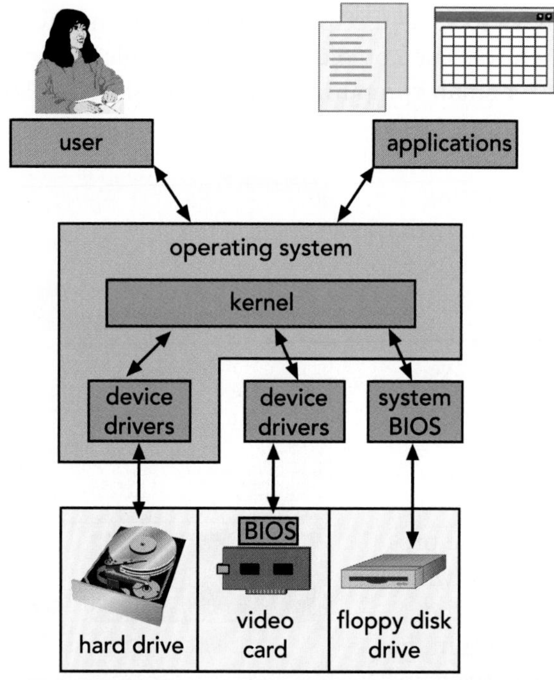

Figure 2-9 An OS relates to hardware devices such as a hard drive, video card, or DVD-ROM drive, by way of BIOS and device drivers.

HOW AN OS USES DEVICE DRIVERS **Device drivers** are small programs stored on the hard drive that tell the computer how to communicate with a specific device such as a printer, network card, or modem. Device drivers are software designed to interface with specific hardware devices — essentially serving as a translator between the device that it controls and programs that use the device. For example, a printer driver translates the commands sent by the printer to something more understandable by the operating system. A device driver is installed when the OS first is installed or when new hardware is added to a system, as shown in Figure 2-10. An operating system provides some device drivers. The manufacturer of a specific hardware device also usually provides device drivers with the hardware device. In either case, unlike BIOS, device drivers usually are written for a particular OS.

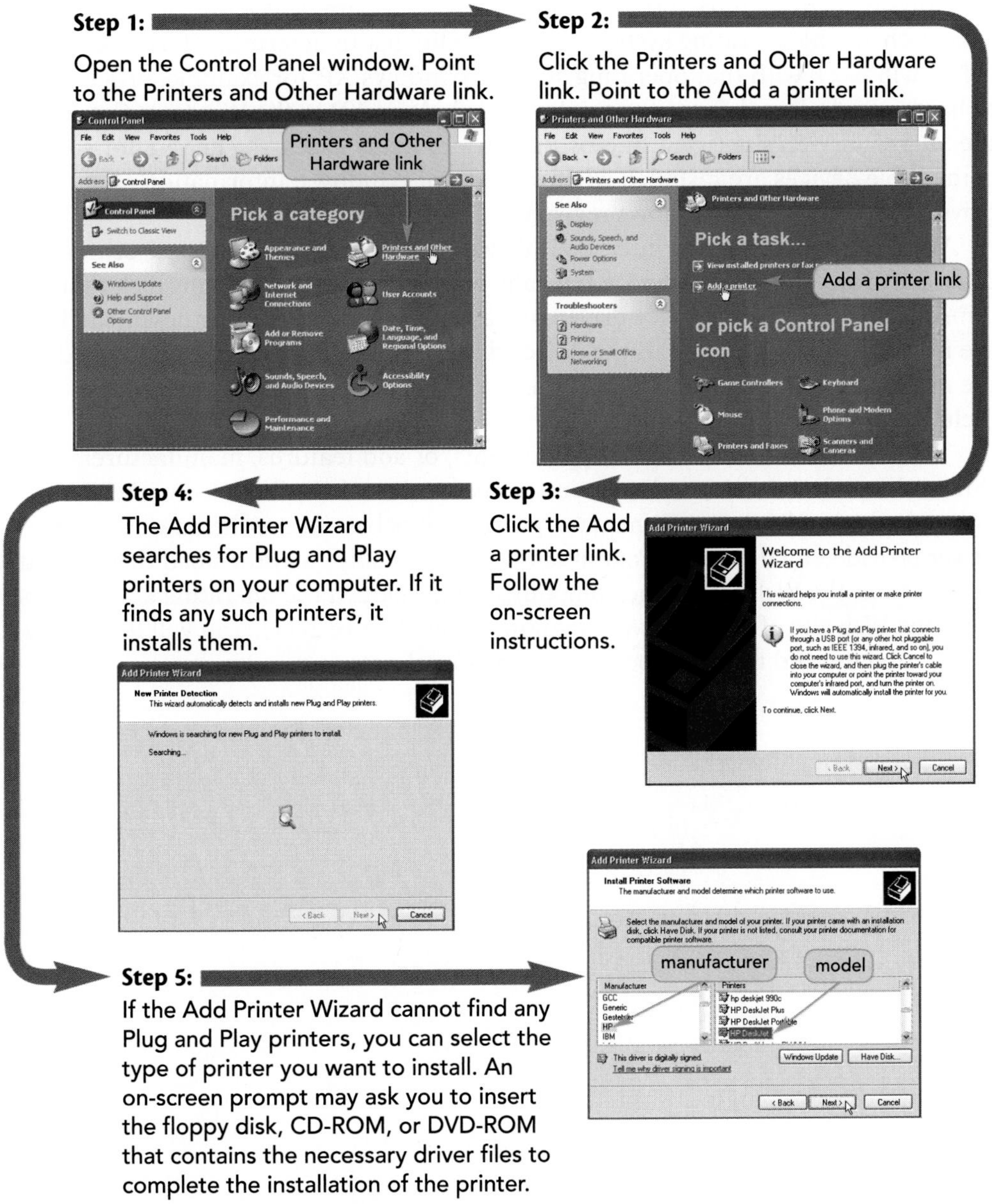

Step 1:
Open the Control Panel window. Point to the Printers and Other Hardware link.

Printers and Other Hardware link

Step 2:
Click the Printers and Other Hardware link. Point to the Add a printer link.

Add a printer link

Step 3:
Click the Add a printer link. Follow the on-screen instructions.

Step 4:
The Add Printer Wizard searches for Plug and Play printers on your computer. If it finds any such printers, it installs them.

Step 5:
If the Add Printer Wizard cannot find any Plug and Play printers, you can select the type of printer you want to install. An on-screen prompt may ask you to insert the floppy disk, CD-ROM, or DVD-ROM that contains the necessary driver files to complete the installation of the printer.

manufacturer

model

Figure 2-10 Steps to install drivers for a printer using Windows XP.

Installing a device in a system that supports Plug and Play usually is a simple process. **Plug and Play (PnP)** is a standard that was designed to make installation of hardware devices easier. PnP applies to the OS, the system BIOS, and the hardware devices themselves. With PnP, if you connect a device to your computer, the operating system recognizes that hardware has been changed since the last time the computer was started or while the computer was running. For example, if you connect a printer to a computer running Windows XP, the OS recognizes the device, determines the system resources needed by each device, and assigns hardware resources appropriately. Windows then determines which drivers are required to support each device and loads those drivers. Windows 9x, Windows 2000, Windows XP, and Windows Server 2003 support Plug and Play, but Windows NT does not.

More About

Device Drivers

To learn more about device drivers for Windows XP, Windows 2000, and Windows 9x, visit the Understanding and Troubleshooting Your PC More About Web page (**scsite.com/understanding/more**) and then click Device Drivers below Chapter 2.

PnP is not entirely foolproof: many devices must have a driver installed before Windows recognizes it. Before installing a new hardware device on your computer, always check the operating system's compatibility list to determine if a device or driver will work with that operating system. Windows XP, for example, provides a list of hardware devices designed to work with Windows XP in the Windows Catalog on the Microsoft Web site (www.microsoft.com). In many cases, the drivers for such compatible devices are installed when you install Windows; information about those drivers is stored in the Windows registry.

When you purchase a printer, DVD drive, Zip® drive, digital camera, scanner, or other hardware device, the device typically comes with a CD or floppy disk that contains the device drivers. Device drivers usually also are available for download from the manufacturer's Web site. If the device drivers for the hardware are provided by the manufacturer, you should install these, rather than relying on the devices included in the operating system.

To address problems, make improvements, or add features, manufacturers sometimes release device drivers that are more recent than those included with Windows or bundled with the device. Whenever possible, it is best to use the latest available driver provided by the device manufacturer. You usually can download these updated drivers from the Web site of the company that developed the operating system or from the Web site of the hardware manufacturer (Figure 2-11). You will learn how to install, update, and troubleshoot drivers in later chapters.

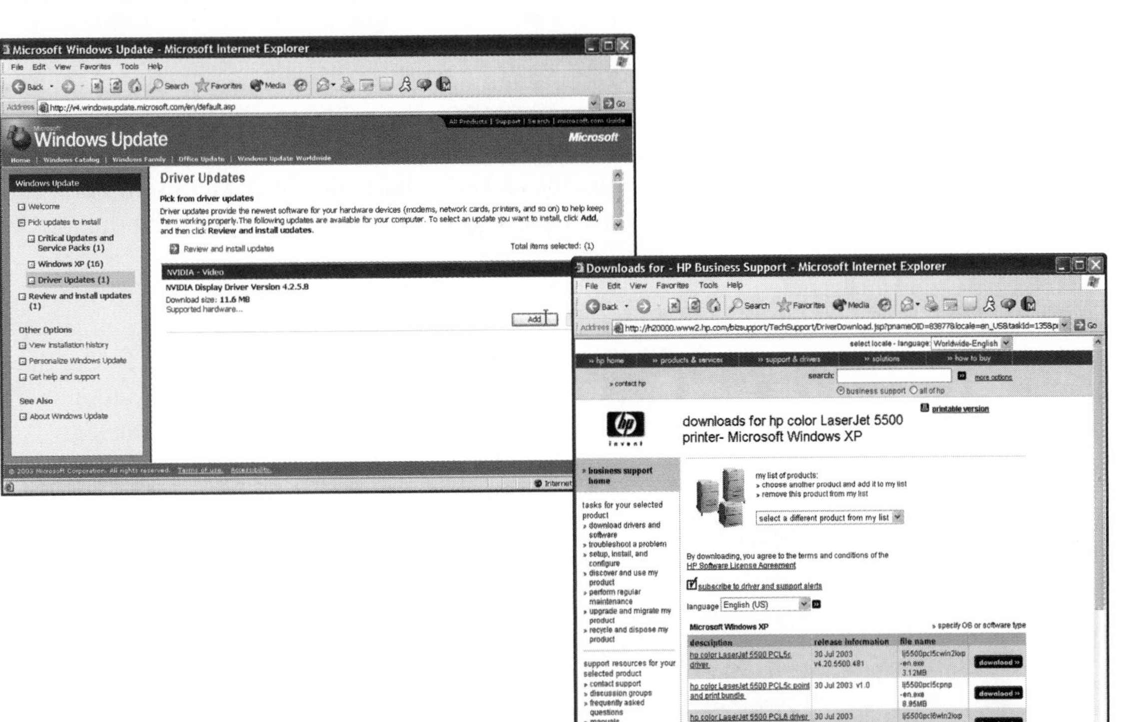

Figure 2-11 Manufacturers often update device drivers to address bugs or provide additional features. You usually can download these updated drivers from the device manufacturer's Web site.

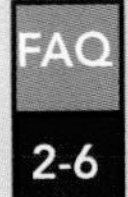

FAQ 2-6

Where can I find device drivers for my new printer (or other device)?

Device drivers come from a number of sources. Some come with and are part of the operating system, some come with hardware devices when they are purchased, and some are provided for downloading from a device manufacturer's Web site.

HOW AN OS USES SYSTEM BIOS TO MANAGE DEVICES Recall from Chapter 1 that the basic input/output system (BIOS) on the motherboard is stored on the ROM BIOS chip. The data and instructions stored on the ROM BIOS chip include:

- the *system BIOS*, which is used to control simple input and output devices
- the *startup BIOS*, which is used to control the startup of a computer
- the *CMOS BIOS* or *CMOS setup* program used to change settings on the motherboard.

The OS communicates with simple devices, such as floppy drives or keyboards, through system BIOS. In addition, system BIOS can be used to access the hard drive. The system BIOS uses the information in CMOS setup to modify or supplement its default programming as needed.

CMOS setup is used to store configuration or setup information about the computer, including which hard drives and floppy drives are present, how the serial and parallel ports are configured, and so on. CMOS setup normally does not need to be changed, except when there is a problem with hardware, a new hard drive or floppy drive is installed, or a power-saving feature needs to be disabled or enabled.

To change the information in CMOS setup, you access the CMOS setup program by pressing a specific key or keys as the computer system is starting up. Different BIOSs use different keystrokes to access CMOS setup; the keystrokes are displayed on the screen during startup (for example, *Press the F2 key to enter setup*). Pressing the indicated key — in this example, the F2 key — launches the CMOS setup program stored on the ROM BIOS chip, which allows you to change the settings in the CMOS setup program.

Once you have entered CMOS setup, you will see a set of text screens with a number of options, as shown in Figure 2-12. Some of these are standard, while others vary according to the BIOS manufacturer. For example, in Figure 2-12a, the Main window for an Award BIOS system lets you configure, or set, the system date and time, the system passwords, floppy disk drives, the hard drive, and the keyboard. Figure 2-12b shows the Advanced window, which allows you to configure serial ports, an infrared port, and a parallel port.

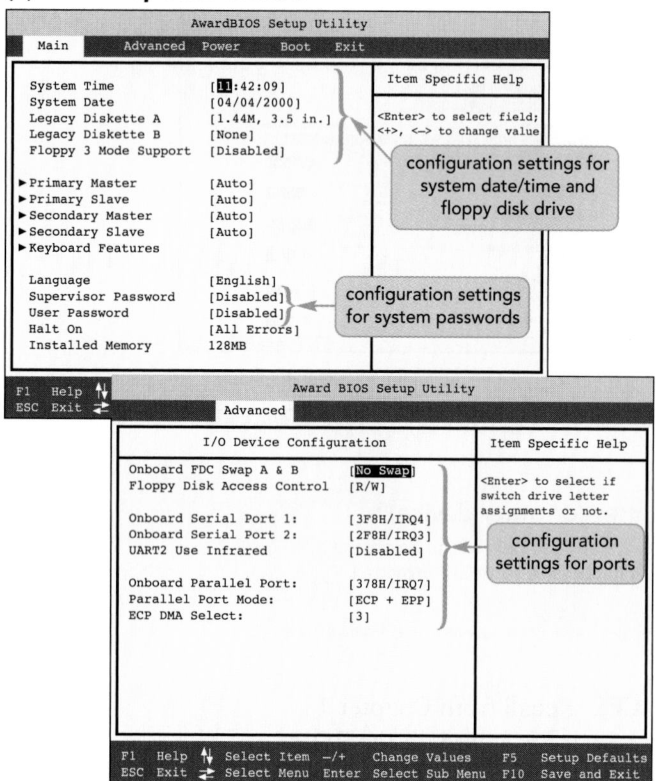

Figure 2-12 The BIOS setup program provides options to configure some of the devices controlled by system BIOS, set system passwords, and configure system resources used by ports.

Recall that the system BIOS is stored in ROM. Data and instructions in ROM take longer to access than data and instructions in RAM. Many newer computers thus shadow the BIOS code — that is, they copy the system BIOS from ROM to RAM at startup, in order to improve performance. **Shadowed BIOS**, also referred to as **shadowed RAM**, allows the operating system to access setup instructions more quickly. Because the system BIOS is not used often, if CMOS setup gives you the option, you might want to disable shadowed BIOS in order to conserve RAM. Further, if your system becomes unstable and crashes at unexpected times, you may want to use the CMOS setup program to disable shadowed BIOS, in an effort to stabilize the system.

 **Your Turn**

Reviewing System BIOS Settings Using CMOS Setup

Boot your PC and look for directions on the screen that tell you how to access CMOS setup on your PC, such as *Press F2 to enter setup*. Press the specified key to access CMOS setup. When the CMOS setup screens display, navigate through the CMOS setup screens and answer these questions about the BIOS:

1. What keystroke(s) did you use to access CMOS setup?
2. What brand and version of BIOS does your motherboard use?
3. List the different CMOS setup windows that you can access from the CMOS main menu window.

Follow the instructions listed at the bottom of the main window to navigate to other windows available in CMOS setup.

4. Access the window that gives information about serial ports. What is the name of that window?
5. What I/O addresses and IRQ does the first serial port use? What I/O addresses and IRQ does the first parallel port use?
6. Does your computer use shadowed BIOS?
7. What are the system date and system time reported by CMOS setup?

When you first start the computer, the system BIOS follows a **boot sequence**, or order of drives listed in the system BIOS, when looking for the operating system to load. The BIOS may be instructed to look for the operating system on the hard disk (drive C) and then the floppy disk (drive A). If the OS is stored in drive C, then the BIOS looks no further; if the BIOS does not find the OS in drive C then it will next look to drive A, and so on depending on the configuration of the boot sequence.

8. Access the window that lists the boot sequence for your computer. What is the current boot sequence? What steps would you take to change the boot sequence to have the BIOS look to the floppy drive (drive A) first?
9. What keys do you press to exit CMOS setup without saving any changes?

Exit CMOS setup without saving any changes you might have made. Your computer then should boot to the Windows desktop.

 **Quiz Yourself 2-1**

To test your knowledge of operating systems and how they work, visit the Understanding and Troubleshooting Your PC Quiz Yourself Web page (scsite.com/understanding/quiz). Click Quiz Yourself 1 below Chapter 2.

System Resources

An OS uses BIOS or device drivers to manage hardware devices. The BIOS or driver communicates with a device by way of system resources on the motherboard. A **system resource** is a tool used by either hardware or software to communicate its requirements. When BIOS or a driver wants to send data to a device (such as when you save a file to the hard drive) or when the device needs attention (such as when you press a key on the keyboard), the device or software uses system resources to communicate. There are four types of system resources used by software and hardware: interrupt requests (IRQs), memory addresses, I/O addresses, and direct memory access (DMA) channels (Figure 2-13 on the next page).

System Resource	Definition
IRQ	A line of a system bus that a hardware device can use to signal the CPU that the device needs attention. Some lines have a higher priority for attention than others. Each IRQ line is assigned a number (0 to 15) to identify it.
I/O addresses	Numbers assigned to hardware devices that software uses to send a command to an input or output device. Each device waits for these numbers and responds to the ones assigned to it. I/O addresses are communicated on the address bus.
memory addresses	Numbers assigned to physical memory located either in RAM or ROM chips. Software can access this memory by using these addresses. Memory addresses are communicated on the address bus.
DMA channel	A number designating a channel on which the device can pass data to memory without involving the CPU. Think of a DMA channel as a shortcut for data moving to and from the device and memory.

Figure 2-13 System resources used by software and hardware.

As outlined in Figure 2-13, all four types of system resources are used for communication between hardware and software. Hardware devices signal the CPU for attention using an IRQ. Software communicates with a device by one of its I/O (input/output) addresses. Software accesses memory using memory addresses, while DMA channels pass data back and forth between a hardware device and memory.

All four system resources depend on certain lines on a bus on the motherboard (Figure 2-14). A bus such as the system bus has three components: the data bus that carries data, the address bus that communicates addresses (both memory addresses and I/O addresses), and the control bus that controls communication via IRQs and DMA channels. The following sections offer a more detailed description of the four system resources and how they work.

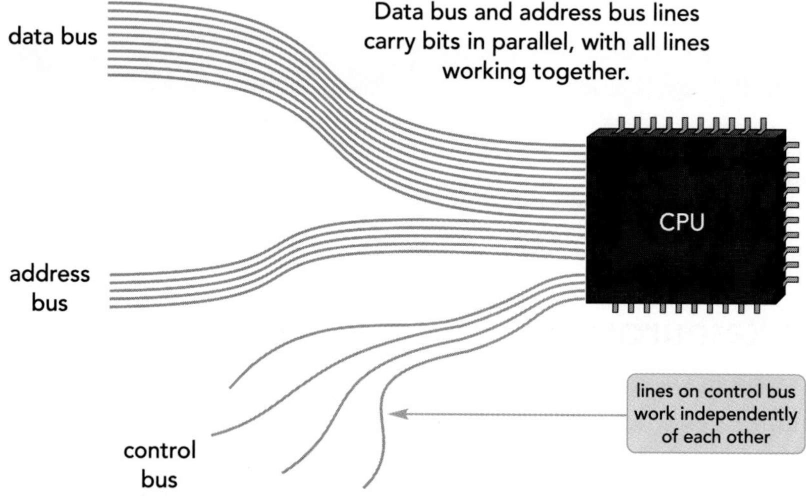

Figure 2-14 A bus consists of a data bus, an address bus, and a control bus.

Interrupt Requests (IRQs)

When a hardware device needs the CPU to do something — for instance, when the keyboard needs the CPU to process a keystroke after a key has been pressed — the device needs a way to get the CPU's attention, and the CPU must know what to do once it turns its attention to the device. These interruptions to the CPU are called **hardware interrupts**. The device initiates a hardware interrupt by placing voltage on the designated **interrupt request** (**IRQ**) **line** assigned to it. This voltage on the IRQ line serves as a signal to the CPU that the device has a request that needs to be serviced — that is, it has a request that needs to be processed. Interrupts initiate many processes that the CPU carries out, and these processes are said to be *interrupt-driven*.

Figure 2-15 lists common uses for the first eight IRQ lines (also called simply IRQs). On motherboards, part of the chip set called the **interrupt controller** manages the IRQs for the CPU. The CPU actually does not know which IRQ is up for processing, because the interrupt controller manages that. If more than one IRQ is up at the same time, the interrupt controller selects the IRQ that has the lowest value to process first. For example, if a user presses a key on the keyboard at the same time that he or she moves the mouse configured to use COM1, the keystroke is processed before the mouse action, because the keyboard is using IRQ 1 and the mouse on COM1 is using IRQ 4. In a sense, the interrupt controller is the doorman for the CPU. All devices wait outside the door for the interrupt controller to let the CPU know what they need.

IRQ	Device
0	system timer *(also referred to as the system clock)*
1	keyboard controller
2	reserved *(used by second IRQ controller to signal the first IRQ controller)*
3	COM2 *(used by serial devices such as modems)*
4	COM1 *(used by serial devices such as modems)*
5	LPT2 *(used by parallel devices such as printers)*
6	floppy drive controller
7	LPT1 *(used by parallel devices such as printers)*

Figure 2-15 Common assignments for the first eight IRQs.

The interrupt controller on early motherboards was designed to handle only eight different IRQs. In order to accommodate more devices, a second group of IRQs was later added (IRQs 8 through 15) and a second interrupt controller was added to manage these new IRQs. This second controller did not have access to the CPU, so it had to communicate with the CPU through the first controller (Figure 2-16 on the next page). To signal the first controller, the second controller used one of the first controller's IRQ values (IRQ 2), which was reserved for a link to a mainframe computer and often was not used. These last eight IRQs plug into the system using IRQ 2. Because of this, the IRQ priority level became: 0, 1, (8, 9, 10, 11, 12, 13, 14, 15), 3, 4, 5, 6, 7. (Later in the chapter, you will learn to use operating system tools, such as Device Manager, to see how the IRQs are assigned on your computer.)

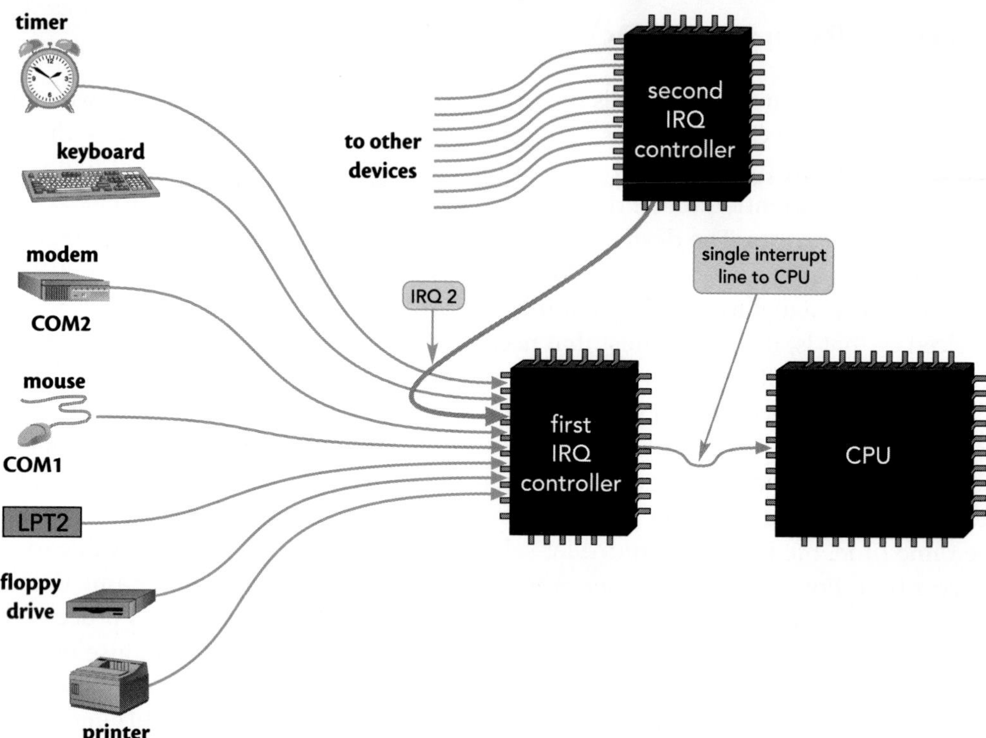

Figure 2-16 The second IRQ controller uses IRQ 2 to signal the first IRQ controller.

With interrupts, the hardware device or the software initiates communication by sending a signal to the CPU. A device also can be serviced using polling. With **polling**, software that is constantly running has the CPU periodically check the hardware device to see if it needs service. Most hardware devices use interrupts as a method of communication, but some devices, such as a joystick, use polling as a way to communicate with the CPU. Software written to manage a joystick has the CPU check the joystick periodically to see if the device has data to communicate, which is why a joystick does not need an IRQ to work.

Memory Addresses

An operating system relates to memory as a long list of cells that it can use to hold data and instructions, somewhat like a one-dimensional table or spreadsheet. When the operating system first is loaded, each memory location or cell is assigned a number beginning with zero. These number assignments are called **memory addresses**. Think of a memory address as a seat number in a theater (Figure 2-17). Each seat is assigned a number regardless of whether someone is sitting in it; the person sitting in a seat can be data or instructions. The OS does not refer to the person in the seat by name; it instead uses the seat number. For example, the OS might send an instruction stating that it wants to print the data in memory addresses 500 through 650.

Figure 2-17 Memory addresses are assigned to each location in memory; these locations can store data or instructions. The OS refers to a location only by memory address (instead of the specific data or instruction). Although each person here only takes up one seat, it normally takes more than a single storage location to hold a program instruction.

Older device drivers, such as those used with DOS and Windows 3.x, required a specified range of memory addresses to work. Newer 32-bit drivers used with Windows 9x and above do not care what memory addresses they use. When thinking about the system resources used by devices, memory addresses no longer are a major consideration.

FAQ 2-7

Why are memory addresses and I/O addresses often shown as numbers such as 78h?

Memory addresses and I/O addresses are most often displayed on the screen as hexadecimal (base 16 or hex) numbers. **Hexadecimal,** often called simply **hex,** is a number system based on 16 values (called base 16). Hexadecimal uses sixteen characters — 0, 1, 2, 3, 4, 5, 6, 7, 8, 9, A, B, C, D, E, and F. Hex numbers often are followed by a lowercase h to indicate they are in hex. Even though computers process binary data, they often display information using the hex system because it is easier for people to read hex numbers than to read binary numbers. For more information about the hexadecimal number system and how it applies to memory addresses and I/O addresses, see Appendix C.

I/O Addresses

Another system resource made available to hardware devices is input/output addresses, or I/O addresses. **I/O addresses**, also called **port addresses** or just ports, are numbers the CPU can use to access hardware devices. The address bus on the motherboard sometimes carries memory addresses and sometimes carries I/O addresses. If the address bus has been set to carry I/O addresses, then each device listens to this bus (Figure 2-18 on the next page). If the address belongs to it, then it responds; otherwise, it ignores the request for information. In short, the CPU knows a hardware device as a group of I/O addresses. If it wants to know the status of a printer or a floppy drive, for example, it places a particular I/O address on the address bus on the motherboard.

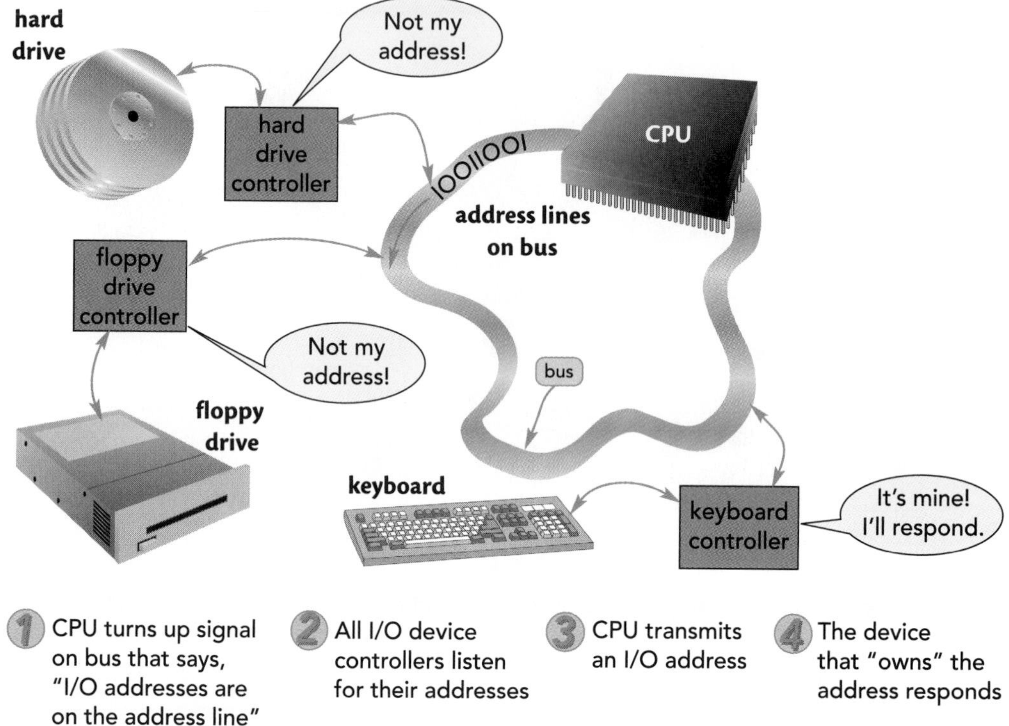
hard drive
Not my address!
hard drive controller
CPU
10011001
address lines on bus
floppy drive controller
Not my address!
bus
floppy drive
keyboard
keyboard controller
It's mine! I'll respond.
1 CPU turns up signal on bus that says, "I/O addresses are on the address line"
2 All I/O device controllers listen for their addresses
3 CPU transmits an I/O address
4 The device that "owns" the address responds

Figure 2-18 All devices hear the addresses on the I/O bus, but only one responds.

Figure 2-19 lists a few common assignments for I/O addresses. Because these addresses are hex numbers, you sometimes see them written with 0x first, such as 0x0040, or with the h last, such as 0040h.

IRQ	I/O Address	Device
0	0040-005F	system timer
1	0060-006F	keyboard controller
2	00A0-00AF	access to IRQs above 7
3	02F8-02FF	serial port COM2
3	02E8-02EF	serial port COM4
4	03F8-03FF	serial port COM1
4	03E8-03EF	serial port COM3
5	0278-027F	sound card or parallel port LPT2
6	03F0-03F7	floppy drive controller
7	0378-037F	printer parallel port LPT1
8	0070-007F	real-time clock

(continued)

IRQ	I/O Address	Device
9-10	Available	
11	SCSI or available	
12	0238-023F	motherboard mouse
13	00F8-00FF	math coprocessor
14	01F0-01F7	IDE hard drive
15	0170-0170	secondary IDE hard drive or available

Figure 2-19 IRQs and I/O addresses for devices.

DMA Channels

Another system resource used by hardware and software is a **direct memory access (DMA) channel**, a shortcut method that lets an I/O device send data directly to memory, bypassing the CPU. A chip on the motherboard contains the DMA logic and manages the process. Earlier computers had four DMA channels numbered 0, 1, 2, and 3 (Figure 2-20). Later, channels 5, 6, and 7 were added. DMA channel 4 is used to connect to the higher DMA channels. As shown in Figure 2-20, DMA channel 4 cascades into the lower DMA channels.

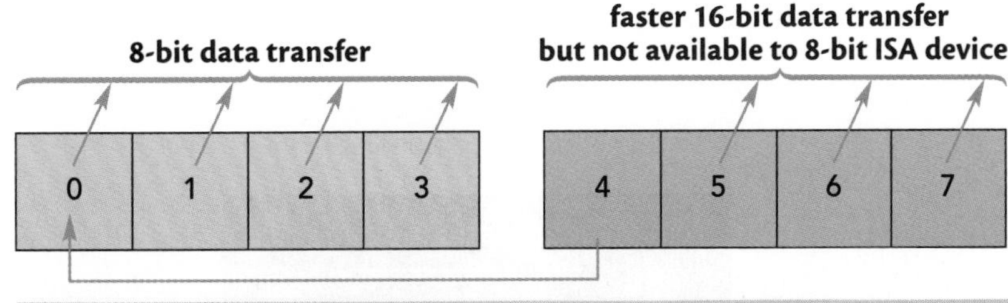

Figure 2-20 DMA channel 4 is not available for I/O use because it is used to cascade into the lower four DMA channels.

Some devices, such as a printer, are designed to use DMA channels, and others, such as the mouse, are not. Those that use the channels might be able to use only a certain channel, such as channel 3, and no other. Alternately, the BIOS might have the option of changing a DMA channel number to avoid conflicts with other devices. Conflicts occur when more than one device uses the same channel. DMA channels are not as popular as they once were, because their design makes them slower than newer methods. Slower devices such as floppy drives, sound cards, and tape drives, however, still might use DMA channels.

Quiz Yourself 2-2

To test your knowledge of system resources used by a computer system, visit the Understanding and Troubleshooting your PC Quiz Yourself Web page (scsite.com/understanding/quiz). Click Quiz Yourself 2 below Chapter 2.

Booting Up Your Computer

Before an operating system can perform its functions or communicate using the system resources outlined here, it must be loaded from disk to random access memory (RAM) when you first start your computer. The process of starting or restarting a computer and loading the operating system is referred to as the **boot process** or **booting**.

> **FAQ 2-8**
>
> **Why is the process of starting or restarting a computer called booting?**
>
> The term booting may be a reference to the phrase, *lifting oneself up by the bootstraps*, which refers to one's ability to improve a situation by one's own efforts, without help from others. In the case of a computer, booting thus refers to the computer bringing itself up to an operable state without user intervention. Others suggest the word booting refers to the bootstrap loader tapes used by early computers, which included a few bytes of instructions for reading in the rest of the tape.

Booting refers to either a cold boot or a warm boot. When you turn on a computer that is powered off completely, you are performing a **cold boot**, or **hard boot**. A cold boot involves turning on the computer with the on/off power button. A **warm boot**, or **soft boot**, is the process of restarting a computer that already is powered on. A warm boot uses the operating system to reboot. With Windows XP, for example, you can perform a warm boot by clicking the Start button, clicking Turn Off Computer (or Shut Down), and then clicking Restart (Figure 2-21).

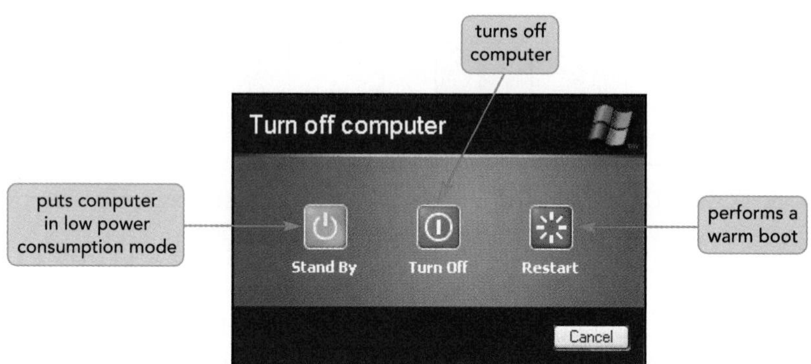

Figure 2-21 With Windows XP, you can perform a warm boot by clicking the Restart button in the Turn off computer window.

> **More About**
>
> **Performing a Warm Boot**
>
> To learn more about the steps used to perform a warm boot using other operating systems, such as Windows 2000, Windows 9x, and DOS, visit the Understanding and Troubleshooting Your PC More About Web page (**scsite.com/understanding/more**) and then click Warm Boot below Chapter 2.

If you need to reboot your computer (for example, if the system freezes up), always try using a warm boot first. A cold boot is more stressful on your machine than a warm boot because of the initial power surge through the equipment. A warm boot also is faster. If the warm boot method does not work and you must perform a cold boot using the on/off power button, avoid immediately turning the computer off and then back on without a pause, because this can damage the machine.

Some PCs also have a reset button on the front of the case. Pressing the reset button starts the boot process at an earlier point than a warm boot. It essentially is the same as powering off and on using a cold boot, except that there is no stress to the system caused by the initial power surge. Pressing the reset button is a little slower than a warm boot, but it might work when a warm boot fails.

The next section addresses what happens when the PC is first turned on and the startup BIOS takes control and then begins the process of loading an OS.

Startup BIOS Controls the Beginning of the Boot

The functions performed during the boot can be divided into four parts, as shown in the following list. Startup BIOS is in control for the first step and the beginning of the second step, when control is turned over to the OS. The following section provides an overview of four major parts of the boot process, before covering the first two parts in detail. (The last steps depend on the OS being used and are covered in later chapters.)

Step 1: Startup BIOS runs a process called the power-on self test and assigns system resources. The ROM BIOS startup program performs a **power-on self test** (**POST**), which involves surveying hardware resources and needs and assigning system resources to meet those needs (Figure 2-22). The ROM BIOS startup program begins the startup process by reading configuration information stored in the CMOS RAM chip, DIP switches, and jumpers, and then comparing that information to the hardware — the CPU, video card, disk drive, hard drive, and so on. Some hardware devices have BIOSs of their own that request resources from startup BIOS, which attempts to assign these system resources as needed.

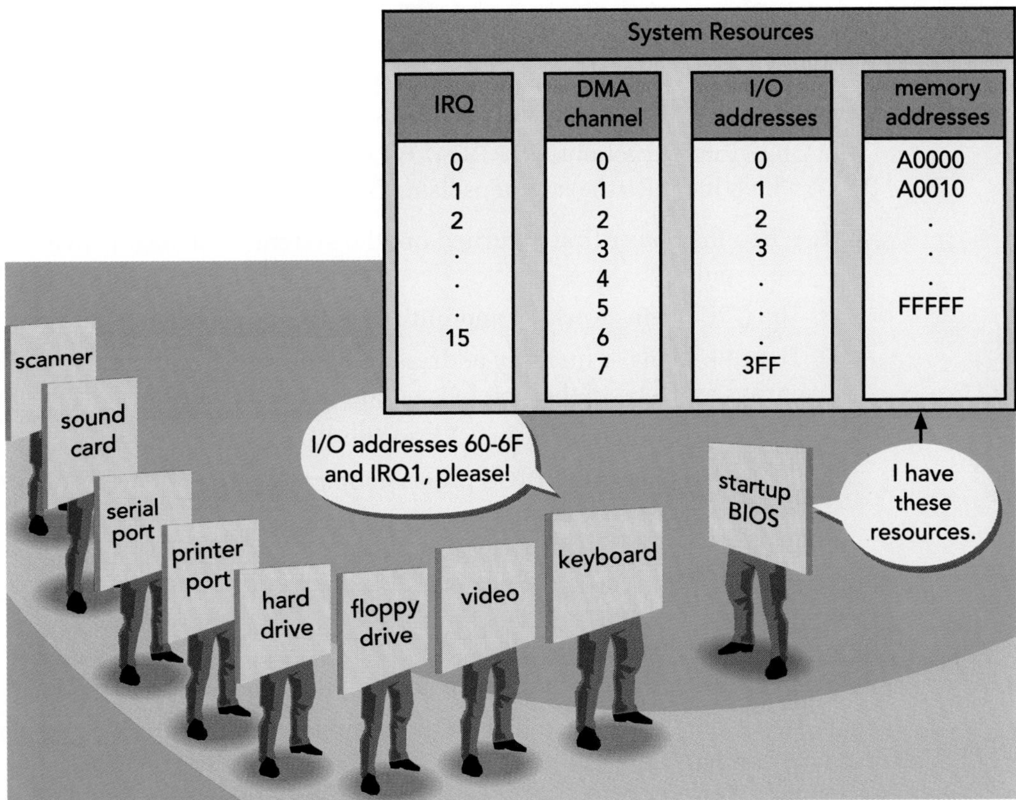

Figure 2-22 During the POST, startup BIOS surveys hardware resources and needs and assigns system resources to satisfy those needs.

Step 2: The ROM BIOS startup program searches for and loads an OS. Most often the OS is loaded from drive C on the hard drive. Configuration information on the CMOS RAM chip tells startup BIOS on which drive to look for the OS. Most new BIOSs support loading the OS from the hard drive, a floppy disk, a CD-ROM drive, or a Zip drive. The BIOS turns to that device, reads the beginning files of the OS, copies them into memory, and then turns control over to the OS. This part of the loading process works the same for any operating system (although the specific OS files being loaded are different).

Step 3: The OS configures the system and completes its own loading. The OS checks some of the same things that startup BIOS checked, such as available memory and whether that memory is reliable. Then the OS loads the software to control a mouse, CD-ROM, scanner, and other peripheral devices. These devices generally have device drivers stored on the hard drive. Next, in the case of the Windows operating system, the Windows desktop is loaded.

Step 4: Application software is loaded and executed. Sometimes an OS is configured to launch application software automatically, as part of the boot process. When you tell the OS to execute an application, the OS first must find the application software on the hard drive, CD-ROM, or other secondary storage device, copy the software into memory, and then turn control over to it. Finally, you can command the application software, which makes requests to the OS, which, in turn, uses the system resources, system BIOS, and device drivers to interface with and control the hardware. At this point, the user is in control.

The following sections review the boot process in more detail, beginning with the POST.

POST AND ASSIGNMENT OF SYSTEM RESOURCES When you turn on the power to a PC, the CPU begins the boot process by initializing itself and then turning to the ROM BIOS for instructions. The ROM BIOS then performs the power on self test or POST, which includes the key steps listed below:

1. When the power first is turned on, the system clock begins to generate clock pulses.
2. The CPU begins working and initializes itself (resetting its internal values).
3. The CPU turns to memory address FFFF0h, which is the memory address always assigned to the first instruction in the ROM BIOS startup program.
4. This instruction directs the CPU to run POST.
5. POST first checks the BIOS program operating it and then tests CMOS RAM.
6. A test determines that there has been no battery failure.
7. Hardware interrupts are disabled. (This means that pressing a key on the keyboard or using another input device at this point does not affect anything.)
8. Tests are run on the CPU, and it is initialized further.
9. A check determines if this is a cold boot. If so, the first 16 KB of RAM is tested.
10. Hardware devices installed on the computer are inventoried and compared to configuration information.
11. The video card is tested and configured. During POST, before the CPU has checked the video system, beeps sometimes communicate errors. Short and long beeps indicate an error; the coding for the beeps depends on the BIOS. After POST checks and verifies the video controller card (note that POST does not check to see if a monitor is present or working), POST can use the monitor to display its progress.
12. POST checks RAM by writing and reading data. The monitor displays a running count of RAM during this phase.
13. Next, the keyboard is checked (if you press and hold any keys at this point, an error occurs with some BIOSs). Secondary storage devices (including floppy disk drives and hard drives), ports, and other hardware devices are

tested and configured. The hardware that POST finds is checked against the data stored in CMOS RAM, jumpers, and/or DIP switches to determine if they agree. IRQ, I/O addresses, and DMA assignments are made; the OS completes this process later.

14. Some devices are set up to go into sleep mode to conserve electricity.
15. The DMA and interrupt controllers are checked.
16. CMOS setup is run if requested.
17. BIOS begins its search for an OS.

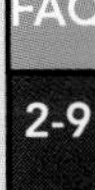
FAQ 2-9

When I started my computer, I got a black screen with the error message, *Non-system disk or disk error, press any key.* What does that mean?

Do not panic. You probably have a floppy disk in the floppy drive. Simply remove the disk and press any key; most likely your computer will boot normally. As you have learned, the BIOS looks to CMOS setup to find out the order in which secondary storage devices should be checked for the OS (the boot sequence). If BIOS looks first to drive A and finds no disk in the drive, it turns to drive C. If it looks first to drive A and finds a disk in the drive, but the disk does not contain the OS, then an error message such as:

- **Non-system disk or disk error, press any key**
- **Bad or missing COMMAND.COM**
- **No operating system found**

appears. You must replace the disk with one that contains the OS or simply remove the disk and press any key to force the BIOS to continue to drive C to find the OS. If desired, you also can change the boot sequence using CMOS setup, so that BIOS is instructed to look to drive C (or another drive) first.

HOW THE BIOS FINDS AND LOADS THE OS Once POST and the first pass at assignment of resources are complete, the next step is to load an OS. Startup BIOS looks to CMOS setup to find out which device is set to be the boot device (Figure 2-23a on the next page). Most often the OS is loaded from logical drive C on the hard drive. The minimum information required on the hard drive to load an OS includes:

- A small sector (512 bytes) at the very beginning of the hard drive, called the **Master Boot Record (MBR)**, which contains two items. The first item is the master boot program, which is needed to locate the beginning of the OS on the drive (Figure 2-23b on the next page).
- The second item in the MBR is a table, called the **partition table**, which contains a map of the logical drives (volumes) on the hard drive. The partition table tells BIOS how many partitions the drive has, how each partition is divided into one or more logical drives, where each logical drive begins and ends, and which partition contains the drive to be used for booting (a partition called the **active partition** or **boot drive**, which usually is logical drive C).
- At the beginning of the boot drive is the OS **boot record**, which loads the first program file of the OS (Figure 2-23c on the next page). For Windows XP, Windows 2000, and Windows NT, that program file is **Ntldr** (NT Loader); for Windows 9x, the program file is **Io.sys**.
- This program file — whether Ntldr or Io.sys — is a boot loader program that contains a list of instructions for the operating system to follow. The boot loader program is responsible for loading the operating system into memory.

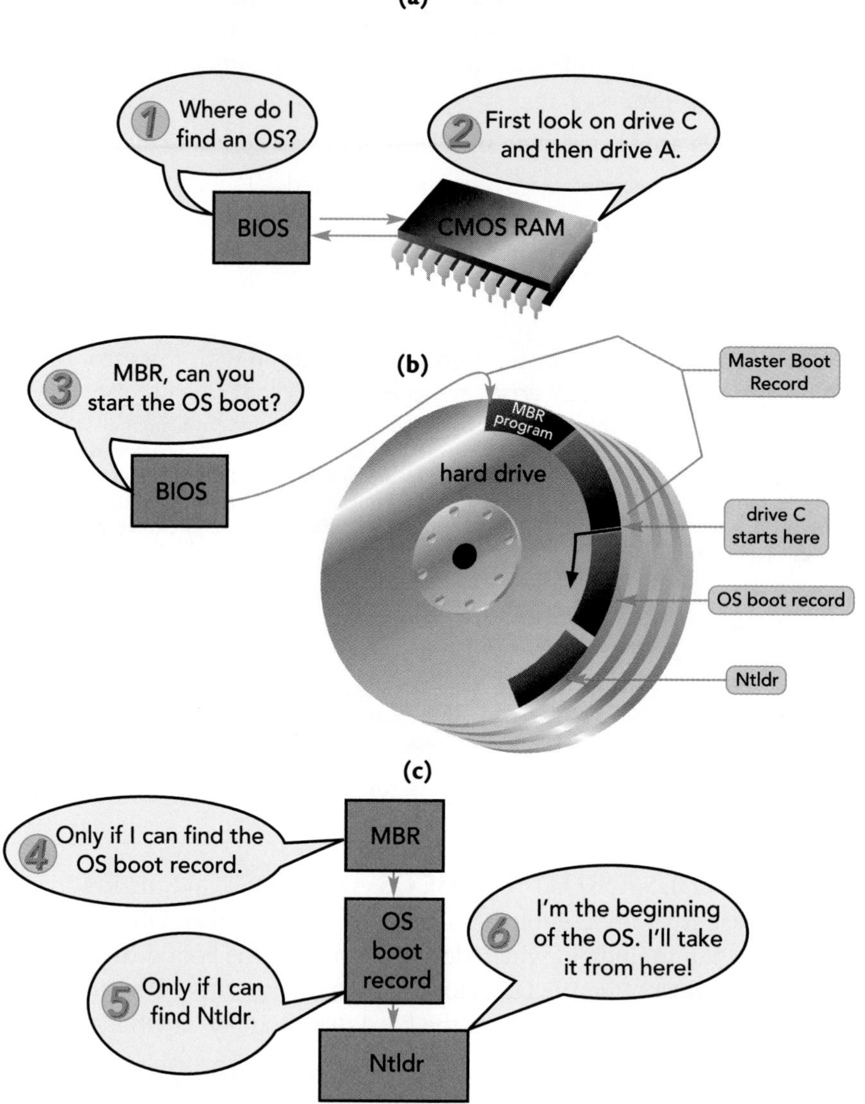

Figure 2-23 BIOS searches for and begins to load an operating system (in this example, Windows XP is the OS and the first program file is Ntldr).

Loading the Core of Windows XP

This section describes what happens during booting when loading Windows XP, as well as Windows 2000 and Windows NT (Figure 2-24). When any of these operating systems is installed, it edits the boot record, or boot sector, of the boot drive, instructing it to load the Windows program Ntldr at startup. The OS boot record thus knows the file name, Ntldr.

Step Performed by	Description
1. Startup BIOS	POST (power-on self test) is executed.
2. Startup BIOS	MBR (Master Boot Record) is loaded, and the master boot program within the MBR is run.
3. MBR program	The program searches for and loads the OS boot record of the active partition. The boot sector from the active partition is loaded, and the program in this boot sector is run.
4. Boot sector program	Ntldr (NT Loader) file is loaded and run.
5. NT Loader (Ntldr)	The processor is changed from real mode to flat memory mode, in which 32-bit code can be executed.
6. NT Loader (Ntldr)	Minifile system drivers (described below) are started so files can be read.
7. NT Loader (Ntldr)	The Boot.ini file is read and the boot loader menu described in the file is built.
8. NT Loader (Ntldr)	If the user chooses Windows NT/2000/XP, then the loader runs Ntdetect.com to detect hardware present; otherwise, it runs Bootsect.dos.
9. NT Loader (Ntldr)	Ntldr reads information from the registry about device drivers and loads them. Also loads the Hal.dll and Ntoskrnl.exe (which are discussed in Chapter 8).
10. NT Loader (Ntldr)	Ntldr passes control to Ntoskrnl.exe. This is the last step performed by the loader; the load is complete.

Figure 2-24 Steps in the process of booting a computer using Windows XP, Windows 2000, and Windows NT.

As noted above, the BIOS first locates the MBR on the hard drive, which looks to the partition table to determine where the boot drive is physically located on the drive. It then runs the boot record stored on the boot drive. The boot record loads Ntldr, the first program file of the operating system.

The boot program then executes the program, Ntldr. With the execution of Ntldr, Windows XP then starts its boot process. This program is responsible for loading Windows XP and performing several chores to complete the loading process, as outlined in the following steps:

- *Ntldr changes the processor mode and loads a file system.* Up to this point, the CPU has been processing in real mode. Because Windows XP, Windows 2000, and Windows NT do not process in real mode, Ntldr begins by changing the CPU mode from real mode to a 32-bit mode called **32-bit flat memory mode** in order to run its 32-bit code. Next a temporary, simplified file system called the **minifile system** is started so that Ntldr can read files from a file system.

More About

The Boot Process under Windows 9x

The process of loading the MS-DOS core of Windows 9x differs from the process of loading Windows XP. It is important for a PC technician to understand this real-mode DOS core because it is often used as a troubleshooting tool when the hard drive fails. To learn more about the boot process that occurs using Windows 9x, visit the Understanding and Troubleshooting Your PC More About Web page (**scsite.com/understanding/more**) and then click Boot Process under Windows 9x below Chapter 2.

- *Ntldr reads and loads the boot loader menu.* Ntldr then is able to read the Boot.ini file, a hidden text file that contains information needed to build the boot loader menu. The user can make a selection from this menu or accept the default selection by waiting for the preset time to expire.
- *Ntldr uses Ntdetect.com.* If Ntldr is to load Windows XP, Windows 2000, or Windows NT as the operating system, Ntldr runs the program Ntdetect.com, which checks the hardware devices present and passes the information back to Ntldr.
- *Ntldr loads the OS and device drivers.* Ntldr then loads Ntoskrnl.exe, Hal.dll, and the System hive. The System hive is a portion of the Windows registry that includes hardware information used to load the proper device drivers for the hardware present. You will learn more about the System hive in Chapter 9.
- *Ntldr passes control to Ntoskrnl.exe.* Ntldr then passes control to Ntoskrnl.exe, and the boot sequence is complete. If an operating system other than Windows NT, Windows 2000, or Windows XP is chosen, such as DOS or Windows 9x, Ntldr loads and passes control to the program Bootsect.dos, which is responsible for loading the other OS.

The files needed to boot Windows NT, Windows 2000, or Windows XP successfully are listed in Figure 2-25. In the table, references to *\winnt_root* or *%SystemRoot%* follow Microsoft documentation conventions and mean the name of the directory where the Windows operating system is stored (the actual directory is \Winnt for Windows NT and Windows 2000; and \Windows for Windows XP).

File	Location
Ntldr	root folder of the system partition (usually C:\)
Boot.ini	root folder of the system partition (usually C:\)
Bootsect.dos	root folder of the system partition (usually C:\)*
Ntdetect.com	root folder of the system partition (usually C:\)
Ntbootdd.sys	root folder of the system partition (usually C:\)*
Ntoskrnl.exe	\winnt_root\system32 folder of the boot partition
Hal.dll	\winnt_root\system32 folder of the boot partition
System key or registry file	\winnt_root\system32\config folder of the boot partition
Device drivers	\winnt_root\system32\drivers folder of the boot partition

Figure 2-25 Files needed to boot Windows XP, Windows 2000, or Windows NT successfully.

**Depending on the startup controllers used or if your system is set up for a dual-boot, these files may not be included on your computer.*

After a system boots and you are working within a Windows operating system, most often you are viewing the Windows desktop. Using Windows Explorer or My Computer, you can copy files, create folders, and even perform some limited troubleshooting tasks. If the OS is not functioning well enough to provide a desktop, however, a PC technician must be able to troubleshoot the system using a command-driven interface. As previously noted, although Windows XP provides a graphical user interface, it also provides a command-line interface in the form of the Command Prompt window. Learning to use the command-line interface is important to help troubleshoot operating system problems. Using the Command Prompt is covered in detail in Appendix B.

FAQ 2-10

What is a program file? What is a hidden file?

A program file can be a part of the OS or an application and have a .com, .sys, .bat, or .exe file extension. (Ntldr is an exception to that rule because it has no file extension.) A hidden file is a file that is not displayed in the directory list. A program file can be a hidden file.

Troubleshooting the Boot Process

In some situations, the boot process might fail. A successful boot depends on the hardware, the BIOS, and the operating system all performing without errors. If errors occur, they might or might not stall or lock up the boot process. Errors are communicated as beeps or as messages on screen. Appendix A, Error Messages and Their Meanings, lists examples of some of the error messages that might occur during the boot process.

If a system will not boot, you may need to try to boot the computer from a floppy disk. Although you normally boot from a hard drive, problems with the hard drive or a virus that has infected the boot record of the hard drive sometimes make booting from a floppy disk necessary. A floppy disk with enough software to load an operating system is called a **boot disk**, or **recovery disk**. A boot disk with some utility programs to troubleshoot a failed hard drive is called a **rescue disk**, **emergency startup disk** (**ESD**), or **startup disk**. Having a rescue disk available for an emergency is very important, and a PC technician should always have one or more on hand.

Each OS provides an automated method to create a boot disk or rescue disk or disks). Windows 9x uses a single boot disk, while Windows 2000 uses a set of four disks. As reviewed in this chapter's High-Tech Talk feature on page 68 and discussed in detail in Chapter 9, Windows XP provides a wizard to help you create a boot disk.

More About

Beep Codes

During the boot process, short beeps are sounded by the BIOS when errors occur, to help you understand and troubleshoot the problem. To learn more about beep codes for different BIOSs, visit the Understanding and Troubleshooting Your PC More About Web page (**scsite.com/understanding/more**) and then click Beep Codes below Chapter 2.

Operating System Tools to Examine a System

You have learned about many hardware devices, OS components, and system resources in this chapter. When installing new components or troubleshooting a system, it is important to know how to use OS tools such as Device Manager and System Information to examine the system.

Device Manager

Using Windows XP, Windows 2000, and Windows 9x, Device Manager is the primary tool used to manage hardware devices. (Windows NT does not have a Device Manager.) To access Device Manager, right-click the My Computer icon on the desktop, select Properties on the shortcut menu, click the Hardware tab, and then click the Device Manager button. Once Device Manager is running, you click the (+) symbol next to an item to expand the view of the item, and click the (-) symbol to minimize the view. To view more detailed information about a device, you can right-click the device and select Properties on the shortcut menu to display the Properties window for that device (Figure 2-26a on the next page).

You also can use Device Manager to see how the IRQs are assigned on your computer. With the Device Manager window displayed, click View on the menu bar and then click Resources by type on the View menu. Click the (+) symbol next to Interrupt request (IRQ) to view the list of assigned IRQs (Figure 2-26b). To return to the original view, click View on the menu bar and then click Devices by type on the View menu.

If a device is problematic, you can use Device Manager to review the properties for that device. As needed, you can also update the driver for a device, enable or disable a device, change a system resource assigned to a device, and uninstall a device from this window.

As you learned in Chapter 1, you also can use Device Manager to generate a printout of system information, which can be useful to document the current status of a system. To print a report, click Action on the menu bar and then click Print. In the Report type area, select the type of report you wish to print: a system summary of all devices, information for just one selected class or device, or a printout listing all devices and a system summary.

System Information

Windows also provides a utility called System Information to provide more detailed information than that provided by Device Manager. For example, System Information lists the BIOS version you are using, the directory where the OS is installed, how system resources are used, information about drivers and their current status, and additional information about the system (Figure 2-27).

(a)

(b)

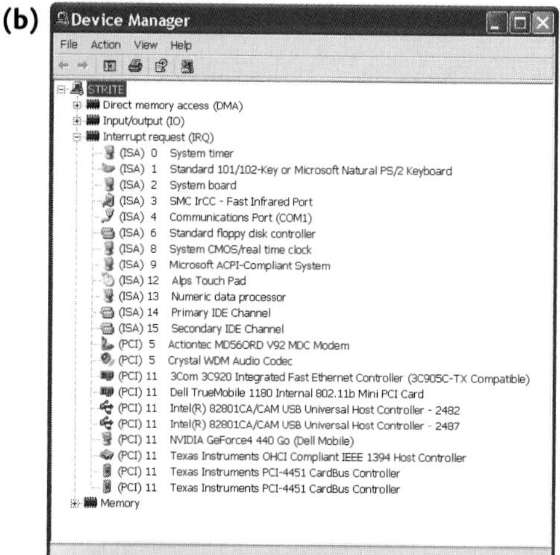

Figure 2-26 Using Device Manager, you can view detailed information about a device, including details on the driver installed for that device. You also can see how the IRQs are assigned on your computer.

To run System Information using Windows XP, Windows 2000, or Windows 9x, click the Start button and then click Run on the Start menu. When Windows displays the Run dialog box, type `Msinfo32.exe` in the Open text box and then click OK to run the System Information utility.

The System Information utility allows you to save or print a report listing system information. This report can be useful when a system is having trouble booting. For instance, you can use System Information to get a list of drivers that loaded successfully. You can then compare this report to a report generated from System Information when the system was starting successfully. Comparing the two reports can help identify the problem device.

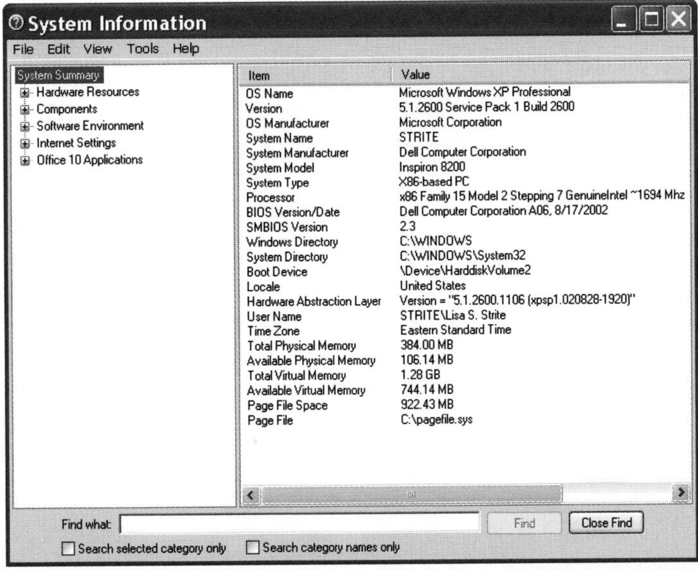

Figure 2-27 The System Information utility lists detailed information about your system.

Quiz Yourself 2-3

To test your knowledge of the boot process and OS tools to examine your system, visit the Understanding and Troubleshooting Your PC Quiz Yourself Web page (scsite.com/understanding/quiz). Click Quiz Yourself 3 below Chapter 2.

More About

Microsoft Diagnostic Utility (MSD)

DOS and Windows 9x include the Microsoft Diagnostic Utility (MSD), a utility useful to view information about a system. To learn more about MSD, visit the Understanding and Troubleshooting Your PC More About Web page (**scsite.com/understanding/more**) and then click MSD below Chapter 2.

High-Tech Talk

Booting 911: Emergency Startup Disk to the Rescue

Each Windows OS provides an automated method to create a rescue disk or set of disks. Windows 98 uses a single boot disk, and Windows 2000 uses a set of four disks. Windows XP provides the Automated System Recovery (ASR) wizard to help you create an emergency startup, which includes information you can use to restore a system in the event it will not boot.

How do you create a recovery disk? As shown in Figure 2-28, the process is simple, requiring you to follow basic steps in the Automated System Recovery wizard.

The Automated System Recovery wizard creates: a backup file the system information and data and files you choose to back up; and a recovery disk, or ASR disk, which stores basic operating system components and information about the backup, the hard disks, and how to restore the system. If your system fails, you can use the ASR disk to restore the hard drive, following the detailed steps outlined in Chapter 9.

When you install an operating system, one of the installation steps involves creating a recovery disk. All too often, however, users do not create a recovery disk because they buy a computer with the operating system already installed. Having a recovery disk, however, is a great tool to bring to the rescue. If you do not already have a recovery disk, now might be a good time to make one.

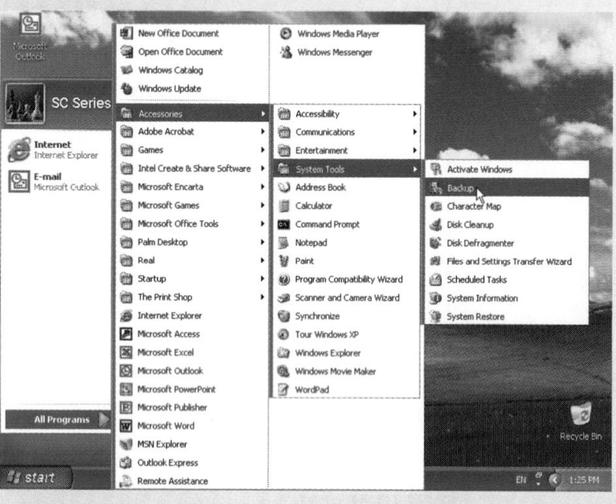

Step 1:

Click the Start button on the taskbar, point to All Programs on the Start menu, point to Accessories on the All Programs submenu, point to System Tools on the Accessories submenu, and then point to Backup.

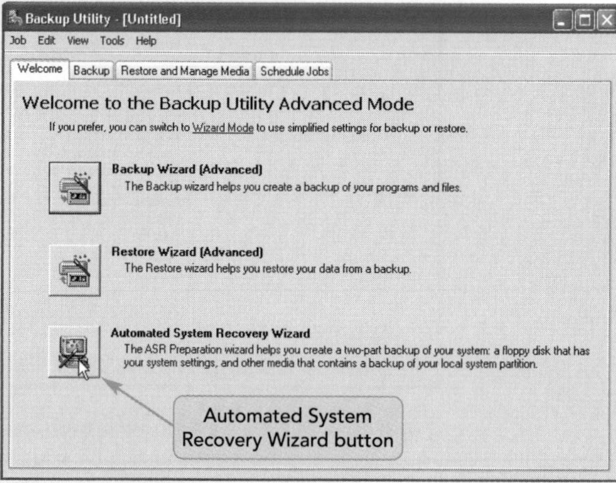

Step 2:

Click Backup on the System Tools submenu to open the Backup Utility window. (If the Backup or Restore Wizard displays, click the Advanced Mode link.) Point to the Automated System Recovery Wizard button.

Step 3:

Click the Automated System Recovery Wizard button to create the recovery disk. Follow the on-screen instructions and insert a disk into the disk drive when prompted.

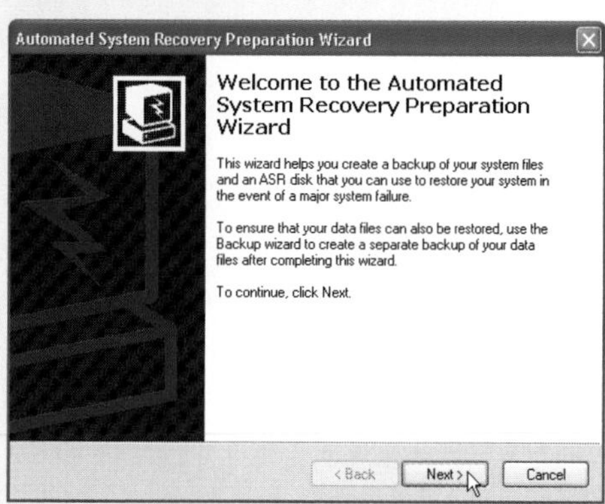

Figure 2-28

CHAPTER SUMMARY

The Chapter Summary reviews the concepts presented in this chapter.

1 Introducing Operating Systems

An operating system (OS) is software that contains instructions that coordinate all the activities among computer hardware resources. Operating systems used for desktop computers include DOS, Windows 9x, Windows NT, Windows 2000, Windows XP, Windows 2003, Unix, Linux, OS/2, and Mac OS. Every OS has a shell, the portion of the OS that relates to the user and to applications, and a kernel, the core of an OS that loads when you first turn on your computer.

2 What an Operating System Does

An OS performs key functions such as providing a user interface, managing files and folders, running applications, and managing hardware. The user interface for an OS can be command-line, menu-driven, or a graphical user interface (GUI). An OS also is responsible for storing and organizing the files on a secondary storage medium such as a hard disk. A hard disk can be divided into regions called partitions, volumes, or logical drives. Each volume then is formatted using a file system. An OS also is responsible for installing and running applications. After an application is installed, an OS provides a way to execute the software. A single tasking OS allows only one program to run at a time. A multitasking OS allows two or more programs to run and reside in memory at the same time. For an OS to support multitasking, the CPU must be running in protected mode, in which the CPU processes 32 bits of data at one time. In real mode, the CPU processes 16 bits of data at one time. An OS also communicates with hardware, using device drivers or the BIOS to interface with hardware. Device drivers are small programs stored on the hard drive that tell the computer how to communicate with a specific hardware device such as a printer. The OS uses the system BIOS to communicate with simple devices, such as keyboards. The system BIOS uses the information in CMOS setup to modify or supplement its default programming as needed.

3 System Resources

There are four types of system resources used by software and hardware: interrupt requests (IRQs), memory addresses, I/O addresses, and direct memory access (DMA) channels. An IRQ is a line on a bus that a device needing service uses to alert the CPU. When the OS is first loaded, each memory location is assigned a memory address so that the CPU can access it. I/O addresses are numbers the CPU can use to access hardware devices. A DMA channel provides a shortcut for a device to send data directly to memory, bypassing the CPU.

4 Booting Up Your Computer

The boot process can be divided into four parts: POST, loading the OS, the OS initializing itself, and loading and executing an application. Startup BIOS is in control when the boot process begins. Then the startup BIOS turns control over to the OS. During the boot, the ROM BIOS startup program performs a power-on self test (POST) and assigns system resources to devices. It then searches secondary storage for an OS. When the OS loads from a hard drive, the BIOS first executes the Master Boot Record (MBR), which turns to the partition table to find the OS boot record. The program in the OS boot record attempts to find a boot loader program for the OS (Ntldr for Windows XP, Windows 2000, and Windows NT; Io.sys for Windows 9x). The boot program then executes the boot loader program, Ntldr, so that Windows XP can start its boot sequence. Ntldr is responsible for loading Windows XP and performing several chores to complete the loading process.

5 OS Tools to Examine a System

Two Windows utilities useful for gathering information about a system are Device Manager and System Information. Device Manager allows you to see the properties for devices, to view IRQ assignments, to enable or disable a device, and more. System Information provides more detailed information, including the BIOS version you are using, the directory where the OS is installed, and how system resources are used.

KEY TERMS

After reading the chapter, you should know each of these Key Terms.

32-bit flat memory mode (*63*)
active partition (*61*)
boot drive (*61*)
boot process (*58*)
boot record (*61*)
boot disk (*65*)
boot sequence (*51*)
booting (*58*)
child directory (*42*)
cold boot (*58*)
command-line interface (*41*)
desktop (*41*)
device driver (*47*)
direct memory access (DMA) channel (*57*)
directory table (*42*)
DOS (Disk Operating System) (*39*)
emergency startup disk (ESD) (*65*)
file extension (*42*)
file system (*42*)
filename (*42*)
folder (*42*)
formatting (*42*)
graphical user interface (GUI) (*41*)
hard boot (*58*)
hardware interrupt (*53*)
hexadecimal (hex) (*55*)
hidden file (*65*)
I/O address (*55*)
Io.sys (*61*)
initialization files (*39*)
interrupt controller (*53*)
interrupt request (IRQ) line (*53*)
Linux (*39*)
kernel (*38*)
logical drive (*42*)
Mac OS (*39*)
Master Boot Record (MBR) (*61*)
memory address (*54*)
menu-driven interface (*41*)
minifile system (*63*)
multitasking (*45*)
Ntldr (*61*)
open source (*39*)
operating system (OS) (*38*)
OS/2 (*39*)
partitioning (*42*)
partition table (*61*)
path (*42*)
Plug and Play (PnP) (*48*)
polling (*54*)
port address (*55*)
power-on self test (POST) (*59*)
preemptive multitasking (*46*)
program file (*65*)
protected mode (*46*)
real mode (*46*)
recovery disk (*65*)
registry (*38*)
rescue disk (*65*)
root directory (*42*)
shadowed BIOS (*50*)
shadowed RAM (*50*)
shell (*38*)
single tasking (*45*)
soft boot (*58*)
startup disk (*65*)
subdirectory (*42*)
system resource (*51*)
Unix (*39*)
volume (*42*)
warm boot (*58*)
Windows (*39*)

Instructions: **To complete the Learn It Online exercises, start your browser, click the Address bar, and then enter the Web address scsite.com/understanding/learn. When the Understanding and Troubleshooting your PC Learn It Online page is displayed, follow the instructions in the exercises below. Each exercise has instructions for printing your results, either for your own records or for submission to your instructor.**

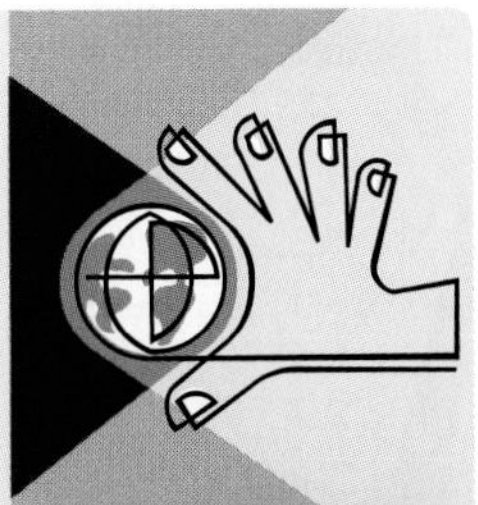

LEARN IT ONLINE

Reinforce your understanding of the chapter concepts and terms with the Learn It Online exercises.

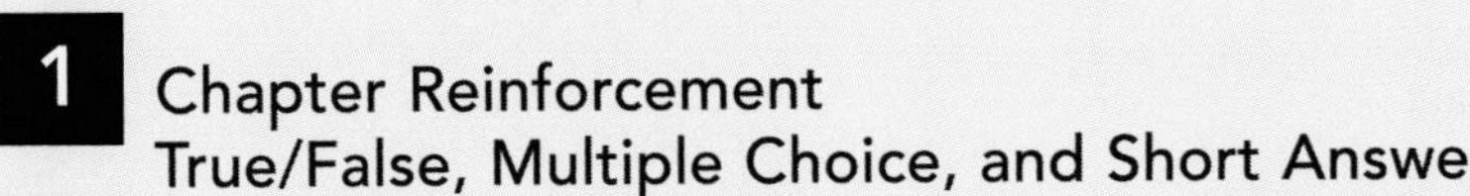

1 Chapter Reinforcement True/False, Multiple Choice, and Short Answer

Below Chapter 2, click the Chapter Reinforcement link. Print the quiz by clicking Print on the File menu for each page. Answer each question.

2 Flash Cards

Below Chapter 2, click the Flash Cards link and read the instructions. Type **20** (or a number specified by your instructor) in the Number of playing cards text box, type your name in the Enter your name text box, and then click the Flip Card button. When the flash card is displayed, read the question and then click the ANSWER box arrow to select an answer. Flip through Flash Cards. If your score is 15 (75%) correct or greater, click Print on the File menu to print your results. If your score is less than 15 (75%) correct, then redo this exercise by clicking the Replay button.

3 Practice Test

Below Chapter 2, click the Practice Test link. Answer each question, enter your first and last name at the bottom of the page, and then click the Grade Test button. When the graded practice test is displayed on your screen, click Print on the File menu to print a hard copy. Continue to take practice tests until you score 80% or better.

4 Who Wants To Be a Computer Genius?

Below Chapter 2, click the Computer Genius link. Read the instructions, enter your first and last name at the bottom of the page, and then click the PLAY button. When your score is displayed, click the PRINT RESULTS link to print a hard copy.

5 Wheel of Terms

Below Chapter 2, click the Wheel of Terms link. Read the instructions, and then enter your first and last name and your school name. Click the PLAY button. When your score is displayed, right-click the score and then click Print on the shortcut menu to print a hard copy.

6 Crossword Puzzle Challenge

Below Chapter 2, click the Crossword Puzzle Challenge link. Read the instructions, and then enter your first and last name. Click the SUBMIT button. Work the crossword puzzle. When you are finished, click the Submit button. When the crossword puzzle is redisplayed, click the Print Puzzle button to print a hard copy.

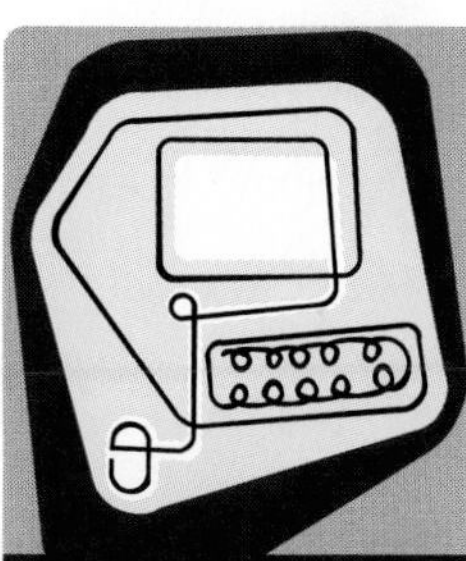

CHAPTER EXERCISES

Complete the Chapter Exercises to solidify what you learned in the chapter.

Multiple Choice

Select the best answer.

1. Which of these types of information is not stored in the Windows registry?
   a. hardware drivers
   b. OS configuration data
   c. application settings
   d. user settings
2. Which of the following types of information is not contained in a hard drive's partition table?
   a. number of partitions present
   b. where each partition begins and ends
   c. which partition is the active partition
   d. which partition lists disable hardware interrupts
3. What is the I/O address range for the keyboard?
   a. AA22-0066
   b. 6660-00FF
   c. 0060-006F
   d. 523F-A006
4. A hardware interrupt is initiated by ________.
   a. a hardware device sending an IRQ to the CPU
   b. a hardware device sending a CPU to the IRQ
   c. the IRQ polling the CPU
   d. a service request being sent to the IRQ
5. A number assigned to physical memory located either in RAM or ROM chips is called a(n) ________.
   a. I/O address
   b. DMA channel
   c. IRQ
   d. memory address

Fill in the Blank

Write the word or phrase to fill in the blank in each of the following questions.

1. The ROM BIOS startup program performs a(n) ________, which involves surveying hardware resources and needs and assigning system resources to meet those needs.
2. The ________ is the core of an operating system and the part of the operating system that loads when you first turn on your computer.
3. A(n) ________ operating system allows you to work with two or more programs that reside in memory at the same time.
4. ________ are small programs stored on the hard drive that tell the computer how to communicate with a specific hardware device.
5. In ________, an application has complete access to all hardware resources, but in ________, the OS controls how an application can access hardware.

Matching Terms

Match the terms with their definitions.

______	1. Device Manager	a.	Windows NT/2000/XP boot loader program
______	2. beep codes	b.	a list of files and subdirectories
______	3. Ntldr	c.	IRQ of the system timer
______	4. 0 (zero)	d.	used by startup BIOS to communicate errors during POST if video is not yet available
______	5. 3 (three)	e.	operating system often used for server applications; scaled-down version of Unix
______	6. Linux	f.	Windows 2000/XP utility that allows you to see the IRQ assignments made to devices
______	7. 4 (four)	g.	program that is needed to locate the beginning of the OS on a drive
______	8. Mac OS	h.	DMA channel used to cascade into the lower four DMA channels
______	9. directory table	i.	operating system only used on Apple Macintosh computers
______	10. MBR (master boot record)	j.	IRQ used by COM2

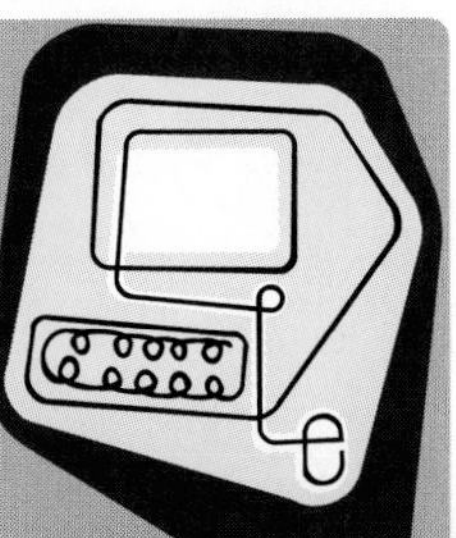

CHAPTER EXERCISES

Complete the Chapter Exercises to solidify what you learned in the chapter.

Short Answer Questions

Write a brief answer to each of the following questions.

1. List four major functions of an OS.
2. List four ways to launch an application from the Windows desktop.
3. What is the difference between a hard boot and a soft boot?
4. What are the four main parts of the boot process?
5. If, during the boot process, a computer first looks on the hard drive for an OS before checking the floppy drive, how do you change this boot sequence so that it first looks on the floppy drive for an OS?

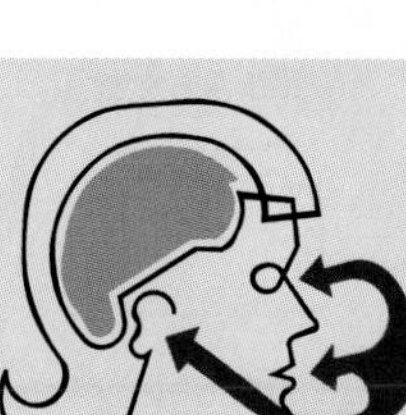

APPLY YOUR KNOWLEDGE

Check your understanding of the chapter with the hands-on Apply Your Knowledge exercises.

1 Using Device Manager

Using Windows XP perform the following steps to use Device Manager to gather information about your computer.

1. Click the Start button and then click My Computer on the Start menu.
2. When the System Properties window is displayed, click the Hardware tab and then click the Device Manager button.
3. Answer the following questions:
   a. Does your computer have a network card installed? If so, what is the name of the card?
   b. What three settings can you change under Device Manager?
   c. What are all the hardware devices that Device Manager recognizes as present?

2 Using the System Information Utility

Using Windows XP or Windows 2000, perform the following steps to run the System Information utility and gather information about your system:

1. Click the Start button on the Windows taskbar, click Run on the Start menu, and then type `Msinfo32.exe` in the Open text box. Click the OK button.
2. When the System Information dialog box appears, browse through the different levels of information in this window and answer the following questions:
   a. What OS and OS version are you using?
   b. What is your CPU speed?
   c. What is your BIOS manufacturer and version?
   d. How much RAM is installed on your video card? Explain how you got this information.
   e. What is the name of the driver file that manages your parallel port? Your serial port?
   f. How is IRQ 4 used on your system? IRQ 10? IRQ 11?
   g. Which DMA channels are used on your system and how are they used?
3. Save one or more reports about your system. Click the System Summary folder in the left pane and then click Export on the File menu. Save the exported file using the name **Ch02-syssumm.txt**. (The export process may take a few minutes.) Use Notepad or Microsoft Word to open the file and then review the information saved in each file.

3 Finding Device Drivers on the Internet

You have just borrowed a HP DeskJet 995c printer from a friend, but you forgot to borrow the CD with the printer drivers on it. Visit the Hewlett-Packard Web site (*www.hp.com*) and search the site to find the driver for the HP DeskJet 995c printer. Visit the Windows Catalog on the Microsoft Web site (*http://www.microsoft.com/windows/catalog*) and search the site to determine if the HP DeskJet 995c printer will work with Windows XP.

4 Observing the Boot Process

1. As needed, save all open files and close any open programs. If your computer has a reset button, press it and then watch what happens. If your computer does not have a reset button, turn it off, wait a few seconds, and then turn it back on. Try to note every beep, every light that goes on or off, and every message you see on the screen. Compare your notes to those of others to verify that you did not overlook something.
2. Answer these questions from observing the boot process:
   a. What type of video card are you using?
   b. Who is the BIOS vendor, and what version of the BIOS are you using?
   c. As the computer boots, memory is counted. Observe the memory count and record the amount of memory detected. What number system is used to count this memory?
3. If possible, unplug the keyboard and reboot the computer. What is different about the boot process? Write down your observations.
4. Plug in the keyboard again, unplug the monitor, and reboot. After you reboot, plug in the monitor. Did the computer know the monitor was missing?
5. Put a floppy disk that is not bootable in the floppy drive (drive A), and reboot. Write down what you observe. If the PC booted to the desktop as usual, why didn't it look to the floppy disk to load the OS?

APPLY YOUR KNOWLEDGE

Check your understanding of the chapter with the hands-on Apply Your Knowledge exercises.

CHAPTER 3

Understanding the Motherboard, the CPU, and Troubleshooting Basics

Introduction

Chapter 1 introduced the basic hardware components of a computer. Chapter 2 showed how hardware and software work together to make a functioning computer system. This chapter begins with a discussion of form factors and computer cases, followed by a detailed review of the motherboard, which is the central site of computer logic circuitry and the location of the CPU. You then learn how to install a motherboard and how to troubleshoot problems with the motherboard and the computer's electrical system.

OBJECTIVES

In this chapter, you will learn:

1. About form factors and types of motherboards
2. About components on the motherboard
3. A basic procedure for building a computer
4. How to install a motherboard
5. How to troubleshoot a motherboard and the electrical system

Up for Discussion

A customer named Joseph Ahn called a few days ago. The clock on his computer was off by about three hours, and he wanted to know how to change the time. You walked him through the simple steps of right-clicking the system tray and then adjusting the date and time in the Date and Time Properties window.

Mr. Ahn came in today, explaining that the clock time was wrong again. He can't figure out why; he's made no changes since he last spoke with you. Your first guess is that the CMOS battery in his computer is getting low on power. As Mr. Ahn watches, you open the computer case to replace the CMOS battery that provides constant power to CMOS RAM. You explain to him how CMOS RAM stores CMOS settings, such as the system date/time, and how the small battery provides enough electricity for the CMOS memory to hold configuration data—even while the main power to the computer is off. Although the CMOS battery appears to be relatively new, you replace it as a precaution and ask him to call you if he continues to have problems.

A few weeks later, Mr. Ahn calls again, this time noting that his computer occasionally freezes at odd times. He asks if he can drop his computer off that day so you can look at it. At first you suspect the problem might be the power supply or overheating. As you review your notes from his last visit, you notice that the BIOS version on his computer is very out of date. You decide to flash the BIOS to see if that will resolve the problems in Mr. Ahn's computer.

Questions:

- What are the key questions to ask when troubleshooting a computer?
- How do you access CMOS setup and what configuration changes can you make there?
- How do you flash the BIOS, and in what situations would you do so?

Form Factors and the Computer Case

The term **form factor** describes the size, shape, and general makeup of a hardware component. The form factor of the motherboard describes its size and shape, the types of cases and power supplies it can use, and its physical organization. When you put together a new computer system, or replace components in an existing system, the form factors of the motherboard, power supply, and case must all match, to ensure that:

- the motherboard fits in the case;
- the power supply cords to the motherboard provide the correct voltage, and the connectors match the connections on the board;
- the holes in the motherboard align with the holes in the case, to firmly anchor the board to the case;
- the holes in the case align with ports coming off the motherboard; and
- any wires for switches and lights on the front of the case match up with connections on the motherboard.

Form Factors

Several form factors apply to power supplies, cases, and motherboards: AT, ATX, LPX, NLX, and backplane (Figure 3-1). Each of these form factors has several variations. The four most common form factors for personal computers are the AT, Baby AT, ATX, and Mini-ATX. Of these, ATX is the form factor most widely used today, although some newer computers are using the NLX form factor.

Form Factor	Description
AT or full AT	• Oldest type of motherboard, still used in some systems • Measures 12" x 13.8" and uses P8 and P9 power connections • Much of the board overlaps with drive bays, making full AT systems difficult to install and service • Design does not allow longer cards to be placed in expansion slots
Baby AT	• Smaller version of AT; motherboard logic is stored on a smaller chip set • Measures 12" x 8.7" and uses P8 and P9 power connections • Was industry standard form factor from about 1993 to 1997 • Fits in many types of cases, including newer ATX cases • Design does not allow longer cards to be placed in expansion slots
ATX	• Most commonly used form factor today • An open, nonproprietary industry specification originally developed by Intel in 1995 • Measures 12" x 9.6" and uses a single P1 power connector • Has a more conveniently accessible layout than AT boards • Includes power connections for extra fans • Requires fewer wires to connect switches/lights on front of case to internal components
	(continued)

Form Factor	Description
NLX	• Used for low-end personal computer motherboards and low-profile cases • Motherboard has only one expansion slot, in which a riser card is mounted • Design allows the motherboard to be removed without tools
LPX and Mini-LPX Form Factors	• Developed by Western Digital; often used in low-cost systems • Has a riser card similar to NLX systems • Difficult to upgrade, they cannot handle the size and operating temperature of today's faster processors

Figure 3-1 Several form factors apply to power supplies, cases, and motherboards, each of which has unique characteristics in terms of size, features, and the position of components.

ATX FORM FACTOR **ATX** is an open, nonproprietary industry specification originally developed by Intel in 1995. An ATX motherboard measures 12" x 9.6" (smaller than a full AT motherboard). On an ATX motherboard, the CPU and memory slots are located so that, instead of sitting in front of the expansion slots, the CPU and memory slots sit beside them, preventing interference with full-length expansion cards (Figure 3-2). With the ATX form factor, components on the motherboard are arranged so they do not interfere with each other.

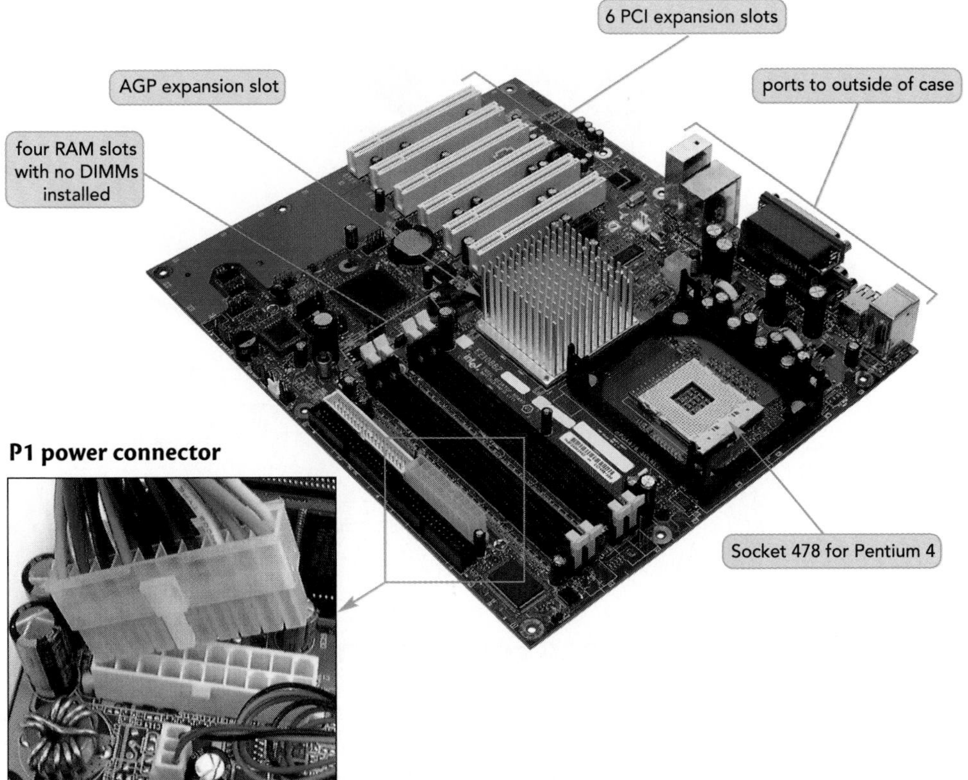

Figure 3-2 The ATX motherboard uses a single P1 power connector, although one or more auxiliary connectors can be used to supply power to the CPU or CPU fan.

The ATX power supply and motherboard use a single power connector called the P1 connector that includes a +3.3-volt circuit for a low-voltage CPU. In addition to the P1 connector, one or more auxiliary connectors can be used to supply power to the CPU or CPU fan.

In addition to regular ATX, several other types of ATX boards exist. Mini-ATX, a smaller ATX board (11.2" x 8.2"), can be used with ATX cases and power supplies. MicroATX boards have fewer expansion slots and thus cost less than standard ATX boards, but still are compatible with cases that require ATX boards. FlexATX allows for maximum flexibility in the design of system cases and boards, and therefore can be a good choice for custom systems.

More About

Form Factors

To learn more about form factors, including the similarities and differences between the AT and ATX form factors, visit the Understanding and Troubleshooting Your PC More About Web page (**scsite.com/understanding/more**) and then click Motherboard Form Factors below Chapter 3.

NLX FORM FACTOR **NLX** is a form factor designed by Intel for low-end personal computer motherboards, and is used with low-profile cases. The NLX form factor is designed to be flexible and to use space efficiently. In NLX systems, the motherboard has only one expansion slot, in which a **riser card**, or **bus riser**, is mounted (Figure 3-3). Expansion cards are mounted on the riser card, which also contains connectors for the floppy and hard drives.

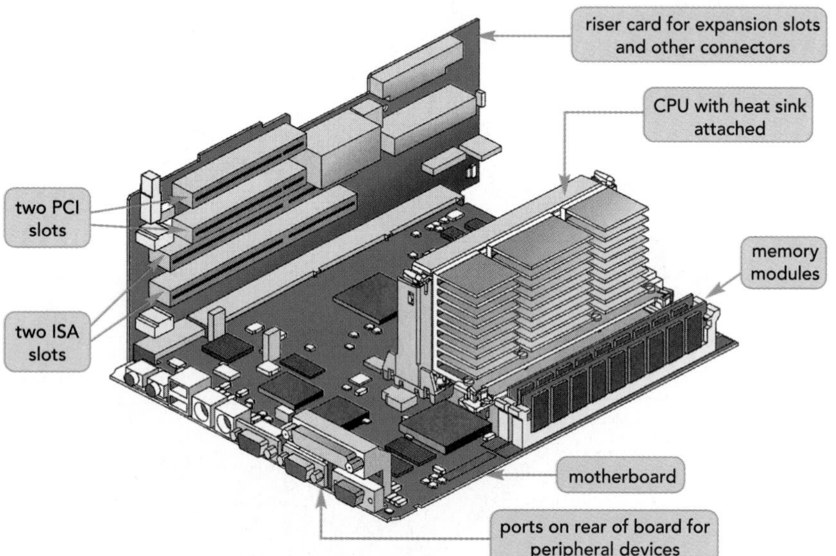

Figure 3-3 The NLX form factor uses a riser card, or bus riser, that connects to the motherboard. The riser card provides slots for expansion cards.

Computer Cases and Form Factors

The form factor also defines the type of computer case, also called a *chassis*, that is used to house the power supply, motherboard, expansion cards, and drives. As you learned in Chapter 1, a computer case falls into one of three major categories: desktop case, tower case, or notebook case (Figure 3-4).

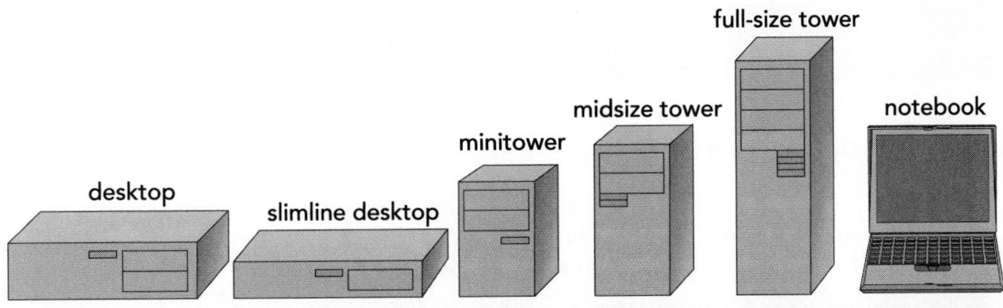

Figure 3-4 Computer cases are available for desktop, tower, and notebook computers.

DESKTOP CASES The **desktop** case sits horizontally on a desktop and often is used as a monitor stand. A desktop case typically has six expansion slots and four **drive bays**, which are rectangular spaces inside the computer case where disk drives can be installed. Most desktops use an ATX, AT, or Baby AT form factor. For low-end desktop systems, compact cases (sometimes called low-profile or slimline cases) use the NLX, LPX, or Mini-LPX form factor. Although slimline cases generally have fewer drive bays, they usually provide for some expansion.

TOWER CASES The **tower** case is one to two feet tall and often is placed vertically under a desk. A tower case has drive bays to allow room for several drives. Full-size towers, which are used for high-end personal computers and servers, usually are built to accommodate ATX, Mini-ATX, and Baby AT form factors. Variations in tower cases include:

- the **midsize tower**, also called a **miditower**, which generally has six expansion slots and four drive bays, providing moderate potential for expansion; and
- the **minitower**, also called a **microtower**, which is the smallest type of tower case and does not provide room for expansion.

NOTEBOOK CASES The **notebook** case is used for portable notebook computers (also referred to as laptop computers), as well as smaller computers called **subnotebooks**. Notebook designs are often highly proprietary, but generally are designed to conserve space, allow portability, use less power, and produce less heat than desktop or tower cases.

CUSTOM CASES Larger computer manufacturers such as Dell, Compaq, IBM, and Hewlett-Packard often use non-standard components and motherboards that require customized computer cases. For example, many Dell computers use custom ATX motherboards with non-standard power connectors and ports in slightly different locations than a standard ATX motherboard. These computers must use custom cases tailored to the motherboard to ensure the holes in the case align with ports coming off the motherboard. Because these computers use non-standard components, you must use parts from the computer manufacturer (which typically are more expensive than those from third-party manufacturers) in order to upgrade the system.

More About

Computer Cases

To learn more about computer cases and manufacturers of cases and power supplies, visit the Understanding and Troubleshooting Your PC More About Web page (**scsite.com/understanding/more**) and then click Computer Cases below Chapter 3.

 Your Turn

Taking Apart and Putting Together a PC

A PC technician needs to be comfortable taking apart a computer and then putting it back together. This exercise focuses on taking apart and putting back together a desktop or a tower computer. In addition to a ground bracelet and other safety equipment, you also will need a Phillips-head screwdriver, a flat-head screwdriver, paper, and a pencil.

1. Be sure to use a ground bracelet as you work and follow the safety precautions described in Chapter 2.
2. Put the computer on a table with plenty of room. Have several plastic bags or other containers to hold screws and label them to indicate which screws are in each. As you remove screws, place them in the correct container so that, as you reassemble the PC, you insert the correct screws back in the same holes.
3. Next, you should write down your CMOS settings, so you can rebuild the settings if your CMOS somehow gets erased. As discussed in Chapter 2, you access the CMOS setup program by pressing a specific key or keys as the computer system is starting up. Navigate through the screens and write down the various settings in a notebook.
4. Make a bootable disk if you do not already have one (for instructions on creating a bootable disk, see the Chapter 2 High-Tech Talk feature).
5. Turn off the computer and unplug it. Next, remove the cover of the computer, following these basic steps:
   a. Unplug the monitor, mouse, and keyboard. Move them out of your way.
   b. For a desktop, locate and remove the screws on the back of the case. Look for screws in each corner and one in the top (Figure 3-5). For tower cases, screws also are located on the back, typically in all four corners and down the sides.
   c. Be careful not to remove any other screws on the case! They likely are holding the power supply in place.
   d. After you remove the desktop cover screws, slide the cover forward and up to remove it from the case, as shown in Figure 3-6. For a tower case, remove the screws and then slide the cover back slightly before lifting it up to remove it. Some tower cases have panels on either side, held in place with screws on the back of the case. Remove the screws and slide each panel toward the rear, then lift the panel off of the case.

   As you complete these steps, remember that computer cases come in a variety of shapes and sizes, which means your case may not conform exactly to the steps listed above. Some Dell computer cases, for example, require no tools to open. Other computer cases require you to remove the front cover to locate the screws. If you have questions on how to remove the cover of your computer, consult your instructor or contact the manufacturer.
6. Once you have removed the cover, identify the following major components:
   a. hard drive
   b. floppy, CD-ROM, or DVD-ROM drives
   c. power supply
   d. motherboard and key components on the motherboard (If possible, leave the computer case open as you read the remainder of the chapter, so that you can identify the motherboard components as they are discussed.)
7. After you have finished, replace the cover and then place the screws back in the holes.
8. Plug in the keyboard, monitor, and mouse.
9. In the classroom, have your instructor check your work before you power up. Turn on the power and check that the computer is working properly.

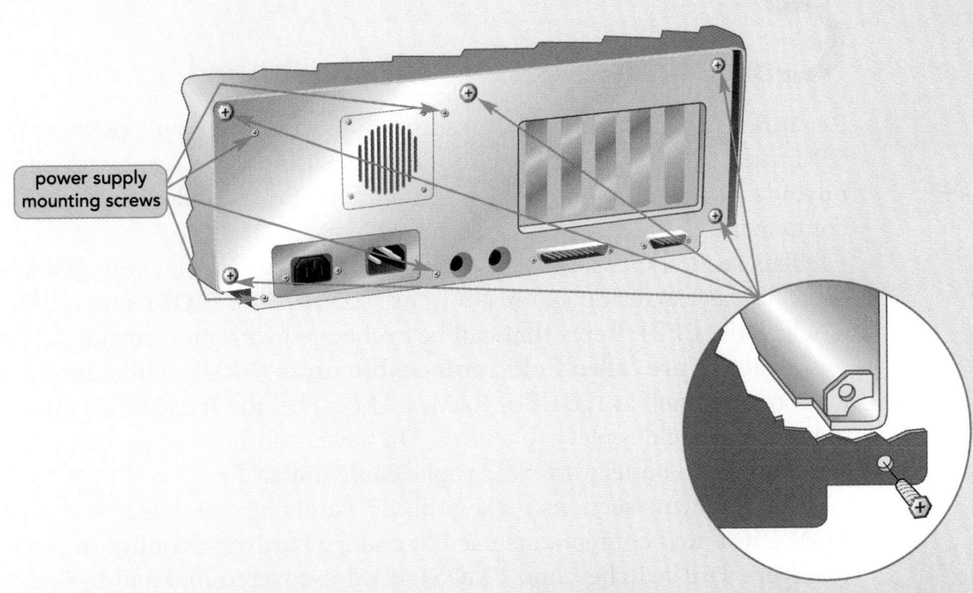

Figure 3-5 Locate the screws that hold the cover in place, as well as the power supply mounting screws. Do not unscrew the power supply mounting screws.

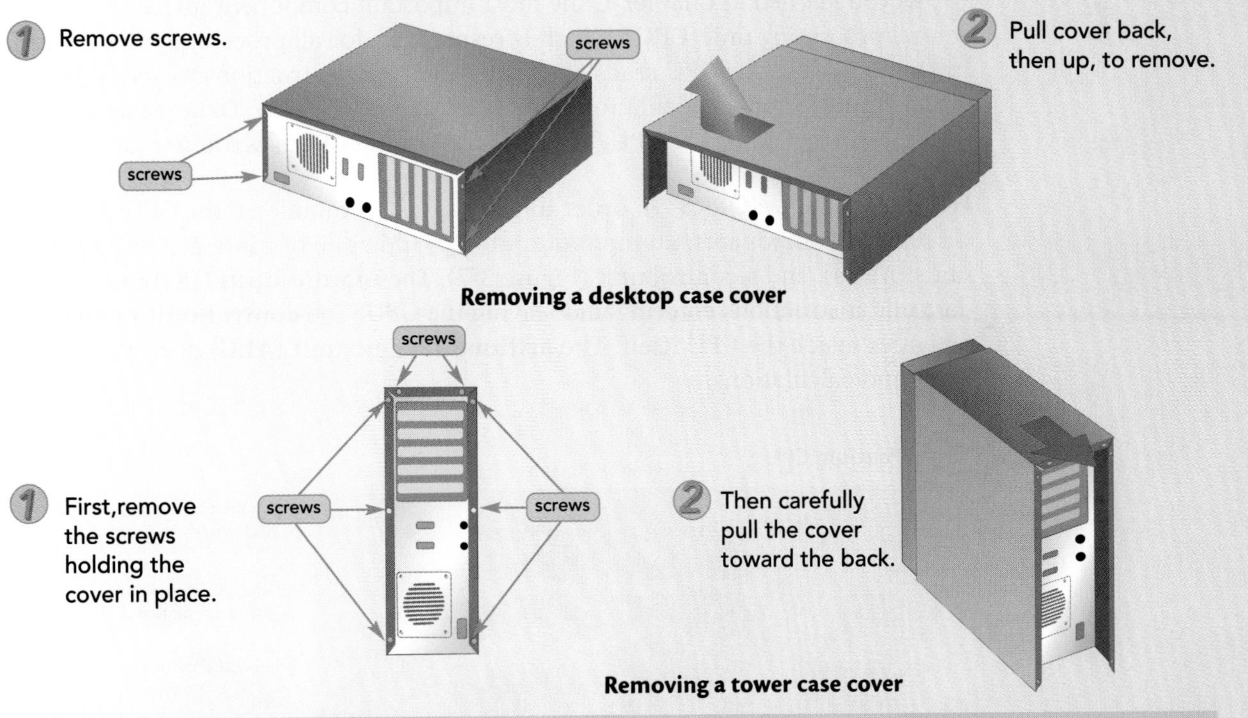

Figure 3-6 Removing a computer case cover.

Components on the Motherboard

Regardless of the form factor, a motherboard's primary purposes are to house the CPU and allow all devices to communicate with the CPU and with each other. When buying a computer, the most important factors to consider are the CPU and other components on the motherboard.

This section focuses on motherboard components that you should know how to use (such as expansion slots), configure (such as the BIOS), and exchange or replace (such as the CPU). Items that can be exchanged without returning the motherboard to the factory are called **field replaceable units** (**FRUs**). On older AT motherboards, components such as the CPU, RAM, RAM cache, the ROM BIOS chip, and the CMOS battery were field replaceable units. On newer motherboards, only the CPU, RAM, and the CMOS battery are field replaceable units.

The following sections review the CPU and chip set, buses and expansion slots, ROM BIOS, and components used to change hardware configuration settings (jumpers, DIP switches, and CMOS). RAM is covered in detail in Chapter 4.

The Central Processing Unit (CPU)

As you learned in Chapter 1, the most important component inside the case is the central processing unit (CPU), which is responsible for all processing tasks completed by the computer. The CPU reads and writes data and instructions to and from storage devices, and performs calculations and other data processing. Data received by input devices also is read by the CPU, and output from the CPU is written to output devices.

HOW THE CPU WORKS In order to perform these functions, the CPU contains three basic components: an input/output (I/O) unit, one or more arithmetic logic units (ALUs), and a control unit (Figure 3-7). The **input/output** (**I/O**) **unit** manages data and instructions entering and leaving the CPU. The **control unit** manages all activities inside the CPU itself. The **arithmetic logic unit** (**ALU**) does all comparisons and calculations.

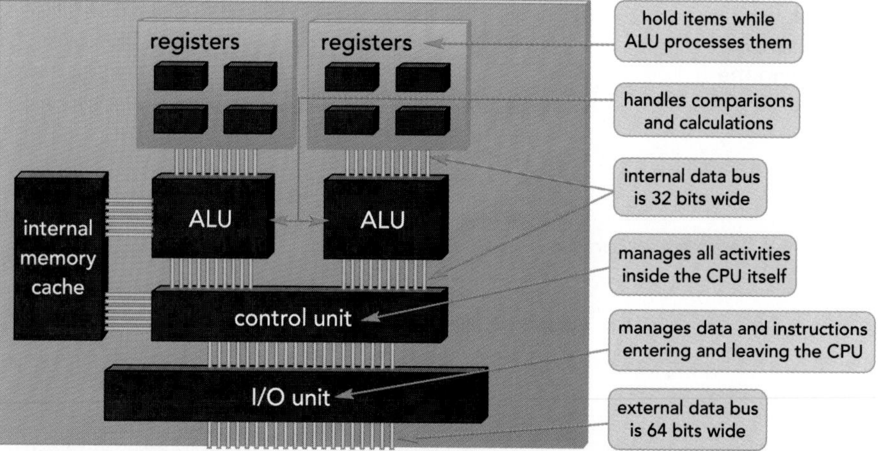

Figure 3-7 The CPU contains three basic components: an input/output (I/O) unit, one or more arithmetic logic units (ALU), and a control unit.

The CPU also needs places to store data and instructions as it works on them. These locations, called **registers**, are small holding areas inside the CPU that work much as RAM does outside the CPU. Registers hold counters, data, instructions, and addresses that the ALU is currently processing. In addition to registers, the CPU has its own internal memory cache that holds data and instructions waiting to be processed by the ALU. A **memory cache** is a small amount of memory that provides faster access to data and instructions than other types of RAM. The CPU has an **internal bus** for communication to the internal memory cache. The CPU's internal bus operates at a much higher frequency than the **external bus**, or system bus, which is used to send data, instructions, addresses, and control signals into and out of the CPU. The industry sometimes calls an internal bus the **back side bus** (**BSB**) and an external bus the **front side bus** (**FSB**).

What does it mean that a processor supports a motherboard speed of 800 MHz?

When you read that a processor supports a motherboard speed of 533 MHz, 800 MHz, or any other speed, the speed refers to the system bus speed. In documentation you sometimes see the system bus speed called the *bus clock*, because the pulses generated on the clock line of the bus determine its speed. Other slower buses connect to the system bus, which serves as the go-between for other buses and the CPU.

Why do some CPUs have one ALU, while others have two or more?

Older CPUs had only a single ALU, but beginning with the Intel Pentium line, CPUs now contain at least two ALUs so the CPU can process two instructions at once. For Pentiums, the front side (external) bus is 64 bits wide, but the back side bus is only 32 bits wide, because of this dual-processing design. This is why the industry calls the Pentium a 32-bit processor; it processes 32 bits at a time internally, even though it uses a 64-bit bus externally. Intel has a 64-bit processor, called the Itanium, which has a 128-bit external data bus.

CHARACTERSTICS OF CPUs As you will learn later, several different companies manufacture CPUs for use in IBM-compatible personal computers. Each of these chips has several basic characteristics, which you can use to identify a CPU installed in a computer, determine what performance to expect from a CPU, and compare it to other CPUs available on the market. Several of these characteristics — processor speed, bus speed, word size and data path size, instruction sets, and memory cache — are discussed in the following sections.

Processor Speed A key characteristic of a CPU is the **processor speed**, which is the speed at which the CPU operates internally. Processor speed is measured in gigahertz (GHz) or billions of cycles per second, based on the pulse of the system clock. The first CPU used in an IBM personal computer, called the 8088, worked at about 4.77 MHz, or 4,770,000 clock pulses per second. An average speed for a new CPU today is about 3 GHz, or 3,000,000,000 pulses per second. To provide a sense of just how fast such a CPU is, in less than one second, a 3 GHz processor beats more times than your heart beats in a lifetime.

Bus Speed The system bus speed that the processor supports also is important. **Bus speed** is the frequency or speed at which data moves on a bus. A motherboard has several buses, including the system bus that transfers data into and out of the CPU.

As you have learned, the system clock synchronizes data transfer into and out of the CPU on the system bus. More than one bit, however, can be transferred in every clock cycle. Thus, if a CPU has a clock speed of 200 MHz and can transfer four bits per cycle, then the **system bus speed** (often referred to as **front side bus speed**) is 800 MHz. With today's CPUs, common speeds for the system bus are 800 MHz, 533 MHz, or 400 MHz. System bus speeds for older CPUs are 200 MHz, 133 MHz, or 100 MHz.

FAQ 3-3

Is the system bus the same as the motherboard bus and the external bus?

Yes. The system bus is referred to by many different names. It is sometimes called the *motherboard bus*, because it is the main bus on the motherboard connecting directly to the CPU, or it is called the *Pentium bus* because it connects directly to the Pentium. It is called the *host bus* because other buses connect to it to get to the CPU, and it is also called the *memory bus* because it connects the CPU to RAM. It is called the *external bus* or the *front side bus* because it connects to the side of the CPU that faces the outside world. Although the name memory bus is the most descriptive, this book uses the more popular term, system bus.

FAQ 3-4

What is a multiplier, when referring to CPU speed?

Suppose you have a CPU with a processor speed of 3.2 GHz, which is the speed at which the CPU operates internally, and a system bus speed of 800 MHz, the speed at which the CPU sends and receives data from external sources. In this case, the CPU operates internally at 4 times the speed of the system bus. This factor of 4 is called the **multiplier** (common multipliers are 1.5, 2, 2.5, 3, 3.5, and 4). Using the multiplier, you can multiply the system bus speed by the multiplier to determine the processor speed of the CPU:

system bus speed x multiplier = processor speed

Older motherboards used jumpers or CMOS setup to set the system bus speed and multiplier, which in turn defined the processor speed. To set the correct motherboard speed and multiplier, you needed to know the speed for which the CPU was designed. Newer motherboards automatically detect the CPU speed and adjust the system bus speed accordingly. Make sure you install a CPU that runs at a speed the motherboard can support.

Word Size and Data Path Size Two other key characteristics that determine the speed of CPU are word size and data path size. **Word size**, sometimes called the **internal data path size**, is the largest number of bits that can be carried on the internal data bus and that the CPU can process in one operation. Word size ranges from 16 bits (2 bytes) to 64 bits (8 bytes). The CPU shown in Figure 3-7 on page 84, for example, has a word size of 32 bits.

The **data path**, sometimes called the **external data path size**, is the largest number of bits that can be transported to and from the CPU on the system bus. Data path size thus is based on the size of the system bus. The data path for the CPU shown in Figure 3-7 is 64 bits wide. As illustrated in this example, word size of a CPU might not be as large as the data path size; some CPUs can receive more bits than they can process at one time.

Instruction Sets The functionality of a chip also is determined by the instruction set used in the CPU. An **instruction set** is a basic set of commands permanently built into the CPU chip to perform fundamental operations, such as comparing or adding two numbers. Older CPUs use one of two types of instruction sets: reduced instruction set computing (RISC) or complex instruction set computing (CISC). **Complex instruction set computing** (**CISC**) processors have larger instruction sets and generally run more slowly, because it takes more steps to accomplish a simple operation.

Reduced instruction set computing (**RISC**) processors have fewer instructions but run more quickly. Until recently, most personal computers used CPUs based on CISC. Newer CPUs, however, are starting to take advantage of RISC to improve performance. Newer CPUs also may include instruction sets tailored for specific functions, such as the ability to multitask, or execute two commands simultaneously.

Memory Cache A CPU's performance also is impacted by the amount of memory included with the chip. A memory cache is a small amount of RAM referred to as static RAM (SRAM), which is much faster than the remaining portion of RAM, which is called dynamic RAM (DRAM). **Dynamic RAM** (**DRAM**) loses data rapidly and must be refreshed often. **Static RAM** (**SRAM**) is faster than DRAM because SRAM does not need refreshing, and can hold its data as long as power is available. When data and instructions are stored temporarily in memory cache that uses SRAM, the CPU can access and process instructions and data faster. Having a large memory cache thus provides faster CPU performance during complex calculations that require a lot of data to be available for processing. (Chapter 4 provides additional detail on different types of memory, such as SRAM and DRAM).

CPUs can have a memory cache on the processor chip, as well as a cache inside the processor housing on a small circuit board. (In documentation, the chip is sometimes called a **die**). A memory cache on the CPU die is called an **internal cache**, **primary cache**, or **Level 1** (**L1**) **cache** (Figure 3-8). A cache outside the CPU microchip or on a small circuit board with the CPU housing is called **external cache**, **secondary cache**, or **Level 2** (**L2**) **cache**. Most of the chips used today have L2 cache directly on the same die as the processor core; this type of L2 cache is referred to as **Advanced Transfer Cache** (**ATC**). ATC makes it possible for the Pentium to fit on a smaller and less expensive form factor, but also makes it difficult to differentiate L1 cache from L2 cache. L2 cache stored on a separate microchip within the CPU housing is called **on-package L2 cache** or **discrete L2 cache**. The back side bus servicing this cache runs at half the speed of the front side bus. In addition, some processors have **Level 3** (**L3**) **cache**, which is additional cache on the motherboard further away from the CPU than L2 cache.

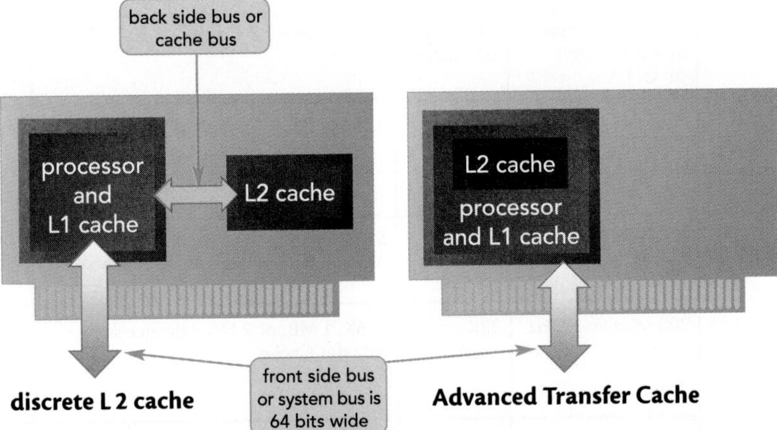

Figure 3-8 Some chips use discrete L2 cache, in which the L2 cache is on a separate die from the processor. Most of today's chips use Advanced Transfer Cache (ATC), in which the L2 cache is on the same die as the processor.

FAQ 3-5

Is it true that L2 cache sometimes is referred to as L3 cache?

As more processors ship with L1 and L2 cache built in, Level 3 cache is more widely used. Because the processor already contains L1 and L2 cache in the processor itself, L3 cache then is the extra cache that sits on the motherboard between the processor and main memory. In short, what was once L2 cache on motherboards is considered to be L3 cache when used with microprocessors containing built-in L1 and L2 caches.

Multiprocessing Some microchips are designed to work in cooperation with other CPUs installed on the same motherboard. Others are really two processors, thus allowing them to do more than one thing at a time. This processing approach, called **multiprocessing** or **parallel processing**, is the simultaneous use of more than one CPU to execute a program. (The terms multitasking and multiprocessing often are used interchangeably, although multiprocessing implies that more than one CPU is involved.) Ideally, parallel processing makes a program run faster because there are more CPUs processing it. However, it can be difficult to divide a program in such a way that separate CPUs can execute different portions without interfering with each other.

TYPES OF CPUS Most IBM and IBM-compatible computers manufactured today use microprocessor chips made by Intel, AMD, or Via Technologies.

Pentium Processors Today, Intel CPUs are the most widely used CPU microchips in personal computers. Early CPUs by Intel were identified by model numbers: 8088, 8086, 80286, 386, and 486. The model numbers can be written with or without the 80 prefix and sometimes are preceded with an i, as in 80486, 486, or i486. After the 486, Intel introduced the Pentium CPU, the first of several in the family of Pentium chips. Pentium chips are sometimes identified simply with a P and a number (for example, P4 for Pentium 4).

Intel processors currently used in today's desktop and notebook computers include Celeron, Pentium III, and Pentium 4 (Figure 3-9). As you will learn later, each type of CPU uses a different slot or socket to connect to the motherboard.

	Processor	Latest Processor Speeds (MHz or GHz)	Primary L1 Cache	Secondary L2 Cache	System Bus Speeds (MHz)
	Celeron *low-end processor for PC multimedia and home market segments*	850 MHz to 2.86 GHz	32K or Execution Trace Cache	128K or 256K Advanced Transfer Cache	Up to 400
	Pentium III *introduced Streaming SIMD Extensions*	450 MHz to 1.33 GHz	32K	512K unified, non-blocking cache or 256K Advanced Transfer Cache	100, 133
	Pentium III Xeon *high-end Pentium III processor designed for mid-range servers*	700 MHz to 1 GHz	32K	256K, 1 MB, or 2 MB Advanced Transfer Cache	100 or 133
	Pentium 4 *increased performance for multimedia applications and Web technologies*	2.6 GHz to 3.2 GHz	Execution Trace Cache	256K or 512K Advanced Transfer Cache (P4 Extreme Edition also includes 2 MB of L3 cache)	400, 533, or 800

Figure 3-9 The Intel Pentium and Xeon family of CPUs. Earlier variations of the Pentium II processor included the Celeron and Xeon. Recently, Intel started referring to the Pentium Xeon as simply the Xeon, making it another group of CPUs that are similar to the Pentiums. The Xeon processors are intended to be used in high-end workstations and servers, but are included in the table to make it complete.

- *Celeron*: The Celeron processor is a Pentium processor that targets the low-end PC multimedia and home market segments. It uses Advanced Transfer Cache for L2 cache and works well with most common Windows applications.
- *Pentium III*: The Pentium III has a 100-MHz or 133-MHz system bus with a processor speed up to 1.4 GHz. The Pentium III introduced Intel's performance enhancement called **Streaming SIMD Extensions** (**SSE**). (**SIMD** stands for single instruction, multiple data and is an instruction set designed to provide better multimedia processing). The Pentium III Xeon is a high-end Pentium III processor designed for midrange servers and high-end workstations.
- *Pentium 4:* The Pentium 4 processor currently can run at up to 3.2 GHz. It provides increased performance for multimedia applications such as digital video, as well as for new Web technologies. It currently uses a 400-, 533-, or 800-MHz system bus. The Pentium 4's improved design provides increased efficiency in creating digital files, faster ways to work with pictures, new ways for the user to interface with the computer (such as through natural speech), and greater responsiveness to Internet applications.

  The Pentium 4 uses a type of Level 1 cache called **Execution Trace Cache**, which contains a list of operations that have been decoded and are waiting to be executed. For example, the Pentium 4 has 8K of Level 1 cache used for data and an additional 12K of Execution Trace Cache. By storing a list of operations ready to be executed, Execution Trace Cache makes the execution process faster.

The Pentium III, Celeron, and Pentium 4 processors also all have versions designed for use in notebook computers. The Pentium 4M (for Mobile) provides the highest performance for notebooks used for multimedia, video, and other data-intensive operations, and is designed to support many low-power features that extend battery life. The Pentium 4M currently is available in speeds up to 2.6 GHz on a 400-MHz system bus.

FAQ 3-6

Is there a type of CPU named Prescott? How is it different than a Pentium 4?

Prescott is the code name for the soon-to-be-released Intel processor that is built to replace the Pentiums. It is designed to improve the multitasking capabilities of the Pentium 4 in response to desktop users who run many applications at the same time. The Prescott uses 32-bit processing.

AMD and Via Processors AMD and VIA Technologies also make processors for use in IBM-compatible personal computers. Figure 3-10 on the next page lists older and current processors made by AMD and VIA Technologies. Many of the AMD processors are popular in the game and hobbyist markets, while newer VIA processors are designed for notebook computers. AMD and VIA processors are generally less expensive than comparable Intel processors.

Processor	Latest Clock Speeds (MHz or GHz)	Pentium Comparison	System Bus Speed (MHz)
AMD PROCESSORS			
AMD-K6-2	166 to 475 MHz	Pentium II, Celeron	66, 95, 100
AMD-K6-III	350 to 450 MHz	Pentium II	100
Duron	1 GHz to 1.3 GHz	Celeron	200
Athlon	Up to 1.9 GHz	Pentium III	200
Athlon Model 4	Up to 1.4 GHz	Pentium III	266
Athlon MP	1.4 GHz to 2.1 GHz	Pentium III	200 to 400+
Athlon XP	Up to 2.2 GHz	Pentium 4	266, 333, 400
VIA (CYRIX) PROCESSORS			
Cyrix M II	300, 333, 350	Pentium II, Celeron	66, 75, 83, 95, 100
Cyrix III	433 to 533	Celeron, Pentium III	66, 100, 133
VIA C3	Up to 1 GHz	Celeron	100 or 133

Figure 3-10 The family of AMD and VIA processors.

64-bit Processors As you learned in Chapter 2, earlier processors operated in real mode using a 16-bit data path, while newer processors operate in protected mode using a 32-bit path. Today, almost all applications use 32-bit protected mode, because most processors for desktop and notebook computers use a 32-bit data path.

Newer computers, however, also can use 64-bit processors that provide even faster performance. Both Intel and AMD have 64-bit processors on the market for use in high-end desktop computers. To take full advantage of a 64-bit processor, such as the Intel Itanium or the AMD Opteron (Figure 3-11), software developers must recompile their applications to use 64-bit processing and write operating systems that use 64-bit data transfers. Microsoft provides a special version of Windows XP, called Windows XP 64 Bit Edition, which works with the Itanium and Opteron processors.

	Processor	Processor Speeds	L1 Cache	L2 Cache	L3 Cache	System Bus Speed
	Intel Itanium	733 and 800 MHz	32K	96K	2 MB or 4 MB	266 MHz
	Intel Itanium 2	900 MHz to 1.5 GHz	32K	256K	1.5 MB to 6 MB	400 MHz
	AMD Opteron	1.4 GHZ to 2.0 GHz	64K	1 MB	N/A	244 MHz

Figure 3-11 Newer 64-bit processors from Intel and AMD have several enhancements to speed processing.

CPU HEAT SINKS AND COOLING FANS Because a CPU generates so much heat, computer systems use a cooling fan to keep temperatures between 90 and 110 degrees Fahrenheit (32 and 43 degrees Celsius). As shown in Figure 3-12, the cooling fan usually fits on top of the CPU with a wire or plastic clip. The cooling fan gets power via a power connector on the motherboard or one of the power cables coming from the power supply.

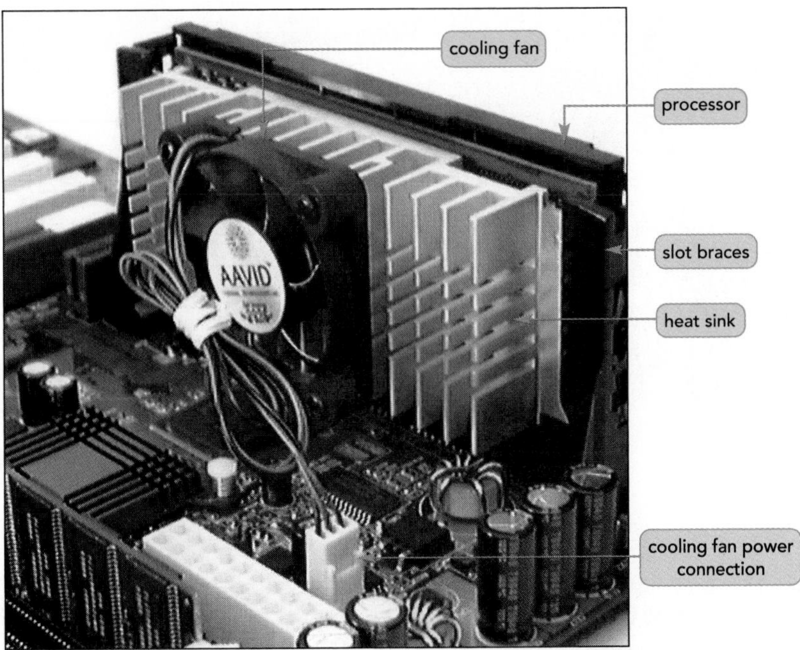

Figure 3-12 A CPU cooling fan mounts on the top or side of the CPU housing and is powered by an electrical connection to the motherboard.

In some computer systems, a cream-like thermal compound, called *thermal grease*, is placed between the fan and the CPU. The thermal grease, which transmits heat better than air, draws heat from the CPU and passes it to the fan. The compound also makes an airtight connection between the fan and the CPU.

Keeping a system cool is important; if the system overheats, components can be damaged. At one time, CPU cooling fans were optional equipment used to prevent system errors and to prolong the life of the CPU. Today's power-intensive CPUs require one or more cooling fans to maintain a temperature that will not damage the CPU. High-end systems can have as many as seven or eight fans mounted inside the computer case.

Older CPUs used a heat sink instead of a cooling fan. A **heat sink** is a clip-on device that mounts on top of the CPU; fingers or fins at its base pull the heat away from the CPU. Today, most cooling fans designed to mount on the CPU housing also have a heat sink, as shown in Figure 3-12. The combination of the heat sink and cooling fan is sometimes called a **cooler** (Figure 3-13 on the next page). The cooler is mounted in a frame to hold it above the chip. Heat sinks sometimes mount on top of other chips to keep them cool. For example, in Figure 3-13, you can see a heat sink mounted on top of a chip sitting behind the Pentium 4 CPU.

More About

Processor Technologies

To learn more about older 16-bit processors, as well as the technology enhancements behind 64-bit processors such as the Itanium and Opteron, visit the Understanding and Troubleshooting Your PC More About Web page (**scsite.com/understanding/more**) and then click Processor Technologies below Chapter 3.

Figure 3-13 A cooler can be made of aluminum or copper. The cooler is mounted in a frame to hold it above the chip.

More About

Cooling a System

In addition to using fans and heat sinks to keep a CPU cool, other options, such as refrigeration, peltiers, and water coolers, are available. To learn more about these options, visit the Understanding and Troubleshooting Your PC More About Web page (**scsite.com/understanding/more**) and then click System Cooling Options below Chapter 3.

CPU PACKAGING, SLOTS, AND SOCKETS Processor chips are small and fragile, which means it can be difficult to connect a CPU to a motherboard without damaging it. For this reason, CPUs and other chips typically are packaged in some type of protective material that also helps dissipate heat. They also have connectors of a standard size and shape. Figure 3-14 lists several of the package types used to house Intel and AMD processors used in personal computers.

The design of a processor's packaging is defined by the socket or slot that the processor uses to connect to the motherboard (shown in Figure 3-15 on page 94 with no processor installed). The type of socket or slot supplied by the motherboard for the processor must match that required by the processor. Figure 3-16 on page 94 lists several types of sockets and slots used by CPUs. Slots 1 and 2 are proprietary Intel slots, and Socket A and Slot A are proprietary AMD connectors.

Current CPU sockets, called **zero insertion force (ZIF) sockets**, have a small lever on the side that lifts the CPU up and out of the socket. Pushing the lever down moves the CPU into its pin connectors with equal force over the entire housing, thus allowing you to remove and replace the CPU more easily, with less chance of damage.

Most processors today are available in one or more package types, so it is important to check the motherboard documentation to determine what processor and processor package matches the socket or slot on the motherboard. It also is important to determine if the motherboard can provide the required voltage to the CPU.

Packaging	Description
SECC (Single Edge Contact Cartridge)	The processor is completely covered with a black plastic housing, and a heat sink and fan are attached to the housing. You cannot see the circuit board or edge connector in a SECC package. The Pentium II and Pentium III use a SECC package in Slot 1 with 242 contacts. The Pentium II Xeon and Pentium III Xeon use a SECC with 330 contacts.
SECC2 (Single Edge Contact Cartridge, version 2)	Similar to the SECC, but it does not have the heat sink thermal plate, and the edge connector on the processor circuit board is visible at the bottom of the housing. The Pentium II and Pentium III use the SECC2 package with 242 contacts.
SEP (Single Edge Processor)	Similar to the SECC package, but the black plastic housing does not completely cover the processor, making the circuit board visible at the bottom of the housing. The first Celeron processors used the SEP package in Slot 1. It has 242 contacts.
PPGA (Plastic Pin Grid Array)	The processor is housed in a square box designed to fit flat into Socket 370. Pins are on the underside of the flat housing, and heat sinks or fans can be attached to the top of the housing by using a thermal plate or heat spreader. The early Celeron processors used this package with 370 pins.
PGA (Pin Grid Array)	Pins on the bottom of this package are staggered and can be inserted only one way into the socket. The Xeon processors use this package with 603 pins.
OOI/OLGA (Organic Land Grid Array)	Used by some Pentium 4s, this 423-pin package is similar to the PGA package, but is designed to dissipate heat faster.
FC-PGA (Flip Chip Pin Grid Array)	Looks like the PPGA package and uses Socket 370. Coolers can be attached directly to the top of the package. Some Pentium III and Celeron processors use this package.
FC-PGA2 (Flip Chip Pin Grid Array 2)	Similar to the FC-PGA package, but has a heat sink attached directly to the die of the processor. When used by a Pentium III or Celeron processor, it has 370 pins. When used by the Pentium 4, it has 478 pins.
PAC (Pin Array Cartridge)	A flat cartridge about the size of an index card, used by Itanium processors. It uses either Socket PAC418, which has 418 pins, or Socket PAC611, which has 611 pins.
CPGA (Ceramic Pin Grid Array)	A flat package with pins on the underside used by several AMD processors including the Duron, AMD-K6-2, and AMD-K6-III. Number of pins varies among processors.
OPGA (Organic Pin Grid Array)	Used by AMD Athlon MP, AMD Athlon XP, and some models of the AMD Duron.
µPGA (Micro Pin Grid Array)	Used by AMD 64-bit processors including the AMD Opteron and Athlon 64.

Figure 3-14 Several of the package types used to house Intel and AMD processors used in personal computers.

Figure 3-15 For Slot 1, which is used by the Pentium II in an SECC package, the motherboard uses universal retention mechanism (URM) arms to receive and hold the CPU (in this photo, the arms are in the upright position).

Connector Name	Used by CPU	Number of Pins	Voltage
Socket 4	Classic Pentium 60/66	273 pins 21 x 21 PGA grid	5 V
Socket 5	Classic Pentium 75/90/100/120/133	320 pins 37 x 37 SPGA grid	3.3 V
Socket 6	Not used	235 pins 19 x 19 PGA grid	3.3 V
Socket 7	Pentium MMX, Fast Classic Pentium, AMD KS, AMD KS, Cyrix M	321 pins 37 x 37 SPGA grid	2.5 V to 3.3 V
Super Socket 7	AMD KS-2, AMD KS-III	321 pins 37 x 37 SPGA grid	2.5 V to 3.3 V
Socket 8	Pentium Pro	387 pins 24 x 26 SPGA grid	3.3 V
Socket 370 PGA370 Socket	Pentium III, Celeron, Cyrix III	370 pins in a 37 x 37 SPGA grid	1.5 V or 2 V
Slot 1 SC242	Pentium II, Pentium III	242 pins in 2 rows, rectangular shape	2.8 V and 3.3 V
Slot A	AMD Athlon	242 pins in 2 rows, rectangular shape	1.3 V to 2.05 V
Socket A Socket 462	AMD Athlon and Duron	462 pins, SPGA grid, rectangular shape	1.5 V to 1.85V
Slot 2 SC330	Pentium II Xeon, Pentium III Xeon	330 pins in 2 rows, rectangular shape	1.5 V to 3.5 V
Socket 423	Pentium 4	423 pins 39 x 39 SPGA grid	1.7 V and 1.75 V
Socket 478	Pentium 4	478 pins in a dense µPGA grid	1.7 V and 1.75 V
Socket PAC418	Itanium	418 pins	3.3 V
PAC611	Itanium 2	611 pins	3.3 V
Socket 603	Xeon DP and MP	603 pins	1.5 and 1.7 V

Figure 3-16 CPU sockets and slots.

CPU Voltage Regulation

As shown in Figure 3-16, different CPUs require different levels of voltage on the motherboard. Some CPUs use a **single-voltage** design, in which the same voltage is used for external (input/output) and internal (core) operations. Many newer CPUs use a **dual-voltage**, or **split rail** design, in which one voltage is used for external operations and another for internal operations.

Older motherboards require that you set jumpers to set the voltage to the CPU, while newer motherboards use a **voltage regulator module (VRM)** to control the amount of voltage to the CPU automatically. The voltage regulator converts the power supplied by the motherboard to the correct core voltage for the processor in the socket. A VRM can be embedded in the motherboard or added later when you upgrade the processor. For example, a Pentium Pro used only a single voltage (3.3 volts), but the Pentium III uses a core voltage of 2.0 volts and an I/O voltage of 3.4 volts. If you upgrade a system from the Classic Pentium to the Pentium MMX, you can use the motherboard's embedded VRM to regulate the 2.0 volts and install another VRM to regulate the 3.4 volts.

Some chips, such as the Pentium 4, receive voltage from the +12-volt power line to the motherboard, rather than the lower-voltage lines used by earlier Pentiums. Some newer motherboards thus have an additional connector, called the ATX12V, to support chips requiring voltage from the motherboard (Figure 3-17). Always read the motherboard and processor documentation to know how to use these auxiliary power connections.

More About

Regulating CPU Voltage Using Jumpers

Some older motherboards require that you set jumpers to determine the voltage to the CPU. To learn more about setting jumpers to regulate CPU voltage, visit the Understanding and Troubleshooting Your PC More About Web page (**scsite.com/understanding/more**) and then click Regulating CPU Voltage below Chapter 3.

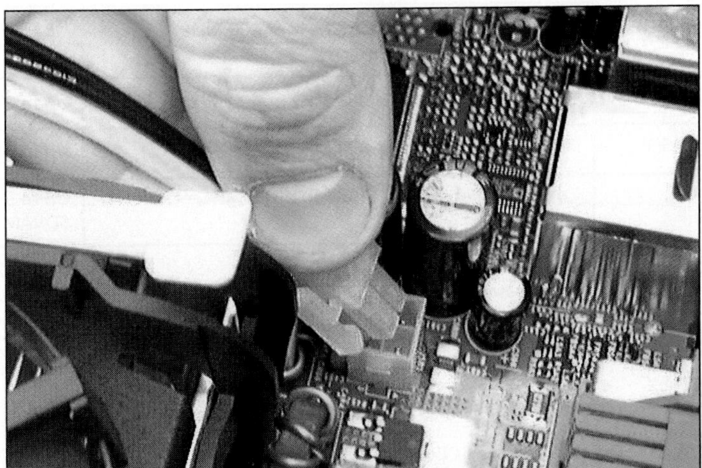

Figure 3-17 An auxiliary 4-pin power cord from the power supply connects to the ATX12V connector on the motherboard to provide power to the Pentium 4 CPU.

The Chip Set

Recall from Chapter 1 that a chip set is a group of chips on the motherboard that controls the flow of data and instructions to and from the CPU, providing careful timing of activities. Collectively, the chip set controls the memory cache, external buses, and some peripherals, as well as providing power management. Intel makes the most popular chip sets; the chip sets currently available from Intel are listed in Figure 3-18. The types of memory supported by each chip set are explained in detail in the next chapter.

Common Name	Model Number	Processors Supported	System Bus Speed Supported	Memory Supported
"E" chip set family	E8870	Up to four Itanium 2 processors	400 MHz	Up to 128 GB on DIMMs
	E7501	Dual Xeon processors	533 MHz	Up to 16 GB on DIMMs
	E7500	Dual Xeon processors	400 MHz	Up to 16 GB on DIMMs
	E7505	Dual Xeon processors	533 MHz or 400 MHz	Up to 16 GB on DIMMs
	E7205	Pentium 4	533 MHz or 400 MHz	Up to 4 GB on DIMMs
Intel i800 Series	875P	Pentium 4	800 MHz or 533 MHz	Up to 4 GB on DIMMs
	865G or 865PE	Pentium 4	800 MHz, 533 MHz or 400 MHz	Up to 4 GB on DIMMs
	865P	Pentium 4	533 MHz or 400 MHz	Up to 4 GB on DIMMs
	860	Dual Xeon processors	400 MHz	Up to 4 GB of memory on up to 8 RIMMs
	850	Pentium 4 or Celeron	400 MHz	Up to 2 GB of memory on up to 4 RIMMs
	850E	Pentium 4 or Celeron	533 MHz or 400 MHz	Up to 2 GB of memory on up to 4 RIMMs
	845PE, 845GE, and 845E	Pentium 4 or Celeron	533 MHz or 400 MHz	Up to 2 GB on DIMMs
	845G and 845GV	Pentium 4 or Celeron	533 MHz or 400 MHz	Up to 2 GB on DIMMs
	845 or 845GL	Pentium 4 or Celeron	400 MHz	Up to 2 GB on DIMMs
	815, 815E, or 815EP	Celeron or Pentium III	133 MHz, 100 MHz, or 66 MHz	Up to 512 MB of SDRAM DIMMs
Orion	460GX	Up to four Itanium 2 processors	400 MHz	Up to 128 GB of SDRAM DIMMs

Figure 3-18 Intel chip sets.

Beginning with the Intel i800 series of chip sets, the buses are connected using a hub interface architecture, called **Accelerated Hub Architecture** (Figure 3-19). In the Accelerated Hub Architecture, all I/O buses connect to a hub, which is called the **hub interface**; the hub in turn connects to the system bus. The fast end of the hub, which contains the graphics and memory controller, connects to the system bus and is called the hub's **North Bridge**. The slower end of the hub, called the **South Bridge**, contains the I/O controller hub. All I/O devices except the display and memory connect to the hub using the slower South Bridge. On a motherboard, when you see two major chips for the chip set, one is controlling the North Bridge and the other is controlling the South Bridge.

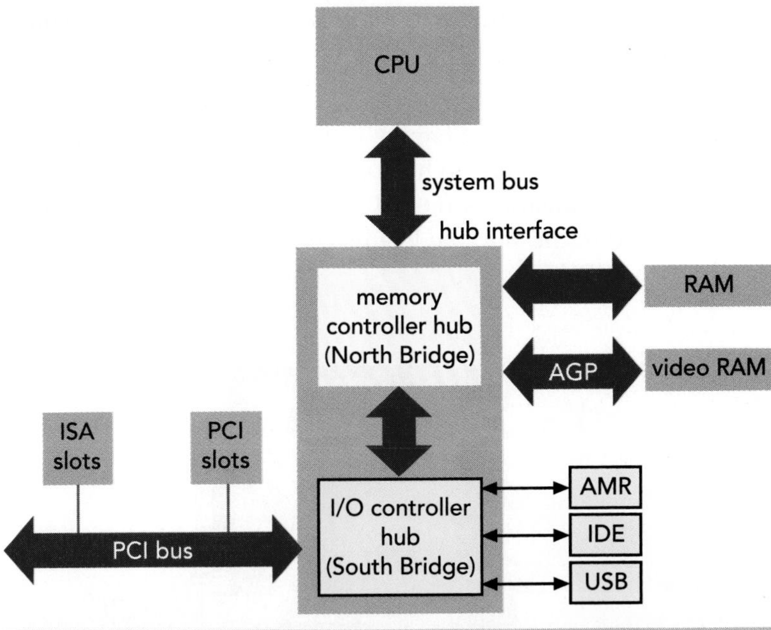

Figure 3-19 In the Accelerated Hub Architecture, a hub interface is used to connect slower I/O buses to the system bus.

Quiz Yourself 3-1

To test your knowledge of the CPU and chip set, visit the Understanding and Troubleshooting Your PC Quiz Yourself Web page (scsite.com/understanding/quiz). Click Quiz Yourself 1 below Chapter 3.

Buses and Expansion Slots

The earliest PC had only a single system bus. Today's personal computers have four or five buses, each with different speeds, access methods, and protocols. As you have seen, backward compatibility dictates that older buses be supported on a motherboard, even when faster, newer buses exist. The net result is a complex system of buses on a motherboard.

WHAT A BUS DOES If you look at the bottom of a motherboard, you will see the maze of circuits that make up a bus. These embedded wires carry four kinds of cargo:

- *Electrical power*. Chips on the motherboard require power to function. These chips tap into a bus's power lines and draw what they need.
- *Control signals*. Some wires on a bus carry control signals that coordinate all the activity.
- *Memory addresses*. Components pass memory addresses to one another, telling each other where to access data or instructions. The number of wires that make up the memory address lines of the bus determines how many bits can be used for a memory address. The number of wires thus limits the amount of memory the bus can address.
- *Data*. Data passes over a bus in a group of wires, just as memory addresses do. The number of lines in the bus used to pass data determines how much data can be passed in parallel at one time. The number of lines depends on the type of processor and determines the number of bits in the data path.

(Remember that a data path is the part of the bus on which the data is placed; it can be 8, 16, 32, 64, or more bits wide.)

BUS EVOLUTION As discussed in Chapter 1, the lines of a bus often extend from the CPU to the expansion slots used to hold expansion cards. Figure 3-20 shows the bus connections for an expansion card used in different types of expansion slots. With the expansion card in the slot, the PCI bus connects to the system bus, which, in turn, connects to the CPU.

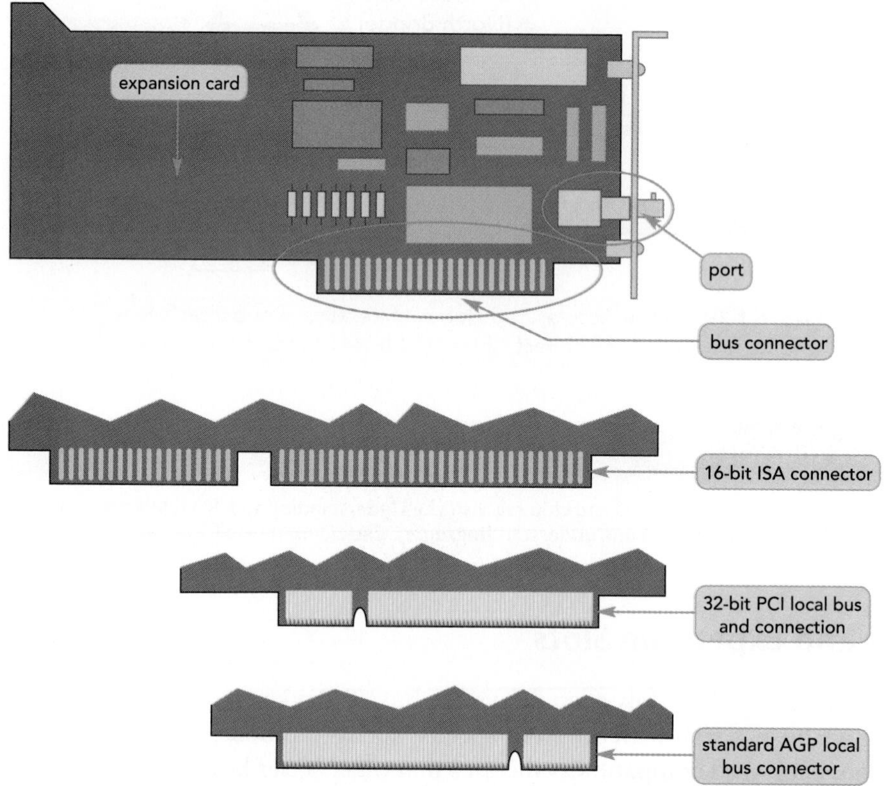

Figure 3-20 Bus connections on expansion cards used in ISA, PCI, and AGP slots.

Depending on the type of slot and the expansion card, buses run at different speeds and provide different features. Over time, buses have evolved to have wider data paths and faster speeds to transfer data faster.

Recall that everything in a computer is digital. Instead of continuously working to perform commands or move data, the CPU, bus, and other devices work in an on-and-off fashion. A bus that works in sync with the CPU and the system clock is called a **local bus.** A bus that works asynchronously with the CPU (at a much slower rate) is called an **expansion bus**. Figure 3-21 lists local and expansion buses, organized by **throughput**, or the amount of data each bus can transfer per second. The following sections review types of local and expansion buses. (As you read, remember that — despite their somewhat confusing names — both local and expansion buses can be used to transfer data between an expansion card and a CPU.)

Bus	Bus Type	Data Path (in bits)	Address Lines	Bus Speed (MHz)	Data Transfer Rate (throughput)
System bus	Local	64	32	800, 533, 400, 133	Up to 3.2 GB/sec
NEWER BUS STANDARDS					
PCI-X	Local I/O	64	32	133	1.06 GB/sec
AGP	Local video	32	NA	66, 75, 100 ...	Up to 528 MB/sec
PCI	Local I/O	32	32	33, 66	264 or 532 MB/sec
FireWire	Local I/O or expansion	1	Addresses are sent serially	NA	Up to 3.2 GB/sec (gigabits)
USB	Expansion	1	Addresses are sent serially	3	Up to 480 MB/sec (megabits)
OLDER BUS STANDARDS					
VESA or VL Bus	Local video or expansion	32	32	Up to 33	Up to 250 MB/sec
MCA	Expansion	32	32	12	Up to 40 MB/sec
EISA	Expansion	32	32	12	Up to 32 MB/sec
16-bit ISA	Expansion	16	24	8.33	8 MB/sec
8-bit ISA	Expansion	8	20	4.77	1 MB/sec

Figure 3-21 Local and expansion buses. Many of the earlier local I/O buses were proprietary designs, which no longer are sold. Others, such as the PCI and AGP buses, are still common.

FAQ 3-7

What does it mean to say some devices work in sync with the CPU and others do not (are asynchronous)?

If a component on the motherboard works by the beat, or clock cycle, then it is synchronized, or in sync, with the CPU. Some components do not attempt to keep in sync with the CPU, instead working at half or a third of clock cycles; these components are said to work asynchronously with the CPU. For example, the back side bus of the Pentium works at half the speed of the CPU. This means that the CPU does something on each clock cycle, but the back side bus is doing something on every other clock cycle. The speed of other components might be determined by the system clock or by another crystal on or off the motherboard. Either way, the frequency is much slower than the CPU's and not in sync with it. If the CPU requests something from a device, but the device is not ready, then the device issues a wait state, a command to the CPU to wait for the slower device to catch up.

Expansion Buses The first expansion slots on early PCs were **Industry Standard Architecture (ISA)** slots, which had an 8-bit data path and ran at 4.77 MHz. Later, 16-bit ISA slots were added that ran at 8.33 MHz to meet the demand for wider data path sizes. The ISA expansion card uses the ISA bus to communicate with the CPU. Most newer computers do not include ISA slots, instead relying on the PCI and AGP slots described below.

A relatively new expansion bus is the **universal serial bus (USB)**, which is used to connect slow input and output devices such as a mouse, digital camera, and scanner.

Local Buses The system bus, which connects directly to the CPU, is synchronized with the CPU and thus is a local bus. As you learned in Chapter 2, a bus such as the system bus has several components:

- the **data bus**, which is the group of lines on the system bus that allow data to flow back-and-forth between devices;
- the **address bus**, which communicates memory addresses and I/O devices to tell devices where data flowing on the data bus should travel; and
- the **control bus**, which coordinates activity between various devices to prevent collisions — that is, the corruption of data resulting from simultaneous use of the data or address bus.

The system bus also includes a line for power, which provides low-current voltage to various system devices. The system bus might be considered the "true" local bus, in the sense that all other buses must connect to the system bus to get to the CPU.

Another type of local bus, called a **local I/O bus**, is designed to support fast input and output devices such as hard drives and video. Local I/O buses did not always exist on a PC. They were created as the need arose for a bus that was synchronized with the system clock, was not as fast as the system bus, but was faster than an expansion bus. Two of the more widely used local I/O buses include the PCI (Peripheral Component Interconnect) bus and the AGP (Accelerated Graphics Port) bus.

The **Peripheral Component Interconnect** (**PCI**) **bus** currently is the most widely used local I/O bus included in most personal computers, including newer versions of the Macintosh computer. The PCI bus is a 32-bit bus with bus speeds of 33 or 66 MHz. A newer version of the PCI bus, called the **PCI-X** (**PCI extended**) **bus**, is a 64-bit bus with speeds of 133 MHz.

The **AGP** (**Accelerated Graphics Port**) **bus** was designed to create a faster, dedicated bus between the chip set on the video card and the CPU. AGP is considered to be a local video bus, because it connects the video card in the AGP slot and the CPU. AGP runs at several times the bus speed of a PCI bus, to support the data transfer needs of a video card supporting 3-D graphics. To help provide additional speed, AGP allows the video processor to access main memory for use while completing processing tasks.

A newer local I/O bus, called the **FireWire bus** or **IEEE 1394 bus**, is a very fast bus with throughput of up to 3.2 gigabits per second. Developed by Apple and Texas Instruments, the FireWire bus often is used for downloading video from a digital video camera to the computer. Also called the *i.Link connector* and the *High Performance Serial Bus (HPSB)*, a FireWire/1394 bus can work either synchronously or asynchronously and thus is classified as either a local or an expansion bus.

ROM BIOS

As you have learned, ROM BIOS and RAM (memory) also are installed on the motherboard. The ROM BIOS chip stores the BIOS, which manages the startup process (startup BIOS), many basic I/O functions of the system (system BIOS), and the settings on the motherboard (CMOS BIOS or CMOS setup). Later in this chapter, you will learn more about troubleshooting issues with the motherboard by configuring and updating BIOS.

Hardware Configuration

Recall from Chapter 1 that you can configure the motherboard in three different ways: DIP switches, jumpers, and CMOS settings. Storing configuration information by physically setting DIP switches or jumpers on the motherboard or peripheral devices is inconvenient, because it often requires you to open the computer case to make a change. Computers today store most configuration information in CMOS RAM, which is combined in a single chip with ROM BIOS. Holding configuration information in CMOS RAM is more convenient, because you can use a setup program to make changes without having to open the computer case.

Changing CMOS Setup Data On newer computers, the data stored in CMOS is usually changed by accessing the setup program stored in ROM BIOS. As you learned in Chapter 2, you access the CMOS setup program by pressing a specific key or keys as the computer system is starting up. The keystrokes are displayed on the screen during startup (for example, *Press the F2 key to enter setup*).

When you press the appropriate key or keys to enter CMOS setup, you will see a set of text screens with a number of menu options and Help features. Although the exact screens and available options depend on the specific BIOS used on your computer, the basic configuration information available in CMOS setup is similar. Typical screens available in CMOS setup include (Figure 3-22 on the next page):

- a main menu to allow changes to system date and time, the keyboard language, the Supervisor and User passwords, and other system features;
- a power menu that allows you to configure automatic power-saving features for your system, such as suspend mode;
- a boot menu that allows you to set the order in which the system tries to boot from certain devices. (Most likely you will want to have the BIOS attempt to boot from the floppy drive first, and if no disk is present, turn to the hard drive.);
- an advanced menu with additional configuration options (not available in all BIOS);
- an exit screen to allow you to save or discard changes and then exit the program, restore default settings, or save changes and remain in the program.

FAQ 3-8

What keystrokes typically are used to enter the CMOS setup program?

The keystrokes used to enter the CMOS setup program are displayed on the screen during startup, typically in a prompt such as *Press DEL to enter setup*. Different BIOSs use different keystrokes to access CMOS setup. For example, newer versions of Phoenix BIOS use the F2 or F1 key, while AMI BIOS uses the DELETE key. Other commonly used keystrokes include CTRL+ALT+S, CTRL+ALT+ESC, and CTRL+ALT+INS. If your computer does not display a prompt showing the correct keystrokes, consult your owner's manual or contact the manufacturer for instructions.

More About

Hardware Configuration

Many older computers require you to set hardware configurations using DIP switches and jumpers, and to make changes to CMOS setup using a program stored on a floppy disk. To learn more about setting hardware configurations using these tools, visit the Understanding and Troubleshooting Your PC More About Web page (**scsite.com/understanding/more**) and then click Hardware Configuration below Chapter 3.

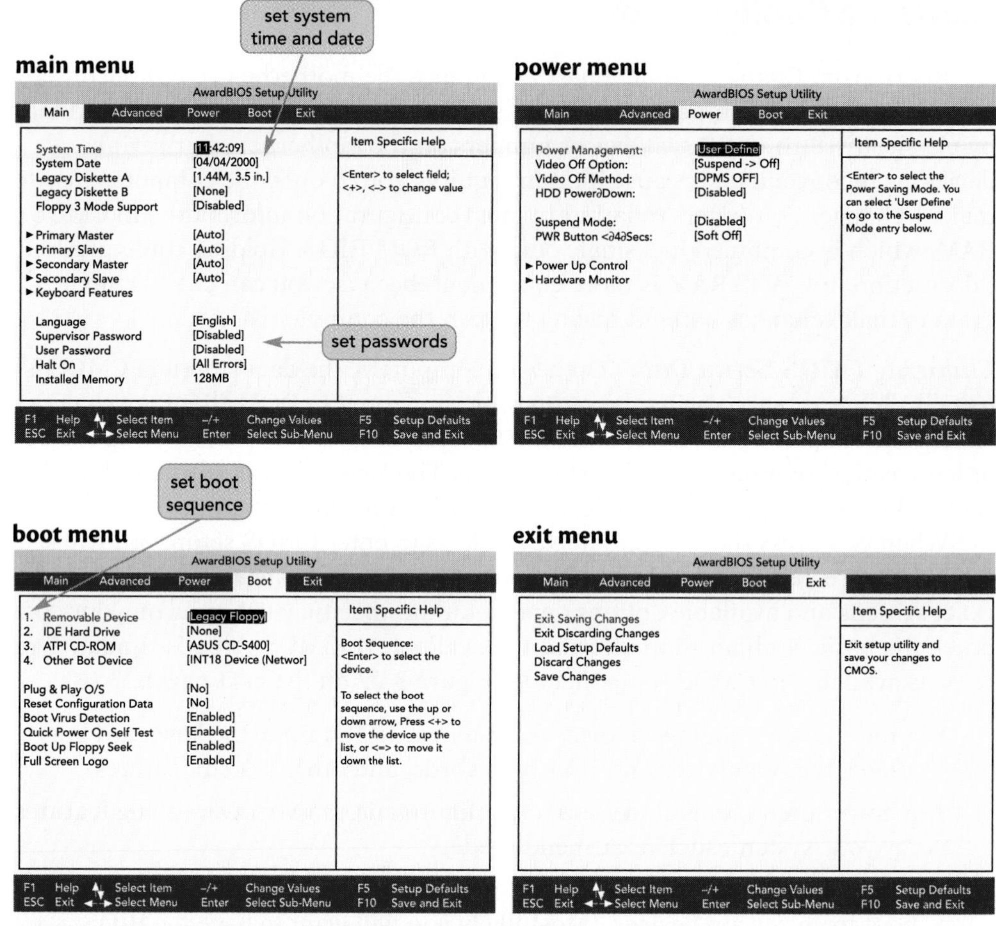

Figure 3-22 Typical screens available in CMOS setup.

Battery Power to CMOS Memory A trickle of electricity from a small battery enables the CMOS memory to hold configuration data even while the main power to the computer is off. If the battery is disconnected or fails, setup information can be lost. An indication that the battery is getting weak is that the system date and time are incorrect after the PC has been turned off.

Several types of CMOS batteries are available:

- a 3.6 volt (also written as 3.6 V) lithium battery with a four-pin connector, which connects using a Velcro strip;
- a 4.5 volt alkaline battery with a four-pin connector, which connects using a Velcro strip;
- a 3.6 volt barrel-style battery with a two-pin connector, which is soldered on to the motherboard; and
- a 3 volt lithium coin-cell battery, which is the most common type of CMOS battery (Figure 3-23).

> **More About**
>
> **CMOS Settings**
>
> To learn more about the settings that can be configured using CMOS setup, visit the Understanding and Troubleshooting Your PC More About Web page (**scsite.com/understanding/more**) and then click CMOS Settings below Chapter 3.

Figure 3-23 The coin cell is the most common type of CMOS RAM battery.

FAQ 3-9

What is the purpose of setting Supervisor and User passwords in CMOS setup?

When a Supervisor password (also called a power-on or startup password) is set, the system prompts a user to enter a password before CMOS setup can be accessed and changed. If a User password is set, the system will prompt for a password when the system boots. If a Supervisor password is set and a user accesses CMOS setup using a User password, the only task the user can complete is to change the User password. In most situations, it is best to leave these passwords disabled, because you may have to erase your CMOS memory if you forget your password. If you have set the password for CMOS and forget it, try these steps:

- Try some of the passwords you commonly use.
- If the manufacturer or another user set the password, try common passwords like *password, user, BIOS, CMOS, setup, award, AMI,* or *Phoenix.*
- Check the documentation that came with your system to see if your motherboard has a jumper for the password set, which can empty the last-stored password.
- If you have no success with the other steps, contact the motherboard manufacturer or your PC manufacturer for assistance.

Quiz Yourself 3-2

To test your knowledge of the buses, expansion slots, and other components on the motherboard, visit the Understanding and Troubleshooting Your PC Quiz Yourself Web page (**scsite.com/understanding/quiz**). Click Quiz Yourself 2 below Chapter 3.

Building a Computer: An Introduction

Now that you have learned how motherboards work and what components they include, you can begin learning how to build your own computer. Earlier in the chapter, you took your first look inside a computer and learned your way around by taking it apart and putting it back together. In this section, you will get an overview of how to put a new computer together from separately purchased parts. This information will be helpful as you learn to install specific components, both in this chapter and the rest of the book. This chapter gives specific steps to install a motherboard, and subsequent chapters give directions for installing other components.

As you read, remember that the following directions are meant to be a general overview of the process. These steps are not meant to include the details of all possible installation scenarios, which can vary according to the components and OS being installed.

The general process for putting together a computer is as follows:

1. *Verify that you have all parts you plan to install.* Check device manufacturer Web sites for updated BIOS and device drivers for your system.
2. *Take necessary safety precautions.* In addition to using a ground bracelet and ground mat, you also should unplug the power cord to the PC before you work inside the case.
3. *Prepare the computer case.* Preparing the case before actually installing components lessens the risk of damaging components as you install them. First, install one or more fans inside the computer case. (Because today's CPUs run at high temperatures, it is a good idea to have at least one case fan, in addition to the power supply fan, to ensure good case ventilation.) Next, remove the plates that cover the drive bays and install the spacers that keep the motherboard from touching the case.
4. *Install drives,* such as the CD-ROM or DVD drive, hard drive, and floppy drive. Have a plan for where to install each drive, to avoid tangling cables or having them interfere with airflow or access to other components. As you install drives, verify jumper settings for each drive.
5. *Determine proper configuration settings for the motherboard.* Especially important are any jumpers, DIP switches, or CMOS settings specifically for the CPU, and RAM speeds and timing. Gather as much information as possible from manufacturer documentation. Read the motherboard manual from cover to cover. You can also check manufacturer Web sites for suggestions for optimizing system settings.
6. *Set any jumpers or DIP switches on the motherboard.* Setting jumpers and DIP switches is much easier to do before you put the board in the case.
7. *Install the CPU and CPU fan or cooler.* The CPU comes already installed on some motherboards, in which case you just need to install the fan or cooler. You might need to add thermal grease.
8. *Install RAM (memory modules)* into the appropriate slots on the motherboard.
9. *Install the motherboard and attach cabling* that goes from the case switches to the motherboard, and from the power supply to the drives. Pay attention to how cables are labeled and to any information in the documentation about where to attach them. (The next section covers motherboard installation.) Position and tie cables neatly together to make sure they do not obstruct the fans.
10. *Install the video card* (which also can be called the display adapter, video adapter, or graphics accelerator) on the motherboard. The video card typically is placed in the AGP slot, as noted earlier.
11. *Plug the computer into a power source, and attach the monitor and keyboard.* Note that you do not attach the mouse now, for the initial setup. Although the mouse generally does not cause problems during setup, avoid initially installing anything you do not absolutely need.

12. *Boot the system and enter CMOS setup* using the keystrokes appropriate for your system. Refer to the documentation for the motherboard to determine the correct keystrokes.
13. *Make sure settings are set to the default*. If components come new from the manufacturer, they probably are already at default settings. If you are reusing a component from another system, you may need to reset settings to the default. Generally a jumper or switch will set all CMOS settings to default settings. While you are in CMOS setup, complete the following tasks:
    - Check the time and date.
    - Check the floppy drive type.
    - Make sure abbreviated POST is disabled. Abbreviated POST, which is what most computers use, offers a shorter version of POST and provides more concise reporting. A full or extensive POST, by contrast, completes many tests and provides many detailed messages. While you are setting up a system, you generally want the POST process to include as many tests as possible. Once you know the system is working, you can choose to abbreviate POST.
    - Set the boot order to drive A, then drive C, if you will be booting the OS from a floppy disk. Set the boot order to CD-ROM, then drive C, if you will be booting the OS from a CD. This determines which drive the system looks to for the OS.
    - Make sure *autodetect hard disk* is enabled so that the system automatically looks for drives.
    - Leave everything else at their defaults unless you know that particular settings should be otherwise.
    - Save and exit.
14. When the computer reboots, *observe the POST process* and listen for beep codes or watch for messages on screen to determine if any errors occur.
15. *Install the operating system.* The system will boot from drive A or drive C, as configured in the CMOS settings. To install an operating system, such as Windows XP, boot the system from the Windows setup CD in drive C and then follow the steps to partition the hard drive and install the operating system.

    Generally, it is best to install the OS before any expansion cards, such as a sound card or a modem card. Installing multiple cards at once can confuse Plug and Play, especially during OS installation. Unless you are very familiar with all components' resource requirements, it is almost always less trouble to install one device at a time on a new system. If you are setting up multiple systems with the same configuration, build the first system one card at a time. If no major errors occur, then try installing all cards at once on a second system, after the OS has been loaded. If this approach is successful, then you can save a little time by installing all hardware devices before you install the OS. However, you should still reboot whenever you have the option, as the OS detects each device.
16. *Change the boot order in CMOS*, if you have it set to boot from CD, so that it does not boot from a CD first. If you set the order as drive A, then drive C, you can boot from a floppy disk later as needed. This is the most common boot order.

17. *Check for conflicts with system resources.* For Windows, use Device Manager to verify that the OS recognizes all devices and that no conflicts are reported. If your motherboard comes with a CD that contains some motherboard drivers, install them now. Remember that the drivers Windows installs for the devices might not be the latest drivers; if your version of Windows is older than some of your components, it might not have the correct or newest drivers for those devices. Using Device Manager, you can see what drivers are installed for a device. If Windows is not using the newest drivers, update them using the latest drivers from the CD that comes with the device or from the device manufacturer's Web site.
18. *Install any other expansion cards and drives*, and install appropriate drivers, one device at a time, rebooting and checking for conflicts after each installation.
19. *Verify that everything is operating properly, and make any final OS and CMOS adjustments*, such as power management settings.

FAQ 3-10

What if I encounter problems when installing/uninstalling software or hardware and need to go back to the original settings?

Whenever you install or uninstall software or hardware, keep a notebook with details about the components you are working on, configuration settings, manufacturer specifications, and other relevant information. This helps if you need to backtrack later, and also can help you document and troubleshoot your computer system. Put all hardware documentation for this system together with your notebook and keep it in a safe place.

Installing the Motherboard

Now that you have learned the general process of putting together a computer, you will learn how to install a motherboard. This section explains how to install and configure a motherboard and how to test the installation. As with any installation, remember the importance of using a ground strap to ground yourself when working inside a computer case, to protect components against ESD.

Preparing the Motherboard to Go into the Case

First, be sure the motherboard you plan to install has a form factor that fits in your computer case. Most newer computers conform to the ATX form factor, but you should check your system documentation or contact the system manufacturer for specifications.

Next, read the manual that comes with the motherboard from beginning to end. The steps included in this section provide a general overview; to install the motherboard, you will need to know information specific to your motherboard. After reading the manual, visually familiarize yourself with the configuration of the case and the motherboard.

SETTING THE JUMPERS The first step in preparing the motherboard to go in the case is to set the jumpers or DIP switches. When doing an installation, read the motherboard documentation carefully, looking for explanations of how jumpers and DIP switches on the board are used. For example, Figure 3-24a shows the documentation for one motherboard that uses three jumpers to configure the BIOS.

The jumper group is shown in Figure 3-24b, with the jumper caps in the normal mode to allow BIOS to use the current configuration for booting. Once set, the jumpers should be changed only if you are trying to recover when the power-up password is lost, or when flashing BIOS has failed.

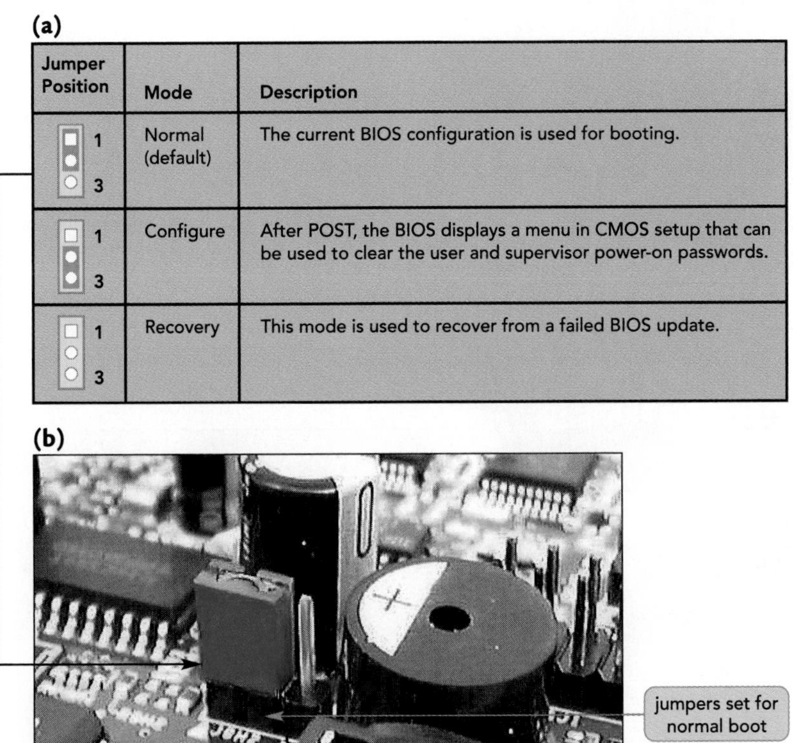
(a)

Jumper Position	Mode	Description
1 3	Normal (default)	The current BIOS configuration is used for booting.
1 3	Configure	After POST, the BIOS displays a menu in CMOS setup that can be used to clear the user and supervisor power-on passwords.
1 3	Recovery	This mode is used to recover from a failed BIOS update.

Figure 3-24 (a) The documentation for a motherboard, such as this one that uses three jumpers to configure the BIOS, lists how jumpers should be set for booting. (b) The jumper caps in the normal mode to allow BIOS to use the current configuration for booting. Notice that the cap covers the first two jumper posts but not the third.

ADDING THE CPU, FAN, AND HEAT SINK Now that you have set the jumpers on the motherboard, you are ready to install the CPU, the fan, and the heat sink. The following section reviews two examples of installing a CPU: a Pentium II installed in Slot 1 and a Pentium 4 installed in Socket 478.

Installing a Pentium II in Slot 1 As shown in Figure 3-15 on page 94, the motherboard uses a universal retention mechanism (URM), which is preinstalled on the board to hold the Pentium II in Slot 1. The following steps allow you to install the fan on the side of the processor first, and then install the processor on the motherboard:

1. Unfold the URM arms. Flip both arms up until they lock into position.
2. Examine the fan and processor to see how the fan brace lines up with holes in the side of the SECC packaging for the Pentium II (Figure 3-25a on the next page).

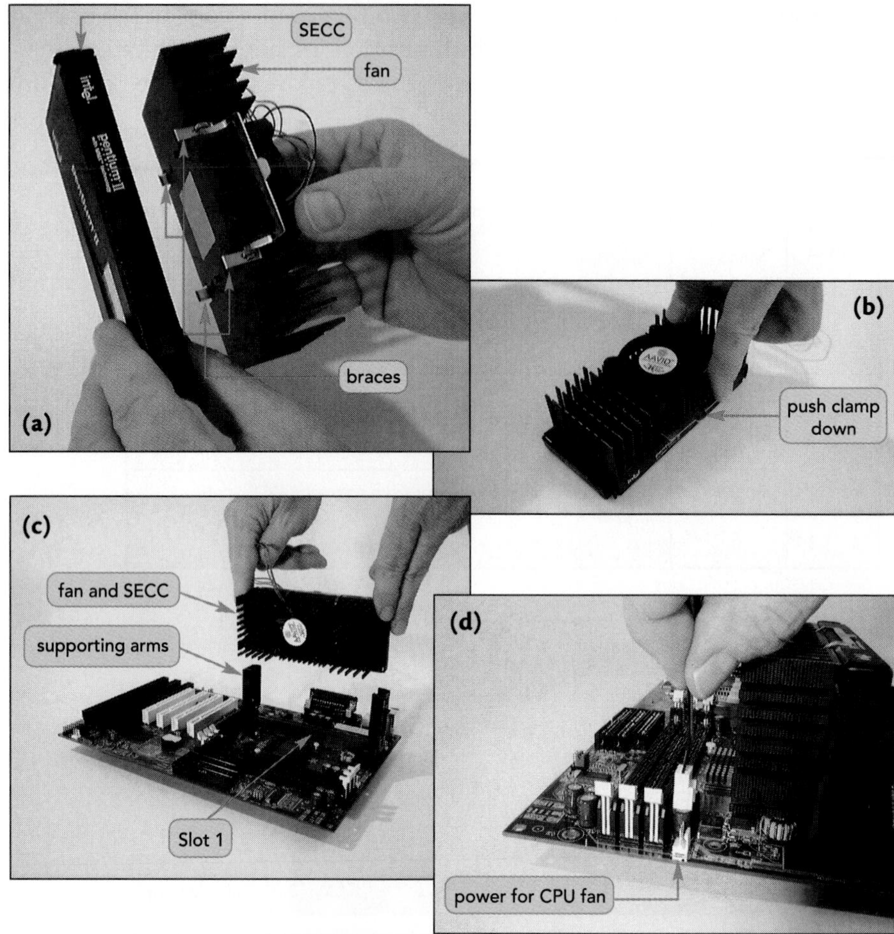

Figure 3-25 Installing a Pentium II in Slot 1. (a) The braces on the fan align with holes in the side of the SECC. (b) Push the clamp on the fan down until it locks in place, locking the fan to the SECC. (c) Insert the fan and SECC into the supporting URM arms and Slot 1. (d) Connect the fan power cord to the motherboard.

3. Place the fan directly on the side of the SECC. The two should fit tightly together, with no space between them.
4. After you fit the fan and SECC together, place the SECC on a table and push the clamp on the fan down and into place, to secure the fan to the SECC (Figure 3-25b).
5. Insert the fan and SECC into the supporting arms (Figure 3-25c). The SECC should fit snugly into Slot 1 and the arms should snap into position when the SECC is fully seated. Be certain you have a good fit.
6. Lock the SECC into position by pulling the SECC locks outward until they lock into the supporting arm lock holes.
7. Look for the power connection near Slot 1 and then connect the power cord coming from the fan to the power connection on the motherboard (Figure 3-25d). If you have trouble locating the power connection, see the motherboard documentation.

Installing a Pentium 4 in Socket 478 If you look back at Figure 3-13 on page 92, you can see the Pentium 4 installed in Socket 478 on a motherboard. Notice the frame or retention mechanism to hold the cooler in place. This frame might be preinstalled or be available separately from the board. If necessary, follow the directions that come with the motherboard to install the frame.

Once the frame is installed, the next step is to install the CPU. Lift the ZIF socket lever as shown in Figure 3-26. Place the processor on the socket so that the corner marked with a triangle is aligned with the connection of the lever to the socket. After the processor is in place, lower the lever to insert the processor firmly into the socket. As you work, be very careful not to force the processor in at a crooked position.

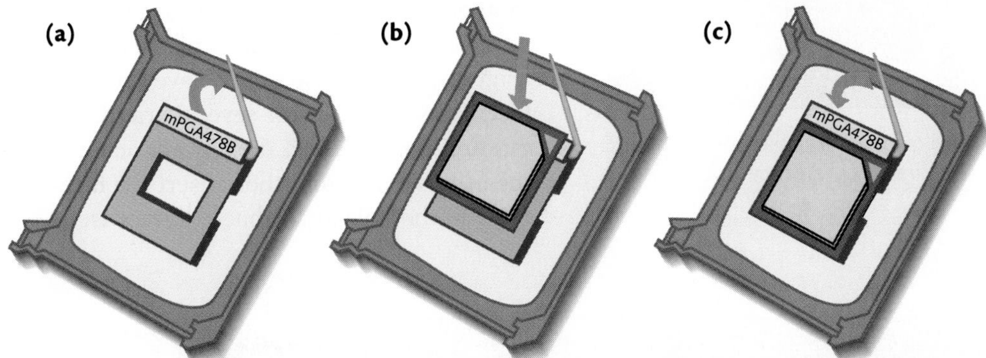

Figure 3-26 Installing a Pentium 4 in Socket 478 (more specifically called the mPGA478B socket). (a) Lift the ZIF socket lever. (b) Place the processor on the socket so that the corner marked with a triangle is aligned with the connection of the lever to the socket. (c) After the processor is in place, lower the lever to insert the processor firmly into the socket.

Before installing the CPU fan over the CPU, place a small amount of thermal grease on top of the processor. The thermal grease helps transfer heat from the processor to the heat sink. (Do not use too much! If you do, it may squish out the sides and interfere with other components.)

A clip assembly surrounds the fan and heat sink. Line up the clip assembly with the retention mechanism already installed on the motherboard, and then press lightly on all four corners to attach it. Once the fan is in place, push down the two clip levers on top of the CPU fan (Figure 3-27 on the next page). Different coolers use different types of clipping mechanisms, so follow the directions that come with the cooler. Sometimes the clipping mechanism is difficult to clip onto the processor, and the plastic levers and housing are flimsy, so work carefully.

The next steps after installing a CPU, fan, and heat sink involve installing the RAM in the memory slots. The steps required to install RAM are covered in detail in Chapter 4.

Figure 3-27 The clip levers attach the cooling assembly to the retention mechanism around the processor.

Installing the Motherboard in the Case

Once the motherboard is prepared and the CPU, fan, heat sink, and memory are in place, the motherboard can be installed in the case. The following section provides an overview of the steps to install the motherboard in the case.

1. Install the faceplate. The **faceplate** or **I/O shield** is a metal plate that comes with the motherboard and fits over the ports to create a well-fitting enclosure around them (Figure 3-28). A case might have several faceplates designed for several brands of motherboards. Select the correct one, put the others aside, and then insert the faceplate in the hole at the back of the case.

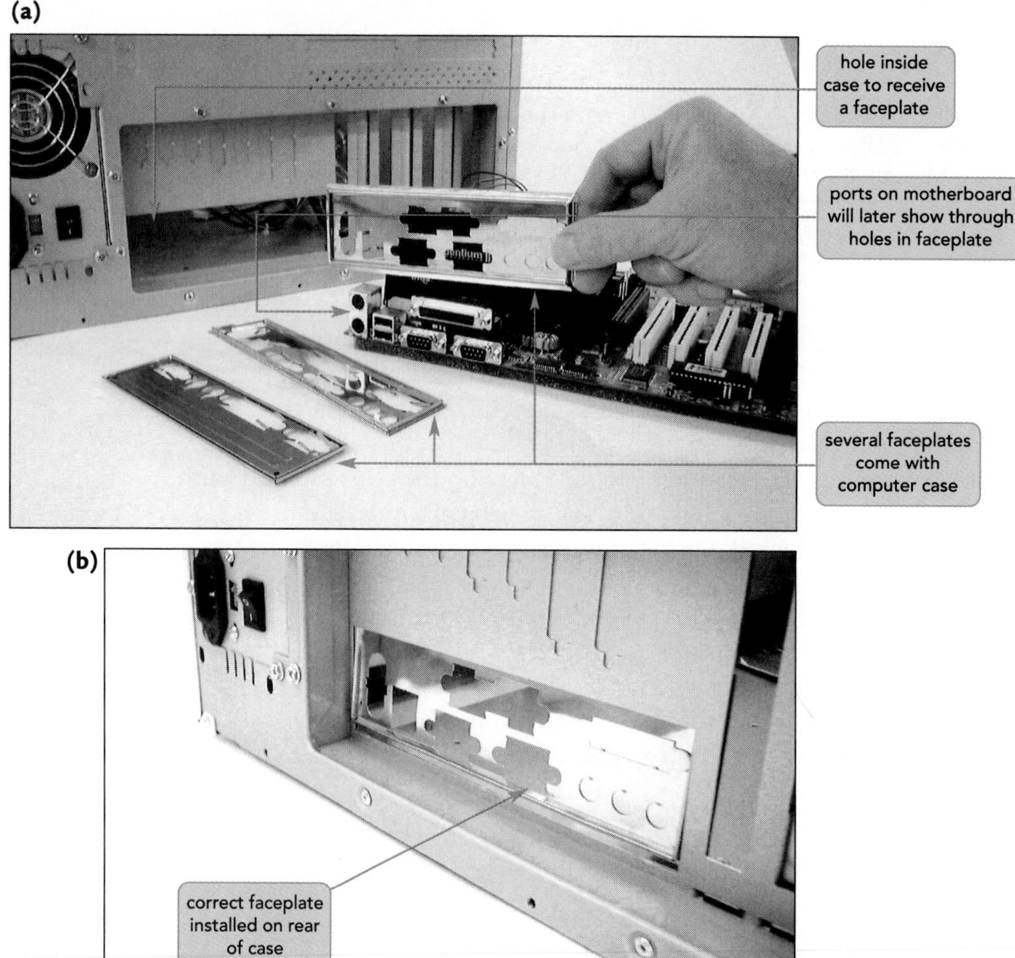

Figure 3-28 A computer case comes with several faceplates. (a) Select the faceplate that fits over the ports that come off the motherboard and (b) install that faceplate in the hole at the rear of the computer case.

2. Install the standoffs and spacers. Standoffs and spacers are round plastic or metal pegs that separate the motherboard from the case, so that components on the back of the motherboard do not touch the case. **Spacers** screw into small holes in the motherboard mounting plate, while **standoffs** typically clip into place. Make sure the locations of the standoffs or spacers match the screw holes on the motherboard. At least one metal standoff must be used to ground the motherboard to the case.

   The case will have more screw holes than you need, in order to support several brands of motherboards. To ensure you are installing the standoffs or spacers in the correct locations, check the computer case and motherboard documentation. If you need to remove a standoff or spacer to move it to a new slot, needle-nose pliers work well to unscrew the standoff.

3. Place the motherboard inside the case, and use screws to attach it to the case. Figure 3-29 shows how you must align the standoffs to the holes on the motherboard. The screws fit into the standoffs you installed earlier. There should be at least four standoff/screw sets, and there may be as many as six. Use as many as there are holes in the motherboard.

Figure 3-29 Three spacers and four screw holes are visible inside this computer case.

4. If you are using an ATX motherboard, connect the power cord from the power supply to the P1 power connection on the motherboard. (If you are using an AT motherboard, you have two power connections, P8 and P9, to connect.)

5. Connect the wire leads from the front panel of the case to the motherboard. These wires are used to connect the switches and lights on the front of the computer to the motherboard. Figure 3-30 shows a computer case that has five wire leads from the front panel that must be connected to the motherboard. The five connectors are:
   - *Reset switch*. Used to warm boot the computer.
   - *HDD LED*. Controls a light on the front panel that lights up when any IDE device is in use. (LED stands for light-emitting diode. An LED is a light on the front panel.)
   - *Speaker*. Controls the speaker.
   - *Power LED*. Light indicating that power is on.
   - *Remote switch*. Controls power to the motherboard. This must be connected for the PC to power up.

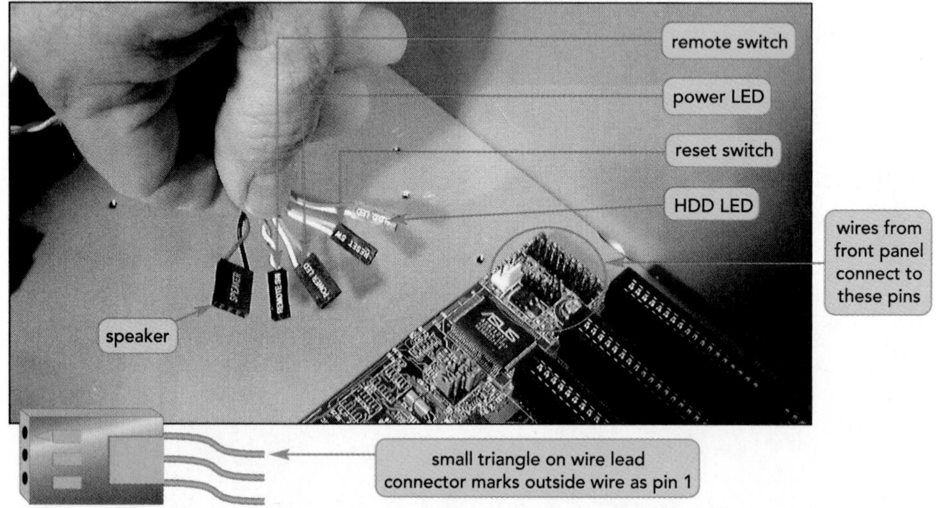

Figure 3-30 Five wires from the front panel connect to the motherboard.

To help orient the connector on the motherboard pins, look for a small triangle embedded on the connector that marks one of the outside wires as pin 1. Look for pin 1 to be labeled on the motherboard as a small 1 embedded to either the right or the left of the group of pins. Also, sometimes the documentation will mark pin 1 as a square pin in the diagram, rather than round like the other pins.

Because the same manufacturer may not have made your case and your motherboard, you need to pay close attention to the source of the wires to determine to which pins they connect on the motherboard. If the documentation is unclear, try and connect the wires as best you can. If it doesn't work, no harm is done and you can reconnect them to resolve the issue.

Completing the Installation

After you install the motherboard, you will install drives and other components, a process that is covered in later chapters. Finally, turn on the system and make sure everything is connected properly. You may need to change some of the hardware configuration settings set in CMOS setup. As you set configuration data, remember to record any changes you make to configurations settings, so that you can restore them to their original settings if something goes wrong.

Introduction to Troubleshooting

If you are still having problems after installing a new component — or find you are having regular problems while simply using your computer — you may need to troubleshoot, or diagnose and fix, the problem.

Troubleshooting a PC problem begins with isolating it into one of two categories: problems that prevent the PC from booting, and problems that occur after a successful boot. To start the troubleshooting process, begin by determining the answers to the following questions, to learn as much as you can about the issue:

- What is the exact nature of the problem? Describe it in detail.
- What error messages, unusual displays, or failures did you see?
- When did the problem start?
- What were you doing on the computer when the problem occurred?
- What programs or software were you using?
- Did you move your computer system recently?
- Has there been a recent thunderstorm or electrical problem?
- Have you made any hardware, software, or configuration changes?
- Has someone else used your computer recently?
- Can you reproduce the problem?

Next, determine if the PC boots properly. This information begins the process of asking a series of questions to help identify the source of the problem (Figure 3-31 on the next page). If the screen is blank and the entire system is dead — that is, it has no lights, no spinning drive, or fan — the issue most likely is the power system. Troubleshooting the power system is covered in detail in Chapter 12.

When you start a computer and POST completes successfully, it sounds a single beep indicating that all is well, regardless of whether the monitor is working or even present. If you hear the beep, it indicates that the source of the problem might be with the computer's video subsystem. If an error message appears on the screen, it indicates that video is working; the next step is to respond to the message. For example, if the error reads "Keyboard not present," the keyboard likely is not plugged in. If you do not hear a beep or you hear more than one, then POST encountered an error and you should proceed to troubleshooting the motherboard.

Troubleshooting the Motherboard and CPU

When troubleshooting the motherboard, use whatever clues POST provides. Before video is checked out, POST reports any error messages as beep codes. When a PC boots, one beep indicates that all is well after POST. If you hear more than one beep, look up the beep code in Appendix A or visit the motherboard manufacturer's Web site (also listed in Appendix A).

In some cases, the problem is as simple as a power-saving feature set in CMOS setup. Many systems can be programmed through CMOS to suspend the monitor or even the hard drive if the keyboard or CPU has been inactive for a few minutes. Pressing any key usually causes operations to resume exactly where the user left off.

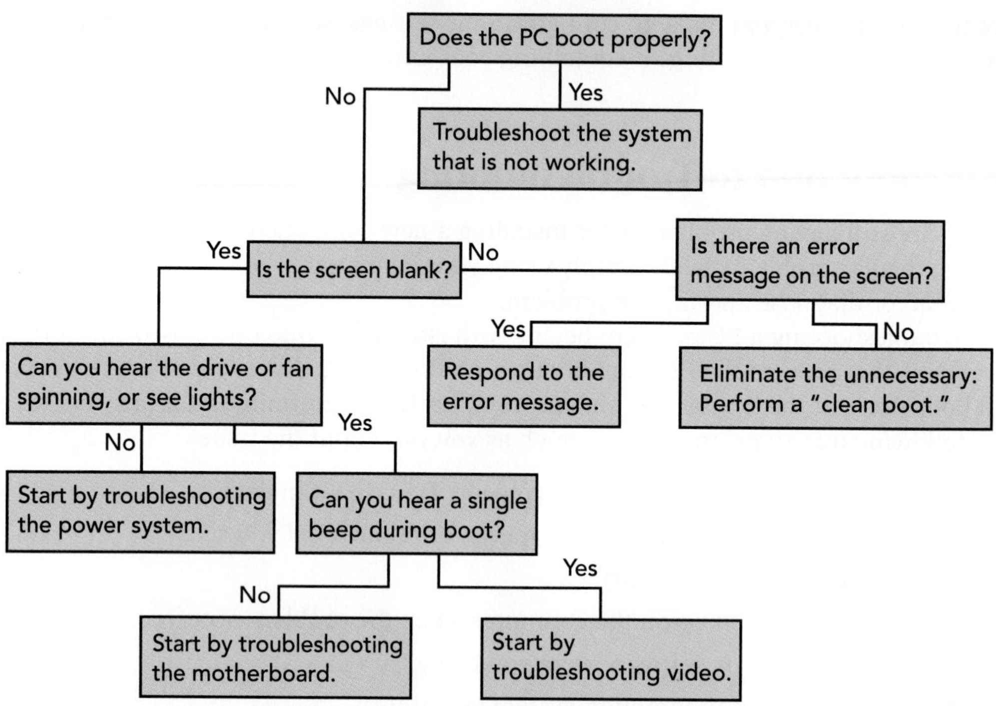

Figure 3-31 Begin PC troubleshooting by asking a series of questions to help identify the source of the issue.

If the motherboard came bundled with a support CD, check the CD for drivers for any motherboard components that are not working. For example, if the USB ports are not working, try updating the USB drivers with those stored on the support CD, using the instructions provided by the CD.

If you have just upgraded the CPU and the system will not boot, reinstall the old CPU, update (flash) BIOS, and then try the new CPU again. Verify that you have installed thermal grease between the CPU and the heat sink. If this does not resolve the problem, try the following:

- If the fan is running, reseat or replace the CPU, BIOS, or RAM. Try installing a DIMM in a different slot (installing memory is covered in Chapter 4). A POST code diagnostic card, covered in Chapter 12, can be a great help.
- Open the computer and reseat cables, adapter cards, socketed chips, and SIMMs, DIMMs, or RIMMs to eliminate or identify issues caused by bad connections and corrosion.
- Look for physical damage on the motherboard.
- Check jumpers, DIP switches, and CMOS settings.
- Check CMOS for a temperature reading that indicates overheating.
- Configure and flash the BIOS, as outlined below.
- Check the battery used to provide power to CMOS RAM. A dead or dying battery may cause problems. A weak battery sometimes causes the CMOS to forget its configuration.
- Reduce the system to essentials. Remove any unnecessary hardware, such as expansion cards, and then try to boot again.
- Exchange the CPU.

- Measure the voltage output of the power supply or simply replace it, in case it is producing too much power and has damaged the board.
- Exchange the motherboard.

You also can try substituting good hardware components for those you suspect are bad. If you choose this option, however, be very cautious as you work and follow the instructions from the manufacturer very carefully.

Configuring and Updating the BIOS

As discussed in the previous section, issues with the BIOS can cause some problems with a computer. When a motherboard becomes unstable or some functions are lost, a possible way to resolve the issue is to refresh or update the BIOS — a process called **flashing BIOS**.

To flash BIOS, you first must accurately identify the BIOS version currently installed on your system. Several methods can be used to identify your motherboard and BIOS:

- Look on the CMOS setup main screen for the BIOS manufacturer and version number.
- Use third-party software, such as BIOS Agent, or an OS utility, such as Windows System Information, to report the BIOS information.
- If the preceding methods do not work, refer to your computer manual or contact the manufacturer.

Once you have identified the version of BIOS installed on your computer, you can flash BIOS. To flash BIOS on the ROM BIOS chip, carefully read the motherboard documentation, as different motherboards use different methods. If you cannot find the documentation, check the motherboard manufacturer's Web site and the directions that came with the upgrade software. The general steps to flash BIOS are as follows:

1. Set a jumper on the motherboard, or change a setting in CMOS setup to tell the BIOS to expect an upgrade.
2. Create a startup disk to allow the system to boot into a command (DOS) prompt. To create a startup disk in Windows XP:
   a. Insert a floppy disk into your computer's floppy drive. Open My Computer and then click the floppy disk drive to select it.
   b. Click Format on the File menu. Under Format options, click Create an MS-DOS startup disk and then click Start. (Note: Creating an MS-DOS startup disk erases all information on the floppy disk.)
3. If needed, download the updated BIOS software from the manufacturer's Web site. The BIOS software update typically includes a flash utility file and the BIOS file. Copy all of the files to the startup disk created in Step 2.
4. Boot from the disk and follow the menu options to upgrade the BIOS. If the menu gives you the option to save the old BIOS to disk, do so in case you need to revert to the old BIOS.
5. Set the jumper back to its original setting, reboot the system, and verify that all is working.

Be *very careful* that you upgrade the BIOS with the correct upgrade version and that you follow the manufacturer's instructions correctly. Upgrading with the wrong file could make your system BIOS useless. If you are not sure that you are using the correct upgrade, *do not guess*. Check with the technical support for your BIOS before moving forward. Before you call technical support, have the information that identifies your BIOS available.

Makers of BIOS code change BIOS frequently to fix problems and add features. You generally can get upgraded BIOS code from manufacturers' Web sites or disks, or from third-party BIOS resellers' Web sites or disks. However, given the potential problems you can cause by updating the BIOS, update your BIOS only if you are having a problem with your motherboard or if there is a new BIOS feature you want to use.

Protecting Documentation and Configuration Settings

One of the most important aspects of managing and maintaining your personal computer is that your documentation and configuration records are organized and in a safe place.

When you purchase a motherboard or a computer, be sure the manual is included. If you do not have the manual, you can sometimes go to the motherboard manufacturer's Web site and download the information you need to understand the components that are compatible with your system, as well as contact information for support. Motherboard manuals also should contain a list of all CMOS settings, an explanation of their meanings, and their recommended values, to use as a reference in the event your CMOS settings are lost.

In addition to having a manual with the CMOS settings, you should keep a written record of all of the changes you make to CMOS, so you have a list of the settings you have changed from the default. If the battery goes bad or is disconnected, you can lose the settings saved in CMOS RAM. If you are using default settings, you can reboot with a good battery and instruct setup to restore the default settings. If you have customized some CMOS settings, however, you can reference your written record and restore your customized CMOS settings.

If you are permanently responsible for a computer, you should consider keeping a written record of any work you have done to maintain it. In addition to recording CMOS settings, use a small notebook or similar document to record hardware and software installed, network settings, and similar information. Keep the documentation well labeled in a safe place. If you have several computers to maintain, you might consider a filing system for each computer. Another method is to tape a cardboard folder to the inside top of the computer case and safely tuck the hardware documentation there.

Regardless of the method you use, it is important that you keep your written record up-to-date and stored with the hardware documentation in a safe place, as the notebook and documentation will be invaluable as you continue to manage, maintain, and troubleshoot problems with that computer.

More About

Flashing BIOS

To learn more about flashing BIOS, including where to find BIOS upgrades and the risks in flashing BIOS, visit the Understanding and Troubleshooting Your PC More About Web page (**scsite.com/understanding/more**) and then click Flashing BIOS below Chapter 3.

Quiz Yourself 3-3

To test your knowledge of how to build a computer, including installing and troubleshooting the motherboard, visit the Understanding and Troubleshooting Your PC Quiz Yourself Web page (scsite.com/understanding/quiz). Click Quiz Yourself 3 below Chapter 3.

High-Tech Talk

ENERGY STAR: Saving Power, Saving the Environment

In 1992 the U.S. Environmental Protection Agency (EPA) introduced ENERGY STAR as a program designed to identify and promote energy-efficient products that can help reduce greenhouse gas emissions. Computers and monitors were the first labeled products. Since then, the ENERGY STAR program has grown to encompass appliances, home electronics, lighting, and other products. In the ENERGY STAR program, manufacturers are encouraged to create energy-efficient devices that use little power when inactive. If a device meets the Energy Star standards, it can display the ENERGY STAR logo.

Computer systems use several different power management methods and features to conserve energy. Most computers and monitors sold today are Energy Star compliant, displaying the ENERGY STAR logo on-screen when the PC is booting. When you access CMOS setup to change settings, it includes a power menu that allows you to configure ENERGY STAR and other automatic power-saving features for your system, such as:

- *Green timer on the motherboard* is a timer that sets the number of minutes of inactivity that must pass before the CPU goes into sleep mode. You can enable or disable the setting and select the number of minutes.
- *Doze time* is the time that elapses before the system reduces 80 percent of its power consumption. Different systems accomplish this in different ways. For example, when one system enters doze mode, the system BIOS slows down the bus clock speed.
- *Standby time* is the time that elapses before the system reduces 92 percent of its power consumption. For example, a system might accomplish this by slowing the system speed and suspending the video signal.
- *Suspend time* is the time that elapses before the system reduces its power consumption by 99 percent. The way this reduction is accomplished varies. The CPU clock might be stopped and the video signal suspended. After entering suspend mode, the system needs warm-up time so that the CPU, monitor, and other components can reach full activity.
- *Hard drive standby time* is the amount of time before a hard drive shuts down.

You also can change ENERGY STAR settings using the operating system. Using Windows XP or 2000, right-click the desktop and select Properties. When the Display Properties dialog box appears, click the Screen Saver tab. If your monitor is ENERGY STAR compliant, you will see the ENERGY STAR logo at the bottom. Click the Power button to display the Power Options Properties dialog box, which provides several options for changing your power (Figure 3-32).

Why worry about purchasing ENERGY STAR-labeled products or about saving power from just your one little computer? For one, power-managed equipment actually may last longer. Because many of the computer's components spend a large portion of time in a low-power sleep mode, mechanical wear on disk drives and heat stress on other components can be reduced. Further, as hard as it may be to believe, the EPA estimates that — in just one year of using ENERGY STAR computers, monitors, and appliances — Americans saved enough energy to power 15 million homes and avoid greenhouse gas emissions equivalent to those from 14 million cars. In the end, that's a win for everyone: you save wear and tear on your computer components, while helping to save the environment.

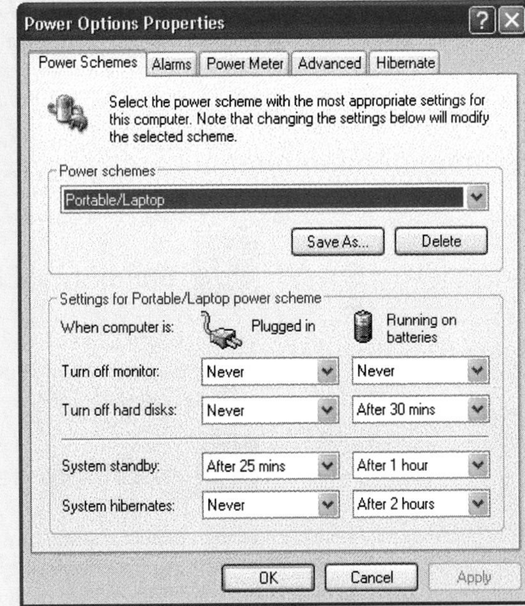

Figure 3-32

CHAPTER SUMMARY

The Chapter Summary reviews the concepts presented in this chapter.

1 Form Factors and the Computer Case

A form factor is a set of specifications for the size and configuration of hardware components such as cases, power supplies, and motherboards. The most common form factor today is ATX. Other form factors include LPX and NLX. Computer case types include desktop, tower, and notebook. The most popular case type in use today is a type of tower case, called the miditower.

2 Components on the Motherboard

A motherboard's primary purpose is to house the CPU and allow all devices to communicate with it and with each other. Components on the motherboard include the CPU and chip set, buses and expansion slots, ROM BIOS, and components used to change hardware configuration settings (jumpers, DIP switches, and CMOS), and RAM.

The CPU contains three basic components: an input/output (I/O) unit, one or more arithmetic logic units (ALU), and a control unit. It also includes registers and memory cache to hold data as it is processed. The CPU has an internal bus for communication to the internal memory cache. Important characteristics of a CPU include processor speed, bus speed, word size, data path size, instruction sets, memory cache, and its ability to support multiprocessing.

Most new IBM and IBM-compatible computers use processor chips made by Intel, including the Celeron, Pentium III, and Pentium 4. AMD and Via Technologies also make processors for use in IBM-compatible personal computers. The design of a processor's packaging is defined by the socket or slot used to connect it to the motherboard. Zero insertion force (ZIF) sockets have a small lever on the side that lifts the CPU up and out of the socket.

A bus is a path on the motherboard that carries electrical power, control signals, memory addresses, and data to different components on the board. A bus that works in sync with the CPU and the system clock is called a local bus. A bus that works asynchronously with the CPU at a much slower rate is called an expansion bus. Buses commonly used today include the AGP, PCI, ISA, FireWire/1394, and USB buses.

Hardware configuration is set on the motherboard using DIP switches or jumpers, or in CMOS. Computers today store most configuration information in CMOS RAM, which can be changed using CMOS setup.

3 Building a Computer: An Introduction

When building a new system, install the drives, motherboard, and expansion cards. Only install essential components before you install the OS. Then add other components one at a time, verifying that each component works before adding another.

4 Installing the Motherboard

When installing a new motherboard, be sure it has the correct form factor. Prepare the motherboard to go into the case by setting the jumpers or DIP switches, and then installing the CPU, the fan, and the heat sink. After you install the motherboard in the case, connect the power cord and the wire leads to complete the installation.

 5 Introduction to Troubleshooting

To start the troubleshooting process, begin by asking questions to learn more about the issue. When troubleshooting the motherboard, use whatever clues POST provides. Other steps to try include reseating components, looking for damage to components, checking CMOS settings and flashing BIOS, and exchanging the CPU or motherboard. When a motherboard becomes unstable or some functions are lost, a possible way to resolve the issue is to flash the BIOS. Be sure to keep documentation and records of your configurations organized and in a safe place.

KEY TERMS

After reading the chapter, you should know each of these Key Terms.

Accelerated Hub Architecture (*96*)
address bus (*100*)
Advanced Transfer Cache (ATC) (*87*)
AGP (Accelerated Graphics Port) bus (*100*)
arithmetic logic unit (ALU) (*84*)
ATX (*79*)
back side bus (BSB) (*85*)
bus riser (*80*)
bus speed (*85*)
complex instruction set computing (CISC) (*86*)
control bus (*100*)
control unit (*84*)
cooler (*91*)
data bus (*100*)
data path (*86*)
desktop (*81*)
die (*87*)
discrete L2 cache (*87*)
drive bays (*81*)
dual-voltage (*95*)
dynamic RAM (DRAM) (*87*)
Execution Trace Cache (*89*)
expansion bus (*98*)
external bus (*85*)
external cache (*87*)
external data path size (*86*)
faceplate (*110*)
field replaceable units (FRUs) (*84*)
FireWire bus (*100*)
flashing BIOS (*115*)
form factor (*78*)
front side bus (FSB) (*85*)
front side bus speed (*86*)
heat sink (*91*)
hub interface (*96*)
I/O shield (*110*)
IEEE 1394 bus (*100*)
Industry Standard Architecture (ISA) bus (*99*)
input/output (I/O) unit (*84*)
instruction set (*86*)
internal bus (*85*)
internal cache (*87*)
internal data path size (*86*)
Level 1 (L1) cache (*87*)
Level 2 (L2) cache (*87*)
Level 3 (L3) cache (*87*)
local bus (*98*)
local I/O bus (*100*)
memory cache (*85*)
microtower (*81*)
miditower (*81*)
midsize tower (*81*)
minitower (*81*)
multiprocessing (*88*)
NLX (*80*)
North Bridge (*96*)
notebook (*81*)
on-package L2 cache (*87*)
parallel processing (*88*)
PCI-X (PCI extended) bus (*100*)
Peripheral Component Interconnect (PCI) bus (*100*)
primary cache (*87*)
processor speed (*85*)
reduced instruction set computing (RISC) (*87*)
registers (*85*)
riser card (*80*)
secondary cache (*87*)
SIMD (*89*)
single-voltage (*95*)
South Bridge (*96*)
spacers (*111*)
split rail (*95*)
standoffs (*111*)
static RAM (SRAM) (*87*)
subnotebooks (*81*)
Streaming SIMD Extensions (SSE) (*89*)
system bus speed (*86*)
throughput (*98*)
tower (*81*)
universal serial bus (USB) (*99*)
voltage regulator module (VRM) (*95*)
word size (*86*)
zero insertion force (ZIF) sockets (*92*)

LEARN IT ONLINE

Reinforce your understanding of the chapter concepts and terms with the Learn It Online exercises.

Instructions: To complete the Learn It Online exercises, start your browser, click the Address bar, and then enter the Web address scsite.com/understanding/learn. When the Understanding and Troubleshooting Your PC Learn It Online page is displayed, follow the instructions in the exercises below. Each exercise has instructions for printing your results, either for your own records or for submission to your instructor.

1 Chapter Reinforcement True/False, Multiple Choice, and Short Answer

Below Chapter 3, click the Chapter Reinforcement link. Print the quiz by clicking Print on the File menu for each page. Answer each question.

2 Flash Cards

Below Chapter 3, click the Flash Cards link and read the instructions. Type **20** (or a number specified by your instructor) in the Number of playing cards text box, type your name in the Enter your Name text box, and then click the Flip Card button. When the flash card is displayed, read the question and then click the ANSWER box arrow to select an answer. Flip through Flash Cards. If your score is 15 (75%) correct or greater, click Print on the File menu to print your results. If your score is less than 15 (75%) correct, then redo this exercise by clicking the Replay button.

3 Practice Test

Below Chapter 3, click the Practice Test link. Answer each question, enter your first and last name at the bottom of the page, and then click the Grade Test button. When the graded practice test is displayed on your screen, click Print on the File menu to print a hard copy. Continue to take practice tests until you score 80% or better.

4 Who Wants To Be a Computer Genius?

Below Chapter 3, click the Computer Genius link. Read the instructions, enter your first and last name at the bottom of the page, and then click the PLAY button. When your score is displayed, click the PRINT RESULTS link to print a hard copy.

5 Wheel of Terms

Below Chapter 3, click the Wheel of Terms link. Read the instructions, and then enter your first and last name and your school name. Click the PLAY button. When your score is displayed, right-click the score and then click Print on the shortcut menu to print a hard copy.

6 Crossword Puzzle Challenge

Below Chapter 3, click the Crossword Puzzle Challenge link. Read the instructions, and then enter your first and last name. Click the SUBMIT button. Work the crossword puzzle. When you are finished, click the Submit button. When the crossword puzzle is redisplayed, click the Print Puzzle button to print a hard copy.

Multiple Choice

Select the best answer.

1. Which item is not a field replaceable unit (FRU) on newer motherboards?
   a. CPU
   b. CMOS battery
   c. system bus
   d. RAM
2. A CPU that uses one voltage for external operations and another for internal operations is considered a(n)________ CPU.
   a. single voltage
   b. cross rail design
   c. expansion voltage
   d. dual voltage
3. ________ is a small amount of static RAM that provides faster access to data and instructions than other types of memory.
   a. Fast memory
   b. Memory cache
   c. Level memory
   d. Dynamic RAM
4. Which of these is not a category of cargo carried over a bus?
   a. control signals
   b. memory addresses
   c. data
   d. IRQs
5. Which of these components is not used to keep a CPU cool?
   a. cool sinks
   b. heat sinks
   c. fans
   d. coolers

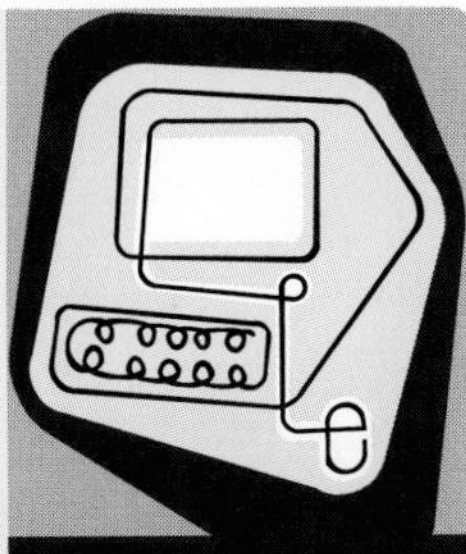

CHAPTER EXERCISES

Complete the Chapter Exercises to solidify what you learned in the chapter.

Fill in the Blank

Write the word or phrase to fill in the blank in each of the following questions.

1. The CPU contains three basic components: a(n)________ unit, one or more ________, and a(n) ________.
2. A bus that works in sync with the CPU and the system clock is called a(n) ________. A bus that works asynchronously with the CPU at a much slower rate is called a(n) ________.
3. A(n) ________ is a basic set of commands permanently built into the CPU chip to perform fundamental operations, such as comparing or adding two numbers.
4. The design of a processor's packaging is defined by the ________ or ________ used to connect it to the motherboard.
5. ________ processors have larger instruction sets and generally run more slowly, because it takes more steps to accomplish a simple operation. ________ processors have fewer instructions but run more quickly.

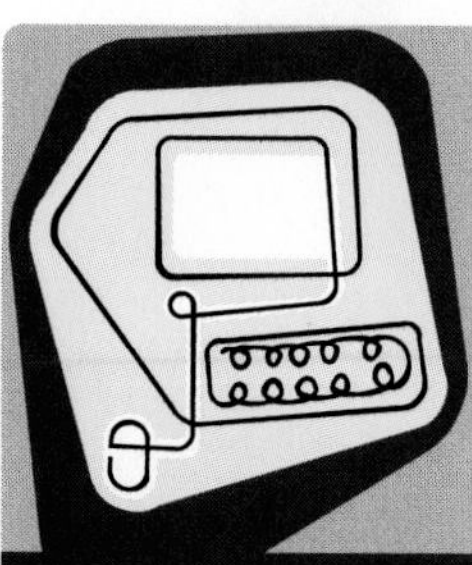

CHAPTER EXERCISES

Complete the Chapter Exercises to solidify what you learned in the chapter.

Matching Terms

Match the terms with their definitions.

_______ 1. ZIF sockets
_______ 2. ISA slots
_______ 3. FireWire bus
_______ 4. USB
_______ 5. faceplate
_______ 6. standoffs
_______ 7. AGP
_______ 8. heat sink
_______ 9. processor speed
_______ 10. packaging

a. the first expansion slots on early PCs
b. metal plate that fits over the ports on the back of a computer case
c. bus used to connect slow I/O devices such as a mouse
d. very fast bus often used for downloading video from a camera to the computer
e. material used to protect chips and provide connectors of a standard size and shape
f. a clip-on device with fingers or fins that pull the heat away from the CPU
g. pegs that separate the motherboard from the case
h. socket with a small lever to lift CPU up and out of the motherboard
i. the speed at which the CPU operates internally, often measured in MHz
j. dedicated bus between the chip set on the video card and the CPU

Short Answer Questions

Write a brief answer to each of the following questions.

1. Name at least eight components that are contained on a motherboard.
2. What is bus speed and how does it relate to the system clock?
3. Why do the buses on a motherboard operate at different speeds?
4. What is one reason to flash BIOS? What is the easiest way to obtain the latest software to upgrade BIOS?
5. List several types of form factors. What is the most popular type of form factor for PCs today?
6. Describe the basic steps required to install a new motherboard in your computer.

1 Recognizing Motherboard Components

Figure 3-33 shows a blank diagram of an ATX motherboard. Using what you learned in this chapter and in previous chapters, label as many components as you can. Next, obtain the manual for a motherboard that uses the ATX form factor. If you do not have a printed manual, your instructor may be able to provide one. Alternatively, search for a motherboard Web site and then download and print a manual. [For Web sites try ASUS at *www.asus.com* or Abit at *www.motherboards.com*]. After reviewing the manual, identify any additional components described in the manual.

APPLY YOUR KNOWLEDGE

Check your understanding of the chapter with the hands-on Apply Your Knowledge exercises.

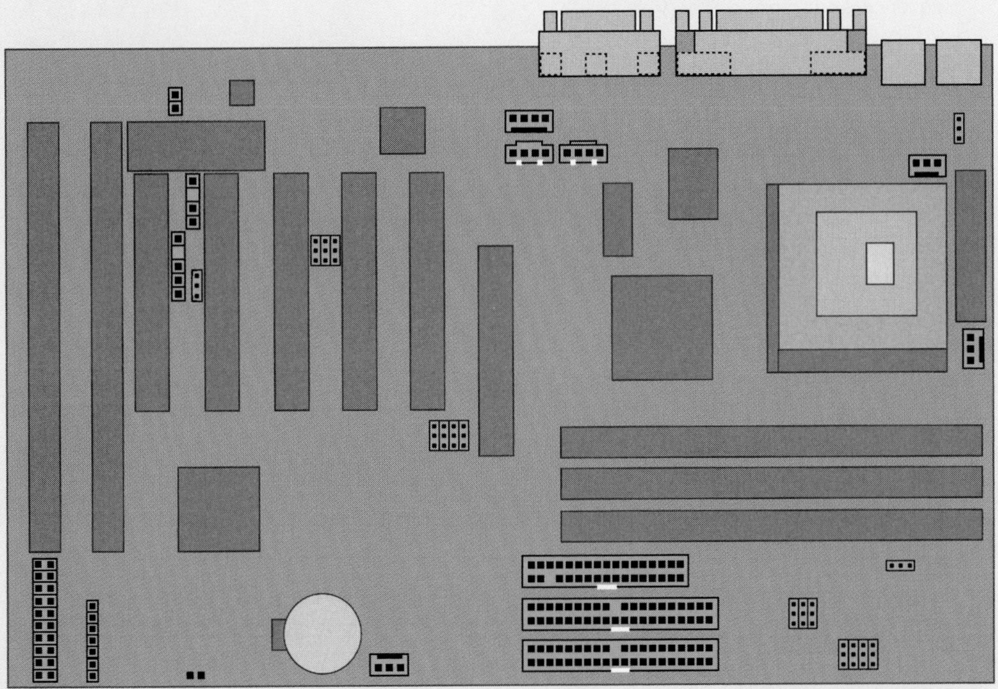

Figure 3-33

2 Recording CMOS settings

As noted in the chapter, having a record of your CMOS settings is important, in the event the settings are lost. The following steps describe the steps to create a written record of your CMOS settings.

1. Boot your PC and look for directions on the screen that tell you how to access CMOS setup on your PC, such as *Press F2 to enter setup*. Press the specified key to access CMOS setup.
2. When the CMOS main screen displays, write down the settings shown. Then follow the instructions on screen to select and navigate to the next screen. (Typically, you can use the arrow keys or TAB key to highlight options. Once you have highlighted your selection, you usually need to press the ENTER key, PAGE DOWN key, or the SPACEBAR. The main screen may or may not display a short summary of the highlighted category.)
3. Continue navigating through screens and writing down settings until you have a complete record of the CMOS settings.

APPLY YOUR KNOWLEDGE

Check your understanding of the chapter with the hands-on Apply Your Knowledge exercises.

3 Changing System Date/Time in CMOS Setup

To help you gain familiarity with how CMOS setup works, the following steps have you change the date and time settings in CMOS setup, reboot the computer and confirm that the changes are reflected in the operating system, and then return the CMOS date and time to the correct settings.

1. Boot your PC and look for directions on the screen that tell you how to access CMOS setup on your PC, such as *Press F2 to enter setup*. Press the specified key to access CMOS setup.
2. Navigate to the standard CMOS Setup screen, which includes settings for date, time, boot sequence, and so on.
3. Highlight the time field(s) and set the time ahead one hour.
4. Move to the date field(s) and set the date ahead one year.
5. Return to the main CMOS setup screen and select the option to Save Settings and Exit. If prompted, verify that you do wish to save the settings.
6. Wait while the system reboots. Allow Windows to load.
7. Once the Windows desktop displays, check the time and date. Are your CMOS setup changes reflected in Windows?
8. Reboot the computer, press the keys required to access CMOS setup, and return the date and time to the correct settings.
9. Repeat Step 8 to confirm that the correct date and time are reflected in Windows.

4 Researching CPUs on the Internet

1. Visit the Intel Web site (*www.intel.com*) and print information on the newest processor available for desktop or notebook computers.
2. Print photographs of at least four different processor packages used by Intel CPUs. List the processor packages that these processors currently use:
   - Celeron
   - Pentium 4
   - Itanium
   - Itanium 2
3. Visit the C|Net News Web site (*www.news.com*) and search for news stories on new chips from Intel and AMD. What is the latest news on chips from these two manufacturers? What types of new chips and new chip technologies are being developed?

5 Researching BIOS Updates on the Internet

1. If you do not already know what brand and version of BIOS your motherboard uses, access CMOS setup to determine this information.
2. Visit the Web site of the manufacturer of your BIOS or another Web site to determine if a BIOS upgrade is available for your computer. Suggested Web sites include:

AMI	*www.ami.com*
Phoenix or Award	*www.phoenix.com*
Any type BIOS	
Motherboards.org	*www.motherboards.org*
Micro Firmware	*www.firmware.com*
Unicore	*www.unicore.com*

3. Print out the Web page(s) listing the steps required to flash BIOS and upgrade to the latest version.

CHAPTER 4

Managing Memory

Introduction

Chapter 3 looked in detail at components on the motherboard, including the CPU and chip set, buses and expansion slots, ROM BIOS, and components used to change hardware configuration settings. This chapter looks at another important component on the motherboard — memory — and how operating systems manage memory. The chapter also reviews how to upgrade and troubleshoot memory to help improve a system's performance.

OBJECTIVES

In this chapter, you will learn:

1. About the different kinds of physical memory (RAM) used on the motherboard
2. About Windows memory management
3. How to upgrade memory modules
4. How to troubleshoot memory

Up for Discussion

Your friend Pamela Smith is a graphics designer who creates direct mail pieces for local companies, including Sunrise Computers. Pamela recently installed Windows XP and the latest version of Adobe Photoshop. Since the upgrade, her computer is running slowly, and she has gotten a few "Not enough memory for operation" errors display on the screen. She is really frustrated and wishes she had never upgraded her software.

After listening to her story, you suggest to Pamela that the real culprit is likely the amount of memory on her system. You explain that if she is running Windows XP, Adobe Photoshop, or other software that requires a lot of memory, she should have 512 MB of RAM on her computer.

You tell her that adding more memory to her system actually is very simple. The first step is determining how much RAM she currently has on her system. Then, after determining what types of RAM her system will support, you can open the computer case and add more memory modules to the motherboard. You explain that upgrading memory will provide a significant boost in her system's performance.

Pamela is thrilled at the idea of having her computer running quickly again, but is worried about the cost. Although you cannot provide an exact cost without knowing more about her system, you assure her that the cost should be relatively low, since RAM prices run about $25 for 128 MB of RAM. Pamela is relieved to hear that the memory upgrade will be easy and inexpensive, and she schedules a time to drop off her computer.

Questions:

- How can you determine the amount of memory installed on a computer?
- How do you determine which memory modules a system can support?
- What are the steps to install memory in a computer?

RAM on the Motherboard

As you have learned, memory temporarily holds data and instructions as the CPU processes them. Memory is divided into two categories: ROM (read-only memory) and RAM (random access memory). ROM retains its data when the computer is turned off. RAM loses all its data when the computer is turned off, because RAM chips need a continuous supply of electrical power to hold data or software stored in them. (The data stored on the CMOS chip is not lost, because the CMOS chip runs on a small battery.)

A computer system has two kinds of memory: a larger amount of main memory to hold data and instructions as they are processed, and a smaller memory cache to help speed up access time to main memory. *Dynamic RAM (DRAM)*, pronounced *dee-ram*, is used for main memory in the computer. DRAM is considered to be dynamic because it needs to be refreshed every few milliseconds. *Static RAM (SRAM)*, pronounced *ess-ram*, is used for memory cache. SRAM is considered static because these memory chips hold data without needing to be refreshed, as long as the power is on. Figure 4-1 summarizes the characteristics of DRAM and SRAM.

Main Memory (DRAM)	Memory Cache (SRAM)
DRAM needs constant refreshing	SRAM does not need refreshing
Slower than SRAM because of refreshing time	Faster than DRAM but more expensive
Physically housed on DIMMs, SIMMs, and RIMMs	Located on the motherboard on COAST modules or single chips, or included inside the processor case

Figure 4-1 Characteristics of main memory (DRAM) and memory cache (SRAM).

Static RAM Technologies

Before reviewing static RAM technologies, it is important to understand how memory caching works. Memory caching is a method used to store data or programs in SRAM for quick retrieval (Figure 4-2). Memory caching relies on SRAM chips to store data and a **cache controller** to manage the storage and retrieval of data from SRAM. When memory caching is used, the cache controller anticipates what data or programming code the CPU will request next and then copies that data or programming code from DRAM to SRAM. Then, if the cache guessed correctly, it can satisfy the CPU request from SRAM without accessing the slower DRAM. Under normal conditions, the cache controller stores the right data or programming code over 90 percent of the time and is an effective way to speed up memory access.

Figure 4-2 A memory cache (SRAM) temporarily holds data in expectation of what the CPU will request next.

Static RAM (SRAM) is used for memory cache because SRAM provides faster access to data than DRAM. SRAM is faster because it does not require that data be rewritten constantly, thus saving the CPU time used to refresh data in DRAM.

As you learned in Chapter 3, CPUs can have memory cache on the processor chip, inside the processor housing on a small circuit board, or directly on the same die as the processor core. Figure 4-3 summarizes the locations of various types of memory cache.

When cache memory is located on the motherboard, it either is located on individual chips or on a memory module called cache on a stick. **Cache on a stick (COAST)**, which was developed by Intel, is a small circuit board with SRAM chips that is attached to the motherboard. COAST is inserted in a special socket on the motherboard. This socket, referred to as a COAST socket or a CELP (card edge low profile), normally is located close to the processor and resembles a PCI expansion slot. COAST is used on older computers to increase the amount of memory cache. Some older motherboards had 256 KB of built-in memory cache and a COAST module for the addition of 256 KB more. This practice is less common, as many manufacturers are creating motherboards with 512 KB of SRAM directly on the motherboard.

More About

SRAM Technologies

To learn more about SRAM technologies such as burst SRAM, pipelined burst SRAM, and other technologies listed in Figure 4-1, visit the Understanding and Troubleshooting Your PC More About Web page (**scsite.com/understanding/more**) and then click SRAM Technologies below Chapter 4.

Memory Cache	Location
L1 cache	• On the CPU die. All CPUs today have L1 cache.
L2 cache	• Inside the CPU housing on newer systems. The first CPU to contain L2 cache was the Intel Pentium Pro. • On the motherboad of older systems.
L3 cache	• On the motherboard when there is L2 cache in the CPU housing. L3 is used with some AMD processors. • Inside the CPU housing, farther away from the CPU than the L2 cache. The Intel Itanium housing contains L3 cache.

Figure 4-3 Different types of memory cache are located in various locations in a system.

Almost all systems today, except for a few that use AMD processors, have memory caches inside the CPU housing. When buying a computer or a new CPU, look for processors that include as much memory cache as possible to get the best performance.

FAQ 4-1

What does it mean when DRAM and SRAM are referred to as synchronous or asynchronous?

Older DRAM and SRAM memory technologies operated asynchronously with the system bus, but newer DRAM and SRAM memory types operate synchronously. To understand the difference between asynchronous and synchronous memory, consider this analogy. Children jump rope with a long rope, and one child on each end turns the rope. A child who cannot keep in step with the turning rope (asynchronous) can only run through on a single pass and must come back around to make another pass. A child who can keep in step with the rope (synchronous) can run into the center and jump awhile, until he or she is tired and runs out. Which child performs the most rope-jumping cycles in a given amount of time? The one who keeps in step with the rope. Similarly, synchronous memory retrieves data faster than asynchronous memory, because it keeps time with the system clock.

Dynamic RAM Technologies

Dynamic RAM (DRAM) needs to be refreshed every few milliseconds. To **refresh** RAM means that the computer must rewrite the data to the chip. DRAM is refreshed by the **memory controller**, which is a circuit in the chip set on the motherboard that generates signals necessary to control the reading and writing of information to and from the memory.

In earlier PCs, DRAM used for main memory was stored on the motherboard as single, socketed chips. Today, DRAM is always stored in DIMM, RIMM, or SIMM modules, which plug directly into a bank on the motherboard. (A **bank** is a location on the motherboard that contains slots for memory modules.) Figure 4-4 shows examples of these different types of memory modules. The major differences among these modules are the width of the data path that each type of module accommodates, and the way data moves from the system bus to the module. In newer computers, DRAM is stored on DIMMs (Figure 4-5) and less commonly on RIMMs.

FAQ 4-2

What types of memory modules are used in notebook computers?

Smaller versions of DIMMs and RIMMs, called SO-DIMMs and SO-RIMMs, are used in notebook computers. (SO stands for "small outline.") MicroDIMMs are used on sub-notebook computers and are smaller than SO-DIMMs.

Type of DRAM Module	Example
SIMM (single inline memory module) Memory module with pins on opposite sides of the circuit board that connect together to form a single set of contacts. A SIMM typically holds SDRAM chips.	 72-pin SIMM  30-pin SIMM
DIMM (Dual inline memory module) Memory module with pins on opposite sides of the circuit board that do not connect and thus form two sets of contacts. A DIMM typically holds SDRAM chips.	 184-pin DDR DIMM  168-pin DIMM
RIMM Memory module that houses Rambus® DRAM (RDRAM®) chips, which are much faster than synchronous DRAM (SDRAM).	 184-pin DIMM

Figure 4-4 Types of DRAM modules.

Figure 4-5 DRAM can be stored on DIMMs that connect to the motherboard via one or more slots.

DRAM and SRAM use several technologies, which are summarized in Figure 4-6. The goal of each new technology is to increase overall throughput while retaining accuracy. The two DRAM technologies currently most used are **Double Data Rate SDRAM** (abbreviated **DDR**, **DDR SDRAM**, or **SDRAM II**) in DIMM modules or **Direct Rambus® DRAM (RDRAM®** or **Direct RDRAM**) in RIMM modules. Some of the other technologies listed in Figure 4-6 are considered obsolete, although you still need to be aware of them in case you see them on older motherboards you support. You will read more about these technologies in the following sections.

Technology	Description	Used with
Fast page (FPM)	Improved access time over conventional memory. FPM is seldom seen today.	• 30-pin or 72-pin SIMM • 168-pin DIMM
Extended data out (EDO)	Refined version of FPM that speeds up access time. Might still see it on older motherboards.	• 72-pin SIMM • 168-pin DIMM
Synchronous DRAM (SDRAM)	SDRAM runs in sync with the system clock and is rated by clock speed, whereas other types of memory run independently of (and slower than) the system clock.	• 66/100/133/150 MHz, 168-pin DIMM • 66/100/133 MHz, 144-pin SO-DIMM
DDR (Double-Data Rate) SDRAM	A faster version of SDRAM and currently the most popular memory type.	• 200/266/300/333/370/400 MHz, 184-pin DIMM • 266 MHz, 200-pin SO-DIMM
Rambus DRAM (RDRAM)	RDRAM uses a faster system bus (800 MHz, 1066 MHz, or 1200 MHz). Currently, a RIMM can use a 16- or 32-bit data path.	• 1200 MHz, 232-pin RIMM using a 32-bit data path • 800 MHz, 232-pin RIMM using a 32-bit data path • 1066 MHz, 184-pin RIMM using a 16-bit data path • 800 MHz, 184-pin RIMM using a 16-bit data path

Figure 4-6 DRAM memory technologies.

SIMM TECHNOLOGIES SIMMs are rated by speed, measured in nanoseconds (ns), which are billionths of a second. This speed is a measure of access time, which is the time the CPU takes to receive a value in response to a request, including the time it takes to refresh the chips. Common SIMM speeds are 60, 70, or 80 ns. An access time of 60 ns is faster than an access time of 70 ns. Therefore, the smaller the speed rating is, the faster the chip.

DIMM TECHNOLOGIES SIMM technologies largely have been replaced by newer and faster DIMM technologies. A DIMM is a memory module that has pins on opposite sides of the circuit board that do not connect and thus form two sets of contacts. DIMMs have 168 or 184 pins on the edge connector of the board and hold between 8 MB and 2 GB of RAM.

Newer DIMMs hold chips that use **synchronous DRAM (SDRAM)**, which is DRAM that runs in sync with the system clock and thus runs faster than other types of DRAM. The speed of SDRAM is rated in MHz rather than in nanoseconds (ns). The SDRAM data path is 64 bits wide.

Several variations of SDRAM exist, the most popular of which is Double Data Rate SDRAM (DDR SDRAM, or SDRAM II), which runs twice as fast as regular SDRAM and can hold up to 2 GB of RAM. Instead of processing data for each beat of the system clock, as regular SDRAM does, DDR SDRAM processes data when the beat rises and again when it falls, doubling the data rate of memory. If a system bus runs at 100 MHz, then DDR SDRAM runs at 200 MHz with a data path of 64 bits.

DDR SDRAM modules have only one notch on the edge connector, whereas regular SDRAM modules have two. After DDR SDRAM was introduced, regular SDRAM became known as Single Data Rate SDRAM (SDR SDRAM).

> **More About**
>
> **DRAM Technologies**
>
> To learn more about older DRAM technologies such as SyncLink DRAM and newer DRAM technologies such as RLDRAM II, visit the Understanding and Troubleshooting Your PC More About Web page (**scsite.com/understanding/more**) and then click DRAM Technologies below Chapter 4.

RIMM TECHNOLOGIES A RIMM is a memory module that houses Rambus DRAM (RDRAM) chips, which are much faster than synchronous DRAM (SDRAM). Direct Rambus DRAM (sometimes called RDRAM or Direct RDRAM or simply Rambus) is named after Rambus, Inc., the company that developed it. Current RDRAM chips use a 16-, 32-, or 64-bit data path. RDRAM can run at internal speeds of 800 MHz to 1200 MHz, using a 400- to 600-MHz system bus.

With RIMMs, each socket must be filled to maintain continuity throughout all sockets. If the socket does not hold a RIMM, then it must hold a placeholder module called a **C-RIMM (Continuity RIMM)** (Figure 4-7). The C-RIMM contains no memory chips.

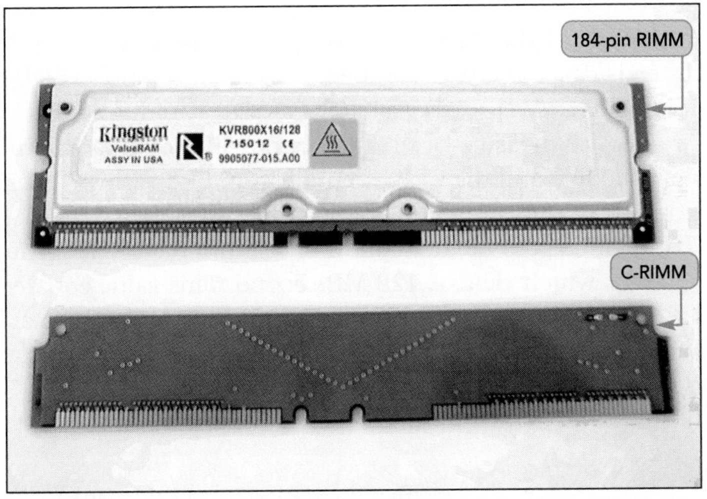

Figure 4-7 A C-RIMM or RIMM must be installed in every RIMM slot on a motherboard.

FAQ 4-3

Why is a 512-MB DIMM likely to cost less than a 512-MB RIMM — even though they provide the same amount of memory?

Rambus designed the RDRAM technology but does not actually manufacture RIMMs; it licenses the technology to memory manufacturers. Because these manufacturers must pay licensing fees to use RDRAM, RIMMs often cost more to cover those fees. Given that, the industry has turned more to SDRAM memory advancements than to Rambus, and particularly to DDR memory because it is faster and cheaper than RIMMs.

Factors Determining Memory Speeds

Several factors contribute to how fast memory runs, and speeds are measured in different ways. Factors to consider when looking at the overall speed of memory are shown in the following list and in Figure 4-8.

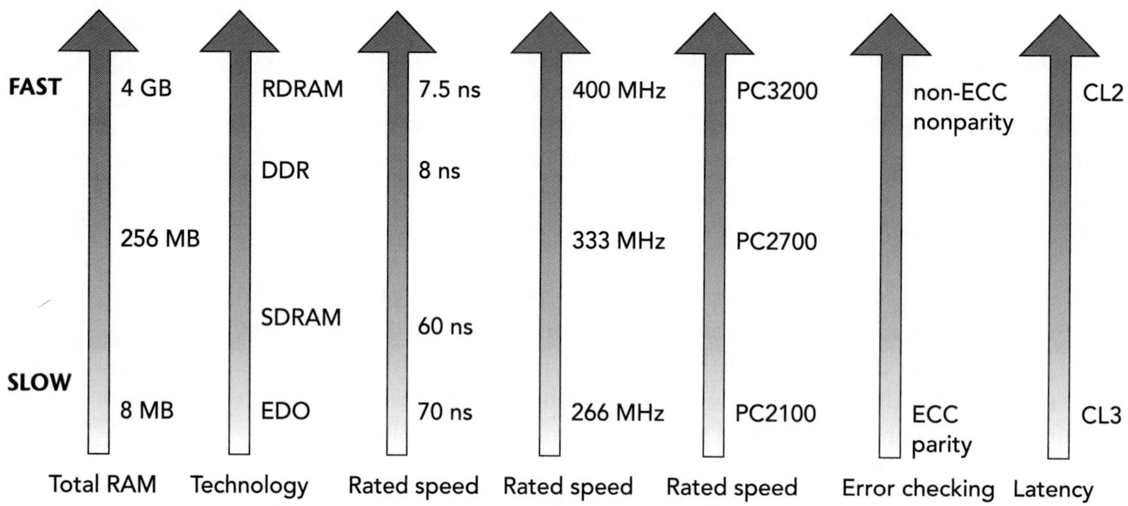

Figure 4-8 Factors that contribute to overall memory speed.

- *Speed of memory.* Memory speeds are measured in ns, MHz, or PC rating. The speed of a SIMM is measured in nanoseconds, while the speed of SDRAM, DDR, and RDRAM is measured in MHz or a PC rating. A DDR module often is described with its speed in the name, such as DDR266 for a DDR running at 266 MHz or DDR333 for a DDR running at 333 MHz.

  A PC rating is a measure of the total bandwidth of data moving between the memory module and the CPU. To understand PC ratings, consider an example of a DDR DIMM module that runs at 266 MHz (DDR266). The module has a 64-bit (8-byte) data path. Therefore, the transfer rate is 8 bytes times 266 MHz, which yields 2,128 MB/second. This value equates to the PC rating of PC2100 for a DDR266 DIMM. Examples of PC ratings are shown in Figure 4-9.

Speed (MHz)	Transfer Rate	PC Rating
200 MHz	1,600 MB/second	PC1600
266 MHz	2,128 MB/second	PC2100
333 MHz	2,664 MB/second	PC2700
400 MHz	3,200 MB/second	PC3200

Figure 4-9 Current PC ratings, as shown for a DDR DIMM module with a 64-bit (8-byte) data path.

- *Memory technology used*. DDR SDRAM is faster than regular SDRAM; RDRAM is faster than SDRAM. When selecting memory, use whatever technology your motherboard supports.
- *Latency rating*. Two other memory features are **CAS Latency** (CAS stands for *column access strobe*) and **RAS Latency** (RAS stands for *row access strobe*). Both features refer to the number of clock cycles it takes to write or read a column or row of data to or from memory. The latency typically is two or three clock cycles. CAS Latency is used more than RAS Latency. CL2 (CAS Latency 2) is a little faster than CL3 (CAS Latency 3). A lower latency rating means memory is faster. When selecting memory, use whatever technology your motherboard supports.
- *Type of error checking used.* In older computers, RAM existed as individual chips socketed to the motherboard in banks of nine chips each. Each bank held eight bytes by storing one bit in each chip, with the ninth chip holding a parity bit (Figure 4-10). **Parity** refers to an error-checking procedure in which a ninth, or parity bit, is added. Using the ninth bit provides a way to test the integrity of the bits stored in RAM and in secondary storage, or sent over a communications device.

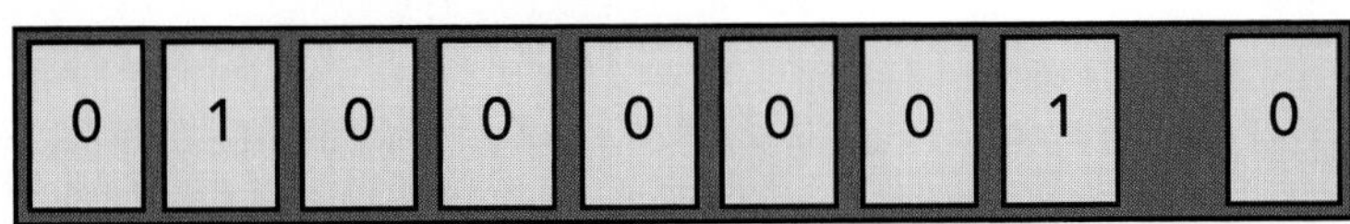

Figure 4-10 Eight chips and a parity chip represent the letter A in ASCII with even parity.

Older DRAM memory used parity checking, but today's memory uses a newer method of error checking called ECC. **ECC (error-correcting code)** memory can detect and correct an error in one bit of the byte. Newer ECC methods also can detect an error in two bits, although the memory cannot correct these double-bit errors.

Memory modules today are either non-ECC or ECC. Some SDRAM, DDR, and RIMM memory modules support ECC. DIMMs that support ECC have an odd number of chips on the module (the odd chip is the ECC chip). A DIMM is normally a 64-bit module; adding an ECC chip to verify the integrity of every 8 bits stored on the module results in a 71- or 72-bit module. ECC memory costs more than regular memory and is slower because of the extra time taken to verify data, but it is more reliable. ECC memory generally is used on servers.

- *Single channel versus dual channel.* Memory can be used in single-channel mode or dual-channel mode. In the past, all memory modules were **single-channel** memory, in which memory modules are accessed through a single channel between the memory controller and the memory module (Figure 4-11 on the next page). The memory controller goes through a single channel to access up to four memory modules. Memory modules can be added one at a time.

  With **dual-channel** memory, the memory controller reads from or writes to two memory modules, each on separate channels, simultaneously. In the most common dual-channel memory layout, the memory controller has up to two

More About

Parity

To learn more about parity checking, visit the Understanding and Troubleshooting Your PC More About Web page (**scsite.com/understanding/more**) and then click Parity below Chapter 4.

memory modules on each of two memory channels. For best performance, all memory modules should have matching capacities and technical specifications and memory modules should be added in matching pairs. Many systems and motherboards will allow for single-channel memory operation if only one memory module is plugged in.

single-channel mode

Memory modules are accessed through a single channel or connection between the memory controller and the memory module.

dual-channel mode

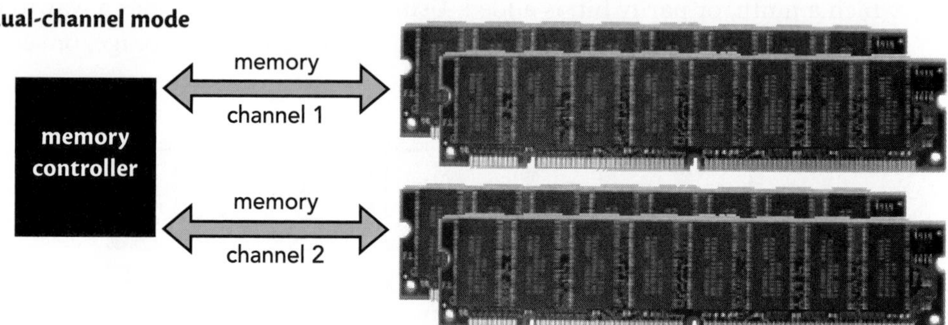

Memory controller reads from or writes to two memory modules, each on separate channels, simultaneously. In the most common dual-channel memory layout, the memory controller has up to two memory modules on each of two memory channels.

Figure 4-11 In the past, all memory modules worked in single-channel mode. Today, many memory modules work in dual-channel mode.

Quiz Yourself 4-1

To test your knowledge of the SRAM and DRAM technologies, visit the Understanding and Troubleshooting Your PC Quiz Yourself Web page (scsite.com/understanding/quiz). Click Quiz Yourself 1 below Chapter 4.

Windows Memory Management

This section discusses how the Windows operating system manages memory. As you learned in Chapter 2, an operating system relates to memory as a long list of cells that it can use to hold data and instructions, somewhat like a one-dimensional table or spreadsheet. When the operating system is first loaded, each memory location or cell is assigned a number beginning with zero. These number assignments are called memory addresses, which generally are expressed using hexadecimal notation. (For additional detail on the hexadecimal number system, see Appendix A.)

When a PC first is booted, many programs demand memory addresses, including ROM BIOS programs on the motherboard and some circuit boards, device drivers, the OS, and applications. This process of assigning memory addresses to programs is called **memory mapping**.

Once memory addresses have been assigned, they can be used for communication with software such as device drivers, the operating system, and application software — all of which are working when a computer is running. As illustrated in Figure 4-12, during output operations, application software must pass information to the OS, which in turn passes that information to a device driver. The device drivers managing input devices must pass information to the OS, which passes it to the application software. These layers of software all identify the data they want to share by referring to the memory address of the data.

Figure 4-12 Applications, the OS, and drivers pass data among them by communicating the address of memory holding the data.

The Evolution of OS Memory Management

The way that the OS manages memory has improved greatly in newer operating systems. Because of the way memory management has evolved over the past 20 years, the process under DOS and Windows 9x can seem complicated. Like an old house that has been added to and remodeled several times, the present-day design is not as efficient as that of a brand new house. Decisions made by IBM and Microsoft in the early 1980s significantly affect, and in some cases limit, the way memory is used under Windows 9x. Because Windows NT, Windows 2000, Windows XP, and Windows Server 2003 have been designed from the ground up, they are free of those limitations.

Early CPUs had only 20 lines on the bus available to handle addresses, so the largest memory address the CPU could use was 11111111111111111111, which is 1,048,575 (decimal), or 1,024K (1 MB) of memory. This 1 MB of memory was used by DOS and divided up according to the scheme shown in Figure 4-13.

Range of Memory Addresses	Type of Memory	Range Using Hexadecimal Notation
0 to 640K	Conventional or base memory	0 to A0000
604K to 1024K	Upper memory (A through F ranges)	A0000 to FFFFF
Above 1024K	Extended memory	100000 and up

Figure 4-13 Division of memory under DOS and Windows 9x. Because the hex numbers in upper memory begin with A through F, the divisions of upper memory often are referred to as the A range, B range, and so on, up to the F range.

> **More About**
>
> **Memory Management in DOS and Windows 9x**
>
> To learn more about how DOS and Windows 9x manage memory, visit the Understanding and Troubleshooting Your PC More About Web page (**scsite.com/understanding/more**) and then click DOS and Windows 9x Memory Management below Chapter 4.

The first 640K of memory (**conventional memory**) was used by DOS and applications, and the addresses from 640K up to 1024K (**upper memory**) were used by the BIOS and device drivers. When newer CPUs and motherboards were developed with 24 or more address lines, memory addresses above 1024K became available. This format is called **extended memory**. Windows 9x still uses these same divisions of memory, although it makes the most use of extended memory.

Recall that for an operating system such as Windows to support multitasking, the CPU must be running in protected mode. In protected mode, the CPU processes 32 bits of data at one time, and more than one program can run at the same time. In real mode, by contrast, the CPU processes 16 bits of data at one time. In real mode, an application has complete access to all hardware resources, but in protected mode, the OS controls how an application can access hardware.

For example, as shown in Figure 4-14, you can see that the 16-bit program running in real mode has direct access to RAM. In protected mode, more than one program can run, and the programs must depend on the OS to access RAM. Using protected mode thus gives the OS some latitude in how it uses RAM. If the OS is low on RAM, it can store some data on the hard drive. This method of using the hard drive as though it were RAM is called **virtual memory**. Data transferred to virtual memory is stored in a file on the hard drive called a **swap file** or **paging file**. The OS manages the entire process, and the applications know nothing about this substitution of the hard drive resources for RAM.

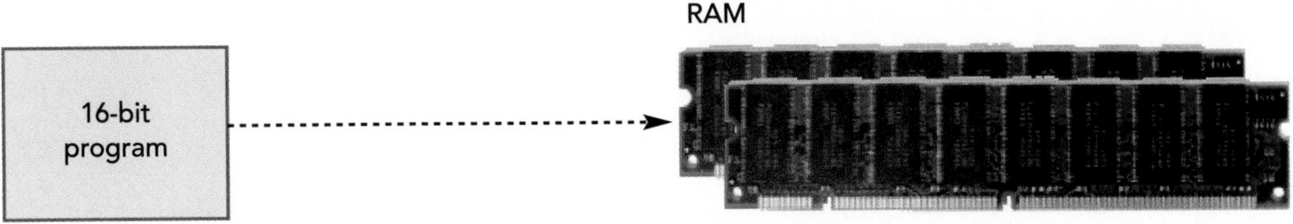
RAM
16-bit
program
real mode: one program has direct access to hardware, including RAM

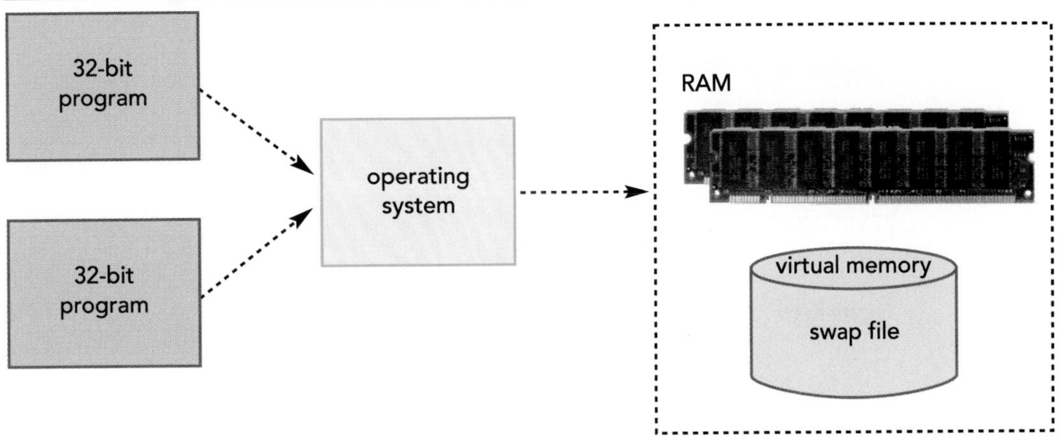
32-bit
program
32-bit
program
operating
system
RAM
virtual memory
swap file
protected mode: multiple programs depend on the OS to access hardware, including RAM

Figure 4-14 Protected mode allows more than one program to run, each protected from the other by the operating system.

Windows 95 was the first Windows operating system to support 32-bit, protected-mode application software, although it still allows 16-bit, real-mode device drivers and software to run. Beginning with Windows NT, the Windows operating system required that all device drivers be 32-bit drivers. This created a much more stable OS than Windows 9x. Further, being able to use virtual memory resolved the 1024K memory limitation imposed by real mode.

> **More About**
>
> **DOS and Windows 9x Utilities that Manage Memory**
>
> To learn more about how Windows 9x manages memory, visit the Understanding and Troubleshooting Your PC More About Web page (**scsite.com/understanding/more**) and then click DOS and Windows 9x Utilities below Chapter 4.

Memory Management in Windows NT, Windows 2000, Windows XP, and Windows Server 2003

With the introduction of Windows NT, the Windows operating system eliminated much of the complexity of memory management that existed with Windows 9x and DOS. The memory management model used by Windows NT, Windows 2000, Windows XP, and Windows Server 2003 is illustrated in Figure 4-15 on the next page. Using this model, an application or device driver indicates that it needs memory, but it does not have to tell Windows which physical memory or which memory addresses it wants, or even the range of addresses it wants to fall within.

Windows uses its virtual memory manager to interface between the application or device driver and the physical and virtual memory that it controls. Memory is allocated in 4K segments or **pages**. Windows assigns a certain number of pages to an application or device driver that needs memory. The application or device drivers know how many pages have been assigned, but do not know the specific memory addresses. Windows virtual memory manager handles managing the memory addresses used for each page and can choose to store these pages in RAM or on the hard drive in the swap file named **Pagefile.sys**.

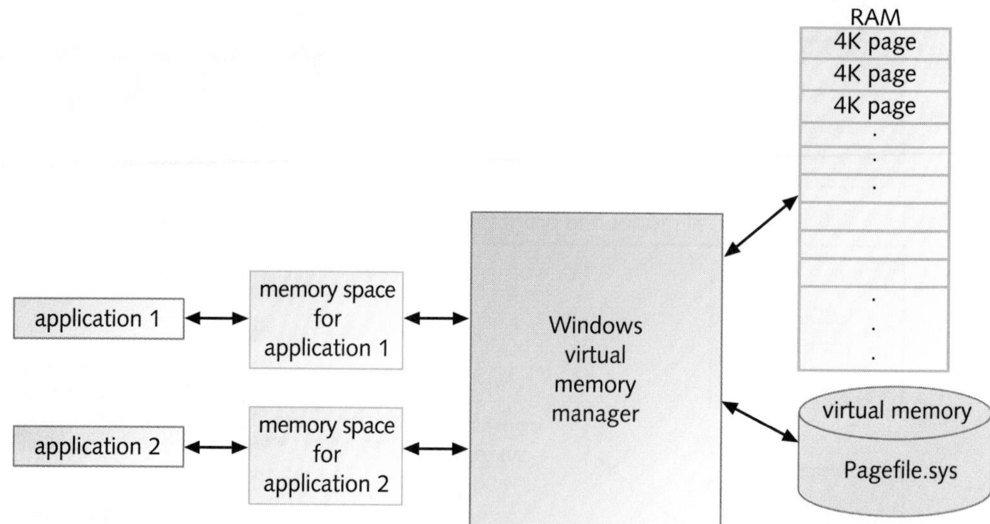

Figure 4-15 Memory management model used by Windows NT, Windows 2000, Windows XP, and Windows Server 2003.

While this approach reduces the complexity of memory management that existed with Windows 9x and DOS, this simpler approach does cause Windows NT, Windows 2000, Windows XP, and Windows Server 2003 to lose some backward compatibility with older software and devices.

> FAQ 4-4
>
> **What is backward compatibility?**
>
> The phrase *backward compatible* refers to hardware or software that works with earlier models or versions of the same product. A backward-compatible spreadsheet program, for example, might allow you to edit spreadsheets created with the previous version of the program. Having hardware or software that is backward compatible can eliminate the need to upgrade other software or hardware on your system to work with your newer product. Most manufacturers try to make products backward compatible, but, as was the case with Windows NT, manufacturers sometimes forfeit backward compatibility to take advantage of a new technology.

Under Windows 2000, Windows XP, and Windows Server 2003, the default size of the paging file is set to 1.5 times the amount of RAM installed. You might need to change the paging file in order to improve system performance. Here are some guidelines to remember in managing paging files:

- Set the initial and maximum sizes of the file to the same value.
- When changing the size of the paging file, remember that you need to balance the file size with disk space usage and that Windows 2000, Windows XP, and Windows Server 2003 each require at least 5 MB of free space on a disk. In other words, do not make the file too large, especially when the disk it is stored on is active or has limited space.

Your Turn

Changing Virtual Memory and Paging File Size

As you have learned, if Windows is low on RAM, it can use a virtual memory method to store some data on the hard drive as though it were RAM. If your system is running slowly when you have many applications open, you may want to optimize virtual memory by changing the size of your paging file.

To estimate how many megabytes should be allocated to a paging file, complete the following steps:

1. Start all of the applications you normally use. Press CTRL+ALT+DELETE to open Windows Task Manager and then click the Performance tab.
   The Total listed in the Commit Charge area is the amount of memory your system currently is using in kilobytes (Figure 4-16a).
2. Divide this number by 1000 to convert it to megabytes (MB) and then add 128 MB to estimate a good starting minimum virtual memory size.
3. Click the Close button on the Windows Task Manager window.

To change virtual memory settings and paging file size in Windows XP, complete the following steps:

1. Click the Start button, right-click My Computer on the Start menu, and then select Properties from the shortcut menu.
2. When the System Properties window is displayed, click the Advanced tab.
3. Click the Settings button in the Performance area on the Advanced tab.
4. When the Performance Options window is displayed, click the Advanced tab.
5. Click the Change button in the Virtual memory area on the Advanced tab.
   Clicking the Change button displays the Virtual Memory window. In this window, you can change the paging file size and view information about the paging file and the registry (Figure 4-16b).

When making changes to the virtual memory paging file, consider the following tips:

- For best performance, set the Initial size and Maximum size to the same size to prevent the OS from resizing the file. Set the Initial size to no less than the recommended size listed in the Total paging file size for all drives area.
- In general, leave the paging file at its recommended size, although you might increase its size if you routinely use programs that require a lot of memory.
- If you decrease the size of either the Initial size or the Maximum size paging file settings, you must restart your computer to see the effects of those changes. Increases generally do not require a restart.

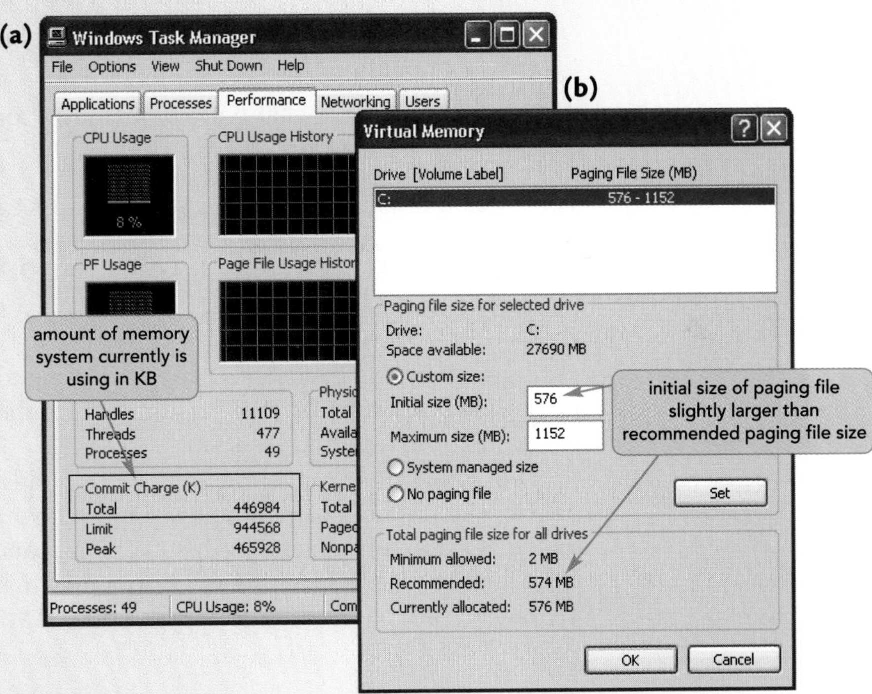

Figure 4-16

Quiz Yourself 4-2

To test your knowledge of the Windows memory management, visit the Understanding and Troubleshooting Your PC Quiz Yourself Web page (scsite.com/understanding/quiz). Click Quiz Yourself 2 below Chapter 4.

Upgrading Memory

If your computer continues to run slowly after you have optimized the paging file, the computer may benefit from a memory upgrade. Upgrading memory — that is, adding more RAM to your system — will make your computer run faster. In fact, in most cases, upgrading memory provides more significant performance improvement than upgrading the CPU or adding a larger hard drive.

When first purchased, many computers have empty slots on the motherboard that allow you to add DIMMs or RIMMs to increase the amount of RAM. This section describes issues you should consider when purchasing and upgrading memory.

> **More About**
>
> **Virtual Memory in Windows 9x**
>
> To learn more about how Windows 9x uses virtual memory, visit the Understanding and Troubleshooting Your PC More About Web page **(scsite.com/understanding/more)** and then click Windows 9x Virtual Memory below Chapter 4.

Determining How Much and What Kind of Memory to Buy

As you start the process of upgrading your system's memory, ask yourself these questions:

- How much memory do I have, and how much memory do I need?
- What size and type of modules should I buy to be compatible with the memory I already have installed?
- How much and what types of memory can I fit on the motherboard?
- How much memory can I afford?

This section discusses in detail how to address each of these questions.

AMOUNT OF EXISTING MEMORY AND ADDITIONAL MEMORY NEEDED To determine how much memory your Windows system has, right-click My Computer on the Start menu and then click Properties on the shortcut menu. When the System Properties window is displayed, click the General tab. The amount of memory or RAM is listed on the General tab, along with other system information (for an example, see Figure 1-12 on page 12 in Chapter 1).

Determining how much memory you need is a fairly simple process. Today's software places high demand on memory, so you want to upgrade your system to the largest amount of memory it can support and that you can afford. For improved performance, install at least 256 MB of RAM in a Windows XP system. If possible, upgrade your system to at least 512 MB of RAM.

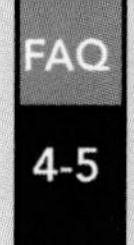

Has the cost of RAM gone up or come down in the last few years?

At one time, RAM was literally worth more than its weight in gold. When building a system several years ago, most people made do with the minimum amount of RAM required for adequate performance. Today, RAM is much cheaper (between $20 and $50 for 128 MB of RAM), which means you can probably buy all the RAM you need to make your system perform at top speed. Users of graphics-editing software, in particular, will benefit from additional RAM.

MATCH MEMORY MODULES TO THE MOTHERBOARD When buying memory to add to a motherboard, know that in most cases, you must match the type of memory to the type supported by the board. Newer motherboards, for example, support either ECC or non-ECC memory. In some cases, you can install ECC memory on a non-ECC board, but error checking will not be enabled. To see if your motherboard supports parity or ECC memory, look for the ability to enable or disable the feature in CMOS setup, or check the motherboard documentation.

Also check the motherboard documentation to determine how your system detects the type of memory installed. Computers use one or two methods to detect memory: **Parallel Presence Detect** (**PPD**), which uses resistors to communicate the type of memory present, or **Serial Presence Detect** (**SPD**), which stores information about the memory type in ROM. When purchasing memory for a system, you must match the method the module uses to what the motherboard expects. If the motherboard documentation does not specify which method your motherboard uses, the system most likely uses PPD.

Finally, as you upgrade memory, you must match the type of memory to the motherboard requirements. For example, if the motherboard documentation says that you must use DDR 300 or DDR 333 DIMMS, then DDR 400 DIMMS will not work.

MEMORY TYPES SUPPORTED BY THE MOTHERBOARD Once you have determined how much memory your system has and reviewed specific details on the memory your motherboard supports, you should determine the specific kind of memory you need and how much memory the system can support. Generally, when upgrading your system, you always should use the fastest memory that your motherboard can support. Read the documentation for your motherboard to determine what memory speed or speeds to use on the board (Figure 4-17). Some boards

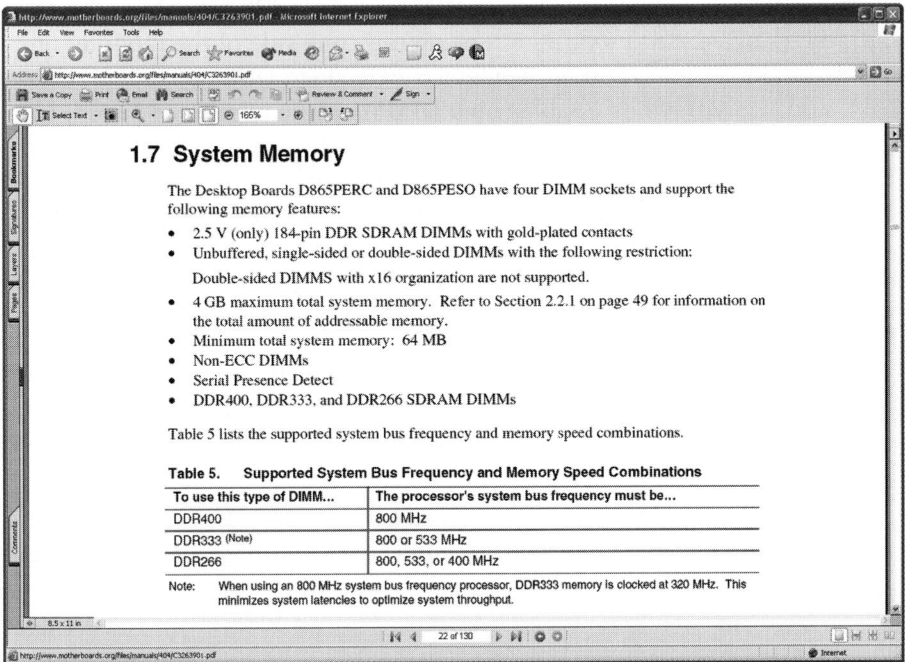

1.7 System Memory

The Desktop Boards D865PERC and D865PESO have four DIMM sockets and support the following memory features:

- 2.5 V (only) 184-pin DDR SDRAM DIMMs with gold-plated contacts
- Unbuffered, single-sided or double-sided DIMMs with the following restriction:
  Double-sided DIMMS with x16 organization are not supported.
- 4 GB maximum total system memory. Refer to Section 2.2.1 on page 49 for information on the total amount of addressable memory.
- Minimum total system memory: 64 MB
- Non-ECC DIMMs
- Serial Presence Detect
- DDR400, DDR333, and DDR266 SDRAM DIMMs

Table 5 lists the supported system bus frequency and memory speed combinations.

Table 5. Supported System Bus Frequency and Memory Speed Combinations

To use this type of DIMM...	The processor's system bus frequency must be...
DDR400	800 MHz
DDR333 (Note)	800 or 533 MHz
DDR266	800, 533, or 400 MHz

Note: When using an 800 MHz system bus frequency processor, DDR333 memory is clocked at 320 MHz. This minimizes system latencies to optimize system throughput.

Figure 4-17 Example of documentation for the Intel D865PERC and D865PESO motherboards.

support only one speed, while others support a variety of speeds. Whenever possible, plan to purchase memory that uses the fastest speed supported by your motherboard. Although it is sometimes possible to mix the speed of memory modules on a motherboard, it is not recommended. (Never use memory chips with different speeds in a single memory bank).

The amount of memory your computer can hold is determined by the number of memory slots on the motherboard and the type and size of memory these slots can support. To determine how much memory your computer physically can hold, read the documentation that comes with your computer. For example, in the documentation shown in Figure 4-17 on the previous page, those two Intel motherboards can hold a maximum of 4 GB of total system memory. You also can open the case and look at the memory sockets to determine how many sockets you have and what size and type of modules are already installed. If all slots are full, sometimes you can take out smaller-capacity modules and replace them with larger-capacity modules, but you only can use the size of modules that the board is designed to support.

Because not all sizes of memory modules fit on any one computer, you must use the right number of SIMMs, DIMMs, or RIMMs with the right amount of memory to fit the memory banks on your motherboard. The following section reviews the types of memory modules used on motherboards.

72-pin SIMMs To accommodate a 64-bit system bus data path, 72-pin SIMMs — which have a 32-bit data path — are installed in groups or banks of two. Most older motherboards that use these SIMMs have one to three banks that can be filled with two, four, or six SIMMs. The two SIMMs in each bank must match in size and speed. For specific information on the sizes and type of SIMMs the board supports, check the motherboard documentation.

DIMMs Most DIMMs have a 64-bit data path and thus can be installed as a single module rather than in pairs (some newer DIMMs have a 128-bit data path). DIMMs come as either single-sided modules (chips on only one side of the module) or double-sided modules (chips on both sides). Single-sided DIMMs come in sizes of 8, 16, 32, 64, and 128 MB, while double-sided DIMMs come in sizes of 32, 64, 128, 256, and 512 MB, 1 GB, and 2 GB.

Reviewing the documentation for your motherboard is critical in determining the right types of DIMMs to purchase, although it may seem slightly complex when you first review it. For example, as shown in Figure 4-17, the documentation for the Intel motherboards states that they use 184-pin DDR SDRAM DIMMs, which should be 2.5V, unbuffered, DDR400 SDRAM. This description can be broken down as:

- *184-pin DDR SDRAM:* DIMMs are listed based on the number of pins. In this case, the slot on the motherboard has 184 pins, so it requires 184-pin DIMMs. The installed DIMM must use Double Data Rate SDRAM, which is standard for newer DIMMs.
- *2.5V:* SDRAM DIMMs often are listed as being powered by either 2.5 volts, 3.3 volts, or 5.0 volts of power. You only should purchase DIMMs that use the voltage supported by your motherboard (in this case, 2.5V).

- *Unbuffered*: Your motherboard also determines if you can use buffered, unbuffered, or registered DIMMs. Older DIMMs used buffers, while newer SDRAM DIMMs use registers. **Registers** and **buffers** hold data and amplify a signal just before the data is written to the module. To determine which feature a DIMM has, check the position of the two notches on the DIMM module (Figure 4-18). As shown in Figure 4-18, the position of the notch on the left identifies the module as registered (RFU), buffered, or unbuffered memory. The notch on the right identifies the voltage used by the module. The position of the notches not only helps identify the type of module, but also prevents the wrong kind of module from being used on a motherboard.

168-pin DIMM notch key definitions (3.3V, unbuffered memory)

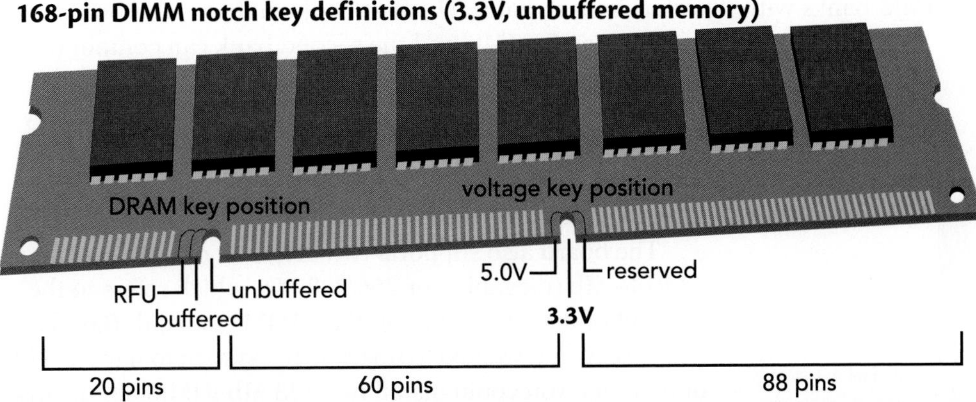

Figure 4-18 The positions of two notches on a DIMM identify the type of DIMM and the voltage requirement, and also prevent the wrong type from being installed on the motherboard.

- *DDR400:* DDR400 refers to the speed of the modules, meaning that the modules should be rated to work with a motherboard that has a system bus that runs at 800 MHz. The speed of memory sometimes also is written as PC3200. (Note that this motherboard also supports DDR333, and DDR266 SDRAM DIMMs).

The motherboard documentation also likely will show possible combinations of modules that can be installed in motherboard sockets. For example, consider a newer Pentium motherboard that allows you to use three different speeds of DDR DIMMs in one to four sockets on the board. The documentation for this motherboard might indicate that it supports up to 4 GB of unbuffered, 184-pin, non-ECC memory running at PC3200, PC2700, or PC2100. The documentation also notes that the system bus can run at 800 MHz, 533 MHz, or 400 MHz depending on the speed of the processor installed. The speed of the processor thus determines the system bus speed, which determines the speed of memory modules you can install.

Figure 4-19 outlines the possible configurations of these modules, showing that you can install one, two, or four DIMMs and which sockets should hold these DIMMS.

As illustrated by these examples, the motherboard documentation is essential when selecting memory. If you cannot find the motherboard manual for your computer, look on the motherboard manufacturer's Web site or contact the manufacturer's technical support.

RIMM Modules When you purchase a system using RIMMs, all RIMM slots will be filled with either RIMMs or C-RIMMs. When you upgrade, you replace one or more C-RIMMs or RIMMs. Be sure to match the new RIMMs with those already on the motherboard, following the recommendations of the motherboard documentation.

The motherboards for most Pentium 4 systems have four RIMM sockets — that is, two RIMM banks with two slots in each bank. The first bank on the motherboard must contain two RIMMs, and the second bank can contain two RIMMs or two C-RIMMs.

Figure 4-20 shows an example of the RDRAM memory configuration for a motherboard with four RIMM sockets. As shown in the figure, each RIMM module can have between 4 and 16 RDRAM chips.

The board also supports two densities of RIMMs, either 128/144 Mb (megabits) or 256/288 Mb, which refers to the amount of data each chip on the RIMM can hold. Based on the table, if you wanted to upgrade the system to have 256 MB of memory, you could install two 128 Mb RIMMs in the first bank of the motherboard and two C-RIMMs in the second bank. To upgrade to 512 MB of memory, you could install four 128 Mb RIMMs — two in the first bank and two in the second bank — or you could install two 256 Mb RIMMS in the first bank and two C-RIMMs in the second bank.

If two RIMMs are placed in one bank, each RIMM must have the same size and density (that is, they must have the same amount of memory and the same number of DRAM chips). If RIMMs are placed in two different banks, the RIMMs in one bank can have a different size and density than the RIMMs in the other bank. All of the RIMMs used in a computer must run at the same speed.

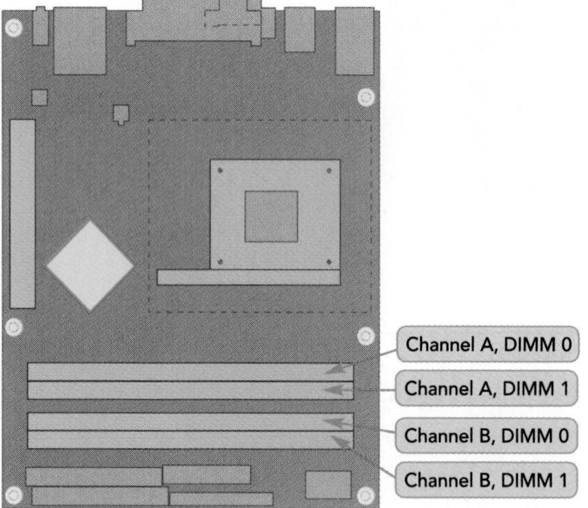

single-channel mode

	Configuration Options			
Sockets	**Option 1**	**Option 2**	**Option 3**	**Option 4**
DIMM_A0	DIMM	—	—	—
DIMM_A1	—	DIMM	—	—
DIMM_B0	—	—	DIMM	—
DIMM_B1	—	—	—	DIMM

dual-channel mode*

	Configuration Options		
Sockets	**Option 1**	**Option 2**	**Option 3**
DIMM_A0	DIMM	—	DIMM
DIMM_A1	—	DIMM	DIMM
DIMM_B0	DIMM	—	DIMM
DIMM_B1	—	DIMM	DIMM

**Use only identical DDR DIMM pairs*

Figure 4-19 Motherboard documentation shows that one, two, or four DIMMs can be installed. Each column refers to a specific channel and bank (for example, DIMM_A0 refers to the DIMM in Channel A, bank 0); each row refers to a possible configuration of DIMMs on the motherboard.

Density	4 RDRAM chips per RIMM	6 RDRAM chips per RIMM	8 RDRAM chips per RIMM	12 RDRAM chips per RIMM	16 RDRAM chips per RIMM
128/144 Mb	64 MB	96 MB	128 MB	192 MB	256 MB
256/288 Mb	128 MB	192 MB	256 MB	384 MB	512 MB

Figure 4-20 Memory configuration for a motherboard using RIMMs.

FAQ 4-6

Why are RIMMs shown with two values, such as 128/144 Mb, with a lowercase b in Mb?

RIMMs are labeled with two values, one showing the value for the ECC version, one showing the value for the non-ECC version. RIMMs often are listed as having a density of either 128/144 Mb or 256/288 Mb. Density is the amount of data each chip on the RIMM can hold, listed as Mb (notice the lowercase b in Mb, as in megabits). Because 8 bits equal one byte, 8 Mb per chip in a RIMM is equal to 1 MB (notice the uppercase MB, as in megabyte) of data. Thus, a 128/144 Mb RIMM with 4 chips actually holds 64 MB of data (4 chips × 128 Mb = 4 chips × 128 Mb / 8 = 4 chips × 16 MB = 64 MB). A chip rated 144 Mb is the ECC version of a non-ECC 128-Mb chip. A 256-Mb RIMM has chips that each hold 32 MB of RAM. Multiply that by the number of devices on the RIMM for the RIMM size. The 288-Mb RIMM is the ECC version of the 256-Mb RIMM.

Purchasing Memory Modules

As previously discussed, memory chips and memory modules come in different sizes, offer different speeds, and use different technologies and features. As you begin to shop for memory chips or modules, you should understand how to read advertisements about memory modules and know how to gauge the quality of a memory module.

Before you start looking for a memory module appropriate for your system, check your system or motherboard manual to determine if you need proprietary memory. Although many computers accept memory chips from a variety of manufacturers, some computers accept only proprietary memory — that is, memory created by the manufacturer of the computer. Proprietary memory typically costs more than memory purchased from a third-party company.

READING ADS FOR MEMORY MODULES Many computer magazines run advertisements for many different types of memory modules. Such ads typically include information about the speed, the size, the type of module, and more. Unfortunately, having all of this information in the ad can be confusing. Figure 4-21 on the next page shows a typical ad for memory modules, listing various types of DIMMs and RIMMs. For each memory module, the ad lists the amount of memory, density, speed, and price.

PC PROGRESS

WWW.PCPROGRESS.COM

MEMORY

68-PIN SDRAM PC100/133			
128MB	16X64	8NS	$19
128MB PC133	16X64	7.5NS	$16
128MB	16X72	8NS	$24
128MB PC133	16X72	7.5NS	$25
256MB	32X64	8NS	$31
256MB PC133	32X64	7.5NS	$30
256MB	32X72	8NS	$47
256MB PC133	32X72	7.5NS	$43
512MB	64X72	8NS	$79
512MB PC133	64X64	7.5NS	$62
512MB PC133	64X72	7.5NS	$73
1024MB PC133	128X72	7.5NS	$214
DDR RAM PC2100/2700/3200			
128MB	16X64	266MHZ	$19
128MB	16X72	266MHZ	$27
256MB	32X64	266MHZ	$32
256MB	32X72	266MHZ	$47
256MB	32X64	333MHZ	$35
256MB	32X64	400MHZ	$56
512MB	64X72	266MHZ	$84
512MB	64X64	333MHZ	$80
512MB	64X64	400MHZ	$102
1024MB	128X72	266MHZ	$299

CORSAIR www.corsairmicro.com

RAMBUS				
CMXR128-1066	128MB	RDRAM	1066MHZ	$57
CM616DR256A-800	256MB	RDRAM	800MHZ	$82
CM618DR256A-800	256MB	RDRAM	800MHZ	$105
CMXR256-1066	256MB	RDRAM	1066MHZ	$109
CM616DR512-800	512MB	RDRAM	800MHZ	$252
CM618DR512-800	512MB	RDRAM	800MHZ	$267

VALUE SELECT MEMORY				
VS256MB100	256MB PC100	32X64 (SDRAM)	8NS	$48
VS256MB133	256MB PC133	32X64 (SDRAM)	7.5NS	$48
VS256MB133A	256MB PC133	32X64 (SDRAM)	7.5NS	$38
VS256REG133	256MB PC133	32X72 (SDRAM)	7.5NS	$68
VS512MB100	512MB PC100	64X64 (SDRAM)	8NS	$71
VS512MB133	512MB PC133	64X64 (SDRAM)	7.5NS	$72
VS512MB133REG	512MB PC133	64X64 (SDRAM)	7.5NS	$98
VS256MB266	256MB PC2100	32X64 (DDR)	2.5CAS	$36
VS256MB333	256MB PC2700	32X64 (DDR)	2.5CAS	$52
VS256MB400	256MB PC3200	32X64 (DDR)	2.5CAS	$73
VS512MB266	512MB PC2100	64X64 (DDR)	2.5CAS	$85
VS512MB333	512MB PC2700	64X64 (DDR)	2.5CAS	$98
VS512MB400	512MB PC3200	64X64 (DDR)	2.5CAS	$134
VS512MBECC266R	512MB PC2100	64X72 (DDR)	2.5CAS	$126
VS256MB800	256MB PC800	RDRAM		$76
VS256MBECC800	256MB PC800	ECC RDRAM		$99
DDR RAM PC2100/2400/2700/3000/3200/3500				
CM72SD256R-2100	256MB (REG)	32X72 ECC DDR	266MHZ	$74
CM72SD512R-2100	512MB (REG)	64X72 ECC DDR	266MHZ	$129
CM73SD512R-2100	512MB (REG)	64X72 ECC DDR	266MHZ	$139
CM73SD512RLP-2100	512MB (REG)	64X72 ECC DDR	266MHZ	$157
CM74SD1024R-2100	1024MB (REG)	128X72 ECC DDR	266MHZ	$319
CM74SD2048R-2100	2048MB (REG)	256X72 ECC DDR	266MHZ	1449
CMX256A-3000C2	256MB (CAS 2)	32X64 DDR	370MHZ	$84
CMX256A-3200C2	256MB (CAS 2)	32X64 DDR	400MHZ	$88
CMX256A-3500C2	256MB (CAS 2)	32X64 DDR	433MHZ	$99
CMX512-2700C2	512MB (CAS 2)	64X64 DDR	333MHZ	$149
CMX512-3000C2	512MB (CAS 2)	64X64 DDR	370MHZ	$157
CMX512-3200C2	512MB (CAS 2)	64X64 DDR	400MHZ	$167
CMX512-3500C2	512MB (CAS 2)	64X64 DDR	433MHZ	$189
XMS LOW LATENCY AND TWIN X DUAL CHANNEL DDR				
CMX256A-2700LL	256MB (LL)	32X64 DDR	XMS2700	$89
CMX256A-3200LL	256MB (LL)	32X64 DDR	XMS3200	$99
CMX512-2700LL	512MB (LL)	64X64 DDR	XMS2700	$167
CMX512-3200LL	512MB (LL)	64X64 DDR	XMS3200	$189
TWINX512-2700LL	512MB (LL)	(2)256MB DDR	XMS2700	$179
TWINX512-3200LL	512MB (LL)	(2)256MB DDR	XMS3200	$199
TWINX1024-2700LL	1024MB (LL)	(2)512MB DDR	XMS2700	$334
TWINX1024-3200LL	1024MB (LL)	(2)512MB DDR	XMS3200	$379

Figure 4-21 Typical ad for memory modules.

Note that, for DIMMs, the ad lists the **density** of the module, which is written as two numbers separated by ×, such as 16×64 (read as *16 by 64*). Density allows you to determine three important things about a memory module: (1) the width of the data bus, (2) whether the module supports error checking, and (3) the size of the module, as follows:

- *Width of the data bus:* The second number listed in the density is 64 or 72. The lower number, 64, represents the width of the data bus in bits, grouped as eight bits to a byte.
- *ECC or non-ECC:* If the second number listed in the density is 64 (the width of the data bus), the memory does not have extra bits for error checking, so this is non-ECC memory. If the number is 72, then it is the width of the data bus plus an extra bit for each byte. This means the memory does have extra bits for error checking and correction and is ECC memory.
- *Module size:* To calculate a memory module's size based on the density, ignore the bits used for error checking and use only the value 64 to calculate. Convert 64 to bytes by dividing it by 8, and then multiply that value (8 = number of bytes) by the number on the left in the density listing. For example, if the density is 16×64, then the size of the module is 16 × (64/8) = 16 × 8 = 128 MB. (Most ads, including this one, list the size of the memory module, so that you do not have to do this calculation).

For Rambus memory or RIMMs, the ad lists the module size in MB (for example, 128 MB, 256 MB, or 512 MB). To determine if a RIMM uses error checking, look at the product code. An 18 in the product code indicates ECC memory, while a 16 indicates non-ECC memory.

Another way to locate memory modules is to browse Web sites that sell memory. Many of these Web sites, such as Kingston Technology's Web site (*www.kingston.com*), include a search utility to help you determine exactly what type of memory modules work with your motherboard (Figure 4-22).

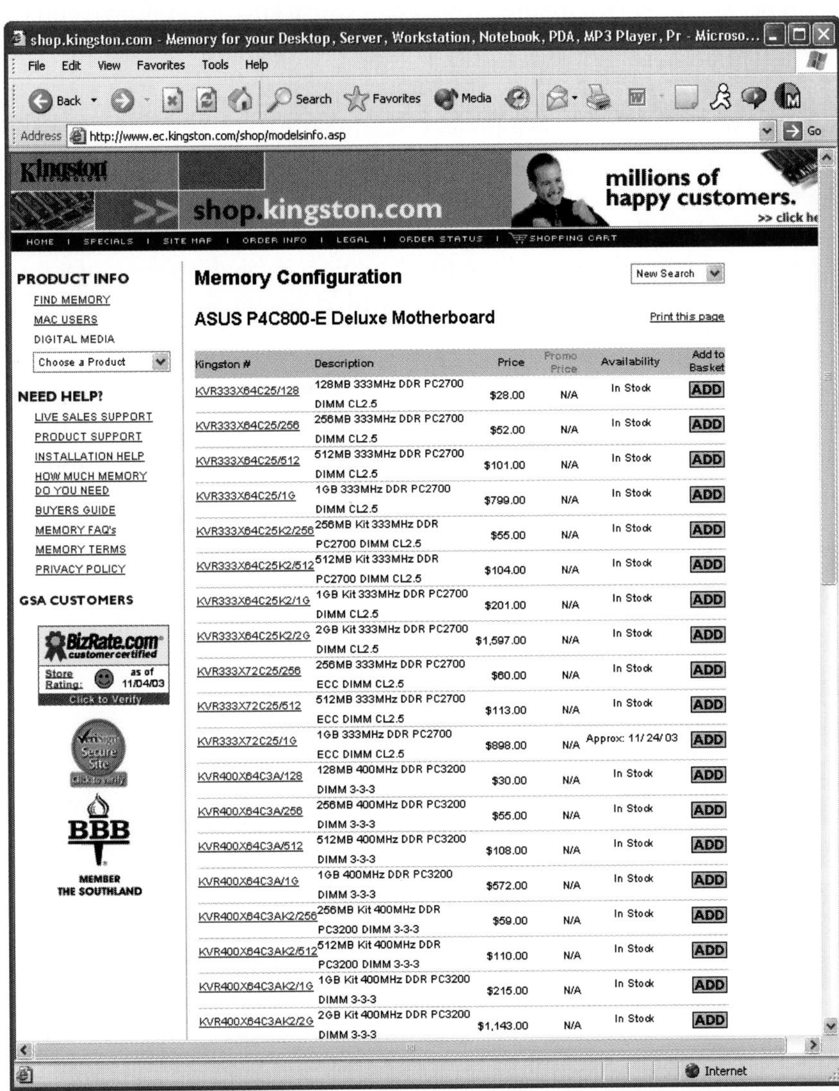

Figure 4-22 Web sites used to purchase memory, often provide tools to help you select the right memory modules for your motherboard.

DETERMINING THE QUALITY OF MEMORY MODULES After you identify the correct memory modules for your system, be aware that memory chips can be high-grade, low-grade, remanufactured, or used. Poor-quality memory chips can cause frequent application errors, errors that cause the system to freeze, and **General Protection Fault** (**GPF**) errors, which is a Windows error that occurs when a program attempts to access a memory address that is not available or no longer is assigned to it.

Given the possible problems caused by poor-quality memory chips, it pays to know the quality and type of memory you are buying. The following guidelines can help you to purchase high-quality memory chips.

Tin or Gold Leads Memory modules and the banks that hold them can be either tin or gold. On a motherboard, the connectors inside the memory slots also are made of tin or gold, as are the edge connectors on the memory modules. Once, all memory sockets were made of gold, but now some are made of tin to reduce cost. You should match tin leads to tin connectors and gold leads to gold connectors to prevent a chemical reaction between the two metals, which can cause corrosion. Corrosion can create intermittent memory errors and even make the PC unable to boot.

Remanufactured and Used Modules Stamped on each chip of a RAM module is a chip ID that identifies the date the chip was manufactured. Look for the date in the YYWW format, where YY is the year the chip was made, and WW is the week of that year. For example, 0410 indicates a chip made in the 10th week of 2004. Date stamps on a chip that are older than one year indicate that the chip is probably used memory. If some chips are old, but some are new, the module is probably remanufactured. When buying memory modules, look for ones with dates on all chips that are relatively close together and less than a year old.

Re-Marked Chips New chips have a protective coating that gives them a polished, reflective surface. If the chip's surface is dull or matted, or you can scratch off the markings with a fingernail or knife, suspect that the chip has been re-marked. **Re-marked chips** have been used, returned to the factory, marked again, and then resold.

Installing Memory

When installing memory (RAM) modules, always take important safety precautions you have learned in previous chapters, including:

- Protect the chips against static electricity.
- Always use a ground bracelet as you work.
- Be sure you have written down CMOS settings, and make a recovery disk if you do not already have one.
- Turn off the computer and unplug it before you remove the cover.

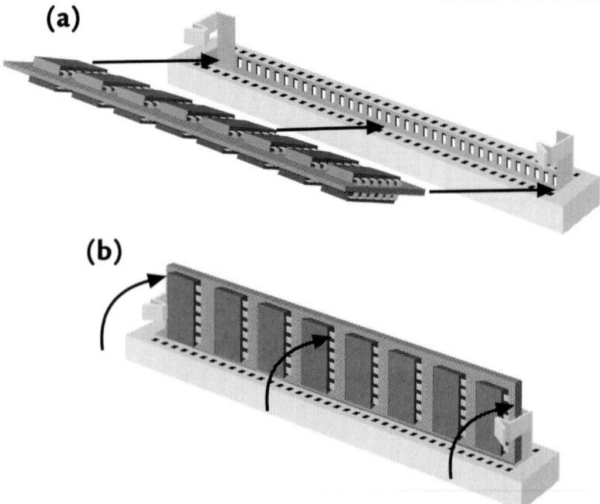

Figure 4-23 To install a SIMM module, (a) slide the module into the slot in an angle and then (b) gently push it to a vertical position between the supporting arms.

Once you have removed the cover to the computer case, you can remove older memory modules and install new ones. As you are working with the memory modules, be sure to handle them with care. Do not stack the modules, because you can loosen a chip.

As you get started, look for the notches that orient the module in the slot on one side or in the middle of the module. Memory modules generally pop into place easily and are secured by spring catches or supporting arms on both ends. You always should check the documentation for any instructions specific to your modules.

For most SIMMs, the module slides into the slot at an angle, as shown in Figure 4-23. For DIMM modules, small latches on each side of the slot hold the module in place, as shown in Figure 4-24. To insert the DIMM in the slot, pull the supporting arms on the sides of the slot outward. Next, look on the DIMM edge connector for the notches, which help you orient the DIMM correctly over the slot, and insert the DIMM straight down into the slot. When the DIMM is fully inserted, the supporting arms should pop back into place. Figure 4-25 shows a DIMM being inserted into a slot on a motherboard.

To install RIMM modules, install the RIMMs beginning with bank 0 and then bank 1. If a C-RIMM is already in the slot, remove the C-RIMM by pulling the supporting arms on the sides of the socket outward and pulling straight up on the C-RIMM. Next, place the RIMM module straight down in the socket (Figure 4-26 on the next page), using the notches on the edge of the RIMM module to help you orient it correctly in the socket. Push down gently to insert the module. When it is fully inserted, the supporting arms should pop back into place.

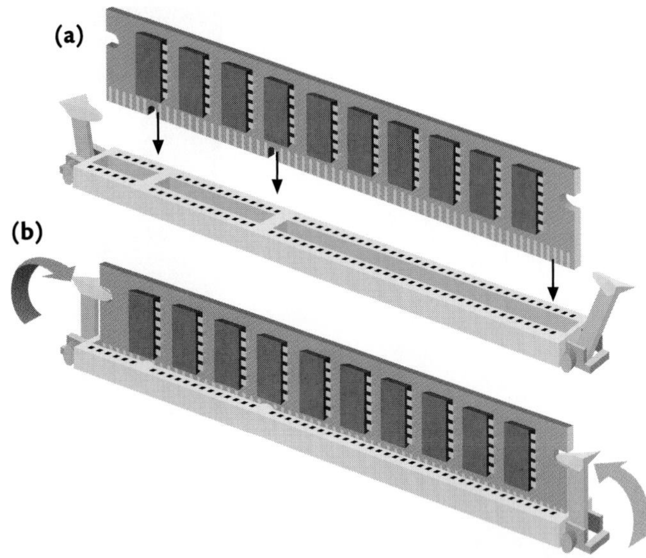

Figure 4-24 To install a DIMM module, (a) pull the supporting arms outward and gently insert the DIMM into the slot, (b) until the supporting arms lock into position.

After you have placed each memory module securely in its slot, turn on the PC and, if possible, watch POST count the amount of memory during the boot process or check the total memory on the system in the System Properties window. If the memory count is not what you expect, power off the system, then carefully remove and reseat each module. To remove a module, release the latches on both sides of the module and gently remove it from the socket.

Finally, update the small notebook or document you use to record information about your computer and note the date of the memory upgrade, the amount of memory installed, type and manufacturer of the modules, and any other relevant information. Be sure to file any manuals or other written documentation you received with the memory modules.

Figure 4-25 Insert the DIMM into the slot by pressing down until the support arms lock into position.

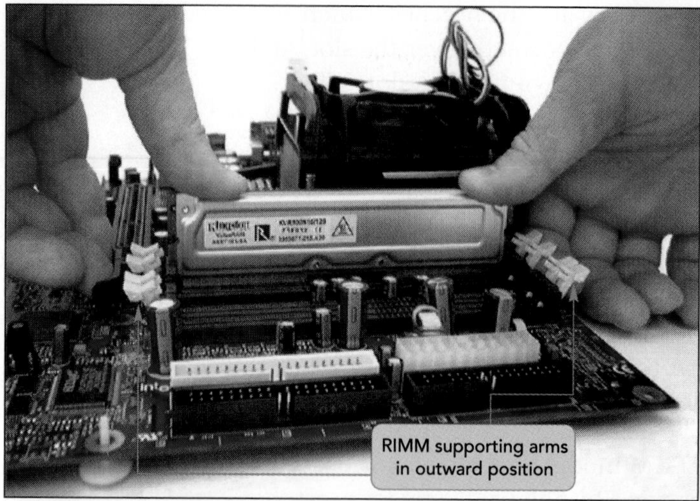

Figure 4-26 Install RIMM modules in banks beginnning with bank 0.

FAQ 4-7

Do I have to change CMOS settings after installing memory?

Most often, placing memory on the motherboard is all that is necessary for installation. When the computer powers up, it counts the memory present without any further instruction and senses the features that the modules support, such as parity or ECC. For some older computers, you must tell CMOS setup the amount of memory present. Read the motherboard documentation to determine if you need to change the CMOS settings.

Troubleshooting Memory

When upgrading memory, if the computer does not recognize new SIMMs, DIMMs, or RIMMs, or if memory error messages appear, do the following:

- Check that you have installed memory modules that are supported by your motherboard.
- Check that you have installed the right module size, as stated in the motherboard documentation.
- Remove and reinstall each module. Confirm that the memory modules are properly seated, and that each module sits in the socket at the same height as other modules.
- Remove the newly installed memory, place the memory in different sockets or slots, and check whether the error message disappears.
- Try installing the new memory without the old installed. If the new memory works without the old, then the new and old modules are not compatible.
- Clean the module edge connectors with a soft cloth or contact cleaner. Blow or vacuum dust from the memory sockets.
- Try flashing your BIOS, using the steps outlined in Chapter 3. It is possible the BIOS has problems with the new memory that a BIOS upgrade can solve.

If you find that you have recurring errors while using your computer for normal operations, it may be a symptom of unreliable memory. For example, if the system locks up — or if you regularly receive error messages about illegal operations and

General Protection Faults occur during normal operation — and you have not just upgraded memory, try the following:

- Run a current version of antivirus software to check for viruses.
- The problem might be with the OS or applications. Download the latest patches for your operating system and application software from the manufacturers' Web sites.
- If you have just installed new hardware, the hardware device might be causing an error, which the OS interprets as a memory error. Try uninstalling the new hardware.
- A Windows error that occurs randomly and generates an error message with *exception fault 0E at >>0137:BFF9z5d0* or similar text is probably a memory error. Test, reseat, or replace RAM.
- Sometimes a problem can result from a bad socket or a broken trace (a fine printed wire or circuit) on the motherboard. Check the motherboard for visible problems. If you find an issue, you might have to replace the entire motherboard.

If errors continue to occur, keep a record of what you are doing when the error message displays or issue occurs, in order to help narrow down the source of the issue.

Quiz Yourself 4-3

To test your knowledge of upgrading and troubleshooting memory, visit the Understanding and Troubleshooting Your PC Quiz Yourself Web page (scsite.com/understanding/quiz). Click Quiz Yourself 3 below Chapter 4.

High-Tech Talk

The Genius of Memory: Transistors, Capacitors, and Electricity

Before you turn on a computer, its RAM is a blank slate. As you start and use your computer, the operating system files, applications, and any data currently being used by the processor are written to and stored in RAM so the processor can access them quickly. How is this data written to and stored in RAM? In the most common form of RAM, dynamic random access memory (DRAM), a *transistor* (as a switch) and a *capacitor* (as a data storage element) are paired to create a *memory cell*, which represents a single bit of data.

Memory cells are etched onto a silicon wafer in a series of columns (bitlines) and rows (wordlines), known as an *array*. The intersection of a column and row constitute the *address* of the memory cell (Figure 4-27). Each memory cell has a unique address that can be found by counting across columns and then counting down by row. Most DRAM chips actually have arrays that are 16 rows deep. To keep it simple, Figure 4-27 only shows the topmost row of memory cells.

To write data to RAM, the processor sends the memory controller the address of a memory cell in which to store data. The *memory controller* organizes the request and sends the column and row address in a burst of electricity along the appropriate address lines, which are very thin electrical lines etched into the RAM chip. This causes the transistors along those address lines to close.

These transistors act as a switch to control the flow of electrical current in either a closed or open circuit. While the transistors are closed, the software sends bursts of electricity along selected data lines. When the electrical pulse traveling down the data line reaches an address line where a transistor is closed, the pulse flows through the closed transistor and charges the capacitor.

A capacitor works as an electronic bucket that holds an electrical charge. Each charged capacitor along the address line represents a 1 bit. An uncharged capacitor represents a 0 bit. The combination of 1s and 0s from eight data lines form a single byte of data. This electrical pulse causes the transistors along the address line to close. At every point along the address line where a capacitor is holding a charge, the capacitor discharges through the circuit created by the closed transistors, sending electrical pulses along the data lines. The process of reading data from RAM uses a similar, but reverse, series of steps.

The capacitors used in dynamic RAM, however, are slightly leaky buckets. The processor or memory controller continuously has to recharge all of the capacitors holding a charge (a 1 bit) before the capacitor discharges. During this *refresh operation*, which happens automatically thousands of times per second, the memory controller reads memory and then immediately rewrites it. This refresh operation is what gives dynamic RAM its name. Dynamic RAM has to be refreshed continually, or it loses the charges that represent bits of data.

As long as your computer is running, data continuously is being written to and read from RAM. As soon as you shut down the computer, RAM loses its data. The next time you turn on your computer, operating system files and other data are again loaded into RAM and the read/write process starts all over again.

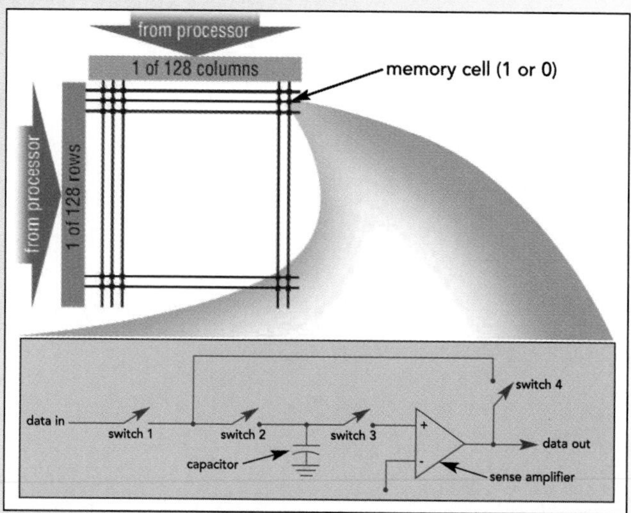

Figure 4-27

CHAPTER SUMMARY

The Chapter Summary reviews the concepts presented in this chapter.

RAM on the Motherboard

SRAM (static RAM) is fast memory used for memory cache, which speeds overall computer performance by holding data and instructions that the CPU may use in the near future. SRAM does not require constant refreshing. DRAM (dynamic RAM), which is used for main memory, is slower than SRAM because it needs constant refreshing. Older motherboards sometimes provided an extra COAST slot to upgrade SRAM, but most systems today come with an optimum amount of SRAM inside the CPU housing.

DRAM is stored on SIMMs, DIMMs, and RIMMs. A SIMM has pins on opposite sides of the circuit board that connect to form one set of contacts. A DIMM has pins on opposite sides of the circuit board that form two sets of contacts. SIMMs and DIMMs typically hold SDRAM chips. A RIMM houses Rambus® DRAM chips, which are much faster than SDRAM. The two DRAM technologies currently most used are Double Data Rate SDRAM in DIMM modules or Direct Rambus DRAM in RIMMs.

Several factors contribute to how fast memory runs, including the speed of memory, the amount of memory installed, the memory technology used, the latency rating, the type of error checking used, and whether memory is single channel or dual channel.

Windows Memory Management

The way that the OS manages memory has improved greatly in newer operating systems. Early limitations on the number of memory addresses available to the CPU resulted from motherboards with 20 lines on the bus for memory addresses, yielding a total of 1 MB of memory addresses. DOS and Windows 9x divide memory into base (conventional), upper, and extended memory. In Windows NT, Windows 2000, Windows XP, and Windows Server 2003 there are no divisions of memory; the 32-bit drivers supported by these operating systems just use memory.

A memory management method of using the hard drive as though it were RAM is called virtual memory. Virtual memory stores data on the hard drive in a swap file or paging file. The OS manages the entire process. You can change the size of the paging file in the System Properties window.

Upgrading Memory

Memory upgrades can help make a computer run faster. To upgrade memory, determine how much memory you need. Next, match the type of memory to the type supported by the motherboard. Be sure to use the right number of SIMMs, DIMMs, or RIMMs with the right amount of memory to fit the memory banks on your motherboard.

As you shop for memory chips or modules, you should understand how to read advertisements about memory modules and how to gauge the quality of a memory module. Buy memory with the right type of connector (gold edge or tin) for your motherboard, and avoid remanufactured and re-marked memory chips.

To install memory, take standard precautions for avoiding ESD and remove the cover to the computer case. Position the module in the slot, based on the notches on the modules. The module should pop into place and be secured by spring catches or supporting arms on both ends. After you have placed each memory module securely in its slot, turn on the PC to ensure the memory is recognized by the system.

Troubleshooting Memory

When upgrading memory, if the computer does not recognize new SIMMs, DIMMs, or RIMMs, or if memory error messages appear, check that you have the right memory modules and that each module is seated correctly. Cleaning the module edge connectors or flashing BIOS also may resolve issues. If you find that you have recurring errors about illegal operations and that General Protection Faults occur during normal operation, it may be a symptom of unreliable memory.

KEY TERMS

After reading the chapter, you should know each of these Key Terms.

bank (*128*)
buffers (*143*)
cache controller (*126*)
cache on a stick (COAST) (*127*)
CAS Latency (*133*)
conventional memory (*136*)
C-RIMM (Continuity RIMM) (*131*)
density (*146*)
Direct Rambus® DRAM (*130*)
Direct RDRAM (*130*)
dual-channel (*133*)
DDR (*130*)
Double Data Rate SDRAM (DDR SDRAM) (*130*)
ECC (error-correcting code) (*133*)
extended memory (*136*)
General Protection Fault (GPF) (*147*)
memory controller (*128*)
memory mapping (*135*)
page (*137*)
paging file (*136*)
Pagefile.sys (*137*)
Parallel Presence Detect (PPD) (*141*)
parity (*133*)
RAS Latency (*133*)
RDRAM® (*130*)
refresh (*128*)
registers (*143*)
re-marked chips (*148*)
Serial Presence Detect (SPD) (*141*)
SDRAM II (*130*)
single-channel (*133*)
swap file (*136*)
synchronous DRAM (SDRAM) (*131*)
upper memory (*136*)
virtual memory (*136*)

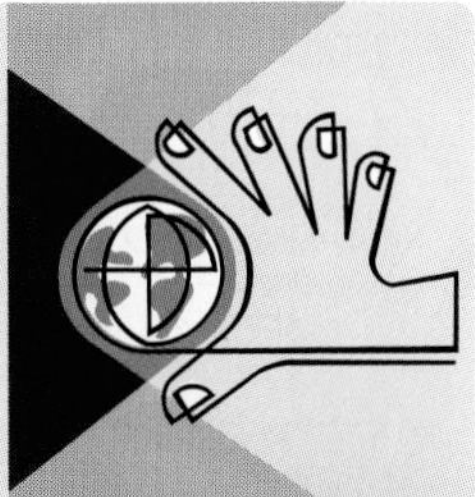

LEARN IT ONLINE

Reinforce your understanding of the chapter concepts and terms with the Learn It Online exercises.

Instructions: To complete the Learn It Online exercises, start your browser, click the Address bar, and then enter the Web address scsite.com/understanding/learn. When the Understanding and Troubleshooting Your PC Learn It Online page is displayed, follow the instructions in the exercises below. Each exercise has instructions for printing your results, either for your own records or for submission to your instructor.

1 Chapter Reinforcement True/False, Multiple Choice, and Short Answer

Below Chapter 4, click the Chapter Reinforcement link. Print the quiz by clicking Print on the File menu for each page. Answer each question.

2 Flash Cards

Below Chapter 4, click the Flash Cards link and read the instructions. Type 20 (or a number specified by your instructor) in the Number of playing cards text box, type your name in the Enter your Name text box, and then click the Flip Card button. When the flash card is displayed, read the question and then click the ANSWER box arrow to select an answer. Flip through Flash Cards. If your score is 15 (75%) correct or greater, click Print on the File menu to print your results. If your score is less than 15 (75%) correct, then redo this exercise by clicking the Replay button.

3 Practice Test

Below Chapter 4, click the Practice Test link. Answer each question, enter your first and last name at the bottom of the page, and then click the Grade Test button. When the graded practice test is displayed on your screen, click Print on the File menu to print a hard copy. Continue to take practice tests until you score 80% or better.

4 Who Wants To Be a Computer Genius?

Below Chapter 4, click the Computer Genius link. Read the instructions, enter your first and last name at the bottom of the page, and then click the PLAY button. When your score is displayed, click the PRINT RESULTS link to print a hard copy.

5 Wheel of Terms

Below Chapter 4, click the Wheel of Terms link. Read the instructions, and then enter your first and last name and your school name. Click the PLAY button. When your score is displayed, right-click the score and then click Print on the shortcut menu to print a hard copy.

6 Crossword Puzzle Challenge

Below Chapter 4, click the Crossword Puzzle Challenge link. Read the instructions, and then enter your first and last name. Click the SUBMIT button. Work the crossword puzzle. When you are finished, click the Submit button. When the crossword puzzle is redisplayed, click the Print Puzzle button to print a hard copy.

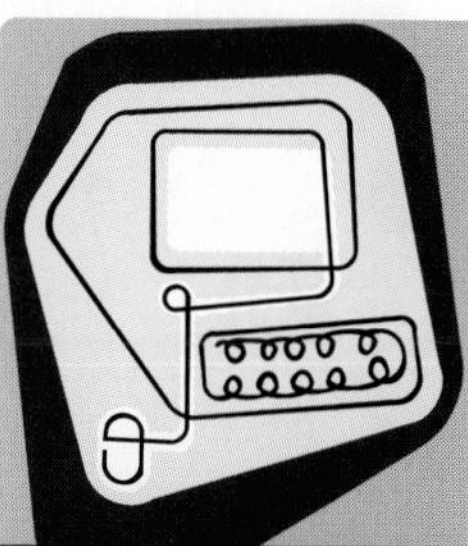

CHAPTER EXERCISES

Complete the Chapter Exercises to solidify what you learned in the chapter.

Multiple Choice

Select the best answer.

1. What are the two possible numbers of pins on a DIMM?
   a. 168 or 184
   b. 30 or 72
   c. 184 or 232
   d. 128 or 256
2. _______________ is DRAM that runs in sync with the system clock and thus runs faster than other types of DRAM.
   a. SIMM
   b. Synchronous DRAM
   c. Asynchronous DRAM
   d. RIMM
3. Instead of using parity checking, newer memory uses a method of error checking called _______________.
   a. mapping
   b. nonparity
   c. non-EKG
   d. ECC (error-correcting code)
4. How many notches are on a DDR SDRAM module?
   a. one
   b. two
   c. four
   d. six
5. In Windows 2000 and Windows XP, the default size of the paging file is set to _______ times the amount of RAM installed.
   a. 128
   b. 2
   c. 1.5
   d. 16

Fill in the Blank

Write the word or phrase to fill in the blank in each of the following questions.

1. Memory caching relies on SRAM chips to store data and a(n) _______________ to manage the storage and retrieval of data from SRAM.
2. Instead of processing data for each beat of the system clock like regular SDRAM, _______________ processes data twice for each beat, thus doubling the data rate of memory.
3. Computers use one or two methods to detect memory: _______________, which uses resistors to communicate the type of memory present, or _______________, which stores information about the memory type in ROM.
4. Ads for DIMMs often list the _______________ of the module, which is written as two numbers separated by an ×, such as 16×64.
5. DRAM is refreshed by the _______________, which is a circuit in the chip set on the motherboard that controls the reading and writing of information to and from the memory.

Matching Terms

Match the terms with their definitions.

________	1. bank	a.	placeholder module used with RIMMs to ensure continuity throughout all slots
________	2. SIMM	b.	memory module that houses RDRAM chips
________	3. refresh	c.	memory above 1024K used in DOS or Windows 9x
________	4. virtual memory	d.	method of using the hard drive as though it were RAM
________	5. DIMM	e.	process of rewriting the data to the RAM chip
________	6. PC100	f.	memory module with pins on opposite sides of the circuit board that form a single set of contacts
________	7. C-RIMM	g.	swap file used by Windows 2000, Windows XP, and Windows Server 2003
________	8. extended memory	h.	memory module with pins on opposite sides of the circuit board that form two sets of contacts
________	9. RIMM	i.	a location on the motherboard that contains slots for memory modules
________	10. Pagefile.sys	j.	speed of memory module that will work with a motherboard that runs at 100 MHz

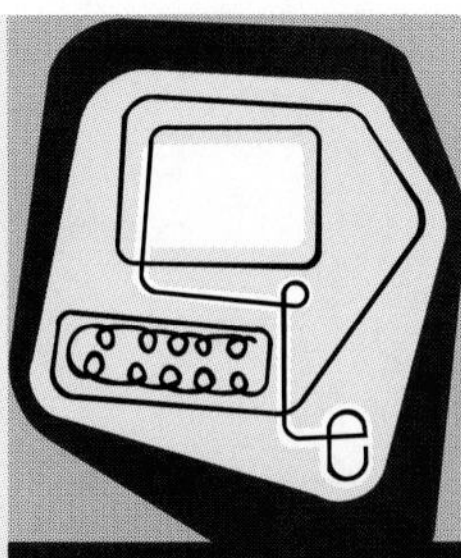

CHAPTER EXERCISES

Complete the Chapter Exercises to solidify what you learned in the chapter.

Short Answer Questions

Write a brief answer to each of the following questions.

1. If your motherboard supports DIMM memory, will RIMM memory work on the motherboard?
2. If your motherboard supports ECC SDRAM memory, can you substitute SDRAM memory that does not support ECC? If your motherboard supports buffered SDRAM memory, can you substitute unbuffered SDRAM modules?
3. List at least four things you can do if you receive memory errors following a memory upgrade.
4. List at least four things you can do if you receive memory errors during normal operation when you have not recently upgraded memory.
5. In addition to speed, what other factors determine how fast memory runs?

APPLY YOUR KNOWLEDGE

Check your understanding of the chapter with the hands-on Apply Your Knowledge exercises.

1 Help Desk Support

A friend calls and asks you to help him determine how much RAM he has on his motherboard. As he starts his computer, he tells you he is running Windows XP.

1. Step him through the process, showing him at least two different ways to determine how much RAM is available on his system.
2. Your friend has discovered he has 128 MB of RAM and wants to upgrade to 256 MB. He is using DIMMs and his motherboard is running at 266 MHz. Looking at Figure 4-21 on page 146, what is the estimated cost of the upgrade?

2 Planning a Memory Upgrade

You need the documentation for your motherboard for this project. If you do not have it, download it from the Web site of the motherboard manufacturer. Use this documentation and the motherboard to answer the following:

1. Determine the amount of RAM currently installed on your computer.
2. What is the maximum amount of memory the banks on your motherboard can accommodate?
3. What type (or types) of memory does your motherboard support?
4. How many slots for memory modules are included on your motherboard?
5. How many memory slots on your motherboard are used and how much RAM is installed in each slot?
6. What is the maximum amount of memory that your motherboard supports?
7. What size and how many memory modules will be needed to upgrade your system to the maximum amount of supported memory?

3 Researching Memory Modules

Based on what you learned about your motherboard in Apply Your Knowledge Question 2, research how to double the amount of RAM currently installed in your computer, using a memory upgrade budget of $200.

Look in a computer magazine, such as *Computer Shopper*, or use a retail Web site such as Kingston Technology (*www.kingston.com*) or Crucial Technology (*www.crucial.com*) to determine how much it will cost to fill the banks on your computer to full capacity. Do not forget to match the speed of the modules already installed, and plan to use only the modules that your computer can accommodate. Answer the following questions:

1. What is the price of the memory modules required to configure your system for maximum memory?
2. Will your budget enable you to install the maximum supported amount of RAM?
3. Can you use the existing memory modules to upgrade to the maximum amount of supported memory?
4. What is the most additional memory that you could install and still stay within your budget (either using existing modules or upgrading to all new modules)?

Next, use resources available on the Internet to research memory modules. Visit Web sites such as *kingston.com, crucial.com, pricewatch.com, memory.shopper.com*, or similar Web sites and answer the following questions:

1. On average, what is the least expensive type of memory that you can find? What is its price per MB (megabyte)?

2. On average, what is the most expensive type of memory that you can find? What is its price per MB?
3. Visit the PC World (*www.pcworld.com*) and PC Magazine (*www.pcmag.com*) Web sites and search for news stories on new DRAM technologies. What types of new DRAM technologies are being developed? How fast is the newest DRAM?

APPLY YOUR KNOWLEDGE

Check your understanding of the chapter with the hands-on Apply Your Knowledge exercises.

4 Upgrading Memory

To practice upgrading memory in a computer, you will install an additional memory module in your computer and then ensure that your computer recognizes it. To complete this exercise, you will need a PC toolkit, an anti-static bracelet, and an additional memory module compatible with your system. Complete the memory upgrade based on the following general steps, as well as what you learned in the chapter:

1. Shut down your system and remove all exterior cabling.
2. Be sure you are wearing your anti-static bracelet and have taken other safety precautions.
3. Open the system case and locate the slots for memory modules.
4. Remove any data cabling and other devices preventing you from getting at the slots. Answer the following questions:
   a. How many modules are currently installed? What is the amount of RAM currently installed on your computer?
   b. Are there any empty slots in which to install an additional module?
5. Notice that the slots have a retaining mechanism at each end to secure the modules in the slot. In current form factors these are typically plastic levers that are spread outward to unseat and remove modules. These modules are inserted and removed straight up and down. Spread the plastic levers apart before inserting or removing the memory modules.
6. Examine an empty slot and note that there are raised ridges that line up with notches on the pin edge of the memory module. Because modules are designed to be inserted in only one orientation, this prevents them from being inserted incorrectly.
7. Insert the SIMMs, DIMMs, or RIMMs from the other computer in the empty slot or slots. With the module correctly oriented, insert the module and gently but firmly push it into the slot.
8. Re-assemble your system.
9. Boot the computer and check that it recognizes the additional memory.
10. When you have finished, remove the additional memory and return the system to its previous configuration.

intel
pentium 4

CHAPTER 5

Understanding, Installing, and Troubleshooting Disk Drives

Introduction

This chapter introduces hard drive technology, explains how a hard drive is organized, and describes how to install and troubleshoot a hard drive. This chapter also examines floppy disk drives, optical storage technologies such as CD-ROMs and DVD-ROMs, and external and removable storage. Finally, the chapter provides an introduction to supporting disk drives to help optimize performance and troubleshoot errors.

OBJECTIVES

In this chapter, you will learn:

1. How hard drives work and organize data
2. How to install a hard drive
3. How floppy drives work and how to install a floppy drive
4. About optical storage technologies and external and removable storage
5. How to manage and troubleshoot hard drives

Up for Discussion

Jennifer Gupta, the superintendent at the local high school, came into Sunrise Computers today to ask for your help with her computer. She noted that lately her computer takes a long time to start up and to load applications. Her applications seem to be running very slowly as well. For example, as she was working on the school budget, the program seemed to be taking a very long time to respond to commands. The problem seems gradually to be getting worse.

After hearing the description of her problem, you wonder if she might need more memory — or if she simply needs to optimize her hard drive. You explain how a disk drive can become fragmented over time, which increases access time. The reason for the computer's sluggishness might be caused by fragmented files that have been updated, modified, and spread over different portions of the disk. You also explain that a Windows utility called Disk Cleanup can be used periodically to remove unnecessary files. You ask Ms. Gupta if you can keep her computer for a few hours while you defragment the drive, remove unneeded files, and check that disk caching is enabled.

The day after getting her computer back, Ms. Gupta calls to thank you. She cannot believe how much better her computer is running — and asks how often she should bring her computer in for you a "tune-up". You explain that she can perform those simple disk maintenance tasks on her own and promise to e-mail her a set of steps she can use every few months to optimize her hard drive.

Questions:

- What are several routine maintenance tasks that help optimize your hard drive?
- What causes a fragmented hard drive and how can you defragment it?
- How does disk caching speed up a hard drive?

How Hard Drives Work

A hard drive is a sealed case containing one or more circular platters or disks that store data, instructions, and information. A hard drive, also called a hard disk drive, stores data magnetically and is a read/write storage medium, meaning it can be read from and written to any number of times.

FAQ 5-1

What is the difference between a storage medium and storage device?

A storage medium is the physical material on which a computer keeps data, instructions, and information. A key characteristic of a storage medium is its capacity, or the number of bytes it can hold, which is measured in kilobytes, megabytes, gigabytes, and so on. A storage device, such as a hard drive, floppy drive, CD-ROM and DVD-ROM drive, or Zip® drive, is the computer hardware that writes and/or reads data to and from storage media.

Hard drives have one, two, or more platters that stack together and spin in unison. Each platter is made of aluminum, glass, or ceramic and is coated with a magnetic material that allows items to be recorded magnetically on its top and bottom surfaces. For each side of the platter, the hard disk has two *read/write heads* — one to write data and one to read data from the surface of the platter. The read/write heads are controlled by an actuator and move in unison across the disk surfaces as the disks rotate on a spindle (Figure 5-1).

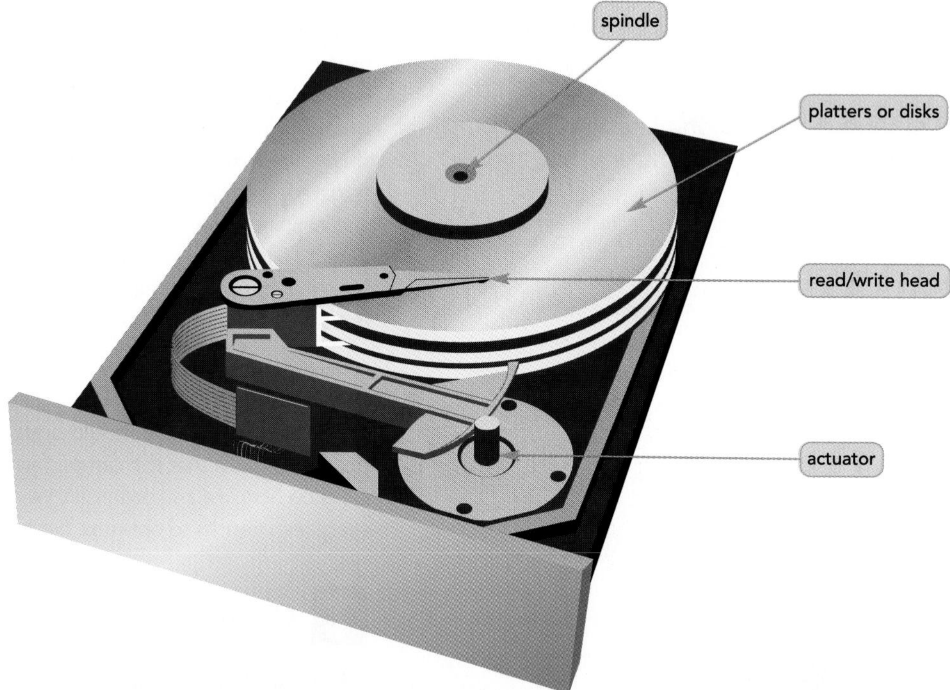

Figure 5-1 Inside a hard drive case. The platters spin on a spindle, while read/write heads are controlled by the actuator.

The drive fits into a bay inside the computer case, where it is securely attached with supports or braces and screws. This helps prevent the drive from being jarred while the disk is spinning and the heads are very close to the disk surface.

FAQ 5-2

What causes a hard drive crash?

On a hard drive, the heads at the ends of the read/write arms get extremely close to the platters, but do not actually touch them. This tiny clearance between the heads and platters (about two millionths of an inch) makes hard drives susceptible to damage from being bumped, or even from the smallest particle of dirt. Should a computer be bumped or moved while the hard drive is operating, a read/write head can easily bump against the platter and scratch the surface. Such an accident causes a hard drive crash, in which the head touches the platter, often making the hard drive unusable.

Figure 5-2 shows a hard drive with two platters. All four sides of the platters are used to store data (although, on some hard drives, the top side of the first platter holds only information used to locate data and manage the disk). Each side is divided into tracks. A **track** is any one of a series of concentric circular rings on one side of the disk. A **cylinder** is the set of tracks that lie at the same distance from the center on all sides of all platters of the hard disk. If a disk has 300 tracks, it also has the same number of cylinders. The entire first cylinder on the outer edge of the platter is written on first, then the read/write heads move inward and begin filling the second cylinder with data. A **sector**, as shown in Figure 5-2, is an arc-shaped area of a track that usually stores 512 bytes of data. The operating system and drive can determine where information is stored on the disk by its track, cylinder, and sector location.

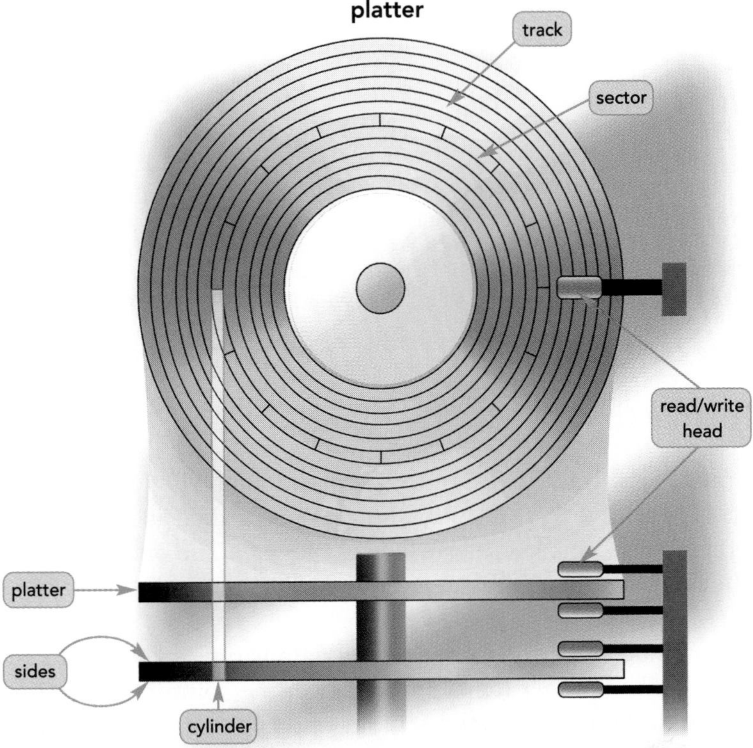

Figure 5-2 A cylinder is the vertical section of a track through all platters on a hard disk.

Data is written to the disk as bits, either 0s or 1s. Each bit is a magnetized, rectangular spot on the disk. Between the tracks and spots are spaces that are not magnetized. This spacing prevents one spot from affecting the magnetism of a nearby spot. The difference between a 0 spot and a 1 spot is the positive or negative magnetic orientation of the spot.

A hard drive requires a **hard disk controller** (also called a **hard drive controller**), which is a special-purpose chip that allows the CPU to communicate with a hard drive. The hard disk controller stores programming that instructs the read/write heads how, where, and when to move across the platters to read or write data. For today's hard drives, the hard drive controller is mounted on a circuit board or is inside the drive housing.

How Data Is Organized on a Hard Disk

Physical storage involves how data is written to and organized on the storage media, while *logical storage* involves how the OS and BIOS organize and view the stored data. This section explains how data is stored physically on a hard disk and then how the operating system logically views the data.

As you learned in Chapter 2, before any files can be stored on a disk, the disk must be formatted. *Formatting* is the process of preparing a disk for reading and writing by defining how files will be organized on the disk. Three main steps are involved in formatting a newly manufactured hard disk:

1. low-level (physical) formatting
2. partitioning
3. high-level (logical) formatting

FAQ 5-3

Do all types of disks — hard disks, floppy disks, and others — need to be formatted?

Formatting a disk can be compared to starting a library. Before any books can be put in place, you must install the bookshelves and a catalog system. Similarly, a disk must have a file system set up to make it ready to receive data. This is true of many different storage media. Floppy disks, hard disks, removable hard disks such as the Zip® disk, and CD-ROMs all must be formatted so that there is a way to organize and find files saved to the disk. Many disks, including floppy disks, CD-ROMs, and DVD-ROMs, come preformatted, so you do not have to format them before use.

Low-Level Formatting

A hard disk must be physically formatted before it can be logically formatted. **Physical formatting** or **low-level formatting** of a hard disk is accomplished by writing a pattern of ones and zeroes on the surface of the disk. The ones and zeroes serve as small electronic markers, which divide the hard drive platter into tracks, sectors, and cylinders.

These three elements define the way in which data is physically written to and read from the disk. As the read/write head moves over the spinning disks, it reads the electronic markers that define the tracks, sectors, and cylinders to determine where it is in relation to the data on the disk's surface.

The hard disk manufacturer usually performs physical or low-level formatting. Older drives used a straightforward method of writing the tracks and sectors on the drive (Figure 5-3a), in which the larger tracks near the outside of the platter contain the same number of bytes as the smaller tracks near the center of the platter. This arrangement makes formatting a drive and accessing data easier, but wastes drive space. Using this approach, the centermost track determines the number of bytes that a track can hold, and all other tracks must follow this restriction.

Today's drives eliminate this restriction by using a formatting system called **zone bit recording** (Figure 5-3b). Using zone bit recording, the number of sectors per track on a drive is not the same throughout the platter. Instead, tracks near the center have the smallest number of sectors per track, and the number of sectors increases as the tracks grow larger. Each track on a hard drive is designed to have the optimum number of sectors appropriate to the size of the track. What makes this arrangement possible, however, is that every sector on the drive stores 512 bytes.

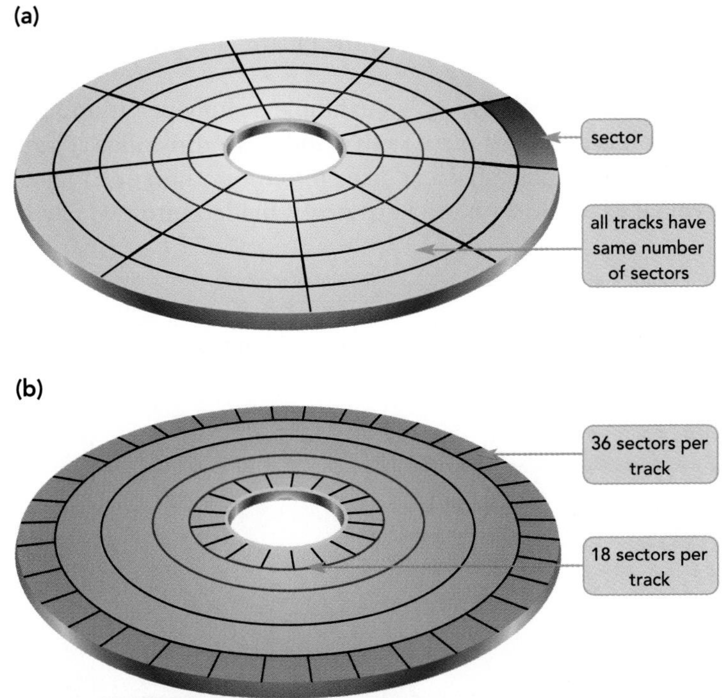

Figure 5-3 (a) Older hard drives and floppy drives use a constant number of sectors per track. (b) Zone bit recording can have more sectors per track as the tracks get larger.

Because the number of sectors per track varies from one track to another with zone bit recording, the OS and system BIOS cannot count on using actual hard drive track, cylinder, and sector locations to access data. Instead, sophisticated methods have been developed so that system BIOS and the operating system communicate with the hard drive controller, which in turn physically locates the data on the hard drive.

More About

Communicating with the Hard Drive Controller

To learn more about the sophisticated methods the system BIOS and OS use to communicate with the hard drive controller, visit the Understanding and Troubleshooting Your PC More About Web page (**scsite.com/understanding/more**) and then click Communicating with the Hard Drive Controller below Chapter 5.

FAQ 5-4

Are there instances where I would need to low-level format my hard drive?

It is highly unlikely that you ever will need to low-level format your hard drive. The track and sector markings created at the factory normally are expected to last for the life of the drive (usually three to five years). As the markings fade and the drive gives many *Bad Sector or Sector Not Found* errors or becomes unusable, you may be able to fix the problem with a low-level format. Hard drive manufacturers sometimes offer a low-level format program specific to their drives. (Some manufacturers only distribute these programs to dealers, resellers, or certified service centers.) Note that it is very risky to low-level format a drive using a format program other than one provided by the manufacturer. Generally, by the time the track and sector markings fade, you may be ready to replace the hard drive with a new, higher capacity drive.

Partitioning

Once a hard disk has been physically formatted, it can be partitioned. As you learned in Chapter 2, *partitioning* is the process of dividing the hard disk into regions called partitions. Each partition occupies a group of adjacent cylinders. Partitioning allows you to organize a hard disk into segments and lets you run multiple operating systems on a single computer. You also can keep the entire hard disk as one partition.

PARTITIONING UNDER WINDOWS 9x As an example of how partitioning works, consider a computer that has one hard drive with Windows 9x installed. Using partitioning, the OS can divide this single physical drive into more than one logical drive. Figure 5-4 shows a typical example with the hard drive divided into two partitions.

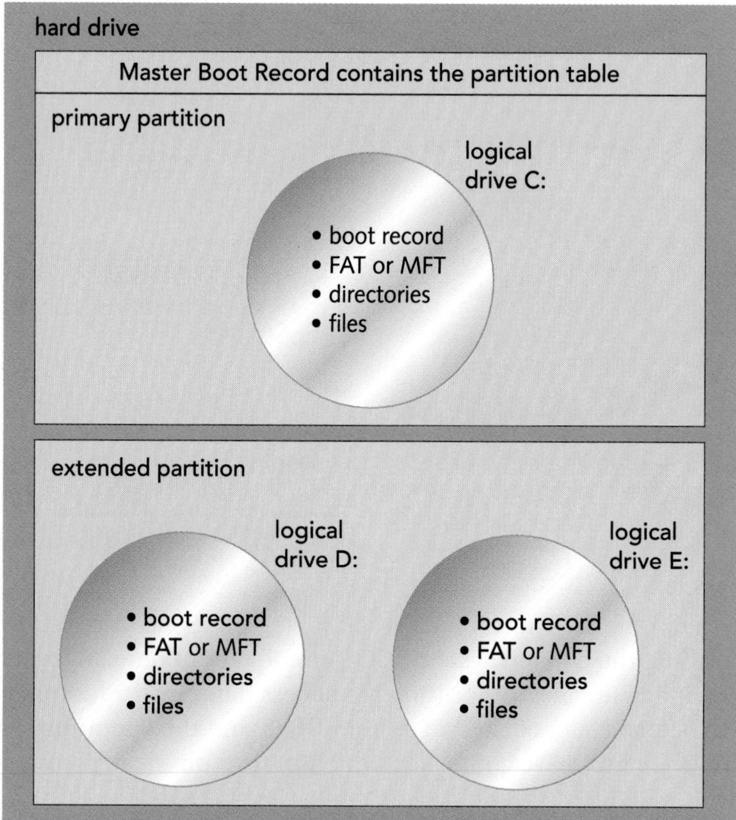

Figure 5-4 A hard drive is divided into one or more partitions that contain logical drives.

The first partition contains one logical drive (drive C), and the second partition is divided into two logical drives (D and E).

The partition table at the beginning of the drive records all these divisions. As you learned in Chapter 2, the first physical sector of the hard drive contains the Master Boot Record (MBR), also known as the **partition sector** or **master boot sector**. The MBR is exactly 512 bytes long and occupies the first sector of the hard drive on head 0, track 0, sector 1. (Do not confuse this first physical sector of the hard drive with sector 1 as Windows knows it. The operating system's sector 1 comes after the physical sector 1 and is the first sector in the logical drive C.).

The MBR contains the master boot program, which is needed to locate the beginning of the OS on the drive, and the partition table, which contains a map of the logical drives (volumes) on the hard drive (Figure 5-5).

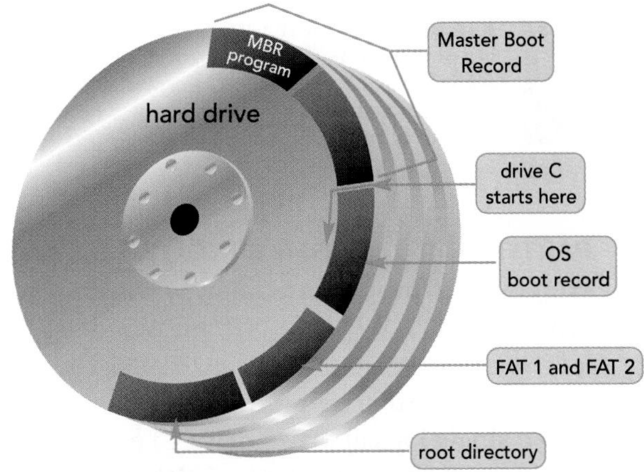

Items in Master Boot Record	Bytes Used	Description
1	**446 bytes**	Master boot program that calls the OS boot record
2	**16 bytes**	Description of the first partition
	1 byte	Is this the active (bootable) partition? (Yes = 90h, No = 00h)
	3 bytes	Beginning location of the partition
	1 byte	System indicator; possible values are: 0 = Not a DOS partition 1 = DOS with a 12-bit FAT 4 = DOS with a 16-bit FAT 5 = Not the first partition 6 = Partition larger than 32 MB
	3 bytes	Ending location of partition
	4 bytes	First sector of the partition table relative to the beginning of the disk
	4 bytes	Number of sectors in the partition
3	**16 bytes**	Describes second partition, using same format as first partition
4	**16 bytes**	Describes third partition, using same format as first partition
5	**16 bytes**	Describes fourth partition, using same format as first partition
6	**2 bytes**	Signature of the partition table, always AA55
Total bytes	**512 bytes**	

Figure 5-5 When using the FAT file system, the first sector of the hard drive on head 0, track 0, sector 1, called the Master Boot Record (MBR), contains the master boot program, which is needed to locate the beginning of the OS on the drive, and partition table, which contains a map of the logical drives (volumes) on the hard drive.

When a hard disk is partitioned, the partition table is created at the beginning of the hard drive. The partition table lists the number of partitions on the drive and their locations. It also identifies the *active partition*, which is the partition used to boot the computer. Within each partition, the operating system creates logical drives and assigns letters, such as drive C or drive D, to each logical drive.

During the boot process, the master boot program stored at the beginning of the Master Boot Record executes and checks the integrity of the partition table itself. If the master boot program finds any corruption, it refuses to continue execution, and the disk is unusable. If the table entries are valid, the master boot program looks in the table to determine which partition is the active partition, and it executes the bootstrap loader program in the boot record of that partition.

 **More About**

Creating Logical Drives

You can partition a hard drive and create logical drives using tools such as the Windows 9x Fdisk program or the Disk Management utility available in Windows 2000 and Windows XP. To learn more about creating logical drives using these tools, visit the Understanding and Troubleshooting Your PC More About Web page (**scsite.com/understanding/more**) and then click Creating Logical Drives below Chapter 5.

FAQ 5-5

Is the Master Boot Record the same as the boot sector?

It is easy to confuse the Master Boot Record (a partition sector) with a boot sector, but they are not the same. The first physical sector on a typical hard disk stores the Master Boot Record (MBR), which lists partition information for the entire disk. The first physical sector in each partition contains a boot sector, which holds information about that partition, such as the number of sectors and number of FATs (file allocation tables).

PARTITIONING UNDER WINDOWS NT AND LATER WINDOWS SYSTEMS

Windows NT incorporated new ways of managing hard drives that are also used in Windows 2000, Windows XP, and Windows Server 2003. In these operating systems, a drive can have up to four partitions. The active partition, or *boot drive,* is the partition on the hard drive used to boot the OS. The active partition most often contains only a single logical drive (drive C) and is usually the first partition on the drive. A partition can be a **primary partition**, which has only one logical drive in the partition, such as drive C, or an **extended partition**, which can have more than one logical drive, such as drive D and drive E. The active partition is always a primary partition. A drive can have only one extended partition.

Windows NT and later versions of Windows assign two different functions to hard drive partitions holding the OS (Figure 5-6). The **system partition**, normally drive C, is the active partition, which contains the OS boot record. Remember that the MBR looks to the OS boot record for the boot program as the first step in turning the PC over to the Windows operating system. The other partition, called the boot partition, is where the Windows operating system is stored.

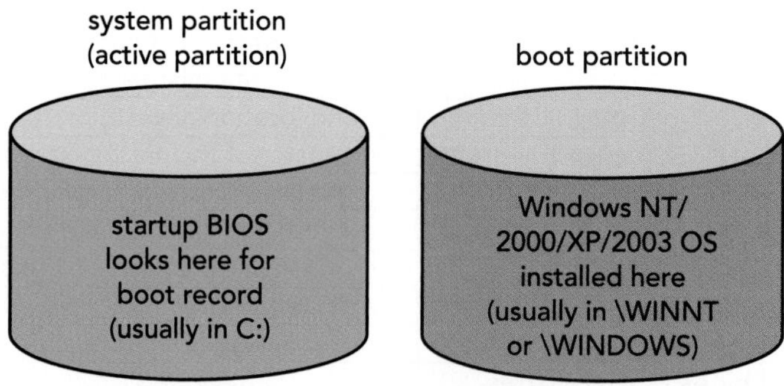

Figure 5-6 Hard drive partitions using Windows NT, Windows 2000, Windows XP, and Windows 2003.

FAQ 5-6

Why is the operating system on the boot partition, while the boot record is on the system partition?

Although it seems somewhat backwards, according to Windows NT, Windows 2000, Windows XP, and Windows Server 2003, the boot partition stores the Windows operating system, while the system partition stores the boot record. A computer boots from the system partition and loads the operating system from the boot partition.

High-Level Formatting

After a hard drive has been physically formatted and partitioned, it must be logically formatted. **Logical formatting** or **high-level formatting** places a file system on the disk for each logical drive. A *file system* allows an operating system, such as DOS or Windows XP, to use the space available on a hard disk to store and retrieve files. The operating system uses the file system to store information about the disk's directory, or folder, structure. DOS and early versions of Windows use the *file allocation table (FAT)* file system, and Windows NT and later versions use the *New Technology file system (NTFS)* by default.

The file system also defines the size of the clusters used to store data on the hard disk. A **cluster**, which also is called a **file allocation unit** or **block,** is made up of two or more sectors on a single track on a hard disk. A cluster is the minimum unit the operating system uses to store information. Even if a file has a size of 1 byte, a cluster as large as 64 kilobytes might be used to store the file on large drives. The number of sectors and tracks and, therefore, the number of clusters that a drive can create on a disk's surface, determine the capacity of the disk.

While creating the file system during logical formatting, the operating system creates a boot record, a root directory, and two copies of the file allocation table (in the FAT file system) or master file table (in NTFS) for each logical drive.

FAQ 5-7

What is the purpose of having a cluster, when the hard disk already has sectors?

A sector refers to the way data is physically stored on a disk, while a cluster describes how data is logically organized on the disk. The BIOS manages the disk as physical sectors, but the OS considers the disk as only a long series of clusters that can each hold a fixed amount of data.

HIGH-LEVEL FORMATTING USING FAT DOS and earlier versions of Windows use the file allocation table (FAT) file system by default. The FAT file system uses three components to manage data on a logical drive: the boot sector, the FAT, and the directories.

The Boot Record As shown in Figure 5-5 on page 167, the first sector of a logical drive is called the **boot sector** or **boot record**. The boot record contains basic information about how the logical drive is organized. This information includes the number of sectors, the number of sectors per cluster, the number of bits in each FAT entry, and other information that an OS or BIOS needs to read the data on the disk. At the end of the boot record is a small program, called the **bootstrap loader**, which can be used to boot from the disk. The boot record indicates the version of DOS or Windows used to format the disk and includes the name of the program it searches for to load an OS. For Windows Server 2003, Windows XP, Windows 2000, and Windows NT, that program file is Ntldr (NT Loader); for Windows 9x, the program file is Io.sys. If this file is on the disk, the disk is bootable and the file loads the rest of the OS files needed to boot the disk.

The File Allocation Table (FAT) After the boot record is created, the next step in formatting a hard disk is to write two copies of the file allocation table to each logical drive. The **file allocation table** (**FAT**) is a one-column table that stores entries that the operating system uses to locate files on a disk. Each entry in the table takes up a certain number of bits, which is why FAT file systems often are referred to as 12-bit, 16-bit, or 32-bit. The content of each entry consists of a whole number, which identifies one or more clusters where the file is stored.

The Root Directory Table The next step in the formatting process creates the **directory table**, or list of files and subdirectories, on the drive. This directory table is called the *root directory*. The root directory contains a fixed number of rows to accommodate a predetermined number of files and subdirectories; the number of available rows depends on the disk type.

As you learned in Chapter 2, the root directory typically is referred to as drive C on a hard drive. This root directory can have subdirectories (also called child directories or folders), which have names such as C:\Tools in which C: indicates the root directory and Tools is the subdirectory. The hard disk thus is organized at several levels, with the operating system managing the files and folders stored on the drive.

The root directory and all subdirectories contain the same information about each file, including the file name, file size, the date the file was created, the date the file was last modified, and so on. Only the root directory has a limitation on the number of entries. Subdirectories can have as many entries as disk space allows.

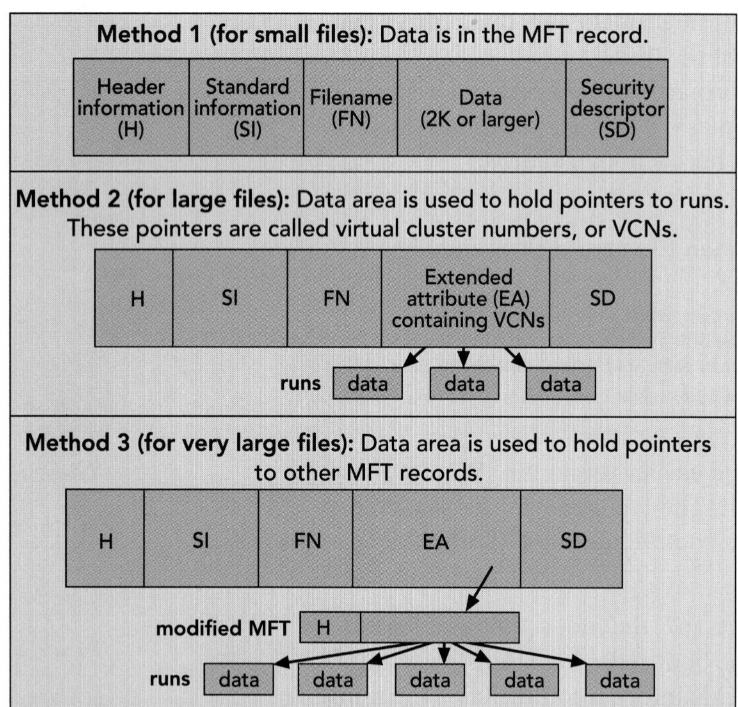

Figure 5-7 The Master File Table uses three methods to store files, depending on the file size.

HIGH-LEVEL FORMATTING USING NTFS

Starting with Windows NT, the Windows operating system has used the *New Technology file system (NTFS)* by default. Instead of using the boot record, FAT, and directories to manage a hard disk, the NTFS file system uses a special file called the **master file table** (**MFT**) to record information about where files are stored on the hard drive. The MFT is a database used to track the contents of a logical drive, using one or more rows in the table for each file or directory on the drive. As shown in Figure 5-7, the MFT contains information about each file in one database record, or row, including header information (abbreviated H in Microsoft documentation); standard information (SI) about the file, including date and time; filename (FN); security information about the file, called the security descriptor (SD); and the file data. Entries in the MFT are ordered alphabetically by filename to speed up a search for a file listed in the table.

As shown in Figure 5-7, the data area in the MFT record is 2K for small hard drives but can be larger for larger hard drives. For small files, if the data can fit into the 2K area, the file and its data are contained fully within the MFT. If the file is moderately large and the data does not fit into the MFT, the data area in the MFT becomes an extended attribute (EA) of the file, which points to the location of the data. The data itself is moved outside the table to clusters called runs. The record in the MFT for this moderately large file contains pointers, called virtual cluster numbers (VCNs), that point to these runs. This mapping is stored in the area of the MFT record that would have contained the data if the file had been small enough. If the file is so large that the pointers cannot be contained in one MFT record, then additional MFT records are used. The first MFT record is called the base file record and holds the location of the other MFT records for this file.

File Systems

Depending on the operating system used to format the disk, the file system can be one of several types. Figure 5-8 summarizes which file systems are supported by which operating systems. Whatever file system is used, the file system is the interface between operating system and drives. When application software asks to read a file from the hard disk, the operating system asks the file system to open the file. Because it is so important to computer operations, the FAT file system stores a second copy of FAT and NTFS stores duplicate records for each record in the MFT, in case the data in the first version becomes corrupted.

File System	Description	Key Features	Total Volume Size	Operating System Support
FAT12	Standard file system for DOS and Windows. FAT also is accessible by Linux, OS/2, Windows NT, and other operating systems.	• used for floppy disks	16 MB	DOS; Windows 95; Windows 98; Windows NT; Windows 2000; Windows XP; Windows Server 2003
FAT16	Standard file system for DOS and Windows. FAT also is accessible by Linux, OS/2, Windows NT, and other operating systems.	• FAT16 used for small to moderate-sized hard disk volumes (up to 2 GB) • FAT16 uses 16 bits for each cluster entry in FAT	4 GB	DOS; Windows 95; Windows 98; Windows NT; Windows 2000; Windows XP; Windows Server 2003
FAT32	A 32-bit version of FAT, introduced with Windows 95 Service Release 2.	• supports long filenames up to 255 characters long • uses 32 bits for each cluster entry in FAT • faster than FAT because computer can read files at least 32 bits at a time	2 GB to 2 TB	Windows 95 (OSR2); Windows 98; Windows 2000; Windows XP; Windows Server 2003

(continued)

File System	Description	Key Features	Total Volume Size	Operating System Support
NTFS (NT File System)	The 32-bit file system currently used for Windows NT, Windows 2000, Windows XP, and Windows Server 2003.	• 32- or 64-bit entries in master file table (Windows 2000 limits to 32-bit entries) • designed to restore consistency after system crash • supports long filenames up to 255 characters long • used for medium-sized to very large hard disk volumes (up to 16 billion GB)	2 TB	Windows NT (service pack 4); Windows 2000; Windows XP; Windows Server 2003

Figure 5-8 Depending on the operating system used to format the disk, the file system can be one of several types. Newer Windows operating systems, such as Windows XP and Windows 2003, use NTFS.

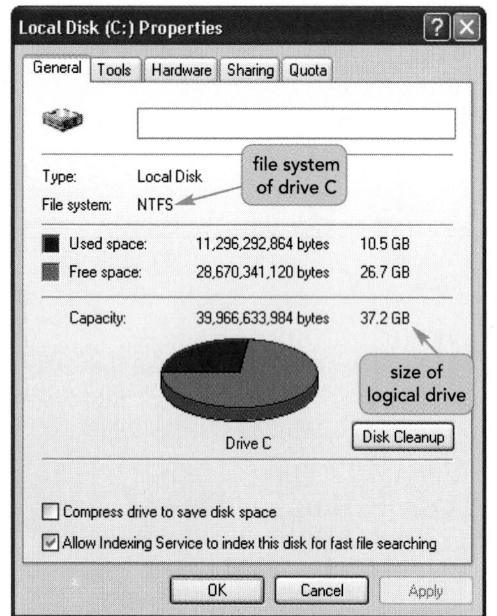

Figure 5-9 This hard drive contains one partition, formatted using the NTFS file system.

In Windows, you can see what file system is being used by right-clicking a drive in Windows Explorer or My Computer and then clicking Properties on the shortcut menu. You also can see the amount of space allotted to this logical drive and how much of it currently is used (Figure 5-9).

FAT16 DOS and all versions of Windows support the **FAT16** file system, which uses 16 bits for each cluster entry in the FAT. Using FAT16, the smallest cluster size is four sectors. Because each sector is 512 bytes, a cluster that contains 4 sectors is 2,048 bytes. Because a cluster is the minimum unit the operating system uses to store information, even a one-character file takes up 2,048 bytes of space on a hard drive. For larger drives, the number of sectors in one cluster is higher. When the drive contains many small files, with cluster size so large, these files can create large amounts of wasted space called **slack**.

FAT32 Beginning with an updated release of Windows 95, Microsoft offered **FAT32**, a file system that contains 32 bits per FAT entry instead of the older 12-bit or 16-bit FAT entries. Only 28 of the 32 bits are used to hold a cluster number; the remaining four bits currently are not used. For logical drives up to 16 GB, FAT32 uses a cluster size of 8K; for drives ranging from 16 GB to 32 GB, the cluster size increases to about 16K. Windows 2000, Windows XP, and Windows Server 2003 only support FAT32 for drives up to 32 GB; for drives larger than 32 GB, you should use NTFS.

NTFS Windows NT, Windows 2000, Windows XP, and Windows Server 2003 support a file system called NTFS. **NTFS (New Technology file system)** is designed to provide more security and more stability than the FAT file system. As mentioned earlier, NTFS uses a database called the master file table (MFT) to store information about files and directories and their locations on the hard drive. For each record, the MFT stores a mirror record so that, if the first MFT record is corrupted, NTFS can read the second record to find the file. If you have a hard drive over 32 GB, use NTFS under Windows NT, Windows 2000, Windows XP, and Windows Server 2003. When you install Windows from the setup CD, it will provide options to allow you to choose NTFS.

More About

NTFS versus FAT

To learn more about the advantages of NTFS over FAT, visit the Understanding and Troubleshooting Your PC More About Web page (**scsite.com/understanding/more**) and then click NTFS versus FAT below Chapter 5.

Hard Drive Interfaces

In addition to understanding the read/write technology used within the hard drive, it is important to understand the technology of how the hard drive interfaces with the system.

As you have learned, the CPU communicates with the hard drive controller, which in turn physically locates the data on the hard drive. The hard drive controller then instructs the read/write heads how, where, and when to move across the platters to read or write data.

In addition to communicating with the CPU, hard drives also physically connect to, or interface with, the motherboard in order to transfer data to memory. A **hard drive interface** is the communication channel over which all the data that is read from or written to the hard disk flows. The standard for a hard drive interface specifies the type of connectors and cables used to connect a hard drive to the motherboard, as well as the speed with which the hard drive can transfer data.

For a hard drive to work in a system, the hard drive interface must be compatible with the hard drive controller, the OS, and the BIOS. In most cases, when installing a drive, you do not need to know which specific hard drive interface standard a hard drive supports, because startup BIOS uses autodetection. With **autodetection**, the BIOS detects the new drive and automatically selects the correct drive capacity and configuration, including the best possible interface standard supported by both the hard drive and the motherboard.

FAQ 5-8

What if my system does not autodetect a new hard drive?

Occasionally, when you install a new hard drive, startup BIOS does not recognize the hard drive, or it detects the drive and reports in CMOS setup that the drive has a smaller capacity than it actually does. In this situation, your older BIOS or IDE controller card does not support the newer IDE standard used by the drive. First check to see if the hard drive came with a floppy disk or CD-ROM with utility software to help with the installation of a hard disk. Alternatively, you can flash BIOS, replace the controller card, or replace the motherboard.

IDE/ATA Interface Standards

As you learned in Chapter 1, the majority of hard drives interface with the motherboard by means of a hard drive interface standard called *Integrated Drive Electronics (IDE)*, in which the controller is integrated into the disk drive. Drives that use IDE standards often are referred to simply as IDE drives.

The IDE interface also is known by other names, including AT Attachment (ATA) or EIDE (Enhanced IDE). Figure 5-10 lists the different interface standards used with IDE drives. Starting with ATA-2, the interface standards allow for up to four IDE devices on the same PC, as illustrated by the computer shown in Figure 5-11.

Standard (may have more than one name)	Speed	Description
• IDE/ATA • ATA	From 2.1 MB/sec to 8.3 MB/sec	The first ANSI hard drive standard for IDE hard drives. Limited to no more than 528 MB. Supports PIO and DMA transfer modes.
• ATA-2 • Fast ATA	Up to 16.6 MB/sec	Breaks the 528-MB barrier. Allows up to four IDE devices. Supports PIO and DMA transfer modes.
• ATA-3	Up to 16.6 MB/sec	Improved version of ATA-2, which provided a small speed increase.
• Ultra ATA • Fast ATA-2 • Ultra DMA • DMA/33	Up to 33.3 MB/sec	Defined a new DMA mode but only supports slower PIO modes.
• Ultra ATA/66 • Ultra DMA/66	Up to 66.6 MB/sec	Uses an 80-conductor cable that provides additional ground lines on the cable to improve signal integrity.
• Ultra ATA/100	Up to 100 MB/sec	Uses the 80-conductor cable with additional grounding.
• Ultra ATA/133	Up to 133 MB/sec	Uses the 80-conductor cable with additional grounding and supports drives larger than 137 GB.
• ATA/ATAPI-6	Up to 133 MB/sec	A part of the ATA/133 standard that supports drives larger than 137 GB.

Figure 5-10 Summary of interface standards for IDE drives. As standards developed, different drive manufacturers called them different names, which can be confusing.

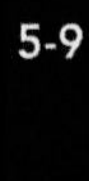

FAQ 5-9

Is the hard drive interface standard abbreviated IDE or EIDE? I have seen it written both ways.

The computer industry often uses the term IDE when it really means EIDE. Technically, for today's computers, EIDE refers to the interface standard, and IDE refers to how the firmware used with the hard drive controller stores data on the drive. Most hardware manufacturers, however, label their EIDE connections as IDE connections. To help eliminate confusion, this chapter also uses IDE to refer to the interface standard although — as noted above — the hard drive interface standard actually is EIDE.

In this computer, the hard drive uses the primary IDE cable, while the CD-ROM drive and Zip drive share the secondary IDE cable. The most widely used IDE interface standard today is Ultra ATA/100, which provides faster data transfer than previous interfaces. Other secondary storage devices, such as CD-ROM drives, DVD-ROM drives, and Zip drives, can use IDE interface if they follow the **ATAPI (Advanced Technology Attachment Packet Interface)** standards.

As shown in Figure 5-10, different hard drive interface standards transfer data at different speeds. If two hard drives share the same IDE cable but use different standards, both drives will run at the speed of the slower drive, unless the motherboard chipset controlling the IDE connections supports a feature called **independent device timing**. Most chipsets today support this feature and the two drives can run at different speeds, as long as the motherboard supports these speeds.

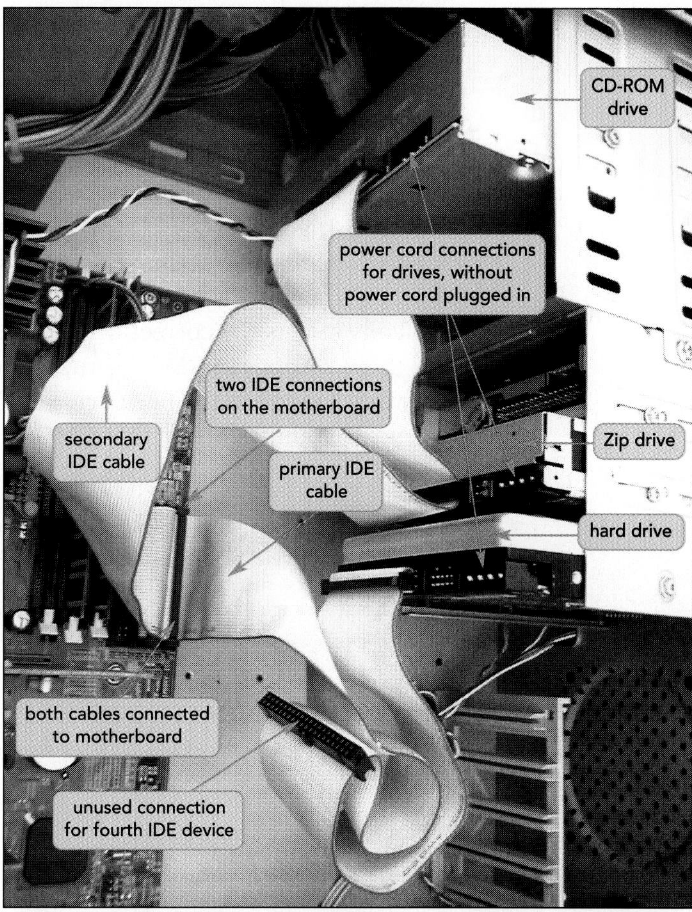

Figure 5-11 In this computer, the hard drive uses the primary IDE cable, while the CD-ROM drive and Zip drive share the secondary IDE cable. (The power cords are not connected, in order to make it easier to see the data cable connections.)

FAQ 5-10

Does it really matter what hard drive interface a computer uses?

The hard drive interface can be a major limiting factor in system performance. The choice of interface also has an essential impact on system configuration, compatibility, upgradeability and other factors. When selecting a drive standard, select the fastest standard appropriate for the price range of your system and size of the drive. Keep in mind that the operating system, system BIOS on the motherboard, and the hard drive controller on the drive must all support this standard. If one of these three does not, the other two probably will revert to a slower standard that all three can use, or the drive will not work.

DMA OR PIO TRANSFER MODES A hard drive uses one of two methods to transfer data between the hard drive and memory: DMA (direct memory access) transfer mode or PIO (Programmed Input/Output) transfer mode. As you learned in Chapter 2, a direct memory access (DMA) channel is a system resource that lets a device send data directly to memory, bypassing the CPU. Hard drives that use a **DMA (direct memory access) transfer mode** can transfer data directly from the drive to memory without involving the CPU. **PIO (programmed input/output) transfer mode** involves the CPU and is slower than DMA. Most new systems use DMA transfer mode.

When a new hard drive is installed in a computer, startup BIOS usually automatically selects the correct transfer mode when it autodetects the drive and records those settings in CMOS setup. If you are having problems with a hard drive, you may want to look in the hard drive documentation to learn which mode the drive supports and then verify that CMOS setup is not set to use a different mode.

FAQ 5-11

What does DMA mode 5 signify in the hard drive documentation?

Several different modes for both PIO and DMA exist, as both standards have been improved several times. PIO mode standards range from 0 (the slowest) to 4 (the fastest). DMA modes range from 0 (the slowest) to 5 (the fastest).

IDE CABLING METHODS Today's hard drives currently use two types of cables to connect to a standard IDE connector: parallel ATA (PATA) or serial ATA (SATA) technology. Parallel ATA technology uses IDE ribbon cables that connect to a standard IDE connector and send signals in parallel along the cable wires. Earlier drives used a **40-conductor IDE cable** that fits a 40-pin IDE connector. The 40-conductor cable, however, does not provide the grounding needed to reduce interference for today's high-speed data transfer. Newer drives, starting with ATA/66, thus use an 80-conductor IDE cable. The **80-conductor IDE cable** is a special 40-pin IDE cable with 40 additional ground wires that reduce interference on the cable. This 80-conductor IDE cable also is called an *ATA/100 cable* or an *UltraDMA100/66 cable*.

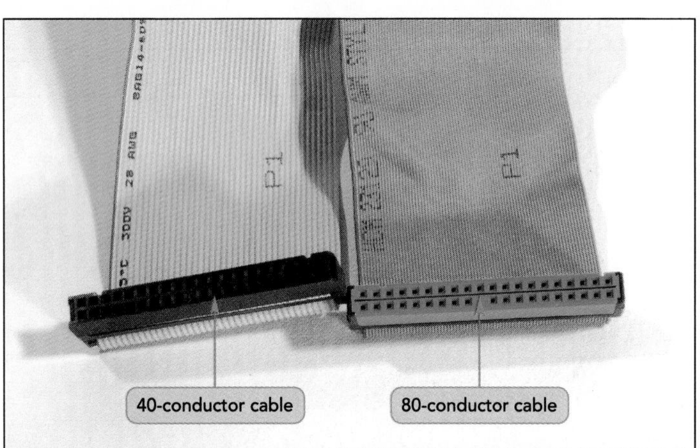

Figure 5-12 In comparing the 80-conductor cable to the 40-conductor cable, note they are about the same width, but the 80-conductor cable has many more and finer wires. Also note the red line down the side of each cable that indicates Pin 1, which should be connected with Pin 1 on the connector.

Figure 5-12 shows a comparison between the 80-conductor cable and the 40-conductor cable. The connectors on each cable are the same, which means you can use an 80-conductor IDE cable in place of a 40-conductor IDE cable to help reduce interference.

A **serial ATA (SATA) cable** is much narrower and has only seven wires (Figure 5-13). A serial ATA cable is faster than an 80-conductor IDE cable, but is currently more expensive because it is a relatively new technology. Serial ATA cabling has been introduced into the industry not so much to handle the speeds of current drives, but to position the industry for the high-performance large drives soon expected to be inexpensive enough for the desktop hard drive market. Some high-end motherboards have both serial ATA connectors and standard IDE connectors for 40-conductor and 80-conductor cables on the same board (Figure 5-14).

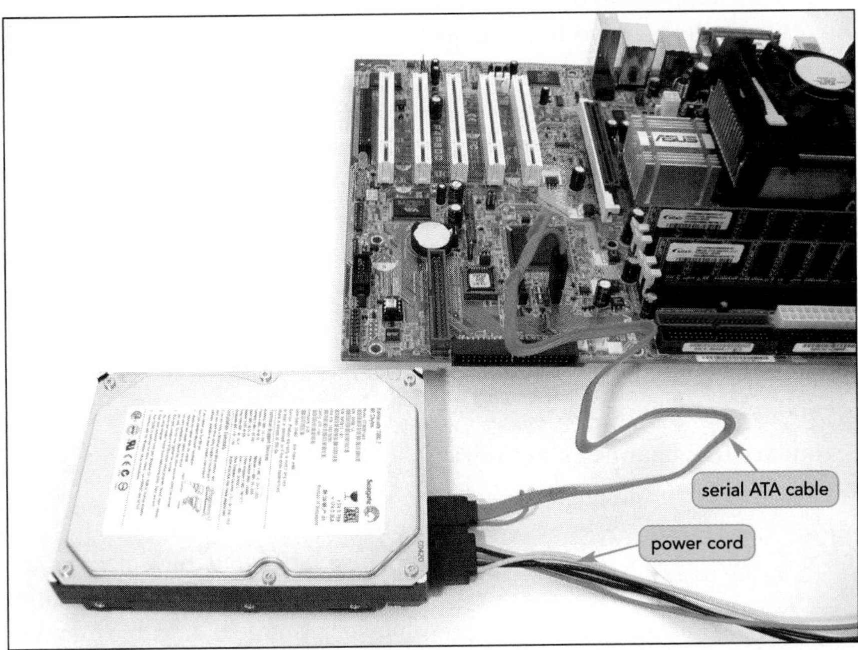

Figure 5-13 A hard drive using a serial ATA data cable.

Figure 5-14 Some newer motherboards have serial ATA and standard IDE connectors.

FAQ 5-12

Why would I want to use a Serial ATA cable, rather than an IDE cable?

Serial ATA cables do provide some practical improvements over IDE cables, which are bulky, inflexible, and often too short. In some cases, wide IDE cable can block airflow inside the computer case, creating additional heat. Serial ATA cables, by contrast, are much thinner, more flexible, and generally are over twice as long as IDE cables. The seven-wire cables use smaller connectors, which saves space on motherboards and hard drives.

CONFIGURING IDE DRIVES IN A SYSTEM Following the IDE standard, a motherboard can support up to four IDE devices using parallel ATA cabling. A motherboard typically has two IDE connectors, or channels. One is the primary IDE channel, the other is the secondary IDE channel. Each channel can accommodate one IDE data cable. The IDE data cable has two connectors: one in the middle of the cable and one at the far end, which allows the cable to connect two IDE devices, such as a hard drive, CD-ROM drive, or other type of drive. If two devices are connected to an IDE cable, one device is configured to act as the master controlling the channel, while the other device is set as the slave (Figure 5-15). If four devices are connected to the IDE cables, each of the devices must be configured as one of the following:

- Primary IDE channel, master device
- Primary IDE channel, slave device
- Secondary IDE channel, master device
- Secondary IDE channel, slave device

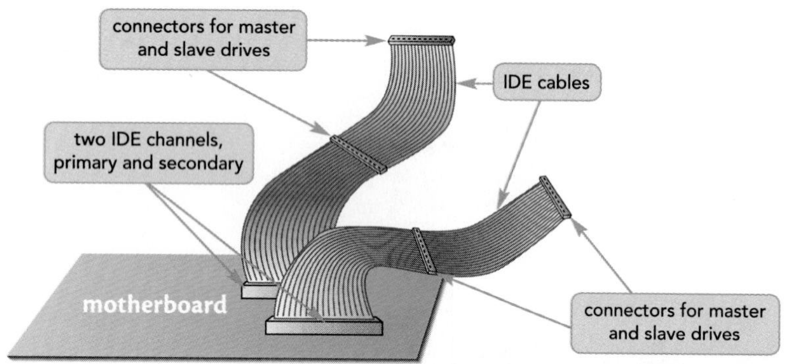

Figure 5-15 A motherboard has two IDE channels; each of which can support a master and slave drive using a single IDE cable.

These designations are made by setting jumpers or DIP switches on the devices or by using a special cable-select data cable, which is recognizable by the small hole somewhere in the data cable. A **cable-select data cable** has two connectors — a master connector and a slave connector. The device attached to the master connector is the master; the device connected to the slave connector is the slave. Sometimes an IDE 80-conductor cable connector is blue to indicate it connects to the primary channel IDE connector on a motherboard, which also can be color-coded, as shown in Figure 5-14 on the previous page.

The hard drive always should be installed as the master device on the primary IDE channel. When installing a hard drive on the same channel with an ATAPI drive such as a CD-ROM drive, always make the hard drive the master and the ATAPI drive the slave. An even better solution is to install the hard drive on the primary channel and the CD drive and any other drive on the secondary channel.

If a motherboard supports serial ATA, it most likely has two serial ATA connectors. A serial ATA cable only can accommodate a single drive. When installing serial ATA drives using Windows 2000 or Windows XP, you can install up to six IDE devices in the system, including up to four parallel ATA devices and up to two serial ATA devices.

Other Interface Standards

The second most popular interface for hard drive, as well as other drives, is SCSI. Other technologies used to interface between the hard drive and the system bus are USB and FireWire.

SCSI **SCSI** (pronounced *scuzzy*) stands for **Small Computer System Interface**, which is a standard for communication between a subsystem of peripheral devices and the system bus. The SCSI bus can contain, and be used by, up to 7 or 15 devices, depending on the SCSI standard. Some computers have a SCSI port, where you can connect a SCSI hard drive, while other computers have a slot that supports a SCSI card.

As described earlier, most IDE/ATA hard drives are controlled by integrated hard drive controllers built into the chipset on the motherboard. With SCSI, if a motherboard does not have an embedded SCSI controller, the gateway from the SCSI bus to the system bus is the **host adapter**, a card inserted into an expansion slot on the motherboard.

The host adapter is responsible for managing all devices on the SCSI bus. A host adapter can support both internal and external SCSI devices, using one connector on the card for a ribbon cable to connect to internal devices, and an external port that supports external devices (Figure 5-16). All the devices and the host adapter form a single **daisy chain** (sometimes called a straight chain).

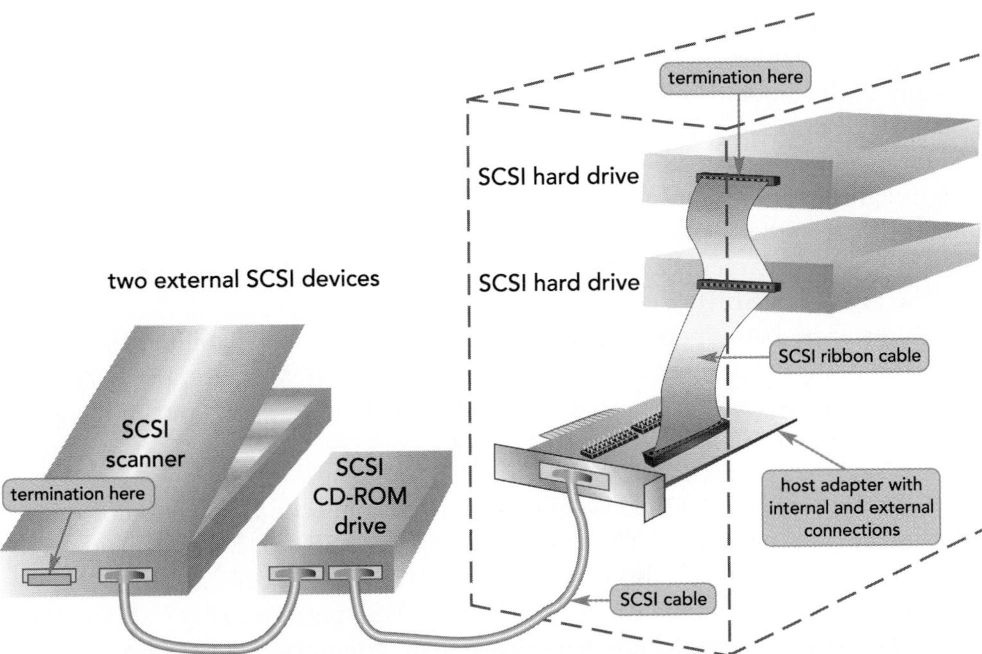

Figure 5-16 Using a SCSI bus, a SCSI host adapter can support internal and external SCSI devices in a daisy chain. This daisy chain has two internal devices and two external devices, with the SCSI host adapter in the middle of the chain.

When a device on the SCSI bus must communicate with the system bus, the data passes through the host adapter. The host adapter keeps up with the interchange between the devices on the SCSI bus and the system bus. SCSI technology has the added advantage of letting two devices on the SCSI bus pass data between them without going through the CPU.

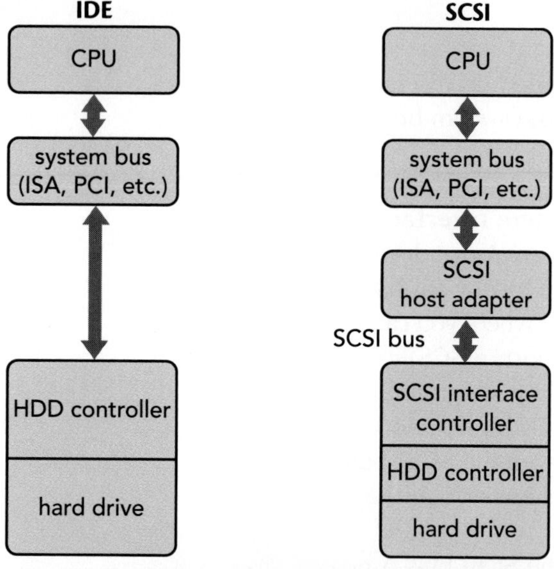

Figure 5-17 SCSI hard drives communicate with the CPU through the SCSI host adapter, but IDE drives communicate directly on the system bus.

Figure 5-17 compares IDE and SCSI communication. With an IDE drive, the CPU communicates with the hard drive controller over the system bus. With a SCSI hard drive, the CPU communicates over the system bus to the SCSI host adapter, which communicates over the SCSI bus to the SCSI interface controller in the hard drive case. This SCSI interface controller communicates with the hard drive controller, which, in turn, communicates with the hard drive.

Each end of a SCSI bus must be terminated properly so commands and data can be transmitted to and from all devices on the bus. **Termination** prevents an echo effect from electrical noise and reflected data at the end of the SCSI daisy chain, which can cause interference with data transmission.

The device at the end of a SCSI chain can be terminated by either setting a switch or plugging a resistor module into an open port on a device. Host adapters typically default to being terminated. If devices are connected both internally and externally, the host adapter termination must be removed and termination must be applied to the ends of both chains. In Figure 5-16 on the previous page, for example, the scanner and hard drive on each end of the SCSI bus are terminated, while termination is disabled for any devices in the middle of the bus, including host adapter.

> **More About**
>
> **SCSI**
>
> To learn more about SCSI and the process of installing a removable hard drive using a SCSI interface, visit the Understanding and Troubleshooting Your PC More About Web page (**scsite.com/understanding/more**) and then click SCSI below Chapter 5.

Many SCSI standards have evolved over several years. The maximum number of devices the SCSI bus can support depends on the SCSI standard being used. Some SCSI buses can link up to seven devices, others up to 15. Each device on the SCSI bus is assigned a number from 0 to 15, called the **SCSI ID**, by means of DIP switches, dials on the device, or software settings. The host adapter generally is assigned a SCSI ID larger than all other devices, either 7 or 15; some come factory-set to the highest SCSI ID.

SCSI provides better performance and greater expansion capabilities for many internal and external devices, including hard drives, CD-ROM drives, DVD drives, and scanners. However, SCSI devices tend to be faster, more expensive, and more difficult to install than similar IDE devices.

USB USB (Universal Serial Bus) is a popular way to connect many external peripheral devices to a system. The first USB standard, USB 1.0, is not fast enough to be used for a hard drive, but the latest standards, USB 1.1 and USB 2.0 (Hi-Speed USB) are. Most computers today have two or more USB ports, making USB an easy way to add a second external hard drive to a system. Windows 2000 supports USB 1.1 and Windows XP supports USB 2.0. Before buying a USB hard drive, verify that your OS and the motherboard USB connection support the same USB standard as the drive.

FIREWIRE (IEEE 1394) FireWire (also known as IEEE 1394 or i.Link as named by Sony) uses serial transmission of data and is popular for multimedia and home entertainment applications. A hard drive designed for home entertainment electronics, for example, likely will use FireWire for the external hard drive interface.

A FireWire device connects to a PC through a FireWire external port or internal connector provided either directly on the motherboard or by way of a FireWire expansion card. Windows 98, Windows 2000, Windows XP, and Windows Server 2003 support FireWire interfaces.

Installing a Hard Drive

Installing an IDE/ATA hard drive using parallel ATA cabling involves the following basic steps:

1. Prepare to install the hard drive by backing up any important data, reading the documentation for the drive and your motherboard, setting up your work area and taking safety precautions.
2. Plan the drive configuration. Remember that you can install up to four IDE devices in a system using only parallel ATA cabling. Determine which drives will use the primary and secondary IDE channels and which will be the master or slave on each channel.
3. Set jumpers on the drive housing.
4. Physically install the drive inside the computer case by mounting the drive in the bay and then attaching the power cord and data cable. To install an IDE drive, you need the drive, a 40-conductor or 80-conductor data cable, and perhaps a kit to make the drive fit into a much larger bay.
5. Change CMOS setup to recognize the new drive or verify that autodetect correctly detected the drive.
6. Format and partition the drive.
   a. If you are installing an OS on the drive, boot from the operating system setup CD and then complete the installation process to partition and complete high-level formatting of the disk.
   b. If the drive is not intended to hold an OS (for example, if it is a second drive in a two-drive system), use the Fdisk utility or Disk Management to create one or more partitions on the drive and then divide the extended partition (if there is one) into logical drives. Next, use the Format command or Disk Management to high-level format each logical drive.

The following sections review each of these steps in detail.

Preparing to Install a Hard Drive

Remember from earlier chapters that keeping notes is a good idea whenever you install new hardware or software or make any other changes to your PC system. Other tips to consider:

- Before you begin installing your hard drive, make sure you know where your starting point is and take notes so you can backtrack later if necessary. Before installing a new device, verify which of your system's devices are working. Later, if a resource conflict causes a device to malfunction, the information will help you isolate the problem.
- When installing hardware and software, do not install too many things at once. If something goes wrong, you will not know what is causing the problem. Install one device, start the system, and confirm that the new device is working before installing another.

- Make sure that you have a good bootable disk or rescue disk.
- Make sure you have a record of your CMOS settings in case you lose setup information in the process. As you work, write down any changes you make.

MAKE A BACKUP OF IMPORTANT DATA If you are upgrading your old hard drive to a new one, be sure to make a copy of any data you later will want to use on the new hard drive. Chapter 12 provides more information on making a copy, or backup, of important data.

READ DOCUMENTATION Before you take anything apart, carefully read all the documentation for the hard drive and the part of your computer's documentation that covers hard drive installation. Check your motherboard documentation to verify that the BIOS accommodates the size and type of hard drive you want to install. If you are not sure which IDE standards your motherboard supports, you can look for different options on the CMOS setup screens.

PREPARE YOUR WORK AREA AND TAKE PRECAUTIONS The next step is to prepare a large, well-lit place to work. Set out your tools, documentation, new hardware, and notebook. Be sure to ground yourself and the computer, and wear a ground bracelet during the installation. Also avoid working on carpet in the winter when there is a lot of static electricity. Some added precautions for working with hard drives are:

- Handle the drive carefully.
- Do not touch any exposed circuitry or chips.
- Prevent other people from touching exposed microchips on the drive.
- When you first take the drive out of the static-protective package, touch the package containing the drive to a screw holding an expansion card or cover, or to a metal part of the computer case, for at least two seconds. This will drain the static electricity from the package and from your body.
- If you must set down the drive outside the static-protective package, place it component-side-up on top of the static-protective package on a flat surface.
- Do not place the drive on the computer case cover or on a metal table.
- Turn off the computer and unplug it. Unplug the monitor and move it to one side. Remove the computer case cover. Check that you have an available power cord from the power supply.

PLAN DRIVE CONFIGURATION Before you start the installation process, plan how you will configure the drives in your system. Remember that the motherboard has a primary and secondary IDE channel. Each channel can support up to two drives, a master and a slave, for a total of up to four IDE drives in a system. When possible, leave the hard drive as the single drive on one channel, so it does not compete with another drive for access to the channel and possibly slow down performance. Be sure to use the primary channel before you use the secondary channel. In addition, put slow devices on the same channel. For example, suppose you have a Zip drive, CD-ROM drive, and two hard drives. Because the two hard drives are faster than the Zip drive and CD-ROM drive, put the two hard drives on the primary channel and the Zip drive and CD-ROM drive on the secondary channel.

To plan the drive configuration further, examine the locations of the drive bays and the length of the data cables. Decide which bay will hold which drive. Bays designed for hard drives do not have access to the outside of the case, unlike bays for Zip drives and other drives in which disks are inserted. Some bays are wider than others to accommodate wide drives such as CD-ROM drives and DVD drives (Figure 5-18). After you determine which drives will go in specific bays, check to see if the data cable will reach the drives and the motherboard connector. If not, you may have to rearrange your plan for locating the drives in the bays or purchase a custom-length data cable. Finally, check the power supply. If there are not enough power cords from a power supply, you can purchase a Y connector that can add an additional power cord.

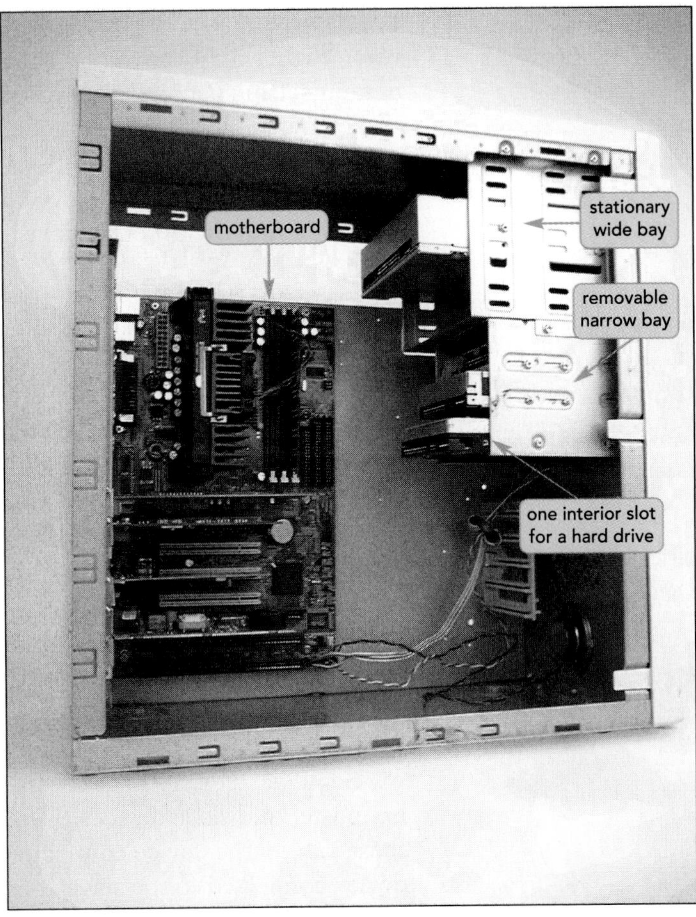

Figure 5-18 Plan for the location of drives within bays.

Set Jumpers

You normally configure a hard drive by setting jumpers on the drive housing. Often, diagrams of the jumper settings are printed on the top of the hard drive housing (Figure 5-19).

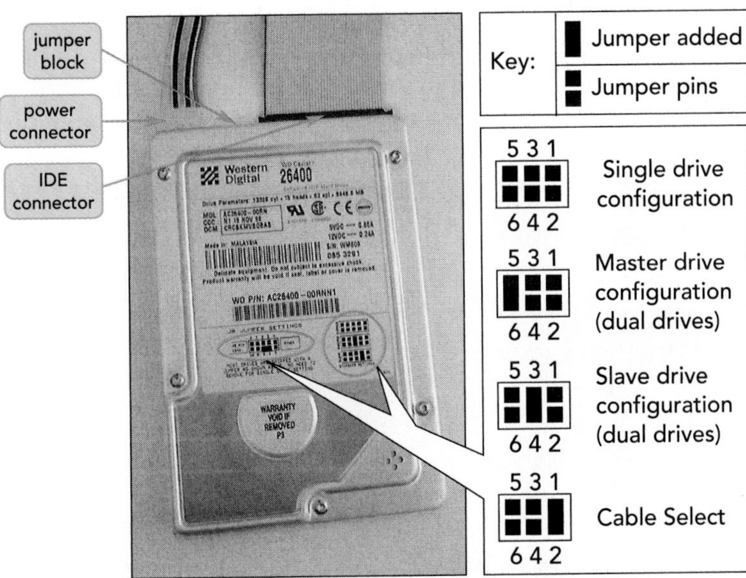

Figure 5-19 An IDE drive often has diagrams of jumper settings for master and slave options printed on the drive housing.

If they are not, see the documentation or visit the Web site of the drive manufacturer. Figure 5-20 lists typical choices for jumper settings for a drive. The factory default setting usually is set for the drive to be the single drive on a system. Before you change any settings, write down the default settings so that, if necessary, you can revert to the original settings and begin again. If a drive is the only drive on a channel, set it to a single-drive configuration. For two drives on a controller, set one to master and the other to slave.

Configuration	Description
Single-drive configuration	This is the only hard drive on this IDE channel. (This is the standard setting.)
Master-drive configuration	This is the first of two drives; it most likely is the boot device.
Slave-drive configuration	This is the second drive using this channel or data cable.
Cable-select configuration	The cable-select data cable determines which of the two drives is the master and which is the slave.

Figure 5-20 Jumper settings on an IDE hard drive.

Some hard drives have a cable-select configuration option that allows you to set up master and slave devices using a cable-select data cable. When you use one of these cables, the device connected to the master connector is the master and the device connected to the slave connector is the slave.

Mount the Drive in the Bay

Next, look at the drive bay that you will use for the drive. The bay can be stationary or removable. Figure 5-21 shows a computer case with a stationary bay for large drives and a removable bay for small drives, including the hard drive. With a removable bay, you first remove the bay from the computer case and mount the

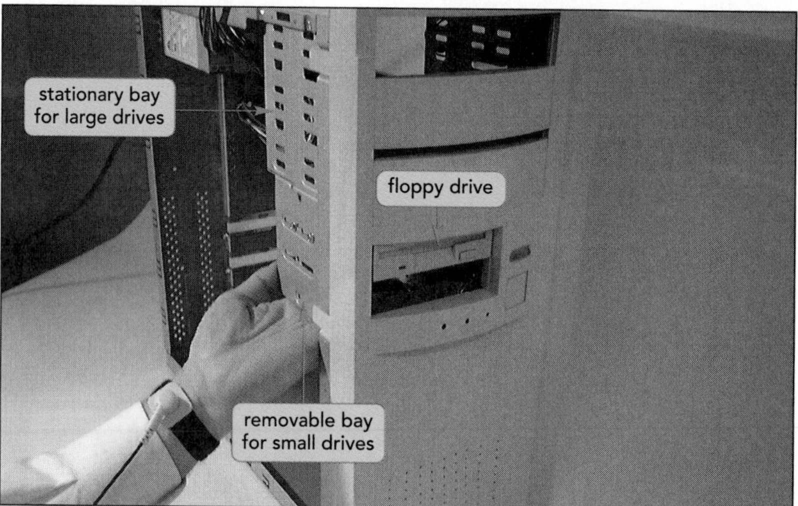

Figure 5-21 Line up the floppy drive in the removable bay so it is flush with the front of the case.

drive in the bay. You then put the bay back into the computer case. In this example, you will see how the hard drive is installed in a computer case that has three other drives: a DVD drive, a Zip drive, and a floppy drive.

Complete the following steps to install the hard drive in the bay:

1. Remove the bay for the hard drive and insert the hard drive in the bay. Put the hard drive in the bay flush with the front of the bay so it will be right against the computer case once the bay is in position (Figure 5-22). Line up other drives in the bay so they are flush with the front of the computer case. In our example, a floppy drive and Zip drive are already in the bay.
2. You must be able to mount the drive in the bay securely; the drive should not move when it is screwed down. Line up the drive and bay screw holes and make sure everything will fit. After checking the position of the drive and determining how screws are placed, install four screws (two on each side) to mount the drive in the bay. Be sure the screws are not too long. If they are, you can screw too far into the drive housing and damage the drive itself. Do not place pressure on the drive. For example, do not force a drive into a space that is too small for it. Also, placing two screws in diagonal positions across the drive can place pressure diagonally on the drive.
3. Decide whether to connect the data cable to the drive before or after you insert the bay inside the computer case, depending on how accessible the connections are. In this example, the data cables are connected to the drives in the removable bay first (Figure 5-23), before the bay is installed inside the computer case.

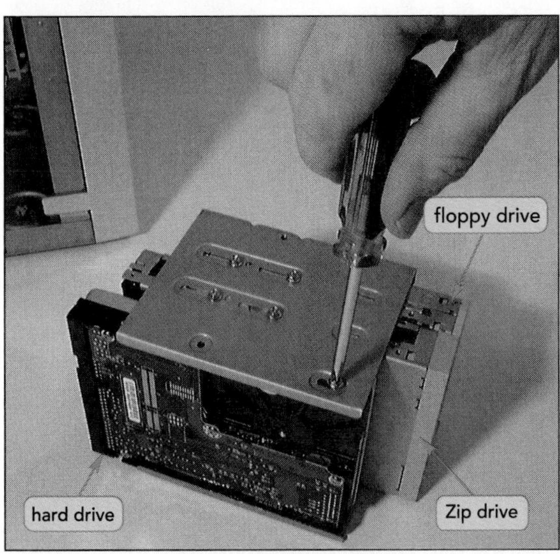

Figure 5-22 Position the hard drive flush with the end of the bay.

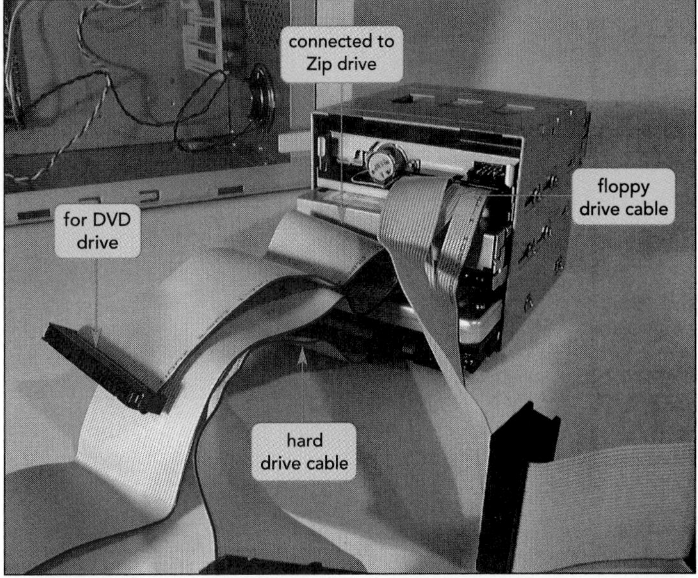

Figure 5-23 Connect the cables to all three drives in the removable bay.

4. Next, place the bay back into position and secure the bay with the bay screw or screws (Figure 5-24).
5. Install a power connection to each drive. As shown in Figure 5-25, the floppy drive uses the small power connection, while the other drives use the large ones. It does not matter which of the power cords you use for the other drives, because they all produce the same voltage.
6. Next, connect the data cable to the IDE connector on the motherboard (Figure 5-26). Make certain pin 1 and the edge color on the cable align correctly at both ends of the cable. Normally, pin 1 is closest to the power connection.
7. If the wire connecting the motherboard to the hard drive light on the front of the case was not connected when the motherboard was installed, connect it now. If you reverse the polarity of the LED wire, the light will not work. Your motherboard manual should tell you the location of the LED wires on the motherboard. If the drive light does not work after you install a new drive, try reversing the LED wire on the motherboard pins.

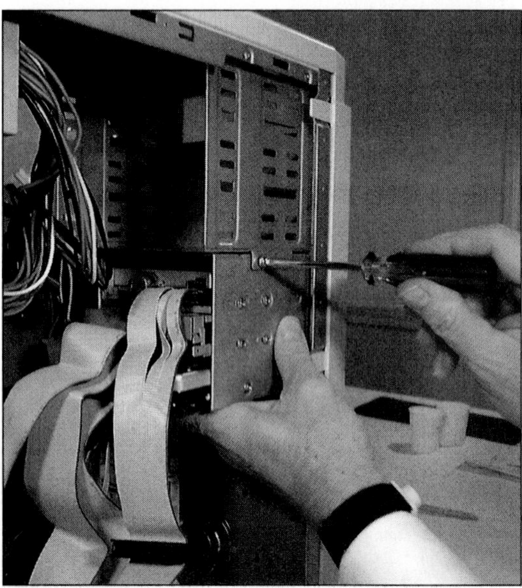

Figure 5-24 Secure the bay with the bay screw.

Figure 5-25 Connect a power cord to each drive.

8. Before you replace the computer case, plug in the monitor and turn on the computer. Verify that your system BIOS can find the drive and that it recognizes the correct size of the drive before you replace the cover. If you encounter problems, refer to the troubleshooting section at the end of this chapter.

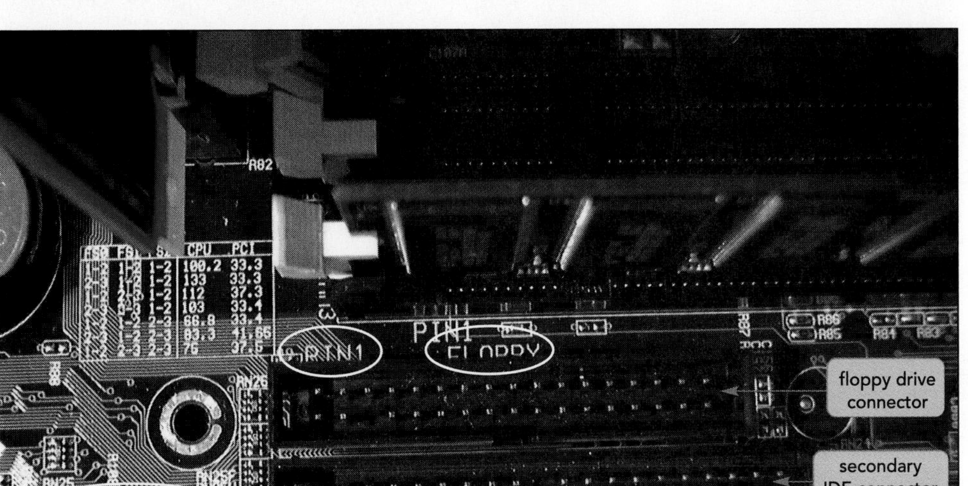

Figure 5-26 Floppy drive and two IDE connectors on the motherboard. Notice the labels that indicate which connectors are used for which drives (circled here).

The preceding steps to install a hard drive assume that you are using a removable bay. However, some computer cases use small stationary bays like the one in Figure 5-27. For these installations, slide the drive into the bay and secure it with four screws, two on each side of the bay.

If you are mounting a hard drive into a bay that is too large, a universal bay kit can help you securely fit the drive into the bay. As shown in Figure 5-28, the adapter spans the distance between the sides of the drive and the bay to help provide a snug fit.

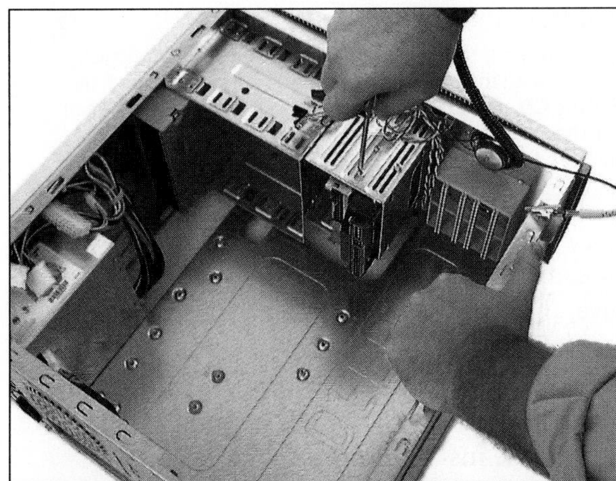

Figure 5-27 To install a drive in a stationary bay, slide the drive in the bay and secure it with four screws.

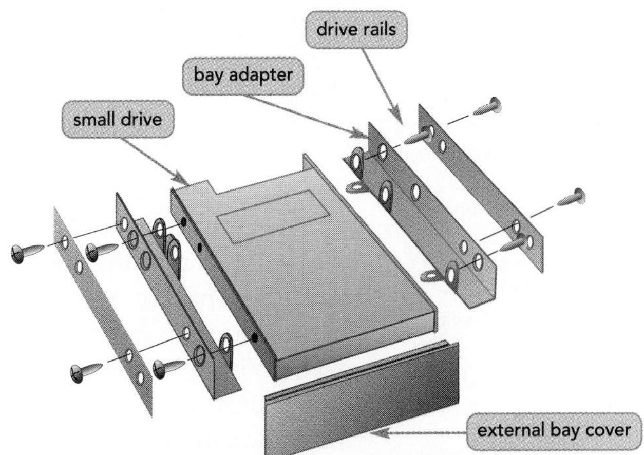

Figure 5-28 Use a universal bay kit to make the drive fit the bay.

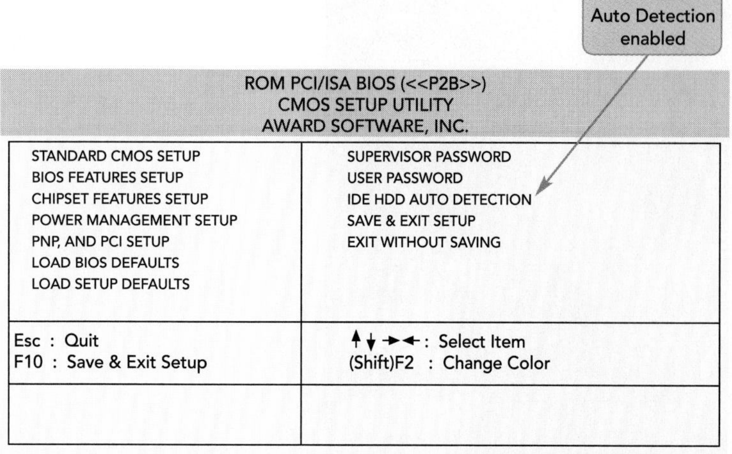

Figure 5-29 Confirm that IDE HDD Auto Detection is enabled in the CMOS setup main (opening) menu.

Use CMOS Setup to Change Hard Drive Settings

When you first boot up after installing a hard drive, go to CMOS setup and verify that the drive has been recognized, that the boot order is set correctly, and that the settings are correct. Also confirm that IDE HDD Auto Detection is enabled (Figure 5-29). If it is not, enable it and then save and exit CMOS setup. When you reboot, the system will detect the new drive. If the system still does not recognize the hard drive, you will have to choose the hard drive in CMOS and then enter information about the hard drive's cylinder, heads, and sectors. Check the hard drive's manual or manufacturer's Web site for this information. Save and exit CMOS setup to save the settings.

Partition and Format a New Drive

After you confirm that your drive is recognized and that all its settings are correct, you can partition and format the drive. The steps to partition and format the drive vary, depending on whether you are installing an OS such as Windows on the drive or if the drive is not intended to hold an OS.

PARTITIONING AND FORMATTING A DRIVE WHILE INSTALLING WINDOWS If you are installing a new hard drive in a system that is to be used for a new Windows installation, boot from the Windows setup CD after you have physically installed the drive and follow the directions on the screen to install Windows on the new drive. The setup process partitions and formats the new drive before it begins the Windows installation (Chapter 8 covers these steps in detail).

FAQ 5-13

Why will my computer not boot from the CD?

Remember that, when you first start the computer, the system BIOS follows a boot sequence, or order of drives listed in the system BIOS, when looking for the operating system to load. In order to have your computer boot from the CD, you may need to access CMOS setup and then change the configuration to ensure that the CD-ROM drive is included in the boot sequence. Be sure to save your changes when you exit CMOS setup.

When you install Windows XP, for example, the Windows Setup screen lists all partitions that it finds on the hard drive, the file system of each partition, and the size of the partition. It also lists any unpartitioned free space on the drive. From this screen, you can create and delete partitions and select the partition on which you want to install Windows XP. If you plan to have more than one partition on the drive, create only one partition at this time. After the installation, you can use Disk Management to create the other partitions.

If you created a partition in Step 2, Windows Setup asks which file system you want to use to format the partition, NTFS or FAT. After you select a file system for the partition, the Windows Setup program formats the drive, completes the text-based

More About

Setup for Large-Capacity Hard Drives

The ATA/ATAPI-6 standard is used to support hard drives over 137 GB. If the hard drive being installed is a large capacity drive, you may need to make additional changes to the BIOS using CMOS setup. To learn more about the ATA/ATAPI-6 standard and setup for large-capacity hard drives, visit the Understanding and Troubleshooting Your PC More About Web page (**scsite.com/ understanding/more**) and then click Setup for Large-Capacity Hard Drives below Chapter 5.

portion of setup, and loads the graphical interface for the rest of the installation, and then restarts the computer.

PARTIONING A DRIVE WITH AN INSTALLED OS If you are installing a second hard drive in a system that already has Windows 2000, Windows XP, or Windows Server 2003 installed on the first hard drive, use Windows to partition and format the second drive. After physically installing the second hard drive, boot into Windows as usual and then use the Disk Management utility to partition and format the hard drive.

The **Disk Management** utility is a graphical, user-friendly utility that allows you to format a hard drive. When Disk Management first loads, it examines the drive configuration for the system and displays all drives in a graphical format so you can see how each drive is allocated. The Disk Management window shown in Figure 5-30 displays three drives. Disk 0 is a basic hard drive using the NTFS file system. Disk 1 is a hard drive that has not yet been allocated into volumes. The third drive is a CD-ROM drive shown with a CD in the drive.

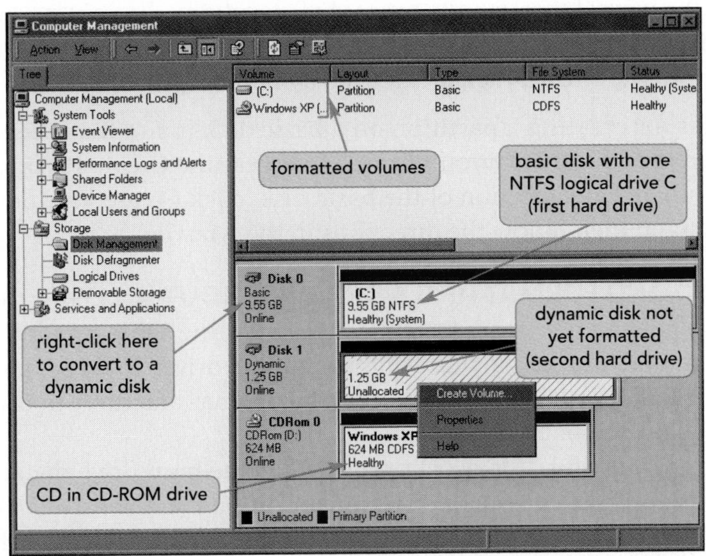

Figure 5-30 Disk Management tools allow you to create a volume on an unallocated dynamic disk.

When you first access Disk Management, it asks if you want to create a basic disk or dynamic disk using the new drive. A **basic disk** is a physical disk that contains primary partitions, extended partitions, or logical drives. By default, Windows 2000, Windows XP, and Windows Server 2003 use basic disk configuration. With basic disk configuration, you generally create partitions of a set size and then do not change them. If you want to change the size of a partition, you either have to reinstall Windows (if Windows is installed on that partition) or use special third-party software that allows you to change the size of a partition without losing your data. Partitions and logical drives on basic disks also are known as basic volumes. You can create up to four primary partitions, or three primary partitions and one extended partition, which contains logical drives.

Dynamic disks do not use partitions or logical drives; instead, they use **dynamic volumes**, which are called dynamic because you can change their size. Data to configure the disk is stored in a disk management database that resides in the last 1 MB of storage space at the end of a hard drive. Dynamic disks are compatible only with Windows 2000, Windows XP, and Windows Server 2003.

After you select an option, Disk Management displays the new disk with unallocated space, as shown in Figure 5-30 on the previous page (in this example, the second hard drive has been designated as a dynamic disk). From that point, you can follow the steps in the Create Volume Wizard to partition the hard drive. To create a volume on a dynamic disk:

1. Right-click an unallocated area of the drive and then click Create Volume on the shortcut menu, as shown in Figure 5-30 on the previous page.
2. When Create Volume Wizard starts, click the Next button to continue.
3. On the next screen, select a volume type (either Simple volume, Spanned volume, or Striped volume). In this example, only Simple volume is available, because the steps are working with only one dynamic drive. You need to have more than one dynamic drive to specify a volume as striped or spanned. Click the Next button to continue.
4. Follow the wizard through the process of specifying the volume size, a drive letter, file system (NTFS, FAT, or FAT32), and allocation unit size (default is 512 bytes). The wizard then creates the dynamic volume.

The process for creating a partition on a basic disk is similar, except that the wizard is called the Create Partition Wizard. To access the Create Partition Wizard, right-click the unallocated portion of the basic disk, click Create Partition on the shortcut menu, and then follow the directions in the wizard.

> **More About**
>
> **Fdisk and the Format Command**
>
> To learn more about using Fdisk and the Format command, visit the Understanding and Troubleshooting Your PC More About Web page **(scsite.com/understanding/more)** and then click Fdisk and the Format Command below Chapter 5.

PARTITIONING AND FORMATTING A DRIVE WITHOUT AN OS If the drive is not intended to hold an operating system, you can use the setup program provided by the drive manufacturer to partition and format the drive. To do so, put the setup floppy disk, CD-ROM, or DVD-ROM provided by the manufacturer in the appropriate drive and follow the instructions.

If a setup program and disk are not provided by the hard drive manufacturer, you can use the Fdisk utility to create one or more partitions on the drive, and divide the extended partition (if there is one) into logical drives. You then can use the Format command to high-level format each logical drive.

> **More About**
>
> **Troubleshooting a Hard Drive Installation**
>
> To learn more about troubleshooting problems that can arise during a hard drive installation, addressing issues that arise during ongoing use, and using third-party software to troubleshoot hard drive problems, visit the Understanding and Troubleshooting Your PC More About Web page **(scsite.com/understanding/more)** and then click Troubleshooting Hard Drives below Chapter 5.

Troubleshooting Hard Drive Installations

After you finish installing a hard drive, you may find that the drive is not recognized by the system or is not working properly. If the computer does not recognize a newly installed hard drive, ask yourself the following questions:

- Has Windows Setup or the Fdisk utility been run successfully?
- Did you format the drive, using the command `Format C: /S`?
- Has the CMOS setup been configured correctly?
- If you are installing a large capacity hard drive, does your system BIOS recognize large drives?
- Are there any DIP switches or jumpers that must be set?
- Have the power cord and data cable been properly connected? Verify that the data cable stripes are connected to pin 1 on the edge connectors of both the motherboard and the drive.
- If the above questions do not help you resolve the issue, check the technical support area of the hard drive manufacturer's Web site to see if they have information that might help fix the problem.

Quiz Yourself 5-1

To test your knowledge of hard drive technologies and the process of installing a hard drive, visit the Understanding and Troubleshooting Your PC Quiz Yourself Web page (scsite.com/understanding/quiz). Click Quiz Yourself 1 below Chapter 5.

How Floppy Drives Work

Once considered essential devices for file storage and installing software on a computer, floppy drives now are used mainly for troubleshooting a failed boot and as a quick and easy way to transfer small files from one computer to another when a network is not available. In this section, you will learn how data is stored on a floppy disk and how to install a floppy disk drive on a PC.

Years ago, floppy disk drives came in two sizes: 5¼ inches and 3½ inches. The 3½-inch disks were formatted as high-density (1.44 MB), extra-high density (2.88 MB), and double density (720K). Today, computers are equipped with drives that read 3½-inch high-density disks that hold 1.44 MB of data (although, as noted in Chapter 1, some newer notebook computers do not have a floppy drive, and some manufacturers offer floppy drives on desktop systems as add-on options only).

FAQ 5-14

If my computer system does not have a floppy drive, can I add one?

In most cases, yes, either inside the system or as an external drive. Check inside your computer case to see if the case has one or two empty bays for a second floppy drive or for a Zip drive. If you have no extra bay and want to add another drive, you can attach an external drive that comes in its own case and has its own power supply. Most external drives today connect to the main system using a USB port.

Figure 5-31 shows the floppy drive, its data cable, and the connector on the motherboard. The data cable used to connect the floppy drive to the motherboard is a 34-pin data cable. Like the IDE cables used to connect hard drives to the motherboard, the 34-pin cable often has a second drive connection placed in the middle of the cable to accommodate a second floppy drive.

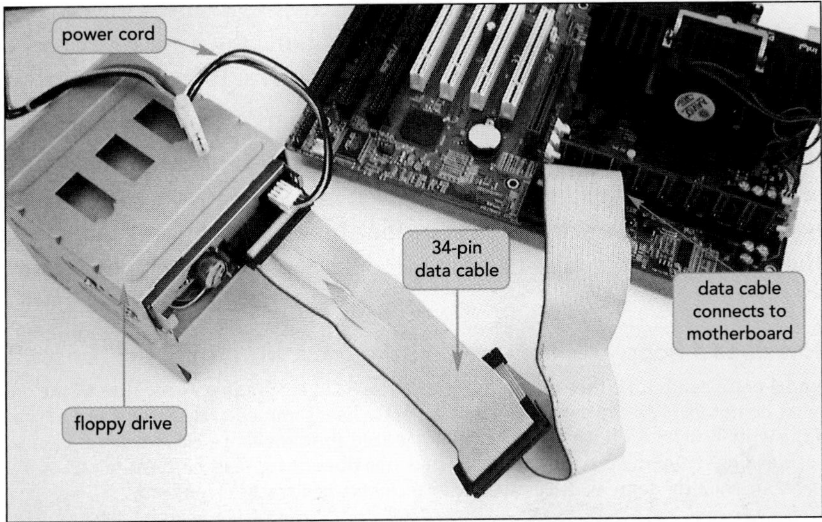

Figure 5-31 Floppy drive, data cable, and power connection.

How Data Is Organized on a Floppy Disk

When floppy disks first are manufactured, the disks are blank sheets of magnetically coated Mylar plastic. Before data can be written on the disk, it first must be formatted to create tracks and sectors (Figure 5-32).

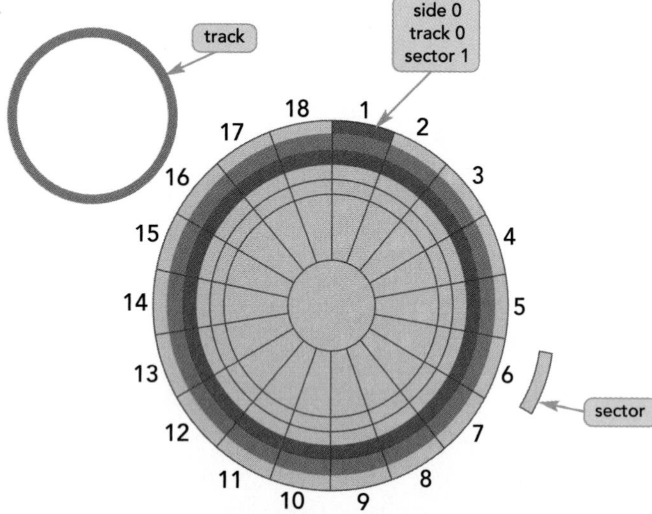

Figure 5-32 3½-inch high-density floppy disk showing tracks and sectors.

Most floppy disks come already formatted, but occasionally you will need to format one. You can format a floppy disk in one of two ways:

1. *Using the Windows Explorer shortcut menu.* To format a disk using Windows Explorer, right-click the 3½ Floppy (A:) icon and select Format from the shortcut menu.
2. *Using the Format command in the Command Prompt window.* Open the Command Prompt window and then enter this command:

```
Format A:
```

(See Appendix B for additional detail on using the Command Prompt window).

Whether you use the Format command or Windows Explorer to do a full format of a floppy disk, the formatting process performs both low-level and high-level formatting of the floppy disk. The following are created during the formatting process for a floppy disk:

- Tracks and sectors, which are created by writing tracks and, as necessary, writing the sector address mark to identify the beginning sector on a track.
- The boot record.
- Two copies of the file allocation table (FAT). Because the width of each entry in the file allocation table is 12 bits, the FAT file system used with floppy disk is called a 12-bit FAT, or FAT12. The FAT lists how each cluster (or file allocation unit) on the disk is currently used and also marks damaged clusters as bad. An extra copy of the FAT immediately follows the first. If the first is damaged, you sometimes can recover your data and files by using the second copy.
- The root directory. After creating the file allocation tables, the formatting process sets up the root directory, or list of files and subdirectories, on the drive.

Figure 5-32 shows a formatted 3½-inch high-density floppy disk. There are 80 tracks, or circles, on the top side of the disk and 80 more tracks on the bottom. The tracks are numbered 0 through 79. Each side of the disk has 18 sectors, numbered 1 through 18. Although the circles, or tracks, on the outside of the disk are larger than the circles closer to the center, all tracks store the same amount of data. A floppy disk also uses

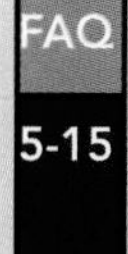
FAQ 5-15

How does a floppy disk ensure that the track widths remain constant?

Tunnel-erase heads on either side of the read/write head ensure that the widths of the data tracks do not vary. As the data is written, the erase heads immediately behind and to the sides of the write head clean both sides of the magnetized spot, making a clean track of data with no "bleeding" from the track. The magnetized area does not spread far from the track. All tracks are then the same width, and the distance between tracks is uniform.

clusters, with one sector per cluster as the smallest unit on a disk used to hold a file or a portion of a file. The OS keeps that list of clusters in the file allocation table.

Optical Storage Technology

CDs and DVDs are popular storage media for distributing software, music, movies, and other multimedia data. Both DVD and CD technologies are considered optical storage technologies because they use laser beams to read and write data. The surface of an optical disc stores data as pits and lands. **Lands** are raised areas and **pits** are recessed areas on the surface; each represents either a 1 or a 0, respectively. The bits are read with a laser beam that distinguishes between a pit and a land by the amount of deflection or scattering that occurs when the light beam hits the surface.

CD drives use the **CDFS (Compact Disc File System)** or the **UDF (Universal Disk Format) file system**, and DVD drives use UDF. Windows supports both file systems, which include several standards used for audio, photographs, video, and other data. In this section, you will learn about the major optical storage technologies, including their similarities and differences, their storage capacities, and variations within each type.

> **More About**
>
> **Installing and Supporting Floppy Drives**
>
> To learn more about installing and supporting floppy drives, visit the Understanding and Troubleshooting Your PC More About Web page (**scsite.com/understanding/more**) and then click Troubleshooting a Floppy Drive Installation below Chapter 5.

CD-ROM

As you have learned, a CD-ROM (compact disc read-only memory) drive uses a laser beam to read data from a CD-ROM, which is a type of optical disc that typically can store 650 MB of data, instructions, and information.

Data can be written to a CD-ROM disc only once, because the data actually is embedded in the surface of the disc. The CD stores data in a single track that spirals from the center of the disc to the edge of the disc. As with a hard disk, this single track is divided into evenly sized sectors in which data is stored (Figure 5-33).

Figure 5-33 The spiral layout of sectors on a CD-ROM surface. If laid out in a straight line, this spiral would be 3.5 miles long.

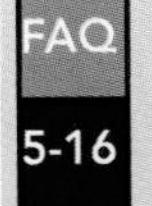

FAQ 5-16

What is the difference between a CD-ROM, a CD-R, and a CD-RW?

The major difference is the method used to read and write data on the disc. A CD-ROM drive only can read data; it cannot write data to a CD-ROM. CD-R (CD-recordable) drives allow you to write data to a recordable CD, but you can write data to the disc only once. A CD-RW (CD-rewritable) drive allows you to overwrite old data on a CD-RW disc with new data.

FAQ 5-17

Does data last longer on magnetic media or optical media?

The half-life (sometimes called the life expectancy or shelf life) of the disk is the time it takes for the magnetic strength of the medium to weaken by half. Magnetic media, including traditional hard drives and floppy disks, have a half-life of five to seven years, but writable optical media such as CD-Rs have a half-life of 30 years.

INSTALLING A CD-ROM DRIVE Once installed, the CD-ROM drive becomes another drive on your system, such as drive D or E. After it is installed, you access it just like any other drive. CD-ROM drives can interface with the motherboard in several ways:

- *Using an IDE interface.* The drive can share an IDE connection and cable with a hard drive. IDE is the most popular interface method for CD-ROM drives. These drives follow the ATAPI (Advanced Technology Attachment Packet Interface) standard, an extension of the IDE/ATA standard that allows tape drives, CD-ROM drives, and other drives to be treated just like another hard drive on the system.
- *Using a SCSI interface with a SCSI host adapter.*
- *As an external drive, by plugging into an external port*, such as a USB port, FireWire port, or SCSI port.

The most popular interface for a CD-ROM drive is IDE, although you will occasionally see a SCSI CD-ROM drive. Figure 5-34 shows the rear of an IDE CD-ROM drive, which has a jumper bank that can be set to cable select, slave, or master. As you have learned, IDE standards provide four choices for drive installations: primary master, primary slave, secondary master, and secondary slave. If the CD-ROM drive will be the second drive installed on the cable, then set the drive to slave. If the drive is the only drive on the cable, choose master. If the CD-ROM drive shares an IDE channel with a hard drive, make the hard drive the master and the CD-ROM drive the slave. The cable select setting is used if a cable-select cable determines which drive is master or slave.

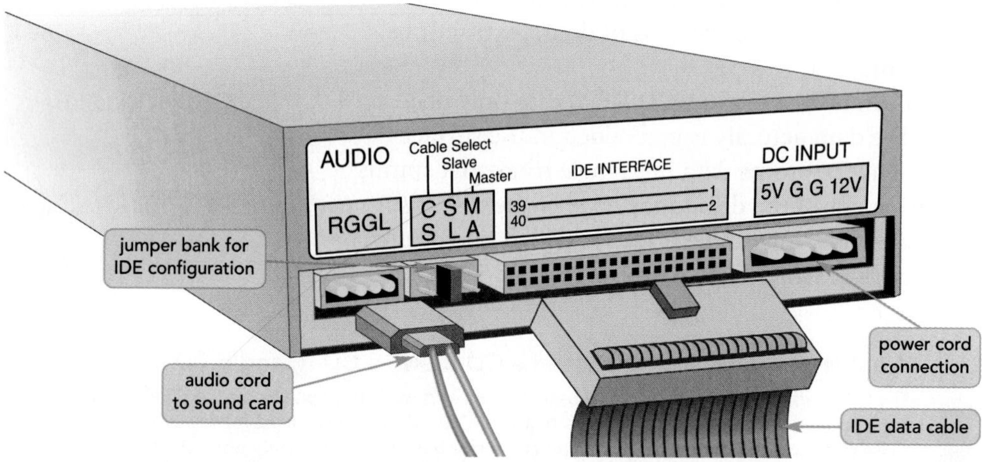

Figure 5-34 Rear view of an IDE CD-ROM drive.

When given the choice of putting the CD-ROM drive on the same cable with a hard drive or on its own cable, choose to use its own cable. A CD-ROM drive that shares a cable with a hard drive can slow down the hard drive's performance. Most systems today have two IDE connections on the motherboard, probably labeled IDE1 and IDE2; you most likely will be able to use IDE2 for the CD-ROM drive.

For ATA/100 hard drives and above, use an 80-conductor IDE cable for the hard drive on one channel and a regular 40-conductor cable for the CD-ROM drive on the other channel.

Follow these general steps to install a CD-ROM drive, using safety precautions to protect the system against ESD:

1. Open the case and slide the drive into an empty bay. If the bay uses rails, screw the rails in place. If you have no rails, then put two screws on each side of the drive, tightening the screws so the drive cannot shift, but avoiding overtightening them. Use the screws that come with the drive; screws that are too long can damage the drive. If necessary, buy a mounting kit to extend the sides of the drive so that it fits into the bay and attaches securely.
2. Connect a power cord to the drive.
3. For IDE drives, connect the 40-pin cable to the IDE motherboard connector and the drive, being careful to follow the pin 1 rule: match the edge color on the cable to pin 1 on both the adapter card and the drive. Generally, the colored edge is closest to the power connector.
4. Attach the audio cord if you have a sound card. Do not make the mistake of attaching a miniature power cord designed for a 3½-inch floppy disk drive to the audio input connector on the sound card. The connections appear to fit, but you probably will destroy the drive by making this connection.
5. Some drives have a ground connection, with one end of the ground cable attaching to the computer case. Follow the directions included with the drive.
6. Check all connections and turn on the power. Press the eject or open button on the front of the drive. If it works, then you know power is getting to the drive. Put the case cover back on.
7. Turn on the PC. If the drive is Plug and Play, Windows launches the Found New Hardware Wizard. Windows supports IDE CD-ROM drives using its own internal 32-bit drivers without add-on drivers, so the installation of drivers requires little intervention on your part. If the Found New Hardware Wizard does not launch, go to the Control Panel and launch the Add New Hardware Wizard. Click Next when you are prompted to begin installing the software for the new device. Complete the installation by following the directions of the Add New Hardware Wizard.
8. The drive is now ready to use. Press the eject button to open the drive shelf, and place a CD in the drive. You can access the CD using Windows Explorer.

If you have a problem reading the CD, verify that you placed the CD in the tray label-side-up and that the format is compatible with your drive. If one CD does not work, try another — the first CD may be defective or scratched.

CD-R and CD-RW

A CD-ROM is a read-only medium, meaning that CD-ROM drives only can read data, but cannot write data to a CD-ROM. In the past, writing to a CD required expensive equipment and was not practical for personal computer use. Now, **CD-R** (**CD-recordable**) drives that allow you to write data to a CD are much more affordable, which makes creating, or burning, your own CDs a viable option. CD-R discs can be read by regular CD-ROM drives and are an excellent way to distribute software or large amounts of data. Another advantage of distributing software and data on a CD-R disc is that no one can edit or overwrite the data written on the disc.

When you purchase and install a CD-R drive, having good software to manage the writing process is important, because some less robust software can make burning a disc difficult. A feature of many CD-R drives, called **multisession** recording, allows you to record data to the same CD-R in several different recording sessions. Multisession recording can help reduce the costs of buying media, because you can continue to add data to a CD-R until it is full, instead of having to use a new CD-R each time you want to record data. (This is extremely important if you want to use the CD-R drive to create backup CDs.)

A slightly more expensive optical drive — a **CD-RW** (**CD-rewritable**) drive — allows you to overwrite old data on a CD-RW disc with new data. The process of creating a CD-RW disc is similar to that used for CD-R discs. The chemicals on the surface of the CD-RW disc are different, allowing a less reflective spot to be written to the disc surface. This process can be reversed so that data can be erased. One drawback to CD-RW discs is that the medium cannot always be read successfully by older CD-ROM drives or by some audio CD players.

The steps to install a CD-R or CD-RW drive are similar to the steps for installing a CD-ROM, as outlined above.

DVD

A DVD (digital video disc or digital versatile disc) is an optical storage medium that can store up to 17 GB of data. DVDs quickly have gained in popularity as an inexpensive way to store huge amounts of digital data. For example, a full-length movie must be stored on up to seven CDs but takes only one DVD. As noted above, DVDs use the Universal Disk Format (UDF) file system to store data.

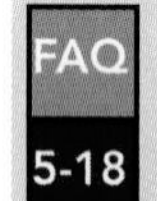

Does a DVD actually hold 17 GB?

When describing storage capacities, the computer industry uses measures where 1 KB = 1,024 bytes. Given that, 1 GB actually is 1,073,741,824 bytes, not one billion bytes (1,000,000,000 bytes). So, although a DVD is defined as holding 17 GB of data, it actually holds 17 billion bytes, which is only 15.9 GB.

When you look at the surface of a CD and a DVD, it is difficult to distinguish between the two. They both have the same 5-inch diameter and 1.2-mm thickness, and the same shiny surface. A DVD can use both the top and bottom surface for data, however. If the top of the disc has no label, data probably is written on it, and it is most likely a DVD.

Because DVD uses a shorter wavelength laser, it can read smaller, more densely packed pits, which increases the disc's capacity. In addition, a second opaque layer is added to DVD that also holds data and almost doubles the capacity of the disc. (One layer on one side of a DVD can hold 4.7 GB of data. If two layers are used, one side can hold 8.5 GB of data.) If both the top and bottom surfaces are used, it can hold 17 GB of data, which is enough for more than eight hours of video storage.

New DVD technologies continually are being introduced. An up-and-coming variation of DVD is **HD-DVD** (**high-density** or **high-definition DVD**), which supports high-definition video encoding using a blue or violet laser. The laser uses smaller pits than normal DVD, thus increasing the capacity of the disc to 30 GB per layer. Regular DVD drives will not read HD-DVD discs, but HD-DVD drives are expected to be backward compatible with older DVD discs.

Besides DVD-ROM, new DVD devices that are read-writable recently have come on the market, as listed in Figure 5-35. Combination drives, such as combination CD and DVD drives and combination DVD+R/W and DVD-R/W drives, are becoming popular as the prices of optical drives continue to drop.

DVD Device	Description
DVD-ROM	Read-only device. A DVD-ROM drive also can read CD-ROMs.
DVD-R	DVD recordable. Uses a similar technology to CD-R drives. Can read DVD-ROM discs.
DVD-RAM	Recordable and erasable. Multifunctional DVD device that can read DVD-RAM, DVD-R, DVD-ROM, and CD-R discs.
DVD-R/W or DVD-ER	Rewritable DVD device, also known as erasable, recordable device. Media can be read by most DVD-ROM drives.
DVD+R/W	A technology similar to and currently competing with DVD-RW. Can read DVD-ROM and CD-ROM discs but is not compatible with DVD-RAM discs.

Figure 5-35 DVD devices. The last three devices all are relatively new and have similar but not identical features. When purchasing one of these devices, pay close attention to compatibility with other media, such as CD-ROMs, and availability and price of discs.

Troubleshooting Optical Storage Drives and Media

One common problem that occurs after installing a new CD-ROM, CD-RW, DVD-ROM, or DVD-RW drive is that the computer does not recognize the drive (for example, no drive D is listed in Windows Explorer). To troubleshoot this issue, ask yourself the following questions:

- Looking at the data cable and power cord connections to the drive, is the stripe on the data cable correctly aligned to pin 1? (Look for an arrow or small 1 printed on the drive. For a best guess, pin 1 is usually next to the power connector.)
- For IDE drives, is the correct master/slave jumper set? For example, if both the hard drive and the CD-ROM or DVD drive are hooked to the same ribbon cable, one must be set to master and the other to slave. If the CD-ROM or DVD drive is the only drive connected to the cable, then it should be set to single or master.
- For an EIDE drive, is the IDE connection on the motherboard disabled in CMOS setup?
- If you are using a SCSI drive, are the proper IDs set? Is the device terminated if it is the last item in the SCSI chain? Are the correct SCSI drivers installed?
- Is another device using the same port settings? Check system resources listed in Device Manager. Is there an IRQ conflict with the IDE primary or secondary channel or the SCSI host that the drive is using?

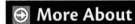

More About

Installing a DVD Drive

Installing a DVD drive is more complicated than installing a CD-ROM drive, because of the need for a decoder to convert video and sound data. To learn more about installing a DVD drive, visit the Understanding and Troubleshooting Your PC More About Web page (**scsite.com/understanding/more**) and then click Installing a DVD Drive below Chapter 5.

Most problems with CD-ROMs, DVD-ROMs, and other optical storage media are caused by dust, fingerprints, scratches, surface defects, or random electrical noise. Figure 5-36 lists several precautions to take when handling optical storage media.

- Hold the disc by the edge; do not touch the bright side of the disc where data is stored.
- Store the disc in a jewel box or other case when not in use.
- To remove dust or fingerprints, use a clean, soft, dry cloth. Do not use cleaners on the disc.
- Do not write or paste paper on the surface of the disc. Do not paste any labels on the top of the disc, because this can imbalance the disc and cause the drive to vibrate.
- Do not subject the disc to excessive heat or leave it in direct sunlight.
- Do not make the center hole larger.
- Do not bend the disc, drop the disc, or subject it to shock.
- If a disc gets stuck in the drive, use the emergency eject hole to remove it. Turn off the power to the PC first. Then insert an instrument such as a straightened paper clip into the hole to eject the tray manually.
- When closing a disc tray, do not push on the tray. Press the close button on the front of the drive.
- Do not use a drive if it is standing vertically, such as when someone turns a desktop PC case on its side to save desk space.

Figure 5-36 Guidelines for the proper care of CD-ROMs, DVD-ROMS, and other optical storage media.

External and Removable Storage

Other types of storage include external hard drives, removable hard drives, and flash memory. An **external hard disk** is a separate, stand-alone hard disk drive that connects to the computer via a cable and a USB, FireWire, or other port. As with an internal hard drive, the entire drive is enclosed in a sealed case that protects the disk. External hard disks generally have capacities of up to 250 GB or higher.

A **removable hard disk**, also called a **disk cartridge**, is a hard disk that you insert and remove from a hard disk drive. A Zip drive, for example, is a widely used type of removable hard disk. As you learned in Chapter 1, a Zip drive is a device that reads from and writes to a removable magnetic medium called a Zip disk. A removable hard disk drive can be installed in a bay inside the computer or it can be an external drive connected via a cable to a USB, FireWire, or other port. This type of disk drive operates much like a floppy drive, reading data from and writing data to the removable hard disk.

As you learned in Chapter 1, flash ROM, which is nonvolatile and holds data even when the power is turned off, is used to store BIOS. Flash ROM, also called **flash memory** or **flash storage**, also is used to store data in small, removable flash memory cards. Flash memory increasingly is popular for use in small storage devices such as the Jump Drive shown in Figure 5-37, as well as media used in digital cameras, MP3 players, and more. One of the main advantages of flash memory is that it is solid-state, which means it has no moving parts. Because flash memory is entirely electronic, rather than mechanical like a hard drive, it is smaller in size, noiseless, and less susceptible to failure. Flash memory does, however, cost more per megabyte than a hard drive. Many different brands and types of flash memory card, and devices are available on the market, including the Jump Drive, CompactFlash, CompactFlash II, SmartMedia, ScanDisk, and Sony Memory Sticks.

More About

Installing an External Hard Drive

To learn more about installing an external hard drive, visit the Understanding and Troubleshooting Your PC More About Web page (**scsite.com/understanding/more**) and then click Installing an External Hard Drive below Chapter 5.

Figure 5-37 shows examples of several external hard drives, removable hard drives, and flash memory. Using one of these types of storage provides several advantages:

- Increases the overall storage capacity of a system
- Makes it easy to move large files from one computer to another
- Serves as a convenient medium for making backups of hard drive data
- Makes it easy to secure important files by keeping the storage device and media locked in a safe when not being used

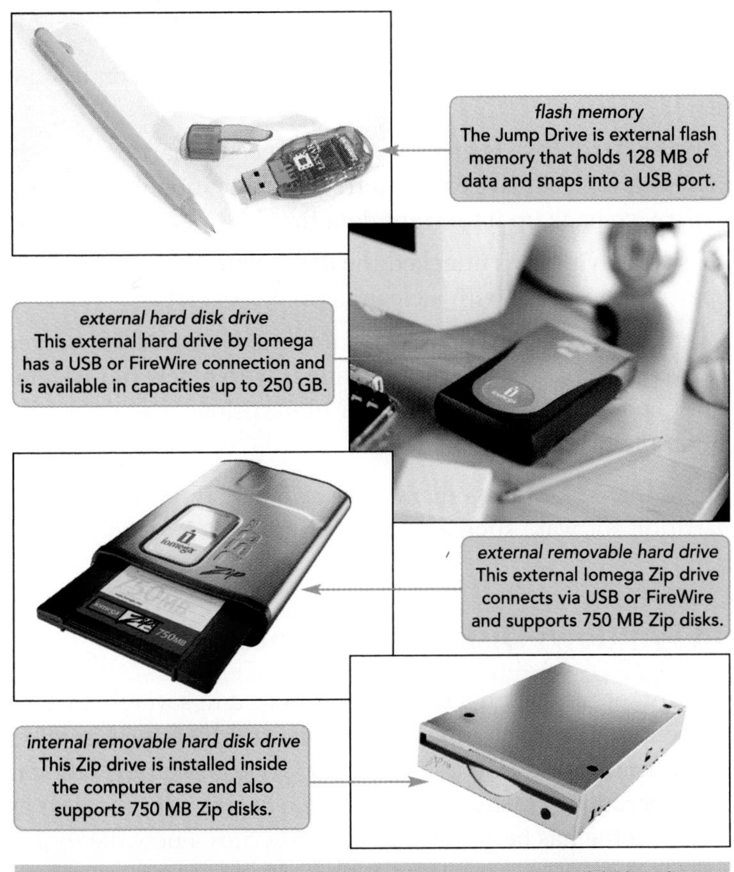

flash memory
The Jump Drive is external flash memory that holds 128 MB of data and snaps into a USB port.
external hard disk drive
This external hard drive by Iomega has a USB or FireWire connection and is available in capacities up to 250 GB.
external removable hard drive
This external Iomega Zip drive connects via USB or FireWire and supports 750 MB Zip disks.
internal removable hard disk drive
This Zip drive is installed inside the computer case and also supports 750 MB Zip disks.

Figure 5-37 Examples of external hard drives, removable hard drives, and flash memory.

Quiz Yourself 5-2

To test your knowledge of floppy drives, optical storage technologies, and external and removable hard disk drives, visit the Understanding and Troubleshooting Your PC Quiz Yourself Web page (scsite.com/understanding/quiz). Click Quiz Yourself 2 below Chapter 5.

Managing Hard Drives

The hard drive is the most important secondary storage device in your computer. In this section, you learn about Windows utilities that protect, optimize, and maintain hard drives. You can access some of these utilities from a command prompt and some from the Windows desktop.

Partitioning a Hard Drive

There are several reasons to partition or repartition a drive:

- When you first install a new hard drive, you must partition it to prepare it for use.
- If an existing hard drive is giving errors, you can repartition the drive and reformat each logical drive to begin fresh. Repartitioning destroys all data on the drive, so back up important data first.
- If you suspect a virus has attacked the drive, you can back up critical data and repartition to begin with a clean drive.
- If you want to wipe a hard drive clean and install a new OS, you can repartition a drive in preparation for formatting it with a new file system. If you do not want to change the size or number of partitions, you do not have to repartition the drive.

In addition to the Disk Management tools available in Windows, you also can use third-party partition software such as Norton Utilities or Partition Magic to partition a hard drive.

Defrag and Windows Disk Defragmenter

Fragmentation occurs when a single file is placed in several cluster locations that are not directly next to each other. When a hard drive is new and freshly formatted, the OS (operating system) writes files to the drive beginning with cluster 2, placing the data in consecutive clusters. Each new file begins with the next available cluster. Later, after a file has been deleted, the OS writes a new file to the drive, beginning with the first available cluster. If the OS encounters used clusters as it writes the file, it simply skips these clusters and uses the next available one. In this way, after many files have been deleted and added to the drive, files become fragmented. On a well-used hard drive, it is possible to have a file stored in clusters at 40 or more locations. Fragmentation is undesirable: when the OS has to access many different locations on the drive to read a file, access time slows down. Further, if the file becomes corrupted, recovering a fragmented file is more complicated than recovering a file from contiguous clusters.

For these reasons, you should **defragment** the hard drive periodically. To do this, you can run the Defrag command from a command prompt or use the graphical Disk Defragmenter utility. When using the Disk Defragmenter utility, you can click an Analyze button to instruct Windows to scan the drive to determine how fragmented it is. When the analysis is complete, you can print a copy of the report or save it as a file. Regardless of the method used, you should defragment your hard drive every six months or so as part of a good maintenance plan.

Disk Cleanup

Disk Cleanup is a Windows utility used to delete temporary and other nonessential files on a hard drive, freeing up space and often improving performance. After reviewing the hard drive for nonessential files to delete, Disk Cleanup allows you to select which types of files to delete in order to save drive space (Figure 5-38). The types of files that can be deleted include files temporarily downloaded to speed Web browsing, deleted files currently stored in the Recycle Bin, program setup files no longer needed, and others. The Disk Cleanup window tells you how much space each type of file is using and the total space you can save on the hard disk by deleting those files. You can select each type of file you wish to delete and then click the OK button to delete the files from the hard disk.

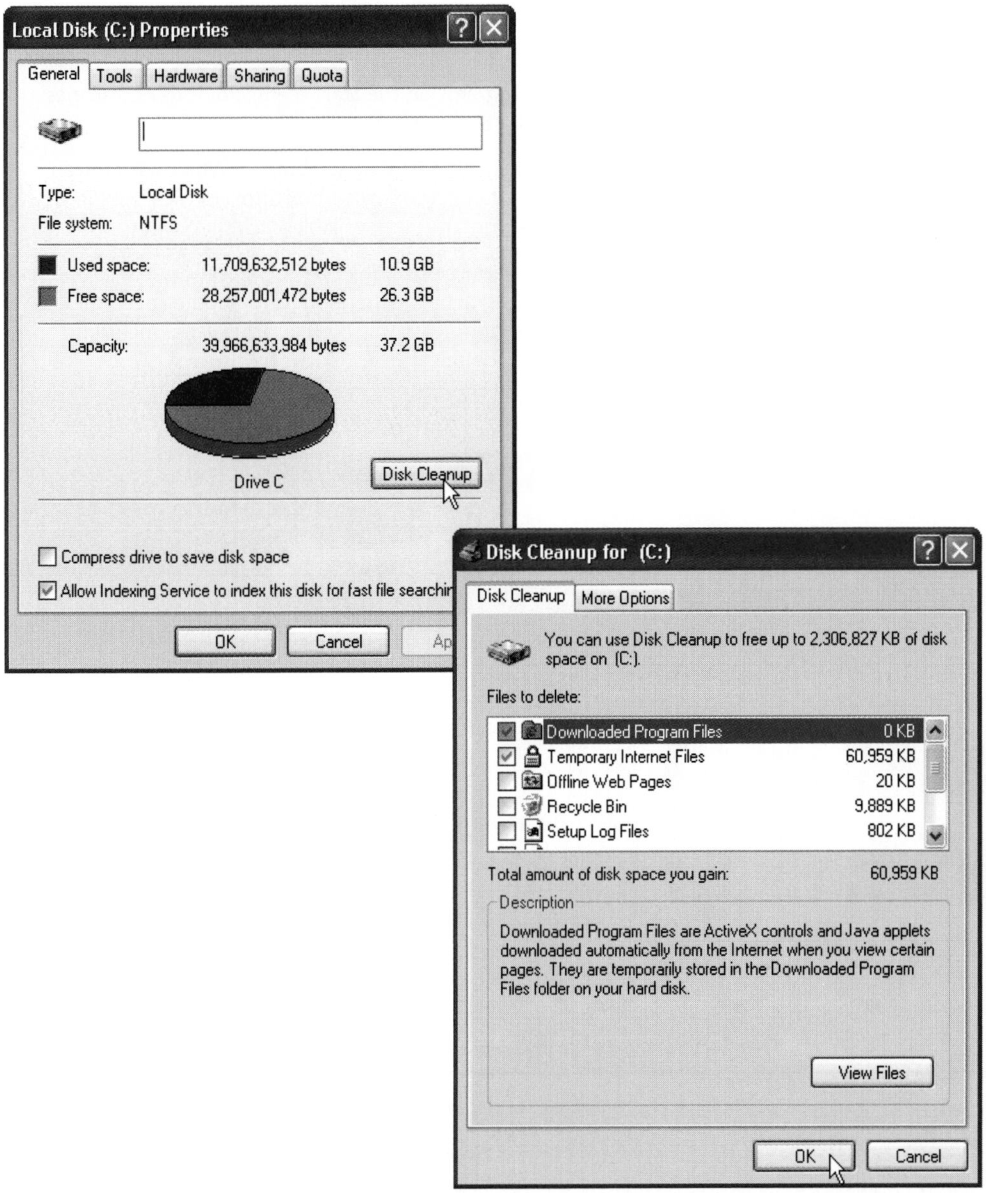

Figure 5-38 The Disk Properties window provides Disk Cleanup, a quick and easy way to delete temporary files on a hard drive.

Your Turn

Using Disk Cleanup and Disk Defragmenter

Running Disk Cleanup and Disk Defragmenter can help optimize the space on your hard drive. Perform the following steps to run these Windows utilities:

1. Open My Computer. In the My Computer window, right-click drive C and then click Properties on the shortcut menu. When the Disk Properties window is displayed, click the General tab and then click the Disk Cleanup button.
2. Disk Cleanup will calculate how many files you can delete to save space, a process that can take a few minutes. Write down the types of files to delete the amount of disk space you will save by deleting them.
3. If necessary, click Temporary Internet files to select it; as needed, click other items in the list to deselect them. Click the OK button and then click the Yes button to confirm the deletion.
4. To use Windows XP Disk Defragmenter, first close all open applications.
5. Click the Start button on the Windows taskbar and then point to All Programs on the Start menu. Point to Accessories on the All Programs submenu, point to System Tools, and then click Disk Defragmenter.
6. When the Disk Defragmenter window is displayed, select drive C and then click the Analyze button. Windows will scan your drive to determine how fragmented the drive is. When the Disk Defragmenter dialog box displays, click the View Report button. Click the Print button to print a copy of the report (if a printer is not available, click the Save As button and save the report as Ch05VolumeC.txt). Click the Close button in the Disk Defragmenter dialog box.
7. Defragmenting a large hard drive may take several hours, so plan to defragment the drive when you do not need the computer for that time (the best time to defragment may be overnight). If time is available, click the Defragment button in the Disk Defragmenter window to defragment the drive. As the utility defragments the drive, it displays its progress in the Disk Defragmenter window (Figure 5-39).

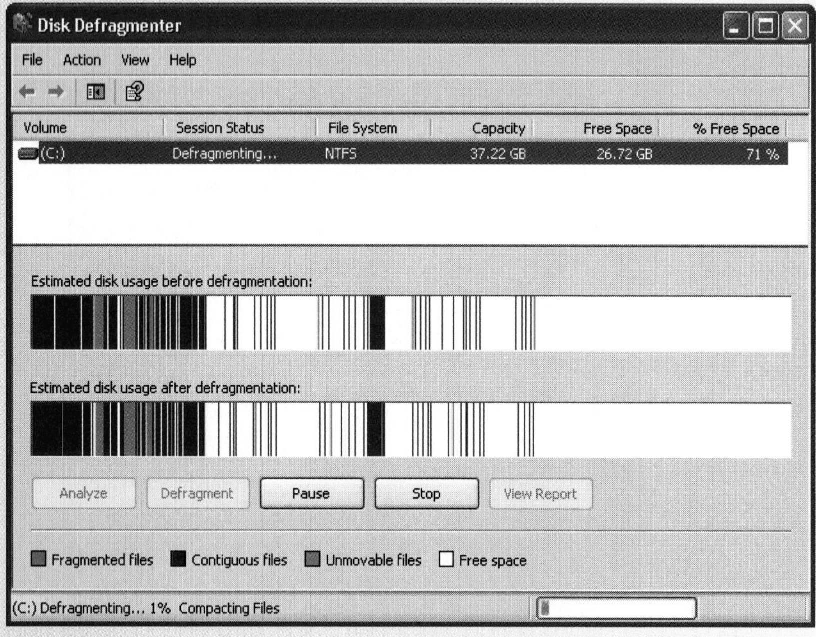

Figure 5-39

Disk Caching

A **disk cache** is a temporary storage area in RAM for data being read from or written to a hard drive, and is used to speed up access time to the drive. The process of disk caching works like this:

1. The CPU asks for data from a hard drive.
2. The hard drive controller sends instructions to the drive to read the data and then sends the data to the CPU.
3. The CPU requests more data, quite often data that immediately follows the previously read data on the hard drive.
4. The controller reads the requested data from the drive and sends it to the CPU. Without a cache, each CPU request requires that data be read from the hard drive, as indicated in the top part of Figure 5-40.

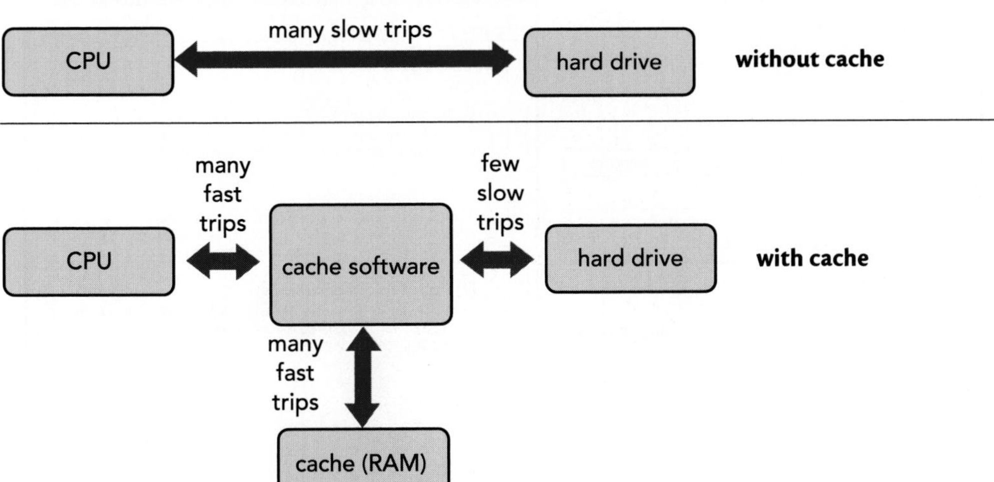

Figure 5-40 A CPU asking a hard drive for data without cache (top) and with cache (bottom).

With a hard drive cache, the cache software handles the requests for data, as shown in the lower part of Figure 5-40. The cache program reads ahead of the CPU requests by guessing what data the CPU will request next. Because most data that the CPU requests is in consecutive areas on the drive, the cache program guesses correctly most of the time. The program stores the read-ahead data in memory (RAM). When the CPU requests the next set of data, if the cache program guessed right, the program can send that data to the CPU from memory without having to go back to the hard drive. Some cache software caches entire tracks at a time; other software caches groups of sectors.

Windows XP relies on software cache to provide caching. A **software cache** is a cache program stored on the hard drive like other software and usually is loaded into memory when a computer is booted. The software cache program uses system RAM to hold the cache. To verify that disk caching is enabled for Windows XP, open My Computer, right-click drive C, and then click Properties on the shortcut menu. When the Properties window is displayed, click the Hardware tab, click the disk drive

More About

Hard Disk Management

To learn more about managing a hard disk using Windows utilities and tools, visit the Understanding and Troubleshooting Your PC More About Web page (**scsite.com/understanding/more**) and then click Hard Disk Management below Chapter 5.

that represents your hard drive, and then click the Properties button (Figure 5-41a). In the drive's Properties window, click the Policies tab and verify that Enable write caching on the disk is checked (Figure 5-41b).

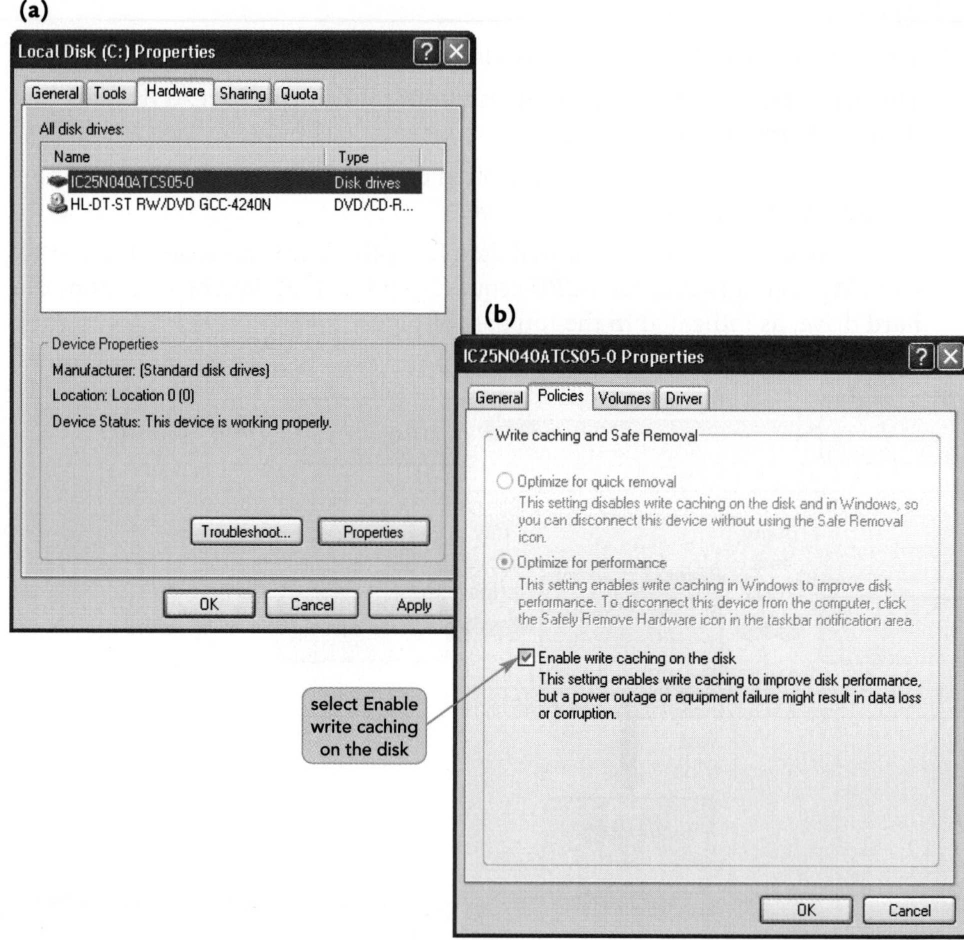

Figure 5-41 Enabling disk caching can help improve hard disk performance.

Making Backups

As you have learned, a backup is an extra copy of a data or software file that you can use if the original file becomes damaged or destroyed. Losing data due to system failure, a virus, file corruption, or some other problem really makes you appreciate the importance of having backups. With data and software, a good rule of thumb is that, if you cannot get along without a file or data, back it up. Windows offers several types of backup tools, which are covered in detail in Chapter 12.

Troubleshooting Hard Drives

An important aspect of computer maintenance is learning how to troubleshoot your hard drive. In this section, you will learn about error messages, tools that you can use to troubleshoot and maintain your hard drive, how to solve common hard drive problems, and some general troubleshooting guidelines.

An Ounce of Prevention

Taking good care of your hard drive is not difficult, but it does require a little time. Some simple precautions can help protect your data and software, as well as the drive itself, and reduce the possibility of future problems.

- *Be gentle with a hard drive.* Do not bump the PC or move it when the drive is spinning.
- *High humidity can be dangerous for hard drives.* If possible, keep your computer in a place with relatively normal to low humidity.
- *Do not smoke around your hard drive.* Although sealed, hard drives are not airtight. To a very sensitive read/write head, a particle of smoke on a hard drive platter can seem as large as a 10-foot boulder. One study showed that smoking near a computer reduced the average life span of a hard drive by 25 percent.
- *Do not leave the PC turned off for weeks or months at a time.* Long spans of inactivity can cause problems on a hard drive (for example, the corruption of the Master Boot Record).
- *Defragment files and scan the hard drive occasionally.* A fragmented hard drive increases access time, and reading and writing files wears out the drive. If you are trying to salvage a damaged file, it is much more difficult to recover a fragmented file than one stored in contiguous clusters.
- *Run antivirus software regularly.* If you lose software or data on your hard drive, the source of the problem most likely is a virus. Your best defense against data and software corruption is to install and run antivirus software. Keep the software current because new viruses are constantly appearing. Chapter 12 provides detail on protecting your computer against viruses.
- *Make backups and keep them current.* As you will learn in Chapter 12, you should keep backups to use if the original data is damaged or deleted. Keep data files in directories separate from the software, to make backing up data easier. Rotate the backup disks or tapes by keeping the last two or three most recent backups.
- *Back up the partition table and boot record.* The partition table and boot record easily are backed up to disk; they do not change unless the drive is repartitioned or reformatted. Always back them up as soon as you can after you buy a new computer or become responsible for a working one. A utility software program such as Norton Utilities provides tools to help you make a backup of the partition table and boot record.

Resolving Common Hard Drive Problems

Although the hard drive itself is a hardware component, problems with hard drives can be caused by software as well. Hardware problems usually show up during POST, unless there is physical damage to an area of the hard drive that is not accessed during POST. Hardware problems often make the hard drive completely inaccessible.

Software problems also can be the root cause of a hard drive problem. For a hard drive and its data to be accessible by DOS or Windows, the following items, listed in the order they are accessed, must be intact: the partition table, the boot record, the FAT or MFT, the root directory, the system files, and data and program files. If any of these items are corrupted, it can make the hard disk inaccessible. In this section, you will learn about hardware and software problems with hard drives.

Drive Retrieves and Saves Data Slowly If the drive retrieves and saves data slowly, run Disk Defragmenter to rewrite fragmented files to contiguous sectors. Slow data retrieval might be caused by fragmented files that have been updated, modified, and spread over different portions of the disk.

Hard Drive Not Spinning Sometimes older drives refuse to spin at POST. Drives that have trouble spinning often whine at startup for several months before they finally refuse to spin altogether. If your drive whines loudly when you first turn on the computer, do not turn off the computer. Leaving the computer off for an extended period of time may make it impossible to start the hard drive the next time you turn on the computer. Do not trust valuable data to a drive that has this kind of trouble. Plan to replace the drive soon. In the meantime, make frequent backups and leave the power on.

As you learned earlier in the chapter, if a read/write head bumps against the platter it can cause a hard drive crash that renders the drive unusable. If the head mechanism is damaged, the drive and its data are probably total losses. However, if the first tracks that contain the partition table, boot record, FAT, or root directory are damaged, the drive might be inaccessible, but the data could be unharmed. To determine this, find a computer with a working hard drive that has the same partition table information as the bad drive. Remove the cover of the computer, place the good drive on top of the bad drive housing, and connect a spare power cord and the IDE data cable to the good drive. (Leave a power cord connected to the bad drive as well). Boot from a floppy disk and access the good drive by entering C: at the A prompt. The C prompt should appear on the monitor.

Without turning off the power, gently remove the data cable from the good drive and connect it to the bad drive. Do not disturb the power cords on either drive or touch chips on the drive logic boards. Immediately copy the data you need from the bad drive to floppy disks using the Copy command in the command prompt window.

Hard Drive Not Found If your system BIOS cannot find your drive and the system displays an error message such as `Hard drive not found`, the reason is most likely a loose cable or adapter card. To troubleshoot this issue, check the following items:

- Boot the computer and look for numeric error codes displayed during POST. Errors in the 1700s or 10400s generally mean fixed disk problems. Check Appendix A or the Web site of the BIOS manufacturer for explanations of these numeric codes.
- Check CMOS setup for errors in the hard drive configuration.

If these steps do not resolve the problem, check the setup inside the computer case, using the following steps:

1. Turn off the computer and monitor before you do anything inside the case.
2. Remove and reattach all drive cables. Check for correct pin 1 orientation.
3. Check the jumper or DIP switch settings on the drive.
4. Inspect the drive for damage such as bent pins on the connection for the cable.
5. Determine if the hard drive is spinning by listening to it or lightly touching the metal drive (with power on).
6. Check the cable for frayed edges or other damage.
7. Check the installation manual for things you might have overlooked. Look for a section about system setup, and carefully follow all directions that apply.
8. Be sure the power cable and disk data cable connections are good.

If the drive still does not boot, try replacing the drive data cable. If the hard drive refuses to work but its light stays on even after the system has fully booted, the problem might be a faulty controller on the hard drive or motherboard. Try replacing the hard drive and then the motherboard.

Invalid Drive or Drive Specification If you get the error message, `Invalid drive or drive specification`, when starting the computer, it indicates that the system BIOS cannot read the partition table information. When the partition table is damaged, BIOS tries to load the OS, first reading the Master Boot Record at the beginning of the partition table information on the hard drive. If the partition table is damaged, BIOS then displays an error message.

The first step is to try to restore the Master Boot Record at the beginning of the partition table. For Windows XP, restoring the Master Boot record involves the following steps:

- Insert the Windows setup CD-ROM and boot the computer. If prompted, select any options required to boot from the CD-ROM.
- Follow the prompts on the Setup screens and then press the R key to choose the repair or recover option and start the Windows Recovery Console.
- If you have a dual-boot or multiple-boot system, choose the installation that you need to access from the Recovery Console. If necessary, type the Administrator password. If the administrator password does not exist, just press the ENTER key.
- At the system prompt, type `Fixmbr` as the command. (For a list of commands, type `help` or type `help commandname` for help on a specific command).
- To exit the Recovery Console and restart the computer, type `exit` as the command.

As you perform these steps, be aware that using the Fixmbr command does have risks. A virus often is the cause of a corrupt or damaged partition table or MBR. Some viruses detect when the MBR is altered or when an attempt is made to repair or alter it — and then do further damage. If you have important data on the drive that is not backed up, try to recover the data before using the Fixmbr command.

If this does not work, you can repartition the drive, but you will lose all data on the drive. If the data is important and is not backed up, try third-party data recovery software to recover the drive and its data before repartitioning. You also can send the hard drive to a third-party service firm that can recover the data from the hard drive.

Restoring the partition table is impossible if the track is damaged physically. The partition table is written on the very first sector of the hard drive. If this first sector is accessible, you can create a primary partition that covers the damaged area, which you will never use. Next, create an extended partition for the remainder of the drive. You will not be able to use this hard drive as your boot device, but it can be used as a secondary hard drive.

Damaged Boot Record If the OS boot record on a hard drive is damaged, you cannot boot from the hard drive. After you boot from a floppy disk and try to access the hard drive, you might get one of these error messages:

```
Invalid media type
Non-DOS disk
Unable to read from Drive C
```

If the OS boot record is damaged and you have a backup copy, you can recover the boot record from that copy. If you do not have a backup, try to repair the boot record using data recovery software such as Norton Disk Doctor, GetDataBack, or SpinRite. If that does not work, you may have to reformat the volume.

Damaged FAT or Root Directory or Bad Sectors Unlike the partition table and the boot record, the FAT and the root directory change often and are more difficult to back up. The success of Windows or third-party utilities in repairing a damaged FAT or root directory depends on the degree of damage to the tables. If these tables are damaged, you may receive this error message:

```
Sector not found reading drive C, Abort, Retry, Ignore, Fail?
Bad Sector
Sector not found
```

First, try using Windows Error-checking tools to repair the damage.

To check the system for and repair file system errors and bad sectors, complete the following steps:

1. Close all open files and programs.
2. Double-click My Computer on the Windows desktop.
3. When the My Computer window is displayed, right-click drive C and then click Properties on the shortcut menu.
4. When the Disk Properties window is displayed, click the Tools tab.
5. Click the Check Now button in the Error-checking area.
6. When the Check Disk window is displayed, check Automatically fix file system errors and Scan for and attempt recovery of bad sectors.
7. Click the Start button. If Windows displays an error message indicating it needs exclusive access to files on the computer and asking if you want to perform the check the next time you restart the computer, click Yes.
8. Close the Properties and My Computer windows. Shut down the computer by clicking the Start button on the taskbar and then clicking Turn Off Computer (Shut Down).

If that does not work and the drive is storing important data that is not backed up, try using the Copy command from a command prompt to copy these files to another medium (if you encounter the error, type `i` to ignore the bad sector and continue copying). Next, try using third-party recovery software, such as Norton Disk Doctor, which might be able to repair the FAT or root directory. If none of these steps work, you may have to reformat the drive.

Data and Program File Corruption Data and program files can become corrupted for many reasons, ranging from power spikes to user error. If the corrupted file is a program file, the simplest solution might be to reinstall the software or recover the file from a previous backup.

To restore a data file that is not backed up, you have three options:

- Use operating system tools and commands to recover the file.
- Use third-party software such as Norton Utilities or SpinRite to recover the file.
- If neither of these approaches works, you can turn to a professional data recovery service. These services can be expensive, but, depending on how valuable the data is, the cost might be justified.

How successfully an OS recovers data depends on how badly damaged the file is. When a data file or program file is damaged, portions of the file still may be intact. Figure 5-42 lists a few examples of how data commonly becomes damaged or erased and what can be done to recover it. Remember that, if a file has been erased accidentally or the disk or hard drive is otherwise damaged, remember not to write anything to the disk or hard drive, because you might overwrite data that you could otherwise recover.

Issue	Description	Resolution
Corrupted file header	If an application cannot open or read one of its data files, the file header might be corrupted. Many applications place a file header at the beginning of the file. The application uses the file header to identify the file and its contents.	You can sometimes recover the contents by treating the file as an ASCII text file. In Windows Explorer, change the file extension to .txt and then import the data into the application. Read your application's documentation to learn how to import a text file (you will lose any formatting).
Lost cluster	A disk can develop lost clusters if a program cannot properly close a file it has opened.	Use Windows Error-checking tools or the Chkdsk command to repair lost clusters.
Erased file	If you accidentally delete a file, the file sometimes can be recovered.	Look for the file in the Recycle Bin. If it is not there, try using the Unerase or Undelete command at a command prompt, which recovers some erased files.
Virus infection	Viruses cause many file system problems, including corrupting system files, program files, or data files.	Run a current version of antivirus software. The software probably will not help recover the file but might prevent other files from becoming infected.
Corrupted data on floppy disk	If your system cannot read data on a floppy disk, the floppy disk might be damaged or the data might be corrupted.	Use Copy Disk in Windows Explorer to make a copy of the disk. If this does not work, try copying the disk with a third-party program such as Norton Utilities.

Figure 5-42 Steps to resolve common issues with corrupt program or data files.

Getting Technical Support

Sometimes you may not be able to solve a hard drive problem on your own. The first step toward getting more help is to check the Web site of the hard drive manufacturer (Figure 5-43). Most of these Web sites have a support section where you can search for information on how to resolve problems with your hard drive.

If you do not find the answer you need and still need more help, you might need to call technical support. To make calls to technical support more effective, be sure to have the following information ready when you call:

- Drive model and description
- Manufacturer and model of your computer
- Exact wording of error message, if any
- Detailed description of the problem
- Hardware and software configuration for your system

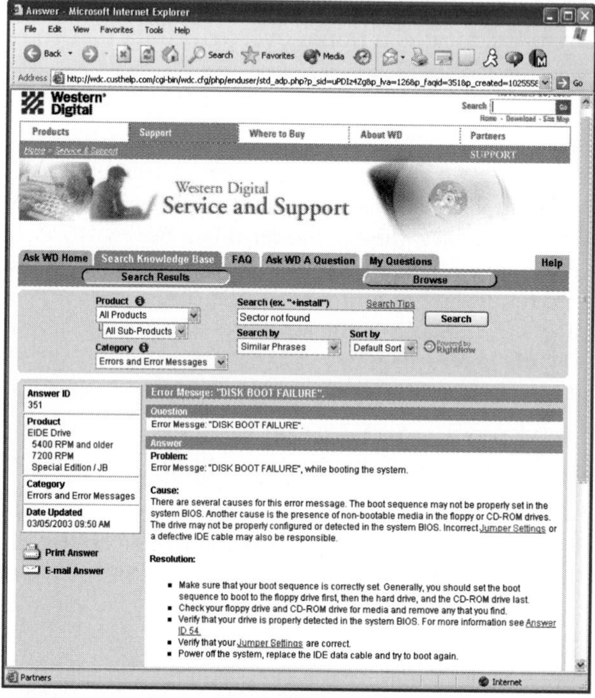

Figure 5-43 Most hard drive manufacturer Web sites will have a support section where you can search for support information.

Before calling, check the manufacturer's Web site to determine if there are charges for calling technical support. As you speak with technical support, ask if there are local service partners where you can take your computer for service.

Quiz Yourself 5-3

To test your knowledge of how to manage and troubleshoot your hard drive, visit the Understanding and Troubleshooting Your PC Quiz Yourself Web page (scsite.com/understanding/quiz). Click Quiz Yourself 3 below Chapter 5.

High-Tech Talk

Backing Up Data: Better Safe than Sorry

The time to prepare for disaster is before it occurs. If you have not prepared, the damage from a hard drive crash, virus, or other event that damages your hard drive may cause you to lose years worth of work. Suppose the hard drive on your PC stopped working today and you lost all of the data on your hard drive. What would be the impact? Are you prepared for this event?

A *backup* is an extra copy of a data or software file that you can use if the original file becomes damaged or destroyed. Losing data due to system failure, a virus, file corruption, or some other problem really makes you appreciate the importance of having backups. Chapter 12 will provide additional detail about the hardware and software needed to make backups of data and software from a hard drive. In general, a good rule of thumb for your data and software is — if you cannot get along without it, back it up.

You can use sophisticated methods to create backups in which the backup process is selective, only backing up files that have changed, files that have not been backed up recently, and so forth. Traditionally, these methods all involve backing up to tapes, because a tape is most likely to be large enough to contain an entire backup of a hard drive, and they are inexpensive. If you do not have a tape drive, you can backup to a DVD±RW, CD±RW, CD-R, or even an external or removable hard drive.

Some backup methods are more efficient because they do not always create a complete backup of all data. A *full backup* backs up all data from the hard drive or an area of the hard drive. An *incremental backup* backs up only files that have changed or been created since the last backup, whether that backup is itself an incremental or full backup. *Differential backups* back up files that have changed or been created since the last full backup.

A basic backup plan might begin by performing a full backup on a Friday. Then, the next time you back up (Monday), you will use the incremental method to back up only files that have changed or been created since the full backup. The second time you perform an incremental backup, you back up only the files that have changed or been created since the last incremental backup (Tuesday through Thursday). Then, on Friday, you again perform a full backup. Alternatively, you can run differential backups Monday through Thursday and then again perform a full backup on Friday.

Backups can be performed manually or can be scheduled to run automatically. A scheduled backup is performed automatically by software when the computer is not commonly in use, such as during the middle of the night. With Windows XP, you can schedule a backup using the Backup utility available in the System Tools shown in Figure 5-44 (you will learn specifics on using this utility in Chapter 12).

Backups are important, but you also should know how to use them to recover lost data. To recover files, folders, or the entire drive from backup using the Windows XP Backup utility, click the Restore and Manage Media tab on the Backup Utility window and then select the backup job to use for the restore process. The Backup Utility window displays the folders and files that were backed up with this job and allows you to select the ones you want to restore.

Backing up your hard drive is one of the most important preventive maintenance tasks you can perform on your computer. Despite its importance, backup plans often are overlooked by computer users — until they have a hard drive problem that causes them to lose important data. Taking the time to backup your data can help ensure you never have to learn that lesson about your hard drive the hard way.

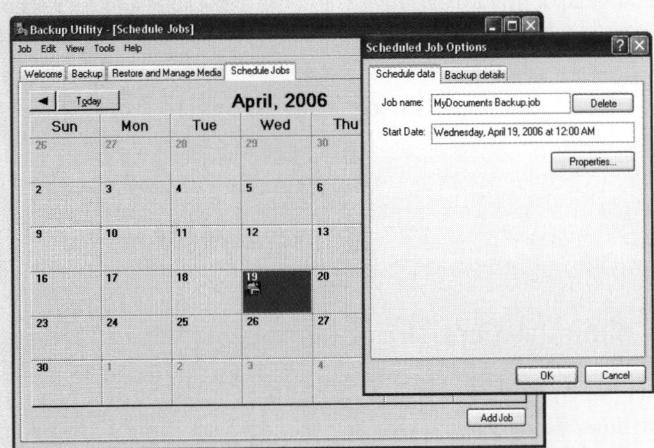

Figure 5-44

CHAPTER SUMMARY

The Chapter Summary reviews the concepts presented in this chapter.

1 How Hard Drives Work and Organize Data

A hard drive, also called a hard disk drive (HDD), stores data magnetically and is a read/write storage medium. Hard drives have platters; each side of the platter is divided into tracks, cylinders, and sectors to identify where data is stored. A hard drive requires a hard disk controller, a special-purpose chip that allows the CPU to communicate with a hard drive. Formatting defines how files will be organized on the disk. Formatting a hard disk involves low-level formatting, partitioning, and high-level formatting. High-level formatting creates a file system, boot record, a root directory, and two copies of the FAT or MFT for each logical drive. File systems used by Windows include FAT12, FAT16, FAT32, and NTFS.

2 Hard Drive Interfaces

Most hard drives today use IDE technology to interface with the system via the system bus. IDE includes several standards, including IDE, ATA, Ultra ATA/100, and Serial ATA. Hard drives can use parallel ATA (PATA) or serial ATA (SATA) connectors. IDE standards support two IDE connections — a primary and a secondary — each of which can support up to two IDE devices for a total of four devices on a system. Other interfaces for hard drives are SCSI (small computer system interface), USB, and FireWire.

3 Installing a Hard Drive

Installing a hard drive includes setting jumpers on the drive, installing the drive and cables, changing CMOS setup (if drive is not autodetected), and partitioning and formatting the drive. Be sure to protect the drive and the PC against static electricity during installation.

4 Working with Floppy Drives

Floppy drives today read 3½-inch high-density 1.44 MB disks. Before a disk can store data, it must be formatted to create tracks and sectors, a boot record, the FAT, and a root directory. Each sector holds 512 bytes of data.

5 Optical Storage Technology

A CD-ROM drive uses a laser beam to read data from a CD-ROM. Internal CD-ROM drives can have an IDE or SCSI interface. External CD-ROM drives can use a USB port, FireWire port, or SCSI port. CD-R drives allow you to write data to a CD-R disc. A CD-RW drive allows you to overwrite old data on a CD-RW disc with new data. A DVD is an optical storage media that can store up to 17 GB of data. To troubleshoot an optical storage drive, check the data cables and connections, and that the proper SCSI ID is set. When handling optical storage media, avoid getting dust, fingerprints, or scratches on the media.

6 External and Removable Storage

An external hard disk is a separate, stand-alone hard disk drive that connects to the computer via a cable and a USB, FireWire, or other port. A removable hard disk, also called a disk cartridge, is a hard disk that you insert and remove from a hard disk drive. A Zip drive, for example, is a widely used type of removable hard disk. Flash memory stores data in small, removable flash memory cards.

7 Managing and Troubleshooting Hard Drives

To protect and maintain your hard drive, use Windows tools to partition the hard drive, defragment the hard drive, clean up nonessential files, and enable automated disk caching. Hard drive problems can be caused by hardware or software problems. Common hard drive problems are drives not spinning or retrieving data slowly, as well as corruption in OS files, the partition table, the boot record, the root directory, the FAT, sector markings, or data itself. If you cannot resolve a problem on your own, check the manufacturer's Web site or call for technical support.

KEY TERMS

After reading the chapter, you should know each of these Key Terms.

- 40-conductor IDE cable (*176*)
- 80-conductor IDE cable (*176*)
- ATAPI (Advanced Technology Attachment Packet Interface) (*175*)
- autodetection (*173*)
- basic disk (*189*)
- block (*169*)
- boot record (*169*)
- boot sector (*169*)
- bootstrap loader (*169*)
- cable-select data cable (*178*)
- CDFS (Compact Disc File System) (*193*)
- CD-R (CD-recordable) (*195*)
- CD-RW (CD-rewritable) (*196*)
- cluster (*169*)
- cylinder (*163*)
- daisy chain (*179*)
- defragment (*200*)
- directory table (*170*)
- disk cache (*203*)
- disk cartridge (*198*)
- disk management (*189*)
- DMA (direct memory access) transfer mode (*176*)
- dynamic disks (*189*)
- dynamic volumes (*189*)
- extended partition (*168*)
- external hard disk (*198*)
- FAT16 (*172*)
- FAT32 (*172*)
- file allocation table (FAT) (*170*)
- file allocation unit (*169*)
- flash memory (*198*)
- flash storage (*198*)
- fragmentation (*200*)
- hard disk controller (*164*)
- hard drive controller (*164*)
- hard drive interface (*173*)
- HD-DVD (high-density or high-definition DVD) (*196*)
- high-level formatting (*169*)
- host adapter (*179*)
- independent device timing (*175*)
- lands (*193*)
- logical formatting (*169*)
- low-level formatting (*164*)
- master boot sector (*167*)
- master file table (MFT) (*170*)
- multisession (*196*)
- NTFS (New Technology file system) (*173*)
- partition sector (*167*)
- physical formatting (*164*)
- PIO (programmed input/output) transfer mode (*176*)
- pits (*193*)
- primary partition (*168*)
- removable hard disk (*198*)
- SCSI ID (*180*)
- sector (*163*)
- serial ATA (SATA) cable (*177*)
- slack (*172*)
- Small Computer System Interface (SCSI) (*179*)
- software cache (*203*)
- system partition (*168*)
- termination (*180*)
- track (*163*)
- UDF (Universal Disk Format) file system (*193*)
- zone bit recording (*165*)

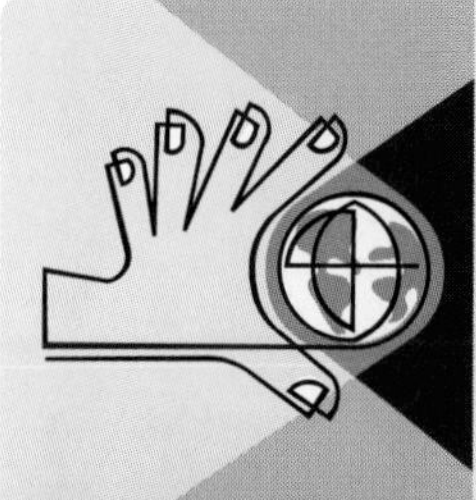

LEARN IT ONLINE

Reinforce your understanding of the chapter concepts and terms with the Learn It Online exercises.

Instructions: To complete the Learn It Online exercises, start your browser, click the Address bar, and then enter the Web address scsite.com/understanding/learn. When the Understanding and Troubleshooting Your PC Learn It Online page is displayed, follow the instructions in the exercises below. Each exercise has instructions for printing your results, either for your own records or for submission to your instructor.

1 Chapter Reinforcement True/False, Multiple Choice, and Short Answer

Below Chapter 5, click the Chapter Reinforcement link. Print the quiz by clicking Print on the File menu for each page. Answer each question.

2 Flash Cards

Below Chapter 5, click the Flash Cards link and read the instructions. Type 20 (or a number specified by your instructor) in the Number of playing cards text box, type your name in the Enter your Name text box, and then click the Flip Card button. When the flash card is displayed, read the question and then click the ANSWER box arrow to select an answer. Flip through Flash Cards. If your score is 15 (75%) correct or greater, click Print on the File menu to print your results. If your score is less than 15 (75%) correct, then redo this exercise by clicking the Replay button.

3 Practice Test

Below Chapter 5, click the Practice Test link. Answer each question, enter your first and last name at the bottom of the page, and then click the Grade Test button. When the graded practice test is displayed on your screen, click Print on the File menu to print a hard copy. Continue to take practice tests until you score 80% or better.

4 Who Wants To Be a Computer Genius?

Below Chapter 5, click the Computer Genius link. Read the instructions, enter your first and last name at the bottom of the page, and then click the PLAY button. When your score is displayed, click the PRINT RESULTS link to print a hard copy.

5 Wheel of Terms

Below Chapter 5, click the Wheel of Terms link. Read the instructions, and then enter your first and last name and your school name. Click the PLAY button. When your score is displayed, right-click the score and then click Print on the shortcut menu to print a hard copy.

6 Crossword Puzzle Challenge

Below Chapter 5, click the Crossword Puzzle Challenge link. Read the instructions, and then enter your first and last name. Click the SUBMIT button. Work the crossword puzzle. When you are finished, click the Submit button. When the crossword puzzle is redisplayed, click the Print Puzzle button to print a hard copy.

Multiple Choice

Select the best answer.

1. The ________, or boot drive, is the partition on the hard drive used to boot the OS.
   a. primary drive
   b. active partition
   c. extended partition
   d. logical drive
2. NTFS (New Technology file system) uses a database called the ________ to store information about files and directories and their locations on the hard drive.
   a. master file table (MFT)
   b. file allocation table (FAT)
   c. partition unit
   d. boot record
3. When connecting a hard drive to an IDE connector, which type of cable is the fastest?
   a. 40-conductor IDE cable
   b. 80-conductor IDE cable
   c. UltraDMA100/66 cable
   d. serial ATA cable
4. Which of these is not a way a CD-ROM drive can interface with a motherboard?
   a. using an IDE interface
   b. using a SCSI interface with a SCSI host adapter
   c. using a DMA interface
   d. via an external port, such as a USB
5. Which of these does a hard drive interface standard not define?
   a. type of connectors used to connect to the motherboard
   b. method used to write data to hard drive
   c. type of cables used to connect to the motherboard
   d. data transfer speed of the hard drive

Fill in the Blank

Write the word or phrase to fill in the blank in each of the following questions.

1. With ________, tracks near the center have the smallest number of sectors per track, and the number of sectors increases as the tracks grow larger.
2. On a CD-ROM, ________ are raised areas and ________ are recessed areas on the surface; each represents either a 1 or a 0, respectively.
3. ________ occurs when a single file is placed in several cluster locations that are not directly next to each other.
4. A(n) ________ is a temporary storage area in RAM for data being read from or written to a hard drive, and is used to speed up access time to the drive.
5. A Zip drive is a type of ________, a hard disk that you insert and remove from a hard disk drive.

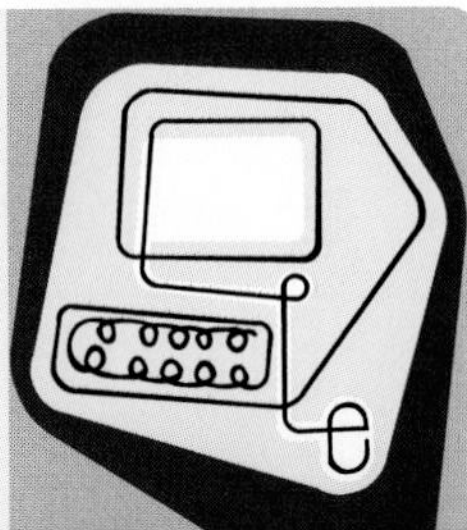

CHAPTER EXERCISES

Complete the Chapter Exercises to solidify what you learned in the chapter.

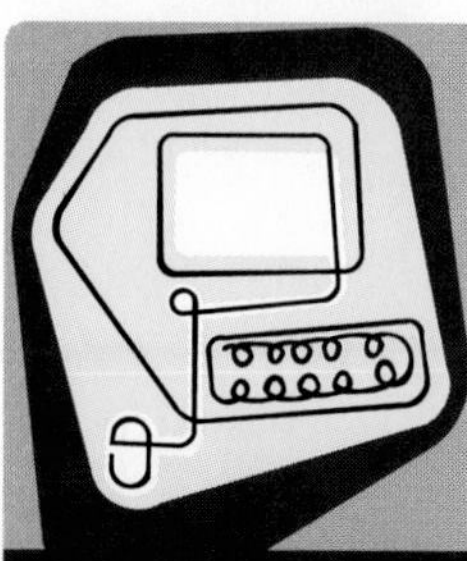

CHAPTER EXERCISES

Complete the Chapter Exercises to solidify what you learned in the chapter.

Matching Terms

Match the terms with their definitions.

________ 1. hard drive controller	a. an arc-shaped area of a track that usually stores 512 bytes of data
________ 2. SCSI ID	b. utility to partition and format a hard drive
________ 3. cylinder	c. set of tracks that lie at the same distance from the center on all sides of all platters of the hard disk
________ 4. CD-RW	d. standard followed by CD-ROM drives, and DVD-ROM drives that use an IDE interface
________ 5. Disk Cleanup	e. number from 0 to 15 assigned to each device on a SCSI bus
________ 6. ATAPI	f. a special-purpose chip that allows the CPU to communicate with a hard drive
________ 7. sector	g. utility used to delete temporary and other nonessential files on a hard drive
________ 8. cluster	h. the minimum unit the operating system uses to store information; made up of two or more sectors
________ 9. Disk Management	i. allows you to overwrite old data on an optical disc with new data
________ 10. multisession	j. allows you to record data to the same CD-R in several different sessions

Short Answer Questions

Write a brief answer to each of the following questions.

1. Describe the formatting process used to take a hard disk from its newly manufactured state to a fully functional storage media.
2. What is the purpose of the boot record on a disk?
3. You install a hard drive and then turn on the PC for the first time. You access CMOS setup and see that the drive is not recognized. What steps should you take next?
4. Describe the steps required to install a new IDE/ATA hard drive.
5. What error message might appear if the partition table is damaged? The boot record? The FAT?

1 Determining the Size of a Cluster

Remember that each entry in a FAT or MFT tracks the use of one cluster. The number of sectors per cluster varies from one file system to another. You can determine the size of one cluster on your computer by using Windows tools or the Chkdsk command. Alternatively, you can determine the size of a cluster by performing the following steps:

1. Click the Start button and then click Run on the Start menu.
2. Enter `cmd` in the Open text box to open the Command Prompt window.
3. If the command prompt is not C:\>, enter `cd c:\` to change the directory to drive C.
4. At the command prompt, enter `dir` to view the amount of space available on your hard drive (listed in bytes). Write down the number of bytes.
5. Click the Start button, point to All Programs on the Start menu, point to Accessories on the All Programs submenu, and then click Notepad on the Accessories menu. When Notepad starts, enter a single character (for example, the letter B) and then save the file as a text file. Click the Close button on the Notepad window.
6. Click the Command Prompt window taskbar button. At the command prompt, enter `dir` to view the amount of space now available on your hard drive. Subtract the number of bytes noted in Step 4 from the number of bytes now reported. The difference in the two values is the size of one cluster, which is the smallest amount that can be allocated to a file like the one-character text file you created in Step 5.
7. Fsutil is a powerful command-line utility that you can use to perform many FAT and NTFS file system related tasks (you must be logged on as a member of the Administrators group in order to use fsutil.) Using fsutil, you can determine the size of a cluster on your computer. Enter `fsutil fsinfo ntfsinfo c:` at the command prompt. The utility will display a report showing the number of bytes per cluster (Figure 5-45). Verify that this matches the number of bytes you calculated in Step 6.
8. Enter `exit` to close the Command Prompt window.

```
C:\WINDOWS\System32\cmd.exe

C:\>fsutil fsinfo ntfsinfo c:
NTFS Volume Serial Number :       0x58b08462b0844908
Version :                         3.1
Number Sectors :                  0x000000004a7193a
Total Clusters :                  0x0000000000094e327
Free Clusters  :                  0x00000000006be100
Total Reserved :                  0x0000000000000150
Bytes Per Sector  :               512
Bytes Per Cluster :               4096
Bytes Per FileRecord Segment    : 1024
Clusters Per FileRecord Segment : 0
Mft Valid Data Length :           0x0000000006531800
Mft Start Lcn  :                  0x00000000000c529a
Mft2 Start Lcn :                  0x000000000004a7193
Mft Zone Start :                  0x0000000000220ba0
Mft Zone End   :                  0x0000000000246360

C:\>
```

bytes per cluster

Figure 5-45 Results of running the fsutil utility.

APPLY YOUR KNOWLEDGE

Check your understanding of the chapter with the hands-on Apply Your Knowledge exercises.

APPLY YOUR KNOWLEDGE

Check your understanding of the chapter with the hands-on Apply Your Knowledge exercises.

2 Examining Disk Drives

This exercise focuses on examining the disk drives inside a desktop or a tower computer with a floppy drive and hard drive. In addition to a ground bracelet and other safety equipment, you also will need a Phillips-head screwdriver, a flat-head screwdriver, and paper and a pencil to take notes as you work. Perform the following steps to examine the drives inside a computer:

1. To open the computer case, follow the instructions as listed in Chapter 3, Your Turn: Taking Apart and Putting Together a PC. Be sure to use a ground bracelet as you work and follow safety precautions.
2. Before removing any cables, note that each cable has a color or stripe down one side. This edge color marks this side of the cable as pin 1. Look on the board or drive to which the cable is attached. You should see that pin 1 or pin 2 is clearly marked.
3. Verify that the edge color is aligned with pin 1. Look at the cable used to connect drive A to the floppy drive controller card. There is a twist in the cable. This twist reverses the leads in the cable, causing the addresses for this cable to be different from the addresses for the cable that does not have the twist. The connector with the twist is attached to drive A. Remove the cables to the floppy drives and the hard drives. Remove the power supply cords from the drives.
4. Remove the expansion cards, following these procedures. (If you are working with a tower case, you can lay it on its side so the motherboard is on the bottom.)
    a. Remove the cables from the card. There is no need to remove the other end of the cable from its component (floppy disk drive, hard drive, or CD-ROM drive). Lay the cable over the top of the component or case.
    b. Remove the screw holding the board to the case.
    c. Grasp the board with both hands and remove it by lifting straight up and rocking the board from end to end (not side to side). Rocking the board from side to side might spread the slot opening and weaken the connection.
    d. As you remove cards, do not put your fingers on the edge connectors or touch a chip, and do not stack the cards on top of one another.
5. Examine the board connector for the cable and identify pin 1. Lay the board aside on a flat surface.
6. Remove the floppy drives next. Some drives have one or two screws on each side of the drive attaching the drive to the drive bay. After you remove the screws, the drive usually slides to the front and out of the case. Sometimes there is a catch underneath the drive that you must lift up as you slide the drive forward. Be careful not to remove screws that hold the circuit card on top of the drive to the drive housing. The whole unit should stay intact.
7. Remove the hard drive next. Look for the screws that hold the drive to the bay. Be careful to remove only these screws, not the screws that hold the drive together. Handle the drive with care.
8. You now are ready to reassemble by reversing the previous steps.
9. Replace the cables, being sure to align the colored edge with pin 1. (In some cases it might work better to connect the cable to the card before you put the card in the expansion slot.)
10. Plug in the keyboard, monitor, and mouse.
11. In the classroom, have your instructor check your work before you power up. Turn on the power and check that the computer is working properly.
12. If everything is working, turn off the PC and replace the cover and its screws. If the PC does not work, turn off the power and go back and check each cable connection and each expansion card. You probably have not solidly seated a card in the slot. After you have double-checked, try again.

3 Installing a Second Hard Drive

This exercise focuses on installing a second hard drive in a computer (in this example, the hard drive is already formatted and partitioned, so you do not have to complete those steps). In addition to a ground bracelet and other safety equipment, you also will need a Phillips-head screwdriver, a flat-head screwdriver, and paper and a pencil to take notes as you work. Perform the following steps to install a second hard drive in a computer:

1. Open the computer case. Examine the inside of the computer and decide where to place the second drive. Consider whether to place the drive on the primary or secondary IDE channel, and if you will need a bay kit to fit a 3½-inch drive into a 5-inch drive bay. In most cases, you should use the primary channel for your hard drive and, if possible, it should be the only drive on that channel.
2. Place the drive in or near the bay to test its position. Make sure that all cables will reach in that position. If the cables will not reach, try a different bay or obtain longer cables.
3. When you are satisfied everything will fit, remove the drive and then set the jumpers to their proper setting. If the drive is to be the only drive on an IDE channel, set it to single. If it is sharing the IDE cable with another drive, set it to master and set the other drive to slave. If the jumpers are not marked on the drive, consult the drive documentation for jumper configuration. You might have to go to the Web site of the drive manufacturer and search for information on the drive.
4. Install the drive in the bay and secure it with screws on each side of the drive.
5. Attach the power cord and data cable and close the case.
6. Now that you have physically installed your hard drive, you need to configure CMOS to recognize the new hard drive. Follow these steps:
   a. Attach the keyboard, monitor, and mouse.
   b. Boot your computer and enter the CMOS setup utility.
   c. If IDE hard drive autodetect is not enabled, enable it now. In CMOS, what is the name of this entry? If you have just enabled autodetect, reboot the system so the drive now can be detected.
   d. Check the drive parameters that were set by autodetect and change them if they were not detected correctly. If your system does not have autodetect, set the drive parameters now (you may need to consult the documentation for the correct drive parameters).
   e. Save and exit CMOS setup.
   f. The system reboots. After the system boots, check My Computer to see if the drive is recognized on the system.
7. After you have finished, you can reverse the steps to remove the hard drive and then reassemble the computer. Replace the cover and then place the screws back in the holes.
8. Plug in the keyboard, monitor, and mouse.
9. In the classroom, have your instructor check your work before you power up. Turn on the power and check that the computer is working properly.

4 Using Disk Management to Partition a Hard Drive

Using Windows XP, you can use Disk Management to partition and format a hard drive. To create a partition on a basic disk, complete the following steps:

1. Click the Start button and then click Control Panel. Double-click Administrative Tools in the Control Panel window, double-click Computer Management in the Administrative Tools window, and then click Disk Management in the left side of the Computer Management window. (Alternatively, you can click the Start button and then click Run. When the Run dialog box is displayed, enter `Diskmgmt.msc` in the Open text box.)
2. In the Disk Management window, right-click unallocated space on the basic disk where you want to create a new partition and then click New Partition. In the New Partition Wizard, click the Next button.

APPLY YOUR KNOWLEDGE

Check your understanding of the chapter with the hands-on Apply Your Knowledge exercises.

APPLY YOUR KNOWLEDGE

Check your understanding of the chapter with the hands-on Apply Your Knowledge exercises.

3. Click the Primary partition and then click the Next button. Specify the size of the partition in the Partition size in MB box, and then click the Next button.
4. Select the option to let the system automatically assign a drive letter to the partition and then click the Next button.
5. Click Format this partition with the following settings. When the Format dialog box is displayed, type a name for the volume in the Volume label text and click the file system to use in the File system box. Click the Next button.
6. Confirm that the options selected are correct, and then click Finish. The new partition or logical drive is created and appears in the appropriate basic disk in the Disk Management window. If you chose to format the volume in Step 5, the format process now starts.
7. Click the OK button when you are prompted to format the volume.
8. To view the properties of the partition, right-click the partition and then click Properties. Click the appropriate tab to view the appropriate property.

CHAPTER 6

Supporting Input, Output, and Multimedia Devices

Introduction

This chapter focuses on how to install and support input and output devices, including how to connect peripherals using ports, wireless connections, and expansion slots. The chapter also covers input and output devices such as keyboards, pointing devices, and monitors, as well as multimedia devices such as digital cameras and MP3 players. Printers are covered in detail in Chapter 7.

OBJECTIVES

In this chapter, you will learn:

1. About how peripherals work
2. How to connect peripherals using ports, wireless connections, and expansion slots
3. About input and output devices
4. About multimedia technologies

Up for Discussion

Jake Weber, the owner of the music store next door to Sunrise Computers, stopped by today to ask for your help installing a new sound card in his computer. Jake also has purchased new speakers and a headset. He plans to put the computer at a listening station in the store, so customers can listen to CDs or MP3s of songs before they decide on a purchase.

You are happy to help and tell Jake that installing a sound card is easier than he might think. It involves three basic steps: installing the sound card in an empty expansion slot on the motherboard, installing the driver, and then installing any applications that came with the sound card. Jake wants to use MusicMatch Jukebox software to play the MP3s, so you also download and install that software.

After you finish installing the sound card, drivers, and software, you connect the speakers to the Rear out ports on the sound card, start MusicMatch, and select an MP3 to play. The software says it is playing the music, but you cannot hear any sound. Jake looks a little concerned, but you reassure him that the problem might be as simple as turning up the volume on the speakers. As it turns out, the speaker volume was fine, but the Windows Master Volume setting was set to *Mute all*. You also plug the headset in the Line out port to ensure that it works as well.

As you and Jake listen to a song on his new speakers, Jake thanks you for your time — and promises you a free CD the next time you visit his store. You assure him that you are just doing your job — and wish him the best of luck with the new listening station.

Questions:

- What are the steps involved in installing a sound card?
- If your computer is not producing sound, what troubleshooting steps should you take?
- What ports are available on a sound card and how can you tell them apart?
- What is an MP3 file and how does the technology work?

An Overview of Peripherals

Input is any data or instructions entered into the memory of a computer. An **input device** is any hardware component that allows users to enter data or instructions. Commonly used input devices include the mouse and the keyboard. **Output** is data that has been processed into a useful form. An **output device** is any hardware component used to convey this information to a user. Commonly used output devices include monitors, printers, and speakers.

As you learned in Chapter 1, many input and output devices are peripheral devices that communicate with the CPU but are not located directly on the motherboard. A peripheral device, also called simply a *peripheral*, can be connected to the computer in an expansion slot, via a cable that connects to a port, or using a wireless connection.

Converting Analog and Digital Data

Recall that data is processed in one of two ways: analog or digital. Humans process data that is analog, in the form of continuous up-and-down wave patterns of light and sound that represent data to the eyes and ears (Figure 6-1a). Personal computers, by contrast, process data that is digital and stored in one of two states: positive (on) and non-positive (off) (Figure 6-1b).

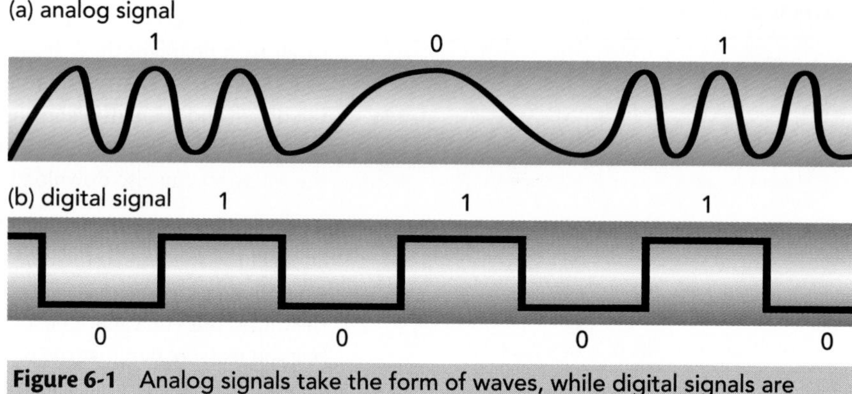

Figure 6-1 Analog signals take the form of waves, while digital signals are discrete on and off states.

A person interacts with a computer in a way that he or she understands, such as inputting analog data and instructions using a keyboard or a mouse or speaking words into a microphone. The computer hardware and software then use **analog-to-digital conversion** to convert all analog input into digital values before processing the data. For example, all letters and characters entered into a computer via a keyboard are converted to a binary code before being stored in the computer. To output the information, the computer performs **digital-to-analog conversion** to convert the digital data back to analog form. Many input and output devices, including multimedia devices such as sound and video cards, perform these conversions. As you learn about specific devices, the chapter will review how that device handles converting analog and digital data.

Installing Peripheral Devices

A peripheral can be internal (installed inside the computer case) or external (installed outside the case). A hard drive connected to the motherboard via an IDE connector is an internal peripheral, as is a sound card or video card installed in an expansion slot. By contrast, a digital camera connected to a FireWire port, a Zip drive connected to a USB port, or a mouse connected to mouse port all are external peripherals.

Whether internal or external, a peripheral essentially is a hardware device controlled by software. When you add a new peripheral to a computer, the hardware device needs software in the form of a device driver or system BIOS; system resources, such as an IRQ, a DMA channel, I/O addresses, and memory addresses; and application software.

The process of installing a new device typically follows three basic steps:

1. Install the device.
2. Install the device driver.
3. Install the application software.

For most devices, you connect the device to the computer before installing the drivers and application software. For some devices, such as a digital camera, scanner, and some printers, however, you install the device driver first and then connect the device.

When adding a new peripheral to a computer, consider the following:

- If the device uses a device driver, the driver must be written specifically for the operating system installed on your PC.
- A peripheral might require different types of software to be installed. For example, a device such as a scanner could require a device driver that interfaces directly with the hardware device and an application software package that interfaces with the driver.

6-1

How do I know if I should connect the device or install the device driver first?

Although you generally connect the device to the computer before installing the device drivers, read the documentation that came with the device before connecting a peripheral device to your computer.

Connecting Peripherals Using Ports

As noted above, peripheral devices can be plugged directly into a port or they can use an expansion card plugged into an expansion slot. Most computers come with one or two serial ports and one parallel port. Newer computers generally have two or more

USB ports and a FireWire (IEEE 1394) port. Figure 6-2 shows several of the ports on the back of a PC. With the exception of the video ports, all of these ports come directly off the motherboard. Figure 6-3 shows the speeds of several ports, from fastest to slowest.

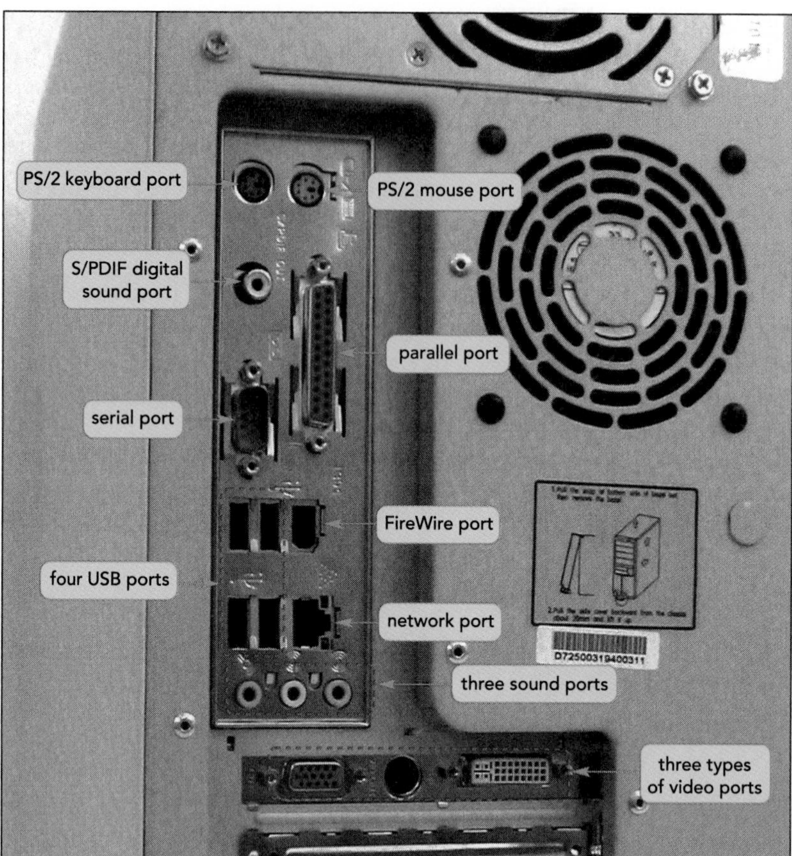

Figure 6-2 Rear of computer case showing ports. With the exception of the video ports, all of the ports come directly off the motherboard.

Port Type	Maximum Data Transmission Speed
FireWire (1394b)	800 Mbps (megabits per second), 1.6 Gbps (gigabits per second), or 3.2 Gbps
USB 2.0	480 Mbps
FireWire (1394a)	400 Mbps
USB 1.1	12 Mbps
Parallel	1.5 Mbps
Serial	115.2 Kbps (kilobits per second)

Figure 6-3 Data transmission speeds for various ports.

Using Serial Ports

Serial ports are used to connect input devices, such as a mouse, or a communication device such as a *modem*, which is used to convert analog and digital data so that a computer can send and receive data over analog telephone lines. (Modems are covered in detail in Chapter 10).

As you learned in Chapter 1, serial ports transmit data in single bits, or serially. You can identify serial ports on the back of a computer case by (1) counting the pins and (2) determining whether the port is male or female. Figure 6-4 shows two serial ports and a parallel port for comparison. On the top are one 25-pin female parallel port and one 9-pin male serial port. On the bottom is one 25-pin male serial port. Serial ports are almost always male ports, while parallel ports are almost always female ports.

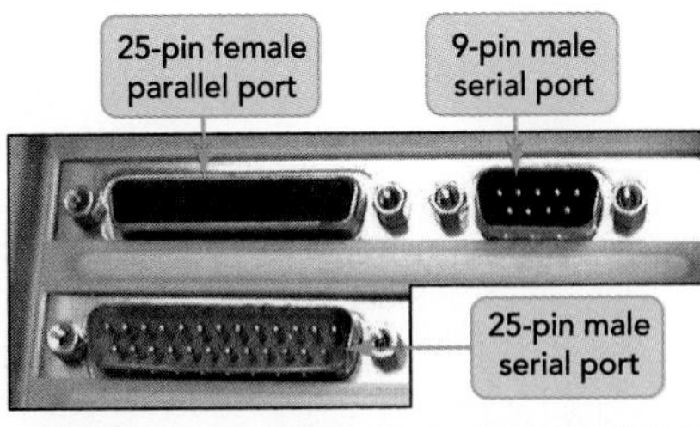

Figure 6-4 Serial and parallel ports.

A serial port conforms to the standard interface called RS-232c (Reference Standard 232 revision c) and thus sometimes also is called an **RS-232 port**. The RS-232c interface standard originally called for 25 pins, but because personal computers only use nine of those pins to transmit data, newer computers often have a modified 9-pin serial port. A 25-pin and a 9-pin port work the same way. Although it has 25 pins, a 25-pin port only uses nine of the pins; the other pins are unused.

Does it matter if my computer has a 9-pin or a 25-pin serial port?

Because the 9-pin and the 25-pin port provide the same functionality, it does not matter which type of port your computer has. Today, some computers have a 9-pin serial port, some have a 25-pin serial port, and some have both. If you have a device such as a modem that has a 25-pin port, but only have a 9-pin port on your computer, you can buy an adapter to convert a 9-pin port to a 25-pin port (and vice versa).

Serial ports rely on a special controller chip, the **Universal Asynchronous Receiver/Transmitter** (**UART**), to function properly. The UART chip takes the parallel output from the computer's system bus and transforms it into serial form for transmission through the serial port.

When the system is using serial ports, one of the devices is called the **DTE** (**Data Terminal Equipment**) and the other device is called the **DCE** (**Data Communications Equipment**). For example, a modem is called the DCE, and the computer on which it is installed is called the DTE.

To simplify the allocation of system resources for devices connected to serial and parallel ports, serial ports are given a port assignment of COM1, COM2, COM3, or COM4, and parallel ports are given a port assignment of LPT1 or LPT2. Each of these port assignments represents a designated configuration of an IRQ and I/O address

More About

Null Modem Connections

When DTE devices, such as two computers, are connected, software can transmit data between the devices over a special cable called a null modem cable, without using a modem. To learn more about null modem connections, visit the Understanding and Troubleshooting Your PC More About Web page (**scsite.com/understanding/more**) and then click Null Modem Connections below Chapter 6.

range, as shown in Figure 6-5. COM1, COM2, COM3, and COM4 are logical assignments to a physical port; COM1 is just a simpler way of expressing that the device connected to the serial port uses IRQ 4 and I/O address 03F8h (remember that the h indicates hexadecimal).

Port	IRQ	I/O Address (in Hex)	Type
COM1	IRQ 4	03F8h – 03FFh	Serial
COM2	IRQ 3	02F8h – 02FFh	Serial
COM3	IRQ 4	03E8h – 03EFh	Serial
COM4	IRQ 3	02E8h – 02EFh	Serial
LPT1	IRQ 7	0378h – 037Fh	Parallel
LPT2	IRQ 5	0278h – 027Fh	Parallel

Figure 6-5 Default port assignments on many computers. Serial port assignments use a label of COM1 through COM4, while parallel port assignments are named LPT1 or LPT2.

DOS, Windows, and most applications that use serial devices comply with these assignments. For example, you can connect your PDA to a serial port using a cable and then tell the PDA software to synchronize data using a serial port assigned COM3. The software then knows that the modem is using IRQ 4 to signal the CPU and is listening for instructions via I/O addresses 03E8h through 03EFh.

Because most serial and parallel ports are connected directly to the motherboard, COM and LPT assignments are made using CMOS setup. Sometimes the setup screen shows the COM assignments, and sometimes you see the actual IRQ and I/O address assignments, as shown in Figure 6-6. The ports also can be enabled and disabled using CMOS setup.

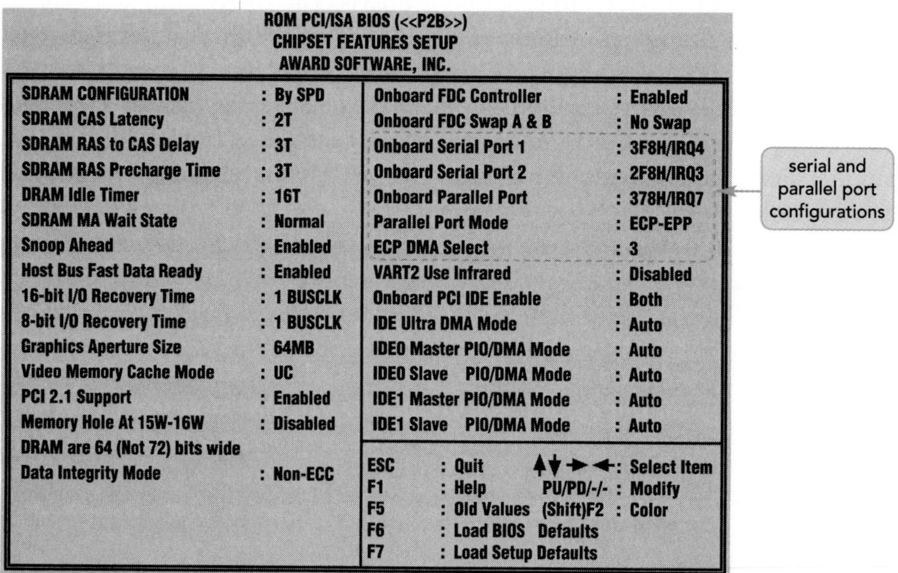

Figure 6-6 CMOS setup allows you to define the configurations for serial and parallel ports.

Using Parallel Ports

A parallel port transmits data in parallel (side by side, as if in lanes), eight bits at a time. Parallel ports most commonly are used by printers, although they also are used by other devices such as scanners and Zip drives. A parallel port generally is used for fast transmission of data over short distances, such as from your computer to the printer sitting on your desk.

A parallel port sometimes is referred to as a **DB-25 connector**, which indicates that it has 25 pins on the connector. As shown earlier in Figure 6-4 on page 225, parallel ports almost always are female ports. Parallel ports are considered *bidirectional*, because the port can send and receive 8 bits of input and output over its 8-bit data bus, which is represented by pins 2 through 7 and 18 through 25.

PARALLEL PORT TECHNOLOGIES Parallel ports fall into three categories: standard parallel port (SPP), enhanced parallel port (EPP), and extended capabilities port (ECP). The **standard parallel port** (**SPP**) is an 8-bit standard port first introduced in 1987 and found on computers today. A standard parallel port also is called a normal parallel port, a bidirectional port, or a Centronics port, which refers to the 36-pin Centronics connection used by printers (Figure 6-7). A standard parallel port is the slowest of the three types of parallel ports.

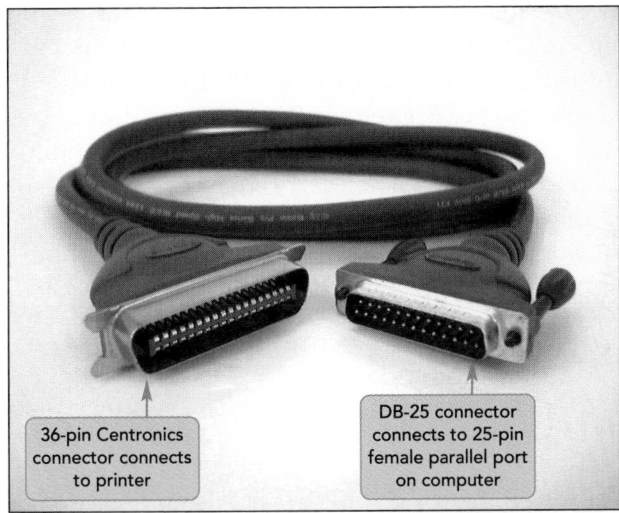

Figure 6-7 This printer cable has a DB-25 connection to connect to the parallel port on the computer and a 36-pin Centronics connection to connect to the printer.

Enhanced parallel port (**EPP**) is a parallel port standard for PCs developed by Intel, Xircom, and Zenith Data Systems in 1991. EPP allows for bidirectional data transfer about 10 times faster than the standard parallel port. The **extended capabilities port** (**ECP**) is a similar parallel port standard developed by Microsoft and Hewlett-Packard in 1992. ECP also allows for bidirectional data transfer at speeds slightly faster than EPP, because it uses a DMA channel to help with data transfer. Because it requires a DMA channel, however, using ECP can cause resource conflicts.

All of these ports adhere to a parallel port standard called IEEE 1284. These standards require that newer parallel port designs such as ECP and EPP are backward compatible with earlier parallel ports, such as the standard parallel port. If you are using an EPP or ECP printer and parallel port, be sure to use a printer cable that is labeled as IEEE 1284 compliant. Older, noncompliant cables will not work properly with these printers.

FAQ 6-3

Is it true that you should not use very long cables to connect your computer to a printer?

The longer the cable connecting your printer to the parallel port, the more likely you will have trouble with your printer. If data is transmitted in parallel over a very long cable, data integrity sometimes can be lost because bits may separate from the byte to which they belong. As a result, most parallel cables are only 6 feet (1.8 meters) long, although no established standard sets maximum cable length. In general, you should avoid using a parallel cable longer than 15 feet (4.6 meters) to ensure data integrity. Hewlett-Packard, one of the larger printer manufacturers, recommends that cables be no longer than 10 feet (3 meters).

CONFIGURING PARALLEL PORTS As previously noted, parallel ports use port assignments of LPT1 or LPT2 to represent a designated configuration of an IRQ and I/O address range, as shown earlier in Figure 6-5 on page 226. Because most parallel ports are connected directly to the motherboard, you configure a parallel port using CMOS setup. CMOS setup includes up to four different settings for parallel ports. For the BIOS in Figure 6-6 on page 226, choices for parallel port mode are Normal, EPP, ECP, and EPP-ECP. If you select ECP or EPP-ECP, you also must select a DMA channel for the parallel port to use (either DMA channel 1 or 3).

To connect a printer or other device to a parallel port, simply connect the device cable to the port and then install any required drivers or software, either manually or using the Add New Hardware wizard for Plug and Play devices. If the parallel port is not working, check CMOS setup to make sure the port is enabled. If you have problems with resource conflicts, try disabling ECP mode for the parallel port. EPP mode provides fast data transfer, without using a DMA channel needed for other devices.

Using USB Ports

As you learned in Chapter 1, a USB (universal serial bus) port can connect to many different input and output devices such as keyboards, printers, scanners, and mice. The USB port, which was created by a group of manufacturers including Compaq, Digital Equipment, IBM, Intel, Microsoft, NEC, and Northern Telecom, was designed to make the installation of peripheral devices as effortless as possible. USB ports provide several advantages over serial and parallel ports. For one, USB provides much faster data transmission than serial and parallel ports. Further, USB uses Plug and Play technology and thus allows for **hot-swapping** or **hot-plugging**, which means you can connect a device to a USB port while the computer is running and it automatically will be configured without your having to restart the computer. Given these advantages, USB is expected to replace both serial and parallel ports as the technology matures and more devices are built to connect to USB ports.

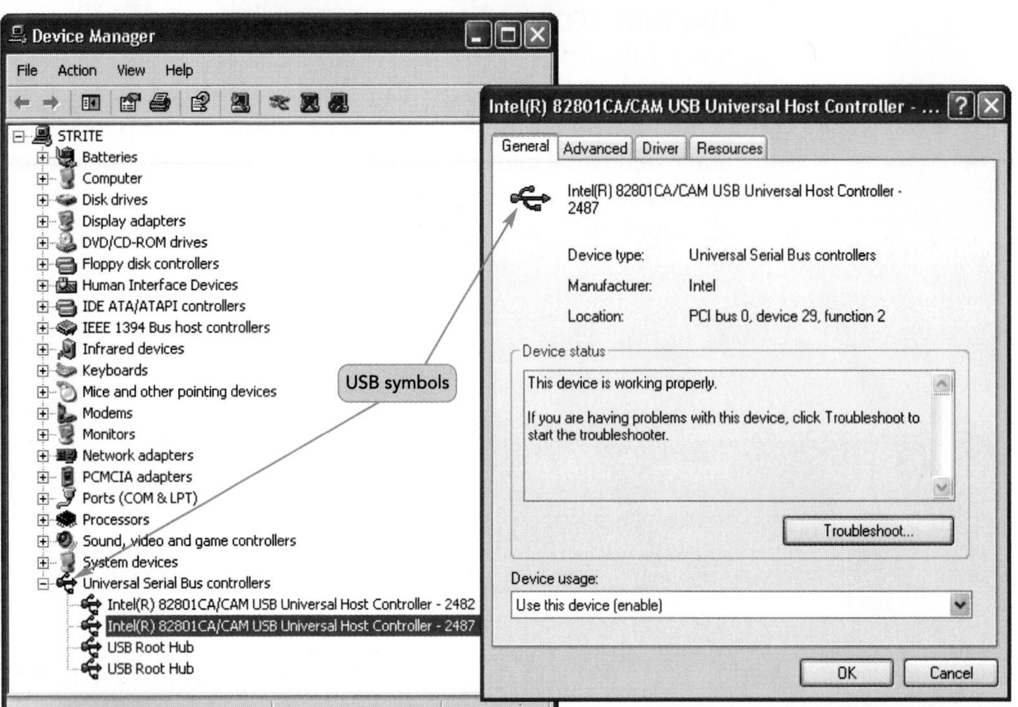

Figure 6-14 Use Device Manager to confirm that the USB host controller is installed and working properly.

4. As needed, install the application software to use the device. For example, scanners often come with application software you can use to scan and edit images.

Using FireWire (IEEE 1394) Ports

As you learned in Chapter 1, a *FireWire port* is used to connect high-speed input, output, and multimedia devices that require large data transfers. FireWire, which also is called IEEE 1394, i.Link, and the High Performance Serial Bus (HPSB), provides data transmission speeds as high as 3.2 gigabits per second — much higher than USB. (The name, IEEE 1394, derives from the Institute of Electrical and Electronics Engineers standards group that originally defined the standard.) While USB is ideal for connecting lower-speed input devices such as keyboards, mice, and joysticks, FireWire is aimed at higher-speed peripherals such as digital video cameras and hard drives. FireWire ports are found on newer high-end motherboards and are expected to become standard ports on all new motherboards.

FAQ 6-6

How do USB and FireWire compare?

FireWire is faster because, unlike USB, it does not rely on the computer to manage the data flow to and from peripherals, which adds system overhead and results in slower data throughput. Because FireWire devices do not have to transfer data via a computer, you can connect two FireWire devices directly — perhaps connecting a stereo to a DVD player to a TV. The widespread use of USB, however, means you are far more likely to have one or more USB ports available on your PC. FireWire ports often are used to connect digital video cameras and other video devices, but they have not yet caught on for other peripherals.

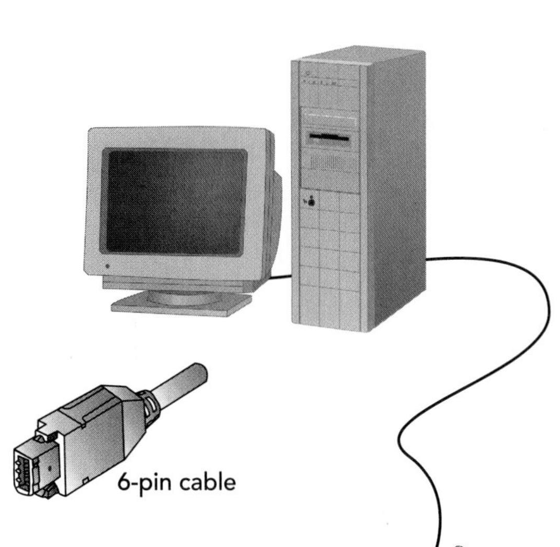

Figure 6-15 A FireWire cable has two types of connectors. The 6-pin connector provides power to a device, while the 4-pin connector does not.

FIREWIRE TECHNOLOGIES The two standards for FireWire are IEEE 1394A and 1394B. 1394A supports speeds up to 400 Mbps and allows for cable lengths up to 15 feet. A newer standard, 1394B, supports speeds from 800 Mbps up to 3.2 Gbps and extends the maximum cable length to 328 feet (100 meters). A FireWire cable can have two different types of connectors, as shown in Figure 6-15. A 4-pin port does not provide voltage to a device, while a 6-pin port does. The two extra pins in the 6-pin port are used to provide voltage to the device and a ground.

FireWire uses **isochronous data transfer**, meaning that data is transferred continuously without breaks over the FireWire bus. For multimedia applications, using isochronous data transfer helps ensure a continuous presentation for the viewer. This works well when transferring real-time data, such as video captured using digital video cameras, VCRs, TVs, and digital cameras.

Devices connected to a FireWire port are controlled by a **FireWire host controller**, which is included in the chipset on the motherboard or on an expansion card that plugs into a PCI expansion slot. Like USB devices, FireWire devices are hot-pluggable. When you plug a device into a FireWire port while the computer is running, the FireWire host controller senses the device and automatically assigns system resources without requiring you to restart the computer. The host controller manages communication to the CPU for all FireWire devices. Up to 63 FireWire devices can be daisy chained together and managed by a FireWire host controller.

FAQ 6-7

How does IEEE 1394.3 relate to the other FireWire standards?

IEEE 1394.3 is a variation of FireWire, which is designed for peer-to-peer data transmission. Using this standard, imaging devices such as scanners and digital cameras can send images and photos directly to printers without involving a computer.

INSTALLING A FIREWIRE DEVICE To install a FireWire device, you need a motherboard or expansion card that provides a FireWire port, a FireWire device and its drivers, and an OS that supports FireWire.

To determine if your computer has a FireWire port, check the ports on the outside of the computer case to locate a FireWire port (FireWire ports often are labeled with the number 1394). Next, determine if your operating system supports FireWire. Windows Server 2003, Windows XP, and Windows 2000 support FireWire; Windows 95 and Windows NT do not. Windows 98 Second Edition supports FireWire storage devices, but not FireWire printers and scanners.

As with a USB device, read the documentation for a FireWire device to determine if you should connect the device or install the drivers first. To install a FireWire device where the device is connected before installing the drivers, you would complete the following steps:

1. Using Device Manager, scroll down and click the expand (+) button next to IEEE 1394 Bus Controller to see the specific host controller on the motherboard. View the properties for the host controller to confirm that it is working properly.

2. Plug the device into the FireWire port. Install the drivers for the device by double-clicking the Add New Hardware icon in the Control Panel and then following the steps in the wizard.
3. Check Device Manager to ensure that the device is listed. For example, after you have installed the drivers for a digital video camera, you should see the device listed in Device Manager under Sound, video, and game controllers. If you do not see the device listed, turn the device off and then on.
4. If necessary, install any application software that came with the device. For example, a digital video camera may come with video-editing software you can use to split the video into scenes, add special effects, and more.

For motherboards that do not support FireWire, you can install a FireWire card in a PCI slot to provide the chipset and FireWire ports. If Step 1 indicates that the host controller is not installed or is not working, reinstall the driver by double-clicking the Add New Hardware icon in the Control Panel and then following the wizard. If you have problems installing the driver, check CMOS setup to confirm that IEEE 1394 support is enabled in setup.

Connecting Peripherals Using Wireless Connections

Input and output devices and other peripherals also can be connected to a computer using wireless technology. Two wireless technologies used to connect peripherals include infrared and radio frequency.

Infrared

Infrared (**IR**) technology uses infrared light waves to transmit signals to other infrared-enabled devices. A common example of an infrared device is a TV remote. Computers also can use infrared technologies to communicate with input and output devices, such as a wireless keyboard, mouse, or printer. Infrared technologies also often are used to transfer data to and from a **PDA** (**personal digital assistant**), a small handheld computer that provides organizer functions.

An **infrared port,** sometimes called an **IrDA** (**Infrared Data Association**) **port** or **infrared transceiver**, supports infrared devices such as wireless keyboards, mice, and printers. An infrared port is a small, plastic-covered port that transmits and receives signals.

Many notebook computers already have infrared ports, but they are less common on desktop computers. If you want to add an infrared port to your computer to use with a device such as a wireless mouse, you can use an infrared adapter that connects to the serial port, parallel port, or USB port. If the transceiver is Plug and Play, automatically will detect the transceiver and use a wizard to step you through installing the drivers. If it is not detected automatically, you can install the drivers by double-clicking the Add New Hardware icon in the Control Panel and then following the wizard. Once installed, the infrared transceiver will be set up with a port assignment for a serial, parallel, or USB port and will use the resources for that port.

Once the infrared adapter is installed, simply position the mouse in front of the infrared port or adapter to transmit signals from the mouse to the infrared port. Infrared technology only can transmit signals approximately 3 feet (1 meter), and the two IrDA ports must be in a direct line with each other to communicate.

More About

PDAs

To learn more about PDAs, visit the Understanding and Troubleshooting Your PC More About Web page (**scsite.com/understanding/more**) and then click PDAs below Chapter 6.

Radio Frequency

In some situations, it is difficult to create an unobstructed view between the infrared device and the infrared transceiver. In these situations, radio frequency (RF) technology is a better option, because radio waves do not require a direct line of sight between the device and the port. With **radio frequency** (**RF**) technology, devices use radio waves to transmit signals. Piles of paper, books, and other desktop items that block the line of sight will not degrade the communications between the computer and an RF device such as a wireless keyboard or mouse.

Connecting a wireless keyboard or mouse using RF technology requires two key parts: a transmitter and a receiver. The radio transmitter is inside the input device — either the keyboard or mouse. The radio receiver plugs into a keyboard port, mouse port, USB port, or other port. Once the receivers are plugged in, the BIOS and operating system detect the radio receivers and use the input as if the devices were connected directly by a cable.

Bluetooth and 802.11 are two widely used radio frequency technologies. **Bluetooth** uses short range radio waves to transmit data between two devices at a rate of up to 1 Mbps. Bluetooth-enabled devices, such as computers, PDAs, cell phones, digital cameras, and printers, contain a small chip that allow them to communicate with other Bluetooth-enabled devices. To communicate with each other, the devices must be within about 33 feet (10 meters) of each other (although additional equipment can extend that to about 328 feet or 100 meters).

802.11 is a group of standards that define how computers and other devices communicate over a network using radio waves. Of the various 802.11 standards, the most widely implemented are 802.11g and 802.11b, which are both referred to as **Wi-Fi** (**wireless fidelity**). 802.11b can transfer data up to 11 Mbps, while 802.11g can transfer data at speeds of 20 Mbps and higher. Windows XP and Windows Server 2003 provide Wi-Fi support, so you can quickly set up a wireless connection to a network. Wi-Fi is covered in more detail in Chapter 10.

Are Wi-Fi and Bluetooth competing technologies?

Not really. Bluetooth is designed for shorter-range communications between two devices, at least one of which usually is portable (for example, a digital camera and a desktop computer, a notebook computer and a printer, or two PDAs). With Wi-Fi, by contrast, users wirelessly network many computers and devices together over a wider area.

Connecting Peripherals Using Expansion Slots

As you have learned, expansion cards are circuit boards designed to provide additional functionality or to provide a connection to a peripheral device. An expansion card is inserted into a PCI, AGP, or ISA expansion slot to provide connections for various types of peripherals. With newer computers, PCI expansion slots typically are used to connect a sound card, network card, FireWire card, or modem card, while an AGP expansion slot is used for a video card that provides a port for the monitor. ISA expansion slots sometimes are used to connect a modem card, although they are used less often on newer computers.

PCI Expansion Slots

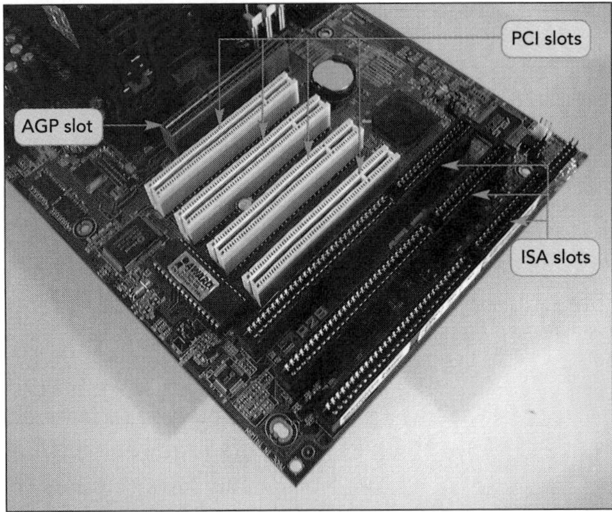

Figure 6-16 In addition to several PCI and ISA slots, a motherboard will have only one AGP slot, which is used to support a video or graphics card.

Recall that the PCI (Peripheral Component Interconnect) bus currently is the most widely used local I/O bus in most personal computers. The original PCI standard has a 32-bit data path and runs at 33 MHz or 66 MHz, depending on the speed of the motherboard (the system bus speed). A newer version of the PCI bus, called PCI-X (PCI extended), is a 64-bit bus with speeds of 133 MHz. The most recent version of the PCI bus, called PCI Express, supports speeds of 2.5 GHz and can transfer data much faster than other PCI buses.

Most new motherboards today come with one AGP slot for the video card, four or five PCI slots for other types of cards, and one or more ISA slots (although some new motherboards have no ISA slots). As shown in Figure 6-16, the PCI expansion slots, which usually are white, are shorter than ISA slots and set a little farther away from the edge of the motherboard.

The PCI bus controller, which is part of the motherboard chip set, manages the PCI bus and the expansion slots. The PCI bus controller assigns IRQ and I/O addresses to a PCI slot, so the card inserted in that slot uses those resources. When installing a PCI card, you most likely will not need to configure the IRQ or I/O address for the card, because the startup BIOS and PCI bus controller do this for you.

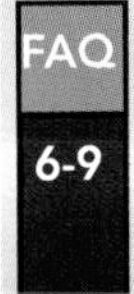
FAQ 6-9

Can two devices in PCI slots share an IRQ?

Yes, although if two devices requiring large data transfers end up sharing an IRQ, they might not work properly. If you suspect this is the case, try moving one of the devices to a different PCI slot, so a device with a heavy demand (such as a FireWire card) is matched with a low-demand device (such as a modem). To see which IRQ has been assigned to a device, view the properties for the expansion card using Device Manager.

AGP Expansion Slots

The AGP (Accelerated Graphics Port) bus was designed to create a faster, dedicated bus between the chip set on the video card and the CPU. AGP is considered to be a local video bus, because it connects the video card in the AGP slot and the CPU. Newer AGP slots can transfer up to 2.1 GB of data per second, to support the data transfer needs of a video card supporting 3-D graphics.

Most motherboards have a single AGP slot to support one AGP video card (although a PCI slot is used for a second video card if a computer uses two monitors). The AGP slot provides faster data transfer than a PCI slot, because the AGP bus connects to and runs at the same speed as the system bus, which is connected directly to the CPU. AGP also offers additional features, such as the ability to share memory with the CPU, that help provide better overall performance for video than PCI. AGP is discussed in more detail in the discussion of monitors.

Installing an Expansion Card in an Expansion Slot

Installing an expansion card in an expansion slot that supports Plug and Play requires a few simple steps. For example, to install an expansion card in a PCI expansion slot, follow these general steps:

1. Protect yourself and the computer from ESD by using an antistatic bracelet and ground mat.
2. Shut down the computer and unplug it. Remove the case cover.
3. Locate the expansion slot in which you want to install the expansion card and then remove the faceplate from the slot. Figure 6-17 shows two PCI slots with the faceplates removed, and two more PCI slots with faceplates in place. Some faceplate covers can be popped out without tools, while others require you to remove a faceplate screw to remove the faceplate or use needle-nose pliers to lift the faceplate off gently.
4. Insert the expansion card in the expansion slot. Be careful to push the card directly into the slot, without rocking it from side to side. Rocking it from side to side can widen the expansion slot, making it more difficult to keep a good contact. If you have a problem getting the card into the slot, you can insert the end away from the side of the case in the slot first and gently rock the card from front to rear into the slot. The card should feel snug in the slot. Insert the screw that connects the card to the case, as shown in Figure 6-17, so the card does not shift out of the slot over time.
5. Replace the cover of the computer case, power cord, and other peripherals. (If you like, you can leave the case cover off until you have tested the device, in case it does not work and you need to reseat the expansion card. Do not leave the cover off too long while running the computer, or it may overheat.)
6. Plug in the device intended to use the port on the rear of the card. For example, for a sound card, plug in the speakers.
7. Reboot the computer. Windows will launch the Found New Hardware Wizard, prompting you to install the device drivers. Follow the steps in the wizard to install the drivers.
8. Test the device. If the device does not work, the expansion card most likely is not seated securely in the slot. If reseating the card does not fix the issue, try installing the expansion card in a different slot.

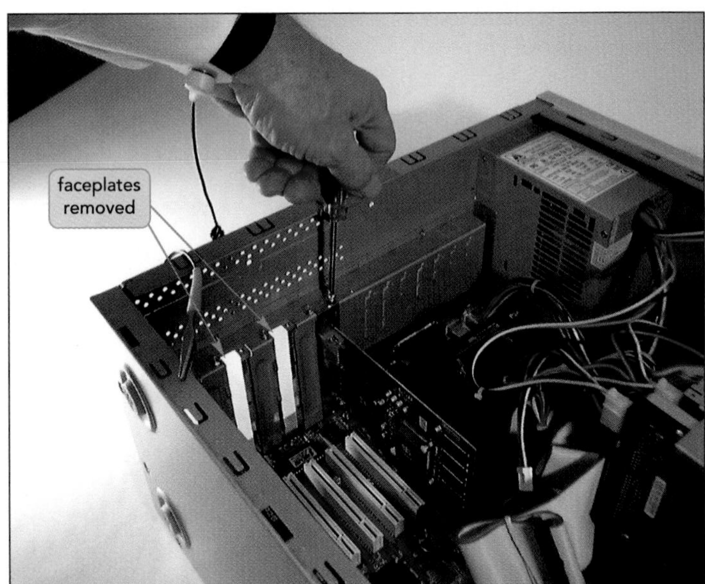

Figure 6-17 Secure an expansion card in the slot with a screw.

Although this example used a PCI slot, the steps to install an expansion card in an AGP slot or an ISA slot are similar. In some cases, even if an expansion card is intended to be Plug and Play, you many have to install device drivers and perform some manual configuration. Further, most ISA slots do not support Plug and Play and may require some manual configuration.

PC Cards and ExpressCards

A popular way to add peripheral devices to a notebook is to use a **PC Card**, also called a **PCMCIA** (**Personal Computer Memory Card International Association**) **Card.** A PC Card is about the size of a credit card, but thicker, and inserts into a **PC Card slot** (Figure 6-18). Once intended only for memory cards, PC Card slots now can be used by many devices, including modems, network cards for wired or wireless networks, CD-ROMs, sound cards, hard disks, and more. Unlike PCs, notebooks do not have the traditional expansion slots that connect to an I/O bus. Instead, notebooks use PC Card slots that connect to the 16-bit PCMCIA I/O bus on the notebook motherboard.

The PCMCIA has developed four standards for these slots. The latest PCMCIA specification, **CardBus**, improves I/O speed and increases the bus width to 32 bits. Earlier standards for PCMCIA slots are named Type I, Type II, and Type III. Type I cards can be up to 3.3-mm thick and primarily are used for adding memory. Type II cards can be up to 5.5-mm thick and often are used as modem cards. Type III cards can be up to 10.5-mm thick, large enough to accommodate a disk drive.

A newer type of card, called an ExpressCard, is smaller, less expensive, and provides data transfer that is almost twice as fast as a PC Card. Similar to PC Cards, ExpressCards can be used to add memory, hard drives, wired and wireless network cards, and more. ExpressCards are either 34-mm wide (ExpressCard/34) or 54-mm wide (ExpressCard/54). Both cards are 75-mm long and 5-mm thick, much like a Type II PC Card. ExpressCard technology uses PCI Express or USB 2.0 buses to transfer data to and from a system.

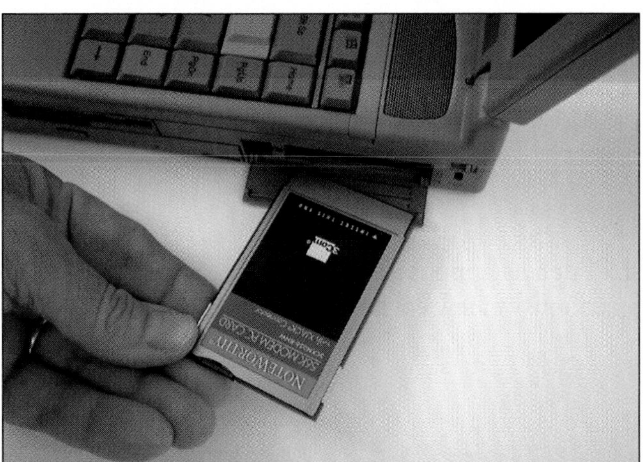

Figure 6-18 Many peripheral devices are added to a notebook using a PC Card slot; here, a modem PC Card is inserted in a PC Card slot.

ExpressCard technology is expected to replace CardBus as the preferred solution for adding devices to notebook and other types of computers. Until that time, a PC Card adapter for ExpressCard/34 is available for notebooks with only PC Card slots.

More About

Expansion Slots

To learn more about installing expansion cards in expansion slots, visit the Understanding and Troubleshooting Your PC More About Web page (**scsite.com/understanding/more**) and then click Expansion Slots below Chapter 6.

More About

Connecting Peripherals to Notebooks

To learn more about connecting peripheral devices to notebook computers, visit the Understanding and Troubleshooting Your PC More About Web page (**scsite.com/understanding/more**) and then click Connecting Peripherals to Notebooks below Chapter 6.

A PC Card or ExpressCard might contain a data cable to an external device, or it might be self-contained. For example, in Figure 6-19, the PC Card on the left is the interface between the notebook PC and an external CD-ROM drive. The card is inserted in the PC Card slot, and the data cable from the PC Card connects to the external CD-ROM drive, which requires its own power supply connected to a wall outlet. The card on the right is a modem card with all of the required technology included inside the card.

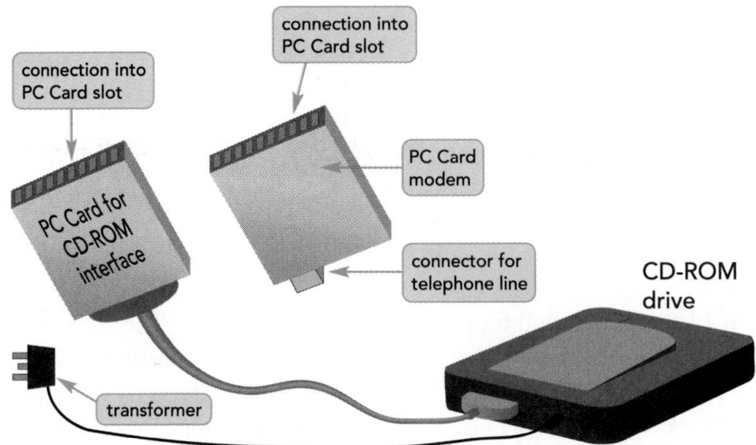

Figure 6-19 Two examples of PC Cards. The modem card is self-contained, while the CD-ROM interface card is connected to an external device (the CD-ROM drive).

Quiz Yourself 6-1

To test your knowledge of adding peripherals to a computer, visit the Understanding and Troubleshooting Your PC Quiz Yourself Web page (scsite.com/understanding/quiz). Click Quiz Yourself 1 below Chapter 6.

Input Devices

The keyboard and a pointing device such as a mouse are two of the more commonly used input devices. The following sections review each of these input devices in greater detail.

Keyboard

As you learned in Chapter 1, a keyboard is an input device with keys that users press to enter data and send instructions to a computer. Most of today's desktop computers use enhanced keyboards with 104 or 105 keys (Figure 6-20). In addition to the typing area with letters, numbers, punctuation, and other basic keys, an **enhanced keyboard** has function keys, a WINDOWS key, and APPLICATION key, and others listed in Figure 6-21.

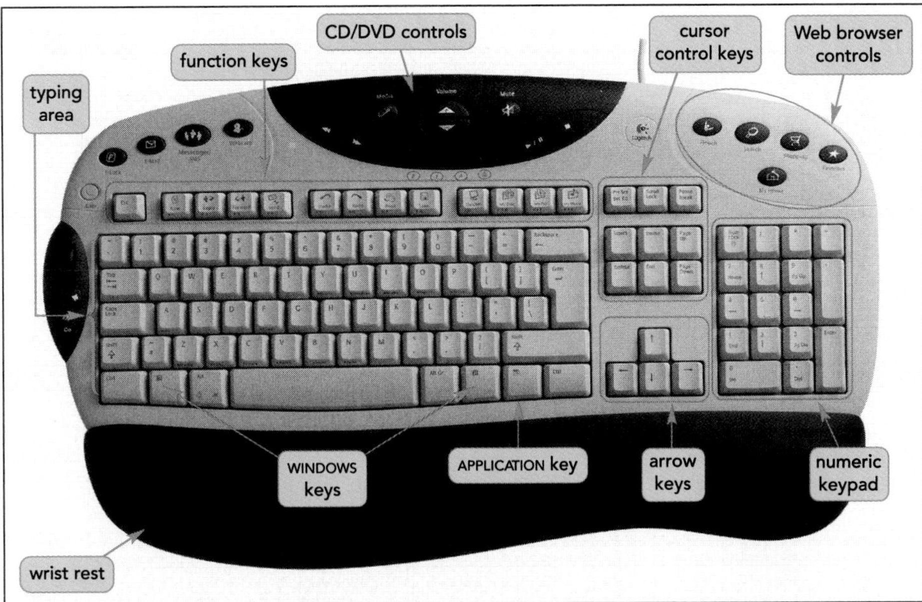

Figure 6-20 Newer enhanced keyboards include many keys in addition to the keys in the typing area.

Example	Key(s)	Description
 F11	function keys	Programmed to issue commands to a computer. F1, for example, tells the application to display Help.
 Home	cursor control keys	Moves the insertion point (or cursor) to top of page, bottom of page, start of document, and so on.
 ↑	arrow keys	Also called navigation keys. Moves the insertion point up, down, right, or left.
	WINDOWS key	Displays the Start menu.
	APPLICATION key	Displays an item's shortcut menu.

Figure 6-21 Special keys on an enhanced keyboard.

More About

Keyboard Technologies and Ergonomics

To learn more about ergonomics, visit the Understanding and Troubleshooting Your PC More About Web page (**scsite.com/understanding/more**) and then click Ergonomics below Chapter 6.

More About

Wireless Input Devices

To learn more about wireless keyboards and mouse units, visit the Understanding and Troubleshooting Your PC More About Web page (**scsite.com/understanding/more**) and then click Wireless Input Devices below Chapter 6.

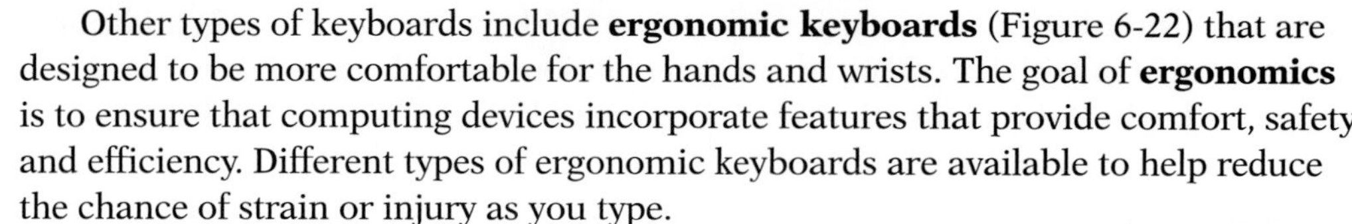

Other types of keyboards include **ergonomic keyboards** (Figure 6-22) that are designed to be more comfortable for the hands and wrists. The goal of **ergonomics** is to ensure that computing devices incorporate features that provide comfort, safety, and efficiency. Different types of ergonomic keyboards are available to help reduce the chance of strain or injury as you type.

Figure 6-22 Ergonomic keyboards and mice are designed to reduce strain and provide comfort.

CONNECTING A KEYBOARD On notebook computers, the keyboard is built into the system unit. For desktop and tower computers, keyboards connect to a PC in one of four ways: a cable with a PS/2 connector, a cable with a DIN connector, a cable with a USB port, or a wireless connection. The **DIN connector**, also called a **keyboard port connector**, is round and has five pins, while the smaller round **PS/2 connector**, sometimes called a **mini-DIN**, has six pins (Figure 6-23). Many newer keyboards use cables with USB ports. Finally, as previously discussed, wireless keyboards are cordless and use radio frequency or infrared technology to communicate with a sensor connected to a keyboard port.

Most often, installing a keyboard simply means plugging it in and turning on the PC. Because the system BIOS manages the keyboard, no keyboard drivers are necessary. The exception to this is a wireless keyboard, which needs a driver to work. With a wireless keyboard, you must use a regular keyboard to install the software to use the wireless keyboard. First, plug the wireless receiver into the correct port, install the drivers and software that came with the device, and then test the wireless keyboard to ensure it is working properly.

6-pin PS/2 connector (mini-DIN)

5-pin DIN connector

Figure 6-23 Two common keyboard connectors are a PS/2 (mini-DIN) connector and a DIN connector (also called a keyboard port connector).

TROUBLESHOOTING KEYBOARDS Often dirt, food, or liquid in the keyboard causes one or more keys to stick or not work properly. Because keyboards typically are not that expensive, the solution for a keyboard that does not work is most often to replace it.

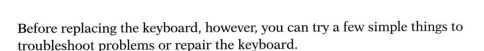

Before replacing the keyboard, however, you can try a few simple things to troubleshoot problems or repair the keyboard.

Several Keys Do Not Work If a few keys do not work, hold the keyboard upside down and blow short sprays from a can of compressed air to loosen and remove debris. Most compressed air cans come with a long straw to attach to the nozzle, which makes it easy to reach in between individual keys. You also can try lightly bumping multiple keys with your flat palm to dislodge any debris.

If that does not work, remove the caps on the bad keys with a **chip extractor**, which is a simple tong-like tool that can be used to remove chips from your computer. Spray contact cleaner into the key and then repeatedly depress the contact in order to clean it. Do not use rubbing alcohol to clean the well under the key, because it can leave a residue on the contact. If this method of cleaning solves the problem, then clean the adjacent keys as well. In work situations where dust and dirt are everywhere, such as a factory or garage, consider using a clear plastic keyboard cover.

If keys are producing the wrong characters when pressed, this problem usually is caused by a bad chip inside the keyboard. You most likely will have to replace the keyboard.

Key Continues to Repeat After Being Released This problem can be caused by a dirty contact: debris beneath the key cap may short the gap between the contacts, and cause the key to repeat. Try cleaning the key switch with contact cleaner, as described above.

Very high humidity and excess moisture sometimes short key switch contacts and cause keys to repeat, because water is an electrical conductor. The problem usually resolves itself when the humidity level decreases. You can hasten the drying process by using a cool fan (not a hot hair dryer) to blow air at the keyboard.

Major Spills on the Keyboard When coffee or sugary drinks spill on the keyboard, you most likely will need to replace the keyboard. You can try to save the keyboard by rinsing it in running water and then letting it dry thoroughly for several days before you use it. Be sure to turn off the computer and disconnect the keyboard before running it under water.

The Keyboard Does Not Work at All If the keyboard does not work at all, first determine that the cable is plugged in or, in the case of a wireless keyboard, that the receiver is connected to the computer. Keyboard cables may become loose or disconnected. If the cable connection is good and the keyboard still does not work, swap it with another keyboard of the same type that you know is in good condition, to verify that the problem is in the keyboard, not the computer.

If the problem is in the keyboard, you may want to turn off the computer, disconnect the keyboard, and then swap the cable with a known good one, perhaps from an old discarded keyboard. Most cables can be detached easily from the keyboard by removing the few screws that hold the keyboard case together, then simply unplugging the cable. Be careful as you work; do not allow the keycaps to fall out. If you continue to have problems, you may want to substitute a keyboard with a USB cable for one with a PS/2 or DIN connector.

Pointing Devices

A **pointing device** allows you to move a pointer on the screen and perform tasks such as executing (clicking) a command. The mouse is the most common pointing device, and other popular devices are the trackball, the touch pad, and a pointing stick embedded in the keyboard (Figure 6-24).

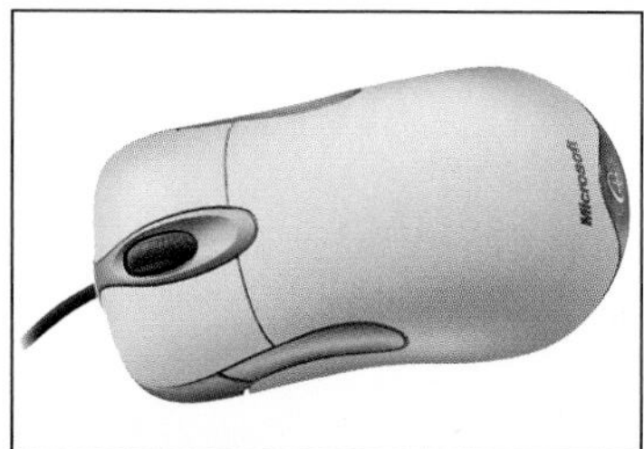

Figure 6-24 The most common pointing devices: a mouse, a trackball, a touch pad, and a pointing stick.

As you learned in Chapter 1, a mouse is an input device used to move a pointer on the screen and to make selections. A mouse typically has one to four buttons you press to complete a task; some also have a small wheel you can use to scroll a document or make selections. You can use Windows tools, or software that comes with the mouse, to program the functions for each button. A **trackball** is a stationary pointing device with a ball on its top, somewhat like an upside down mouse. You move the ball on top to turn rollers that turn a wheel sensed by a light beam. In addition to the ball, a trackball usually has one or more buttons that work just like mouse buttons.

A **touch pad** is a small, flat, rectangular pointing device that is sensitive to pressure and motion. A touch pad allows you to duplicate the mouse function, moving the pointer by applying light pressure with one finger on a pad that senses the movement. Touch pads are popular on notebook computers, because they work well in situations where space is limited.

A **pointing stick** is a pressure-sensitive pointing device shaped like a pencil eraser that is positioned between keys on a keyboard. To move the pointer using a pointing stick, you push the pointing stick with a finger; the pointer on the screen moves in the direction that you push the pointing stick.

Users who play games on their PC also may use a joystick or wheel as an input device. A **joystick** is a vertical lever mounted on a base. You move the lever in different directions to control the actions of the item on screen. A **wheel** is a steering-wheel-type input device. You turn the wheel to simulate driving a car, truck, or other vehicle. A joystick and wheel typically attach via a cable to a port on a sound card or a USB port.

Because the mouse is the most popular pointing device, the rest of this section focuses on mouse units.

TYPES OF MOUSE UNITS Two basic types of mouse units exist: a mechanical or wheel mouse and the optical mouse (Figure 6-25). A mechanical mouse or wheel mouse has a rubber or metal ball inside, which moves freely as you drag the mouse on a surface, such as a mouse pad. As shown in Figure 6-26, two or more rollers on the sides of the ball housing turn as the ball rolls against them. Each roller turns a wheel. The turning of the wheel is sensed by a small light beam as the wheel cuts the light beam when it turns. The cuts in the light beams are interpreted as mouse movement and sent to the CPU. One of two rollers tracks the x-axis (horizontal) movement of the mouse, and a second roller tracks the y-axis (vertical) movement.

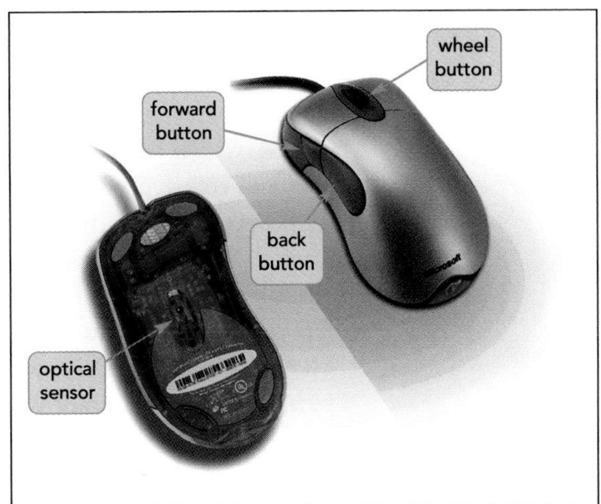

Figure 6-25 Two basic types of mouse units exist: a mechanical or wheel mouse and an optical mouse.

An optical mouse replaces the ball in a standard mouse with a microchip, miniature red light, and camera. The bottom of an optical mouse has a tiny hole for the camera, rather than a ball. As you move the mouse, the red light illuminates the work surface, the camera takes 1,500 snapshots every second, and the microchip reports the tiniest changes to the computer. An optical mouse works on most surfaces and does not require a mouse pad.

CONNECTING A MOUSE A mouse can connect to the computer using one of several ports, including the serial port, a USB port, or the round **mouse port** or **PS/2 port** coming directly from the motherboard. Finally, as previously discussed, a wireless mouse can be connected using radio frequency, such as Bluetooth, or infrared technologies to send a signal to a receiver on the computer.

If a mouse (PS/2) port is available and the mouse will connect to it, use the mouse port, rather than serial or USB port that other devices could use. The motherboard mouse port most likely uses IRQ 12. If you are not using a mouse on this port, the motherboard might release IRQ 12 so other devices can use it. If a computer does not have a mouse port, you can use a serial port or USB port to connect a mouse.

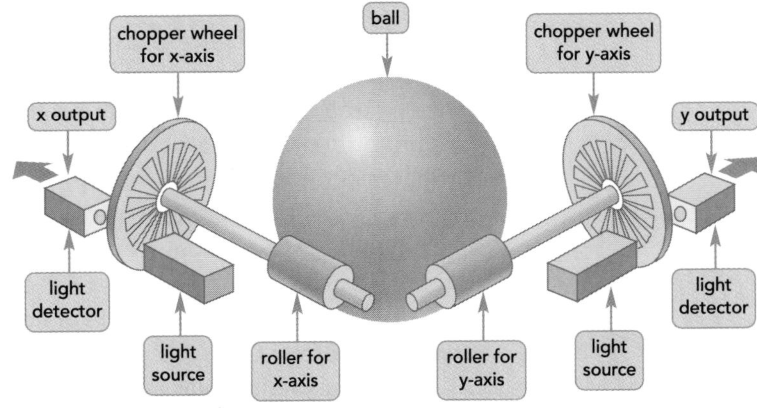

Figure 6-26 How a mechanical mouse works.

FAQ 6-10

The keyboard and mouse ports look exactly alike! How can I tell them apart?

As shown earlier in Figure 6-2 on page 224, the PS/2 port used by a mouse looks very similar to the PS/2 port used by a keyboard. These ports are not interchangeable, however. You can identify the different ports by the color: mouse ports are green and keyboard ports are purple. Many computer cases also put symbols above the ports to indicate which port is which.

MAINTAINING AND TROUBLESHOOTING A MOUSE Although a mechanical mouse is a relatively simple device, the rollers inside the wheel mouse housing do collect dirt and dust and occasionally need cleaning. To clean a mechanical mouse, remove the cover of the mouse ball from the bottom of the mouse (the cover usually comes off with a simple turning motion). After you have removed the cover, clean the rollers with a cotton swab dipped in a very small amount of water.

If the mouse does not work or the mouse pointer is moving erratically on the screen, try the following to troubleshoot the mouse:

- Close any open applications and restart the computer.
- Check the mouse port connection. Is it secure and is the mouse plugged into the appropriate port (for example, is the mouse accidentally plugged into the keyboard port?)
- Using Device Manager and the Add New Hardware icon in the Control Panel, first uninstall and then reinstall the mouse driver. Restart the computer and check to see if the mouse is behaving correctly.

Output Devices

The monitor and the printer are the two most widely used output devices. The following section reviews monitors in greater detail. Printers are covered in detail in the next chapter.

CRT and Flat-Panel Monitors

A monitor (also called a *display* or *screen*) is a plastic or metal case that houses a device that visually displays the output of the computer. The two necessary components for output from a monitor are the video card and the monitor itself. The video card not only provides a port for the monitor, it serves as the interface between the computer and the monitor — taking program output and instructing the monitor how to display it on the screen. Video cards are referred to by several different names, including video controller card, graphic adapter, video board, graphics card, or display card.

Before discussing video cards in detail, the following sections review the two types of monitors: CRT (cathode-ray tube) monitors and flat-panel monitors that use LCD (liquid crystal display) technology.

CRT MONITORS A **CRT monitor** is a desktop monitor that is similar to a standard television because it contains a cathode ray tube. A *cathode-ray tube (CRT)* is a large, sealed glass tube. Filaments at the back of the cathode-ray tube shoot a beam of electrons to the screen at the front of the tube, as illustrated in Figure 6-27. Plates on the top, bottom, and sides of the tube control the direction of the beam. The beam is directed by these plates to start at the top of the screen, move from left to right to make one line, and then move down to the next line, again moving from left to right. As the beam moves vertically down the screen, it builds the image.

By turning the beam on and off and selecting the correct color combination, the grid in front of the filaments controls what goes on the screen when the beam hits that portion of the line or a single dot on the screen. When hit, special phosphors on the back of the monitor screen light up and produce colors. The grid controls which one of three electron guns fires, each gun targeting a different color (red, green, or blue) positioned on the back of the screen.

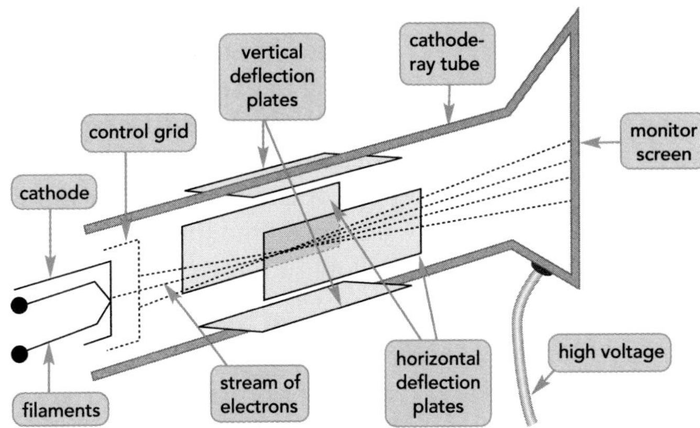

Figure 6-27 How a CRT monitor works.

When purchasing a CRT monitor, you should understand that quality and price of a CRT monitor is based on several features — screen size, refresh rate, interlace features, dot pitch, and resolution (Figure 6-28). The following sections discuss these features in detail.

Monitor Characteristic	Description
Screen size	Diagonal length of the screen surface.
Refresh rate (vertical scan rate)	The number of times in one second that an electronic beam fills a video screen with lines from top to bottom in one second. *Multiscan* monitors offer a variety of refresh rates so they can support several video cards.
Interlaced	The electronic beam draws every other line with each pass, which lessens the overall effect of a lower refresh rate.
Dot pitch	The distance between adjacent dots on the screen.
Resolution	The number of spots, or pixels, on a screen that can be addressed by software.

Figure 6-28 Features of a monitor.

Can I open a monitor to look at the parts inside?

It is not advisable. As you learned in Chapter 1, computer monitors contain capacitors that can store dangerous electrical charges even when the device is unplugged. You never should open the case on a power supply or monitor unless you are working with an expert or are qualified to do so, and know exactly what you are doing. If you are working with a power supply or monitor, be careful NOT to ground yourself or wear a ground bracelet — otherwise you will provide a path for the voltage to discharge through your body.

Screen Size The screen size of a monitor is the one feature that most affects price. The larger the screen size, the more expensive the monitor. Common screen sizes in inches are 15, 17, 19, 21, and 22. Monitor sizes are measured diagonally from one corner of the case to the other. In addition to the monitor, a monitor also has a viewable size. The **viewable size** is the actual size of the lighted screen in the monitor. A 21-inch monitor, for example, may have a viewable size of only 20 inches.

Refresh Rate The **refresh rate**, or **vertical scan rate**, is the number of times in one second an electronic beam can fill the screen with lines from top to bottom. Refresh rates differ among monitors. Slower refresh rates make the image appear to flicker, while faster refresh rates make the image appear solid and stable. You can set the refresh rate by double-clicking the Display icon in the Control Panel and then clicking the Settings tab (in Category view, click Appearance and Themes and then click Display). **Multiscan** monitors offer a variety of vertical and horizontal refresh rates so they can support a variety of video cards. They cost more, but are much more versatile than other monitors. If you spend many hours in front of a computer, use a good monitor with a higher refresh rate (above 70 Hz). The lower refresh rates (below 70 Hz) cause monitor flicker that can tire your eyes.

Interlaced or Noninterlaced **Interlaced** monitors draw a screen by making two passes. On the first pass, the electronic beam strikes only the even lines, and on the second pass, the beam strikes only the odd lines. The result is that a monitor can have a slow refresh rate with a less noticeable overall effect than there would be if the beam hit all lines for each pass. Interlaced monitors generally have slightly less flicker than **noninterlaced** monitors, which always draw the entire screen on each pass. An interlaced monitor is easier on the eyes, especially if you plan to spend many hours looking at the screen.

Dot Pitch **Dot pitch** is the distance between the spots, or dots, on the screen that the electronic beam hits. Remember that three beams build the screen, one for each of three colors (red, green, and blue). Each composite location on the screen is really made up of three dots and is called a triad. The distance between a color dot in one triad and the same color dot in the next triad is the dot pitch. The smaller the pitch is, the sharper the image. Dot pitches of .20 or .22 mm give the best results and cost more. Although less expensive monitors can have a dot pitch of .35 mm or .38 mm, they still can create a fuzzy image, even with the best video cards.

Resolution *Resolution* describes the sharpness and clarity of an image, which, for a monitor, is defined by how many spots on the screen are addressable by software. Each addressable location is called a *pixel* (short for *picture element*), which is composed of several triads. Manufacturers state the resolution of a monitor in pixels. For example, a monitor set at 800 × 600 pixels displays up to 800 pixels per horizontal inch and 600 pixels per vertical inch, for a total of 480,000 pixels to create a screen image.

Most monitors support a number of resolutions. Standard CRT monitors usually display a maximum of 1600 × 1200 pixels, with 800 × 600 pixels as the overall baseline. High-end monitors may even display up to 2048 × 1356. You can set the resolution for a monitor by double-clicking the Display icon in the Control Panel and then clicking the Settings tab. The video card and drivers installed in the computer must support the resolution.

Why does setting the monitor to a higher resolution make items look smaller on screen?

As resolution increases, the overall screen size increases — which means you can see more items on the screen, but each individual item appears smaller. In general, smaller monitors look better at a lower resolution and larger monitors look better at a higher resolution. The display resolution you choose, however, is a matter of personal preference and you should set the resolution to a size that makes it comfortable for you to read text on the screen.

FLAT PANEL MONITORS A **flat panel monitor**, also called an **LCD monitor**, uses a liquid crystal display instead of a cathode-ray tube to produce images on the screen. An LCD panel produces an image using a liquid crystal material made of large, easily polarized molecules. Figure 6-29 shows the layers of the LCD panel that together create the image. At the center of the layers is the liquid crystal material. Next to it is the layer responsible for providing color to the image. These two layers are sandwiched between two grids of electrodes. One grid of electrodes is aligned in columns, and the other electrodes are aligned in rows. The two layers of electrodes make up the electrode matrix. Each intersection of a row electrode and a column electrode forms one pixel on the LCD panel. Software can manipulate each pixel by activating the electrodes that form it. The image is formed by scanning the column and row electrodes, much as the electronic beam scans a CRT monitor screen.

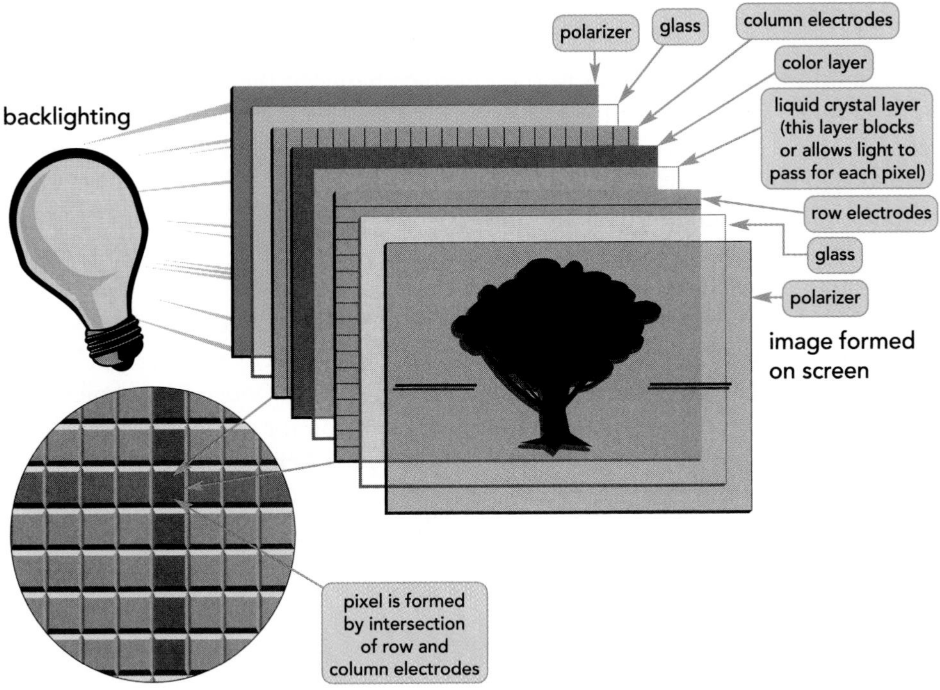

Figure 6-29 How the layers of an LCD monitor work.

The polarizer layers outside the glass layers in Figure 6-29 are responsible for preventing light from passing through the pixels when the electrodes are not activated. When the electrodes are activated, light on the back side of the LCD panel can pass through one pixel on the screen, picking up color from the color layer as it passes through.

Two kinds of LCD panels are on the market today: active-matrix and dual-scan passive matrix displays. With a dual-scan **passive matrix display**, two columns of electrodes are activated at the same time. With **active-matrix display**, also known as a **TFT (thin-film transistor) display**, a transistor that amplifies the signal is placed at every intersection in the grid, which further enhances the pixel quality. Although a dual-scan passive matrix display is less expensive than an active-matrix display, the active-matrix display provides a much higher quality image.

Flat panel monitors support resolution differently than CRTs. While a CRT can display a range of resolutions by using larger and smaller pixels to fit the resolution, an LCD panel has a fixed number of pixels (the intersections of row and column electrodes) based on the highest resolution supported. A flat panel monitor displays the highest resolution at full-screen size, using one cell per pixel. Lower resolutions are displayed using only a proportion of the screen or are scaled to fit the full screen. For

> **More About**
>
> **Installing Dual Monitors**
>
> To learn more about installing dual monitors for your computer, visit the Understanding and Troubleshooting Your PC More About Web page (**scsite.com/understanding/more**) and then click Installing Dual Monitors below Chapter 6.

example, if you send an 800 × 600 image to a flat panel designed to display 1280 × 1024 resolution, the image either will be scaled up to fit the full screen or appear as a rectangle in the middle of the screen.

Notebook computers use flat panel monitors built into the computer case. More and more desktop computer users are choosing to use stand-alone flat panel monitors because they take up much less desk space than CRT monitors, are lighter, emit less radiation, and require less electricity to operate. Although they continue to drop in price, flat panel monitors still cost much more than comparable CRT monitors.

Video Cards

Recall that the video card serves as the interface between the computer and the monitor — taking program output and instructing the monitor how to display it on the screen. For a CRT, a video card converts digital output from the computer into an analog video signal and sends the signal through the cable to the monitor, which displays output on the screen. Flat panel monitors have two ports to accommodate an analog or digital signal from the video card. If the signal is analog, it must be converted to digital before the monitor can process it.

Over the years, several video card standards have been developed to define the resolution, number of colors, and other display properties supported by video cards. These standards, which are listed in Figure 6-30, are defined by VESA (Video Electronics Standard Association), which consists of video card and monitor manufacturers. Most current video cards support **SVGA (Super Video Graphics Array)** and beyond for CRTs; newer video cards are providing support for DVI and several other digital LCD standards. For a monitor to display images using the resolution and number of colors defined by a standard, the video card and the monitor both must support the standard.

CRT Standard	Example of Resolution	Maximum Possible Colors
VGA (Video Graphics Array)	640 × 480 320 × 200	16 256
XGA (Extended Graphics Array)	1024 × 768 640 × 480	256 65,536
SVGA (Super Video Graphics Array)	800 × 600 1024 × 768 1280 × 1024 1600 × 1200	16.7 million 16.7 million 16.7 million 16.7 million
Beyond SVGA	1920 × 1440 2048 × 1536	16.7 million 16.7 million

Figure 6-30 Video standards. Most current video cards support SVGA for CRTs.

A video card can pass data to a monitor or other display device such as a television in one of four ways, which determines the type of port on the back of the video card that connects to the monitor or television cable. Figure 6-31 shows a video card that has three of the four ports. The four methods of data transfer are:

- *RGB video port*. This is the standard method of passing three separate signals for red, green, and blue, which most video cards and CRT monitors use. The card shown in Figure 6-31 has a regular 15-pin SVGA port (commonly called a VGA port).

- *DVI (Digital Video Interface) port*. This method is the digital interface standard used by digital monitors such as flat panel monitors and digital TVs (HDTV). For a video card that only has a DVI port, you can purchase a VGA converter so you can connect a standard VGA video cable to use a regular analog CRT monitor.
- *S-Video (Super-Video)*. This method sends two signals over the cable, one for color and the other for brightness, and is used by some high-end TVs and video equipment. It uses a 4-pin round port. The television or video equipment and the video card must support this method, and you must use a special S-Video cable like the one in Figure 6-32. This standard is not as good as RGB for monitors, but is better than Composite video when output to a television.
- *Composite video*. Using this method, the red, green, and blue are mixed together in the same signal. This is the method used by television, and can be used by a video card that is designed to send output to a TV. This method uses a Composite Out port, which is round and is the same size as the S-Video Out port showing in Figure 6-31, but has only a single pin in the center of the port. Composite video does not produce as sharp an image as RGB video or S-Video.

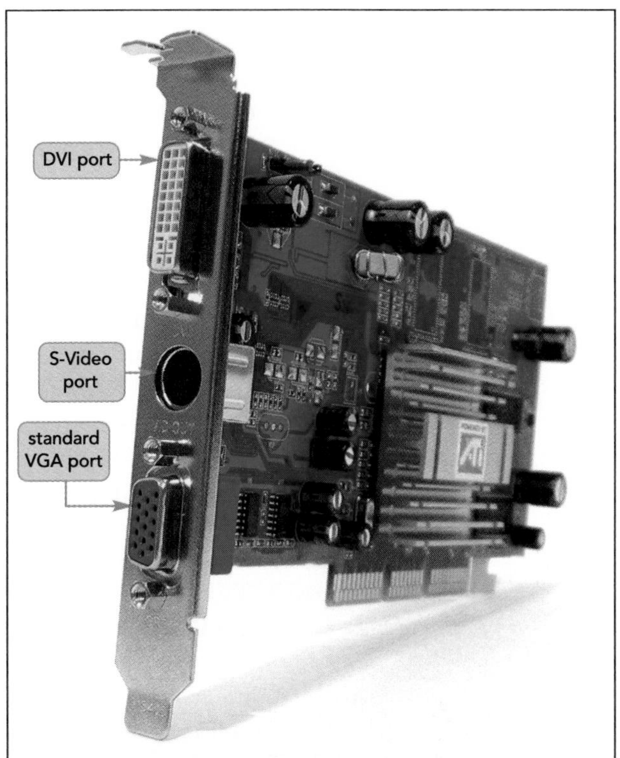

Figure 6-31 This video card has three video ports: DVI, S-Video, and a standard VGA port as the RGB video port.

The quality of a video subsystem is rated according to how it affects overall system performance, video quality (including resolution and color), power-saving features, and ease of use and installation. Two main features to look for in a video card are the type of video RAM it has or can support and the bus it uses.

VIDEO RAM Older video cards had no memory, but today they need memory to handle the large volume of data generated by increased resolution and color. Video memory is stored on video cards as memory chips. The first video cards to have memory used DRAM chips, but now video memory chips can use several technologies.

Current types of video memory include VRAM, SGRAM, WRAM, and 3-D RAM. **Video RAM**, or **VRAM**, is a form of RAM used to store image data for a computer display. Most forms of video RAM are **dual-ported**, which means that while the CPU is writing a new image to video RAM, the monitor is reading from video RAM to refresh its current display content. The dual-port design is the main difference between main RAM and video RAM. The amount of data a video card receives from the CPU for each frame (or screen) of data is determined by the screen resolution (measured in pixels), the number of colors (called color depth and

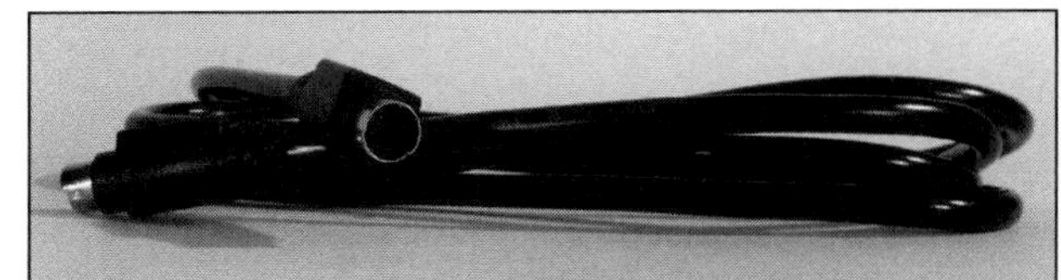

Figure 6-32 An S-Video cable used to connect a video card to an S-Video port on a television.

measured in bits), and enhancements to color information (called alpha blending). The more data required to generate a single screen of data, the more memory is required to hold that data. The video RAM holds one frame of data before it is sent to the monitor and thus is called the frame buffer.

SGRAM (synchronous graphics RAM) is similar to SDRAM, but is designed specifically for video card processing. Like SDRAM, SGRAM can synchronize itself with the CPU bus clock, which makes the memory faster. SGRAM also uses other methods to increase overall performance for graphics-intensive processing but is not dual-ported memory. It is used on moderate to high-end cards when the very highest resolutions are not required.

WRAM (window RAM) is a type of dual-ported RAM that is faster and less expensive than VRAM. WRAM's increased speed is primarily due to its own internal bus on the chip, which has a data path that is 256 bits wide. WRAM is used on high-end graphics cards with very high resolutions and true color. **3-D RAM** specifically was designed to improve performance for video processing that involves simulating 3-D graphics.

AGP TECHNOLOGIES Three buses have been used for video cards in the last 10 years or so: the VESA bus, the PCI bus, and the AGP bus. The VESA and AGP buses were developed specifically for video cards, and the PCI bus is used for many types of cards, including a video card. As previously discussed, today's video cards use the AGP bus, because it is designed to provide fast access to video and offers additional features that help provide better overall performance for video than PCI.

AGP technologies have evolved over the years. The AGP 2X specification allowed AGP to transfer two cycles of data during a single AGP clock beat. The latest AGP standard is AGP 8X that runs at eight cycles of data per clock cycle (2.1 GB/sec). In order for AGP to work at its full potential, the motherboard must run at a minimum of 100 MHz, and the operating system must support AGP. Windows 98, Windows 2000, Windows XP, and Windows Server 2003 all support AGP.

Once of the unique features of AGP is **direct memory execute (DIME)**, which is its ability to share system memory with the CPU. Because it can share memory with the CPU to perform calculations, AGP does not always have to first copy data from system memory to video memory on the graphics card. DIME is probably the most powerful feature of AGP.

GRAPHICS ACCELERATORS One of the more important advances made in video cards in recent years is the introduction of graphics accelerators. A **graphics accelerator** is a type of video card that has its own processor to boost performance. The processor on a graphics accelerator card is similar to a CPU but specifically designed to manage video and graphics.

Some features of graphics accelerators are support for 3-D graphics, digital output to flat panel display monitors, and support for high-intensity graphics software such as AutoCAD and Quark. All these features are designed to reduce the burden on the motherboard CPU and to perform the video and graphics functions much faster than the motherboard CPU. With the demands that graphics applications make in the multimedia environment, graphics accelerators are standard equipment on high-end computers.

Troubleshooting Monitors and Video Cards

Monitors and video cards may start to have problems for any number of reasons, although many monitor problems are caused by poor cable connections or bad contrast/brightness adjustments. For example, if the power light does not go on and the monitor has no picture, confirm that the monitor is turned on and plugged in. If necessary, verify that the wall outlet works by plugging in a lamp or radio. If the monitor power cord is plugged into the back of the computer, verify that the connection is tight and the computer is turned on.

If the monitor has power, but is not displaying a picture, try the following:

- Check the contrast and brightness adjustments on the monitor.
- In addition, check that the cable from the monitor is connected securely to the correct port on the computer. If the monitor cable can be detached, exchange it for a cable you know is good to determine if the cable is the source of the problem.
- You also might want to check the CMOS settings or software configuration on the computer by booting into Safe Mode. Using Windows Server 2003, Windows XP, or Windows 2000, you can boot into safe mode by pressing F8 during the boot (press F5 is you are using Windows 9x). Booting into Safe Mode allows the OS to select a generic display driver and low resolution. If this works, change the driver and resolution.
- If the system still does not work, open the computer and reseat the video card. For a PCI card, move the card to a different expansion slot. Before reseating the card, clean the card's edge connectors, using a contact cleaner or a white eraser. Do not let crumbs from the eraser fall into the expansion slot.

If the monitor is flickering, try the following:

- Check that the cable connections are snug.
- Also check if something in the work area is causing a high amount of electrical noise. For example, you might be able to stop a flicker by moving the office fan to a different outlet. Fluorescent lights or large speakers also can produce interference. Two monitors placed very close together also can cause problems.
- Finally, if the refresh rate of the monitor is set below 60 Hz, a screen flicker may appear. Check the settings for the monitor and set if to the highest refresh rate available.

More About

Troubleshooting Monitors

To learn more about troubleshooting issues with a monitor, visit the Understanding and Troubleshooting Your PC More About Web page (**scsite.com/understanding/more**) and then click Troubleshooting Monitors below Chapter 6.

Quiz Yourself 6-2

To test your knowledge of input and output devices, visit the Understanding and Troubleshooting Your PC Quiz Yourself Web page (scsite.com/understanding/quiz). Click Quiz Yourself 2 below Chapter 6.

Multimedia Technologies

The goal of multimedia technology is to create or reproduce lifelike representations for audio, video, and animation. Remember that computers store data digitally and ultimately as a stream of only two numbers: 0 and 1. In contrast, sights and sounds have an infinite number of variations and are analog in nature. The challenge for multimedia technology is to bridge these two worlds.

Many multimedia capabilities are added to a system using sound cards and other adapter cards. There also are externally attached devices such as digital cameras or MP3 players. In this section, you will learn about these and other devices, as well as CPU technologies designed to provide better multimedia support.

CPU Technologies for Multimedia

As the use of multimedia became more widespread, Intel updated their CPUs with new technologies to support multimedia applications. Multimedia applications tend to require more data-intense input and output operations, as they do complex computations. The Pentium MMX introduced **MMX (Multimedia Extensions)** and the Pentium III introduced Intel's performance enhancement called *Streaming SIMD Extensions (SSE)*. Both MMX and SSE were designed to speed up the repetitive looping of multimedia software and manage the high-volume input/output of graphics, motion video, animation, and sound.

MMX technology added new instructions designed for repetitive processing, more efficient ways to pass those instructions to the CPU, and increased CPU cache. SSE relies on *SIMD (single instruction, multiple data)*, which is a process that allows the CPU to receive a single instruction and then execute it on multiple pieces of data rather than receiving the same instruction each time the data is received.

Audio Input and Output

An audio input device allows a user to enter any sound into the computer, such as speech, music, and sound effects. Users input sound via audio input devices such as microphones, CD and DVD players, tape players, and even musical instruments such as electronic keyboards. To input high-quality sound, a personal computer must have a sound card. An audio output device produces audio output such as music, speech, and beeps. Two commonly used audio output devices — speakers and headsets — connect to a port on the sound card to receive audio output from the computer.

SOUND CARDS A *sound card* is an expansion card that records sound, saves it in a file on your hard drive, and plays it back. Some cards give you the ability to mix and edit sounds, and even to edit the sounds using standard music score notation. Sound cards have at least three ports — Line in, Line out, and Microphone — that allow you to attach an external sound source, such as a music keyboard, external stereo speakers, and a microphone, respectively. A computer's CD-ROM or DVD-ROM drive is attached to the sound card internally.

A sound card can be an expansion card installed in the PCI expansion slot, or can come built into a few chips on a motherboard with embedded or integrated sound capability. For example, the computer shown earlier in Figure 6-2 on page 224 has three regular sound ports (Line in, Line out, and Microphone) and an S/PDIF port. An **S/PDIF port**, short for Sony/Philips Digital Interface port, is a specialized port that allows the transfer of digital audio data from one device to another, without the data first having to be converted to analog format. If onboard sound is problematic or you simply want to upgrade to a better sound, you can use CMOS setup to disable the onboard sound and then install a sound card.

Sound cards often are referred to as **Sound Blaster-compatible**, meaning that they understand the commands sent to them that have been written for a Sound Blaster card, which generally is considered the standard for PC sound cards.

SAMPLING AND DIGITIZING THE SOUND Speakers, headsets, and other audio output devices all rely on a sound card to produce audio output such as music, voices, beeps, and chimes. A sound card contains the circuitry for recording and reproducing sound.

To record a sound, an input device, such as a microphone or audio CD player, must be connected to a port on the sound card. The input device sends the sound to the sound card as an analog signal. The analog signal flows to the sound card's analog-to-digital-converter. The **analog-to-digital-converter** (**ADC**) converts the signal into digital (binary) data of 1s and 0s by sampling the signal at set intervals.

The analog sound is a continuous waveform. To represent the waveform in a recording, the computer would have to store the value of the waveform at every instant in time. Because this is not possible, the sound is recorded using a sampling process. **Sampling** consists of breaking up the waveform into set intervals and representing all values during that interval with a single value.

Several factors in the sampling process affect the quality of the sound during playback. These include sampling rate, audio resolution, and mono or stereo recording.

- *Sampling rate,* also called *sampling frequency*, refers to the number of times per second the sound will be recorded (Figure 6-33). The more frequently a sound is recorded per second, the smaller the intervals and the better the quality. The sampling frequency used for audio CDs, for example, is 44,100 times per second, which is expressed in hertz (Hz) as 44,100 Hz. A sampling rate of 22,050 Hz is used for lower quality multimedia files with the quality of a cassette tape or FM radio; a sampling rate of 11,024 Hz is used for basic sounds like Windows chimes.
- *Audio resolution* — defined as 8-bit, 16-bit, or 24-bit — refers to the number of bytes used to represent the sound at any one interval. A sound card using 8-bit resolution can represent a sound with 1 of 256 values. A 16-bit sound card can use any 1 of 65,536 values for each interval. The resolution directly relates to the range of sound (the difference between the softest and loudest sounds) that can be represented. Simply put, the higher the audio resolution, the more accurate the representation of the level of each sample and, consequently, the better the sound. With 8-bit resolution, the sound quality is like that of an AM radio; 16-bit sound is CD quality. High quality digital audio editing uses 24-bit sampling.

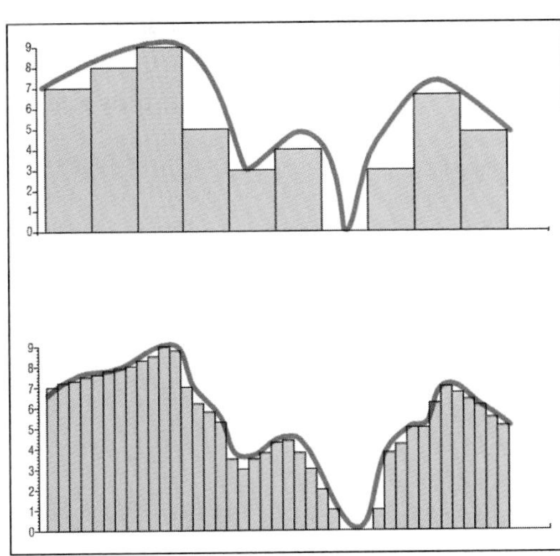

Figure 6-33 Comparison of low versus high sampling rates.

- *Mono or stereo recording* refers to the number of channels used during recording. Mono means that the same sound will come from both the left and right speaker during playback. Stereo means that there are two separate channels in the recording: one for the right speaker and one for the left. Most sound cards can handle more than one signal at a time, allowing you to record sounds in stereo, which provides more realistic playback of complex sounds.

After the ADC converts the analog sound through sampling, the digital data flows to the **digital signal processor** (**DSP**), which gets instructions on how to handle the data from a memory chip on the sound card. The memory chip — either ROM or flash memory — contains the instructions that tell the DSP how to process the digital signal. Typically, the DSP compresses the digital data to save space. Finally, the DSP sends the compressed data to the computer's main processor, which stores the data in audio file format, such as WAV or MP3.

To play a recorded sound, such as a WAV or MP3 file, or a CD track, the processor retrieves the file that contains the compressed digital data from a hard drive, CD-ROM, or other storage device. The processor then sends the digital data to the DSP, which decompresses the data and looks to the memory chip to determine how to recreate the sound.

The DSP then sends the digital signals to the sound card's **digital-to-analog converter** (**DAC**), which converts the digital data back to an analog electrical voltage. An amplifier built into the speakers strengthens the electrical voltage and causes the speaker's cone to vibrate, recreating the sound.

INSTALLING A SOUND CARD When you purchase a sound card, it most likely will come with device drivers and application software. The three main steps in the following example are to install the card in an empty PCI slot on the motherboard, install the driver, and then install the applications stored on the CD-ROM or DVD-ROM that comes with the sound card.

The Sound Blaster card shown in Figure 6-34 has several ports that are labeled in the figure. The sound card has three internal connections (connections to something inside the case) and one jumper group that enables or disables a speaker amplifier. If you are using a speaker system with an external amplifier, disable the amplifier on the card by setting the jumper on the sound card to disable the amplifier.

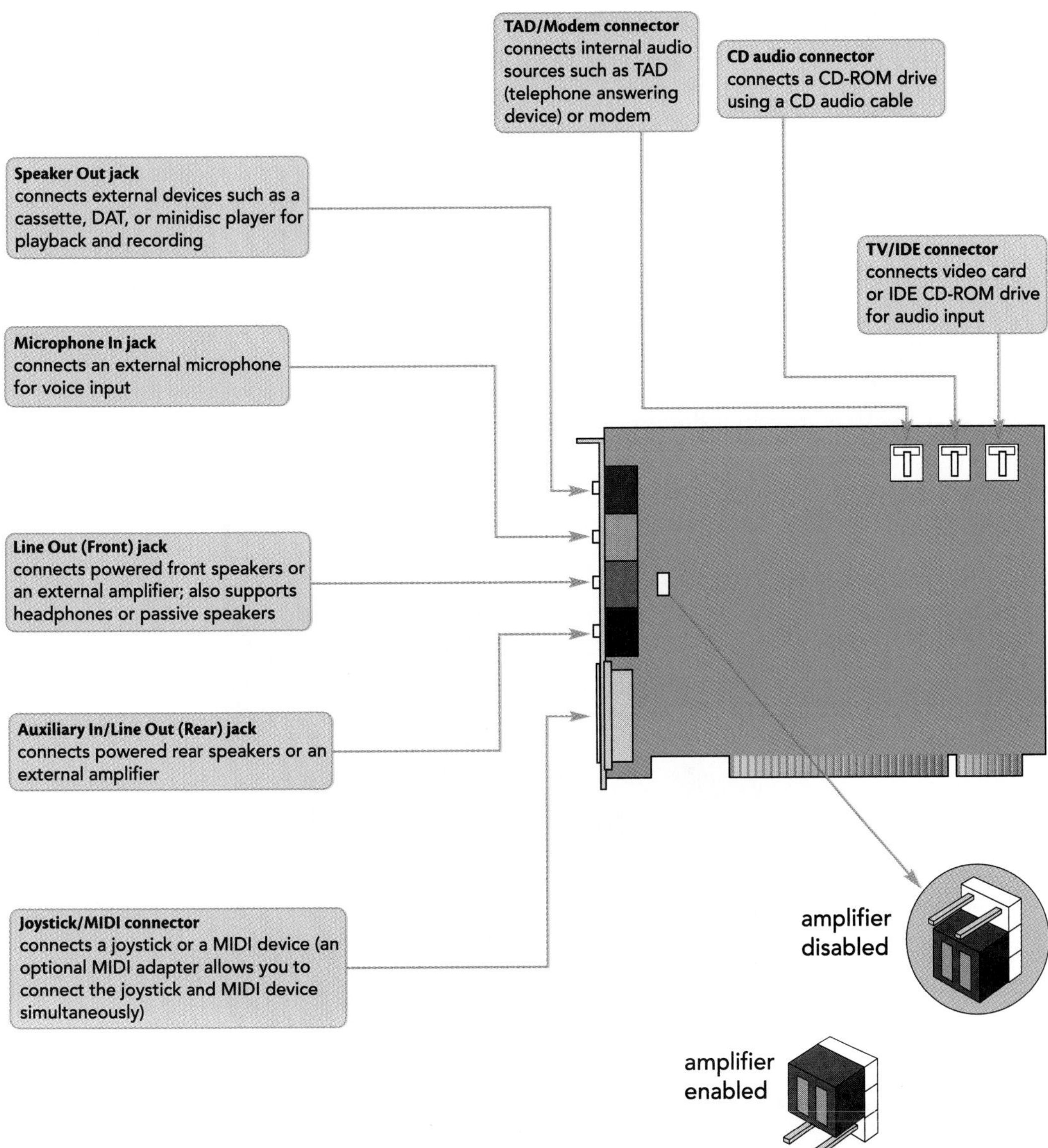
TAD/Modem connector
connects internal audio sources such as TAD (telephone answering device) or modem
CD audio connector
connects a CD-ROM drive using a CD audio cable
Speaker Out jack
connects external devices such as a cassette, DAT, or minidisc player for playback and recording
TV/IDE connector
connects video card or IDE CD-ROM drive for audio input
Microphone In jack
connects an external microphone for voice input
Line Out (Front) jack
connects powered front speakers or an external amplifier; also supports headphones or passive speakers
Auxiliary In/Line Out (Rear) jack
connects powered rear speakers or an external amplifier
Joystick/MIDI connector
connects a joystick or a MIDI device (an optional MIDI adapter allows you to connect the joystick and MIDI device simultaneously)
amplifier disabled
amplifier enabled

Figure 6-34 This Sound Blaster sound card has three internal connections and one jumper group that controls amplifier support.

Follow these steps to install a sound card:

1. Make sure that you are grounded properly. Wear a ground bracelet and follow other procedures to guard against ESD.
2. Turn off the PC, remove the cover, and locate an empty expansion slot for the card. Because this installation uses the connecting wire from the sound card to the CD-ROM drive (the wire comes with the sound card), place the sound card near enough to the CD-ROM drive so the wire can reach between them.

3. Attach the wire to the sound card and to the CD-ROM drive (Figure 6-35).
4. Remove the cover from the slot opening at the rear of the PC case and place the card into the PCI slot, making sure that the card is seated firmly. Use the screw taken from the slot cover to secure the card to the back of the PC case.
5. Check again that both ends of the wire still are connected securely and that the wire is not hampering the CPU fan, and then replace the case cover. Note that some high-end sound cards have a power connector to provide extra power to the card. For this type of card, connect a power cable with a miniature 4-pin connector to the card.
6. Plug in the speakers to the ports at the back of the sound card, and turn on the PC. The speakers may or may not require their own power source. Check the product documentation or manufacturer's Web site for more information.

Figure 6-35 Connect the wire to the sound card that will make the direct audio connection from the CD.

After the card is installed, the device drivers must be installed. With Windows 2000, Windows XP, or Windows Server 2003, restart the computer and Windows will detect the sound card and start the Found New Hardware Wizard. If your sound card came with a CD-ROM or DVD-ROM, insert it in the drive and follow the steps to install the driver from the disc. If you downloaded the driver from the Internet, Windows XP should detect it on your computer, but you may need to select Install from a list or specific location on the Found New Hardware Wizard window and then navigate to the file. Follow the instructions on the wizard to finish installing the driver.

When the driver installation is complete, restart your PC and then access Device Manager to confirm that the sound card and its drivers are listed in Device Manager under Sound, video, and game controllers (Figure 6-36). To see the resources used by the card, right click the sound card in the list and then click Properties on the shortcut menu.

With most sound cards, the CD containing the sound card driver has application software for the special features offered by the card. Sometimes, as with the previous example, the software is installed at the same time as the drivers, so you can use the

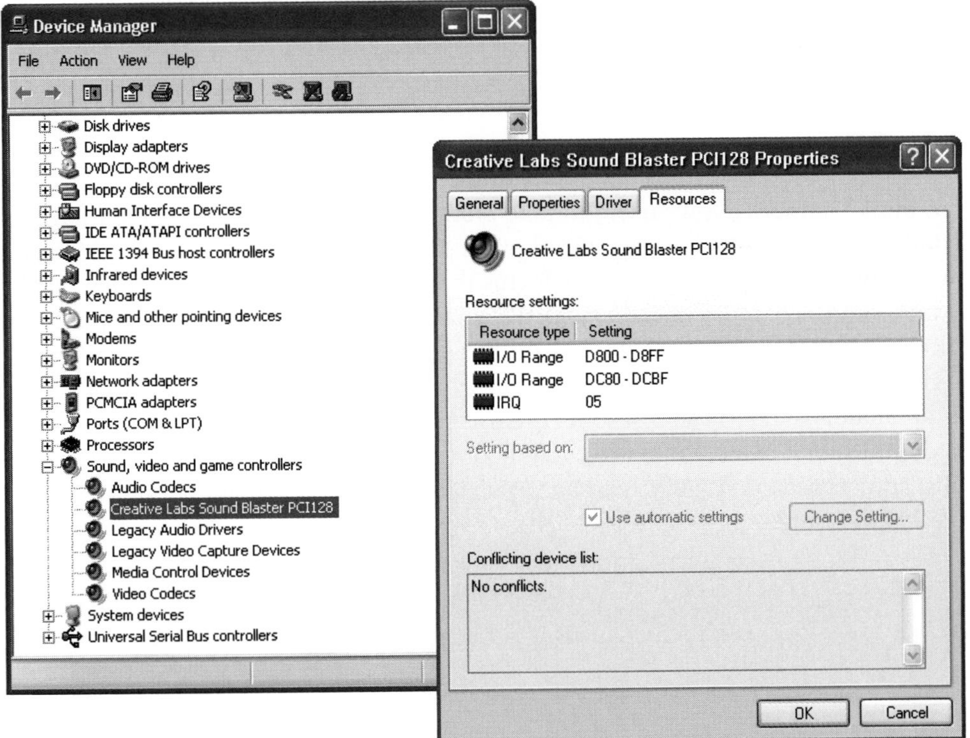

Figure 6-36 Device Manager shows the installed sound card and the resources it is using.

software at this point in the installation. For other sound cards, you can install the additional software after the driver is installed and the sound card is working. Before installing a sound card, read the documentation that comes with it to learn if application software is present, and how and when to install it.

TROUBLESHOOTING SOUND PROBLEMS Problems with sound can be caused by a problem with the sound card itself, but they also can be a result of system settings, bad connections, or a number of other factors. If your sound card is not producing sound, ask yourself the following questions:

- Is the sound cable attached between the drive and the analog audio connector on the sound card?
- Are the speakers turned on? Is the speaker volume turned down? Is the volume control for Windows turned down?
- Are the speakers plugged into the line “Out” or the “Spkr” port of the sound card?
- Is the transformer for the speaker plugged into an electrical outlet on one end and into the speakers on the other end?
- Is Device Manager displaying a red X to indicate the card is disabled or an exclamation point symbol to indicate a problem with the card? If the card is disabled, enable it. If another device is using the same I/O addresses or IRQ number, assign new resources to the card.
- Is the sound card properly seated? To check for a bad connection, turn off the computer, and then remove and reinstall the sound card. If you think the sound card is the source of the problem, replace the card with one you know is good.

If none of these approaches solves the problem, try using Device Manager to uninstall the sound card and then reinstall it using the Add New Hardware applet in the Control Panel.

Digital Cameras

A digital camera allows users to take pictures and store the electronic images digitally on a storage medium, instead of on traditional film. Figure 6-37 illustrates how one type of digital camera transforms the captured image into a screen display. As you point the camera lens towards the image you want to photograph and then click the button to take the picture, light passes into the lens of the camera. The image is focused on a chip called a **charge-coupled device** (**CCD**). The CCD generates an analog signal that represents the image. The analog signal then is converted to a digital signal by an analog-to-digital converter (ADC). A digital signal processor (DSP) adjusts the quality of the image and stores the digital imaging on the storage media in the camera.

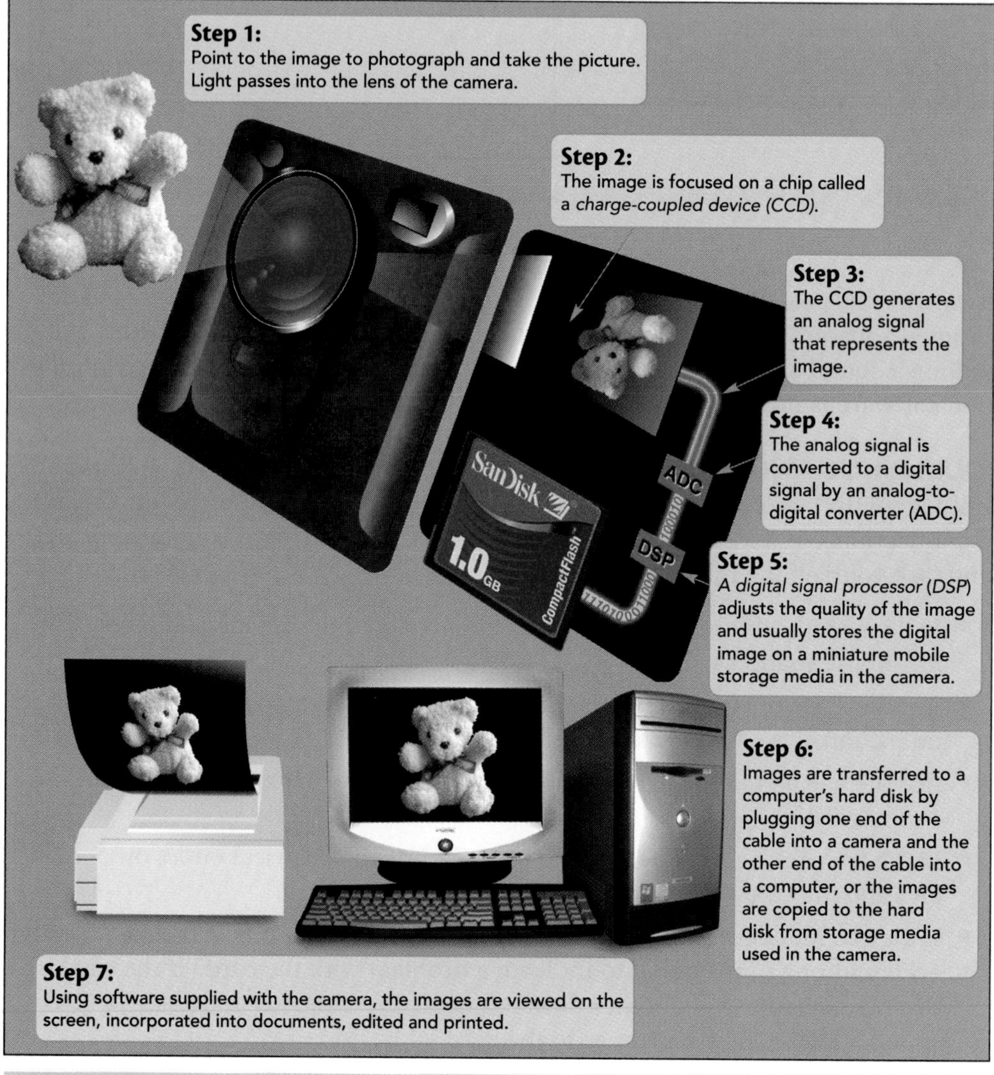

Step 1:
Point to the image to photograph and take the picture. Light passes into the lens of the camera.
Step 2:
The image is focused on a chip called a *charge-coupled device (CCD)*.
Step 3:
The CCD generates an analog signal that represents the image.
Step 4:
The analog signal is converted to a digital signal by an analog-to-digital converter (ADC).
ADC
DSP
SanDisk
1.0GB
CompactFlash
Step 5:
A digital signal processor (DSP) adjusts the quality of the image and usually stores the digital image on a miniature mobile storage media in the camera.
Step 6:
Images are transferred to a computer's hard disk by plugging one end of the cable into a camera and the other end of the cable into a computer, or the images are copied to the hard disk from storage media used in the camera.
Step 7:
Using software supplied with the camera, the images are viewed on the screen, incorporated into documents, edited and printed.

Figure 6-37 How a digital camera works.

The picture file usually is stored in **JPEG (Joint Photographic Experts Group)** format, which is a standard used to compress image files to make them smaller. Most JPEG files have a .jpg file extension. In addition, a high-end camera might support the uncompressed TIFF format. **TIFF (Tagged Image File Format)** files are larger, but retain more image information and give better results when printing photographs. Most TIFF files have a .tif extension.

Digital cameras use a variety of media to store image, including more common storage media such as floppy disks and CD-ROMs, and miniature storage media, such as a **flash memory card**. CompactFlash, CompactFlash II, SmartMedia, Secure Digital (SD), and Sony Memory Sticks are different types of flash memory cards. Once captured, the images are transferred from the camera to a computer's hard disk by copying the images from the storage medium to the hard disk, or by directly connecting the camera to a computer using a cable supplied with the camera. The cable might attach directly to the camera or connect to a cradle the camera sits in to recharge. The cable can use a serial, parallel, USB, or FireWire connection. Alternatively, you can connect a card reader to the computer via a USB port, FireWire port, or parallel port. The **card reader** is a device that reads data from information stored on flash memory cards.

To transfer images to your PC, first install the software bundled with your camera or other device that contains the images. After the images are on the PC, you can use the camera's image-editing software, or another program such as Adobe PhotoShop, to view, touch up, and print the picture.

Most digital cameras also have a video-out port that allows you to attach the camera also to any TV, using a cable provided with the camera. You then can display pictures on TV or copy them to videotape.

Video Cameras and Digital Video Cameras

Video input is the process of capturing full motion images into a computer and storing them on a storage medium, such as a hard disk or DVD. Many video devices, such as video cameras or VCRs, capture analog data. To input video from these analog devices into a computer, the analog video must be converted to a digital signal via a video capture card.

A **video capture card** converts the analog signals from a video camera, VCR, or television for storage. Most video capture cards include a FireWire port that connects to an input device, such as a video camera; an antenna or cable TV port for input; and a TV or VCR port for output.

Most new computers are not equipped with video capture cards, because most users do not need this type of expansion card. If you want to install a video capture card, purchase a card that will fit in an AGP slot and take the place of your existing video card.

The newest generation of video cameras, called **digital video (DV) cameras**, record video as digital signals instead of analog signals. In addition to capturing live full-motion video, many digital video cameras also can capture still frames. Capturing digital video works in much the same way as capturing digital photos. As you point the camera lens towards the scene and press a button to record the video, light passes into the lens of the camera, and the image is focused on a charge-coupled device (CCD). For the best picture quality, processional digital video cameras have three CCDs to capture three different light spectrums (red, green, and blue). The CCDs generate an analog signal that represents the image. The analog signal then is converted to a digital signal by an analog-to-digital converter (ADC). A digital signal processor (DSP) adjusts the quality of the image and stores the digital imaging on the storage media in the camera.

As you record digital video, the digital data is stored on one of several different types of media, including MiniDV or DVCAM tapes. To transfer the images from the tape to a computer hard drive, you connect the DV camera to a FireWire port on the system unit and start the software used to support the video transfer. Because the video output already is digital, the computer does not need to have a video capture card to convert the data from analog to digital format.

MP3 Players

A popular audio compression method is **MP3**, a method that can reduce the size of a sound file to make it significantly smaller and easier to transfer to and from computers and audio devices, without much loss of quality. An **MP3 player** is a device that plays MP3 files. MP3 players typically are small, but can store many gigabytes of data (Figure 6-38). An 40 GB MP3 player, for example, can store around 10,000 songs.

The MP3 format is possible because it cuts out or drastically reduces sound that is not normally heard by the human ear. In the regular audio CD format (uncompressed), one minute of music takes up about 10 MB of storage. The same minute of music in MP3 format takes only about 1 MB of storage. This makes it possible to download music in minutes rather than hours. Sound files downloaded from the Internet are most often MP3 files, which have a file extension of .mp3.

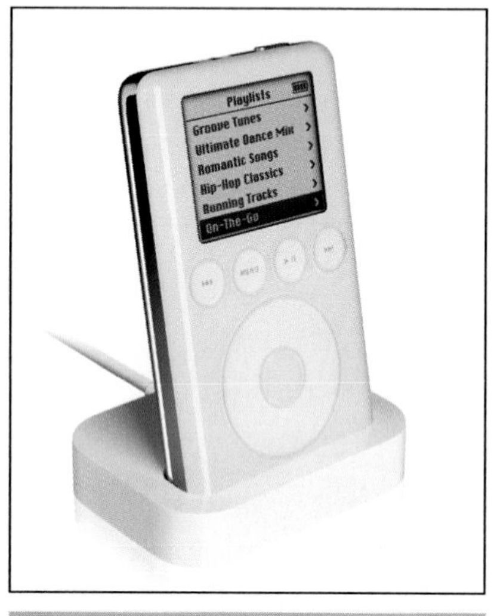

Figure 6-38 The Apple iPod MP3 Player has a cradle that connects to your computer using a FireWire or USB cable.

You can download and purchase MP3 music files from Web sites such as iTunes (*www.itunes.com*), Napster (*www.napster.com*), and Rhapsody (*www.listen.com*). Once the files are downloaded to your PC, you can play them on your PC using MP3 player software such as iTunes, Windows Media Player, or MusicMatch Jukebox. You also can transfer them to a portable MP3 player, or convert them into an audio CD if your computer has a rewritable CD drive. MP3 files are generally transferred to portable devices using a USB or FireWire cable. The Apple iPod, for example, has a charger base that comes with a USB and a FireWire cable.

Most portable MP3 players today store MP3 files in onboard memory or hard drives. The capacity of some MP3 players can be expanded using an add-on flash memory card such as SmartMedia, CompactFlash, or Memory Stick.

Quiz Yourself 6-3

To test your knowledge of multimedia devices, visit the Understanding and Troubleshooting Your PC Quiz Yourself Web page (scsite.com/understanding/quiz). Click Quiz Yourself 3 below Chapter 6.

High-Tech Talk

Ergonomics: Smart and Safe Computing

While computers and technology have had many positive impacts on the work world, using a computer also creates some new health issues and safety hazards. Problems such as repetitive stress injuries are examples of potential health problems caused by using computers for long stretches.

The goal of *ergonomics* is to incorporate comfort, efficiency, and safety into the design of items in the workplace. Employees can be injured or develop disorders of the muscles, nerves, tendons, ligaments, and joints from working in an area that is not designed ergonomically.

Ergonomic studies have shown that using the correct type and configuration of chair, keyboard, display device, and work surface helps you work more comfortably and efficiently, while protecting your health. For the computer work area, experts recommend an area of at least two feet by four feet.

Be sure to organize the elements of your workplace to help you work comfortably. You should have sufficient desk space to position a keyboard, mouse, monitor, document holder, and other items in a way that works for you. Organize your desk so the things you use most regularly, such as a mouse or telephone, are within easy reach. Above all, vary your tasks and take periodic breaks to help reduce the possibility of discomfort or fatigue.

Repetitive stress injury (RSI), such as carpal tunnel syndrome, is caused when muscle groups complete the same repetitive actions, over and over again. Keyboards, mice, and trackballs are a major source of RSIs, resulting from constant movement and typing at fast speeds. Today, many input and output devices are designed to address ergonomic issues. For example, some keyboards have built in wrist-rests, while others have a design specifically intended to prevent RSIs. Correct typing technique and posture, the right equipment setup, and good work habits, as listed in Figure 6-39, are important for prevention of RSIs.

As more and more people use computers, ergonomics increasingly is recognized as an important part of computing. Understanding the possible health risks of computing — and how to prevent them — is a key step in having a safe work environment and a healthy and productive you.

TIP	DESCRIPTION
Use correct posture.	You should not have to slouch or stretch to reach the keys or read the screen. Anything that creates awkward reaches or angles in the body will create problems. Relax and shift positions frequently.
Get a good chair.	Select a chair that is adjustable, provides good back support, and is comfortable. Your feet should rest flat on the floor when you are seated and using your keyboard; if they are not, lower the chair or use a footrest.
Position your monitor to reduce eye strain.	Position the monitor to a comfortable viewing distance, of 20 to 24 inches away from your eyes. Adjust the monitor so the top of the screen is slightly below eye level. Put the monitor in a location to reduce glare and reflections from windows and other light sources.
Increase your font sizes and use easy colors.	Small fonts encourage you to hunch forward to read. Use color schemes easy on the eyes, particularly shades of grey for text documents.
Position your keyboard correctly.	Position the keyboard so your forearms are almost horizontal to the floor as you type and are relaxed and comfortable. Your shoulders should be relaxed, not hunched, and your wrists should be straight, not bent up or down.
Type gently.	Do not press hard on the keyboard; use a light touch. Also, use two hands to perform operations with two keys (such as CTRL+X).
Keep a light grip on the mouse.	Hold the mouse lightly; do not grip it or squeeze it hard. Place the pointing device where you do not have to reach up or over to use it (close to the keyboard is best).
Take a break.	Take time to stretch and relax. This means both momentary breaks every few minutes and longer breaks every hour or so. Place and plan your computer work.
Listen to your body.	If you are experiencing pain, it could be a first sign that your work area is unfriendly. Stop and evaluate the pain; take time to learn what is comfortable for you as you work.

Figure 6-39 Simple practices can help you avoid RSIs and other injuries.

CHAPTER SUMMARY

The Chapter Summary reviews the concepts presented in this chapter.

1 An Overview of Peripherals

Most input and output devices are peripheral devices that communicate with the CPU but are not located directly on the motherboard. Many input and output devices perform analog-to-digital and digital-to-analog conversions to allow a user or a multimedia device to communicate with a computer. The process of installing a new input or output device requires installing the device, the device driver, and any required application software.

2 Connecting Peripherals Using Ports, Wireless Connections, and Expansion Slots

A peripheral device can be connected to the computer using a cable that connects to a port, using a wireless connection, or via an expansion slot. Serial ports transmit data serially and are used to connect devices, such as a mouse or modem. Parallel ports transmit data in parallel and often are used to connect printers. Serial ports are configured as COM1, COM2, COM3, or COM4. Parallel ports can be configured as LPT1, LPT2, or LPT3. A USB port, which supports hot-swapping and hot-plugging, is a faster port that can connect to many different input and output devices. A FireWire port connects high-speed devices that require large data transfers. Wireless peripherals can be connected using infrared technology that uses infrared light waves to transmit signals, or radio frequency technology that uses radio waves. Expansion cards are circuit boards designed to provide additional functionality or to provide a connection to a peripheral device. An expansion card is inserted into a PCI, AGP, or ISA expansion slot to provide connections for various types of peripherals.

3 Input and Output Devices

A keyboard is an input device that has keys that users press to enter data and send instructions to a computer. A keyboard can use a DIN, PS/2, USB, or wireless connection. A pointing device allows you to move a pointer on the screen and perform tasks such as executing a command. Common pointing devices are the mouse, trackball, touch pad, and a pointing stick embedded in the keyboard. Users who play games on their computer also may use a joystick or wheel as an input device. A monitor is a plastic or metal case that houses a display device that visually shows the output of the computer. Two common types of monitors are CRT and LCD. CRT costs less but LCD takes less desktop space. Features to consider when purchasing a monitor are screen size, refresh rate, interlacing, dot pitch, and resolution. The two necessary components for output from a monitor are the video card and the monitor itself. A video card is rated by the bus that it uses and the amount of video RAM on the card. Both features affect the overall speed and performance of the card. Some types of video memory are SGRAM, WRAM, and 3-D RAM.

4 Multimedia Technologies

Multimedia technology is used to create or reproduce representations for audio, video, and animation. CPU technologies such as MMX and SSE were designed to speed up processing of graphics, motion video, animation, and sound. To input or output audio, a computer needs a sound card. Connecting a sound card includes physically seating the card in an expansion slot, then installing the sound card driver and sound application software. A digital camera uses light sensors to detect light and then stores the electronic images digitally on a storage medium. Video input involves capturing full motion images into a computer and storing them on a storage medium. A video capture card converts the analog signals from a video camera, VCR, or television. A digital video camera does not require a video capture card, as it captures video digitally. MP3 is a popular audio compression method that reduces sound file size without sacrificing quality. An MP3 player is a device that plays MP3 files.

KEY TERMS

After reading the chapter, you should know each of these Key Terms.

3-D RAM *(252)*
802.11 *(236)*
active-matrix display *(249)*
analog-to-digital-conversion *(222)*
analog-to-digital-converter (ADC) *(255)*
Bluetooth *(236)*
card reader *(261)*
CardBus *(239)*
charge-coupled device (CCD) *(260)*
chip extractor *(243)*
CRT monitor *(246)*
DB-25 connector (227)
DCE (Data Communications Equipment) *(225)*
digital signal processor (DSP) *(256)*
digital video (DV) camera *(261)*
digital-to-analog conversion *(222)*
digital-to-analog converter (DAC) *(256)*
DIN connector *(242)*
direct memory execute (DIME) *(252)*
dot pitch (248)
DTE (Data Terminal Equipment) *(225)*
dual-ported *(251)*
enhanced keyboard *(241)*
enhanced parallel port (EPP) *(227)*
ergonomic keyboards *(242)*
ergonomics (242)
extended capabilities port (ECP) *(227)*
FireWire host controller *(234)*
flash memory card *(261)*
flat panel monitor *(248)*
graphics accelerator *(252)*
hot-plugging *(228)*
hot-swapping *(228)*
infrared (IR) (235)
infrared port *(235)*
infrared transceiver *(235)*
input *(222)*
input device (222)
interlaced (248)
IrDA (Infrared Data Association) port *(235)*
isochronous data transfer *(234)*
joystick *(244)*
JPEG (Joint Photographic Experts Group) *(261)*
keyboard port connector *(242)*
LCD monitor *(248)*
mini-DIN *(242)*
MMX (Multimedia Extensions) *(254)*
mouse port *(245)*
MP3 *(262)*
MP3 player *(262)*
multiscan *(248)*
noninterlaced *(248)*
output *(222)*
output device *(222)*
passive matrix display *(249)*
PC Card *(239)*
PC Card slot *(239)*
PCMCIA (Personal Computer Memory Card International Association) Card *(239)*
PDA (personal digital assistant) *(235)*
pointing device *(244)*
pointing stick *(244)*
PS/2 connector *(242)*
PS/2 port *(245)*
radio frequency (RF) *(236)*
refresh rate *(247)*
RS-232 port *(225)*
S/PDIF port *(255)*
sampling *(255)*
SGRAM (synchronous graphics RAM) *(252)*
Sound Blaster-compatible *(255)*
standard parallel port (SPP) *(227)*
SVGA (Super Video Graphics Array) *(250)*
TFT (thin-film transistor) display *(249)*
TIFF (Tagged Image File Format) *(261)*
touch pad *(244)*
trackball *(244)*
Universal Asynchronous Receiver/Transmitter (UART) *(225)*
USB host controller *(230)*
vertical scan rate *(247)*
video capture card *(261)*
video input *(261)*
video RAM *(251)*
viewable size *(247)*
VRAM *(251)*
wheel *(244)*
Wi-Fi (wireless fidelity) *(236)*
WRAM (window RAM) (252)

LEARN IT ONLINE

Reinforce your understanding of the chapter concepts and terms with the Learn It Online exercises.

Instructions: To complete the Learn It Online exercises, start your browser, click the Address bar, and then enter the Web address scsite.com/understanding/learn. When the Understanding and Troubleshooting Your PC Learn It Online page is displayed, follow the instructions in the exercises below. Each exercise has instructions for printing your results, either for your own records or for submission to your instructor.

1 Chapter Reinforcement True/False, Multiple Choice, and Short Answer

Below Chapter 6, click the Chapter Reinforcement link. Print the quiz by clicking Print on the File menu for each page. Answer each question.

2 Flash Cards

Below Chapter 6, click the Flash Cards link and read the instructions. Type 20 (or a number specified by your instructor) in the Number of playing cards text box, type your name in the Enter your Name text box, and then click the Flip Card button. When the flash card is displayed, read the question and then click the ANSWER box arrow to select an answer. Flip through Flash Cards. If your score is 15 (75%) correct or greater, click Print on the File menu to print your results. If your score is less than 15 (75%) correct, then redo this exercise by clicking the Replay button.

3 Practice Test

Below Chapter 6, click the Practice Test link. Answer each question, enter your first and last name at the bottom of the page, and then click the Grade Test button. When the graded practice test is displayed on your screen, click Print on the File menu to print a hard copy. Continue to take practice tests until you score 80% or better.

4 Who Wants To Be a Computer Genius?

Below Chapter 6, click the Computer Genius link. Read the instructions, enter your first and last name at the bottom of the page, and then click the PLAY button. When your score is displayed, click the PRINT RESULTS link to print a hard copy.

5 Wheel of Terms

Below Chapter 6, click the Wheel of Terms link. Read the instructions, and then enter your first and last name and your school name. Click the PLAY button. When your score is displayed, right-click the score and then click Print on the shortcut menu to print a hard copy.

6 Crossword Puzzle Challenge

Below Chapter 6, click the Crossword Puzzle Challenge link. Read the instructions, and then enter your first and last name. Click the SUBMIT button. Work the crossword puzzle. When you are finished, click the Submit button. When the crossword puzzle is redisplayed, click the Print Puzzle button to print a hard copy.

Multiple Choice

Select the best answer.

1. Most current video cards support the video standard called ________.
   a. VGA (video graphics array)
   b. SVGA (super video graphics array)
   c. XGA (extended graphics array)
   d. MGA (monochrome graphics array)
2. Which of these ports provides a faster data transmission speed?
   a. USB 2.0
   b. parallel
   c. serial
   d. FireWire (1394b)
3. When connecting a video card, in which expansion slot should you install it?
   a. AGP
   b. ISA
   c. USB
   d. VESA
4. Which of these is not a parallel port technology?
   a. standard parallel port
   b. extended printer port (EPP)
   c. extended capabilities port (ECP)
   d. enhanced parallel port
5. Which of the following monitors provides a better image quality?
   a. .38-mm dot pitch monitor
   b. .32-mm dot pitch monitor
   c. .20-mm dot pitch monitor
   d. .25-mm dot pitch monitor

Fill in the Blank

Write the word or phrase to fill in the blank in each of the following questions.

1. The ________ is the number of times in one second an electronic beam can fill the screen with lines from top to bottom.
2. FireWire uses ________, meaning that data is transferred continuously without breaks over the FireWire bus.
3. Wireless devices that use ________ require a direct line of sight between devices, while ________ devices do not.
4. A port assignment such as LPT1 or COM3 represents a designated configuration of a(n) ________ and a(n) ________.
5. USB allows for ________, which means you can connect a device to a USB port and it automatically will be configured without your having to restart the computer.

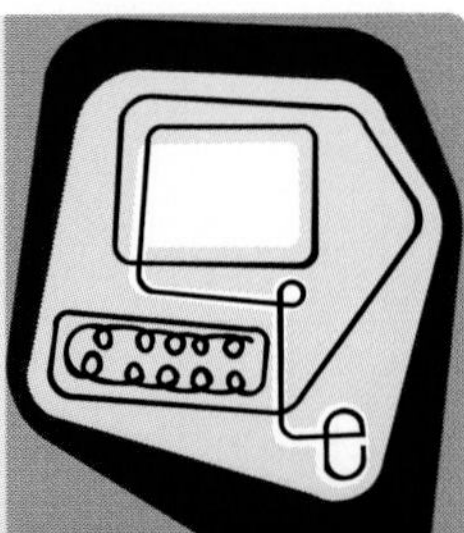

CHAPTER EXERCISES

Complete the Chapter Exercises to solidify what you learned in the chapter.

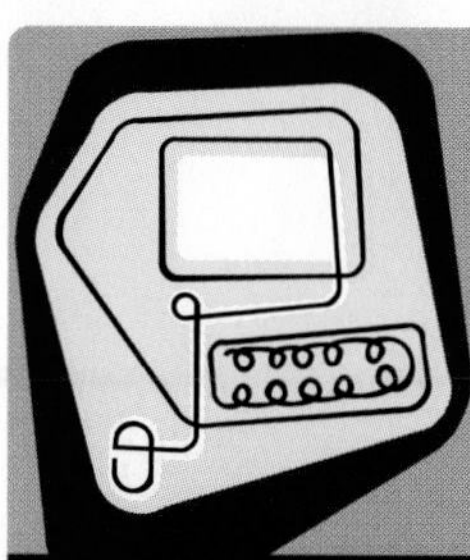

CHAPTER EXERCISES

Complete the Chapter Exercises to solidify what you learned in the chapter.

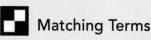

Matching Terms

Match the terms with their definitions.

______ 1. isochronous data transfer	a. AGP feature that involves sharing memory with the CPU
______ 2. MP3	b. number of bytes used to represent the sound at any one interval
______ 3. touch pad	c. small, flat rectangular pointing device that is sensitive to pressure and motion
______ 4. direct memory execute	d. data is transferred continuously without breaks; used by FireWire
______ 5. DIN connector	e. uses short range radio waves to transmit data between two devices
______ 6. Bluetooth	f. video card with its own processor to boost performance
______ 7. viewable size	g. actual size of the lighted screen in the monitor
______ 8. graphics accelerator	h. also called a keyboard port connector
______ 9. sampling rate	i. the number of times per second a sound is recorded
______ 10. audio resolution	j. popular audio compression method

Short Answer Questions

Write a brief answer to each of the following questions.

1. The quality and price of a CRT monitor is based on several features — screen size, refresh rate, dot pitch, interlacing, and resolution. Briefly explain each of these features.
2. If a mouse is not working properly, what troubleshooting steps should you take?
3. Explain why sampling is used when recording sound, and list factors in the sampling process that affect the quality of the sound during playback.
4. Describe the steps required to install a new sound card.
5. List and explain the various types of video RAM used by a video card.

1 Understanding Ports

Draw a diagram for the back, front, or either side of your computer that has ports. Label each of the ports with the correct name and then provide one or more examples of devices that could be connected using those ports. For each port, indicate whether the port comes directly off the motherboard or is a port from an expansion card.

2 Working with a Monitor

Windows provides several tools that allow you to change resolution, refresh rate, and other properties of your computer monitor. Perform the following steps using Windows XP to explore and change the properties of a monitor.

1. Click the Start button and then click Control Panel on the Start Menu.
2. When the Control Panel window is displayed, if necessary, click Switch to Classic View to view the Control Panel in Classic view. Double-click the Display icon to open the Display Properties window. Click the Settings tab.
3. Write down the current color quality and resolution settings used on your monitor. In the screen resolution area, move the slider to the left to reduce the screen resolution. Click the Apply button. (If Windows displays a Warning error message, click OK. If Windows displays a Monitor Settings message box, click Yes to keep the settings.) Describe the appearance of the display on your monitor using this lower resolution. Move the slider back to the original settings and then click the Apply button.
4. Click the Advanced button on the Settings sheet. Click each of the sheet tabs in the monitor Properties window to answer the following questions:
   a. What video card (adapter) is used on the computer? How much memory does it have?
   b. What is the dot per inch (DPI) setting for the monitor?
   c. What is the refresh rate for the monitor? Is a higher refresh rate available?
   d. What level of hardware acceleration is used by the monitor? What is the recommended setting?

   When you have finished, click the Cancel button to return to the Display Properties window.
5. Click the Appearance tab. Write down the existing settings for Windows and buttons, Color scheme, and Font size. Next, change the settings and then click the Apply button to view how the Windows desktop changes. If you are not using your own computer, make sure to restore each setting after making changes.
6. Problems with a monitor often are caused by loose cables or a loose video card. To better understand how the monitor behaves when such issues occur, try each of the following:
   a. Loosen or disconnect the computer monitor cable from the port on the computer.
   b. Turn the contrast and brightness all the way down.
   c. Turn off the computer, remove the case, and loosen the video card.

   After trying each step, write down the problem as a user would describe it. After you have described the problem, return the monitor to its original state.

3 Installing a USB Device

Installing a USB device such as a printer, digital camera, or keyboard generally is simple, because USB is Plug and Play and supports hot-swapping. If your computer has a USB port, perform the following steps to install a new USB device.

1. Check the connectors on either end of the cable. Are they Type A or Type B?
2. With the computer running, connect the USB cable to the device and then insert the cable in the USB port on your computer.

APPLY YOUR KNOWLEDGE

Check your understanding of the chapter with the hands-on Apply Your Knowledge exercises.

APPLY YOUR KNOWLEDGE

Check your understanding of the chapter with the hands-on Apply Your Knowledge exercises.

3. Windows detects the devices and starts the Found New Hardware Wizard. Follow the steps in the wizard to install the device drivers. (If the wizard does not launch, click the Start button, click Control Panel on the Start menu, double-click the Add New Hardware icon, and then follow the steps in the wizard.)
4. Open Device Manager and check that the USB device is listed in Device Manager. Verify that Windows sees the device with no conflicts and no errors.
5. If needed, install the application software to use the device.

4 Installing a Sound Card

To input and output audio, a computer must have a sound card. Perform the following steps to install a sound card in a computer to be used by the CD-ROM:

1. Wear a ground bracelet and follow other procedures to guard against ESD.
2. Turn off the PC, remove the cover, and locate an empty expansion slot for the card. Place the sound card near enough to the CD-ROM drive so the wire can reach between them.
3. Attach the wire to the sound card and to the CD-ROM drive.
4. Remove the cover from the slot opening at the rear of the PC case, and firmly seat the card into the PCI slot. Use the screw taken from the slot cover to secure the card to the back of the PC case.
5. Check again that both ends of the wire are still securely connected and that the wire is not hampering the CPU fan, and then replace the case cover.
6. Plug in the speakers to the ports at the back of the sound card, and turn on the PC.
7. Restart the computer. Windows will detect the sound card and start the Found New Hardware Wizard. Follow the steps in the wizard to install the driver from the CD-ROM.
8. When the driver installation is complete, restart your PC and then access Device Manager to ensure that the sound card and its drivers are listed.
9. Verify that the card works by playing a music CD or an MP3 file. Double-click the Volume icon in the taskbar and then change various volume settings until the sound levels are to your liking.

5 Researching Multimedia Devices on the Web

Using the Internet, create a presentation or write a paper about digital cameras, digital video cameras, or MP3 players. Summarize the features to look for when buying the device, the average price, and how to compare quality from one device to another. Web sites that may help with your research include:

- *www.pcworld.com*
- *www.pcmag.com*
- *www.cnet.com*
- *reviews-zdnet.com.com*

In the final presentation or paper, include citations from any Web sites you used in your research.

CHAPTER 7

Supporting Printers

Introduction

This chapter discusses laser printers, inkjet printers, dot-matrix printers, thermal printers, and solid ink printers; how they work; and how to support them. After reviewing how to install a local printer or share a printer with others on a network, the chapter discusses how Windows handles print jobs. Finally, you will learn how to maintain a printer and troubleshoot printer problems.

OBJECTIVES

In this chapter, you will learn:

1. About characteristics of printers
2. About various types of printers and how they work
3. How to install printers and share them over a local area network
4. How to maintain printers and troubleshoot printer problems

Up for Discussion

Jennifer Nguyen called Sunrise Computers this morning to ask for your help with a new printer. Jennifer works across town at Viking Press, a small print shop that creates flyers, cards, and brochures for many area businesses. Viking just purchased a new, high-end color laser printer, which they plan to use to print smaller jobs.

Jennifer tells you that she can install the printer locally, for one person to use it. But all five designers at Viking need to have access to the printer, and she does not know how to set that up.

You assure Jennifer that setting the printer up should be simple enough to do over the phone, and you walk her through the steps. First you have Jennifer install the printer on one computer by attaching the printer cable to the correct port, installing the printer drivers, and then printing a test page to ensure that it is set up correctly. Next, you explain how to set the printer up for sharing over a network. Finally, Jennifer installs the printer on the other computers on the network, using the same steps used to install the printer locally. When the last test page prints, Jennifer happily reports that all of the designers can print to the new printer from their computers.

About a month later, Jennifer calls to let you know they have hired a new designer. She followed your instructions to install the printer on his computer but, for some reason, it will not print. You ask Jennifer a few questions about the problem and realize that the designer is using an older computer with Windows NT — and you did not set up the shared printer with the drivers for that OS. You walk Jennifer through the steps to install the additional drivers and then have her print a test page, which prints correctly. Jennifer thanks you for all of your help, and promises that the print job for Sunrise Computers' new business cards will move to the top of the list.

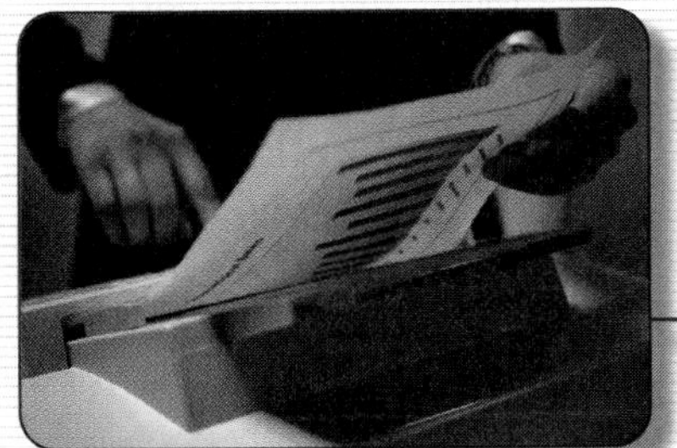

Questions:

- What are the steps to install a local printer?
- What steps are required to set up a shared printer and install it on remote computers?
- How can you update printer drivers on a computer?

Printer Characteristics

As you have learned, a *printer* is an output device that produces text and graphics on a physical medium, such as paper. The printed information output from a printer often is referred to as a **printout** or **hard copy**, because it physically exists. Information displayed on a monitor or stored in an electronic file, by contrast, is considered **soft copy**, because it only exists electronically.

Printers often are described based on several features: resolution, print quality, speed, memory, and the ability to print color (Figure 7-1). The following sections discuss these features in detail.

Printer Characteristic	Description
Resolution	Clarity of printer output, measured in dots per inch (dpi), which describes the density of ink dots used to create printed output.
Print quality	The quality of the printed output, often described as being letter quality, near letter quality, or draft quality.
Speed	Speed at which the printer creates output, measured in characters per second or pages per minute (ppm). Another measure of speed, called graphics pages per minute (gppm), describes the speed at which a printer can print non-text pages.
Memory	Used to store the text or image information before printing the document. The more memory a printer has, the more efficiently it can print out pages.
Color	Printer's capability to print in color and black and white, or just black and white.

Figure 7-1 Characteristics of a printer.

Resolution *Resolution* describes the sharpness and clarity of printed text and images. For a printer, resolution is measured in **dots per inch** (**dpi**), which describes the density of ink dots used to create printed output. A 600 dpi printer, for example, prints 600 dots across and 600 dots down, for a total of 360,000 dots per inch. A higher number of dots per inch results in a higher resolution or clarity of image. A 1200 dpi printer, which prints 1,440,000 dots per inch, would output a higher quality printout than a 600 dpi printer.

Print Quality The quality of a printout generated from a printer often is described as being letter quality, near letter quality, or draft quality. **Letter quality** refers to the highest quality of printout, such as that used in business correspondence or other professional documents. **Near letter quality** is a slightly lower quality printout than letter quality, in which the letters are less crisply defined on the paper. **Draft quality** is the lowest quality printout and often is used to save ink or allow a user to see what a print job might look like before printing the final copy. In general, the higher the resolution (dpi), the better the print quality.

Speed Depending on the type of printer, printer speed often is measured in characters per second or pages per minute. **Characters per second** (**cps**) is used to measure the speed of printers that produce text output using some mechanism that physically contacts the paper. **Pages per minute** (**ppm**) is used to measure the speed of printers that produce text output a page at a time. Another measure of speed, called **graphics pages per minute (gppm)**, describes the speed at which a printer can print non-text pages. A printer's gppm measure always is lower than the ppm. If you plan to do a lot of printing, the printer speed is very important. In general, more expensive printers are faster than less expensive ones. If you plan to print graphics-rich documents, also be sure to consider the gppm speed.

Memory Most printers come with a small amount of memory to store the text or image information before printing the document. The more memory a printer has, the more efficiently it can print out pages with large images or tables with lines around them. If a printer needs more memory, you typically can upgrade the printer's memory to add more megabytes.

Color Some printers print only in black and white, while others also can print in color. Color printers allow users to create a wide range of high-quality color documents, including presentations, maps, and photos. Color printers are more expensive to operate, however, because they use two types of ink (color inks and black inks). Users who do not need to print color documents will find that a black-and-white printer costs much less to operate.

More About

Purchasing a Printer

To learn more about what to consider when purchasing a printer, visit the Understanding and Troubleshooting Your PC More About Web page (**scsite.com/understanding/more**) and then click Purchasing a Printer below Chapter 7.

Types of Printers

Many types of printers are available on the market, each of which has different characteristics and offers different types of features. The two major categories of printers are impact printers and non-impact printers. An **impact printer** forms characters and graphics on a printed page by using some mechanism that physically contacts the paper. A **non-impact printer** forms characters and graphics without using a mechanism that physically contacts the paper. A dot-matrix printer is an impact printer, while laser, ink-jet, solid ink, dye-sublimation, and thermal printers are non-impact printers. Ink-jet printers currently are most widely used in homes and small businesses, while laser printers are widely used in businesses of all types. The following sections discuss each of these types of printers in detail.

Dot-Matrix Printers

A **dot-matrix printer** is an impact printer with a print head that moves across the width of the paper to print a matrix of dots on the page. The print head on a dot-matrix printer has 9 to 24 pins that strike an inked ribbon; in turn, the ribbon hits the paper, depositing the ink in dots, forming characters and graphics (Figure 7-2). A higher number of pins produces a higher print quality.

While dot-matrix printers are less expensive than other types of printers, they can provide only near letter quality printouts. The speed of a dot-matrix printer is measured in characters per second (cps). Speeds range from 300 to 1,100 characters per second, depending on print quality.

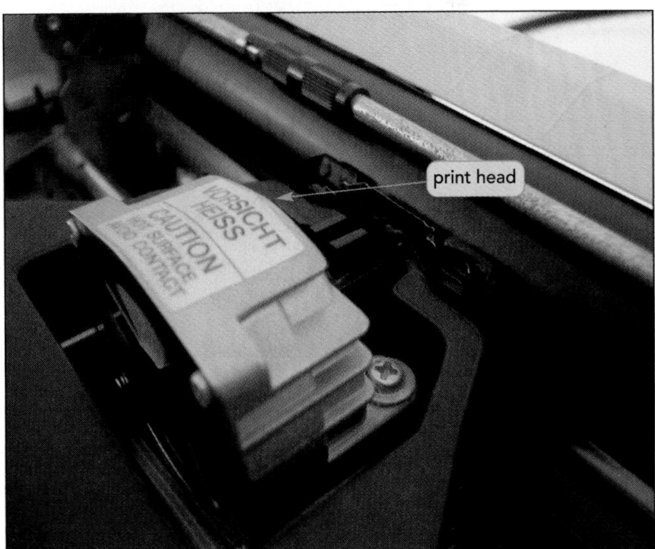

Figure 7-2 The print head on a dot-matrix printer has 9 to 24 pins.

Dot-matrix printers use continuous form paper, in which thousands of sheets of paper are connected together and have holes along the sides to help guide the paper through the printer. Dot-matrix printers once were used for a wide range of printing needs; most PC users no longer use them for home or personal use. Businesses, however, continue to use dot-matrix printers for applications where multipart forms or labels must be printed.

Dot-matrix printers do not require a significant amount of maintenance, although the ribbon should be replaced when the print starts to fade. Overheating also can damage the printer's print head, so keep the printer in a cool, well-ventilated area, and do not use it to print more than 50 to 75 pages without allowing the head to cool down. The print head also can wear out over time and can be replaced. (Replacing the print head generally is not cost-effective, because it can cost almost as much as the dot-matrix printer itself. If the print head fails, check on the cost of replacing the head versus the cost of buying a new printer.)

Ink-jet Printers

An **ink-jet printer** (Figure 7-3) is a non-impact printer that forms characters and graphics by spraying tiny drops of liquid ink onto paper. An ink-jet printer uses a print head that moves across the paper, creating one line of text with each pass. The printer puts ink on the paper using a matrix of small dots. Different types of ink-jet printers form their droplets of ink using different technologies, the most popular of which is bubble-jet. A **bubble-jet printer** uses tubes of ink that have tiny resistors near the end of each tube (Figure 7-4). These resistors heat up and cause the ink to boil. Then, a tiny air bubble of ionized ink — that is, ink with an electrical charge — is ejected onto the paper. A typical bubble-jet print head has 64 or 128 tiny nozzles, all of which can fire a droplet simultaneously. (High-end printers can have as many as 3,000 nozzles.) Plates carrying a magnetic charge direct the path of ink onto the paper to form shapes.

Figure 7-3 Ink-jet printers can produce quality color output at a reasonable price.

Most ink-jet printers range from 300 to 2400 dpi, although high-end ink-jet printers may have a higher dpi. Ink-jet printers generally can print between 3 and 19 pages per minute for black and white printouts. Graphics and color printouts print more slowly.

In order to create color printouts, ink-jet printers include one or more ink cartridges, as shown in Figure 7-5. The cartridges are placed in a print head assemblage. Most commonly, one cartridge contains black ink, while another cartridge contains three colors of ink (magenta, cyan, and yellow), though some ink-jet printers use more than three colors. When a cartridge runs out of ink, you can open the top cover of the printer so the print head assemblage moves to the center of the printing area. You then can remove

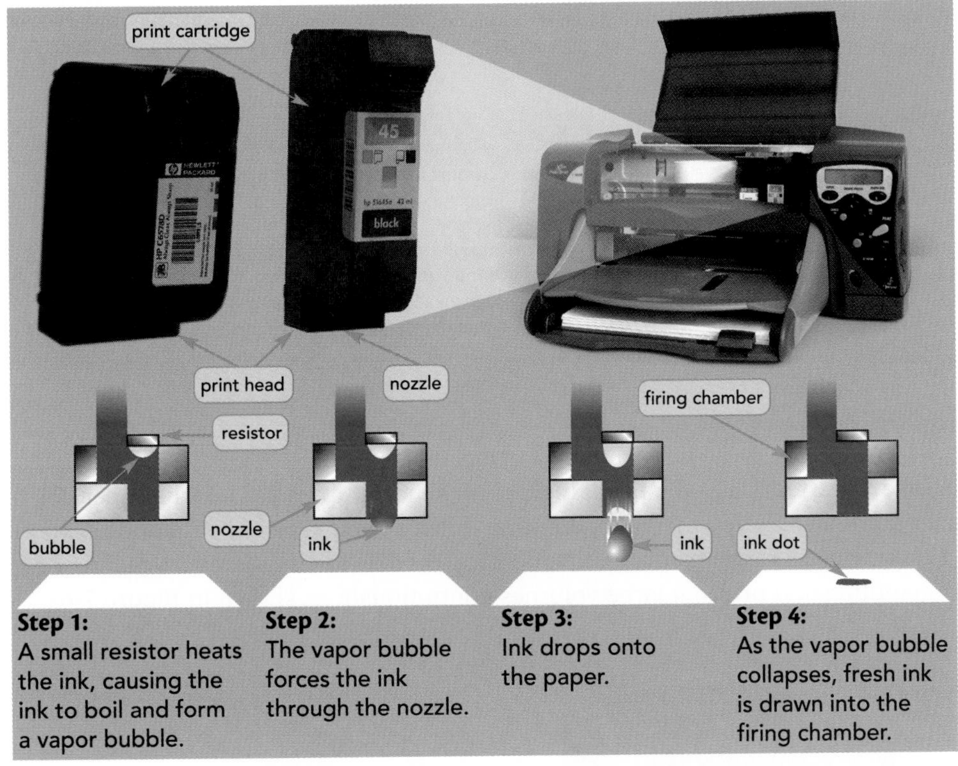
print cartridge
print head
nozzle
resistor
bubble
nozzle
ink
ink
firing chamber
ink dot
Step 1:
A small resistor heats the ink, causing the ink to boil and form a vapor bubble.
Step 2:
The vapor bubble forces the ink through the nozzle.
Step 3:
Ink drops onto the paper.
Step 4:
As the vapor bubble collapses, fresh ink is drawn into the firing chamber.

Figure 7-4 How a bubble-jet printer works.

the ink cartridge and replace it with a new one. After the new cartridge is in place and you close the top cover, the print head assemblage will move to the side of the printing area — a position called the home position — which helps to protect the ink in the cartridges from drying out.

When purchasing an ink-jet printer, look for the kind that uses two separate cartridges, one for black ink and one for three-color printing. If an ink-jet printer does not have a black ink cartridge, then it combines all colors of ink to produce a dull black. Having a separate cartridge for black ink means that it prints true black and, more importantly, does not use the more expensive colored ink to create a black color. You can replace the black cartridge without also replacing the colored ink cartridge.

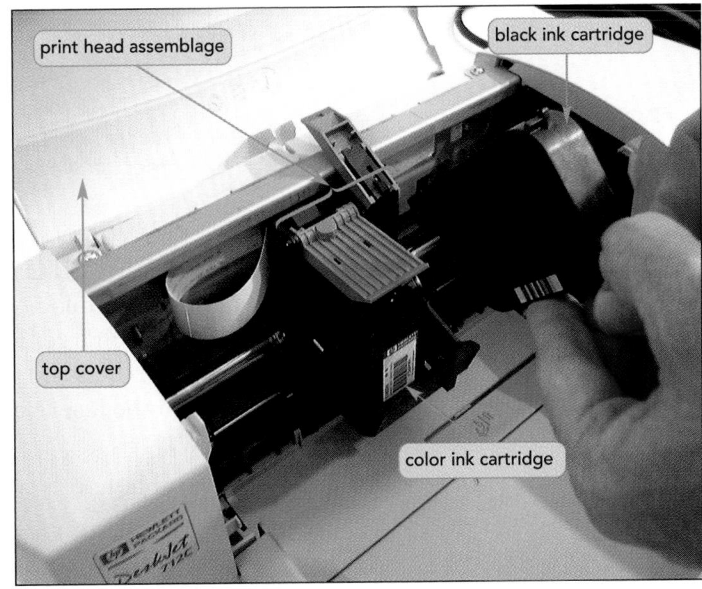
print head assemblage
black ink cartridge
top cover
color ink cartridge

Figure 7-5 An ink-jet printer uses two or more ink cartridges.

Ink-jet printers have become the most popular type of color printer for home use because they are small and relatively inexpensive, they can output near letter quality print, and they can produce color printouts cost effectively. Ink-jet printers typically use individual sheets of paper stored in one or two removable or stationary trays. The quality of the paper used with ink-jet printers significantly affects the quality of printed output. For example, if you use photo paper, most ink-jet printers can print photo-quality images. By contrast, if you use very inexpensive paper, ink-jet printers tend to smudge.

Can ink-jet cartridges be refilled?

Yes. If you want to save money on ink, you can purchase an ink-jet refill kit, which costs about half the price of a new cartridge. Along with instructions, a refill kit typically comes with bottles of ink, a tool to open the ink cartridge, and a refill tool. The kit often includes enough ink to refill the ink cartridge two to eight times. Before opting to refill your ink cartridges, check to be sure using refills will not void the manufacturer's warranty. Also note that head clogging is more prevalent when refilling your own cartridges with ink, and that the print quality from refilled cartridges can be lower than from regular cartridges.

Laser Printers

A **laser printer** is a high-speed, high-quality, non-impact printer that operates in a manner similar to a copy machine, creating images using a laser beam and powdered ink. Laser printers range from smaller, desktop models to large network printers capable of handling and printing large volumes continuously, as shown in Figure 7-6.

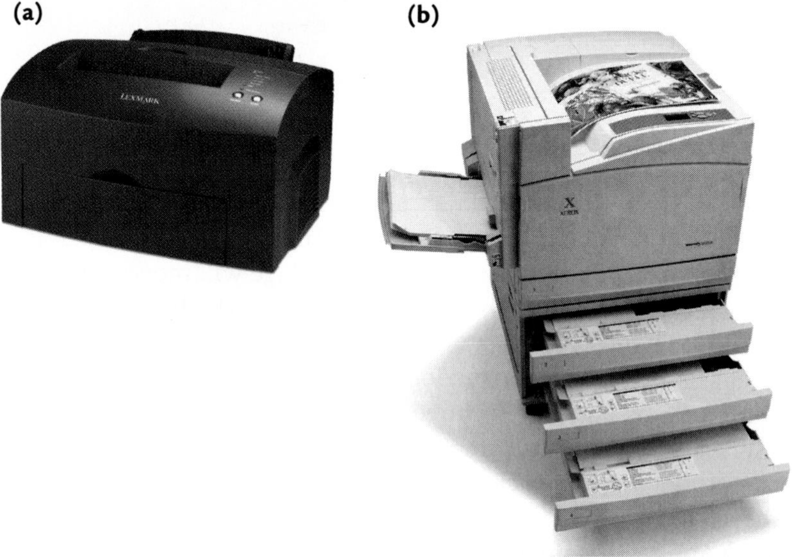

Figure 7-6 Laser printers range from (a) smaller, desktop models to (b) larger, network printers.

HOW A LASER PRINTER WORKS Laser printers require the interaction of mechanical, electrical, and optical technologies. They work by placing powdered ink, called **toner**, on an electrically charged rotating drum and then depositing the toner on the paper it moves through the system at the same speed the drum is turning. Figure 7-7 illustrates the steps in the laser printing process, which include:

1. *Cleaning.* During the cleaning step, the drum is cleaned of any residual toner and electrical charge.
2. *Conditioning.* The drum is conditioned to contain a high electrical charge.
3. *Writing.* A laser beam discharges a lower charge only to places where toner should go.
4. *Developing.* Toner is placed on the drum where the charge has been reduced.

5. *Transferring.* A strong electrical charge draws the toner off the drum onto the paper.
6. *Fusing.* Heat and pressure fuse the toner to the paper.

The first four steps produce the most wear on printer components, so these components are contained within the removable toner cartridge to increase the printer's life. The last two steps are performed outside the cartridge.

More About

How Laser Printers Work

To learn more about how laser printers output text and graphics to a page, visit the Understanding and Troubleshooting Your PC More About Web page (**scsite.com/understanding/more**) and then click How Laser Printers Work below Chapter 7.

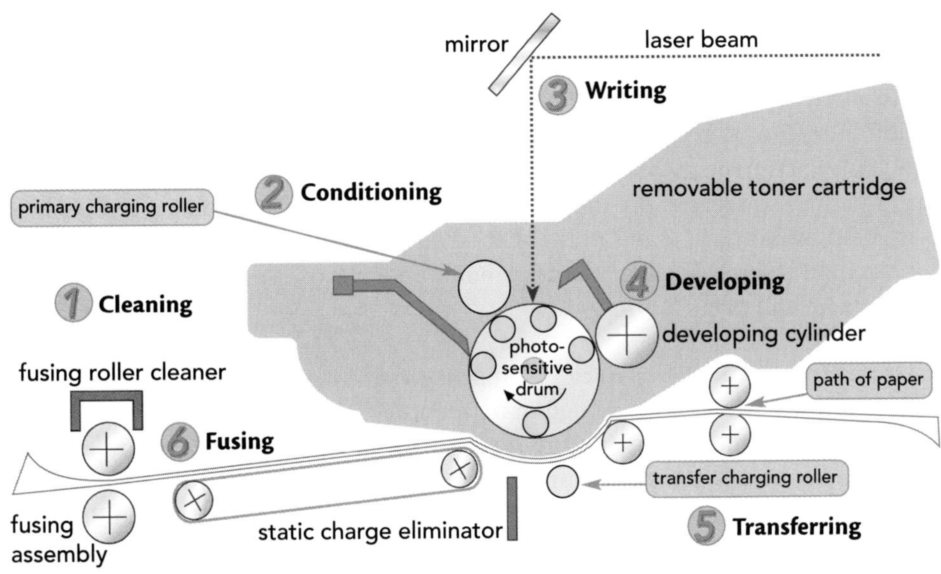

Figure 7-7 Six steps are involved in the laser printing process.

The result of this series of steps is a printout of data from the computer. Color laser printers work in a similar way, but the writing process repeats four times, one for each toner color of cyan (a bright blue color), magenta, yellow, and black. Then the paper passes to the fusing stage, when the fuser bonds all toner to the paper and aids in blending the four tones to form specific colors.

Note that Figure 7-7 shows only a cross-section of a laser printer. The drum, roller, and other mechanisms are as wide as the sheet of paper. The toner used as ink for a laser printer is stored in a toner cartridge (Figure 7-8). Toner responds to a charge and moves from one surface to another if the second surface has a more positive charge than the first. Like the ink cartridges used with ink-jet printers, a toner cartridge can be replaced or refilled when it is empty.

Figure 7-8 Laser printers use toner cartridges to store the powdered ink called toner. When empty, a toner cartridge can be replaced or refilled.

FEATURES OF A LASER PRINTER Most laser printers can print letter-quality text and graphics in very high resolutions, ranging from 600 to 2400 dpi. Laser printers also are faster than ink-jet printers. A desktop laser printer, for example, might print 9 to 30 pages per minute, while a high-end network printer may print up to 150 ppm.

Laser printers range in cost from a few hundred to several thousand dollars for a black and white printer. In general, the higher the resolution and speed, the more expensive the printer. Color laser printers also are available, but cost more than a black and white printer.

Laser printers also are called **page printers**, because they process and store an entire page before printing the page. To store the information about the page, a laser printer needs to have a certain amount of memory (which often is referred to as onboard memory). Most laser printers have at least 2 MB of onboard memory, which is enough to print black and white text. Printing high-resolution graphics requires significantly more memory. To print a full-page graphic at 600 dpi, for example, you need at least 16 MB of memory in the printer. For example, the desktop laser printer shown in Figure 7-6 on page 276 has up to 16 MB of onboard memory to allow a few users to print documents, while the network laser printer has up to 416 MB of onboard memory so it can store pages with very high resolution color graphics before printing them. As you will learn later in the chapter, if a printer does not have enough memory to hold the entire page of a document, an error message may display or only part of the page will print.

> **More About**
>
> **Ink-jet versus Laser**
>
> To learn more about the advantages and disadvantages of using an ink-jet printer versus a laser printer, visit the Understanding and Troubleshooting Your PC More About Web page (**scsite.com/understanding/more**) and then click Ink-jet versus Laser below Chapter 7.

PAGE DESCRIPTION LANGUAGES As discussed above, a laser printer needs to have all the information about a page in its memory before it can start printing. This data is sent to the printer using a **page description language (PDL)** that describes the layout and contents of a page sent to the printer. Most laser printers support at least one of two most widely used PDLs: Hewlett-Packard PCL and Adobe PostScript. **PCL (Printer Control Language)** supports the fonts and layouts used in standard business documents and is considered a de facto standard in the printing industry. **PostScript** supports complex graphics, fonts, and numerous colors and thus is used in the fields of desktop publishing and graphic arts (and is the PDL used by the Macintosh OS). Some printers support only one of the two PDLs, while others support both PCL and PostScript. Depending on the PDL used by a printer, software may require different drivers to communicate with the printer. Windows XP includes drivers for both PCL and PostScript printers.

> **FAQ 7-2**
>
> **Why is it that, even if a dot-matrix printer and a laser printer have the same dpi, the laser printer produces a higher quality image?**
>
> Even when printing at the same dpi, a laser printer can produce better-quality printouts than a dot-matrix printer, because it can vary the size of the dots it prints. This technology, called REt (Resolution Enhancement technology), was created by Hewlett-Packard to allow printers to vary the size of dots on a page, thus creating a sharp, clear image.

Thermal Printers and Solid Ink Printers

Similar printer technologies are used by thermal printers and solid ink printers. A **thermal printer** uses wax-based ink that is heated by pins that melt the ink onto paper (Figure 7-9). The print head containing these pins is as wide as the paper. The internal logic of the printer determines which pins get heated to produce the printed image. Thermal printers are popular in retail applications for printing bar codes, price tags, and receipts (gasoline dispensers, for example, typically use thermal printers to print receipts). A thermal printer can burn dots onto special paper, as done by older fax machines (called direct thermal printing), or the printer can use a ribbon that contains the wax-based ink (called thermal wax transfer printing).

Figure 7-9 Other types of printers provide functionality specific to the user's needs.

One variation of thermal printing uses thermal dye sublimation technology to print photos, identification cards, and access cards. A **dye-sublimation printer** uses solid dyes embedded on different transparent films. As the print head passes over each color film, it heats up, causing the dye to vaporize onto the glossy surface of the paper. Because the dye is vaporized onto the paper rather than jetted at it, the results are more photo-lab quality than with ink-jet printing.

A **solid ink printer**, such as the one shown in Figure 7-9, uses ink stored in solid blocks. The sticks or blocks are easy to handle and several can be inserted in the printer to be used as needed, avoiding the problem of running out of ink in the middle of a large print job. The solid ink is melted into the print head, which spans the width of the paper. The head jets the liquid ink onto the paper as it passes by on a drum. Solid ink printers are easy to set up and maintain and the print quality is excellent. The greatest disadvantage to solid ink printing is the time it takes for the print head to heat up to begin a print job, which is about 15 minutes. For this reason, some solid ink printers anticipate that a print job might be coming based on previous use of the printer, and automatically heat up. Solid ink printers generally are low-cost to purchase and operate. A solid ink printer costs about the same as a black-and-white laser printer, has a cost per page similar to a laser printer, and does not require the more expensive ink-jet paper required to achieve high-quality color prints from an ink-jet printer.

Photo Printers

A **photo printer** is a color printer that can print photographs at a quality equal to photos developed at a photo lab (Figure 7-9). Photo printers include features aimed at creating high-quality prints in a range of sizes, including photos without white borders. If you anticipate that you will print more photos than text-based documents, a photo printer might be a good option.

Photo printers use ink-jet or dye-sublimation technologies specifically designed to print photographs. An ink-jet photo printer works much like a regular ink-jet printer, but often uses six or seven shades of ink (rather than three or four) to provide more realistic color in complex photographs. Ink-jet printers are reasonably priced, typically ranging from eighty to eight hundred dollars, depending on the speed, resolution, and other features. A dye-sublimation photo printer uses the dye-sublimation process to generate prints that are even higher quality than with ink-jet photo printers. These printers typically are more expensive than ink-jet photo printers and generally are designed only for printing photos of a specific size. This makes them somewhat impractical for the typical user who may want to use the printer to output photos in a range of sizes.

The paper used in a photo printer significantly impacts the quality of the printout. Many types of photo paper are available, providing different finishes, brightness, and weight. Professional quality photo papers have the highest weight and quality (rated from 44 to 58 pounds) and cost about 50 cents per sheet. Premium and standard photo papers provide slightly lower weight and can cost between 5 to 15 cents per sheet.

Many photo printers provide unique photography-related features not found on standard printers. For example, many of them include a slot for flash memory cards and other storage media used to store digital photos. To print photos, you insert the media card in the slot and then push buttons on the printer to select the desired photos, specify the number of copies and the size, and then print the images. Other printers allow you to connect the digital camera to the printer, so you can print directly from the camera without going through your computer.

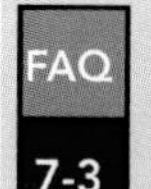

FAQ 7-3

What are the seven shades of ink used in an ink-jet photo printer?

The seven shades of ink used in an ink-jet photo printer are light cyan, light magenta, light black, and photo black, in addition to the standard cyan, magenta, and yellow. Many also include a matte black cartridge for printing black and white photos and fine art photo prints on matte paper.

Multifunction Peripherals

A **multifunction peripheral** (**MFP**), also called a **multifunction device** (**MFD**) or an **all-in-one device**, is a single device that serves several functions, including printing. Typically, a multifunction peripheral such as the one shown in Figure 7-9 on the previous page can act as a printer, a scanner, a fax machine, and a copier.

Multifunction peripherals often are used in small home offices, because they require less space and eliminate the cost of buying three or four separate devices. Using an MFP also reduces ongoing operating costs, as all of the devices use the same ink or toner. Typically, however, you only can perform one operation at a time — that is, you cannot fax one document and print another document simultaneously. The downside of multifunction peripherals is that, if the device breaks, you may lose all of its functions at once.

If you can afford it, the best practice is to purchase one machine for one purpose instead of bundling many functions into a single machine. For example, if you need a scanner and a printer, purchase a good printer and a good scanner rather than a multifunction peripheral. Routine maintenance and troubleshooting are easier and less expensive on single-purpose machines, although the initial cost is higher.

More About

Other Types of Printers

To learn more about other types of printers, such as label and postage printers, visit the Understanding and Troubleshooting Your PC More About Web page (**scsite.com/understanding/more**) and then click Other Types of Printers below Chapter 7.

Quiz Yourself 7-1

To test your knowledge of printer types, visit the Understanding and Troubleshooting Your PC Quiz Yourself Web page (scsite.com/understanding/quiz). Click Quiz Yourself 1 below Chapter 7.

Installing and Sharing a Printer

Like other peripheral devices, a printer can be connected to a computer or network using a cable connected to a port, or via a wireless connection. The following section reviews how Windows handles print jobs and then explains how to install a printer on a computer and share it with others on the network.

How Windows Handles Print Jobs

As described above, most printers support one or more page description languages, including PCL and PostScript. Depending on the PDL used by a printer, software may require different drivers to communicate with the printer.

An operating system, such as Windows, manages the order in which print jobs are processed (a *job* is any operation managed by the processor, including receiving data from an input device and sending information to an output device such as a printer). When you execute a print command in an application, such as a word processor or e-mail software, the application combines data objects including text, fonts, and graphics and then uses a printer driver to send that information to the printer using the correct PDL. For Windows using a PostScript printer, the print job data is converted to PostScript. For Windows using a PCL printer, the print job data is converted to PCL.

When the data is received by the printer, it places the job in a buffer (Figure 7-10 on the next page). As you learned in an earlier chapter, a *buffer* is a segment of memory or storage in which items are placed while waiting to be transferred to an input or output device. Windows sends print jobs to a buffer, instead of sending them to the printer immediately. The buffer holds the information waiting to print, while the printer prints from the buffer at its own rate of speed. If several print jobs are sent to the printer at one time, the print jobs accumulate in a **queue** (pronounced "Q") in the buffer and are released to the printer as soon as possible. This process is called **spooling**. Using spooling allows you to continue to work on other tasks while your document is printing. If you send one or more documents to a printer, you can view the queue in the Printers window.

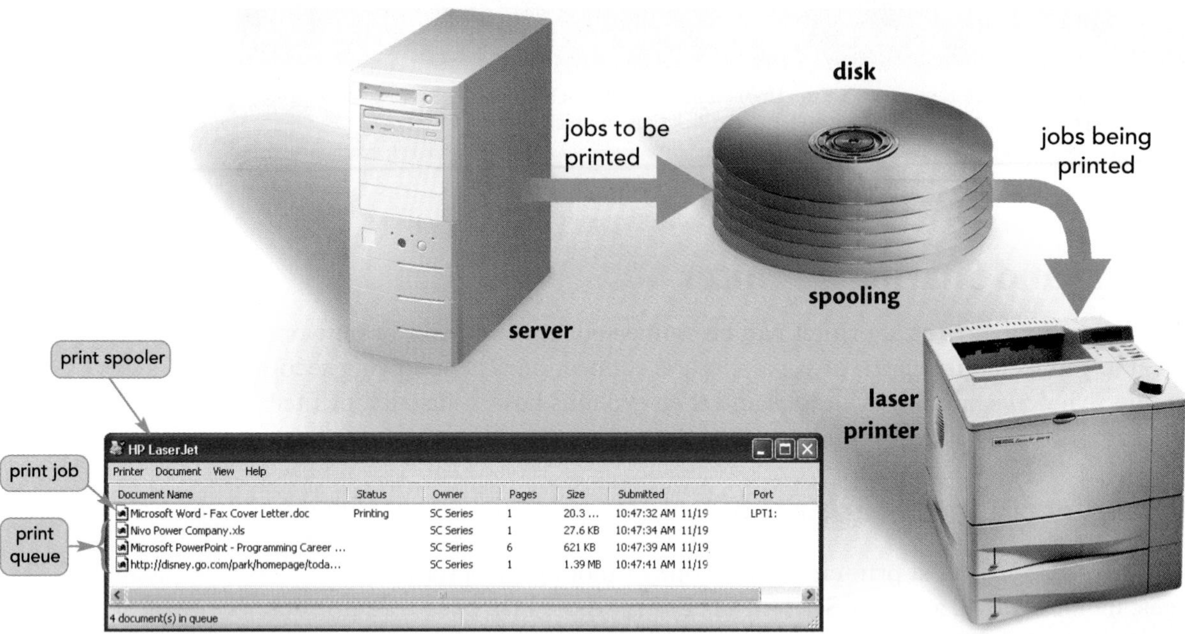

Figure 7-10 Spooling increases process and printer efficiency by placing print jobs in a buffer on disk, before they are printed. As shown here, three jobs are in the queue and one is printing.

FAQ 7-4

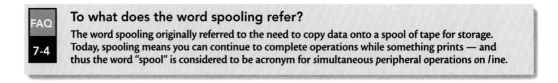

To what does the word spooling refer?

The word spooling originally referred to the need to copy data onto a spool of tape for storage. Today, spooling means you can continue to complete operations while something prints — and thus the word "spool" is considered to be acronym for *s*imultaneous *p*eripheral *o*perations *o*n *l*ine.

Local and Network Printers

Printers often are described as local or network, depending on how they are connected to a PC. A **local printer** is connected directly to a computer by way of a wireless connection or by a cable that connects to a parallel, serial, USB, SCSI, or FireWire port.

A **network printer** is a device that can be connected to a network and is accessible to a computer by way of a network. (Networks are covered in detail in Chapter 10.) Each computer on the network that uses the printer must have printer drivers installed, so the OS on each computer can communicate with the printer and provide the interface between the applications it supports and the printer.

A computer can have several printers installed, including a local printer and one or more network printers. Windows designates one printer to be the **default printer** for each computer, which is the one Windows prints to unless another is selected. This section covers how to install a local printer, how to share that printer with others on the network, and how a remote computer on the network can use a shared printer.

Installing a Local Printer Using a Cable

Recall from Chapter 6 that installing a new peripheral (such as a printer) typically follows three basic steps: installing the device, installing the device driver, and installing the application software. For most devices, you connect the device to the computer before installing the device driver and application software.

Using Windows XP Professional, follow these steps to install a local printer using a cable:

1. Physically attach the printer cable to the computer by way of a parallel port, serial port, FireWire port, or USB port. (Recall from Chapter 6 that you should use an IEEE 1284-compliant printer cable for a parallel port connection.)
2. Install the printer driver, either by having Windows install the driver or by using the printer manufacturer's installation software, which comes on a CD-ROM or DVD-ROM with the printer.
   a. To use the manufacturer's installation software to install the printer drivers, insert the CD-ROM or DVD-ROM bundled with the printer in the correct drive and then follow directions onscreen.
   b. To use Windows to install the printer driver using Plug and Play technology, open the Printers and Faxes window by clicking the Start button and then clicking Printers and Faxes on the Start menu. When the Printers and Faxes window opens, click Add a Printer and follow the Add Printer Wizard to install the printer driver. When prompted to select a local or network printer, select Local printer attached to this computer. To instruct Windows to try to identify and install the correct driver automatically using Plug and Play, click Automatically detect and install my Plug and Play printer. If Windows cannot locate the printer driver, it will give you the option to install the printer manually.

   In most cases, it is best to use the drivers provided by the printer manufacturer. The exception to this rule is if you have several similar printers installed. Windows does a better job of preventing files used by one printer installation from being overwritten by files from another installation.
3. Many printers also come with printer management software that provides tools to monitor ink levels, set print quality, download updated drivers, and troubleshoot any issues (Figure 7-11). If your printer came with printer management software, insert the CD-ROM or floppy disk into the correct drive and follow the instructions in the user guide to install the software.

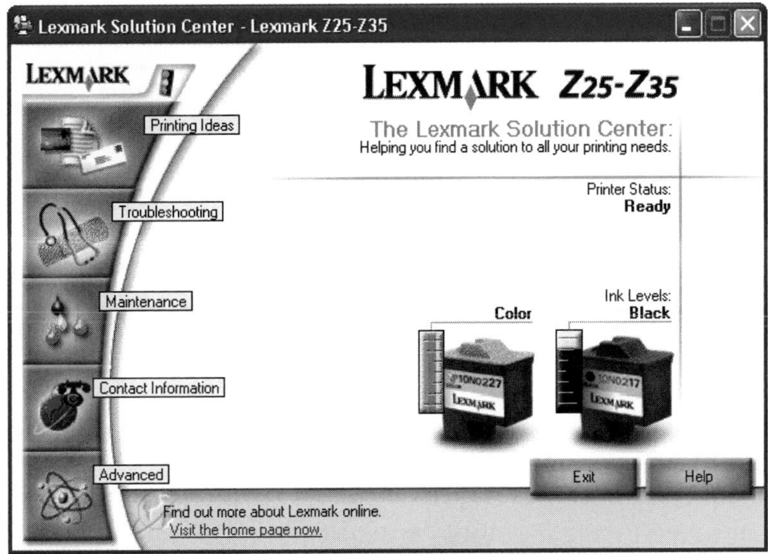

Figure 7-11 Many printers include printer management software that provides tools for setting print options, updating drivers, and maintaining and troubleshooting the printer.

4. After you install the printer driver and any printer management software, you should print a test page to confirm that the driver is installed properly. To print a test page, open the Printers and Faxes window and then right-click the printer you just installed. Click Properties on the shortcut menu and then click the General tab in the Properties window. Click the Print Test Page button to print a test page (Figure 7-12).

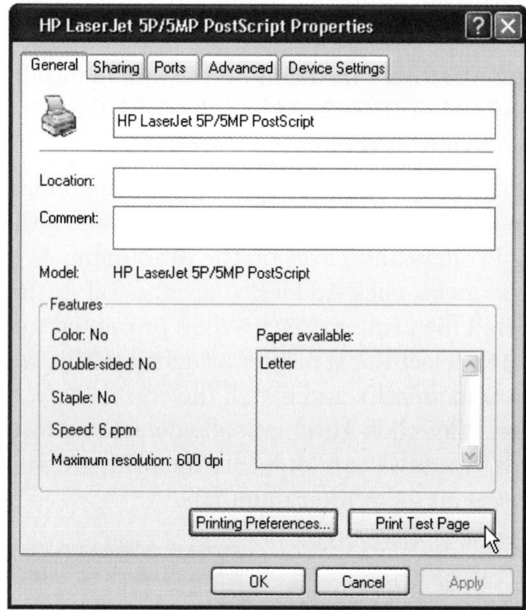

Figure 7-12 After you have installed the printer drivers, print a test page to verify that the drivers are installed properly.

The options and features available in the Printers and Faxes window also allow you to delete printers, change the Windows default printer, purge print jobs to troubleshoot failed printing, update printer drivers, and perform other printer maintenance tasks. Because printer manufacturers frequently update printer drivers to resolve problems, you should download and install the latest printer drivers from the manufacturer on a regular basis.

7-5

I just plugged the printer cable into the port and Windows automatically found the printer and installed the drivers. Is that OK?

Yes. If you have a Plug and Play printer that connects through any hot-pluggable port, such as a USB or FireWire port, simply connect the printer and turn it on. Windows automatically will install the printer for you. If you later want to install the drivers provided by the manufacturer (as opposed to built-in Windows drivers), you can use the Add Printer Driver wizard to update them.

Your Turn

Reviewing Printer Properties and Setting a Default Printer

The Properties window for a printer provides detailed information about the printer, including the resolution, speed, and the amount of memory installed. Using Windows XP, perform the following steps to learn more about an installed printer and then set a default printer:

1. Turn on the printer, if needed, and print a document to a printer installed on your computer.
2. Click the Start button and then click Printers and Faxes on the Start menu. When the Printers and Faxes window opens, right-click the printer from which you just printed the document.
3. When the printer's Properties window is displayed, click the Print Test Page button. If prompted, click OK after the test page prints. What information is listed on the test page?
4. Review the values in the Features area, as shown earlier in Figure 7-12. Answer the following questions:
   a. What is the printer speed?
   b. What is the printer's maximum resolution?
   c. Does the printer print in color?
5. Click the Printing Preferences button. On the Layout sheet, click the Advanced button. (Depending on your printer model, you may access the Advanced Options window using different steps.)
6. When the Advanced Options window is displayed, select a lower dpi setting in the Print Quality list (Figure 7-13). (Your Advanced Options window may differ, depending on your printer model).
7. Click OK three times to close the windows and then print the same document you printed in Step 1. Compare the quality of the two documents and then repeat Steps 2 through 5 to return the Print Quality setting to its original value.
8. Explore the tabs of the printer's Properties window to answer the following questions:
   a. How much onboard memory does the printer have?
   b. What page description languages does the printer support?
   (The Properties window for older printers may not include this information.)
   c. What port is used by the printer?
9. Click the OK button to close the Properties window.
10. When the Printers and Faxes window is displayed, note that the printer set as the default printer appears with a small black checkmark icon. If the printer does not already display a checkmark, right-click the printer and then click Set as Default Printer on the shortcut menu.

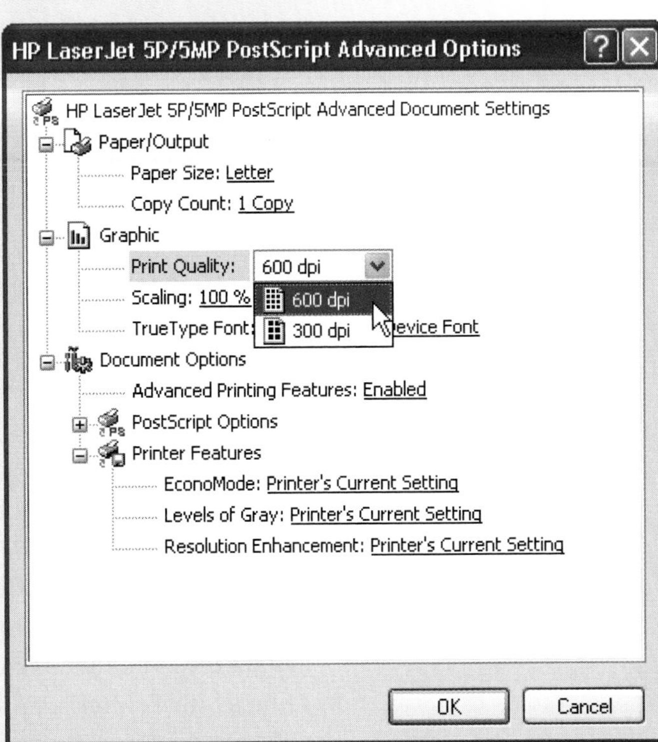

Figure 7-13

Installing a Local Printer Using a Wireless Connection

The steps to install a wireless printer are similar to the steps for installing a printer that uses a cable. Most wireless printers use Bluetooth technology, which, as you learned in Chapter 6, uses short-range radio waves to transmit data between two devices, such as a computer and a printer. To communicate with each other, the computer and printer must be within about 33 feet (10 meters) of each other. (Although infrared wireless printers are available, Bluetooth printing is more convenient than infrared connections because infrared requires a clear line of sight between the IrDA port and the printer.)

Some printers already are Bluetooth enabled and have a radio receiver built into the printer. A Bluetooth wireless printing kit typically comes with a Bluetooth adapter that plugs into the USB slot or PC Card slot on your computer, a printer adapter that connects to your printer's parallel port, and a power cable, in case the printer does not have enough power to support the printer adapter (Figure 7-14).

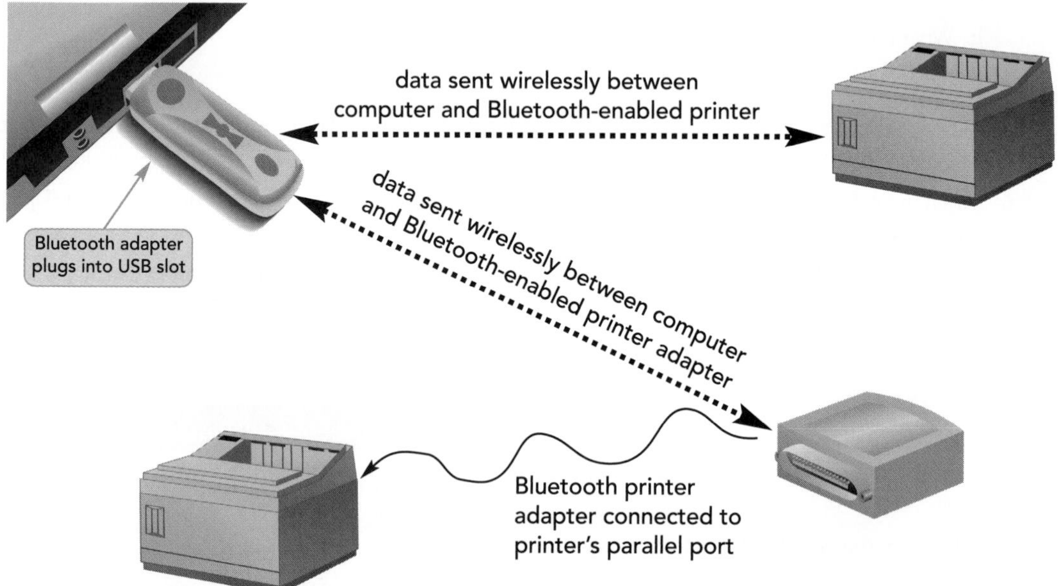

Figure 7-14 Bluetooth allows computers and other devices to transmit data wirelessly to a printer from distances of up to 10 meters.

Follow these steps to install a local printer using a Bluetooth wireless connection:

1. Turn the printer off.
2. Install the printer drivers using the manufacturer's installation software. Insert the CD-ROM or DVD-ROM bundled with the printer or wireless Bluetooth printing kit in the correct drive and then follow directions on the screen.
3. If you are using a wireless Bluetooth printing kit,
   a. Plug the Bluetooth adapter into the USB port or insert it into the PC Card slot on the computer.
   b. Connect the printer adapter to the printer's parallel port and, if needed, connect the power supply and plug it in.

4. Turn the printer on. Windows automatically will identify the printer using Plug and Play. If Windows cannot locate the printer, it will give you the option to install the printer manually.
5. Many printer adapters have a button, such as a TEST button, that allows you to print a test page. Press the button to print a test page and verify that the printer was installed correctly. If your adapter does not have such a button, open the Printers and Faxes window and then right-click the printer you just installed. Click Properties on the shortcut menu and then click the General tab in the Properties window (as shown in Figure 7-12). Click the Print Test Page button to print a test page.

More About

Installing Printers Using Windows 9x

To learn more about installing, sharing, and connecting to printers using Windows 9x, visit the Understanding and Troubleshooting Your PC More About Web page (**scsite.com/understanding/more**) and then click Installing Printers using Windows 9x below Chapter 7.

Sharing and Installing a Network Printer

When a network printer is shared, it means that more than one computer or other device on a network can send print jobs to the printer. To share a network printer using Windows, a Windows component called File and Printer Sharing must be installed on the computer to which the printer is attached — and a Windows component called Client for Microsoft Networks must be installed on the remote computer using the printer. These two components are installed by default when you install Windows Server 2003, Windows XP, or Windows 2000.

SHARING A NETWORK PRINTER To share a network printer, complete the following steps using Windows XP Professional:

1. Open the Printers and Faxes window by clicking the Start button and then clicking Printers and Faxes on the Start menu. When the Printers and Faxes window opens (Figure 7-15a), right-click the printer you want to share and then click Sharing on the shortcut menu.
2. When the printer's Properties window is displayed, click Share this printer and then enter a name for the printer in the Share name text box (Figure 7-15b). Note that your Properties window may differ, depending on the printer model.

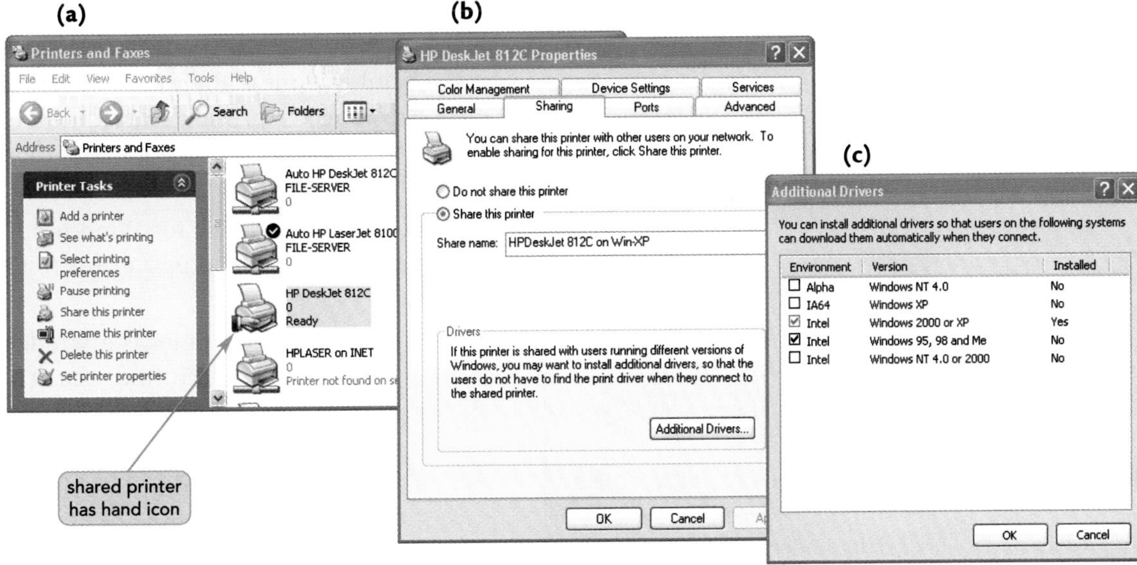

Figure 7-15 Setting up a shared printer using Windows XP.

3. If you want to make a driver for the printer available to remote users who are using an operating system other than the OS used on the computer to which the printer is connected, then click the Additional Drivers button. For example, if the printer is connected to a computer running Windows XP, but a computer running Windows 98 will need to use the printer, you should make additional drivers available.
4. The Additional Drivers window is displayed, as shown in Figure 7-15c on the previous page. Select the operating systems used by computers that will use the printer, so these computers will have access to the correct printer drivers (you might be asked for the Windows or printer manufacturer's CD or other access to the installation files). Click OK twice to close both windows. A shared printer shows a hand icon under it in the Printers and Faxes window.

CONNECTING TO A SHARED PRINTER Recall that for a remote PC to connect to and use a shared network printer, the driver for that printer must be installed on the remote PC. There are two approaches to installing shared network printer drivers on a remote PC. You can perform the installation using the drivers on CD (either the Windows CD or printer manufacturer's CD), or you can perform the installation using the printer drivers on the host PC. While the following steps show how to install the drivers using Windows XP, the installations work about the same way for Windows Server 2003, Windows 2000, and Windows 98.

To connect to a shared printer on the network by installing the manufacturer's printer driver from CD, complete the following using Windows XP:

1. Open the Printers and Faxes window, and then click Add a printer. When the Add Printer Wizard starts, follow the Add Printer Wizard to install the printer driver. When prompted to select a local or network printer, click A network printer, or a printer attached to another computer and then click the Next button.
2. Enter the name of the **host computer** (that is, the computer connected to the printer) and printer name. Start entering the name with two backslashes and separate the computer name from the printer name with a single backslash (for example, \\lisapc\hpdeskjet, where lisapc is the computer name and hpdeskjet is the printer name). Alternatively, you can click Browse for a printer, search the list of shared printers on the network, and then select the printer to install (Figure 7-16).
3. Windows XP searches for Windows XP drivers on the host computer for this printer.
   a. If the host computer is a Windows XP machine and it finds the driver, then the wizard skips to Step 4.
   b. If the host computer is not a Windows XP machine and it cannot find the driver, Windows displays a message to ask if you want to search for the proper driver. Click the OK button. Click Have Disk to use the manufacturer's driver, or to use

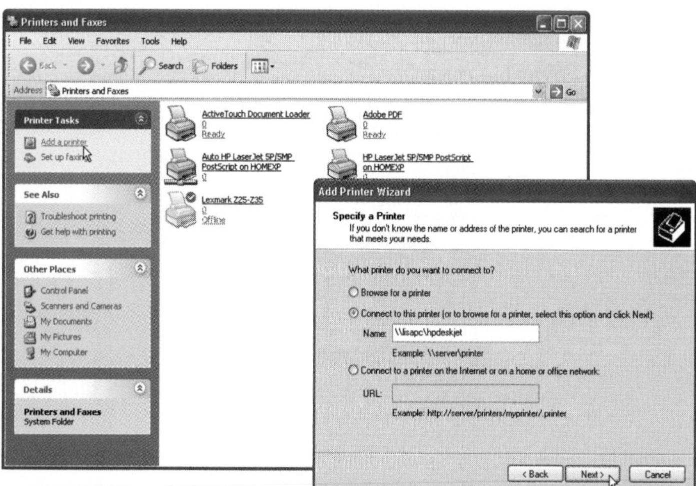

Figure 7-16 To use a network printer under Windows XP, enter the host computer name followed by the printer name or have Windows XP browse the network for shared printers.

Windows drivers, select the printer manufacturer and then the printer model from the list of supported printers. Click OK when you finish.

4. When the wizard asks if you want to use this printer as the default printer, click Yes if you want Windows to send documents to this printer by default. Click the Next button and then the Finish button to complete the wizard.
5. The printer icon appears in the Printers and Faxes window. To test the printer installation, right-click the icon and select Properties from the shortcut menu. Click the General tab and then click the Print Test Page button.

More About

Sharing Printers on a Network

To learn more about ways to share printers on a network, visit the Understanding and Troubleshooting Your PC More About Web page (**scsite.com/understanding/more**) and then click Sharing Printers on a Network below Chapter 7.

Quiz Yourself 7-2

To test your knowledge of installing printers, visit the Understanding and Troubleshooting Your PC Quiz Yourself Web page (scsite.com/understanding/quiz). Click Quiz Yourself 2 below Chapter 7.

Maintaining and Troubleshooting Printers

This section first discusses general printer maintenance and then explains how to troubleshoot problems specific to each of the three major types of printers. As a general rule, to help prevent problems with printers, follow the manufacturer's instructions when using the printer and perform routine printer maintenance.

Printer Maintenance

Routine printer maintenance procedures vary widely based on the specific printer type and the manufacturer of the printer. A basic maintenance step, however, is to ensure that the **consumables**, or items used by the printer, such as paper, ink ribbons, color sticks, toner cartridges, and ink cartridges, are on hand.

Also, for each printer you support, research the printer documentation or the manufacturer's Web site for specific maintenance procedures and how often you should perform them. For example, the maintenance plan for a color laser printer might instruct you to replace the transfer roller assembly after printing 120,000 pages and replace the fusing assembly after 150,000 pages. (The printer documentation includes instructions to command the printer to report how many pages have printed since each maintenance task was performed.) When you are ready to replace these components, you can purchase a kit called a **printer maintenance kit**, which includes the specific printer components you need to replace, step-by-step instructions for performing maintenance, and any special tools or equipment you need to complete the maintenance.

When you perform routine maintenance on a printer, clean the inside and outside of the printer. You can clean the outside of the printer with a damp cloth; do not use ammonia-based cleaners. The inside of the printer can be cleaned with a dry cloth to remove dust, bits of paper, and stray toner (do not use an antistatic vacuum cleaner). For a laser printer, wipe the rollers from side to side with a dry cloth to remove loose dirt (but be sure to not touch the soft black roller (the transfer roller) or you might affect the print quality). If you get toner on your hands while cleaning a laser printer, wash your hands thoroughly with soap and water. If toner gets on your clothes, dust it off and clean your clothes with cold water. Hot water will set the toner.

A printer manufacturer's Web site is an important resource when supporting printers (Figure 7-17). Here are some things to look for:

- *Online documentation.* The Web sites of most printer manufacturers include documentation on installing, configuring, troubleshooting, using, upgrading, and maintaining the printer. Also look for information on printer parts and warranty, compatibility information, specifications and features of your printer, a way to register your printer, and how to recycle or dispose of a printer.

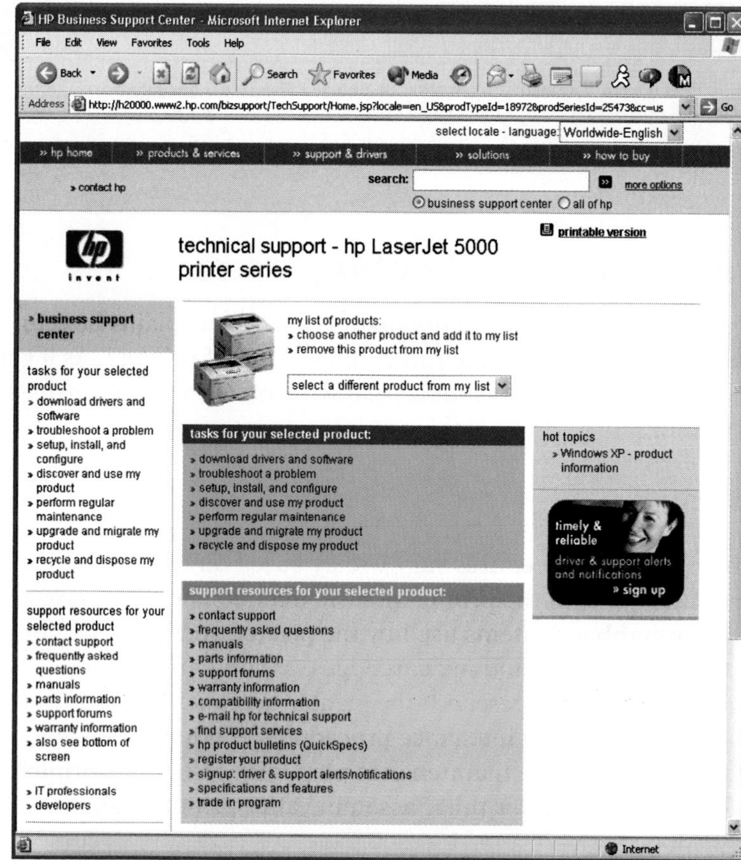

Figure 7-17 A printer manufacturer's Web site is an important resource when supporting printers.

- *A knowledge base of common problems and what to do about them.* Some Web sites also offer a newsgroup service or discussion group where you can communicate with others responsible for supporting a particular printer. You also may be able to e-mail your questions to technical support.
- *Updated device drivers.* Printer problems sometimes can be resolved by downloading and installing the latest drivers. You also may want to look for and download new drivers regularly to take advantage of new features and options available through these drivers. Be sure you download files for the correct printer and operating system. Download the drivers to a folder on the hard drive such as C:\Downloads\Printer and then double-click the driver file to extract files and launch the installation program to update the printer drivers.

- *Flash BIOS updates.* Some high-end printers have firmware that can be flashed to solve problems and add features. Be careful to verify that you download the correct update for your printer.
- *Catalog of options and upgrades.* As you browse the printer manufacturer's Web site, look for memory upgrades, optional trays, feeders, sorters, staplers, printer stands, and other equipment to upgrade your printer. You also should check if new software, such as software to produce greeting cards or edit photographs, is available for use with your printer.
- *Printer maintenance kits.* The best practice is to buy everything you need for routine maintenance either from the printer manufacturer or from an approved vendor.
- *Replacement parts.* When a printer part breaks, buy only parts made by or approved by the printer manufacturer. Manufacturers generally also sell consumable supplies such as toner and ink cartridges.

General Printer Troubleshooting

Printing problems can be caused by the printer, the PC hardware or operating system, the application using the printer, the printer cable, or the network. Figure 7-18 outlines some basic questions to ask and steps to follow, in order to isolate the problem.

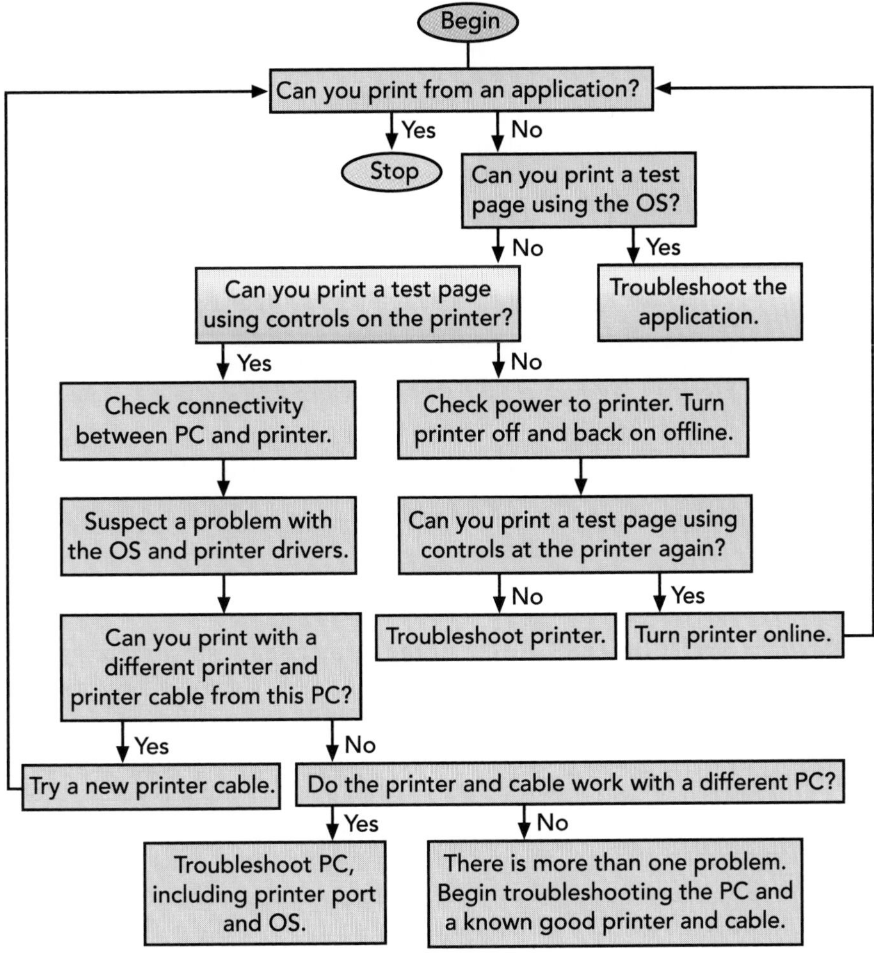

Figure 7-18 Steps to isolate a printer problem.

The sections that follow address printer problems caused by all of these categories. If the printer port, printer cable, and printer all support bidirectional communication, the printer can communicate with Windows and may be able to display error messages on the screen, such as an out-of-paper or paper-jam message.

PROBLEMS WITH THE PRINTER ITSELF To eliminate the printer as the problem, first check that the printer is on and then print a self-test page. The directions on how to print a self-test page should be listed in the printer's user guide (for example, you might need to hold down a button or buttons on the printer's front panel). If the self-test page prints correctly, then the printer works correctly.

A printer self-test page generally prints some text, some graphics, and some information about the printer, such as the printer resolution and how much memory is installed. Verify that the information on the test page is correct. For example, if you know that the printer should have 16 MB of onboard printer memory, but the test only reports 8 MB, the printer may have a memory problem.

If the self-test page does not print or prints incorrectly (for example, it has missing dots or smudged streaks through the page), then troubleshoot the printer by asking the questions listed in Figure 7-19 until it prints correctly. If none of these steps works, check the printer user guide or manufacturer's Web site for troubleshooting suggestions and documentation. The printer documentation can be very helpful and most often contains a phone number for technical support. If you still cannot resolve the issue, try contacting the manufacturer or taking the printer to a certified repair shop.

Area	Questions to ask
Paper	• Does the printer have paper? • Is the paper installed correctly? • Is there a paper jam? Is the paper damp or wrinkled, causing it to refuse to feed?
Printer cover	• Are the printer cover and rear access doors properly closed and locked?
Ink and toner cartridges	• For a laser printer, check that a toner cartridge is installed. For an ink-jet printer, check that ink cartridges are installed. • Has the protective tape been removed from the print cartridge? • For a laser printer, replace the toner cartridge. For ink-jet printers, replace the ink cartridge.
Power	• Check that power is getting to the printer. Try another power source.

Figure 7-19 If the self-test page does not print or prints incorrectly, ask these questions to help troubleshoot the problem.

PROBLEMS WITH THE PRINTER CABLE If the printer self-test worked, try printing a test page from the printer Properties window. If the test page does not print, the problem might be with the printer cable. First, check that the cable is connected firmly at both ends. Then, try printing using the same printer and printer cable but a different PC. If that still does not work, verify that a parallel cable is IEEE 1284-compliant and then try connecting a different, shorter printer cable to the original computer (cables longer than 10 feet or 3.05 meters can sometimes cause problems). Next, enter CMOS setup and check how the parallel port is configured. Make sure it is not disabled. If it is set to ECP, which requires the use of a DMA channel, try setting the port to EPP or bidirectional.

PROBLEMS WITH THE WIRELESS CONNECTION If you are having difficulty printing from a local printer using a wireless connection, such as Bluetooth, first try to print a test page by pressing the TEST button on the print adapter. If the test page prints, the printer and printer adapter are communicating. Next, try to reduce the distance between the printer and the Bluetooth adapter. In most cases, the range is at least 33 feet (10 meters) from the printer adapter, but steel buildings and other types of construction can interfere with the signal.

If the test page does not print, check that the printer adapter is connected to the printer securely via a parallel or USB port, but not to both connections simultaneously; also check that the power supply for the printer adapter is plugged in. Next, try a cold reset on the printer adapter by temporarily removing power and then restoring power while holding down the TEST button.

If you still cannot print a test page, then verify that the printer is powered on and review the questions listed in Figure 7-19 to eliminate other issues with the printer. Next, confirm that the printer works when not using a wireless connection, by connecting the printer directly to your computer and printing a page from your computer. As noted above, if none of these steps works, look for troubleshooting suggestions and documentation in the user guides or manufacturer's Web sites for the printer and the printer adapter. If you still cannot resolve the issue, try contacting the manufacturer or taking the printer to a certified repair shop.

Problems with Laser Printers

This section covers some problems that can occur with laser printers, including poor print quality, toner problems, paper jams, too little memory, and trouble communicating with the computer. For more specific guidelines on troubleshooting issues with your printer, refer to the printer documentation or the manufacturer's Web site for information on your printer model.

ISSUES WITH PRINT QUALITY Poor print quality, including faded, smeared, wavy, speckled, or streaked printouts, often indicates that the toner is low. The printer also may display a message indicating that toner is low. All major mechanical printer components that normally create problems conveniently are contained within the replaceable toner cartridge. In most cases, the solution to poor-quality printing or a low toner situation is to replace this cartridge. When replacing a toner cartridge, follow these general guidelines:

- If you suspect the printer is overheated, unplug it and allow it to cool.
- Remove the toner cartridge and gently rock it from side to side to redistribute the toner (to avoid flying toner, do not shake the cartridge too hard). Replace the toner cartridge. This may solve the problem temporarily, but you should plan to replace the toner cartridge soon.
- If this does not solve the problem, try replacing the toner cartridge.
- Also be aware that extreme humidity may cause the toner to clump in the cartridge and give a toner low message. If this is a consistent problem, you might want to invest in a dehumidifier for the room where your printer is located.

Low-grade paper also can result in poor print quality. First, try a new sheet of the same paper or, if you think the paper quality may not be high enough, try a different brand of paper. In general, try to use only paper recommended for use with a laser printer. EconoMode, a mode that uses less toner, may be on. Turning it off also can help improve print quality.

Poor print quality also may indicate that you need to clean the printer. First, clean the inside of the printer with a dry, lint-free cloth, being careful not to touch the transfer roller. On some laser printers, you also can clean the mirror (check the printer user guide for directions). If the transfer roller is dirty, the problem will probably correct itself after several sheets print. If not, then take the printer to an authorized service center.

Also consider whether or not the printer requires routine maintenance. Check the Web site of the printer manufacturer for how often to perform the maintenance and to purchase the required printer maintenance kit.

What is EconoMode?

EconoMode is a technology that uses substantially less toner than normal printing. The printed image is much lighter, but it is adequate for printing drafts or proofs. To set EconoMode settings, click the Printing Preferences button in the General tab of the printer's Properties window.

A PAPER JAM OCCURS OR PAPER OUT MESSAGE APPEARS If paper is jammed inside the printer, do not jerk the paper from the printer mechanism. First, read the directions in the printer documentation on how to remove the paper and, when you do pull out the paper, pull evenly on the paper. When a paper jam occurs, other steps to take include the following:

- Check for jammed paper from both the paper tray and the output bin.
- If there is no jammed paper, then remove the tray and check the metal plate at the bottom of the tray. If it cannot move up and down freely, replace the tray.
- When you insert the tray in the printer, check to see if the printer lifts the metal plate as the tray is inserted. If it does not, the lift mechanism might need repair.

Also be sure that the paper inserted in a printer is not damp, as a result of high humidity. Damp paper can cause paper jams.

PRINTER STAYS IN WARM-UP MODE The warming up message on the front panel of the printer should turn off as soon as the printer establishes communication with the computer. If this does not happen, try the following:

- Turn off the printer and disconnect the cable to the computer. Turn on the printer. If it now displays a Ready message, the problem is communication between the printer and computer.
- Verify that the cable is connected to the correct printer port, for example to a parallel port or USB port.

- Verify that data to the installed printer is being sent to the correct port. For example, open the Properties dialog box of the installed printer. If the printer is using a parallel cable, verify that the print job is being sent to LPT1, as shown in Figure 7-20. Check that the printer port is enabled in CMOS setup and set to the correct mode.
- Replace the cable.

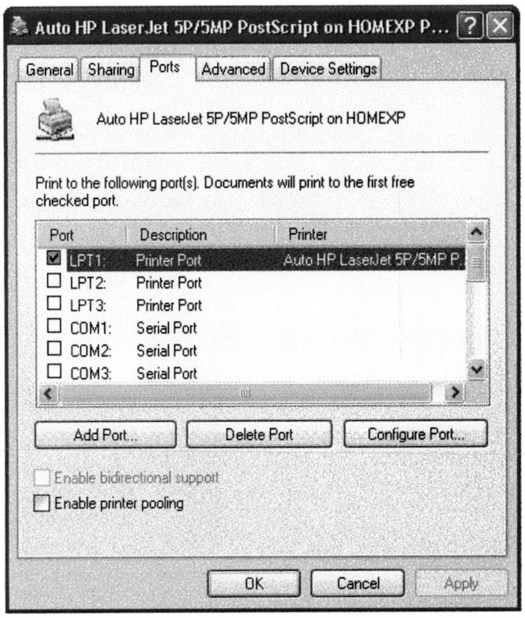

Figure 7-20 Verify that print data is being sent to the correct port.

PRINTING IS SLOW Laser printers are rated by two speed properties: the time it takes to print the first page (measured in seconds) and the print speed (measured in pages per minute). Try the following if the printer is slow:

- Space is needed on the hard drive of the computer that queues and manages print jobs. Clean unneeded files from the drive or, if necessary, install a larger drive.
- Add more memory to the printer, following the directions in the printer manual.
- Lower the printer resolution and the print quality.

A PORTION OF THE PAGE DOES NOT PRINT For some laser printers, an error occurs if the printer does not have enough memory to hold the entire page. For other printers, only a part of the page prints. Some may signal this problem by flashing a light or displaying an error message, such as 20 Mem Overflow, on their display panels or on the printout. The solution is to install more memory. Print a self-test page to verify how much memory is installed and then check the printer guide to determine how much memory the printer can support and what kind of memory to buy. Follow the directions in the printer manual to install additional memory.

> **More About**
>
> **Upgrading Printer Memory**
>
> To learn more about the steps to upgrade printer memory, visit the Understanding and Troubleshooting Your PC More About Web page (**scsite.com/understanding/more**) and then click Upgrading Printer Memory below Chapter 7.

Problems with Ink-jet Printers

This section covers some problems that can occur with ink-jet printers, including poor print quality and intermittent printing. As with the laser printer, you should refer to the printer documentation or the manufacturer's Web site for information when troubleshooting your ink-jet printer.

If the print quality of an ink-jet printer is poor, check the quality of the paper being used. The paper quality determines the final print quality, especially with ink-jet printers. Other steps to take include the following:

- Check if the ink supply is low or if any of the cartridges have a partially clogged nozzle. If necessary, remove and reinstall the cartridge or follow the printer's documentation to clean each nozzle. Note that some ink-jet printer cartridges just replace the ink, while some actually replace the ink and the print head. The cost for replacement cartridges that include the print head is a little higher, but provide the option of replacing the cartridge if the print head becomes irreparably clogged.
- Open the Printers and Faxes window and right-click the printer. When the Properties window is displayed, click the Printing Preferences button on the General tab. Change the Print Quality selection to a higher dpi. Try different settings until you find a quality that is acceptable. If your printer came with

printer management software to allow you to manage settings, change the print quality using the software and again print sample pages using different settings until you find an acceptable quality.

- Check that the print head is at the correct distance (not too close to or too far from the paper).
- Some printers have a little sponge near the carriage rest that can become clogged with ink. Remove and clean the sponge.
- If you are printing transparencies, try changing the fill pattern in your application.

What grade or quality of paper should I use in a printer?

The quality of paper determines the final print quality, especially with ink-jet printers. In general, the better the quality of the paper used, the better the print quality. If you do not need professional quality printouts, you can save costs by using a lower grade paper for drafts and a higher-grade paper for the final printed copy. Do not use less than 20-lb. paper in any type of printer, unless the printer documentation specifically says that a lower weight is satisfactory.

Sometimes dust or dirt gets down into the print head assemblage, causing streaks or lines on the printed page. Follow the manufacturer's instructions to clean the print cartridge assemblage. Use clean distilled water and cotton swabs to clean the cartridge cradle and the face and edges of the print cartridge, being careful not to touch the nozzle plate. To prevent the ink-jet nozzles from drying out, do not leave the print cartridges out of their cradle for longer than 30 minutes.

Newer printers often allow you to use software or buttons on the front panel of the printer to clean the nozzles automatically or calibrate or align the ink cartridges on ink-jet printers (Figure 7-21). To access the printer software, open the Printer and Faxes windows, right-click the printer icon, and then click Properties on the shortcut menu. In the Properties window, click the Printing Preferences button on the General tab. When the printer software starts, follow the instructions for your printer management software to clear the print cartridges or calibrate or align the ink cartridges.

When you have finished, print a test page. If the page prints sharply with no missing dots or lines, then you are finished. If the page does not print correctly, perform the auto-clean again. You might need to perform the auto-clean procedure six or seven times to clean the nozzles completely. If the problem persists, do not attempt to clean the nozzles manually; contact the manufacturer or vendor for service.

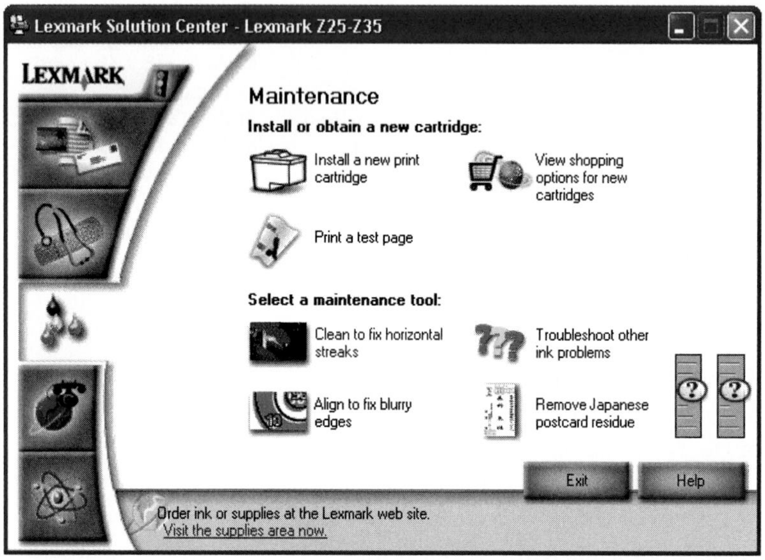

Figure 7-21 The printer management software provided with newer printers often provides features to clean the ink-jet nozzles or calibrate or align the ink cartridges.

Troubleshooting Problems Printing from Windows and Application Software

As outlined above, problems with a printer may result from problems with the operating system or application software attempting to use the printer.

TROUBLESHOOTING PRINTING FROM WINDOWS If a self-test page works, but you still cannot print to a local printer from Windows, try the following troubleshooting steps:

- The print spool might be stalled. Try deleting all print jobs in the printer's queue by double-clicking the printer icon in the Printers window. Click Purge Print Documents on the Printer menu. It may take a moment for the print jobs to disappear.
- Try to print a test page using the Printers window. Right-click the printer you want to test and then click Properties on the shortcut menu. Click the Print Test Page button to send a test page to the printer. Verify that the correct default printer is selected.
- Verify that the printer is online, or ready to accept print jobs. See the printer documentation for information on how to determine the status from the control panel of the printer.
- If you still cannot print, verify that the printer cable or cable connections are tight and reboot the PC.
- Try removing and reinstalling the printer and printer drivers. To uninstall the printer driver, right-click the printer icon in the Printers window and then select Delete. Reinstall the printer using the steps described above.

You also should check the port settings for the printer to verify that they are not the source of the problem. First, check to see if the printer is configured for the correct port. Next, access CMOS setup and check the configuration of the USB, serial, or parallel port that the printer is using and be sure it is enabled. If the printer is using the parallel port, check the parallel port mode in CMOS setup. If ECP mode is selected, verify that a DMA channel is available and not conflicting with another device; you also can try setting the port to EPP or bidirectional. Finally, check the resources assigned to the printer port. Open Device Manager, select the port being used by the printer, and then click Properties. Verify that the resources are assigned correctly for LPT1 (I/O addresses are 0378 to 037B) and that Device Manager reports no conflicts.

TROUBLESHOOTING PRINTING FROM APPLICATION SOFTWARE If you can print a Windows test page, but you cannot print from an application, try the following troubleshooting steps:

- Verify that the correct printer is selected in the Print Setup dialog box.
- Try printing a file from a different application.
- Delete any files in the print spool. From the Printers window, double-click the printer icon. Click Printer on the menu bar of the window that appears, and then click Purge Print Documents.
- Reboot the PC. Immediately enter Notepad or WordPad, type some text, and print.

- Reopen the application giving the print error and attempt to print again.
- Try creating data in a new file and printing it. Keep the data simple.
- If you can print from other applications, consider reinstalling or upgrading the problem application.
- Close any applications that are not being used.
- Add more memory to the printer.
- Remove and reinstall the printer drivers.

Troubleshooting Networked Printers

If you have problems printing to a network printer, try the following troubleshooting steps:

- First, be sure you are printing to the correct printer. Check to see if the printer is online.
- Check to see if you can print to another network printer. If so, there may be a problem with the printer.
- Try printing a test page from the computer that has the printer attached to it locally. In the Printer and Faxes window, right-click the printer you want to test and click Properties on the shortcut menu. Click the Print Test Page button to send a test page to the printer. If you cannot print from the local printer, troubleshoot the issue with the local printer before attempting to print over the network.
- Return to the remote computer. Using the Printers window, delete the printer, and then use My Network Places to reconnect the printer.
- Verify that you can access the computer to which the printer is attached. Open the My Network Places window and attempt to open shared folders on the printer's computer. Perhaps you have not entered a correct user ID and password to access this computer; if so, you will be unable to use the computer's resources.

More About

Troubleshooting Printers

To learn more about troubleshooting printers, visit the Understanding and Troubleshooting Your PC More About Web page (**scsite.com/understanding/more**) and then click Troubleshooting Printers below Chapter 7.

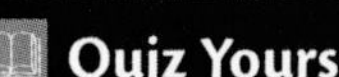

Quiz Yourself 7-3

To test your knowledge of troubleshooting printers, visit the Understanding and Troubleshooting Your PC Quiz Yourself Web page (scsite.com/understanding/quiz). Click Quiz Yourself 3 below Chapter 7.

High-Tech Talk

Printing in Black and White, Color — and Green?

Printers can print in a wide range of colors, to provide a full spectrum of hues for printing photos, documents, and more. One color that often comes up in discussions of printers, however, has nothing to do with ink. That color — green — refers to the impact that printers can have on our environment. With many printers, unfortunately, the environmental impact is negative. The amount of waste and pollution created by printers, along with the energy they use, are of concern to many.

- *Waste*: As you have learned, printers rely on a lot of consumables in the printing process, including paper, ink ribbons, color sticks, toner cartridges, ink cartridges, and more. The result is that each year, tons of paper and millions of empty toner and ink-jet cartridges are thrown in the trash, destined for landfills or incinerators. Most laser printers use a toner cartridge that integrates a photosensitive drum, developer, and toner into a single, disposable unit. When the toner runs out, the entire cartridge is disposed of and replaced with a new unit, even though the other components in the cartridge may still be usable. Color printers often create more waste, because they have separate cartridges for each color of ink.
- *Pollution*: The technology used in laser printers makes ozone pollution as a by-product of the printing process. The level of emission depends on where and how a printer is kept. Areas with large concentrations of dust; small, enclosed offices; or poorly ventilated rooms can cause high ozone intensity.
- *Energy use*: Energy conservation also is becoming important in printer design. In many homes and offices, printers always are left on, so they continually use energy, even when no one is around to print a document.

What can you do to help make printing just a bit greener? One obvious way is simply to print fewer documents. Before you print a document, ask yourself if you need to print it — or if you can read it on the monitor. Use e-mail to share documents, instead of printed copies. Next, try to reduce the consumables you create by using ink-jet or toner refills and recycling the cartridges (only after confirming that this will not void your manufacturer's warranty). Try to purchase recycled or remanufactured products, such as paper, ink cartridges, or toner cartridges. A properly remanufactured toner cartridge will perform at least as well as a new one.

To help ensure a healthy working environment, look for a laser printer with a filter to reduce the ozone and follow the manufacturer's recommendations for cleaning the printer, as well as replacing the filter. Place a laser printer in a well-ventilated area, to ensure an acceptable standard of air quality. When you are looking to buy a printer, consider an environmentally friendly printer, such as the ECOSYS cartridge-free printer from Kyocera. With the ECOSYS printer, the toner is separate from the other printer parts and thus does not require you to throw out the other components just to replace the toner (Figure 7-22). ECOSYS printers also use high-quality drums and developer that can print 500,000 pages before bring replaced (as opposed to a normal drum, which typically is replaced every 6,000 to 14,000 pages). The long-life drum eliminates the need for replacement toner cartridges, allowing simple replacement of only the toner container.

Finally, be sure the printer you purchase is ENERGY STAR rated and has power-saving features to reduce power consumption when it is not being used. The power saver usually works by warming up the printer only when it is sent a job. If the printer is left idle for a certain period of time, the printer's power consumption is reduced.

Taking these simple steps can help ensure that your printer not only prints in black and white and color, but in a green, environmentally friendly way.

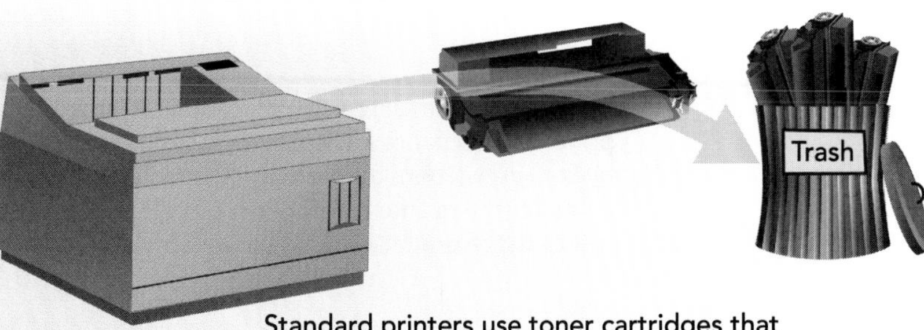

Standard printers use toner cartridges that must be replaced often, which creates waste.

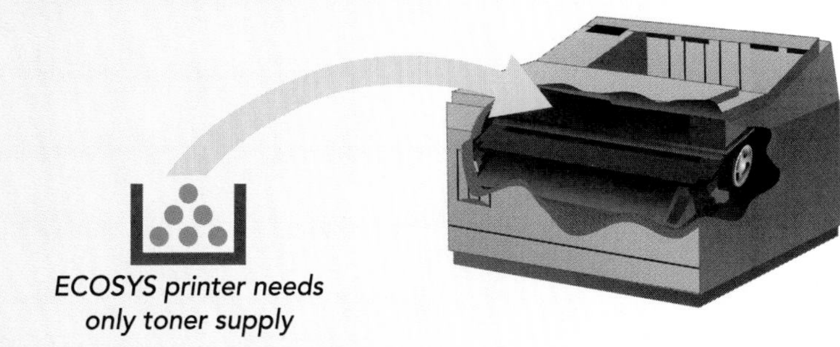

ECOSYS printer needs only toner supply

Figure 7-22

CHAPTER SUMMARY

The Chapter Summary reviews the concepts presented in this chapter.

1 Printer Characteristics

Printed output often is referred to as a printout or hard copy; information displayed on a monitor is considered soft copy. Printers are described based on several features: resolution, print quality, speed, memory, and the ability to print color. Printer resolution is measured in dots per inch (dpi), the density of ink dots used to create printed output. Print quality is described as letter quality, near letter quality, or draft quality. Printer speed can be measured in characters per second or pages per minute. Most printers come with a small amount of memory to store text or image information before printing the document. Some printers can print in color.

2 Types of Printers

An impact printer forms characters and graphics on a printed page using some mechanism that physically contacts the paper. A non-impact printer forms characters and graphics without a mechanism that contacts the paper. The three most popular types of printers are laser, ink-jet, and dot-matrix. Dot-matrix printers are impact printers that can print multicopy documents. Ink-jet printers print by shooting ionized ink at a sheet of paper. Laser printers produce high-quality output using six steps: cleaning, conditioning, writing, developing, transferring, and fusing. Data is sent to the printer using a page description language (PDL) such as PCL or PostScript, which describes the layout and contents of a page sent to the printer.

3 Installing and Sharing a Printer

Windows manages the order in which print jobs are processed. When data is received by the printer, it places the job in a buffer. Print jobs accumulate in a queue in the buffer and are released to the printer, as part of a process called spooling. A local printer is connected directly to a computer by way of a cable that connects to a port or a wireless connection. A network printer is accessible to a computer by way of a network. Installing a local printer involves connecting the printer and then installing the device driver and any application software or setting up a wireless connection. Once a local printer is connected to a computer, it can be shared, so that more than one computer or other device on a network can send print jobs to the printer.

4 Maintaining and Troubleshooting Printers

Routine printer maintenance procedures involve having spare consumables on hand and using a printer maintenance kit, which includes the specific printer components you need to replace, step-by-step instructions for performing maintenance, and any special tools or equipment you need to complete the maintenance. When troubleshooting printers, first isolate the problem by narrowing the source to the printer, cable, OS or device drivers, or the application.

KEY TERMS

After reading the chapter, you should know each of these Key Terms.

all-in-one device *(280)*
bubble-jet printer *(274)*
characters per second (cps) *(272)*
consumables *(289)*
default printer *(282)*
dot-matrix printer *(273)*
dots per inch (dpi) *(272)*
draft quality *(272)*
dye-sublimation printer *(279)*
graphics pages per minute (gppm) *(273)*
hard copy *(272)*
host computer *(288)*
impact printer *(273)*
ink-jet printer *(274)*
laser printer *(276)*
letter quality *(272)*
local printer *(282)*
multifunction peripheral (MFP) *(280)*
multifunction device (MFD) *(280)*
near letter quality *(272)*
network printer *(282)*
non-impact printer *(273)*
page description language (PDL) *(278)*
page printers *(278)*
pages per minute (ppm) *(272)*
PCL (Printer Control Language) *(278)*
photo printer *(279)*
PostScript *(278)*
printer maintenance kit *(289)*
printout *(272)*
queue *(281)*
soft copy *(272)*
solid ink printer *(279)*
spooling *(281)*
thermal printer *(278)*
toner *(276)*

LEARN IT ONLINE

Reinforce your understanding of the chapter concepts and terms with the Learn It Online exercises.

Instructions: **To complete the Learn It Online exercises, start your browser, click the Address bar, and then enter the Web address scsite.com/understanding/learn. When the Understanding and Troubleshooting Your PC Learn It Online page is displayed, follow the instructions in the exercises below. Each exercise has instructions for printing your results, either for your own records or for submission to your instructor.**

1 Chapter Reinforcement True/False, Multiple Choice, and Short Answer

Below Chapter 7, click the Chapter Reinforcement link. Print the quiz by clicking Print on the File menu for each page. Answer each question.

2 Flash Cards

Below Chapter 7, click the Flash Cards link and read the instructions. Type 20 (or a number specified by your instructor) in the Number of playing cards text box, type your name in the Enter your Name text box, and then click the Flip Card button. When the flash card is displayed, read the question and then click the ANSWER box arrow to select an answer. Flip through Flash Cards. If your score is 15 (75%) correct or greater, click Print on the File menu to print your results. If your score is less than 15 (75%) correct, then redo this exercise by clicking the Replay button.

3 Practice Test

Below Chapter 7, click the Practice Test link. Answer each question, enter your first and last name at the bottom of the page, and then click the Grade Test button. When the graded practice test is displayed on your screen, click Print on the File menu to print a hard copy. Continue to take practice tests until you score 80% or better.

4 Who Wants To Be a Computer Genius?

Below Chapter 7, click the Computer Genius link. Read the instructions, enter your first and last name at the bottom of the page, and then click the PLAY button. When your score is displayed, click the PRINT RESULTS link to print a hard copy.

5 Wheel of Terms

Below Chapter 7, click the Wheel of Terms link. Read the instructions, and then enter your first and last name and your school name. Click the PLAY button. When your score is displayed, right-click the score and then click Print on the shortcut menu to print a hard copy.

6 Crossword Puzzle Challenge

Below Chapter 7, click the Crossword Puzzle Challenge link. Read the instructions, and then enter your first and last name. Click the SUBMIT button. Work the crossword puzzle. When you are finished, click the Submit button. When the crossword puzzle is redisplayed, click the Print Puzzle button to print a hard copy.

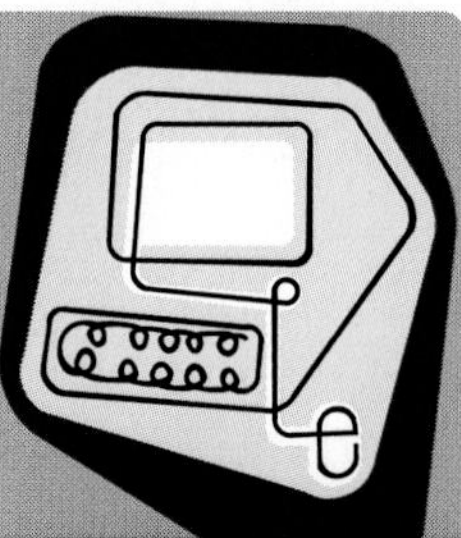

CHAPTER EXERCISES

Complete the Chapter Exercises to solidify what you learned in the chapter.

Multiple Choice

Select the best answer.

1. A 600 dpi printer would output a higher quality printout than a ________ printer.
   a. 1200 dpi
   b. 300 dpi
   c. 2400 dpi
   d. 1600 dpi
2. A ________ uses tubes of ink that have tiny resistors near the end of each tube.
   a. laser printer
   b. dot-matrix printer
   c. bubble-jet printer
   d. thermal printer
3. When a printer is ________ more than one computer on a network can send print jobs to that printer.
   a. shared
   b. local
   c. impact
   d. resident
4. Which of these is *not* a measure of printer speed?
   a. graphics pages per minute
   b. pages per minute
   c. characters per second
   d. graphics characters per second
5. During the writing step with a laser printer, a ________ discharges a lower charge only to places where toner should go.
   a. laser beam
   b. beam detect
   c. formatter
   d. scanning mirror

Fill in the Blank

Write the word or phrase to fill in the blank in each of the following questions.

1. Laser printers also are called ________, because they process and store an entire page before printing the page.
2. A(n) ________ such as PCL, is a language that describes the layout and contents of a page sent to the printer.
3. If several print jobs are sent to the printer at one time, the print jobs accumulate in a(n) ________ in the buffer.
4. While a(n) ________uses wax-based ink that is heated by heat pins that melt the ink onto paper, a(n) ________ uses ink stored in solid blocks.
5. Windows designates one printer to be the ________ which is the one Windows prints to by default, unless another is selected.

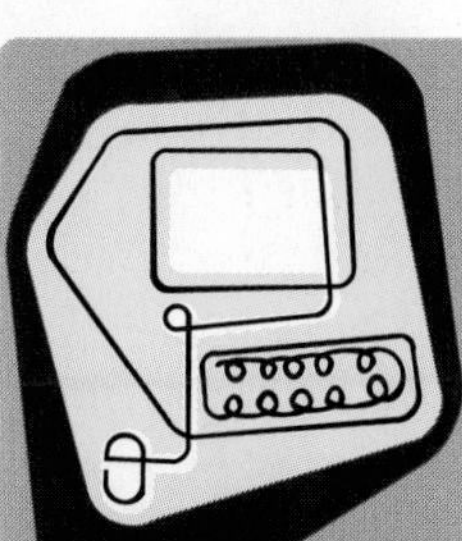

CHAPTER EXERCISES

Complete the Chapter Exercises to solidify what you learned in the chapter.

Matching Terms

Match the terms with their definitions.

______	1. hard copy	a.	de facto PDL standard in the printing industry
______	2. local printer	b.	allows you to work on other tasks while a document is printing
______	3. non-impact printer	c.	measure of resolution; the number of ink dots used to create printed output
______	4. dpi	d.	printed information output from a printer
______	5. PostScript	e.	printer connected to and accessible via a network
______	6. network computer	f.	forms characters and graphics without physically contacting the paper
______	7. multifunction peripheral	g.	PDL that supports complex graphics and colors; used in desktop publishing
______	8. spooling	h.	printer connected directly to a computer by way of a cable or a wireless connection
______	9. impact printer	i.	also called an all-in-one device
______	10. PCL	j.	forms characters and graphics using mechanism that physically contacts the paper

Short Answer Questions

Write a brief answer to each of the following questions.

1. List the six steps used by a laser printer to print a page.
2. What are the characteristics used to describe a printer? Briefly explain each characteristic.
3. When you are isolating a printer problem, what are the four major possible sources of the problem?
4. If a printer is not working correctly, what troubleshooting questions should you ask to eliminate the printer as the source of the problem?
5. Briefly describe how Windows and the printer handle print jobs when several documents are printed to the same printer.

APPLY YOUR KNOWLEDGE

Check your understanding of the chapter with the hands-on Apply Your Knowledge exercises.

1 Installing a Local Printer

Follow the steps described in the chapter and those outlined below to install a local printer on your computer, using a cable.

1. Physically attach the printer cable to the computer by way of a parallel port, serial port, FireWire port, or USB port.
2. Install the printer driver, either by having Windows install the driver or by using the printer manufacturer's installation software, which comes on a CD-ROM or DVD-ROM with the printer.
3. To confirm that the drivers are installed properly, print a test page by opening the Printers and Faxes window and then right-clicking the printer you just installed. Click Properties on the shortcut menu and then click the General tab in the Properties window. Click the Print Test Page button.
4. Print a self-test page from the printer. If you are not sure how to do this, read the printer user guide or research the printer documentation on the manufacturer's Web site to determine how to print a self-test page from the printer.

2 Updating Printer Drivers

Printer problems sometimes can be resolved by downloading and installing the latest drivers. Perform the following steps to update the drivers for a printer:

1. Search the printer manufacturer's Web site for the latest drivers for your printer and operating system. Be sure you download files for the correct printer and operating system.
2. Download the drivers to a folder on the hard drive such as C:\Downloads\Printer.
3. Using Windows Explorer, navigate to that folder.
   a. If the driver files are included in an .exe (executable) file, double-click the driver file to extract files and launch the installation program to update the printer drivers.
   b. If the drivers from the printer manufacturer's Web site are not an executable file, click the Start button and then click Printers and Faxes on the Start menu.
   c. When the Printers and Faxes window is displayed, right-click the printer for which you want to update the drivers. Click Properties on the shortcut menu.
   d. Click the Advanced tab and then click the New Driver button.
   e. When the Add Printer Driver Wizard starts, click the Next button.
   f. In the Printer Driver Selection page, select the manufacturer and model of your printer (check the user's guide if you are unsure of the model). Click the Next button and then click the Finish button. Windows will complete the update of the drivers.

3 Sharing a Local Printer

Once a printer is installed, you can share the printer so others on the network can use the device. Perform the following steps to share any printer already installed on your computer:

1. Open the Printers and Faxes window by clicking the Start button and then clicking Printers and Faxes on the Start menu. When the Printers and Faxes window opens, right-click the printer and then click Sharing on the shortcut menu.
2. When the printer's Properties window is displayed, click Share this printer and then enter a name for the printer in the Share name text box, as shown in Figure 7-15 on page 287.
3. Click the Additional Drivers button. Select the operating systems used by computers that will use the printer, so these computers will have access to the correct printer drivers (you might be asked for the Windows installation CD or other access to the installation files).

APPLY YOUR KNOWLEDGE

Check your understanding of the chapter with the hands-on Apply Your Knowledge exercises.

4. Click OK twice to close both windows. Check to see that the printer has a hand icon displayed under it in the Printers and Faxes window.
5. If a remote computer on the same network is available, install the shared printer on that remote computer following the steps outlined in the chapter. Print a test page to verify that the remote PC can print to the printer.

4 Researching a Printer Maintenance Plan

You have been asked to recommend a maintenance plan for a laser printer. Search a printer manufacturer's Web site for information and then write a maintenance plan. In the plan, include maintenance tasks that need to be done, how often they need doing, and what tools and components are needed to perform the tasks. Use the Hewlett-Packard LaserJet 8100 DN printer, unless your instructor tells you to use a different printer.

CHAPTER 8

Installing and Using Windows XP Professional

Introduction

Windows XP is a newer generation of the Microsoft Windows operating system, which is the most widely used operating system in the world. This chapter focuses on Windows XP Professional, including how it uses memory and how it manages hard drives using partitions and NTFS. It also covers how to install and use Windows XP and how to install hardware and applications using Windows XP. This chapter builds the foundation you will need to manage and provide technical support for Windows XP, the focus of the next chapter.

OBJECTIVES

In this chapter, you will learn:

1. About the features and architecture of Windows XP
2. How to install Windows XP
3. How to use Windows XP
4. How to install hardware and applications with Windows XP

Up for Discussion

Paul Cormier, a photographer for a national news service, stopped in to Sunrise Computers to check prices for Windows XP Professional and ask your advice on moving to the new OS. Paul explains that, when he bought his computer, it came with Windows 2000 Professional already installed. Although he has been thinking about upgrading, he has many questions. For one, he is not sure his computer can support Windows XP. He also wants to be sure his digital cameras, printers, and scanner will work with Windows XP, because they are the core equipment for his business.

You reassure Paul that moving to a new OS only involves some planning and a few basic steps. First, you will help him determine if his computer meets the system requirements for installing Windows XP and decide whether to perform an upgrade or a clean install. After checking to see that his hardware and software will work with Windows XP, you will check to see if he has available space on the hard drive and review how he will connect to the news service network. Finally, you will create a checklist to confirm that you are ready to begin the installation. After installing the OS software and activating it, he will be ready to work.

After reviewing Paul's hardware and applications, you determine that he will only need the upgrade version of Windows XP. He purchases the upgrade and you set up an on-site visit to his office to walk him through the installation process and spend some time showing him how to use Windows XP. He thanks you for your help and says he will clean up his hard drive by running Disk Cleanup and moving some older digital photo files to CD-R.

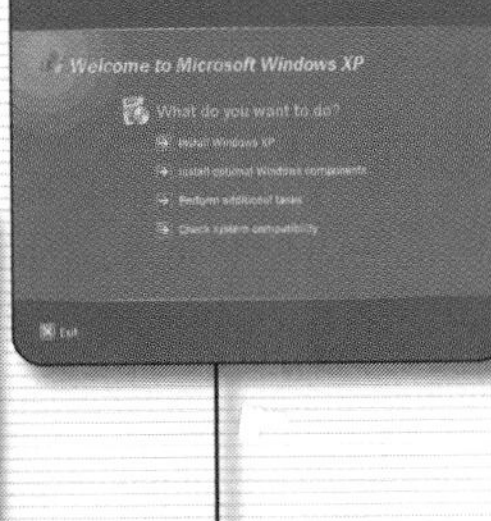

Questions:

- What steps should you take to prepare for installing Windows XP?
- How do you choose between a clean install and an upgrade install?
- What tools can you use to check for hardware and software compatibility for Windows XP?

Features and Architecture of Windows XP

Windows XP comes in several versions, as listed in Figure 8-1, for home and business users alike. All these versions of Windows XP integrate features of many previous versions of Windows, such as Windows 9x and Windows 2000, while providing added support for multimedia and networking technologies. The look and feel of Windows XP differs slightly from its predecessors, and utilities and functions are organized differently under menus and windows.

Windows XP Version	Unique Features
Windows XP Professional	An upgrade to Windows 2000 Professional. Includes all features of Windows XP Home Edition, plus provides greater security through file and folder encryption, remote access to a computer, simpler administration of groups of users, and a user interface that supports multiple languages.
Windows XP Home Edition	An upgrade to Windows Me (Millennium Edition). Provides features targeted to home users, such as the capability to organize and share digital pictures, create and edit videos using Windows Movie Maker, and tools to help simplify home network setup.
Windows XP Media Center Edition	Includes additional support for digital entertainment hardware such as video recording integrated with TV input. Designed for the high-end PC home market and only is available when preinstalled on a high-end PC manufactured by a Microsoft partner.
Windows XP Tablet PC Edition	Provides support for tablet PCs, which are a special type of notebook computer that allow you to write on the screen using a special pen.
Windows XP 64-Bit Edition	For use with a high-end 64-bit CPU such as the Intel Itanium or AMD Opteron. Designed for servers or heavily technical workstations that run scientific and engineering applications and need greater amounts of memory and higher performance than standard desktop PCs.

Figure 8-1 Windows XP comes in several versions, with features targeted to different user types.

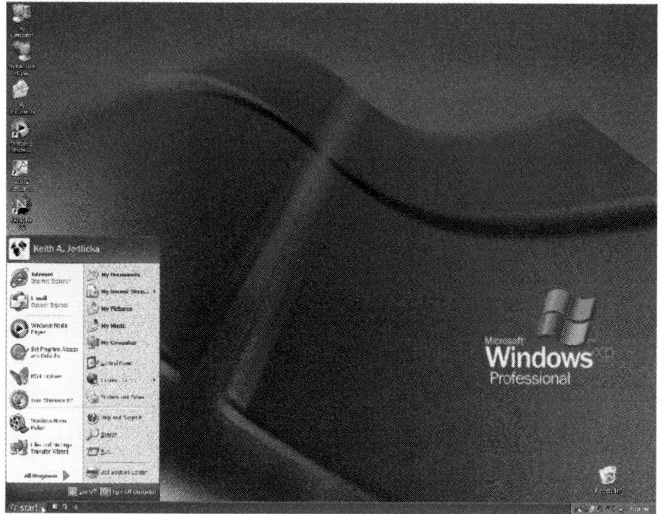

Figure 8-2 Windows XP desktop and Start menu.

Windows XP Features

Since the first version of Windows, Microsoft continually has updated the Windows operating system, incorporating new features and functions with each new version. Windows XP Professional was designed to provide a cleaner user interface that is easy to use (Figure 8-2), as well as better reliability and performance than any previous versions of Windows. Figure 8-3 highlights features of Windows XP.

Appearance and Performance

- New look and feel to the user interface
- Redesigned Start menu and Control Panel
- Increased reliability and security
- Increased performance to run programs faster
- Improved battery-life management for notebook computers
- Support for multiple languages*

Administration

- Improved interface for creating and switching among multiple user accounts. Each user has a separate profile, and Windows XP can switch between users, keeping a separate set of applications open for each user
- Enhanced system recovery with System Restore helps reduce possibility of data loss
- Easy to install home or office network
- Advanced networking for multiple PC environments*
- Improved wireless network support
- Internet Connection Firewall to protect a home or small office network from unauthorized access or hackers
- Encrypting File System (EFS) to encrypt files and folders that contain sensitive data

Help and Support

- Comprehensive Help and Support system
- Remote Assistance that allows another person to control the computer remotely to help demonstrate a process or solve a problem

Communication and the Web

- New version of Windows Messenger for instant messaging, conferencing, and application sharing
- New version of Internet Explorer with improved look and feel
- Remote Desktop to access data and applications on the desktop computer while away from the computer using another Windows-based computer with a network or Internet connection*
- Publish, store, and share text, graphics, photographs, and other items on the Web
- Internet Information Services (IIS), a Windows XP Professional feature that lets users host and manage personal Web sites*

Digital Media

- New version of Windows Media Player to listen to Internet radio stations, play MP3 and Microsoft WMA format music, write music and data to blank CDs, and watch DVD movies
- The capability to burn a CD simply by dragging and dropping a folder or file onto the CD-R or CD-RW device icon
- New version of Microsoft Movie Maker
- Easier to transfer images from a digital camera or scanner to a computer

Figure 8-3 Key features of Windows XP Professional and Home Edition. Items with asterisks are available in Windows XP Professional only (not included in Home Edition).

Windows XP is integrated tightly with several other Microsoft products, including the Internet Explorer browser, Windows Media Player, and Internet Connection Firewall, a software **firewall** that protects a computer or network from unauthorized access. Some users see this integration as a disadvantage, and others see it as an advantage. Tight integration allows applications to interact easily with other applications and the OS, but makes it more difficult for third-party software to compete with Microsoft applications.

Windows XP provides several enhancements over Windows 2000 and earlier versions of Windows. Figure 8-4 summarizes the advantages and disadvantages of Windows XP.

Advantages	Disadvantages
Provides better integration of Windows 9x and NT than Windows 2000 did	Minimum requirements are 1.5 GB of free hard drive space and at least a 233 MHz processor with 64 MB of RAM
Offers significant GUI enhancements over earlier versions of Windows	Programs used with Windows XP may need more than the minimum system requirements for the operating system
Adds features but uses only slightly more total memory for the OS than Windows 2000	Nearly eliminates support for device drivers not approved by Microsoft
Adds advanced file sorting options, such as sorting pictures by dimensions (size) or sound files by artist	Security concerns with centralized storage of online information in Microsoft Passport, a repository of the user IDs and passwords you use on the Internet
Includes built-in support for compressed files	
Has improved troubleshooting tools and generally is more stable than previous Windows operating systems	

Figure 8-4 Advantages and disadvantages of Windows XP.

Windows XP Architecture

Windows XP, along with Windows NT and Windows 2000, operates in two modes: user mode or kernel mode (Figure 8-5). Each mode takes advantage of different CPU functionality and abilities.

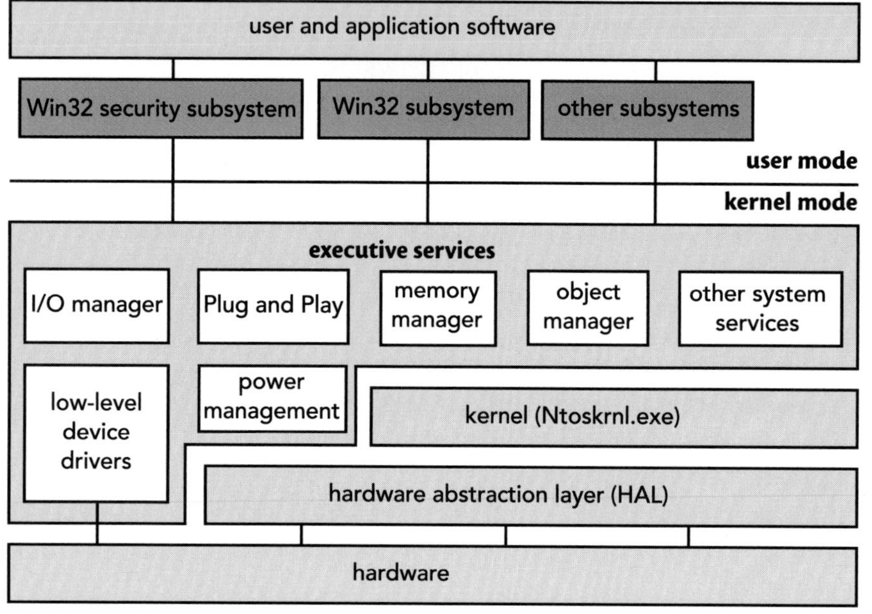

Figure 8-5 The Windows XP architecture supports user mode and kernel mode.

USER MODE **User mode** is a processor mode in which programs have only limited access to system information and can access hardware only through OS services. The OS has several subsystems, or OS modules, that use this mode and interface with the user and with applications. As shown in Figure 8-5, user mode relies on two key subsystems: the Win32 security subsystem and the Win32 subsystem. The Win32 security subsystem provides logon to the system and other security functions, including privileges for file access. The Win32 subsystem is the most important user mode subsystem, because it manages and provides an environment for all 32-bit programs, such as the Windows user interface and Windows Explorer. All applications relate to Windows XP by way of the Win32 subsystem, either directly or indirectly.

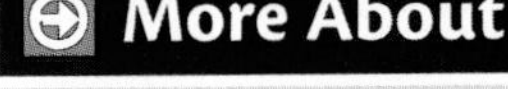

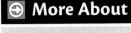

More About

Win32 Subsystem

To learn more about the Win32 subsystem, visit the Understanding and Troubleshooting Your PC More About Web page (**scsite.com/understanding/more**) and then click Win32 Subsystem below Chapter 8.

KERNEL MODE **Kernel mode** is a processor mode in which programs have extensive access to system information and hardware. Kernel mode is used by two main components: the HAL and a group of components collectively called executive services, both shown in Figure 8-5. The **HAL (hardware abstraction layer)** is the layer between the OS and the hardware. The HAL is available in different versions, each designed to address the specifics of a particular CPU technology. **Executive services** interface between the subsystems in user mode and the HAL. Executive services components manage hardware resources by way of the HAL and device drivers.

Applications in user mode have no access to hardware resources. In kernel mode, executive services have limited access to hardware resources, but the HAL primarily interacts with hardware. Limiting access to hardware mainly to the HAL increases OS integrity because more control is possible. With this isolation, an application cannot cause a system to hang by making illegal demands on hardware. Overall performance is increased because the HAL and executive services can operate independently of the slower, less efficient applications using them.

Figure 8-5 shows how the different OS components relate. Notice that some low-level device drivers, such as those that access the hard drive, have direct access to hardware. All 16-bit and 32-bit applications relate to the kernel by way of the Win32 subsystem operating in user mode.

Windows XP generally is more stable than Windows 9x, Windows NT, and Windows 2000. It was designed to avoid situations in which conflicts with drivers and applications crashed these earlier systems.

More About

Windows 9x Architecture

To learn more about Windows 9x architecture, visit the Understanding and Troubleshooting Your PC More About Web page (**scsite.com/understanding/more**) and then click Windows 9x Architecture below Chapter 8.

Windows XP Networking Features

A workstation running Windows XP can be configured to work as one node in a workgroup or one node on a domain. A **workgroup** is a logical group of computers and users that share resources (Figure 8-6), where administration, resources, and security on each workstation are controlled by that workstation. A workgroup uses a **peer-to-peer** networking model, in which each computer, or peer, on the network has equal responsibilities and capabilities. Each computer maintains a list of users and their rights on that particular PC.

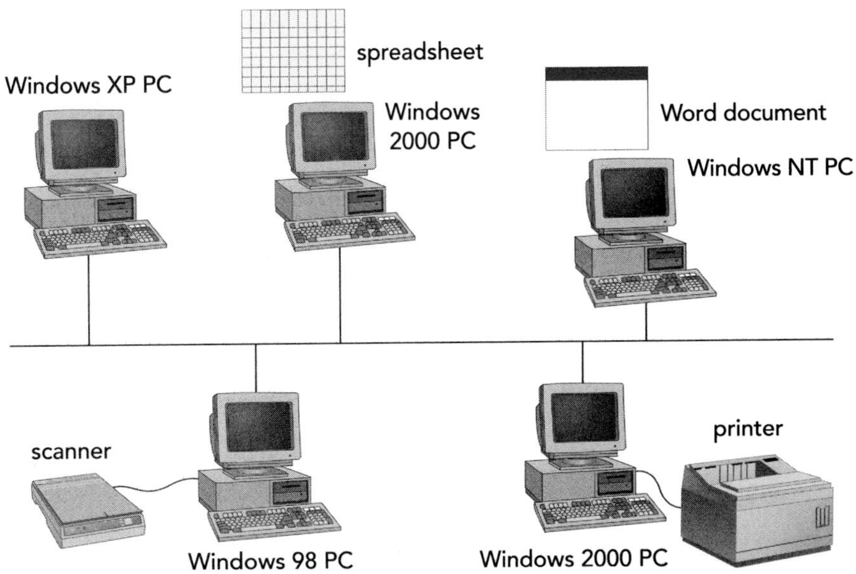

Figure 8-6 In a workgroup, no single computer controls the network and each computer controls its own resources.

A Windows **domain** is a group of networked computers that share a centralized directory database of user account information and security for the entire set of computers (Figure 8-7). A domain uses a **client/server** networking model, in which one or more computers acts as a server and the other computers on the network request services from the server. A server, sometimes called the host computer, controls access to the hardware, software, and other resources on the network and provides a centralized storage area for programs, data, and information.

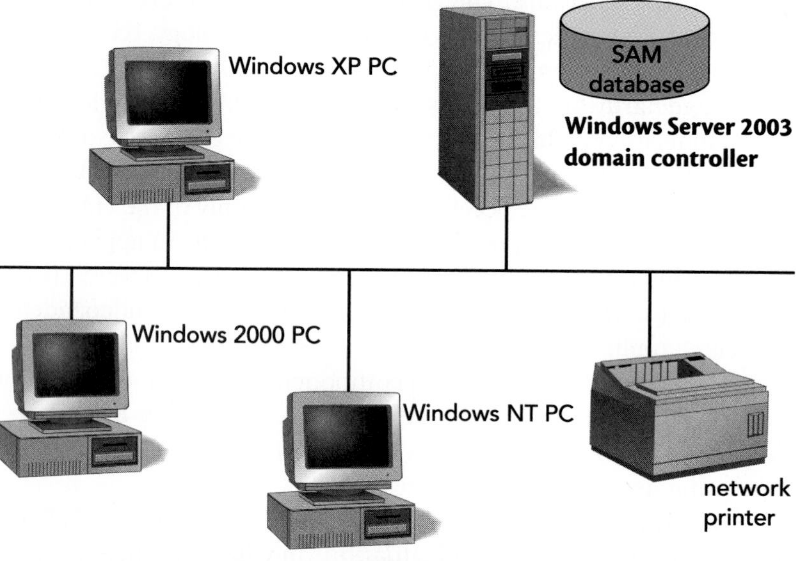

Figure 8-7 A Windows domain is a network where security on each PC or other device is controlled by a centralized domain controller.

Figure 8-7 shows the different components of a Windows domain. Every domain has at least one server set up as the domain controller. The **domain controller** stores and controls a database of user accounts, group accounts, and computer accounts. This database is called the **directory database** or the **security accounts manager (SAM) database**. The security accounts manager database is controlled by a **network operating system (NOS)**, which is an operating system specifically designed to support a network. Popular NOSs include Windows Server 2003, Windows 2000 Server, Novell NetWare, Unix, Linux, and Mac OS; NOSs are discussed in more detail in Chapter 10.

In a domain, a network administrator manages access to the network through the SAM database stored on the domain controller. Because the SAM database is so important, Windows allows backup copies of the database to exist on more than one computer in the domain. With Windows XP (and Windows 2000 and Windows Server 2003), a network can have any number of domain controllers, each keeping a copy of the directory that can be edited. An administrator can update the directory on any one of these domain controllers, which then will communicate the change to the other domain controllers.

Windows XP User Accounts

Regardless of whether Windows XP computers are networked or not, any user of the computer has a user account. A **user account** defines the actions a user can perform in Windows. Windows XP has two types of accounts: administrator and limited. An **administrator** has rights and permissions to all computer software and hardware resources and is responsible for setting up other user accounts and assigning them privileges. Windows XP allows more than one administrator to be set up on the same computer. A **limited account** cannot change most settings or delete important files. Figure 8-8 lists the characteristics of administrator and limited accounts.

Administrator account	Limited account
• Intended for someone who can make system-wide changes to the computer, install programs, and access all files on the computer. • Can create and delete user accounts on the computer. • Can create account passwords for other user accounts on the computer. • Can change other people's account names, pictures, passwords, and account types. • Cannot change his or her own account type to a limited account type unless there is at least one other user with a computer administrator account type on the computer. This ensures that there is always at least one user with a computer administrator account on the computer.	• Intended for someone who should be prohibited from changing most computer settings and deleting important files. • Cannot install software or hardware, but can access programs that already have been installed on the computer. • Can change his or her account picture and also can create, change, or delete his or her password. • Cannot change his or her account name or account type. A user with a computer administrator account must make these types of changes.

Figure 8-8 Characteristics of Windows XP user accounts.

During the Windows XP installation, you enter a password to the default administrator account. When the workstation is part of a Windows workgroup, you can log on as an administrator after the OS is installed and create limited accounts that apply only to that computer. If the workstation is part of a domain, a network administrator sets up global user accounts that apply to an entire domain, including giving access to computers connected in that domain.

When Windows XP starts up, a user either must log on with a user name and password or click the correct user name on the Welcome screen. If Windows XP is set up to use the Welcome screen, a user logs on to the computer by clicking his or her user account name. If a password is assigned to the account, the user is prompted to enter it. If Windows XP is not set up to use the Welcome screen, a user logs on to the computer by typing a user name and password (if needed) into the standard Log On to Windows dialog box. If a valid account name and password are not entered, Windows XP does not allow access to the system. Windows XP tracks which user is logged on to the system and grants rights and permissions according to the user's account, or to specific permissions granted this user by the administrator.

Quiz Yourself 8-1

To test your knowledge of Windows XP features and architecture, visit the Understanding and Troubleshooting Your PC Quiz Yourself Web page (scsite.com/understanding/quiz). Click Quiz Yourself 1 below Chapter 8.

Installing Windows XP

Installing Windows XP involves several important considerations, as described in this section. One consideration is whether you will install Windows XP as a clean install or as an upgrade. With a **clean install**, you have to erase all data, reformat the hard disk, and then install the new operating system. A clean install ignores any settings in the currently installed OS, including information about installed hardware or software. After a clean install, you must reinstall all hardware and applications. An **upgrade install**, which sometimes is called an *upgrade in-place*, installs the new operating system and carries forward information about installed hardware and software, user preferences, and other settings (unless they are not compatible with Windows XP).

In this section, you learn how to install Windows XP as a clean install and as an upgrade install, as well as how to set up a dual boot. With a **dual boot**, or *multiboot*, the operating systems are configured so a user can boot the computer from two or more different operating systems that are both installed on the same or different hard drives on the computer.

Planning the Installation

When installing Windows XP as a clean or upgrade install, you first should plan for the installation. Before installing Windows XP, do the following:

- Verify that the system at least meets the minimum system requirements for installing Windows XP. If possible, use a system that meets or exceeds recommended requirements (Figure 8-9).

Component or Device	Minimum Requirement	Recommended Requirement
One or two CPUs*	Pentium II 233 MHz	Pentium II 300 MHz or faster
RAM	64 MB; may limit performance and some features	128 MB or higher
Hard drive partition	2 GB	2 GB or more
Free space on the hard drive partition	1.5 GB	2 GB or more
Monitor	Super VGA (800 × 600) or higher-resolution video adapter and monitor	Super VGA (800 × 600) or higher-resolution video adapter and monitor
CD-ROM drive	12x	12x or faster
Accessories	Keyboard and mouse or other pointing device	Keyboard and mouse or other pointing device

* Intel Pentium/Celeron family, or AMD K6/Athlon/Duron family, or compatible processor recommended

Figure 8-9 Minimum and recommended system requirements for Windows XP Professional.

- Determine if you will perform an upgrade or a clean install.
- Use Upgrade Advisor or check the Windows Catalog as described below to verify that all installed hardware components and software are compatible with Windows XP. Be sure you have Windows XP drivers for any hardware you will install or connect to the system.
- Decide how you will partition your hard drive and what file system you will use.
- For a PC on a network, decide whether the PC will be configured as a workstation in a workgroup or as part of a domain.
- Make a final checklist to verify that you have done all of the above and are ready to begin the installation.

SYSTEM REQUIREMENTS To determine if your computer meets recommended system requirements for installing Windows XP, check to see what CPU the computer is using and the amount of available RAM and hard drive space. With Windows XP, you can determine the current CPU and available RAM by right-clicking My Computer on the Windows desktop, clicking Properties on the shortcut menu, and then reviewing the information on the General tab. (If the My Computer icon does not display on your desktop, click the Start button, right-click My Computer on the Start menu, and then click Properties on the shortcut menu.) To see how much hard drive space is available, double-click My Computer, right-click the drive where Windows XP will be installed (usually drive C), and then click Properties on the shortcut menu. The Properties window for the drive displays how much free space is available on the hard drive. Note that, even though Windows XP requires only 640 MB to install, the system will have lowered performance unless you have at least 1.5 GB of free hard drive space (preferably 2 GB free space) on the volume that holds Windows XP. Also remember that, although Microsoft recommends certain system requirements, the performance of your computer may vary depending on which Windows XP version you have installed and what applications and hardware you have installed with it.

8-1

How can I determine CPU speed and the amount of RAM on a Windows 98 or Windows NT computer?

To view this information on a Windows 98 computer, click the Start button, point to Programs, point to Accessories, point to System Tools, and then click System Information. The amount of RAM is displayed in the System Information window. Click Windows Report Tool on the Tools menu. In the Windows Report Tool window, click Change System File Selections. The "COMPSPEED" (CPU speed) is displayed in the System Settings to Copy window. For Windows NT, click the Start button, point to Programs, point to Accessories, point to Administrative Tools (Common), and then click Windows NT Diagnostics. In the Windows NT Diagnostics window, click the System tab to view the CPU speed and the Memory tab to view the RAM on the computer.

UPGRADE OR CLEAN INSTALL? If you plan to set up a dual boot, then you will perform a clean install for Windows XP. If you already have an OS installed and you do not plan a dual boot, then you have a choice between an upgrade and a clean install. Things to consider when making this decision include the following:

- The operating system version on your computer may or may not support an upgrade to Windows XP. If it does, as shown in Figure 8-10, you can install the less expensive Windows XP Upgrade. If it does not, you must complete a clean install using the more expensive full version of Windows XP. Both the upgrade and full versions of the software can be purchased directly from Microsoft or other third-party retailers (Figure 8-11).

Current OS Version	Can be upgraded to Windows XP Home Edition	Can be upgraded to Windows XP Professional
Windows 3.1	no	no
Windows 95	no	no
Windows 98/Windows 98 SE	yes	yes
Windows Me	yes	yes
Windows NT Workstation 3.51	no	no
Windows NT Workstation 4.0	no	yes
Windows 2000 Professional	no	yes
Windows XP Home Edition	--	yes
Windows XP Professional	no	--

Figure 8-10 Certain versions of Windows allow you to perform an upgrade using the Upgrade version of Windows XP. If the OS version on your computer does not support an upgrade, you must perform a clean install using a full version of Windows XP.

- An upgrade is faster than a clean install because you do not need to reinstall software and hardware. If you are having problems with your current operating system and applications, however, consider doing a clean install rather than an upgrade. Problems with an old installation sometimes carry forward into the upgrade.
- Before deciding to do a clean install, verify that you have all the application software installation CDs or floppy disks, and then back up all data on the drive. Also take time to verify that the backups are good and that you have all device driver software.
- Regardless of whether you have an OS currently installed, you still can choose to do a clean install if you want a fresh start. Unless you erase your hard drive, reformat it, or delete partitions before the upgrade, data on the hard drive is not erased even if you convert to a new file system during the installation. OS settings and installed software, however, do not carry forward into the new installation.

HARDWARE COMPATIBILITY After confirming that the system meets the recommended system requirements, you should verify that software and hardware currently installed on the computer are compatible with Windows XP. Microsoft provides two tools to help you check hardware and software compatibility to make sure your system is ready for upgrade to Windows XP: the Upgrade Advisor and the Windows Catalog.

The **Upgrade Advisor** is a tool you can use to check if your system hardware and software are ready for upgrade to Windows XP (Figure 8-12 on the next page). The Upgrade Advisor, which is available on the Windows XP CD and the Microsoft Web site, checks your system hardware and software to determine if it is compatible with Windows XP, displays any possible problems, and then allows you to save a hardware and software compatibility report for your system. The report is important if you have software or hardware you are not sure will work under Windows XP. To run Upgrade Advisor from the Windows XP CD, place the Windows XP CD in your CD-ROM or DVD-ROM drive. Your PC automatically should detect the CD and display Windows XP Setup menu. Click Check system compatibility to start Upgrade Advisor. If you run Upgrade Advisor while you are connected to the Internet, Upgrade Advisor will find required updates (such as new device drivers) from the Windows Update Web site and step you through the process of installing the updates.

Another way to determine if your hardware is compatible with Windows XP is to use the **Windows Catalog**, which is a section of the Microsoft Web site that lists products that are compatible with Windows XP. The Windows Catalog allows you to search for hardware devices by type to determine if specific hardware or software is compatible with Windows XP (Figure 8-13 on page 319).

Figure 8-11 The upgrade and full versions of the software can be purchased directly from Microsoft or other third-party retailers. The upgrade version costs less than the full version.

If the Upgrade Advisor or Windows Catalog reports that your software will not work under Windows XP, you might choose to upgrade the software or set up a dual boot with your old OS and Windows XP. If your hardware is not compatible with Windows XP, check the hardware manufacturer's Web site for an upgrade and download the upgraded drivers before you begin the installation. If the hardware is not Windows XP-compatible, even with updated drivers, you may need to purchase new hardware.

It is especially important to know that your network card or modem card is compatible with Windows XP before you install the operating system, because you need a network connection to access the Internet to get the latest upgrades. If you are not sure that an important hardware component qualifies, install Windows XP as a dual boot with your current OS. Later, when you get the component working under Windows XP, you can uninstall the other OS.

More About

Upgrade Advisor and Windows Catalog

To learn more about Upgrade Advisor and the Windows Catalog, visit the Understanding and Troubleshooting Your PC More About Web page (**scsite.com/understanding/more**) and then click Upgrade Advisor and the Windows Catalog below Chapter 8.

FAQ 8-2

What determines if a product is listed in the Windows Catalog?

Any software or hardware listed in the Windows Catalog meets minimum requirements for compatibility with Windows XP, as determined by Microsoft or by the product manufacturer. Many products in the catalog feature the Designed for Windows XP logo, which means they are specifically created to take advantage of the great new features in Windows XP and can reduce the number of problems you might have using your computer.

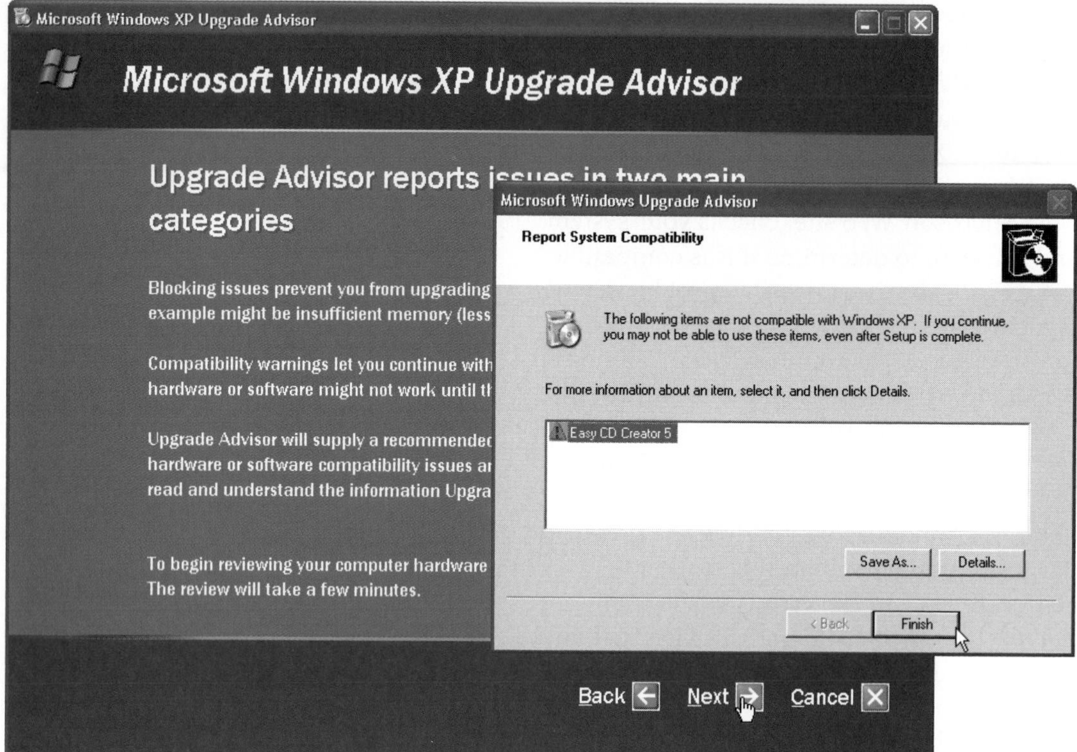

Figure 8-12 Upgrade Advisor checks your system hardware and software to determine if it is compatible with Windows XP and reports any possible problems.

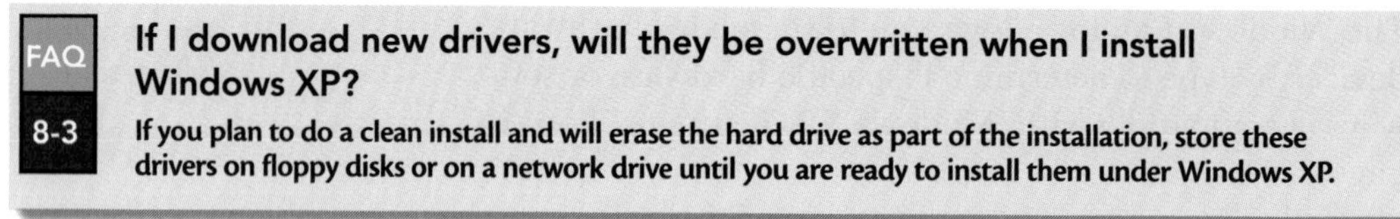
FAQ 8-3

If I download new drivers, will they be overwritten when I install Windows XP?

If you plan to do a clean install and will erase the hard drive as part of the installation, store these drivers on floppy disks or on a network drive until you are ready to install them under Windows XP.

HARD DRIVE PARTITIONS AND FILE SYSTEMS Next, you should decide on which partition you will install Windows XP and what file system you will use. Windows XP needs at least a 2 GB partition for the installation. This partition should have at least 1.5 GB of free space for regular use of Windows XP. Follow these general directions to ensure that partitions on the hard drive are adequate to install Windows XP:

- For Windows 9x, use Fdisk at the command prompt, and for Windows 2000, use Disk Management to determine what partitions are on the drive, how large they are, what logical drives are assigned to them, and how much free space on the drive is not yet partitioned.
- If you have a 2 GB partition that already has another operating system installed, you can install Windows XP on that partition, but Windows XP will overwrite the existing OS on that partition.
- If existing partitions are too small, look at the free space on the drive. If the hard drive has enough free space that is not yet partitioned, use that free space to create a new partition that is at least 2 GB.
- If you cannot create a 2 GB or larger partition, back up your data, delete the smaller partitions, and create a 2 GB or larger active partition on the drive. Deleting a partition erases all data on it, so be sure to create backups first.

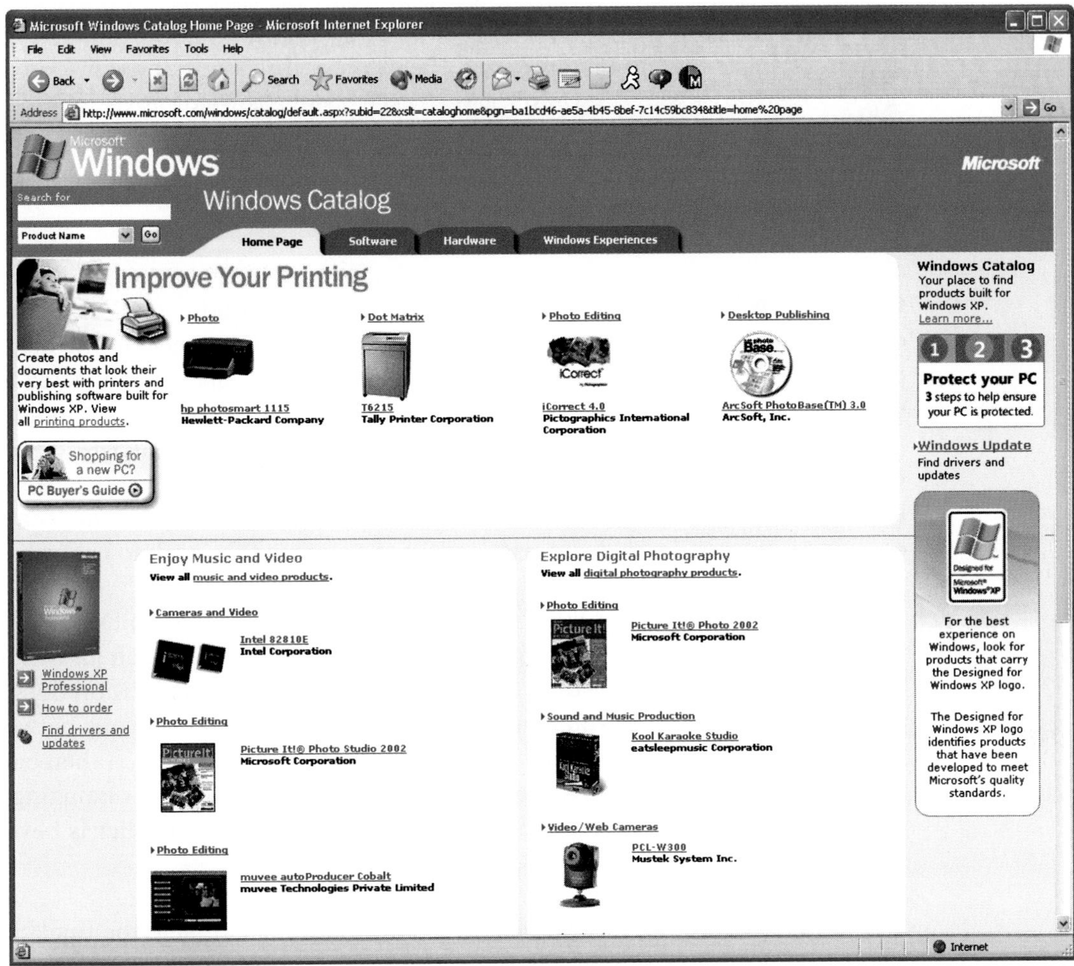

Figure 8-13 To see if your hardware device is compatible with Windows XP, search by hardware category, manufacturer name, or product name.

- If you have free space on the drive for other partitions, do not partition them at this time. First install Windows XP and then use the Disk Management tools available in Windows XP to partition the remaining free space on the drive.

Next, you should decide what file system to use when you install Windows XP. As you learned in Chapter 5, Windows XP uses NTFS by default, but also supports FAT16 and FAT32. For most users installing and running Windows XP, NTFS is the obvious choice, because it offers better file and folder security, file compression, control over how much disk space a user is allowed, and file encryption, which is the process of converting readable data into unreadable characters to prevent unauthorized access. The only time not to use NTFS is if you are setting up a dual boot system. In that situation, use the FAT16 or FAT32 file system if you are setting up a dual boot with Windows 9x and each OS must access all partitions. (When using FAT 16, be sure to make the partition no larger than 2 GB so it will be compatible with Windows 9x.) Use the FAT16 file system if you are setting up a dual boot with MS-DOS or Windows NT and each OS must access all partitions.

FAQ 8-4

If I am setting up a dual boot with NT or Windows 2000, should I use NTFS as the file system?

The NTFS file system used by Windows XP and Windows 2000 is incompatible with the Windows NT NTFS file system, causing a potential problem when installing Windows XP and Windows NT on the same PC as a dual boot. Because the Windows XP NTFS file system is the same as the Windows 2000 NTFS file system, a dual boot between these two operating systems should be no problem.

CONNECTING TO A NETWORK If you are installing Windows XP on a networked computer, you must decide if you will configure the PC to connect to the network as part of a workgroup or via a domain. If your computer is already connected to a network, record your network configuration so you easily can configure Windows XP.

If you have fewer than ten computers networked together, Microsoft recommends that you join these computers in a workgroup, in which each computer controls its own resources. In this case, each user account is set up on the local computer, independently from user accounts on other PCs, and no centralized control of resources is established.

For more than ten computers, Microsoft recommends that you set up a network with a domain controller running a network operating system such as Windows Server 2003 to control network resources. Windows XP Home Edition does not support joining a domain. If you plan to use a domain controller on your network, install Windows XP Professional on a workstation computer, which then can be connected to the domain on a Windows network. (Chapter 10 covers managing workgroups in more detail. Setting up and managing a domain controller is beyond the scope of this book.)

FINAL CHECKLIST Before you begin the installation, complete the final checklist shown in Figure 8-14 to verify that you are ready.

Things to Do	Further Information
Does the PC meet the minimum or recommended hardware requirement?	CPU: RAM: Hard drive size: Free space on the hard drive:
Have you run the Upgrade Advisor or checked the Windows Catalog to determine needed hardware and software upgrades?	List hardware and software that need to be upgraded:
Do you have the product key available?	Product key:
Have you decided how you will join a network?	Workgroup name: Domain name: Computer name:
Will you do an upgrade or clean install?	Current operating system: Does the current OS qualify for an upgrade?
Is your hard drive ready?	Size of the hard drive partition: Free space on the partition: File system you plan to use:
	(continued)

Things to Do	Further Information
For a clean install, will you set up a dual boot?	List reasons for a dual boot: Size of the second partition: Free space on the second partition: File system you plan to use:
Have you backed up important data on your hard drive?	Location of backup:

Figure 8-14 Checklist to complete before installing Windows XP.

The **product key** is a unique identification number included on the product packaging (usually on the outside of the CD-ROM) that you enter during installation to verify that you do not have a counterfeit copy of Windows XP and that you are not installing Windows XP on more than one PC without purchasing additional licenses.

Also note that, during the installation process, you will be asked to read and accept a license agreement. The most common type of license included with software purchases by individual users is a single-user license agreement, also called an end-user license agreement. An **end-user license agreement (EULA)** includes conditions that specify a user's responsibility upon acceptance of the agreement. Under most end-user license agreements, users are permitted to:

- Install the software only on one computer (some agreements allow users to install the software on one desktop computer and one notebook computer)
- Make a copy of the software as a backup
- Give or sell the software to another individual, but only if the software is removed from the user's computer first

Users are not permitted to:

- Install the software on a network, such as a school computer lab
- Give copies to friends or colleagues while continuing to use the software
- Export, rent, or lease the software

Unless otherwise specified by a license agreement, you do not have the right to copy or in any way distribute software.

Installation Process

The following section reviews the installation process for four different types of installations: (1) a clean install of Windows XP on a PC that does not already have an operating system installed; (2) a clean install on a PC that already has an OS installed; (3) an upgrade install to Windows XP; and (4) setting up a dual boot with Windows XP and another operating system. During the Windows XP installation process, Windows XP setup will reboot the system several times.

CLEAN INSTALL ON A PC WITH NO OS INSTALLED After you have completed the planning steps, follow these general instructions to perform a clean install of Windows XP on a PC that does not already have an operating system installed:

1. Start your computer and place the Windows XP CD in your CD-ROM or DVD-ROM drive.
   a. Your PC should detect the CD automatically and display a message instructing you to press any key to boot from the CD. Press any key and Windows XP setup will begin and start copying preliminary setup files to your computer.
   b. If your PC does not boot from the CD-ROM, you may need to access CMOS setup and add the CD-ROM drive to the boot sequence.
2. The Windows Setup menu appears, providing a list of menu options for you to perform a new installation, repair an existing installation, or quit (Figure 8-15).

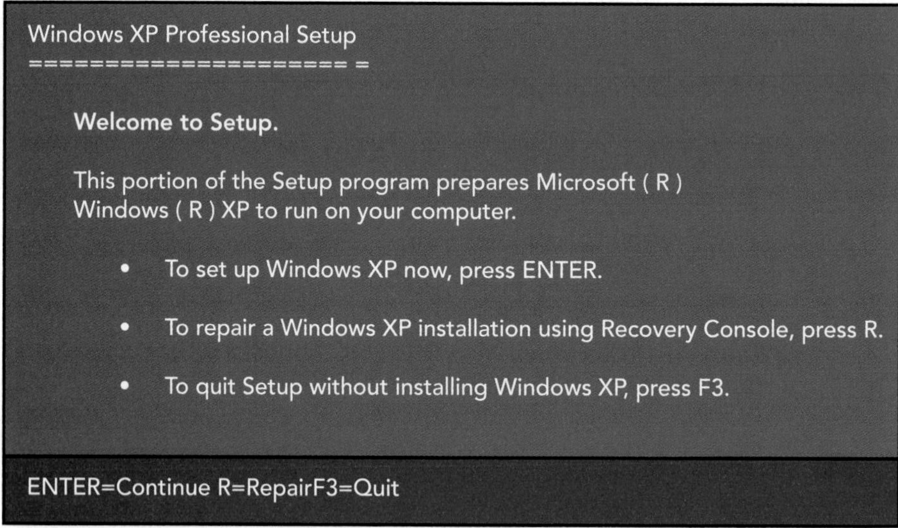

Windows XP Professional Setup
===================== =
Welcome to Setup.
This portion of the Setup program prepares Microsoft (R)
Windows (R) XP to run on your computer.
• To set up Windows XP now, press ENTER.
• To repair a Windows XP installation using Recovery Console, press R.
• To quit Setup without installing Windows XP, press F3.
ENTER=Continue R=RepairF3=Quit

Figure 8-15 Windows XP Setup opening menu. The menu may be slightly different, depending on the Windows XP release.

3. Select the option to set up Windows XP now and then press the ENTER key. When the End-User License Agreement is displayed, read and accept the agreement.
4. Windows Setup lists all partitions that it finds on the hard drive, the file system of each partition, and the size of the partition (Figure 8-16). It also lists any unpartitioned free space on the drive. From this screen, you can create and delete partitions and select the partition on which you want to install Windows XP. Even if you plan to have more than one partition on the drive, create only one partition at this time. The partition must be at least 2 GB in size and have 1.5 GB free. After the installation, you can use Disk Management to create the other partitions.
5. If you created a partition in Step 2, Setup asks which file system you want to use to format the partition, NTFS or FAT. Select NTFS. The Setup program formats the drive, which completes the text-based portion of setup.

6. At this point, the computer will restart. Leave the Windows XP CD in the CD-ROM or DVD-ROM drive, but this time do not press any key if the Press any key to boot from CD message is displayed. In a few seconds, setup will load the graphical user interface (GUI) for the remainder of the installation.
7. The GUI Windows XP Setup wizard will guide you through the setup process of gathering information about your computer. Select your geographical location from the list provided. Windows XP will use it to decide how to display dates, times, numbers, and currency.
8. Select your keyboard layout. Different keyboards can be used to accommodate special characters for other languages.
9. Enter your name, the name of your organization, and your product key.
10. Enter the computer name and the password for the Administrator account. If you are joining a workgroup, you can create your own computer name — for example, using your first initial and last name (JSMITH) or the type of computer (HOMELAPTOP). If you are joining a domain, the computer name is the name assigned to this computer by the network administrator managing the domain controller. Note that it is *very* important that you remember the Administrator password, as you cannot log on to the system without it. This password is stored in the security accounts manager database on this PC.
11. Select the date, time, and time zone. The PC might reboot.
12. If you are connected to a network, you will be asked to choose between a Typical or Custom setting to configure your network settings. The Typical setting installs Client for Microsoft Networks, File and Printer Sharing, and other settings. The Custom setting allows you to configure the network differently. If you are not sure which to use, choose Typical; you can change the settings later. Chapter 10 discusses network configurations in more detail.
13. Enter a workgroup or domain name. If you are joining a domain, the network administrator will have given you specific directions on how to configure user accounts on the domain.

```
Windows XP Professional Setup
======================= =

   The following list shows the existing partitions and
   unpartitioned space on this computer.

   Use the UP and DOWN ARROW keys to select an item
   in the list.

      •  To set up Windows XP on the selected item,
         press ENTER.

      •  To create a partition in the unpartitioned
         space, press C.

      •  To delete the selected partition, press D.

   28663 MB Disk 0 at Id 0 on bus 0 on atapi [MBR]

      Unpartitioned space                    28663 MB

ENTER=Install   C=Create Partition   F3=Quit
```

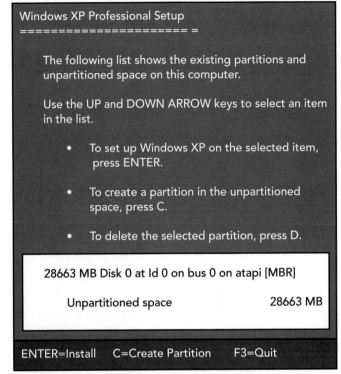

Figure 8-16 During Setup, you can create and delete partitions and select a partition on which to install Windows XP. In this example, the entire hard drive has not yet been partitioned.

FAQ 8-5

How do I install Windows XP if I cannot boot from a CD-ROM?

If your computer (or the BIOS) will not allow you to boot from a CD-ROM, you should download the Windows XP startup disk from the Microsoft Web site. The Windows XP startup disk allows computers without a bootable CD-ROM to perform a new installation of Windows XP. The startup disk automatically loads the correct drivers to gain access to the CD-ROM drive and then start a new installation of Setup. When you download the startup disk, be sure to get the disk for the correct version of Windows XP. Windows XP Professional startup disks will not work for Windows XP Home Edition installations and vice-versa. Also be aware that you only can perform a clean install (not an upgrade) from a Windows XP startup disk.

CLEAN INSTALL ON A PC WITH OS INSTALLED For a clean install on a PC that already has a previous version of the Windows OS installed, follow these general directions:

1. Close any open applications. Close any software that might be running in the background, such as an antivirus software package.
2. Insert the Windows XP CD in the CD-ROM or DVD-ROM drive. Your PC automatically should detect the CD and Autorun will start the Setup program and display the Windows Setup menu (Figure 8-17).

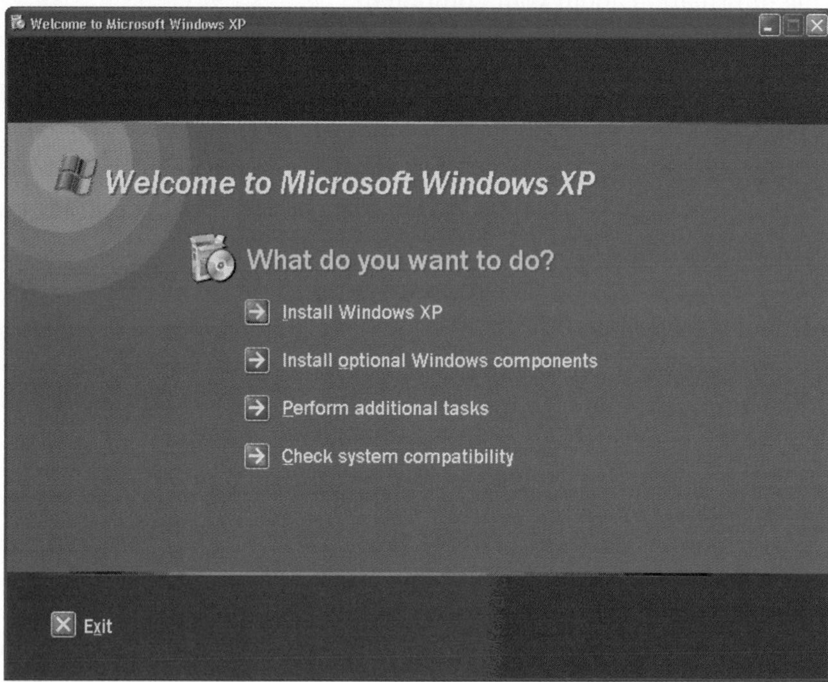

Figure 8-17 Windows XP Setup menu.

3. Click Install Windows XP. On the next screen, click New Installation under Installation Type. When the End-User License Agreement is displayed, read and accept the agreement.
4. From this point forward, continue the installation process, starting with Step 7 of the previous procedure.

UPGRADE INSTALL OF WINDOWS XP When performing an upgrade from a previous version of Windows to Windows XP, follow these general directions:

1. Before you begin the installation, do the following to prepare the system:
   a. Clean up the hard drive. Delete any unneeded or temporary files using Disk Cleanup and run Disk Defragmenter.
   b. If you have determined that you must upgrade hardware or software and that these upgrades are compatible with your old OS, perform the upgrades now and verify that the hardware or software is working.
   c. If you do not have the latest BIOS for your motherboard, flash your BIOS.
   d. Back up important files.

e. Scan the hard drive for viruses using a current version of antivirus software.

f. If you have a compressed hard drive, uncompress the drive. The only exception is that if you are using Windows NT file compression on an NTFS drive, you do not need to uncompress it.

g. Uninstall any hardware or software that you know is not compatible with Windows XP and for which you have no available upgrade.

2. Insert the Windows XP Upgrade CD in the CD-ROM or DVD-ROM drive. Autorun starts the Setup program and displays the Windows Setup menu (Figure 8-17). Click Install Windows XP. If the Windows Setup menu does not appear, open the Command Prompt window and enter `D:\Setup.exe`, substituting the drive letter of your CD-ROM drive for D, if necessary.

3. When you are prompted to choose an installation type on the next screen, select Upgrade. The following menu gives you two options:

   a. *Express Upgrade*, which uses existing Windows folders and all existing settings that are compatible with the upgrade.

   b. *Custom Upgrade*, which allows you to change the installation folder, set language options, and change the file system to NTFS.

   Select the desired upgrade and then read and accept the license agreement. If you are not sure which option to use, choose Express Upgrade.

4. Select the partition on which to install Windows XP. If the drive is configured as FAT and you want to convert to NTFS, specify that now. (Note that Windows XP has an uninstall utility that allows you to revert to Windows 98, if necessary. This uninstall tool does not work if you convert FAT to NTFS.)

5. Setup performs an analysis of the system and reports any compatibility problems. Stop the installation if the problems indicate that you will not be able to operate the system after the installation.

6. For an upgrade from Windows 98 or Windows Me to Windows XP, the Setup program converts whatever information it can in the registry to Windows XP. At the end of the installation process, you are given the opportunity to join a domain. For Windows NT and Windows 2000 upgrades, almost all registry entries are carried forward into the new OS; the information about a domain is not requested because it is copied from the old OS into Windows XP.

Upgrading from Windows NT or Windows 2000 to Windows XP is the easiest type of upgrade because these operating systems all have similar registries and support applications and devices in the same way. Nearly all applications that run on Windows NT or Windows 2000 will run on Windows XP. When you upgrade from Windows NT to Windows XP, the NTFS file system is automatically converted to the Windows XP version.

FAQ 8-5

Why does the antivirus software used on my Windows NT system not work with Windows XP?

Antivirus software designed to be used with the Windows NT NTFS file system might not run under the Windows XP NTFS file system because of the way some antivirus programs filter software as it accesses the file system. You might have to upgrade your antivirus software after Windows XP is installed.

SETTING UP A DUAL BOOT To configure Windows XP to set up a dual boot with another operating system, follow these general directions:

1. Start the installation as you would for a clean install on a PC with another operating system already installed.
2. Windows XP Setup recognizes that another OS is installed and displays an option to allow you to select a partition on which to install Windows XP. Choose to install Windows XP on a different partition than the other OS.
3. After the installation, when you boot with a dual boot, the **boot loader menu** automatically appears and asks you to select an operating system (Figure 8-18).

When setting up a dual boot, be sure that the first active partition (drive C) is set up with a file system that both operating systems understand. For example, for a dual boot with Windows 98 and Windows XP, use the FAT32 file system. For a dual boot with Windows 2000 and Windows XP, use either the FAT32 or the NTFS file system. In general, you always should install the most recent operating system last. For example, for a dual boot with Windows 2000 and Windows XP, install Windows 2000 and then install Windows XP.

When you install Windows XP on another active partition or an extended partition, it places only the files necessary to boot in the first active partition, which it calls the system partition. This causes Windows XP to initiate the boot rather than the other OS. The rest of Windows XP is installed on a second partition, which Windows XP calls the boot partition.

```
Please select the operating system to start:

    Microsoft Windows XP Professional
    Microsoft Windows 2000 Professional

Use the up and down arrow keys to move the highlight to your choice.
Seconds until highlighted choice will be started automatically: xx
Press ENTER to choose.

For troubleshooting and advanced startup options for Windows, press F8.
```

Figure 8-18 Boot loader menu displayed for a dual boot.

FAQ 8-7

Why would I want to create a dual boot?

Do not create a dual boot unless you need two operating systems, such as when you need to verify that applications and hardware work under Windows XP before you delete the old OS. Windows NT and Windows 2000 do not support running a second operating system on the same partition, so you must have at least two partitions on the hard drive. All applications must be installed on each partition to be used by each OS.

FAQ 8-8

When setting up a dual-boot, what do I do if the hard disk only has one partition?

When you install Windows on a hard disk, the Setup program does not partition your hard disk automatically. To create multiple partitions (one for each OS), choose Advanced Options during Setup and follow the instructions to create and name multiple partitions. You also can create partitions using Fdisk.

After the Installation

After you have installed Windows XP, you must complete several additional steps to activate the operating system and transfer files and user preferences from an old computer to a new computer.

PRODUCT ACTIVATION With Windows XP and other software products, Microsoft uses a set of technologies, collectively referred to as **Product Activation**, to prevent copying and sharing of the Windows XP CD in a way that infringes on the license agreement.

With Windows XP, the first time you log on to the system after the installation, the Activate Windows dialog box appears with three options (Figure 8-19). If you choose to activate Windows over the Internet and are connected to the Internet at the time, the process almost is instant. Windows XP sends a numeric identifier to a Microsoft server, which sends a certificate activating the product on your PC. Windows keeps track of the number of days since you first logged on to Windows and gives a grace period of up to 30 days after installation to activate Windows XP. After the grace period, all features of Windows XP except the Product Activation feature will stop working.

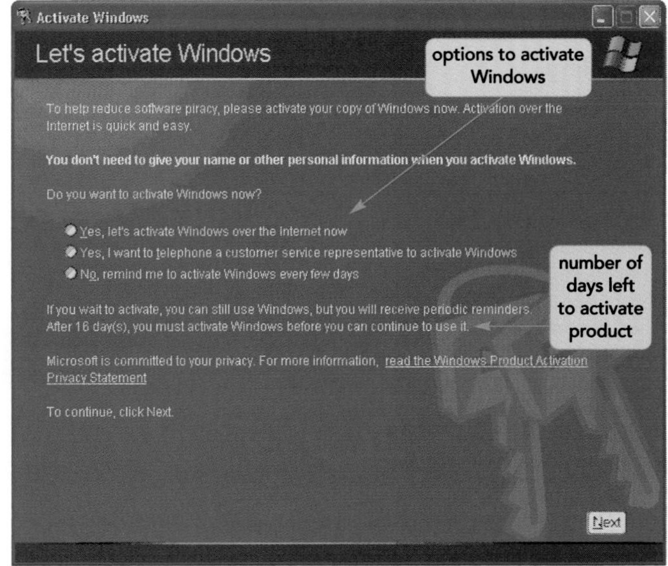

Figure 8-19 Product Activation is a strategy used by Microsoft to prevent software piracy.

If you install Windows XP from the same CD on a different computer and you attempt to activate Windows from the new PC, a dialog box appears telling you of the suspected violation of the license agreement. You can call a Microsoft operator and explain what caused the discrepancy. If your explanation is reasonable (for example, you uninstalled Windows XP from one PC and installed it on another), the operator can issue you a valid certificate. You then can type the certificate value into a dialog box to complete the boot process.

TRANSFERRING FILES AND SETTINGS TO A NEW PC Windows XP offers a utility called **Files and Settings Transfer Wizard** (Figure 8-20) that helps you transfer files and user preferences from one computer to another computer that has just had Windows XP installed. The Files and Settings Transfer Wizard transfers personalized settings for Microsoft Internet Explorer and Microsoft Outlook Express, as well as desktop, display, and dial-up connection settings from a Windows 9x, Windows NT, Windows 2000 Professional, or Windows XP computer to a Windows XP computer. Transferring these settings helps minimize the time required to

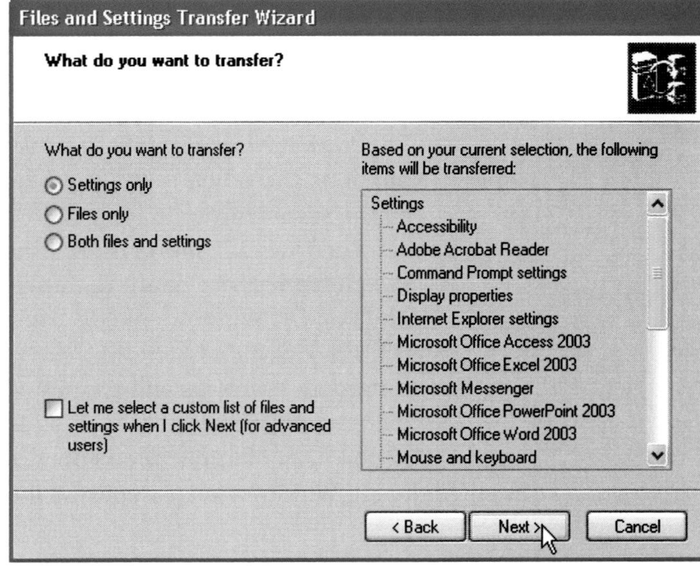

Figure 8-20 The Files and Settings Transfer Wizard allows you to transfer files, settings, or both to a new computer.

reconfigure operating system settings on a new computer. The basic steps involved in using the Files and Settings Transfer Wizard involve:

1. Collecting files and settings from the old (source) computer by using the Windows XP CD or a disk created with the wizard file. Run the wizard and copy the desired files and settings to a floppy drive, CD-R, Zip drive, or another removable medium.
2. Transferring the files and settings to the new computer using the Files and Settings Transfer Wizard.

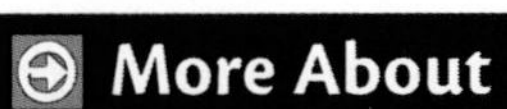

Installing Windows 9x and Windows 2000

To learn more about installing Windows 9x and Windows 2000, visit the Understanding and Troubleshooting Your PC More About Web page (**scsite.com/understanding/more**) and then click Installing Windows 9x and 2000 below Chapter 8.

Detailed steps to use the Files and Settings Transfer Wizard are outlined in Apply Your Knowledge 3. After you have completed the steps, you may find that some settings are not transferred to your Windows XP computer. If the computer from which the files and settings have been transferred contained settings for devices that are incompatible with Windows XP, those settings will not be transferred. For example, device drivers for devices not installed on the Windows XP computer will not be transferred. A list of files or folders that could not be restored to their original locations appears on the Completing the Files and Settings Transfer Wizard screen of the Files and Settings Transfer Wizard.

 **Quiz Yourself 8-2**

To test your knowledge of installing Windows XP, visit the Understanding and Troubleshooting Your PC Quiz Yourself Web page (scsite.com/understanding/quiz). Click Quiz Yourself 2 below Chapter 8.

Using Windows XP

After completing the installation, activating Windows XP, and transferring any files or settings, you can start to use Windows XP by logging on and then customizing your Windows desktop and settings.

Logging On

As you have learned, when Windows XP starts up, a user either must log on with a user name and password or click the correct user name on the Welcome screen. Windows XP tracks which user is logged on to the system and grants rights and permissions according to the user's account or to specific permissions granted this user by the administrator.

Windows XP allows more than one user to be logged on at the same time. To switch from one account to another, click the Start button and then click Log Off. The Log Off Windows dialog box opens, giving you two choices: Switch User and Log Off. Click Switch User and then select a new account from the list of user accounts. If needed, Windows will prompt you for a password. The screen will go blank and then the desktop configuration for the new user appears. Each user can have his or her own set of applications open at the same time. When users switch back and forth, Windows keeps separate instances of applications open for each user.

Using Windows Explorer, My Computer, and My Documents

Windows Explorer, My Computer, and My Documents are Windows tools that display the hierarchical structure of files, folders, and drives on your computer. **Windows Explorer** provides a quick way to see all the files and folders on your computer and provides a simple way to copy or move files from one folder to another. **My Computer** provides a simpler view of the folders on your computer. My Computer is a good tool to use if you want to work with a number of files in one folder, or if you want to reorganize the contents of a folder by creating new subfolders or renaming subfolders. **My Documents** actually is a folder on the computer, which can be used to store documents, graphics, or other files you want to access quickly. The My Documents folder is designed to make it easy to locate and back up your files, because they all are stored in one central location. If multiple users have accounts on a Windows XP computer, each user has his or her own My Documents folder.

FAQ 8-9

Where can I find my My Documents folder?

In earlier versions of Windows, such as Windows 98, all documents were stored in a common *C:\My Documents* directory for all users that logged on to the system. In Microsoft Windows XP, user-specific documents and data is stored in separate locations for each user under that user's profile, in the following location: *C:\Documents and Settings\username\My Documents*. For example, if you are logged in as Dave Fisher, your My Documents folder is located at *C:\Documents and Settings\Dave Fisher\My Documents*. If you want to view the documents for another user on the computer, go to My Computer and then click the other user's My Documents folder in the Files Stored on This Computer area.

Using Windows Explorer, My Computer, and My Documents, you can copy, move, rename, and search for files and folders. For example, you can open a folder that contains a file you want to copy, copy the file, and then paste it in another folder.

Using and Customizing the Windows XP Desktop

If you have used previous versions of Windows, learning to use Windows XP is easy and intuitive. The Windows XP GUI does have several new features, including the Windows desktop and Start menu (Figure 8-21 on the next page). When Windows XP is first installed, the Recycle Bin is the only shortcut on the desktop. The Start menu is organized with a more graphical look and the user name for the person currently logged on shows at the top of the Start menu. Applications at the top of the Start menu are said to be **pinned** to the menu and are permanently listed there until you change them in a Start menu setting. Applications that are used often are listed below the pinned applications and can change based on which applications you use often. When you click the Start button and then point to All Programs on the Start menu, the All Programs menu lists any software currently installed on the computer.

Windows XP provides many tools to allow you to customize your desktop. This section looks at several ways to make the desktop look and work the way you want it to. Each user account has a different desktop configuration, so if you want to create a customized desktop for a user, you first must log on to the system under that user account.

Working with Files and Folders

To learn more about working with files and folders using Windows XP tools, visit the Understanding and Troubleshooting Your PC More About Web page (**scsite.com/understanding/more**) and then click Working with Files and Folders below Chapter 8.

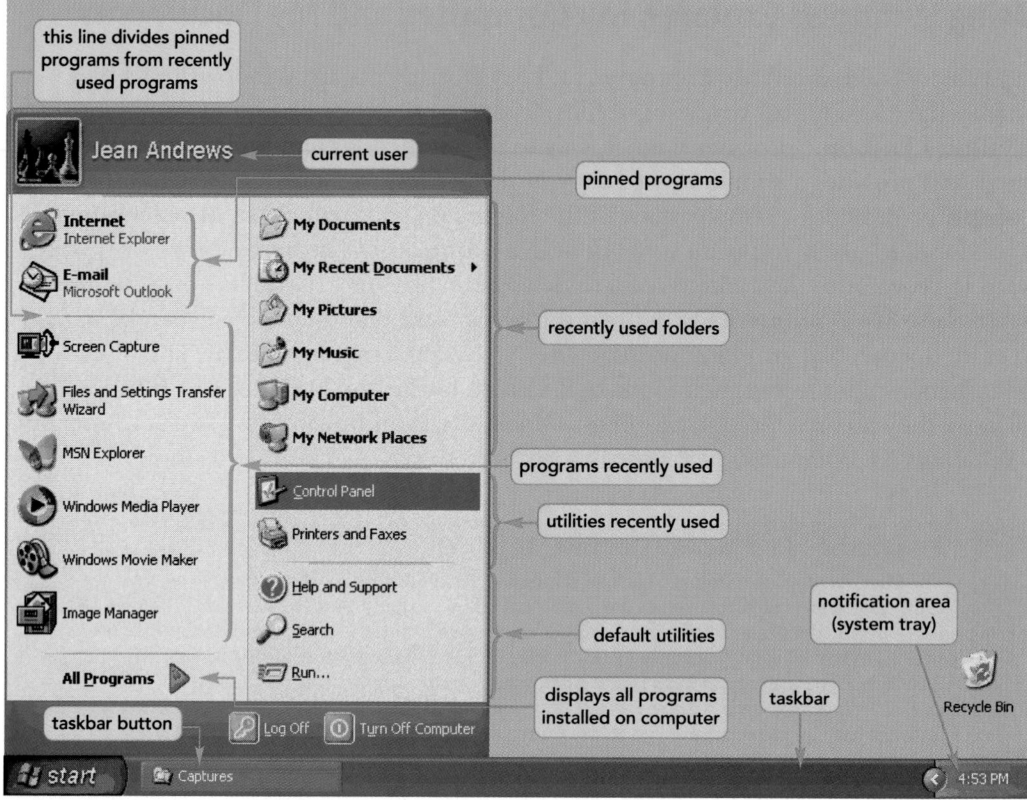

Figure 8-21 The Windows XP desktop and Start menu.

CHANGING THE TASKBAR You can customize how the Windows taskbar displays by right-clicking the taskbar and then clicking Properties on the shortcut menu. When the Taskbar and Start Menu Properties window is displayed (Figure 8-22), you can add items to and remove items from the Start menu, control how the taskbar manages items in the notification area, and specify how the taskbar appears.

If you want to display frequently used programs as icons in the taskbar, click Show Quick Launch and then click the OK button. (Alternatively, you can select Toolbars on the taskbar's shortcut menu and then click Quick Launch on the Toolbars menu.) The Quick Launch bar makes it easy to access frequently used programs such as your e-mail program or Internet Explorer. Windows XP automatically includes several icons on the Quick Launch toolbar, including the Show Desktop icon that you click to minimize or restore all of the programs on your desktop.

The Taskbar and Start Menu Properties window also allows you to choose to hide inactive icons in the notification area. The **notification area** (also called the **system tray**) is the area on the taskbar that displays the time and contains shortcuts that provide quick access to programs, such as Volume Control. Other shortcuts can appear temporarily, providing information about the status of activities. For example, an e-mail icon appears when a new message is received. As you work, the notification area can become cluttered with icons for various programs. You can hide any inactive icons by clicking Hide inactive icons in the Taskbar and Start Menu Properties window, as shown in Figure 8-22. If you need to display the icons, click the left arrow on the left side of the notification area.

MANAGING ICONS AND SHORTCUTS An **icon** is a small image displayed on a computer screen that represents a program, a document, or some other object. An icon often represents a **shortcut**, which is an icon on the desktop that points to a program that can be executed or to a file, folder, or Web page. A shortcut provides a quicker way to access a program, document, or other file that otherwise would require you to navigate through several menus. If an icon is a shortcut, it displays with a small, bent-arrow shortcut symbol (Figure 8-23). In Figure 8-23, the icon on the right represents the document file, report12.21.05.doc, stored in the C:\Documents and Settings\User\Desktop. The icon on the left is a shortcut to the Microsoft Word executable file, which can be stored anywhere on the drive.

If you delete a document icon, such as the report12.21.05.doc icon shown in Figure 8-23, the document itself is deleted. If you delete a shortcut icon from the desktop, the shortcut is deleted, but the actual file that the shortcut points to is not deleted.

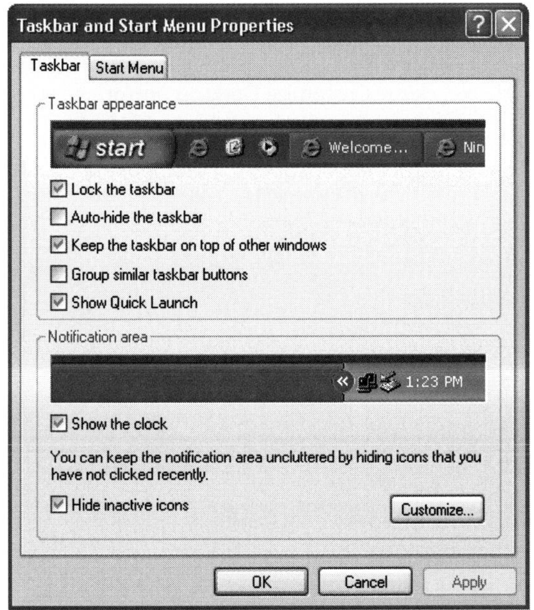

Figure 8-22 The Taskbar and Start Menu Properties window provides options to control what appears in the Start menu and taskbar.

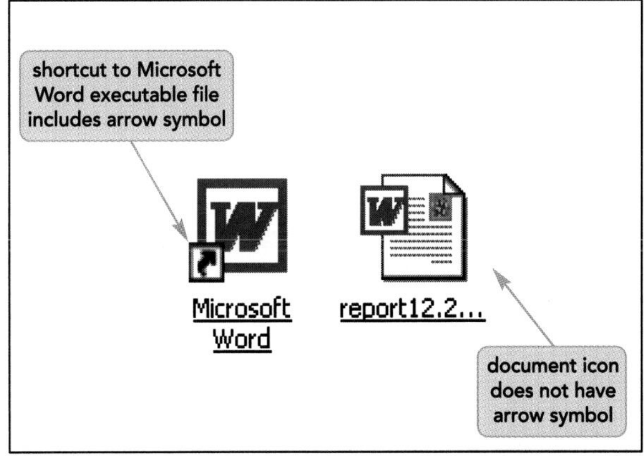

Figure 8-23 If an icon is a shortcut, it displays with a small, bent-arrow shortcut symbol on the icon.

Your Turn

Customizing Windows XP Settings

Windows XP uses a more graphical user interface than previous versions of Windows. While many users like the new look, others prefer to have the user interface look more like previous versions of Windows. For example, you can customize the Control Panel to use a new look specific to Windows XP or to use a more classic view. Using Windows XP, perform the following steps to change the view used by the operating system:

1. Click the Start button and then click Control Panel on the Start menu.
2. Control Panel is displayed in Category View or Classic View. If necessary, click Switch to Category View to change to Category View. Click several categories to review the customization options available in each category. Close any category windows that open.
3. Click Switch to Classic View to change the Control Panel interface to one more closely resembling previous versions of Windows.
4. Click Switch to Category View.

In addition to changing the views of windows, you can customize shortcuts on the Windows desktop. When you first install Windows XP, only the Recycle Bin shows on the desktop by default. Using Windows XP, perform the following steps to add new shortcuts to the Windows desktop:

1. Right-click anywhere on the Windows desktop and then click Properties on the shortcut menu.
2. When the Display Properties window opens, click the Desktop tab and then click the Customize Desktop button.
3. If they are not selected, My Documents, My Computer, My Network Places, and Internet Explorer. Click the OK button twice to close both windows to add these shortcuts to the desktop.

Perform the following steps to add other program shortcuts to your Windows XP desktop:

1. Click the Start button and then point to All Programs. Right-click any program name in the All Programs menu and then click Copy in the shortcut menu. (Be sure to pick a program and not a menu name.)
2. Right-click anywhere on the desktop and click Paste on the shortcut menu.

You also can use Windows Explorer, My Computer, or My Documents to create a shortcut.

1. Click My Documents on the Windows desktop.
2. Minimize any open programs to view the Windows desktop.
3. Double-click My Computer. When the My Computer window is displayed, right-click the file name of a document, program, or other data file. Click Send To on the shortcut menu and then click Desktop (create shortcut) on the Send To menu (Figure 8-24).

A shortcut is created and placed on the desktop. To delete the shortcut, simply select the shortcut and then press the DELETE key. If Windows displays a confirmation dialog box, click the appropriate button to confirm that you want to delete the shortcut.

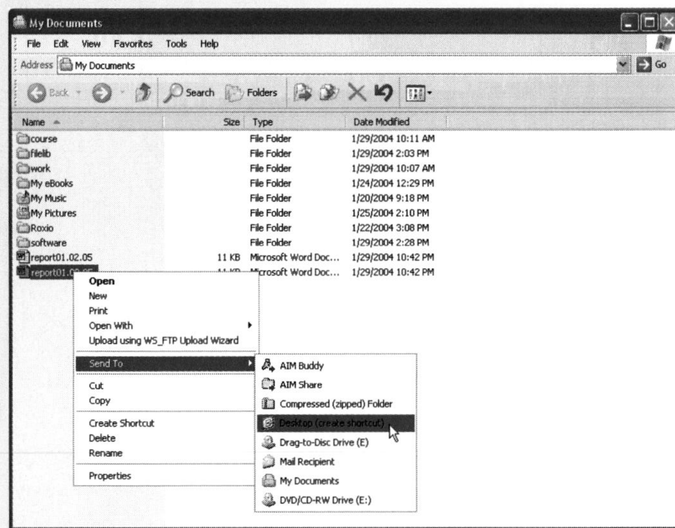

Figure 8-24

FAQ 8-10

Windows XP automatically starts Windows Messenger when I log on. How can I keep it from starting automatically?

Windows Messenger automatically is installed when you install Windows XP. When Windows XP starts, it loads Windows Messenger by default, which consumes system resources even if you are not using it. To stop Windows Messenger from loading at startup, click the Start button, point to All Programs, and then click Windows Messenger. When Windows Messenger starts, click Tools on the menu bar and then click Options. When the Options window is displayed, click the Preferences tab and deselect Run this program when Windows starts. Click the OK button and then click the Windows Messenger close button to close the program.

Installing Hardware and Software Using Windows XP

Once Windows XP is installed and you are comfortable working with its features, you can install hardware and software applications under Windows XP. You also must learn how to troubleshoot issues with hardware and software installations. In the following section and the next chapter, you will learn about more tools and procedures you can use to troubleshoot a failed system, program, or hardware device.

Installing Hardware

As you have learned, installing hardware, such as an input, output, or multimedia device, typically involves connecting the device, installing any required drivers, and then installing any software that came with the device. Windows XP often automatically identifies the new device after it is connected and automatically launches the Found New Hardware Wizard. If the wizard does not automatically launch when you start Windows, you can start it using the Add Hardware icon in the Control Panel.

As discussed in Chapters 6 and 7, if your hardware device comes bundled with drivers for Windows XP on CD or floppy disk, use those drivers. If the drivers are not written for Windows XP, go to the manufacturer's Web site to download Windows XP drivers or visit the Microsoft Web site and search for the driver or device.

USING DEVICE MANAGER As you have learned, Device Manager is a powerful utility that offers several important tools to support Windows XP. After a hardware device is installed, Device Manager offers several ways to help solve problems with a device:

- Providing a way to find an update automatically for a driver
- Rolling back a driver in case an updated driver fails
- Verifying that the driver is certified by Microsoft

To start Device Manager, click the Start button, right-click My Computer on the Start menu, and then click Manage on the shortcut menu. When the Computer Management window is displayed, click Device Manager in the left side of the Computer Management window (Figure 8-25). (Alternatively, you can (1) click the Start button and then click Run. When the Run dialog box is

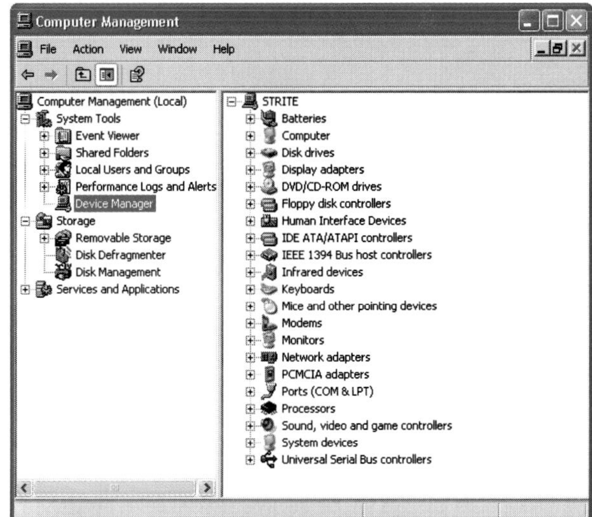

Figure 8-25 Device Manager is one tool available in the Computer Management window.

displayed, enter `Devmgmt.msc` in the Open text box or (2) right-click My Computer, click Properties on the shortcut menu, click the Hardware tab, and then click the Device Manager button.)

After a device is installed, you can use Device Manager to verify that Windows XP sees no resource conflicts with the device and that it works properly. If a device appears to have a problem, you can update a driver using the Update Device Driver Wizard. To update the driver, perform the following steps:

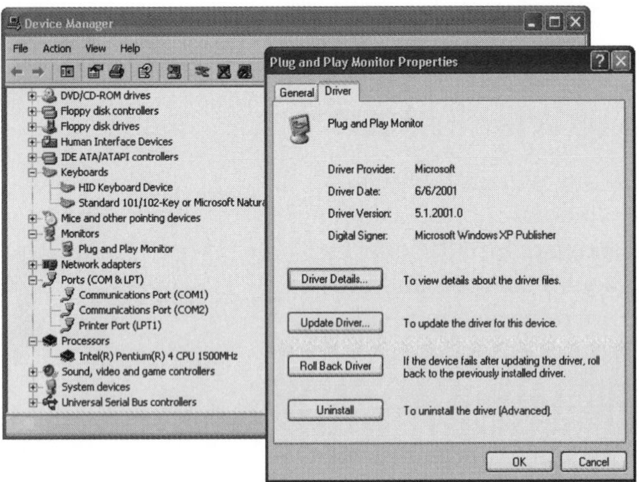

Figure 8-26 The Properties window allows you to obtain updated device drivers from the Microsoft Web site.

1. Right-click the device in Device Manager and then click Properties on the shortcut menu. The Properties window for that device appears.
2. Click the Driver tab (Figure 8-26) and then click the Update Driver button. (If you do not have an always-on connection to the Internet, connect to the Internet before you click the Update Driver button).
3. When the Hardware Update Wizard starts, follow the steps on the screen. The wizard goes to the Microsoft Web site, searches for updates to the driver, informs you if there is an update, and asks permission to install the update. Windows XP only suggests an update if the hardware ID of the device exactly matches the hardware ID of the update. A hardware ID is a number assigned to a device by the manufacturer that uniquely identifies the product.

If you update a driver and the new driver does not perform as expected, you can revert to the old driver by opening the Properties window for the device and then clicking the Roll Back Driver button. If a previous driver is available, it will be installed. In many cases, when a driver is updated, Windows saves the old driver in case you want to revert to it. (Windows does not save printer drivers when they are updated and does not save drivers that are not functioning properly at the time of an update.)

More About

Digital Signatures for Drivers

To learn more about Microsoft's use of digital signatures to verify drivers, visit the Understanding and Troubleshooting Your PC More About Web page (**scsite.com/understanding/more**) and then click Digital Signatures for Drivers below Chaper 8.

FAQ 8-11

I have an older hardware device installed on my computer, but I do not see it in Device Manager. Why is that?

By default, Device Manager hides older (legacy) devices that are not Plug and Play. The View menu of Device Manager, however, allows you to control how you view devices and resources. To view installed legacy devices, click the View menu of Device Manager and then select Show hidden devices so a check mark displays next to the menu option.

Installing and Uninstalling Software

To install software using Windows XP, you can run the software's setup program, much as you ran the Windows Setup program to install Windows XP. Many software programs are distributed on CD-ROMs or DVD-ROMs and will start automatically when the disc is placed in the drive. If the setup program does not start automatically, you can browse the files on the disc to locate the setup.exe or install.exe program and double-click it to start the installation process.

Windows XP also allows you to install programs using the Add or Remove Program window. To open the window, click the Start button, click Control Panel on the Start menu, and then click Add or Remove Programs in the Control Panel window. Click the Add New Programs button on the left side of the window to start the installation process. An installed program normally is made available to all users on a computer when they log on. If a program is not available to all users, try installing the program files in the C:\Documents and Settings\All Users folder.

If you use a program almost every time you use your computer, you can set it to launch automatically each time you start Windows by putting a shortcut to the program in the Startup menu folder for the user. The Startup folder for each user on a Windows XP computer is C:\Documents and Settings*username*\ Start Menu\Programs\Startup. If you want the software to start up automatically for all users, put the shortcut in this folder: C:\Documents and Settings\All Users\Start Menu\Programs\Startup. You should limit the number of programs included in the Startup folder. Adding many programs can slow the process of starting your computer significantly.

To uninstall software, click Add or Remove Programs in the Control Panel window and select the software to uninstall in the Currently installed programs list and then click the Change/Remove button (Figure 8-27). Most programs will display a confirmation dialog box to verify that you want to uninstall the program. If other users are logged on to the system, a warning message is displayed to indicate that the program might not uninstall completely if other users are running the program. Be sure all other users are logged off and then again complete steps to uninstall the software.

More About

Installing Legacy Software

To learn more about installing older (legacy) software under Windows XP, visit the Understanding and Troubleshooting Your PC More About Web page (**scsite.com/understanding/more**) and then click Installing Legacy Hardware below Chapter 8.

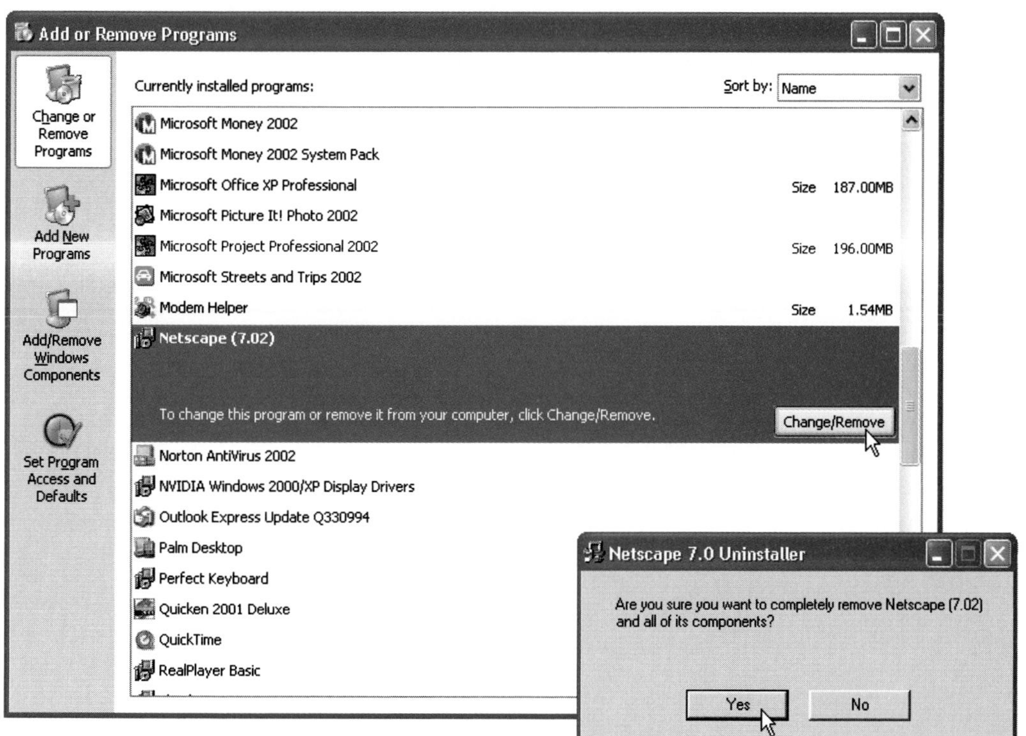

Figure 8-27 To uninstall software, click Add or Remove Programs in the Control Panel window and select the software to uninstall in the Currently installed programs list.

FAQ 8-12

Why will Windows XP not allow me to install software?

Recall from earlier in the chapter that Windows XP supports two types of user accounts: administrator and limited. You only can install software if you are logged on as an administrator. Check to see if the user account you used to log on is a limited or administrator account. If it is a limited account, log off and log back on as an administrator. If you already are logged on as an administrator, check the manufacturer's Web site or the user's guide for the software to look for troubleshooting suggestions.

 Quiz Yourself 8-3

To test your knowledge of using Windows XP, visit the Understanding and Troubleshooting Your PC Quiz Yourself Web page (scsite.com/understanding/quiz). Click Quiz Yourself 3 below Chapter 8.

High-Tech Talk

Making Software Piracy Walk the Plank

Look around at your classmates. Most likely, you would not expect any of them to be thieves — but you might be surprised how many of them have stolen or used stolen software. You also might be a guilty party! *Software theft* occurs when someone steals software media, intentionally erases software programs, or illegally copies a software program. For example, a dishonest student might steal the Microsoft Encarta CD-ROM from the library reference desk — or a software programmer might intentionally remove programs he or she has written from company computers.

Software also can be stolen from software manufacturers. This type of theft, called *software piracy*, is the unauthorized and illegal duplication of copyrighted software. Software piracy is by far the most common form of software theft. Even after you have purchased a software package and agreed to the license agreement, you do not have the right to copy, loan, rent, or in any way distribute the software. Doing so not only is a violation of copyright law, it also is a federal crime. Despite this, recent statistics show that 40 percent of the world's software is pirated.

Software companies take piracy very seriously, and increasingly are using Product Activation technology to help thwart software pirates. Microsoft is using Product Activation in newer versions of Windows, Office, and Visio. With Product Activation, to use their software, users must complete a simple, straightforward, and anonymous activation process that takes less than one minute when completed over the Internet. Product Activation works by validating that the software's product key, required as part of product installation, has not been used on more PCs than are allowed by the software's end user license agreement (EULA). Product Activation discourages piracy by limiting the number of times a product key can be activated on different PCs.

During the installation process, the user is prompted to activate the software within a specific grace period (for example, 30 days from first boot for Windows XP or 50 launches of Office XP). The user then can activate the product directly via the Internet or by a telephone call to a customer service representative (Figure 8-28). During the activation process, product key information in the form of the product ID is sent along with a *hardware hash* (a non-unique number generated from the PC's hardware configuration) to Microsoft's activation system. Activations on the same PC using the same product key are unlimited, but activations on more than two different PCs using the same product key are in violation of most EULAs.

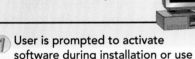

User/User's Computer	Microsoft Activation Server
1 User is prompted to activate software during installation or use (each software package has a grace period during which they will operate without being activated)	
2 User starts activation process directly via Internet or by contacting customer service via telephone — sends product ID and hardware hash →	3 Microsoft activation server processes the activation
	4 Activation server confirms that product ID and hardware hash are unique and software is being used within terms of EULA
6 Confirmation is processed, either behind the scenes for Internet confirmation or user enters confirmation ID provided over telephone	← 5 Activation server returns activation confirmation to user or user's computer
7 Software is activated	

Figure 8-28

When Product Activation was first brought to market, many users expressed concern about their privacy. Microsoft, however, is quick to point out that Product Activation is *not* the same as voluntary product registration. No personally identifiable information is required to activate a software product. The only information exchanged during activation is the Installation ID created by the software and possibly the country in which the software is being installed.

In the end, Microsoft designed Product Activation not to create problems for honest users, but as a way to help sink software pirates. Although many anti-piracy measures often are cracked by the pirates themselves, Product Activation thus far has proved a solid defense against some forms of piracy, and manufacturers are continuing to work on new measures to stay one step ahead of the swashbucklers stealing software, raising prices, and getting away with theft.

CHAPTER SUMMARY

The Chapter Summary reviews the concepts presented in this chapter.

1 Features and Architecture of Windows XP

Windows XP comes in five versions, each of which has many new features, including a new user interface and added support for multimedia and networking technologies. The two architectural modes of Windows XP are user mode and kernel mode. User mode is a processor mode in which programs have only limited access to system information and can access hardware only through other OS services. Kernel mode is further divided into two components: executive services and the hardware abstraction layer (HAL). A workgroup is a group of computers and users sharing resources. Each computer maintains a list of users and their rights on that particular PC. A domain is a group of networked computers that share a centralized directory database of user account information and security. Windows XP supports two types of user accounts, administrator and limited. An administrator has rights and permissions to all computer software and hardware resources and is responsible for setting up other user accounts and assigning them privileges. A limited account cannot change most settings or delete important files.

2 Installing Windows XP

With a clean install, you have to erase and/or backup all data, reformat the hard disk, and then install the new operating system. An upgrade install installs the new operating system and carries forward information about installed hardware and software, user preferences, and other settings from the existing operating system. Perform an upgrade if you have another version of Windows installed and you do not plan to dual boot, in which the OSs are configured so a user can boot the computer from one of two different operating systems that are both installed on the same hard drive.

Before installing Windows XP, verify that the system at least meets the minimum system requirements and determine if you will perform an upgrade or a clean install. Use Upgrade Advisor or check the Windows Catalog to verify that all installed hardware components and software are compatible with Windows XP. Decide how you will partition your hard drive and what file system you will use. Determine whether the PC will be configured as a workstation in a workgroup or as part of a domain. Make a final checklist to verify that you have done all of the above. After you have installed Windows XP, you must complete several additional steps to activate the operating system and use the File Settings and Transfer Wizard to transfer files and user preferences from an old computer to a new computer.

3 Using Windows XP

Differences in the Windows XP desktop from earlier versions include the absence (by default) of any shortcuts other than the Recycle Bin and a more graphical organization of the Start menu. Windows XP allows more than one user to be logged on at the same time, each with their own instances of open applications. Windows Explorer, My Computer, and My Documents all are Windows tools that display the hierarchical structure of files, folders, and drives on your computer. Windows XP also provides tools to customize your desktop.

4 Installing Hardware and Software Using Windows XP

Installing hardware typically involves connecting the device, installing any required drivers, and then installing any software that came with the device. Windows XP offers processes to help find updates for a driver and roll back a driver if an update fails. To install or uninstall software using Windows XP, you can run the software's setup program or use the Add or Remove Programs window.

KEY TERMS

After reading the chapter, you should know each of these Key Terms.

administrator (*312*)
boot loader menu (*326*)
clean install (*314*)
client/server (*312*)
directory database (*312*)
domain (*312*)
domain controller (*312*)
dual boot (*314*)
end-user license agreement (EULA) (*321*)
executive services (*311*)
Files and Settings Transfer Wizard (*327*)
firewall (*309*)
HAL (hardware abstraction layer) (*311*)
icon (*331*)
kernel mode (*311*)
limited account (*313*)
My Computer (*329*)
My Documents (*329*)
network operating system (NOS) (*312*)
notification area (*330*)
peer-to-peer (*311*)
pinned (*329*)
Product Activation (*327*)
product key (*321*)
security accounts manager (SAM) database (*312*)
shortcut (*331*)
system tray (*330*)
Upgrade Advisor (*317*)
upgrade install (*314*)
user account (*312*)
user mode (*310*)
Windows Catalog (*317*)
Windows Explorer (*329*)
workgroup (*311*)

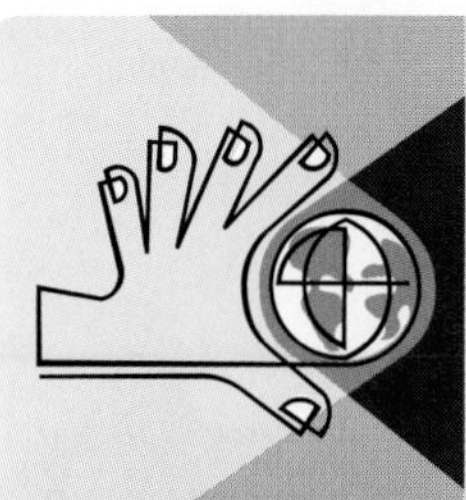

LEARN IT ONLINE

Reinforce your understanding of the chapter concepts and terms with the Learn It Online exercises.

Instructions: To complete the Learn It Online exercises, start your browser, click the Address bar, and then enter the Web address **scsite.com/understanding/learn.** When the Understanding and Troubleshooting Your PC Learn It Online page is displayed, follow the instructions in the exercises below. Each exercise has instructions for printing your results, either for your own records or for submission to your instructor.

1 Chapter Reinforcement True/False, Multiple Choice, and Short Answer

Below Chapter 8, click the Chapter Reinforcement link. Print the quiz by clicking Print on the File menu for each page. Answer each question.

2 Flash Cards

Below Chapter 8, click the Flash Cards link and read the instructions. Type 20 (or a number specified by your instructor) in the Number of playing cards text box, type your name in the Enter your Name text box, and then click the Flip Card button. When the flash card is displayed, read the question and then click the ANSWER box arrow to select an answer. Flip through Flash Cards. If your score is 15 (75%) correct or greater, click Print on the File menu to print your results. If your score is less than 15 (75%) correct, then redo this exercise by clicking the Replay button.

3 Practice Test

Below Chapter 8, click the Practice Test link. Answer each question, enter your first and last name at the bottom of the page, and then click the Grade Test button. When the graded practice test is displayed on your screen, click Print on the File menu to print a hard copy. Continue to take practice tests until you score 80% or better.

4 Who Wants To Be a Computer Genius?

Below Chapter 8, click the Computer Genius link. Read the instructions, enter your first and last name at the bottom of the page, and then click the PLAY button. When your score is displayed, click the PRINT RESULTS link to print a hard copy.

5 Wheel of Terms

Below Chapter 8, click the Wheel of Terms link. Read the instructions, and then enter your first and last name and your school name. Click the PLAY button. When your score is displayed, right-click the score and then click Print on the shortcut menu to print a hard copy.

6 Crossword Puzzle Challenge

Below Chapter 8, click the Crossword Puzzle Challenge link. Read the instructions, and then enter your first and last name. Click the SUBMIT button. Work the crossword puzzle. When you are finished, click the Submit button. When the crossword puzzle is redisplayed, click the Print Puzzle button to print a hard copy.

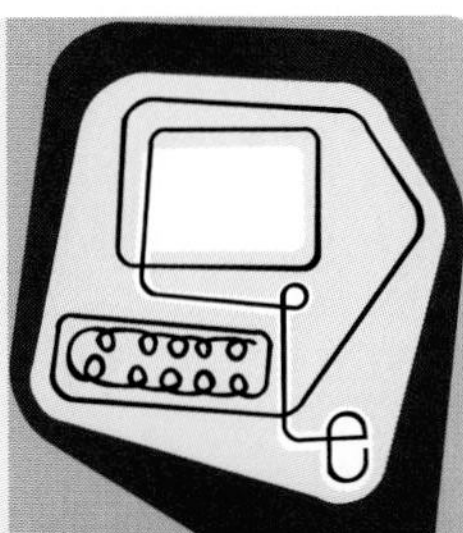

CHAPTER EXERCISES

Complete the Chapter Exercises to solidify what you learned in the chapter.

Multiple Choice

Select the best answer.

1. Which of these is not a system requirement for a Windows XP installation?
   a. 64 MB or higher of RAM
   b. 2 GB free space on a hard drive
   c. 1,200 dpi laser printer
   d. Pentium II 300 MHz CPU
2. Which of the following operating systems cannot be upgraded to Windows XP Professional using the upgrade version of the software?
   a. Windows XP Home Edition
   b. Windows 2000 Professional
   c. Windows Me
   d. Windows 95
3. In which of these situations would you not perform a clean install?
   a. Your current OS, Windows 2000 Professional, has no known issues.
   b. You do not currently have an operating system installed.
   c. You are having problems with your current installation of Windows Me.
   d. You are planning a dual boot setup.
4. Which of the following tasks is not possible using Device Manager?
   a. find an update for a driver
   b. roll back a driver in case an updated driver fails
   c. determine if new models are available from the manufacturer
   d. verify that the driver is certified by Microsoft
5. Which file system does Windows XP not support?
   a. FAT12
   b. FAT16
   c. FAT32
   d. NTFS

Fill in the Blank

Write the word or phrase to fill in the blank in each of the following questions.

1. The domain controller stores and controls a database of user accounts, group accounts, and computer accounts called the ________________.
2. A(n) ____________ is a logical group of computers and users that share resources, where administration, resources, and security on a workstation are controlled by that workstation.
3. When a computer is set up for a(n) ______, the operating systems are configured so a user can boot the computer from one of two different operating systems that are both installed on the same hard drive.
4. A(n) _________ has rights and permissions to all computer software and hardware resources and is responsible for setting up other user accounts and assigning them privileges. A user under a(n) ___________ cannot change most settings or delete important files.
5. A(n) __________________ is a single task that the process requests from the kernel, such as printing a file. A(n) ___________ is a program or group of programs that is running, together with the system resources assigned to it.

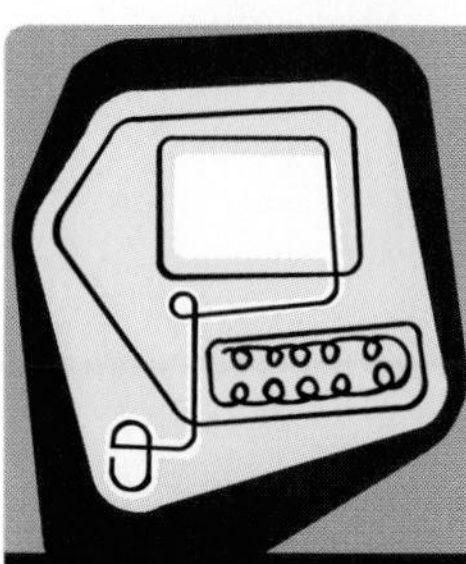

CHAPTER EXERCISES

Complete the Chapter Exercises to solidify what you learned in the chapter.

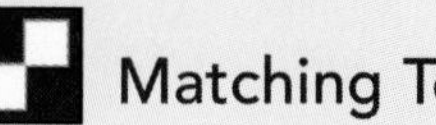

Matching Terms

Match the terms with their definitions.

______	1. Product Activation	a.	an icon on the desktop that points to a program that can be executed or to a file or folder
______	2. firewall	b.	unique identification number included on the product packaging
______	3. pinned	c.	the area on the taskbar to the right of the taskbar buttons; also called the system tray
______	4. product key	d.	displays the structure of files, folders, and drives on your computer
______	5. icon	e.	small image on a computer screen that represents a program, a document, or some other object
______	6. boot loader menu	f.	hardware or software that protects a computer or network from unauthorized access
______	7. My Computer	g.	describes applications listed at the top of the Start menu
______	8. notification area	h.	a group of networked computers that share a centralized directory database of user account information and security
______	9. shortcut	i.	asks you to select an operating system on system set up with a dual boot
______	10. domain	j.	used to prevent copying and sharing of a Microsoft software product

Short Answer Questions

Write a brief answer to each of the following questions.

1. Describe at least ten features of Windows XP.
2. List at least five things you should do before installing Windows XP.
3. Explain the purpose of the Files and Settings Transfer Wizard, and briefly describe the steps involved in using it.
4. Briefly define and describe a clean install and an upgrade install.
5. Describe two ways to check hardware and software compatibility for Windows XP. What steps should you take if you learn that software or a hardware device is not Windows XP compatible?

APPLY YOUR KNOWLEDGE

Check your understanding of the chapter with the hands-on Apply Your Knowledge exercises.

1 Changing the Desktop Background

Another way to customize your Windows desktop is to change the desktop background, which often is referred to as wallpaper. Perform the following steps to change the wallpaper using Windows XP:

1. Right-click the Windows desktop and click Properties in the shortcut menu.
2. When the Display Properties window is displayed, click the Desktop tab, if necessary, and note what image currently is used for the background.
3. Scroll through the Background list and click on several backgrounds to see how they will appear on the desktop.
4. Select a background and then click the three items in the Position list to see how that changes the display of the background on the desktop.
5. When you are satisfied with your selection, click the OK button.
6. Open the My Documents window and find any graphics or photographs you have stored in C:\Documents and Settings*username*\My Documents\My Pictures, or in any other folders on your hard drive.
7. Right-click the file and click Set as Desktop Background from the shortcut menu. Close the My Documents window and view the new background.
8. Right-click the Windows desktop and click Properties in the shortcut menu. When the Display Properties window is displayed, set the background back to its original state.

2 Preparing for an Upgrade to Windows XP

On a PC with Windows 2000 or an earlier version of Windows installed, use Upgrade Advisor to determine whether the PC is ready for Windows XP installation. If a Windows XP CD is not available, download the Windows XP Upgrade Advisor from the Microsoft Web site (*www.microsoft.com/windowsxp/home/howtobuy/upgrading/advisor.asp*). When you click the link to download the Upgrade Advisor, click Open in the File Download dialog box to run the program from the Web site.

Next, search the Windows Catalog to verify that the following hardware and software are compatible with Windows XP:

- Quicken 2001 Suite
- HP LaserJet 4100
- Digimax 350SE

What does it mean when something is labeled Compatible with Windows XP versus being labeled as Designed for Windows XP? Based on the results from Upgrade Advisor and the Windows Catalog, make a list of any hardware or software components found incompatible with Windows XP and draw up a plan for getting the system ready for an XP upgrade.

3 Using the Files and Settings Transfer Wizard

Using Windows XP, perform the following steps to use the Files and Settings Transfer Wizard to collect settings from an old computer and transfer them to a new computer. First, you must collect files and settings from the old computer.

1. If the old computer has a CD-ROM or DVD-ROM drive, insert the Windows XP CD-ROM into the CD-ROM or DVD-ROM drive of the old computer. Right-click Start, click Explore, and then open the Support\Tools folder on the Windows XP CD-ROM. Double-click the Fastwiz.exe file to start the Files and Settings Transfer Wizard.
2. When the wizard launches, click the Next button to start the wizard, click Old Computer, and then click the Next button.

APPLY YOUR KNOWLEDGE

Check your understanding of the chapter with the hands-on Apply Your Knowledge exercises.

3. Click Floppy drive or other removable media as the transfer method, and then click Next.
4. On the What do you want to transfer? screen, click Settings only and then click Next.
5. The wizard collects your settings. When prompted, insert the floppy disk in drive A and then click OK.
6. Click Finish. Remove the floppy disk from drive A.

   Next, you must transfer files and settings to the new computer.
7. Log on to the new Windows XP computer to which you want to transfer settings.
8. Click the Start button and then point to All Programs on the Start menu. Point to Accessories, then point to System Tools, and then click Files and Settings Transfer Wizard on the System Tools menu. Click Next.
9. On the Which computer is this screen, click New computer and then click Next.
10. Click I don't need the Wizard Disk. I have already collected my files and settings from my old computer and then click Next.
11. On the Where are the files and settings screen, click Floppy drive or other removable media.
12. Click Next. If you selected Floppy drive or other removable media, insert the floppy disk from the previous steps in drive A and then click OK. Click Finish.
13. Click Yes when prompted to log off for the changes to take effect. Log on to the computer to apply your transferred settings.

If the old computer does not have a CD-ROM drive, instead of completing Step 1, use a Windows XP computer to create a floppy disk that contains the Files and Settings Transfer Wizard file. To access the wizard, click the Start button and then point to All Programs on the Start menu. Point to Accessories, then point to System Tools, and then click Files and Settings Transfer Wizard on the System Tools menu. Click Next after the wizard's Welcome window opens. When the wizard asks if this is the New computer or Old computer, click New computer and then click Next. On the next screen, click the first option to create a Wizard Disk on the floppy disk in drive A. Insert the disk in drive A of the old computer, browse to and double-click the Fastwiz.exe file. Continue with Step 2.

4 Installing Windows XP

Complete an upgrade install or a clean install (with or without another operating system previously installed) of Windows XP Professional, following the steps outlined in the chapter. As you complete the installation, write down each decision you had to make as you performed the installation. If you get any error messages during the installation, write them down and list the steps you took to recover from the error. How long did the installation take from start to finish?

CHAPTER 9
Managing and Supporting Windows XP

Introduction

In Chapter 8, you learned how to install and use Windows XP Professional. This chapter provides information on supporting this OS. You will learn about security features that protect the Windows XP system, its users, and their data. You also will learn how the Windows XP registry is organized and how to edit it, and about many troubleshooting tools available under Windows XP. Finally, you will learn how to troubleshoot the Windows XP boot process. In later chapters, you will learn more about how Windows XP Professional is used on networks and about additional security features it has when networked.

OBJECTIVES

In this chapter, you will learn:

1. About consoles and snap-ins in Windows XP
2. How to use Windows XP features to secure the PC and protect users and their data
3. About the Windows XP registry
4. How to troubleshoot the Windows XP boot process
5. About tools for troubleshooting and maintaining Windows XP

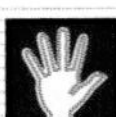

Up for Discussion

Reed Jacques, the owner of Sunrise Computers, is planning to offer evening computer courses to the public. He has decided that one of the first courses should cover how to use and troubleshoot problems with Windows XP. Reed developed specific course objectives for installing Windows XP and using the interface, but he asked if you could help him define course objectives related to maintaining and troubleshooting a Windows XP machine.

After some consideration, you suggest adding objectives on troubleshooting the Windows XP boot process and accessing additional Windows XP help on the Microsoft Web site. When Reed asks you for more detail, you explain that Windows includes many tools to help troubleshoot the boot process, including the Advanced Options menu, System Restore, the Recovery Console, and Automated System Recovery.

Reed admits he has never used any of those tools and asks you to show him how they work. You sit down at his computer and begin to explain the various troubleshooting tools Windows XP provides. You also reassure him that he does not need to remember how every utility works, because the help and support resources available in Windows XP and on the Microsoft Web site provide detailed descriptions and steps for how to use the various tools.

Questions:

- What tools does Windows XP provide to help you troubleshoot the boot process?
- What other maintenance and troubleshooting tools are available in Windows XP?
- What help and support tools are available in Windows XP and online to help you learn more about a feature or problem?

Using Consoles in Windows XP

When Windows XP combines several administrative tools in a single window, the window is called a **console**. Each individual tool within the console is called a **snap-in**. The Disk Defragmenter, Disk Management, System Information, and Computer Management tools used in earlier chapters all are examples of a console. Other consoles and snap-ins, such as Event Viewer, Local Users and Groups, and Group Policy, will be discussed later in this chapter.

Computer Management

Computer Management is a console that consolidates several Windows XP administrative tools for managing the local computer or other computers on the network. To use most of these tools, you must be logged on as an administrator, although you can view certain settings and configurations in Computer Management if you are logged on with lesser privileges.

You can access the Computer Management console in one of two ways:

- Click the Start button and then click Control Panel on the Start menu. With the Control Panel in Classic View, double-click Administrative Tools and then double-click Computer Management in the Administrative Tools window. With the Control Panel in Category View, click Performance and Maintenance, click Administrative Tools, and then double-click Computer Management.
- Click the Start button and then right-click My Computer on the Start menu. Click Manage on the shortcut menu.

The Computer Management window (Figure 9-1) allows you to perform such tasks as monitoring problems with hardware, software, and security. You can share folders, view device configurations, add new device drivers, start and stop services, and manage server applications.

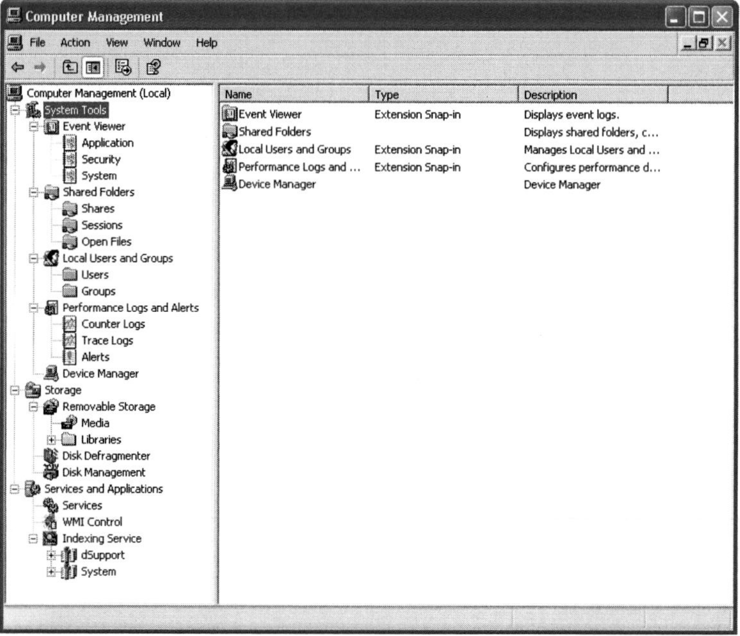

Figure 9-1 Windows XP Computer Management console combines several administrative tools in a single window.

> **FAQ 9-1**
>
> **Can I add a shortcut to Computer Management so I can access it without accessing Control Panel?**
>
> Yes. By default, Administrative Tools is located in the Control Panel. You also can have Administrative Tools appear as a shortcut on the desktop, however. To do so, click the Start button and then click Control Panel on the Start menu. When the Control Panel window is displayed, right-click Administrative Tools and then click Create Shortcut on the shortcut menu. When the Shortcut dialog box is displayed, click Yes to place a shortcut to Administrative Tools on the desktop.

Microsoft Management Console (MMC)

Windows XP offers a way for you to create your own customized consoles using the **Microsoft Management Console** (**MMC**) utility. As with the Computer Management console, you must have administrative privileges to perform most tasks from the MMC. You can use MMC to create your own custom consoles, by adding any of the snap-ins listed in Figure 9-2.

Snap-in	Description
Active X Control	Enables you to add Active X controls to your system
Certificates	Provides certificate management at the user, service, or computer level
Component Services	Links to the Component Services management tool, which is located on the Control Panel
Computer Management	Links to the Computer Management tools on the Control Panel
Device Manager	Lets you see what hardware devices you have on your system and configure device properties
Disk Defragmenter	Links to the Disk Defragmenter utility
Disk Management	Links to the Disk Management tool
Event Viewer	Links to the Event Viewer tool, which displays event logs for the system
Fax Service Management	Enables you to manage fax settings and devices
Folder	Enables you to add a folder to manage from MMC
Group Policy	Provides a tool to manage group policy settings
Indexing Service	Searches files and folders using specified parameters
IP Security Policy Management	Manages Internet communication security
Link to Web Address	Enables you to link to a specified Web site
Local Users and Groups	Provides a tool to manage settings for local users and groups
Performance Logs and Alerts	Gives you an interface from which to set up and manage logs of performance information and alerts about system performance
Removable Storage Management	Enables you to manage settings and configuration information for removable storage devices such as Zip drives and tape backup drives
Security Configuration and Analysis	Enables you to manage configuration of security settings for computers that use security template files
Services	Provides a centralized interface for starting, stopping, and configuring system services
Shared Folders	Provides information about shared folders, open files, and current sessions
System Information	Contains information about the system that you can use when troubleshooting

Figure 9-2 Some MMC snap-ins that can be added to a custom console.

Perform the following steps to open MMC and create a console that contains several snap-ins:

1. Click Start and then click Run on the Start menu. When the Run window is displayed, enter `MMC` in the Open text box and then click the OK button. An empty console window appears.
2. Click File on the menu bar and then click Add/Remove Snap-in on the File menu. The Add/Remove Snap-in window is displayed as an empty window, because no snap-ins have been added to the console.
3. Click the Add button to view a list of snap-ins that can be added to the console (Figure 9-3). Select a snap-in and then click the Add button.
4. Windows XP opens a window that allows you to set the parameters for the snap-in (the options available in the window differ, depending on the snap-in being added). When you have made your selections, click Finish. The new snap-in appears in the Add/Remove Snap-in window.
5. Repeat Steps 3 and 4 to add other snap-ins to the console. When you finish, click the Close button in the Add Standalone Snap-in window. Click OK in the Add/Remove Snap-in window and the console is created, with the snap-ins added (Figure 9-4).

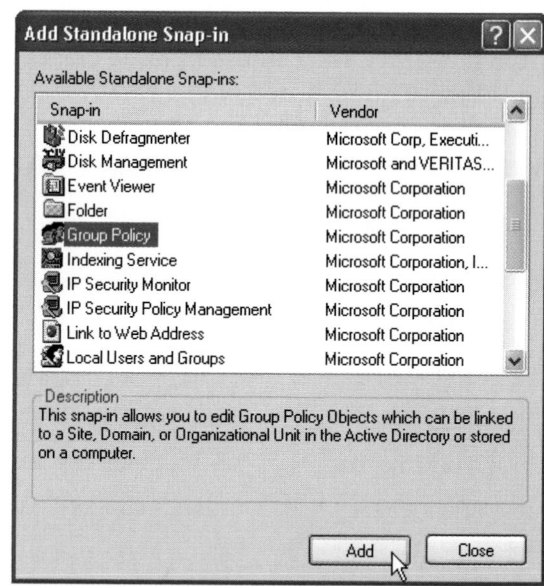

Figure 9-3 The Add Standalone Snap-in window allows you to select snap-ins to add to a custom console.

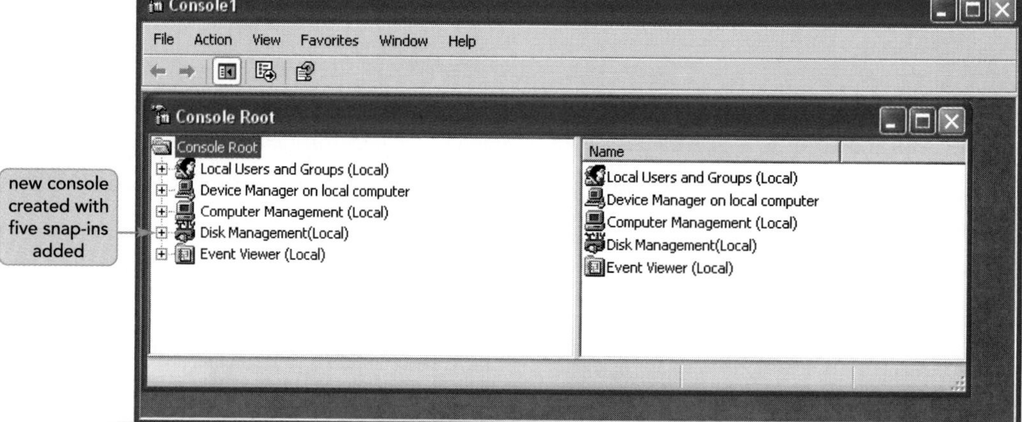

Figure 9-4 After (a) adding the snap-ins to the console in the Add/Remove Snap-in window, click the OK button to (b) create the new console with those snap-ins added.

You also can save a customized console in a Microsoft Management Console file with an .msc file extension. The default file location for the console file set is C:\Documents and Settings*username*\Start Menu\Programs\Administrative Tools folder. Saving the console file in this location ensures that the console appears as an option under Administrative Tools on the Start menu. To save the console:

1. Click File on the menu bar and then click Save As. The Save As dialog box is displayed, with the default file location and file name.
2. Change the file name from the default file name and then click the Save button. The new console is saved. Click the Close button to close the console window.

To use the console, click the Start button, point to All Programs on the Start menu, point to Administrative Tools on the All Programs submenu, and then select the console from the Administrative Tools menu (Figure 9-5).

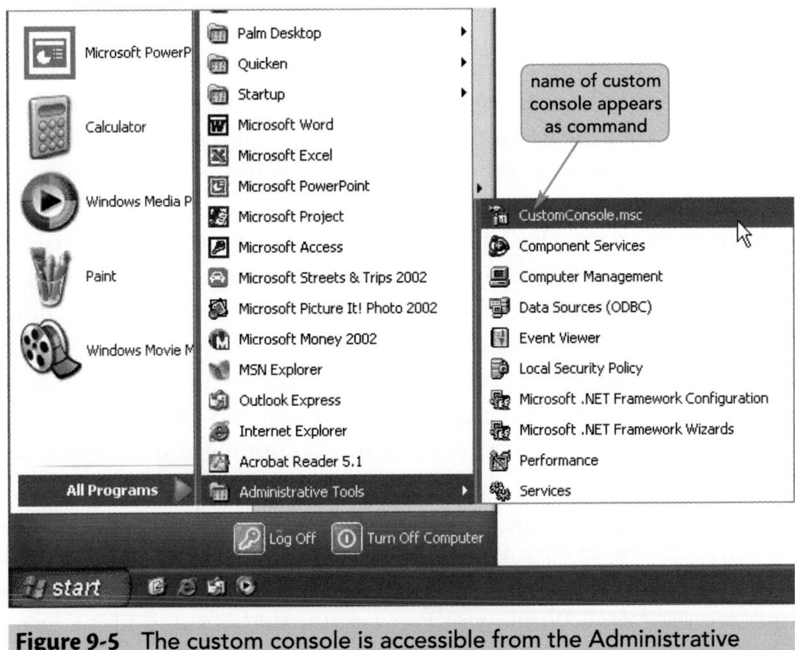

Figure 9-5 The custom console is accessible from the Administrative Tools submenu.

FAQ 9-2

Can I create a shortcut to my custom console?

Yes. Once the console is saved as a file, you can place a shortcut to the .msc file on the desktop. Creating a shortcut to the console is just like creating a shortcut to any other file.

Security Using Windows XP

Consoles, such as the Computer Management console, provide access to various security settings available in Windows XP. Security under Windows XP is much improved over previous versions of Windows and has two goals: to secure the system resources,

More About

Consoles and Snap-Ins

To learn more about consoles and snap-ins that you can add to consoles, visit the Understanding and Troubleshooting Your PC More About Web page (**scsite.com/understanding/more**) and then click Consoles and Snap-Ins below Chapter 9.

including hardware and software, from improper use; and to secure users' data from improper access. In this section you will learn about some security features of Windows XP Professional. Although the discussion is focused on Windows XP Professional, Windows Server 2003 and Windows 2000 Professional provide similar security features.

User Accounts and Profiles

At the heart of Windows XP security is the concept of user accounts. As you learned in Chapter 8, a user account defines a user to Windows and records information about the user including the user name, password, groups that the account belongs to, and the rights and permissions assigned to the account. Permissions assigned to a user account control what the user can and cannot do and access in Windows.

The way in which user accounts are set up depends on whether the computer is a stand-alone workstation (that is, not connected to a network), belongs to a workgroup, or belongs to a domain. User accounts fall into two groups: local user accounts or domain user accounts. A **local user account** enables users to log on to a single, specific computer, so that the account has access to resources on that computer. Information on a local user account physically resides in the SAM (Security Accounts Manager) database on that computer.

A **domain user account**, also called a **global user account**, allows users to log on to a computer, just like a local user account, except that the account is recognized by all of the computers in the domain. A domain user account is used at the domain level, created by an administrator, and stored in the SAM (security accounts manager) database on a domain controller. This is convenient for both users and administrators, as the user only has to remember one login and password, and administrators can grant permission to the resources (files, printers) of any computer in the domain to the domain user account.

This chapter focuses on using Windows XP Professional to set up security for stand-alone workstations and for workstations in a workgroup, rather than addressing how to manage user accounts at the domain level. Several different types of local user accounts are used on a Windows XP computer that is stand-alone or part of a workgroup:

- *Built-in user accounts.* As described in Chapter 8, every Windows XP workstation has two built-in user accounts that are set up when the OS is first installed: an administrator account and a guest account. An *administrator* has rights and permissions to all computer software, data, and hardware resources. Under Windows XP, the administrator can create other user accounts and assign corresponding rights and permissions to individual accounts, to groups of selected accounts, or to all accounts that use the computer. A *guest account* has very limited privileges and provides access to a computer for someone who does not have a user account. The guest account is useful in a business environment where many people use a single computer for limited purposes and it is not practical for all of them to have unique user accounts.
- *Limited account.* A *limited account* is created on a local computer and allows a user to complete only limited functions, such as modifying the account password or changing the account picture. A limited account cannot

change most settings or delete important files. On a stand-alone computer, a limited account is set up by the administrator for each person that uses the computer. A limited account is designed for a person who uses a single stand-alone computer or a computer connected to a peer-to-peer network or workgroup.

In a workgroup, each computer manages the security for its own resources. Each local user account is set up on the local computer independent of other accounts on other PCs, and there is no centralized control of resources.

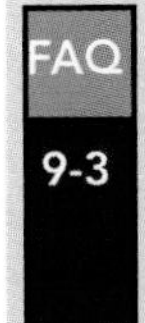

How do you know what type of user account to set up for a user?

As a general rule, a user account should have no more rights than a user needs to do his or her job. For example, an administrator responsible for setting up and maintaining user accounts in an office workgroup can set the permissions on a limited account to deny a user the right to install a printer, install software, or do any other tasks that change the PC software or hardware environment.

Each user account on a computer or network is associated with a user profile. A **user profile** stores customized desktop settings, application settings, network and printer connections settings, and more. When the user changes settings to customize his or her computer and then logs off, the user profile is updated so that settings can be restored the next time the user logs on.

The first time you log on to a computer, the system creates a **local user profile**, which is stored on the computer's hard disk. Any changes made to your local user profile are specific to the computer on which the changes are made.

If the computer is networked to other computers in a Windows workgroup, then the administrator may create a roaming user profile. A **roaming user profile** is created by your system administrator and stored on a server on the network, so the profile is available every time you log on to any computer on the network. Without a roaming user profile, you would have to reestablish the user profile at each computer, recreating desktop settings and application settings for each computer, each time you logged on to a computer in a workgroup. With roaming user profiles, any changes made to your profile are updated on the server. When you log on to another computer in the workgroup using your user account, the computer accesses the roaming profile from the network so you do not have to recreate settings at each computer.

A **mandatory user profile** is a roaming user profile that can be used to specify particular settings for individuals or an entire group of users. When defined for a group, a mandatory user profile often is called a **group profile**. Mandatory user profiles often are used in situations where a group of users only need to perform specific job-related tasks. Individual users cannot change a mandatory user profile; only system administrators can make changes to mandatory user profiles.

To view all profiles stored on a Windows XP computer, perform the following steps:

1. Click the Start button, right-click My Computer on the Start menu, and then click Properties on the shortcut menu.
2. When the System Properties window is displayed, click the Advanced tab. Click the Settings button in the User Profiles area (Figure 9-6).

The User Profiles window appears, showing all users with profiles on the system. A user who has an account but never has logged on to the system will not have a user profile.

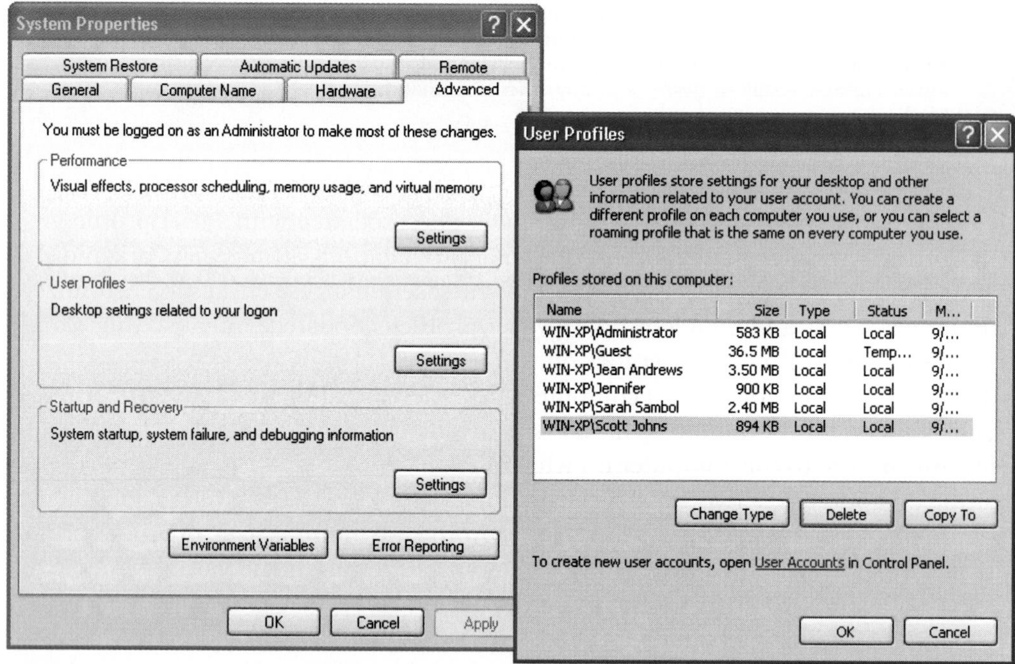

Figure 9-6 All user profiles stored on a computer are listed in the User Profiles window.

ADMINISTERING LOCAL USER ACCOUNTS An administrator can create and administer local user accounts using the Computer Management console or the User Accounts window, both of which are accessible from the Control Panel. If the account is created using the Computer Management console, it will be set up as a limited account. If it is created using the User Accounts window, it will be set up as an administrator account.

To create a limited account using the Computer Management console, follow these steps using Windows XP Professional:

1. Log on to the computer using an account set up as an administrator.
2. Click the Start button, right-click My Computer on the Start menu, and then click Manage on the shortcut menu.
3. When the Computer Management window is displayed, click the expand (+) symbols to view all items under Local Users and Groups.

4. Right-click the Users folder and then click New User on the shortcut menu. When the New User window is displayed (Figure 9-7), enter the User name, enter the password twice, and check the boxes to define how and when the password can be changed. You also can enter values for the Full name and Description to help identify the user.

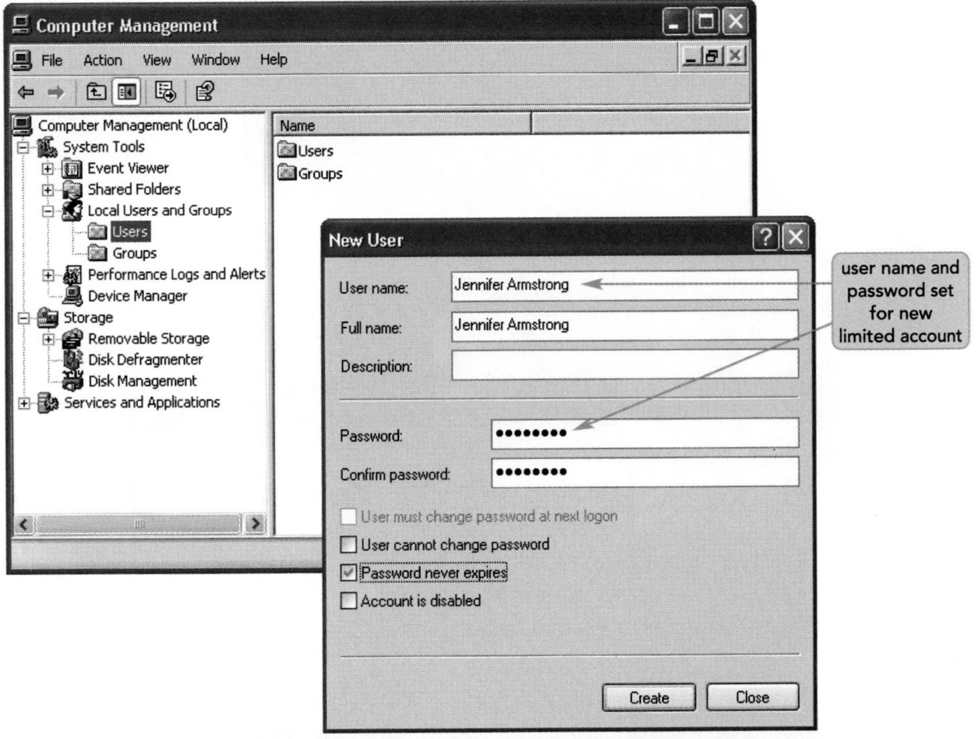

Figure 9-7 You can create a user account using Computer Management or the User Account window accessible via the Control Panel.

5. When you have finished, click the Create button and then click the Close button. Windows creates the new account as a limited account, which means the account cannot create, delete, or change other accounts; make system-wide changes; or install software.
6. If you want to give the account Administrator privileges, click the Start button and then click Control Panel on the Start menu.
7. Click User Accounts in the Control Panel window. The User Accounts window opens, listing all accounts (Figure 9-8a on the next page). To make changes to an account, click the account you want to change.
8. In the next window, you can choose to change the name of the account, change the password, remove a password, change the picture icon associated with the account, change the account type, or delete the account (Figure 9-8b on the next page). Click Change the account type.

9. In the next window, select Computer administrator and then click the Change Account Type button (Figure 9-8c). Click the Back button on the menu bar to return to the main User Accounts screen. Click the Close button to close the User Accounts window.

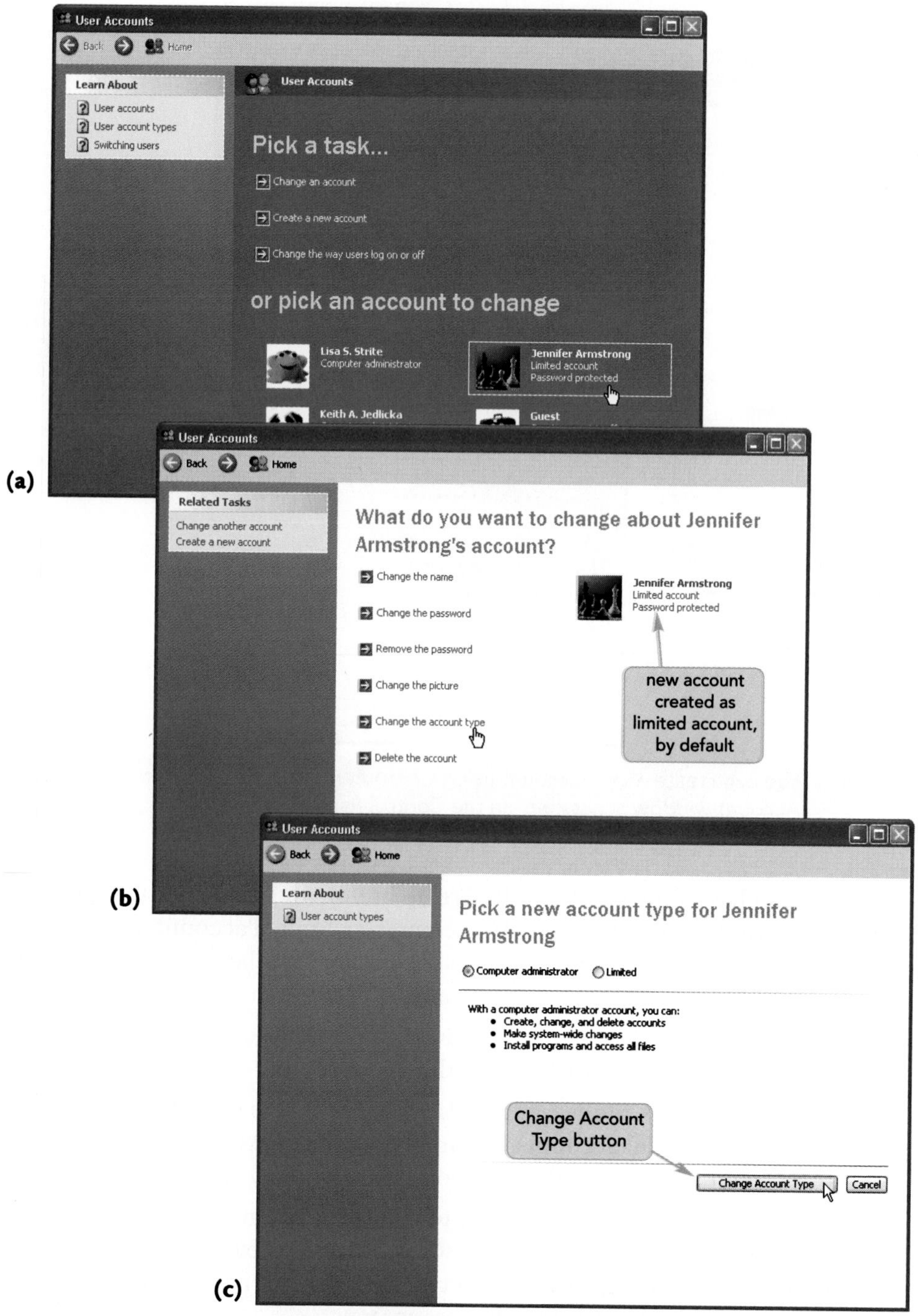

Figure 9-8 After creating a user account, you can modify the settings associated with that account using the User Accounts window.

FAQ 9-4

My Computer Management console does not have a Local Users and Groups folder. Why not?

If you are running Windows XP Home Edition, you will not have a Local Users and Groups folder. As discussed in Chapter 8, Windows XP Home Edition may not include all of the administrative and security features of Windows XP Professional, such as EFS, Remote Desktop, and advanced networking for multiple PC environments. The Local Users and Groups tool is available in Windows XP Professional, Windows 2000 Professional, and Windows Server 2003 and can be accessed via the Computer Management console or added as a snap-in to a custom console.

User accounts can be set up with or without passwords, although passwords provide greater security. Where security is a concern, you always should set a password for any administrator accounts. When defining user names and passwords, you should follow a few guidelines for administrators and other types of accounts:

- A user name cannot be identical to any other user or group name on the computer. It can contain up to 20 uppercase or lowercase characters except for the following: " / \ [ ] : ; | = , + * ? < >
- A user name cannot consist solely of periods (.) or spaces.
- Passwords can be up to 127 characters.
- A password should not be easy to guess, such as one consisting of real words, your telephone number, or the name of your pet.
- The most secure type of password is a combination of letters, numbers, and even non-alphanumeric characters.

Given all the possible ways another user can obtain your password, you should select a password carefully and try to create one that no one can guess. Longer passwords provide greater security than shorter ones; the password should include letters and numbers and, if possible, be at least eight characters long. Figure 9-9 offers some tips on how to choose a good, secure password. Initially, passwords can be set by the administrator, but users generally should be allowed to change their own passwords so they are less likely to forget them.

Do	Do Not
• Make the password at least eight characters long • Use uppercase and lowercase letters throughout the password (for example, CoFFeeKup2) • Use numbers and punctuation in the password at random locations (for example, Co3FfEKup) • Choose a password you can type quickly • Change your password every few months • Keep your password private; do not share it with anyone • Memorize your password so you do not have to write it down	• Use any word in the dictionary • Use two short words together (fluffycat) or separated by a symbol or numbers (surf_wave) • Use any proper name, such as the name of a geographical location or famous person • Use a sequence of letters or numbers from the keyboard (for example, CVBNM or 56789) • Use personal information in your password, such as your last name, pet's name, birthday, or words related to hobbies you enjoy • Post your password near your computer

Figure 9-9 Tips for choosing a good, secure password.

Sometimes a user forgets his or her password or the password is compromised. If this happens and you have administrator privileges, you can access the account through the Control Panel or the Computer Management window to set a new password for that user account. Another approach is to create a **forgotten password disk** (also called a *password reset disk*) for each user, in the event a user forgets his or her password. To create the disk, open the Control Panel window and then click user accounts. Click the account for which to create a forgotten password disk and then click Prevent a forgotten password under Related Tasks in the left pane of this window. Follow the wizard to create the disk. If a user enters a wrong password at logon, he or she has the opportunity to use the forgotten password floppy disk to log on. The forgotten password floppy disk should be kept in a protected place so others cannot use it to gain unauthorized access to the computer.

FAQ 9-5

What should I do if I do not know the password for any user accounts — and have not created a forgotten password disk?

If you have forgotten the password for all user accounts on a computer and have not created a password reset disk, Windows will not allow you to log on (nor will Windows allow you to start Windows in Safe Mode or use the Recovery Console). You will have to perform a clean install of Windows XP, set up all of the user accounts again, and reinstall all of your programs. Given the amount of work required to resolve the problem, making a forgotten password disk is a simple step that can help you avoid the time-consuming steps outlined above.

CONTROLLING HOW A USER LOGS ON With Windows XP Professional, you can define settings to determine how a user logs on to the computer. For a stand alone computer or a computer connected to a workgroup, you can change the way users log on to the computer to use a Welcome screen, Fast User Switching, or a Log On to Windows window by changing these options in the User Accounts window:

- *Welcome screen.* The default option is a Welcome screen that appears when the computer is first booted or comes out of a sleep state. All users are listed on the Welcome screen along with a picture. To log on to the computer, a user clicks his or her user name and enters the password if a password has been set. The Welcome screen is not an available option if your computer is connected to a domain.
- *Fast User Switching.* Fast User Switching makes it possible to switch quickly between users without actually logging one user off the computer and then logging the second user on. Instead, multiple users can share a computer, switching back and forth between users without closing the programs they are running. If Fast User Switching is enabled, when a user clicks the Log Off button on the Start menu, the Log Off Windows dialog box includes a Switch User button. Clicking the Switch User button returns the user to the Welcome screen, where a user can click another user name and log on using that account. When Fast User Switching is disabled, the Switch User option does not appear.

FAQ 9-6

In what situations would I want to disable Fast User Switching?

Fast User Switching definitely saves the time required to log users on and off. You may want to disable Fast User Switching when you want to conserve resources, however, because performance is poor when several users leave applications open. Also keep in mind that the Fast User Switching feature of Windows XP is available only for stand-alone computers or computers in a workgroup (it is not available for computers that are part of a domain).

 Your Turn

Changing How Users Log On

Using Windows XP, perform the following steps to change the way users log on to a computer:

1. Click the Start button and then click Control Panel in the Start menu.
2. Double-click User Accounts and then click Change the way users log on or off. Click Use the Welcome screen and Use Fast User Switching to select them (Figure 9-10). Click the Apply Options button.

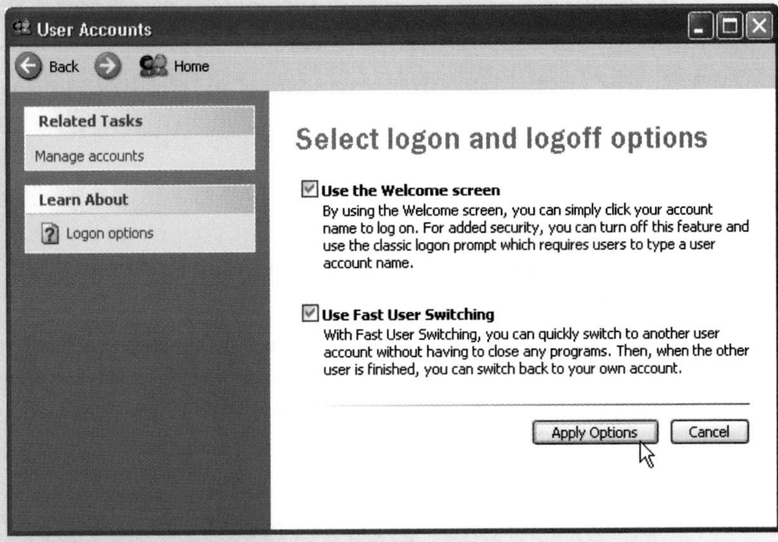

Figure 9-10 The User Accounts window allows you to change logon and logoff options.

3. Click the Start button and then click Log Off on the Start menu. Note that three buttons (Switch User, Log Off, and Cancel) display in the Log Off Windows window. Click the Switch User button. When the Welcome screen displays, click your user name to log on to the computer again.
4. Click the User Accounts taskbar button to return to the User Accounts window and then click Change the way users log on or off.
5. Click Use Fast User Switching to deselect it. Click the Apply Options button.
6. Click the Start button and then click the Log Off button on the Start menu. Note that only two buttons (Log Off and Cancel) display on the Log Off Windows window. Click the Cancel button.
7. Click the User Accounts taskbar button to return to the User Accounts window and then click Change the way users log on or off. Click Use the Welcome Screen to deselect it (note that Use Fast User Switching no longer is available as an option). Click the Apply Options button. Click the Close button to close the User Accounts window and then click the Close button to close the Control Panel window.
8. Click the Start button and then click the Log Off button. When Log Off Windows is displayed, click the Log Off button. Windows XP logs you out of the system and then displays the Log On to Windows window. Enter your user name and password, if needed, and then click the OK button.
9. After you are logged on to Windows XP, click the Start button and then click Control Panel in the Start menu. Double-click User Accounts and then click Change the way users log on or off.
10. Change settings so the logon process is set back to its original settings.

User Groups

User groups are an efficient way for an administrator to manage multiple user accounts that require the same privileges and similar profiles. Each group has a specific set of security settings that define what the user can do on a computer system or a network. When installed, Windows XP Professional sets up several user groups including:

- **Administrators**, a group of users who have access to all parts of the system, can install or uninstall devices and applications, and can perform all administrative tasks.
- **Backup Operators**, a group of users who can back up and restore any files on the system regardless of their access privileges to these files.
- **Power Users**, a group of users who can read from and write to parts of the system other than their own local drive, install applications, and perform limited administrative tasks.
- **Limited Users**, a group of users who have read-write access only on their own folders, read-only access to most system folders, and no access to other users' data. They cannot install applications or carry out any administrative responsibilities.
- **Guests**, a group of users who use a workstation occasionally and have limited access to files and resources. Any account set up as part of the guest user group has permission to shut down a computer.

CREATING A NEW USER GROUP You also can create your own user group and customize the permissions and profiles for this group of users. Perform the following steps to create a new group:

1. Click the Start button, right-click My Computer on the Start menu, and then click Manage on the shortcut menu.
2. When the Computer Management window is displayed, click the expand (+) symbol to view all items under Local Users and Groups.
3. Right-click the Groups folder and then select New Group on the shortcut menu.
4. The New Group window opens, as shown in Figure 9-11. In the New Group window, enter a name and description of the new group and click the Add button to find and select users to add to this group.
5. When you have added all of the users to the group, click Create to finish creating the group.

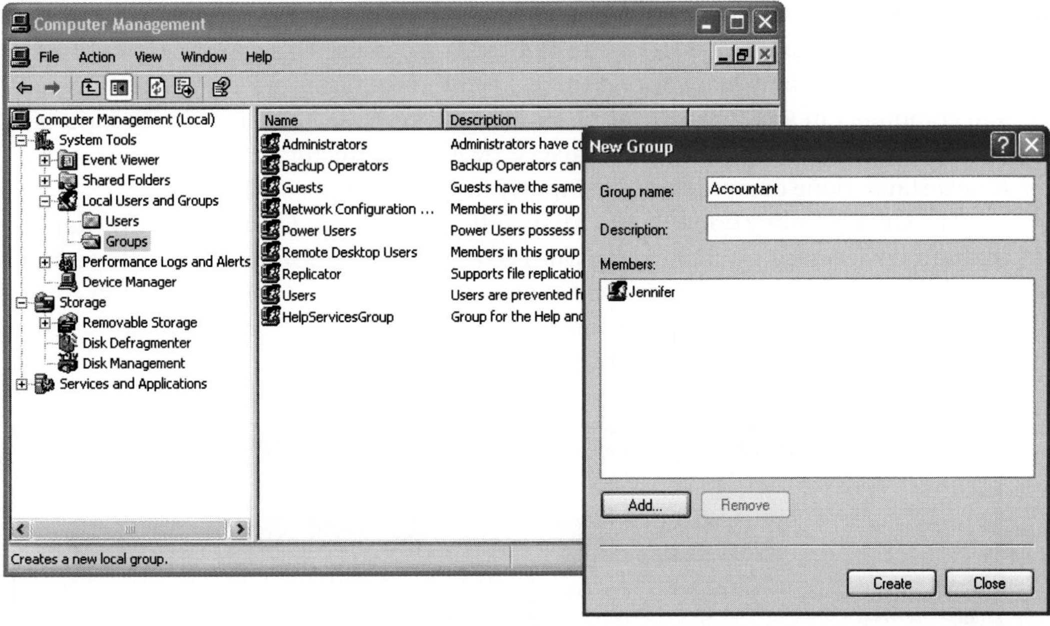

Figure 9-11 Creating a new user group.

You then can change the profile settings assigned to users in a group. For example, to control what a user or a user group can do, open Administrative Tools in the Control Panel. When the Administrative Tools window opens, double-click Local Security Policy. When the Local Security Settings window is displayed (Figure 9-12), click the expand (+) symbols to view all items under Local Policies, and then click the User Rights Assignment group folder. The window displays a list of tasks, each of which can be assigned to one or more user groups to give them the right to do these activities. For example, if you right-click Change the system time and then select Properties on the shortcut menu, the Change the system time Properties window is displayed. From this window, you can add and remove the user groups that have the right to change the system time.

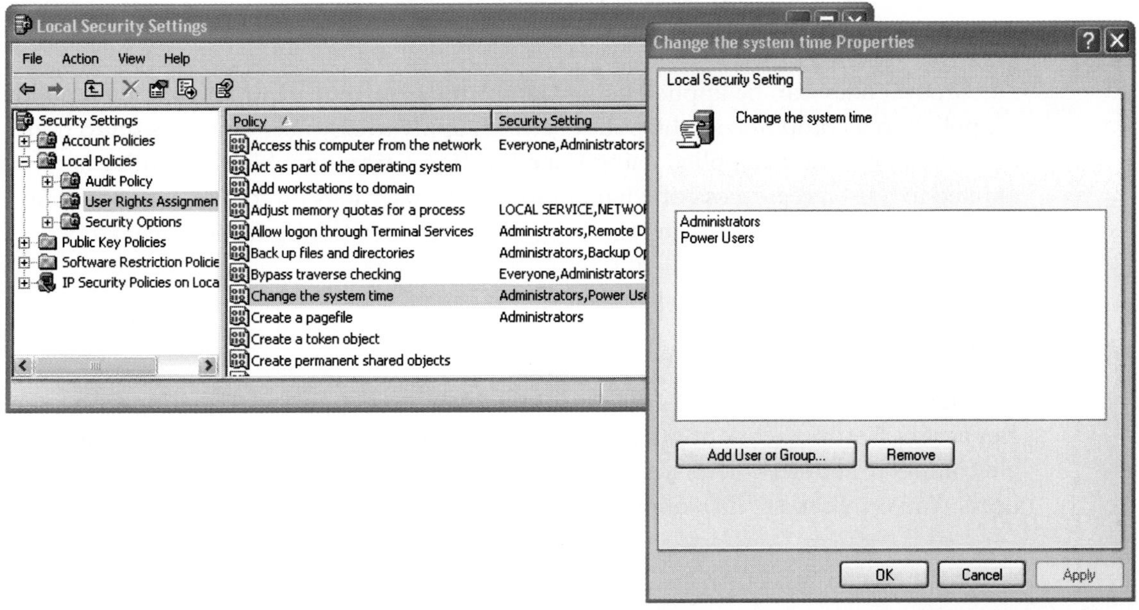

Figure 9-12 Local policies can be assigned to a user group, affecting all users in the group.

More About

User Groups and Group Policies

To learn more about user groups and group policies, visit the Understanding and Troubleshooting Your PC More About Web page (**scsite.com/understanding/more**) and then click User Groups and Group Policies below Chapter 9.

GROUP POLICY Another way to control the tasks a user can perform on a computer is by applying settings called a **Group Policy**. You can use Group Policy to define and control how programs, network resources, and the operating system behave for users and computers in an organization. Group Policy normally is intended to be used on a domain where group policies are managed by Active Directory, although you can use it on a stand-alone computer or a computer in a workgroup.

The **Group Policy console** is a Microsoft Management Console (MMC) snap-in that can be accessed by clicking the Start button, clicking Run on the Start menu, and then typing `gpedit.msc` in the Open text box. From the console you can control such things as how Media Player, Internet Explorer, and NetMeeting work, as well as many Windows settings and components (Figure 9-13).

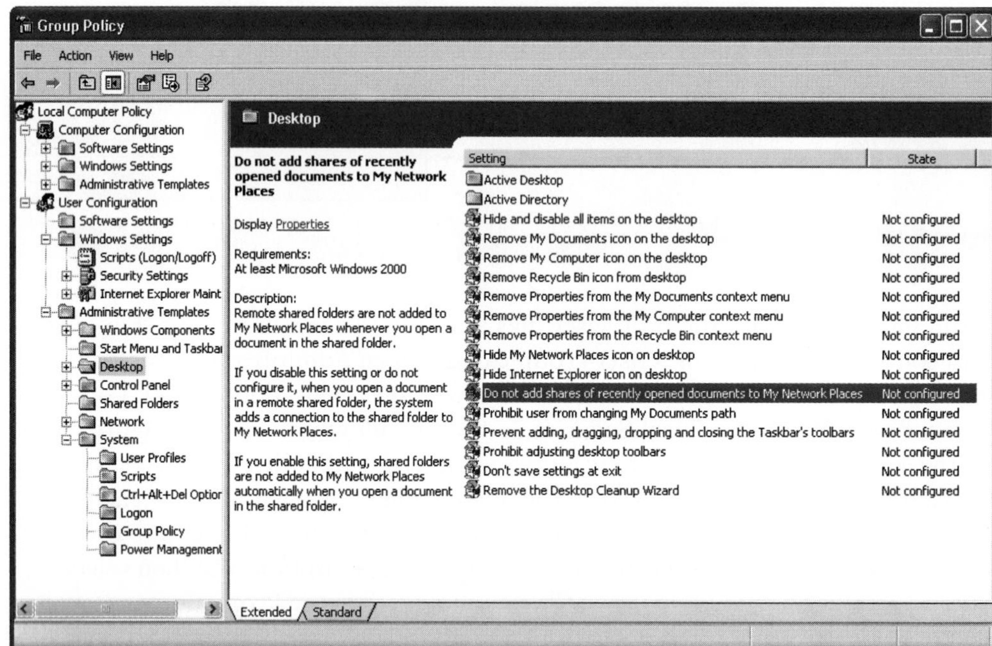

Figure 9-13 From the Group Policy window, you can control Windows settings and components for specific users or computers.

Group Policy can be applied using **Computer Configuration**, in which the policy is applied to a computer, so the policy settings apply to any user who logs on to that computer, or it can be applied using **User Configuration**, in which the policy is applied to a user, regardless of what computer the user logs on to. For a stand-alone computer or a computer in a workgroup, use Computer Configuration instead of User Configuration to implement Group Policy settings.

Disk Quotas

An administrator can set a **disk quota**, which limits how much disk space a user can access. Setting a disk quota is important when two or more users are using a single computer and need to share its storage capacity. The disk quota set applies to all users. You only can set disk quotas if you are using NTFS.

To set a disk quota, you must be logged on to the computer as an administrator. Perform the following steps to set a disk quota.

1. Click the Start button and then click My Computer on the Start menu.
2. Right-click the volume for which you want to set a disk quota and then click Properties on the shortcut menu.
3. Click the Quota tab and then click Enable quota management to select it (Figure 9-14). You use the choices in the Quota tab to enable or disable quotas on a volume, set the amount of space for users, deny disk space to a user who has exceeded the disk space limit, or set a level of disk space used that will trigger a warning message to a user.
4. You then can select the options:
   a. *Do not limit disk usage*, which tracks disk space usage without limiting disk space; or
   b. *Limit disk space to*, which limits disk space to a specific amount and allows you to set a warning level to warn users when they have used that amount of their allotted space.

A disk quota does not specify where a user's files must be located; it only specifies how much total space the user can take up on a volume.

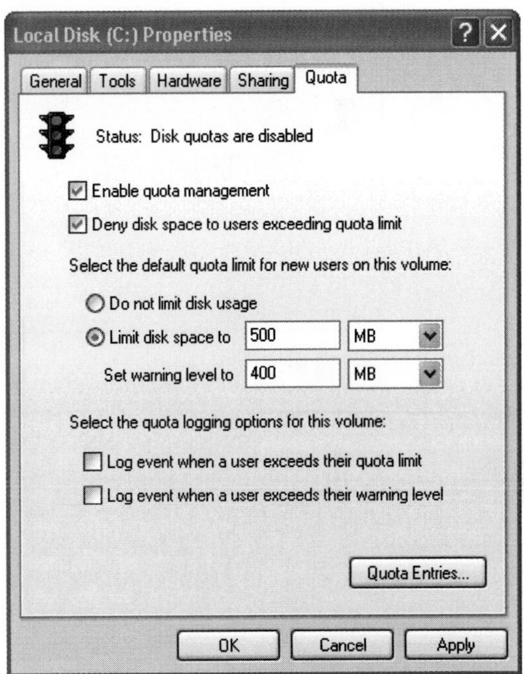

Figure 9-14 Setting disk quotas limits how much disk space a user can access.

EFS (Encrypted File System)

Another Windows XP security feature is the Encrypted File System. **Encrypted File System** (**EFS**) is a technology supported by the file system, NTFS, which allows users to store their data in encrypted format. **Encryption** is the process of putting readable data (plaintext) into code (ciphertext) that must be translated before it can be accessed. The encryption process typically uses a **key** that encrypts the data and also provides a way to decrypt it, or translate it back into readable data. **Decryption** is the process of converting data from encrypted format back to its original format.

In the past, it was possible to bypass an existing operating system's security measures by installing a new operating system or booting from a startup disk. Encrypting sensitive files using EFS prevents such breaches, by protecting encrypted data even when someone who is not authorized to view those files or folders has full access to a computer's data storage. When an unauthorized user attempts to access a file encrypted using EFS, the user receives an Access Denied error message.

From a user's perspective, using EFS simply requires the user to place a file in a folder marked for encryption. Encryption can be implemented at either the folder or file level. If a folder is marked for encryption, every file created in the folder or copied to the folder will be encrypted. At the file level, each file must be encrypted individually. To encrypt a folder:

1. Right-click the folder name in the Windows Explorer, My Computer, or My Documents window and then click Properties on the shortcut menu.

2. When the Properties window is displayed, click the General tab, if necessary, and then click the Advanced button. The Advanced Attributes window appears.
3. Click Encrypt contents to secure data and then click the OK button (Figure 9-15).
4. Click the Apply button in the Properties window. If the Confirm Attribute Changes dialog box displays, select whether to encrypt only the folder or to encrypt all existing files or folders within the selected folder.

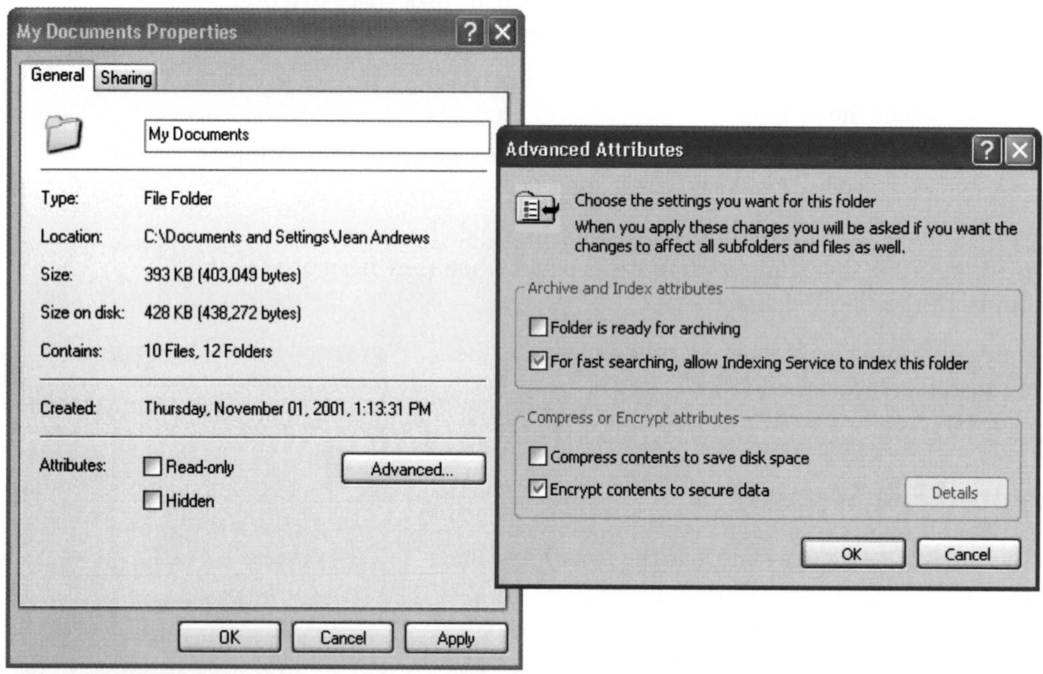

Figure 9-15 Encrypting folder contents helps secure files from unauthorized users.

> **More About**
>
> **Using Cipher**
>
> To learn more about using command-line Cipher utility to decrypt files, visit the Understanding and Troubleshooting Your PC More About Web page (**scsite.com/understanding/more**) and then click Using Cipher below Chapter 9.

Encrypting with EFS at the folder level is encouraged and considered a best practice because it provides greater security. Any file placed in an encrypted folder is automatically encrypted so the user does not have to remember to encrypt it. An encrypted file remains encrypted if you move it from an encrypted folder to an unencrypted folder on the same or another NTFS logical drive.

To decrypt a file or folder to allow others to view it, right-click the file name and then click Properties on the shortcut menu. When the Properties window is displayed, click the General tab, if necessary, and then click the Advanced button. In the Advanced Attributes window, click Encrypt contents to secure data to deselect it and decrypt the file.

Before encrypting a file or folder, remember that encrypting a file always creates a risk that it cannot be read again. For example, a user's profile might be damaged or deleted, meaning that the user no longer has the key needed to decrypt the file. To ensure that a file can be accessed if a user is not available or forgets the password to log on to the system, an administrator for the operating system can decrypt a file. In this case, the administrator is called a data recovery agent (DRA).

> **More About**
>
> **Windows XP Security Features**
>
> To learn more about additional Windows XP security features such as Internet Connection Firewall, visit the Understanding and Troubleshooting Your PC More About Web page (**scsite.com/understanding/more**) and then click Windows XP Security Features below Chapter 9.

The Windows XP Registry

When troubleshooting issues with Windows XP, you may need to edit the Windows XP registry. The **registry** is a hierarchical database containing information about all the hardware, software, device drivers, network protocols, profiles for each user of the computer, and user configuration needed by the OS and applications. Many components depend on this information, and the registry provides a secure and stable location for it. Figure 9-16 lists ways in which some components use the registry. Windows XP continually references the information in the registry during its operation.

Component	Description
Setup programs for devices and applications	Setup programs can record configuration information in the registry and query the registry for information needed to install drivers and applications.
User profiles maintained and used by the OS	Windows maintains a profile for each user that determines the user's environment. User profiles are kept in files, but, when a user logs on, the profile information is written to the registry, where changes are recorded, and then later written back to the user profile file. The OS uses this profile to control user settings and other configuration information specific to this user.
Files active when Ntldr is loading the OS	During the boot process, NTDetect.com surveys present hardware devices and records that information in the registry. Ntldr loads and initializes device drivers using information from the registry, including the order in which to load them.
Device drivers	Device drivers read and write configuration information from and to the registry each time they load. The drivers write hardware configuration information to the registry and read it to determine the proper way to load.
Hardware profiles	Windows can maintain more than one set of hardware configuration information (called a hardware profile) for one PC. The data is kept in the registry. An example of a computer that has more than one hardware profile is a notebook that has a docking station. Two hardware profiles describe the notebook, one docked and the other undocked. This information is kept in the registry.
Application programs	Many application programs read the registry for information about the location of files and various other parameters.

Figure 9-16 Components that use the Windows XP registry.

The next section looks at how the registry is organized, how to view the contents of the registry, and how to back up and edit the registry.

How the Registry Is Organized

When studying how the registry is organized, keep in mind that there are two ways to look at this organization: logical and physical.

LOGICAL ORGANIZATION OF THE REGISTRY Logically, the organization of the registry looks like an upside-down tree with five branches, called **keys** or **subtrees**, which are categories of information stored in the registry (Figure 9-17). Each key is made up of several **subkeys** that also may have subkeys. Subkeys hold, or contain, values. Each **value** has a name and data assigned to it. Data in the registry is always stored in a value, the lowest level of the tree.

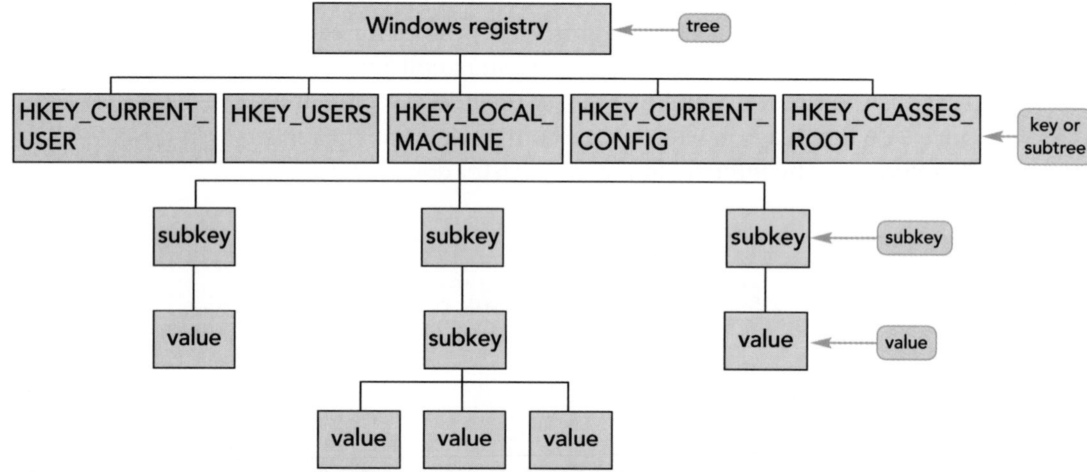

Figure 9-17 The Windows XP registry is organized logically in an upside-down tree structure of keys, subkeys, and values.

The five keys in the registry are listed in Figure 9-18, along with their primary functions. The most important key in the registry is the HKEY_LOCAL_MACHINE key, which contains all configuration data about the computer, including information about device drivers and devices used at startup.

Key (Subtree)	Primary Function
HKEY_CURRENT_USER	Contains information about the currently logged-on user.
HKEY_USERS	Contains information used to build the logon screen and the ID of the currently logged-on user.
HKEY_LOCAL_MACHINE	Contains all configuration data about the computer, including information about device drivers and devices used at startup. The information in this key does not change when different users log on.
HKEY_CURRENT_CONFIG	Contains information about the active hardware configuration, which is extracted from the data stored in the HKEY_LOCAL_ MACHINE subkeys called SOFTWARE and SYSTEM.
HKEY_CLASSES_ROOT	Contains information about software and the way software is configured. This key points to data stored in HKEY_LOCAL_MACHINE.

Figure 9-18 The five main keys, or subtrees, of the Windows XP registry.

PHYSICAL ORGANIZATION OF THE REGISTRY The physical organization of the registry is different from the logical organization. Physically, the registry is stored in five files called **hives**. In a physical sense, each hive is a file. The registry hives are stored in the \%SystemRoot%\system32\config folder as a group of files. Each hive is backed up with a log file and a backup file, which also are stored in the \%SystemRoot%\system32\config folder.

Although there are five keys and five hives, a one-to-one relationship between keys and files does not exist. Figure 9-19 shows the way the keys are stored in hives.

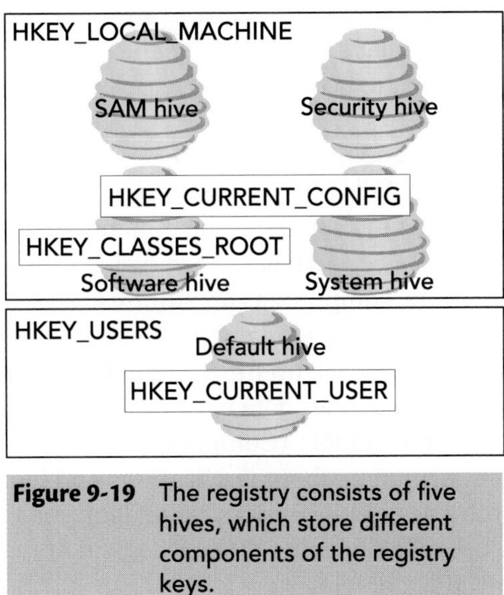

Figure 9-19 The registry consists of five hives, which store different components of the registry keys.

- HKEY_LOCAL_MACHINE data is stored in four hives: the SAM hive, the Security hive, the Software hive, and the System hive.
- HKEY_CURRENT_CONFIG data is kept in portions of two hives: the Software hive and the System hive.
- HKEY_CLASSES_ROOT data is kept in a portion of the Software hive.
- HKEY_USERS data is kept in the Default hive.
- HKEY_CURRENT_USER data is kept in a portion of the Default hive.

As shown in Figure 9-19, some keys use data contained in other subtrees. For instance, the HKEY_CURRENT_USER data is a subset of the data in the HKEY_USERS subtree. HKEY_CURRENT_CONFIG and HKEY_CLASSES_ROOT subtrees use data contained in the HKEY_LOCAL_MACHINE keys. Do not, however, let this physical relationship cloud your view of the logical relationship among these keys. Although data is shared among the different keys, when considered logically, none of the five keys is subordinate to any other.

Backing Up and Editing the Registry

When you make a change in the Control Panel, Device Manager, or many other places in Windows XP, Windows XP automatically modifies the registry. On rare occasions, however, you might need to edit the registry manually — for example, when you are following the directions of Microsoft technical support staff to delete references in the registry to viruses or worms.

Incorrectly editing the registry may severely damage your system. Because changes to the registry take effect immediately and are permanent, new users should not make changes to the registry without help from a more experienced user. Before you edit the registry, you should back it up so you can restore it if something goes wrong. Backing up the system state is one way to back up the registry.

BACKING UP THE REGISTRY The Backup tool in Windows XP helps you protect your data in case your hard disk fails or files are erased accidentally. By using Backup, you can create a duplicate copy of all the data on your hard disk and then archive it on another storage device, such as a hard disk or a tape.

You must be logged on to the computer as an administrator to back up files and folders. In order to back up the registry, along with the other data and files on the computer, you must select the option to back up the System State data during the backup process. The **System State data** includes data such as the registry, all files necessary to boot the operating system, and the COM+ (Component Object Model) Registration database, which contains information about applications and includes files in the Windows folders. When you back up the System State data, you cannot select which files you want to back up because Windows XP backs up all of them. To back up the System State data, perform the following steps:

1. Click the Start button, point to All Programs, point to Accessories, point to System Tools, and then click Backup.
2. If the backup process starts by launching the Backup or Restore Wizard window, click Advanced mode.
3. When the Backup Utility window opens, click the Backup tab.
4. Click System State to select it.
5. Click System State in the list of items you can back up to insert a check mark in its check box.
6. Select the destination for the backup. You can back up to any media, including a folder on the hard drive, Zip drive, tape drive, or network drive. Click the Start Backup button to begin the process.
7. A Backup Progress dialog box appears and the backup starts. When the backup is complete, click the Close button.

Later, if you have problems with a corrupted Windows XP installation, you can click the Restore and Manage Media tab in the Backup window to restore the system to its state at the last backup.

When the system state is backed up, the Backup utility puts a copy of the registry files in the \%SystemRoot%\repair folder. If you later have a corrupted registry, you can copy files from this folder to the folder where the registry resides, which is \%SystemRoot%\system32\Config.

EDITING THE REGISTRY Figure 9-20 shows the **Registry Editor**, a tool for viewing and changing settings in your system registry. Registry Editor has a look and feel similar to Windows Explorer. When you first open the Registry Editor, the five keys display in the left pane. Each key can have several subkeys. For example, as shown in the figure, the HKEY_CURRENT_USER key has been opened to show subkeys under it. If you click a subkey that has a value assigned to it, that value appears on the right side of the window.

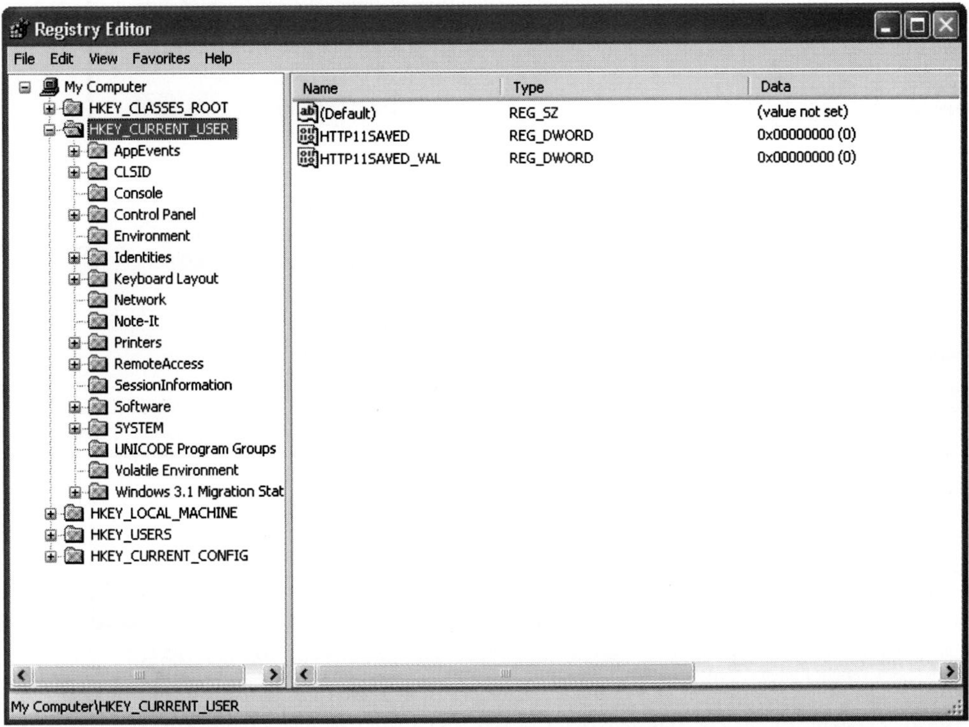

Figure 9-20 Registry Editor shows the five high-level keys in the Windows XP registry.

The executable file for the Registry Editor, regedit.exe, is located in the \%SystemRoot% folder. The following example outlines the steps to open the Registry Editor, view the registry, look at registry values, and then change the name of the Recycle Bin on the Windows XP desktop for the currently logged on user.

1. Click the Start button and then click Run on the Start menu. Type `Regedit` in the Open text box and then click the OK button.
2. When the Registry Editor window is displayed, locate the subkey, `HKEY_CURRENT_USER\Software\Microsoft\Windows\CurrentVersion\Explorer\CLSID\645FF040-5081-101B-9F08-00AA002F954E` which is the name of the Recycle Bin on the Windows desktop. To navigate to the subkey, double-click the folder icon of each subkey, moving down through the tree to the lowest subkey value. As you move down the tree, if the currently selected subkey has a value, that value appears in the right pane of the window.

3. When you click the subkey, the right pane shows (value not set) listed under Data, which indicates the default value (Recycle Bin) is used (Figure 9-21). Position the window on the screen so you can see the Recycle Bin icon.

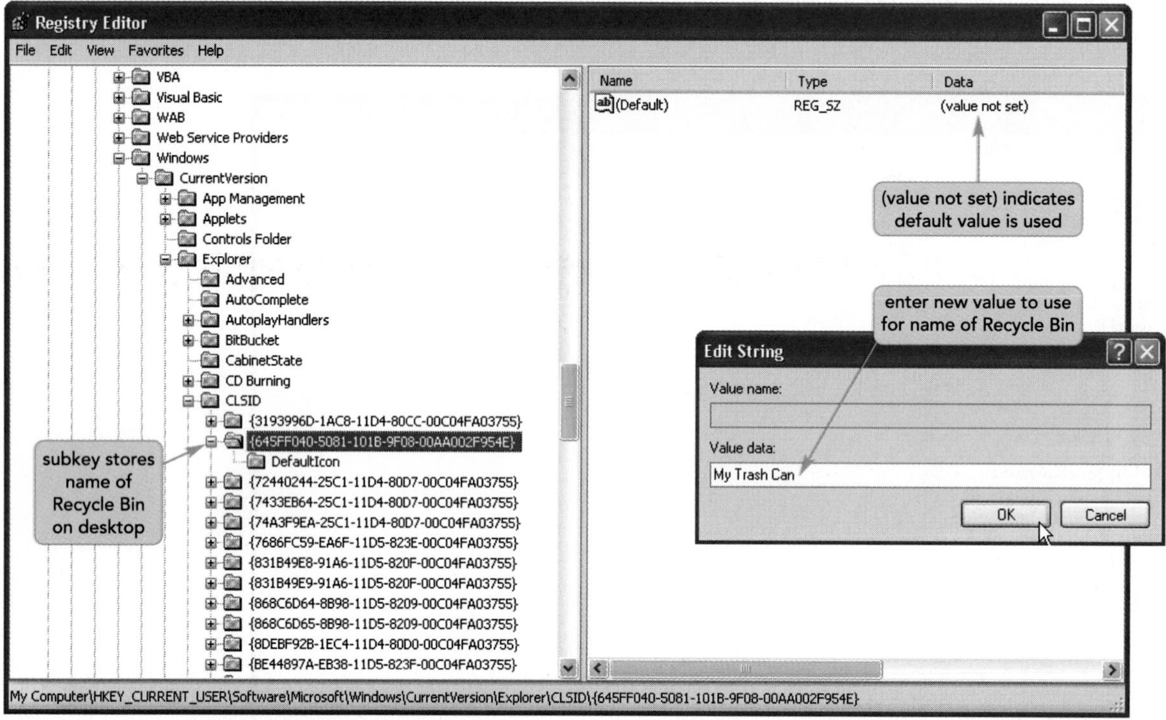

Figure 9-21 Registry Editor allows you to edit subkey values, including the name of the Recycle Bin on the desktop.

4. Double-click the name of the value in the right pane. The Edit String dialog box appears. The Value data should be empty in the dialog box. If a value is present, you may have selected the wrong subkey in the left pane.
5. Enter a new name for the Recycle Bin, such as My Trash Can. Click the OK button.
6. To see your change, minimize the Registry Editor window, right-click the desktop, and click Refresh on the shortcut menu. The name of the Recycle Bin changes.
7. To restore the name to the default value, click the Registry Editor button on the taskbar and then again double-click the name of the value in the right pane. The Edit String dialog box appears. Delete your entry and click the OK button. Close the Registry Editor window.
8. To verify that the change has been made, right-click the desktop and select Refresh on the shortcut menu. The Recycle Bin name should return to its default value.

As illustrated in these steps, changes made to the registry take effect immediately, so you should take great care when editing the registry. If you make a mistake and do not know how to correct a problem you create, you then can restore the system state to restore the registry.

Quiz Yourself 9-1

To test your knowledge of Windows XP consoles, security features, and the registry, visit the Understanding and Troubleshooting Your PC Quiz Yourself Web page (scsite.com/understanding/quiz). Click Quiz Yourself 1 below Chapter 9.

Troubleshooting the Boot Process

Chapter 2 introduced you to the Windows XP boot process, providing an overview of the steps involved and the files required for a successful boot. If problems arise with the boot process, try the simple things first. Turn off the power and restart the system. Check for loose cables, switches that are not on, stuck keys on the keyboard, a wall outlet switch that has been turned off, and similar easy-to-solve problems. The next step is to determine at what point in the boot process the system fails and then consider what changes have been made to the system since the last successful boot. (For example, new hardware or software has been installed; a power surge or electrical storm; or another user modified system settings.)

If you cannot pinpoint the source of the problem, then you can try using one of the tools Windows XP provides to help solve problems with the boot process, including:

- Advanced Options Menu
- System Restore
- Windows XP Boot Disk
- Recovery Console
- Automated System Recovery
- Reinstall Windows XP using the Windows XP CD

These tools are listed in the order you should try them, as each tool is more powerful than the one before it and affects more of the system, installed hardware and software, and user data. The following sections review these tools in detail.

Advanced Options Menu

Windows XP offers an Advanced Options menu, which allows you to start the computer using the Last Known Good Configuration or in Safe Mode to troubleshoot the boot process. As the computer boots and the Starting Windows message appears at the bottom of the screen, press the F8 key to display the Windows XP Advanced Options menu (Figure 9-22 on the next page). This menu provides options that can be used to diagnose and fix problems when booting Windows XP. You then can use the ARROW keys to navigate to the desired menu option.

```
Windows Advanced Options Menu
Please select an option:

    Safe Mode
    Safe Mode with Networking
    Safe Mode with Command Prompt

    Enable Boot Logging
    Enable VGA Mode
    Last Known Good Configuration (your most recent settings that worked)
    Directory Services Restore Mode (Windows domain controllers only)
    Debugging Mode

    Start Windows Normally
    Reboot
    Return to OS Choices Menu

Use the up and down arrow keys to move the highlight to your choice.
```

Advanced Options Menu Option	Description
Safe Mode	This option uses a minimal set of device drivers and services to start Windows.
Safe Mode with Networking	This option uses a minimal set of device drivers and services to start Windows, plus the drivers that you need to load networking.
Safe Mode with Command Prompt	This option is the same as Safe mode, except that Cmd.exe starts instead of Windows Explorer.
Enable Boot Logging	This option enables logging when the computer is started with any of the Safe Boot options except Last Known Good Configuration. The Boot Logging text is recorded in the Ntbtlog.txt file in the \%SystemRoot% folder.
Enable VGA Mode	This option starts Windows in 640 × 480 mode, using the current video driver (not Vga.sys). This mode is useful if the display is configured for a setting that the monitor cannot display. Note that Safe mode and Safe mode with Networking load the Vga.sys driver instead.
Last Known Good Configuration	This option starts Windows by using a previous good configuration.
Directory Services Restore Mode	This mode is valid only for Windows-based domain controllers. This mode performs a directory service repair.
Debugging Mode	This option turns on debug mode in Windows. Debugging information can be sent across a serial cable to another computer that is running a debugger. This mode is configured to use COM2.
Start Windows Normally	This option starts Windows in its normal mode.
Reboot	This option reboots the computer.
Return to OS Choices Menu	On a computer that is configured for booting to more than one operating system, this option returns to the Boot menu.

Figure 9-22 Windows XP Advanced Options menu.

LAST KNOWN GOOD CONFIGURATION If Windows does not start when you try to boot, first restart Windows by using the **Last Known Good Configuration** option. Each time the system boots completely and the user logs on, the Last Known Good Configuration is saved in the registry. If you suspect the system was configured incorrectly, using the Last Known Good Configuration option restores Windows XP to the settings of the last successful boot and all system setting changes made after this last successful boot are lost. If you have booted several times since a problem started, the Last Known Good Configuration will not help you recover from the problem, because all saved versions of the Last Known Good Configuration reflect the problem.

SAFE MODE **Safe Mode** boots the OS with a minimum configuration and prevents many of the device drivers and system services that normally load during the boot process from loading. Safe Mode can be used to solve problems with a new hardware installation or problems caused by user settings. Safe Mode boots with the mouse, monitor (with basic video), keyboard, and secondary storage drivers loaded. It uses the default system services and does not provide network access. When you boot in Safe Mode, Windows XP uses a slightly modified version of the graphical user interface, in which the screen resolution is 600 × 800, the desktop background is black, and the text, Safe Mode, is displayed in all four corners of your screen. After Windows XP loads in Safe Mode, you can disable the problem device, scan for viruses, run diagnostic software, or take other appropriate action to diagnose and solve problems. When you load Windows XP in Safe Mode, all files used for the load are recorded in the Ntbtlog.txt file.

SAFE MODE WITH NETWORKING **Safe Mode with Networking** also boots the computer into Safe Mode, but provides network connections. Safe Mode with Networking is helpful when you are solving a problem with booting and need access to the network to solve the problem. For example, if the operating system hangs when you boot and you have just attempted to install a printer with drivers on the network, boot into Safe Mode with networking, uninstall the printer, and then install it again from the network. You also should use Safe Mode with networking when Windows XP installation files are available on the network, rather than on the Windows XP CD, and you need to access these files.

SAFE MODE WITH COMMAND PROMPT **Safe Mode with Command Prompt** also boots the computer into Safe Mode, but loads a command prompt, instead of automatically loading the GUI desktop. If the Safe Mode or Safe Mode with Networking does not load Windows XP, then try this option.

ENABLE BOOT LOGGING When you select **Enable Boot Logging** and then boot the computer, Windows XP loads normally and you have access to the regular desktop. All files used during the load process, however, are recorded in the Ntbtlog.txt file, which is stored in the \%SystemRoot% folder. Using Enable Boot Logging allows you to see what did and did not load during the boot process. For example, if you have a problem getting a device to work, check Ntbtlog.txt to see what driver files loaded. Boot logging is much more effective if you have a copy of Ntbtlog.txt that was made when everything worked as it should. You should make a copy of the Ntbtlog.txt after you successfully install any new hardware or software, which you then can use to compare the good load to the bad load, looking for differences.

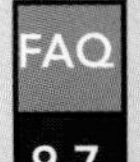
FAQ 9-7

When I boot using Last Known Good Configuration, the boot log does not change. Why is that?

The Enable Boot Logging option enables logging when the computer is started with any of the options listed on the Advanced Option menu, except Last Known Good Configuration.

ENABLE VGA MODE You should use the **Enable VGA Mode** option when the video setting does not allow you to see the screen well enough to fix a bad setting. This can happen because of a corrupted video driver or when a user creates a desktop with black fonts on a black background, or something similar. Booting in this mode gives you a very plain VGA video display which allows you to go to the Display settings, correct the problem, and then reboot normally.

DIRECTORY SERVICES RESTORE MODE (WINDOWS DOMAIN CONTROLLERS ONLY) The Active Directory is the domain database managed by a domain controller to track users and resources on the domain. **Directory Services Restore Mode** applies only to domain controllers and is used as a step in the process of recovering from a corrupted Active Directory.

DEBUGGING MODE **Debugging mode** gives you the opportunity to move system boot logs from a failing computer to another computer for evaluation. To use debugging mode, connect a working computer to the failing computer using a serial cable. Windows XP then sends all of the boot information via the serial port to the other computer, where you can diagnose the source of the issue.

System Restore

If the options available on the Advanced Options menu do not resolve the issue, you should try the System Restore utility, which is a new utility introduced in Windows XP. If you can load Windows XP, then you can use **System Restore** to restore the system state to its condition at the time a snapshot was taken of the system settings and configuration. The restore process does not affect user data on the hard drive, but can affect installed software and hardware, user settings, and OS configuration settings. Unfortunately, the restore process cannot help you recover from a virus or worm infection.

How does System Restore differ from Automated System Recovery?

The main difference between System Restore and Automated System Recovery is that System Restore does not affect user data on the hard drive, but Automated System Recovery does. To recover a failed system without destroying data, make it a habit to create a restore point every time, just before you make a change to the system.

When using System Restore, the restoration is taken from a snapshot of the system state, called a **restore point**, which was created earlier. The system automatically creates a restore point before you install new software or hardware or make other changes to the system. You also can manually create a restore point at any time. To create a restore point manually, perform the following steps:

1. Click the Start button, point to All Programs, point to Accessories, point to System Tools, and then click System Restore.
2. The System Restore window appears and provides two choices: Restore my computer to an earlier time and Create a restore point. Click Create a restore point and then click the Next button.

3. Enter a description of the restore point, such as *Before updating video driver*. The system automatically assigns the current date and time to the restore point.
4. Click the Create button. After the restore point is created, click the Close button. Windows XP saves the restore point.

Before using System Restore to undo a change, try rolling back the driver as described in Chapter 8, so as few changes as possible to the system are lost. To roll back a device driver, open the Computer Management console and then click Device Manager in the left side of the Computer Management window. Right-click the device, click Properties on the shortcut menu, click the Driver tab, and then click the Roll Back Driver button.

If rolling back the driver does not work or is not appropriate, perform the following steps to revert the system back to the restore point:

1. Click the Start button, point to All Programs, point to Accessories, point to System Tools, and then click System Restore.
2. If necessary, click Restore my computer to an earlier time and then click the Next button. When the Select a Restore Point window appears (Figure 9-23), select the date and time and the specific restore point. A bold date on the calendar indicates a restore point was created on that day, either manually or automatically.

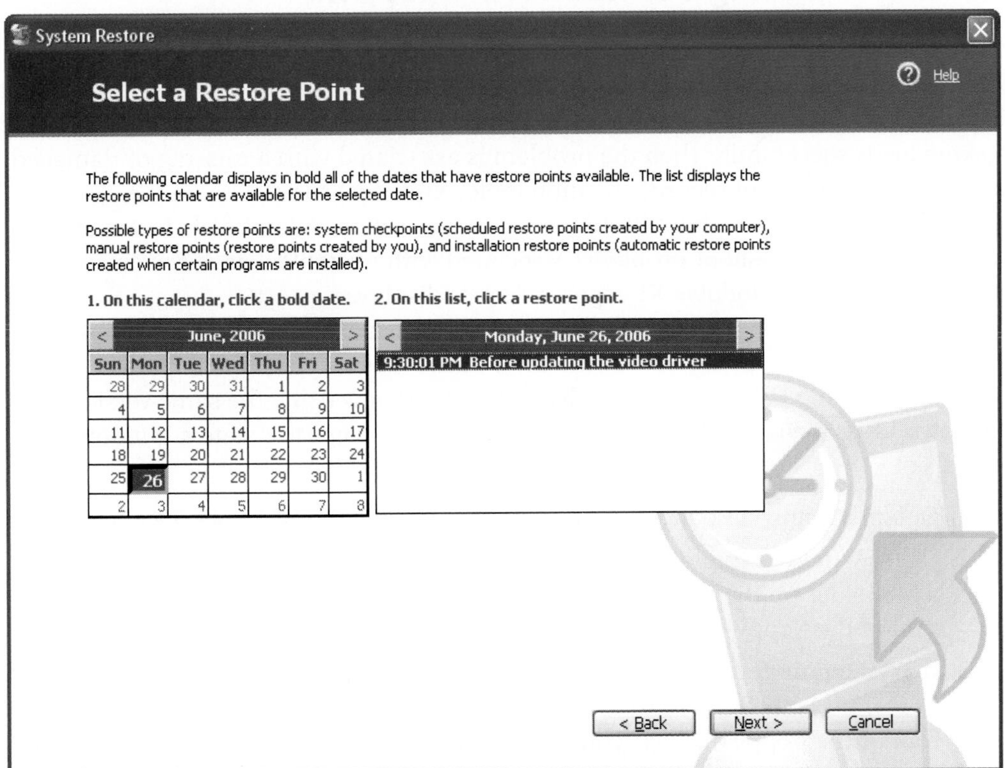

Figure 9-23 Restore points are created automatically, as well as every time software or hardware is installed.

3. Click the Next button twice to complete the System Restore process.
4. Windows XP reboots and restores the system state to the settings saved in the restore point. Changes to user data are not affected, but any installation or configuration changes made after the restore point are lost.

When selecting a restore point, select a point as close to the present as you can so that as few changes to the system as possible are lost. Note that the previous steps assume you can access System Restore by booting to a Windows desktop. If that does not work, try booting to the Advanced Options menu. From the Advanced Options menu, select Safe Mode. When Windows XP asks if you want to go directly to System Restore rather than to Safe Mode, choose to go directly to System Restore.

FAQ 9-9

Are there other tools that allow you to restore the system if you cannot boot from the hard drive?

Rolling back the system to a Windows XP System Restore point requires that you can boot from the hard drive. If you cannot boot from the hard drive, you can try third-party utility software, such as ERD Commander 2003 by Winternals (*www.winternals.com*). You can boot the computer from the ERD Commander 2003 CD, which loads a Windows XP-like interface with tools that allow you to access the registry, event logs, and disk management console and reset a forgotten administrator password. You also can roll back the Windows XP system to a System Restore point.

Creating and Using a Windows XP Boot Disk

If System Restore does not work when troubleshooting a failed boot and your computer will not boot from the CD-ROM, the next tool to try is the Windows XP boot disk that boots from the floppy disk drive. If you boot from the disk and the Windows XP desktop loads successfully, then the problem is associated with a missing or damaged boot sector, master boot record, partition table, Ntldr file, Ntdetect.com file, Ntbootdd.sys (if it exists), boot.ini file, or a virus infection. A boot disk, however, cannot be used to troubleshoot problems associated with unstable device drivers or those that occur after the Windows XP logon screen is displayed.

You first create the boot disk by formatting the disk using a working Windows XP computer and then copying files to the disk. These files can be copied from a Windows XP setup CD or a Windows XP computer that is using the same version of Windows XP as the problem PC. Perform the following steps to create a Windows XP boot disk:

1. Obtain a floppy disk and, if needed, format it using the Windows XP computer.
2. Using Windows Explorer, copy the files Ntldr and Ntdetect.com from the \i386 folder on the Windows XP setup CD or a Windows XP computer to the root of the floppy disk.
3. If your computer boots from a SCSI hard drive, then obtain a device driver (*.sys) for your SCSI hard drive, rename it Ntbootdd.sys, and copy it to the root of the floppy disk. (If you used an incorrect device driver, then you will receive an error after booting from the floppy disk. The error will mention a "computer disk hardware configuration problem" and that it "could not

read from the selected boot disk." If this occurs, contact your computer manufacturer for the correct version of the SCSI hard drive device driver for your computer.)

4. View the Boot.ini file on the problem computer. To review the file, click the Start button, right-click My Computer on the Start menu, and then click Properties on the shortcut menu. Click the Advanced tab and then click the Settings button in the Startup and Recovery area. Click the Edit button in the System Startup area. The Boot.ini file opens in Notepad. If the problem computer is booting from an IDE hard drive, then its Boot.ini should be similar to:

   ```
   [boot loader]
   timeout=30
   default=multi(0)disk(0)rdisk(0)partition(1)\WINDOWS
   [operating systems]
   multi(0)disk(0)rdisk(0)partition(1)\WINDOWS="Microsoft
   Windows XP Professional" /fastdetect
   ```

   Obtain an identical copy of the Boot.ini file from another known good computer or create an exact copy of the file and save it to the root of the floppy disk.

5. The Windows XP boot disk is complete. Write-protect the floppy disk so it cannot become infected with a virus.

After you have created the Windows XP boot disk, check CMOS setup to make sure the first boot device is set to the floppy disk and then insert the boot disk and reboot your computer. If you were not able to boot Windows XP successfully using the boot disk, then the next tool to try is the Recovery Console.

> **More About**
>
> **Windows XP Boot and MS-DOS Startup Disks**
>
> To learn more about creating a Windows XP boot disk and an MS-DOS startup disk that can be used to boot into MS-DOS mode, visit the Understanding and Troubleshooting Your PC More About Web page (**scsite.com/understanding/more**) and then click Windows XP Boot and MS-DOS Startup Disks below Chapter 9.

Recovery Console

The Recovery Console provides tools to help when Windows XP does not start properly or hangs during the load. The **Recovery Console** is a command-driven operating system that does not use a GUI. With it you can access the FAT16, FAT32, and NTFS file systems. The Recovery Console provides a long list of commands that you can use to troubleshoot or fix your computer when your computer does not start properly or does not start at all.

In the Windows Recovery Console, you can:

- Use, copy, rename, or replace operating system files and folders
- Repair the file system boot sector or the Master Boot Record (MBR)
- Enable or disable service or device startup when you next start your computer
- Create and format partitions on drives

The purpose of the Recovery Console is to allow you to repair a damaged registry, system files, or file system on the hard drive. You must enter the Administrator password in order to use the Recovery Console and access an NTFS volume. You are not allowed into all folders, and you cannot copy files from the hard drive to a floppy disk without setting certain parameters. If the registry is so corrupted that the Recovery Console cannot read the password in order to validate it, you are not asked for the password, but you are limited in what you can do at the Console.

The Recovery Console software is on the Windows XP CD. You can launch the Recovery Console from the CD or manually install the Recovery Console on the hard drive and launch it from there. Perform the following steps to load the Recovery Console from the Windows XP CD:

1. Insert the Windows XP CD in the drive and then restart the computer. When the Setup screen appears, press the F10 key or press the R key to repair and start the Windows Recovery Console.
2. The Windows XP Recovery Console window opens and displays the menu as shown in Figure 9-24. In this example, the Recovery Console looked at the hard drive and determined that only a single Windows XP installation was on the drive installed in the C:\Windows folder. Press the 1 (number) key and then press the ENTER key to select that installation.

```
Microsoft Windows(R) Recovery Console
==============
The Recovery Console provides system repair and recovery functionality.

Type EXIT to quit the Recovery Console and restart the computer.

1: C:\WINDOWS

Which Windows Installation would you like to log onto
(To cancel, press ENTER)? 1
Type the Administrator Password:
C:\WINDOWS>
```

Figure 9-24 The Windows Recovery Console displays a command prompt to allow you to enter commands.

3. Enter the administrator password and press the ENTER key. Note that, if you do not know the password, you cannot use the Recovery Console.
4. A command prompt displays, at which point you can enter a limited group of DOS-like commands listed in Figure 9-25 to recover a failed system. To retrieve the last command, press the F3 key at the command prompt. To retrieve the command one character at a time, press the F1 key.
5. To exit the Recovery Console and start Windows XP, type **Exit** at the command prompt.

Command	Description and Sample Commands
Attrib	Changes the attributes of a file or folder. For example, `attrib -r -h -s —c filename` clears the read, hidden, system, and compressed file attributes from the file.
Batch	Carries out commands stored in a batch file. For example, `batch file1 file2` executes the commands stored in file1 and the results are written to file2. If no file2 is specified, results are written to the screen.
Bootcfg	Used for boot configuration and recovery (boot.ini for most computers). For example, `bootcfg /default` sets the default boot entry; `bootcfg /add` adds a Windows installation to the boot list; and `bootcfg /rebuild` allows a user to choose which Windows installation to add.
Chdir or Cd	Displays or changes the current directory. For example, `chdir c:\windows` or `cd c:\windows` changes the directory to the Windows folder on the root drive.
Chkdsk	Checks a disk and repairs or recovers the data.
Cls	Clears the screen.
Copy	Copies a single uncompressed file. For example, `copy a:\file1 c:\winnt\file2` copies the file named file1 on the floppy disk to the hard drive's Windows folder, naming the file file2. Use the command to replace corrupted files.
Delete or Del	Deletes a file. For example, `delete file1` or `Del file1` deletes file1.
Dir	Lists files and folders.
Disable	Used when a service or driver starts and prevents the system from booting properly. For example, `disable servicename` disables a Windows system service or driver, restarts the computer without it, and helps you determine the problem.
Diskpart	Creates and deletes partitions on the hard drive. To display a command-based version of diskpart, enter the command with no parameters.
Enable	Enables a Windows system service or driver. For example, `enable eventlog` enables the eventlog service.
Exit	Quits the Recovery Console and restarts the computer.
Expand	Expands a compressed file and copies it from a floppy disk or a CD to the destination folder. For example, `Expand a:\file1 c:\windows` expands the file on the floppy disk and copies it to the hard drive.
Fixboot	Rewrites the OS boot sector on the hard drive. For example, the `fixboot C`: command will help repair a damaged boot sector.
Fixmbr	Rewrites the Master Boot Record of the boot disk. For example, `Fixmbr` writes a new master boot record to drive C.
Format	Formats a logical drive. If no file system is specified, NTFS is assumed. Enter `format c:/fs:FAT32` to use the FAT32 file system. Enter `format c:/fs:FAT` to use the FAT16 file system.
Help	Displays a list of the commands you can use in the Recovery Console. If a specific command is entered as a parameter (for example, `Help Fixboot` or `Help Delete`), Help displays information for that specific command.
Listsvc	Lists all available services.
Logon	Allows you to log on to an installation with the Administrator password.
Map	Lists all drive letters and file system types.
Mkdir or Md	Creates a directory. For example, `mkdir c:\temp` creates a TEMP directory on drive C.
More or Type	Displays the contents of a text file on screen; user can view but not modify it. For example the command `More c:\documents and settings\`*`username`*`\my documents\filename.txt` will display the contents of filename.txt in the My Documents folder for user name.
Rename or Ren	Renames a file. For example, `rename file1.txt file2.txt` changes the name of file1.txt to file2.txt.
Rmdir or Rd	Deletes a directory. For example, `rmdir c:\temp` deletes the TEMP directory from drive C.
Set	Displays or sets Recovery Console environmental variables.
Systemroot	Sets the current directory to the directory where Windows is installed.

Figure 9-25 Commands available from the Recovery Console.

More About

Using the Recovery Console

To learn more about installing the Recovery Console and using it to restore the registry, visit the Understanding and Troubleshooting Your PC More About Web page (**scsite.com/understanding/more**) and then click Using the Recovery Console below Chapter 9.

Automated System Recovery

If using the Recovery Console does not solve the problem, you can use the Automated System Recovery tool to try to resolve the problem. Windows XP offers a utility called **Automated System Recovery** (**ASR**) that allows you to restore an entire hard drive volume to its state at the time the backup of the volume was made. This process creates the ASR backup that backs up the system state, system services, and all the disks that are associated with the operating system components. It also creates the ASR restore floppy disk, which includes a file that lists information about the backup and disk configurations, which you can use to recover the system and restore the backup. ASR should be a last resort for system recovery, used only after you have exhausted other options described in this chapter.

You should regularly create Automated System Recovery (ASR) backup and disks as part of an overall plan for system recovery so you are prepared if the system fails. The backup file created will be just as large as the contents of the hard drive volume, so you will need a large capacity backup medium such as a removable hard drive, file server, a tape drive, or a writeable CD-R or CD-RW drive.

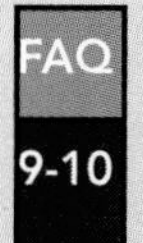

Can I back up a volume to the same volume?

Do not back up the logical drive or volume to a folder on the same volume. While the ASR backup process will allow you to back a volume up to the same volume, restoring data from this backup will not work if that volume is the problem. To better protect your installation, back up to a different hard drive or a removable medium.

Creating an ASR disk and a backup follows steps similar to those used to back up the System State or to back up the registry. You will need a storage medium, such as a Zip drive, tape drive, network drive, or other removable medium, to store the backed up files and a blank 1.44 MB floppy disk to store the system settings. This floppy disk will be used as the ASR disk. Perform the following steps to create the ASR disk and the backup:

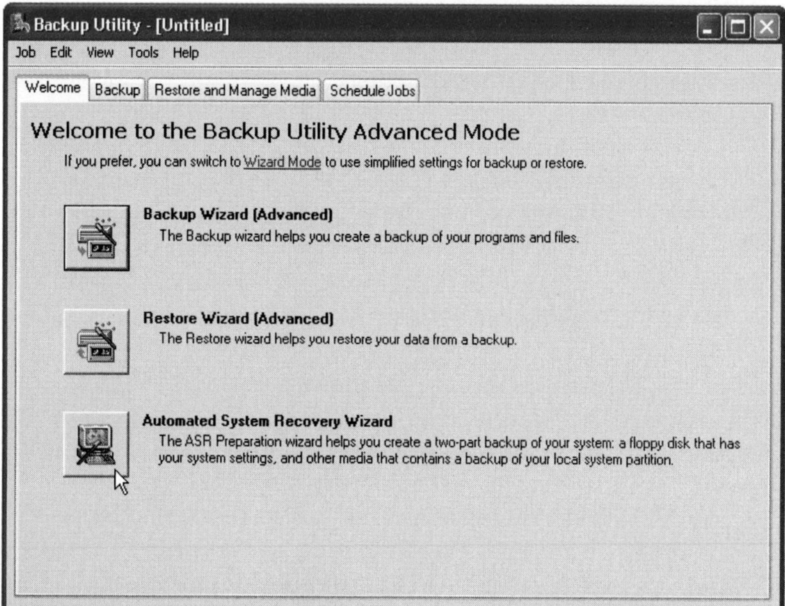

Figure 9-26 The Backup utility can create a backup of drive C and an ASR disk to be used later for the Automated System Recovery utility.

1. Click the Start button, point to All Programs, point to Accessories, point to System Tools, and then click Backup.
2. If the backup process starts by launching the Backup or Restore Wizard window, click the Advanced Mode link.
3. When the Backup Utility window opens (Figure 9-26), click the Welcome tab, if necessary, and then click the Automated System Recovery Wizard button. If a dialog box displays, click the No button to clear any selections before starting the wizard. Click the Next button on the Welcome to the Automated System Recovery Preparation Wizard window.

4. In the Backup Destination window, enter a drive or directory on which to store the backed up files. Enter a descriptive file name in the Backup media or file name text box (for example, 26Jun2006.bkf). Click the Next button.
5. The Completing the Automated System Recovery Preparation Wizard window explains that when you click Finish, the wizard creates a backup of your system files and that you then will be asked to insert a floppy disk. Click the Finish button.
6. The Backup utility will copy all of the important system files and settings to the backup file on the storage medium you specified in the Backup Destination window. The utility provides an estimate and status bar to show progress, as the backup process can take some time, especially for a large-capacity hard drive with numerous files.
7. After the backup is complete, a Backup Utility window will prompt you to insert a blank, 1.44 MB formatted diskette in drive A. Insert a floppy disk in drive A and then click the OK button. The Backup utility displays a status bar to show progress. (If the floppy disk becomes full during the backup process, Windows will display a message. Insert a new disk and then click the OK button.)
8. When the process is complete, a Backup Utility window will prompt you to remove the floppy disk and label it as a Windows Automated System Recovery Disk for the file created on that date and time. It also will remind you to keep the ASR disk in a safe place in case your system needs to be restored using the ASR disk.

I am running Windows XP Home Edition and cannot find the Backup utility installed on my computer. How can I find it?

By default, Windows XP Home Edition does not include the Backup utility. To install it manually, go to the \VALUEADD\MSFT\NTBACKUP folder on your Windows XP setup CD and double-click Ntbackup.msi. The installation wizard will complete the installation.

After you have created the Automated System Recovery disk set, you can use the most recent set of recovery disks to restore a hard drive volume to its state when the backup was made. As noted above, using Automated System Recovery should be a last step in troubleshooting issues with Windows XP. If you back up the system state when you complete an installation and a failure occurs in the future, you can restore the system state without overwriting user data on the hard drive. If you use the Automated System Recovery process to restore the entire volume, you will lose any changes made to the volume since the backup, including software and device drivers installed, user data, and any changes to the system configuration. For this reason, it is a good idea to make fresh copies of the ASR disk set periodically.

To restore the hard drive to its state when the last ASR disk set was made, do the following:

1. Insert the Windows XP CD in the CD-ROM drive and perform a cold boot of the computer.
2. When the message appears saying, Press any key to boot from CD, press any key.

3. When a blue screen appears with the message, Press F2 to run the Automated System Recovery process, at the bottom of the screen, press F2. (Note that, if your system uses RAID or a SCSI hard drive, you first will press F6 to load RAID or SCSI drivers.)
4. The screen shown in Figure 9-27a appears, instructing you to insert the ASR floppy disk. Insert the disk and then press the ENTER key.

Windows XP Setup then completes the following steps:

- Loads files it needs to run.
- Repartitions and reformats the drive (Figure 9-27b).
- Installs Windows from the Windows XP CD.
- Launches the Automatic System Recovery Wizard to restore the Windows system state, applications, and data to what they were at the time of the last ASR backup.

Because it reformats the logical drive just before the Windows XP installation process begins, the ASR recovery process erases everything on the volume being restored.

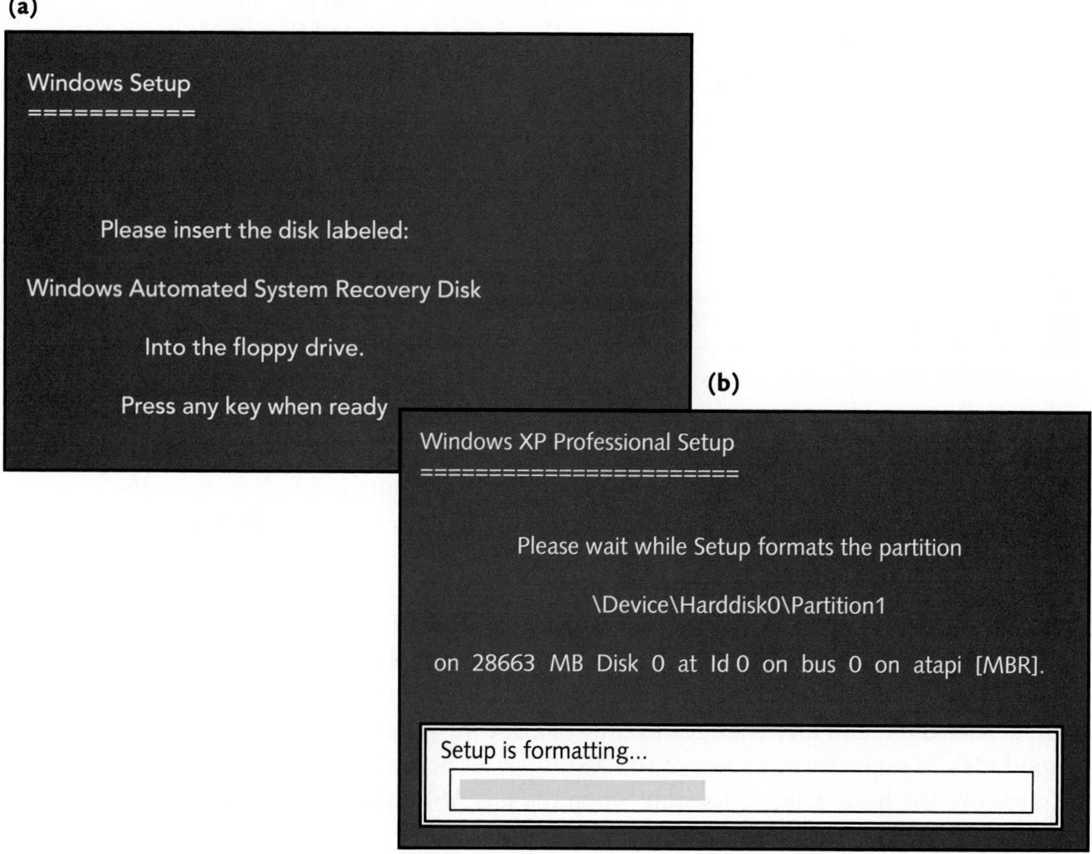

(a)
Windows Setup
===========
Please insert the disk labeled:
Windows Automated System Recovery Disk
Into the floppy drive.
Press any key when ready
(b)
Windows XP Professional Setup
=======================
Please wait while Setup formats the partition
\Device\Harddisk0\Partition1
on 28663 MB Disk 0 at Id 0 on bus 0 on atapi [MBR].
Setup is formatting...

Figure 9-27 (a) Automatic System Recovery process must have the ASR floppy disk. (b) As part of the Automatic System Recovery process, Windows XP Setup repartitions and reformats the volume holding Windows XP.

Quiz Yourself 9-2

To test your knowledge of troubleshooting the Windows XP boot process, visit the Understanding and Troubleshooting Your PC Quiz Yourself Web page (scsite.com/understanding/quiz). Click Quiz Yourself 2 below Chapter 9.

Additional Windows XP Maintenance and Troubleshooting Tools

Windows XP provides many tools for maintenance and troubleshooting, several of which are listed in Figure 9-28. Some of these tools or utilities can be executed from a command line (.exe file extension), others are Microsoft Management Console snap-ins (.msc file extension), and others are graphical tools built into Windows XP (such as Device Manager). Many tools listed in the table have been discussed in previous chapters; several others are discussed in the following sections. For more extensive information about any of these tools, click Start, then click Help and Support on your Windows XP computer, or search the online Microsoft Knowledge Base at *support.microsoft.com.*

More About

Windows XP Maintenance and Troubleshooting Tools

To learn more about Windows XP tools listed in Figure 9-28, visit the Understanding and Troubleshooting Your PC More About Web page (**scsite.com/ understanding/more**) and then click Windows XP Maintenance and Troubleshooting Tools below Chapter 9.

Tool	Description
Add or Remove Programs	Allows user to install or uninstall software.
Automated System Recovery (ASR)	Recovers a failed system by restoring from the most recent backup. ASR is a last step in the recovery process, as all data and applications written to the drive since the last backup are lost.
Backup (Ntbackup.exe)	Backs up and restores data and software.
Boot logging	An option on the Advanced Options startup menu; logs events to Ntbtlog.txt file.
Chkdsk (Chkdsk.exe)	Checks and repairs errors on a logical drive.
Computer Management (Compmgmt.msc)	Provides access to several snap-ins used to manage and troubleshoot a system.
Device Driver Roll Back	Replaces a driver with the one that worked before the current driver was installed.
Device Manager	Displays and changes device drivers and other hardware settings.
Disk Cleanup (Cleanmgr.exe)	Deletes unused files to make more disk space available.
Disk Defragmenter and Defrag.exe	Defragments a logical drive or floppy disk. Defrag.exe is a command-line tool to defragment a logical drive or floppy disk; it is similar to the graphic tool, Disk Defragmenter.
Disk Management (Diskmgmt.msc)	Displays and changes partitions on hard drives and formats drives.
Dr. Watson (Drwtsn32.exe)	Records errors and information about those errors when applications fail. Errors are recorded in a log file named Drwatson.log.

(continued)

Tool	Description
Driver Signing and Digital Signatures (Sigverif.exe)	Verifies that drivers, system files, and software have been approved by Microsoft.
Error Reporting	Produces an error report and sends it to Microsoft when the error occurs and the PC is connected to the Internet.
Event Viewer (Eventvwr.msc)	Records and displays system problems.
Help and Support	Provides helpful information, connects to Windows newsgroups, enables Remote Assistance, and steps users though many other troubleshooting tasks.
Last Known Good Configuration	A startup option used when normal booting does not work. Allows a user to revert a system back to before a driver or application that is causing problems was installed.
Performance Monitor (Perfmon.msc)	Reports information about performance problems.
Program Compatibility Wizard	Looks at legacy software and attempts to resolve issues that prevent the software from working in Windows XP.
Recovery Console	Provides a command line to perform troubleshooting tasks when the desktop will not load.
Registry Editor (Regedit.exe)	Displays and changes entries in the registry.
Remote Assistance	Allows a user to share his computer with a support technician at a remote location so the technician can control the computer.
Remote Desktop	Allows a support technician to control a Windows XP computer remotely.
Safe Mode	Loads the Windows desktop with a minimum configuration and then used to troubleshoot problems with device drivers, display settings, and other startup options that are causing problems.
System Information (Msinfo32.exe)	Displays information about hardware, applications, and Windows, which can be useful when troubleshooting.
System Information (Systeminfo.exe)	A command-line version of System Information, which lists information on screen as text only. To store that information in a file, enter the command `systeminfo.exe >myfile.txt`; the stored information can be used to document information about the system.
System Restore	Used to restore the system to a previously working condition, it restores the registry, some system files, and some application files.
Task Killing Utility (Tskill.exe)	Stops a process or program currently running. Useful when managing background services such as an e-mail server or Web server.
Task Lister (Tasklist.exe)	Lists currently running processes similar to the list provided by Task Manager.
Task Manager (Taskman.exe)	Lists and stops currently running processes, as well as stalled processes.
	(continued)

Tool	Description
Uninstall Windows XP Professional	Used to uninstall Windows XP and revert back to a previously installed OS.
Windows Update (Wupdmgr.exe)	Updates Windows by examining the system, comparing it to available updates on the Microsoft Web site, and recommending appropriate updates.

Figure 9-28 Windows XP maintenance and troubleshooting tools.

FAQ 9-12

It is hard to remember the parameters for a command-line tool. Is there a quick way to get a listing of the parameters?

Yes. To view a list of the parameters most often used with a command-line tool, along with a description of each parameter, enter the command name followed by /?. For example, to get help about the Defrag utility, enter `Defrag /?` in the Command Prompt window. You also can enter the command name in the Help and Support window available in Windows XP. To view a list of available commands you can use in the Command Prompt window, enter `help` at the command prompt.

Event Viewer

The Event Viewer MMC snap-in connects to the **Event Viewer** tool, which displays logs about significant system events that occur in Windows XP or in applications running under the operating system, such as a hardware or network failure, OS error messages, a device or service that has failed to start, or General Protection Faults. As shown in Figure 9-29 on the next page, Event Viewer displays three different logs:

- The **application log**, which records application events that the developer of an application set to trigger a log entry. One type of event recorded in this log is an error recorded by the Dr. Watson utility, which you will learn about later in the chapter.
- The **security log**, which records events based on audit policies set by an administrator to monitor user activity such as successful or unsuccessful attempts to access a file or log on to the system. Only an administrator can view this log.
- The **system log**, which records events triggered by Windows components, such as a device driver failing to load during the boot process. Windows XP sets which events are recorded in this log. All users can access this log file.

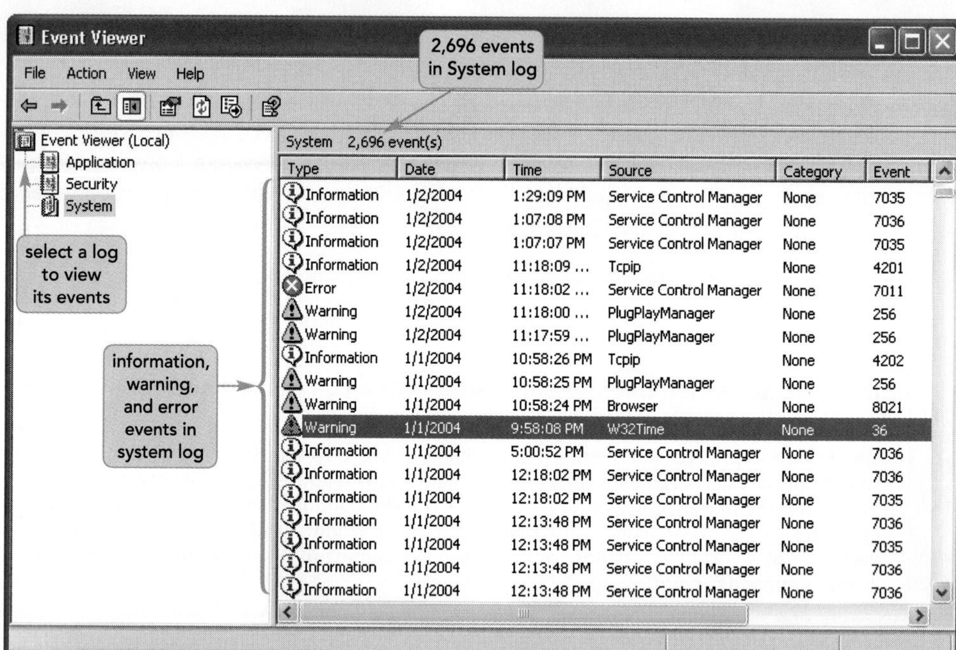

Figure 9-29 Event Viewer captures information about security audits in the security log and information, warning, or error events for the application and system logs.

Three types of events are recorded in the application and system logs:

- An **information event** is recorded when a driver, service, or application functions successfully.
- A **warning event** is recorded when something happens that may indicate a future problem, but does not necessarily indicate that something is presently wrong with the system. For example, low disk space might trigger a warning event.
- An **error event** is recorded when something goes wrong with the system, such as a necessary component failing to load, data getting lost or becoming corrupted, or a system or application function ceasing to operate.

You can open Event Viewer from the Computer Management console or you can open Control Panel, double-click Administrative Tools, and then locate Event Viewer in the left pane of the Administrative Tools windows. To view a log within Event Viewer, click the name of the log you want to view in the left pane; the right pane displays a list of events in that log. To view the details for a specific event, double-click the event in the list.

The number of events listed in the three logs can grow quickly, which makes it hard to find specific events in the log and uses hard drive space. For example, as shown in Figure 9-29, the system log lists 2,696 events. If you want to view only certain events, instead of the entire list, right-click the log name in the left pane, click View on the shortcut menu, and then click Filter on the View submenu. When the System Properties window is displayed, you then can enter several criteria to filter the view of events listed in the log (Figure 9-30).

Property	Description
Event type	The type of event, such as information, error, or warning
Event source	The application, driver, or service that triggered the event
Category	The category that the event falls under, such as an attempt to log on to the system or access a program
Event ID	A number that identifies the event and makes tracking events easier for support personnel
User	The logon name for a user
Computer	The name of a computer on the system
From: / To:	The range of events that you want to view. You can view the events from first to last event, or you can view all events that occurred on a specific date and in a specific time range.

Figure 9-30 Event Viewer log properties that can be used to filter events.

Another way to avoid an increasingly large log file is to set a size limit and specify what happens when the log reaches this limit. To set a size limit for a log, right-click the log name in the left pane, select Properties on the shortcut menu, and then click the General tab. From this tab, you can set the maximum size of the log in megabytes. You also can set the log to overwrite events as needed, overwrite events that are more than a specified number of days old, or not overwrite events at all. If you select this option, the system simply stops recording events when the log file reaches the maximum size (Figure 9-31).

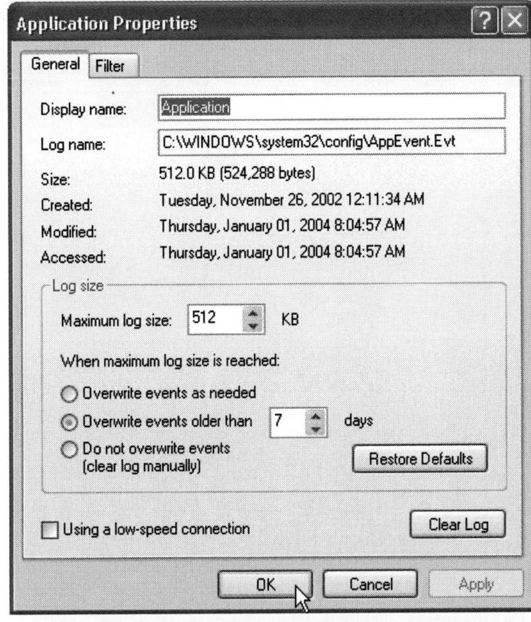

Figure 9-31 The log Properties window displays information about a log, including maximum size of the log file.

To allow the system to record events in the log after a log reaches maximum size, you have to review the events and clear the log manually, either by clicking the Clear Log button on the Properties dialog box or selecting Clear All Events from the Action menu. Before clearing the log, Event Viewer gives you a chance to save the event log for future reference.

Task Manager

> **More About**
>
> **Performance Monitoring and Optimization**
>
> To learn more about using the Performance tab and performance monitoring and optimization using Windows XP, visit the Understanding and Troubleshooting Your PC More About Web page (**scsite.com/understanding/more**) and then click Performance Monitoring and Optimization below Chapter 9.

Task Manager allows you to view the applications and processes running on your computer, as well as performance information for the processor and the memory. There are three ways that you can access Task Manager:

- Press CTRL+ALT+DELETE and then click Task Manager.
- Press CTRL+SHIFT+ESC.
- Right-click a blank area on the taskbar and then click Task Manager on the shortcut menu.

Task Manager has several tabs, including Applications, Processes, and Performance. On the Applications tab (Figure 9-32a), each application loaded can have one of two states: Running or Not Responding. If an application is listed as Not Responding, it likely has stalled. You can end it by selecting it and clicking the End Task button at the bottom of the window. You will lose any unsaved information in the application.

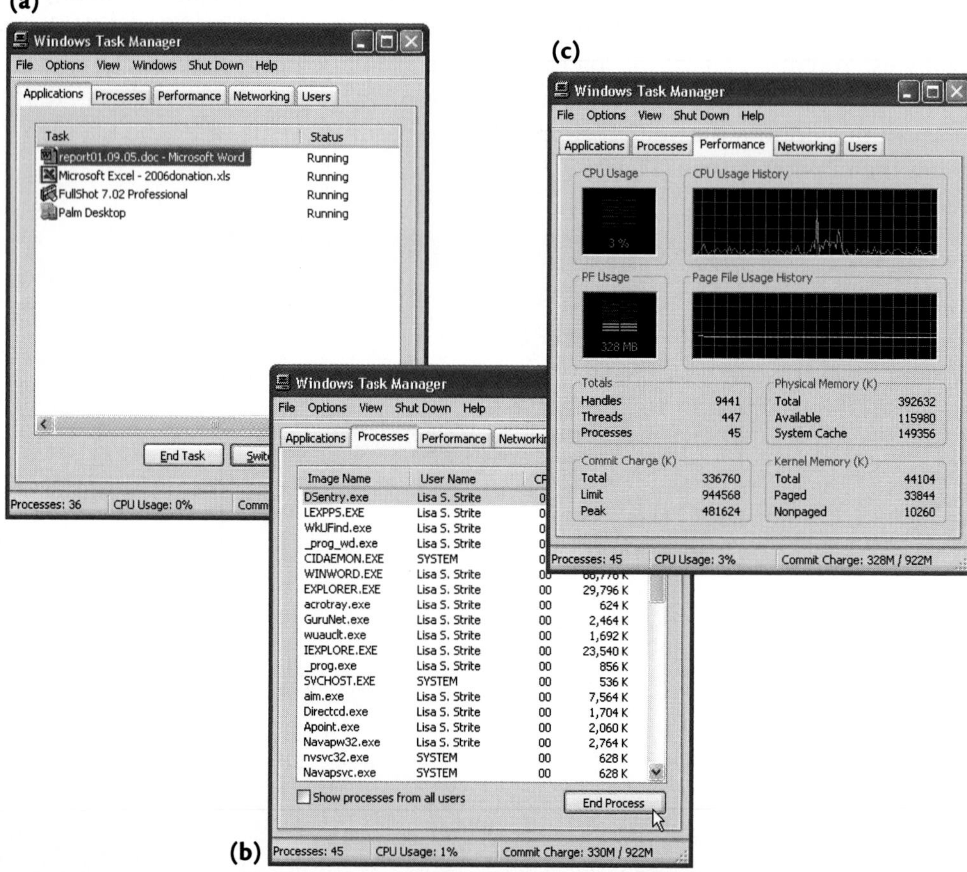

Figure 9-32 Task Manager has several tabs, including Applications (a), Processes (b), and Performance (c). The Applications tab shows the status of active applications.

The Processes tab (Figure 9-32b) lists system services and other processes associated with applications, together with how much CPU time and memory the process uses. This information can help you determine which applications are slowing down your system. If your desktop locks up, you can use Task Manager to shut down (or *kill*) any applications that might not be responding or refreshing the process that provides the desktop. As an example, press CTRL+ALT+DELETE, click the Task Manager button, and then click the Processes tab. Scroll through the list, click EXPLORER.EXE (the process that provides the desktop), and then click the End Process button. When prompted, click the Yes button. Click the Applications tab and then click the New Task button. When the Create New Task window displays, enter `Explorer.exe` in the Open text box and then click the OK button. Your desktop will be refreshed and any running programs still will be open. Be aware that shutting down some processes may cause the computer to become unstable; other processes are protected and cannot be shut down using Task Manager.

The Performance tab (Figure 9-32c) provides more detail about how a program uses system resources. You can use these views to identify which applications and processes use the most CPU time.

Dr. Watson and Memory Dumps

Two tools that can produce text output useful in diagnosing problems with the operating system and applications are Dr. Watson and memory dumps. **Dr. Watson** is used to debug errors in applications by recording error events to a log file (Figure 9-33). It can help log problems such as when an application fails to install or load, when the system locks, or when error messages appear. In Windows XP, these events are recorded in the Drwtsn32.log file.

Dr. Watson automatically starts behind the scenes when an application error occurs, or you can launch it manually by clicking the Start button, clicking Run on the Start menu, and then entering `drwtsn32` in the Open text box. Dr. Watson cannot prevent errors from occurring, but the information recorded in the log file can be used by technical support personnel to diagnose the problem. The log file is written to the path specified in the Log File Path text box in the Dr. Watson for Windows window.

Another tool that helps you understand what happened when an error occurs is a **memory dump**. It saves the contents of memory at the time a stop error halts the system, in a file called a **dump file**. A **stop error** is an error so severe that the operating system stops all processes. A stop error also often is called a **blue screen**, because the error typically displays in text against a blue screen and then thesystem halts.

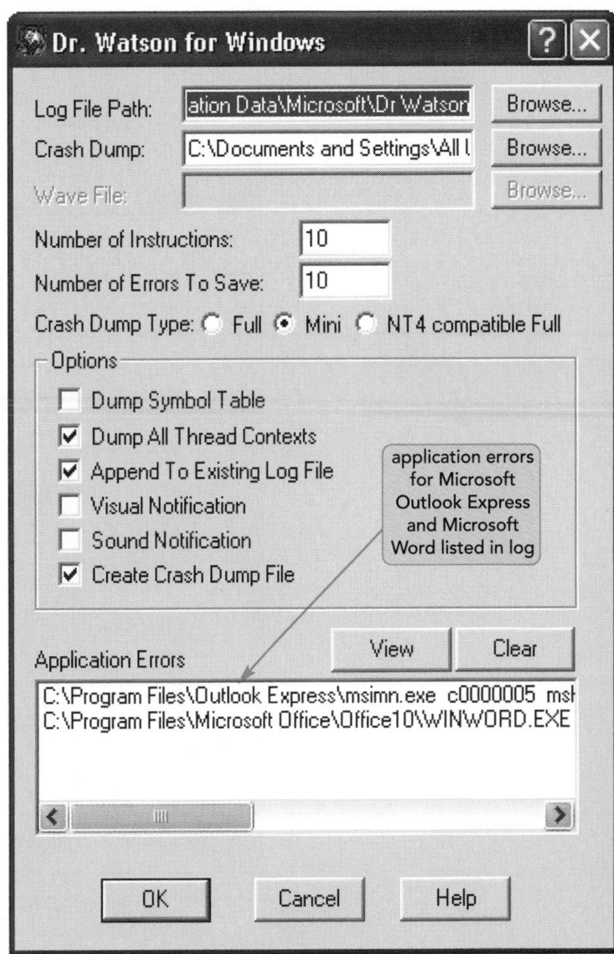

Figure 9-33 Dr. Watson can help log problems such as when an application fails to install or load.

Windows Update

Windows XP includes a tool called **Windows Update** that provides an automated way to update the OS, applications, and device drivers made available on the Microsoft Web site. If no user interaction is required, anyone can perform the update, but if decisions must be made during the update, only someone with administrator privileges can perform the update.

To start Windows Update to update the operating system, software, and drivers, first be sure the computer is connected to the Internet. Then click the Start button, point to All Programs on the Start menu, and then click Windows Update. The Update Wizard takes you to the Microsoft Windows Update Web site (Figure 9-34a). Click Scan for updates and follow the directions on screen.

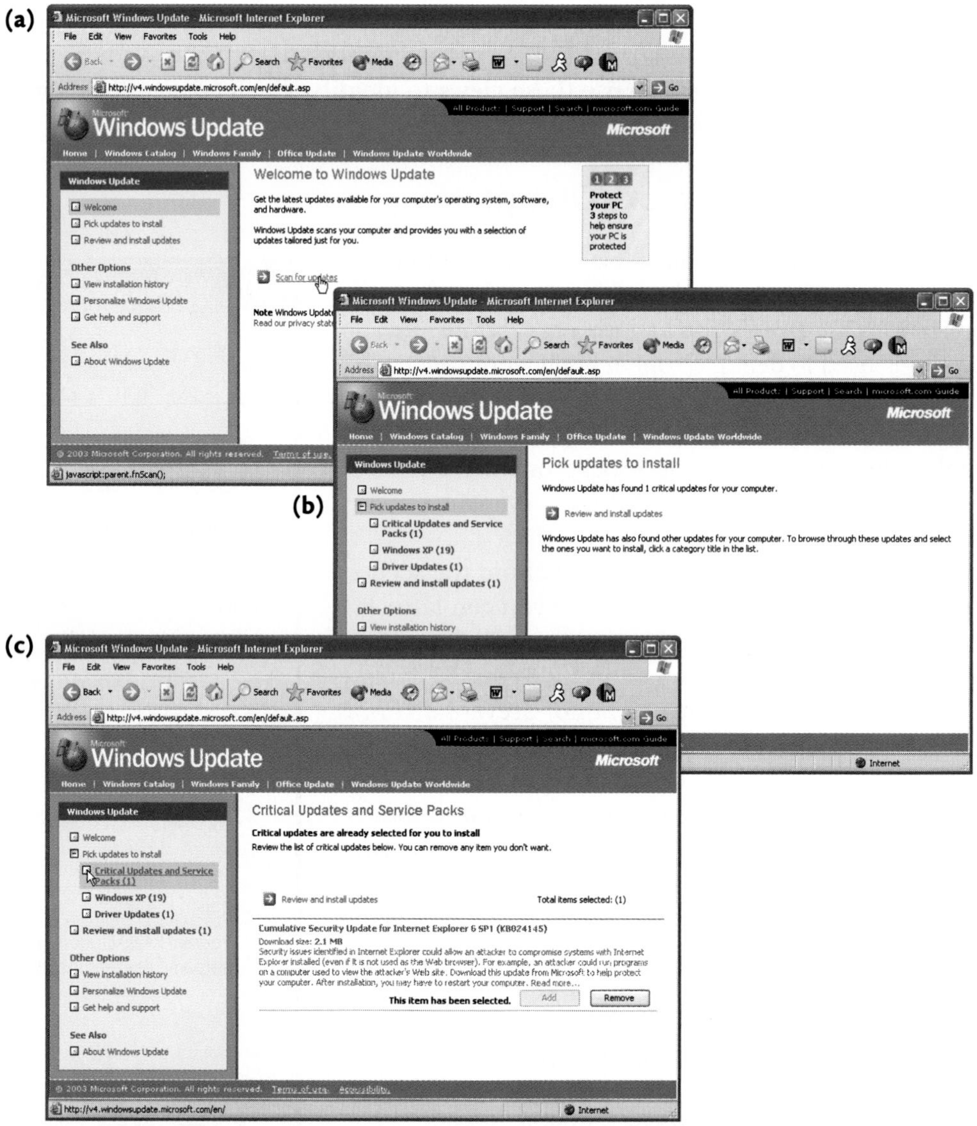

(a)

(b)

(c)

Figure 9-34 The Windows Update utility manages the process of downloading updates from the Microsoft Web site.

If an update is available for your computer, the Web site displays a list of updates (Figure 9-34b). Note in the figure that the update process found 1 critical update, 19 updates to Windows XP that it does not consider critical, and 1 update for drivers. To view information about these updates, click the category in the left pane and review the details about each update in the right pane. For example, the one critical update was designed to solve a problem with security in Internet Explorer (Figure 9-34c). To install other updates, click the Add button below each update you want to install. After you have selected what to update, click Review and install updates in the left pane and follow directions on the screen.

Additional Help and Support Resources

Microsoft offers additional help and support resources for Windows XP and on the Microsoft Web site, in the Microsoft Knowledge Base and Windows Newsgroups. In addition to the Microsoft Web site, many good Windows support Web sites exist. To view a list of these sites, go to a search engine on the Web, such as Google or Yahoo!, and enter `Windows XP Help` as the phrase in the Search box.

WINDOWS HELP AND SUPPORT Windows **Help and Support** is an electronic, interactive user guide that can provide useful information when you are learning to use a new feature or trying to resolve a problem. To access Help and Support, click the Start button and then click Help and Support on the Start menu to display the Help and Support menu (Figure 9-35a on the next page).

With Help and Support, you can enter a phrase or terms in the Search box to look for information on a specific topic, or you can browse through topics by clicking a topic on the left side of the Window. Help and Support also provides several unique tools, called Troubleshooters, which walk through questions and provide suggestions that can lead you to a solution. To access a Troubleshooter tool, start Help and Support and then click the Fixing a problem link in the main screen. When the Fixing a problem window displays, click the problem listed in the left side of the window and Help and Support will display a list of topics in the left pane. For example, as shown in Figure 9-35b on the next page, if you click Printing problems in the left pane and then click Printing Troubleshooter in the right pane, Help and Support displays a series of questions designed to help narrow and identify the source of the problem.

MICROSOFT WEB SITE In previous chapters, you have learned about valuable tools available on the Microsoft Web site, including the Windows Catalog and Upgrade Advisor. The Microsoft Help and Support Web site (*support.microsoft.com*) also is a valuable source of information to help you find updates and comprehensive resources

 **More About**

Windows XP Support Online

To learn more about using online Help and Support tools for use with Windows XP, visit the Understanding and Troubleshooting Your PC More About Web page (**scsite.com/understanding/more**) and then click Windows XP Support Online below Chapter 9.

FAQ 9-13

When I start Help and Support, I do not see a Get support, or Find information in Windows XP newsgroups link on the main page. Why not?

If you are using a computer with a customized version of Help and Support, such as the Dell version of Help and Support, this link may not be available. If it is not, you can access a Windows newsgroup through Help and Support by entering the search phrase, windows newsgroup, in the Search box and then pressing the ENTER key. When the search results display, click Go to a Windows newsgroup in the left pane and then click the Go to Windows Newsgroups link in the right pane.

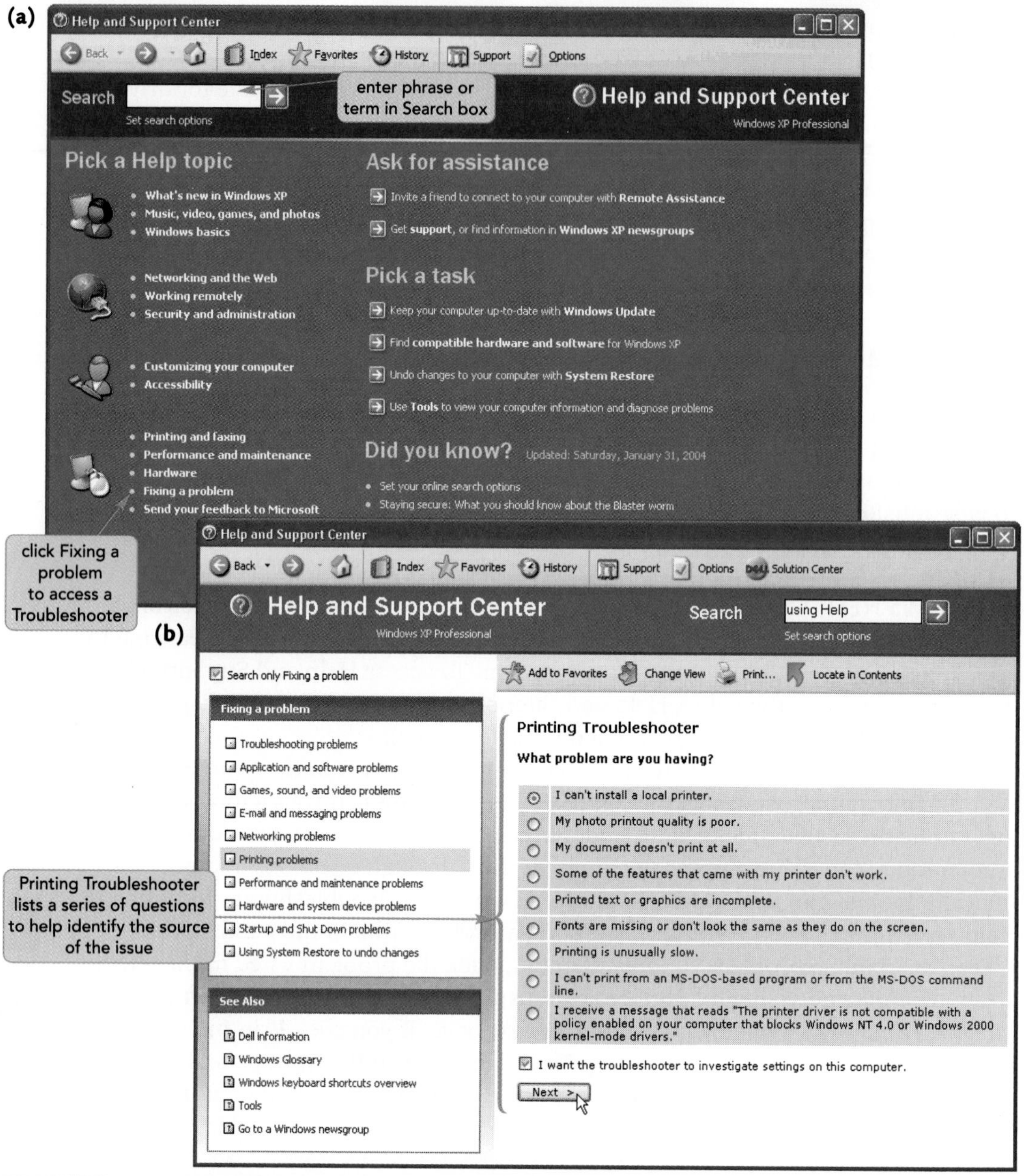

(a)

enter phrase or term in Search box

click Fixing a problem to access a Troubleshooter

(b)

Printing Troubleshooter lists a series of questions to help identify the source of the issue

Figure 9-35 The Help and Support window provides access to information and troubleshooting tools.

on technical issues related to Windows XP and other Microsoft products. From the Help and Support home page, you can link to the Knowledge Base, which allows you to perform powerful searches on a device name, an error message, a Windows utility, a symptom, a software application, an update version number, or key words that lead you to articles about problems and solutions.

WINDOWS NEWSGROUPS If you have exhausted your sources of information and still have not resolved a problem, sometimes you can get help from a Windows newsgroup. To access a newsgroup, click the Start button and then click Help and Support on the Start menu. In the Help and Support window, click Get support, or find information in Windows XP newsgroups. When the Windows Newsgroups article displays, click Go to Windows Newsgroups to start your browser and view the Windows XP newsgroups (Figure 9-36).

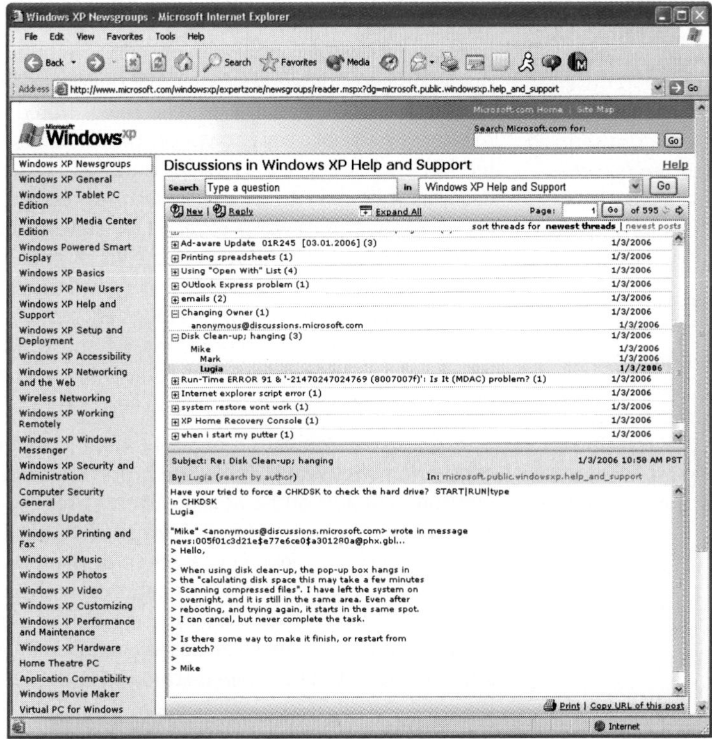

Figure 9-36 Windows XP Newsgroups provide forums for users to communicate with other users to seek help or answer questions.

The Windows XP Newsgroups are user forums in which you can find other Windows XP users, seek help, or answer questions from other users. Before starting to use the newsgroups, you may want to read the Frequently Asked Questions and information on how to use the newsgroups. In the forum, you can post a question or read questions and answers posted by other users. Microsoft does not monitor the accuracy of information exchanged in this forum, so be careful about following the advice of users posting answers to questions on the forum.

FAQ 9-14

Do I need special software to use a Windows XP newsgroup?

Probably not. If you have a Web browser such as Internet Explorer, you can access newsgroups with your Web browser by clicking the Use Web-based reader link on the Windows XP Newsgroups main page. Alternatively, you can access newsgroups using newsreader software included in such programs as Outlook Express by clicking the Open with newsreader link on the Windows XP Newsgroups main page.

Quiz Yourself 9-3

To test your knowledge of troubleshooting and maintaining Windows XP, visit the Understanding and Troubleshooting Your PC Quiz Yourself Web page (scsite.com/understanding/quiz). Click Quiz Yourself 3 below Chapter 9.

High-Tech Talk

The Key(s) to Making Encryption Work

Every day hundreds of thousands of people carry laptop computers to and from work, even as other computer users interact electronically, via e-mail, Web sites, ATM machines, and cellular phones. The increase of electronically transmitted information has led to an increased reliance on encryption, which helps ensure that unauthorized individuals cannot obtain the contents of these electronic transmissions.

In the encryption process, the unencrypted, readable data is called *plaintext*. The encrypted data is called *ciphertext*. To encrypt the data, the originator of the data converts the plain text into ciphertext using an *encryption algorithm*, which is a mathematical procedure for performing encryption on data to convert plaintext into meaningless ciphertext. To decrypt the data, the recipient uses an encryption key to transform the data back into its original form. In its simplest form, an *encryption key* is a programmed formula that the recipient of the data uses to decrypt the ciphertext.

The two basic types of encryption are private key and public key. With *private key encryption*, also called *symmetric key encryption*, both the originator and recipient use the same secret key to encrypt and decrypt the data. The most popular private key encryption system and algorithm is *advanced encryption standard (AES)*, which was adopted officially as the U.S. Government standard in May 2002.

Public key encryption, also called *asymmetric key encryption*, uses two encryption keys: a public key and a private key. Public key encryption software generates both your private key and public key. A message encrypted with your public key only can be decrypted with your private key, and vice versa.

The public key is made known to those with whom you communicate. For example, public keys are posted on a Web page or e-mailed. A central administrator can publish a list of public keys on a public-key server. The private key, by contrast, should be kept confidential. To send an encrypted e-mail message with public key encryption, the sender uses the receiver's public key to encrypt the message. Then, the receiver users his or her private key to decrypt the message (Figure 9-37). For example, if Sylvia wants to send Doug an encrypted message, she would use Doug's public key to encrypt the message. When Doug receives the encrypted message, he would use his private key to decrypt it. Doug's encryption software generated his public and private keys. Sylvia used Doug's public key to encrypt the message. Thus, only Doug will be able to decrypt the message with his private key.

EFS uses a combination of public key and symmetric key encryption to ensure that files are protected from almost any method of unauthorized access. When a user encrypts a file, EFS generates a random number for the file that EFS calls the file's file encryption key (FEK) to encrypt the data. EFS then uses the FEK to encrypt the file's contents with an encryption algorithm. The FEK then is encrypted with the user's public key using the RSA public key-based encryption algorithm, and the encrypted FEK then is stored with the file. Of course, the entire encryption process happens behind the scenes for the user, who simply completes a few mouse clicks to encrypt a folder or file. That is part of the elegance of EFS: while it is simple for a user, it is very difficult for any unauthorized user without the correct keys to crack the encryption. In the end, that is the key to keeping your data safe and sound.

Step 1:
The sender creates a document to be e-mailed to the receiver.
Step 2:
The sender uses the receiver's public key to encrypt a message.
Step 3:
The receiver uses his or her private key to decrypt the message.
Step 4:
The receiver can read or print the decrypted message.
CONFIDENTIAL
The new plant will be located . . .
message to be sent
public key
private key
sender (Sylvia)
AA311C253
43025OC
4CAD078
32EC8EF
encrypted message
receiver (Doug)
CONFIDENTIAL
The new plant will be located . . .
decrypted message

Figure 9-37

1 Using Consoles in Windows XP

A console combines several administrative tools, called snap-ins, in a single window. Computer Management is a console that consolidates several Windows XP administrative tools that you can use to manage the local computer or other computers on the network. The Microsoft Management Console (MMC) utility allows you to create your own customized consoles.

CHAPTER SUMMARY

The Chapter Summary reviews the concepts presented in this chapter.

2 Security Using Windows XP

User accounts are a key part of Windows XP security. Local user accounts apply to a stand-alone computer or a single computer in a workgroup. Global user accounts are managed from a domain controller and apply to every computer in the domain. Local user accounts include administrator, guest, and limited accounts. When a user makes changes to the system, the changes often are recorded in the user profile so the next time the user logs on, these changes automatically take effect. An administrator can set up several types of user profiles, including local user, roaming user, mandatory user, and group profiles. User accounts can be set up with or without passwords, although passwords provide greater security. You can define settings to determine how a user logs on to the computer either using the logon window, Welcome screen, or Fast User Switching. Windows XP user groups include Administrators, Backup Operators, Power Users, Limited Users, and Guests. Group Policy allows you to define and control how programs, network resources, and the operating system behave for a group of users and computers. Using disk quotas, an administrator can limit the amount of hard drive space a user can use. Encrypted File System allows you to encrypt files and folders on a Windows XP computer to provide added security.

3 The Windows XP Registry

The Windows XP registry is organized logically into five subtrees or keys, and organized physically into five files called hives. The registry is edited using the Registry Editor, which is accessed by entering `Regedit` in the Open text box of the Run window. Changes to the registry are immediate, so always make a backup of the system state before editing the registry.

4 Troubleshooting the Boot Process

If Windows XP will not boot, the Advanced Options menu allows you to boot using the Last Known Good Configuration, or Safe Mode, or other options to try to troubleshoot the issue. System Restore allows you to restore the system state using a backup of the system settings and configuration. Next, you can try to boot the computer from the Windows XP boot disk. If that does not work, try the Recovery Console, a command-driven operating system that helps repair a damaged registry, system files, or file system on the hard drive. Automated System Recovery (ASR) creates a backup and an ASR floppy disk that can be used to restore the backup of the volume or logical drive holding Windows XP. ASR should be a last resort for system recovery, because you will lose all data prior to the last backup.

5 Additional Windows XP Maintenance and Troubleshooting Tools

The Event Viewer tool displays logs about significant system events that occur in Windows XP or an application, such as a hardware or network failure. Task Manager allows you to view the applications and processes running on your computer, as well as performance information for the processor and the memory. Dr. Watson is used to debug errors in applications by recording error events to a log file, while a memory dump saves the contents of memory at the time a stop error halts the system in a file called a dump file. Windows XP includes the Windows Update tool to update the OS, applications, and device drivers automatically. Microsoft offers additional help and support resources, including Help and Support in Windows XP, the Microsoft Web site, the Microsoft Knowledge Base, and Windows Newsgroups.

KEY TERMS

After reading the chapter, you should know each of these Key Terms.

Administrators (*358*)
application log (*383*)
Automated System Recovery (ASR) (*378*)
Backup Operators (*358*)
blue screen (*387*)
Computer Configuration (*360*)
console (*346*)
debugging mode (*372*)
decryption (*361*)
Directory Services Restore Mode (*372*)
disk quota (*360*)
domain user account (*350*)
Dr. Watson (*387*)
dump file (*387*)
Enable Boot Logging (*371*)
Enable VGA Mode (*372*)
encryption (*361*)
Encrypted File System (EFS) (*361*)
Event Viewer (*383*)
error event (*384*)
forgotten password disk (*356*)
global user account (*350*)
Group Policy (*360*)
Group Policy console (*360*)
group profile (*351*)
Guests (*358*)
Help and Support (*389*)
hives (*365*)
information event (*384*)
key (*361*)
keys (*364*)
Last Known Good Configuration (*370*)
Limited Users (*358*)
local user account (*350*)
local user profile (*351*)
mandatory user profile (*351*)
memory dump (*387*)
Microsoft Management Console (MMC) (*347*)
Power Users (*358*)
Recovery Console (*375*)
registry (*363*)
Registry Editor (*367*)
restore point (*372*)
roaming user profile (*351*)
Safe Mode (*371*)
Safe Mode with Command Prompt (*371*)
Safe Mode with Networking (*371*)
security log (*383*)
snap-in (*346*)
stop error (*387*)
subkeys (*364*)
subtrees (*364*)
system log (*383*)
System Restore (*372*)
System State data (*366*)
Task Manager (*386*)
User Configuration (*360*)
user profile (*351*)
value (*364*)
warning event (*384*)
Windows Update (*388*)

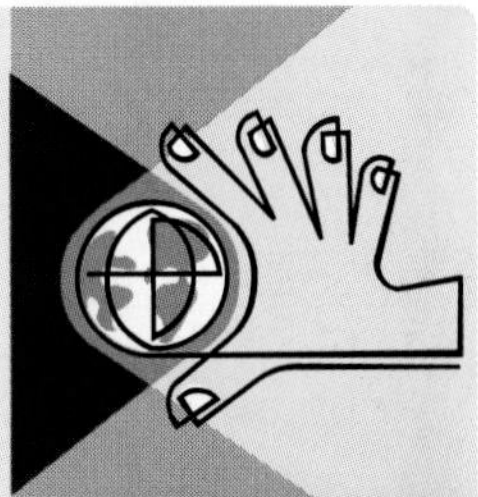

LEARN IT ONLINE

Reinforce your understanding of the chapter concepts and terms with the Learn It Online exercises.

Instructions: To complete the Learn It Online exercises, start your browser, click the Address bar, and then enter the Web address scsite.com/understanding/learn. When the Understanding and Troubleshooting Your PC Learn It Online page is displayed, follow the instructions in the exercises below. Each exercise has instructions for printing your results, either for your own records or for submission to your instructor.

1 Chapter Reinforcement True/False, Multiple Choice, and Short Answer

Below Chapter 9, click the Chapter Reinforcement link. Print the quiz by clicking Print on the File menu for each page. Answer each question.

2 Flash Cards

Below Chapter 9, click the Flash Cards link and read the instructions. Type 20 (or a number specified by your instructor) in the Number of playing cards text box, type your name in the Enter your Name text box, and then click the Flip Card button. When the flash card is displayed, read the question and then click the ANSWER box arrow to select an answer. Flip through Flash Cards. If your score is 15 (75%) correct or greater, click Print on the File menu to print your results. If your score is less than 15 (75%) correct, then redo this exercise by clicking the Replay button.

3 Practice Test

Below Chapter 9, click the Practice Test link. Answer each question, enter your first and last name at the bottom of the page, and then click the Grade Test button. When the graded practice test is displayed on your screen, click Print on the File menu to print a hard copy. Continue to take practice tests until you score 80% or better.

4 Who Wants To Be a Computer Genius?

Below Chapter 9, click the Computer Genius link. Read the instructions, enter your first and last name at the bottom of the page, and then click the PLAY button. When your score is displayed, click the PRINT RESULTS link to print a hard copy.

5 Wheel of Terms

Below Chapter 9, click the Wheel of Terms link. Read the instructions, and then enter your first and last name and your school name. Click the PLAY button. When your score is displayed, right-click the score and then click Print on the shortcut menu to print a hard copy.

6 Crossword Puzzle Challenge

Below Chapter 9, click the Crossword Puzzle Challenge link. Read the instructions, and then enter your first and last name. Click the SUBMIT button. Work the crossword puzzle. When you are finished, click the Submit button. When the crossword puzzle is redisplayed, click the Print Puzzle button to print a hard copy.

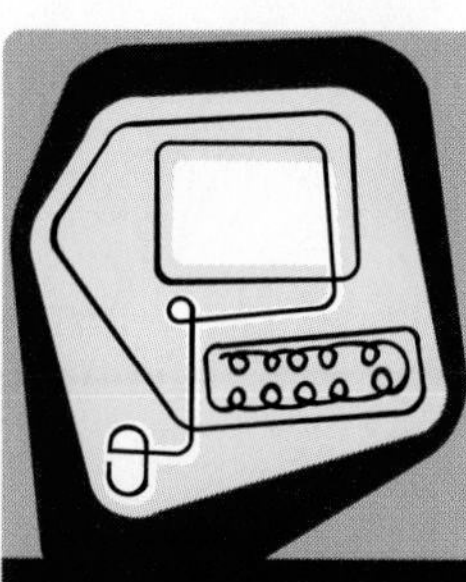

CHAPTER EXERCISES

Complete the Chapter Exercises to solidify what you learned in the chapter.

Multiple Choice

Select the best answer.

1. Which of the following is not an option for defining how users log on to Windows XP?
   a. Active Directory window
   b. Welcome screen
   c. Log On to Windows window
   d. Fast User Switching
2. ________ allows you to view the applications and processes running on your computer, along with performance information for the processor and the memory.
   a. Recovery Console
   b. Dr. Watson
   c. Event Viewer
   d. Task Manager
3. The ________ data includes the registry, all files necessary to boot the operating system, and the COM+ Registration Database.
   a. Windows Registry
   b. System State
   c. user profile
   d. System Restore
4. Which of the following is not a log recorded by Event Viewer?
   a. application log
   b. security log
   c. dump log
   d. system log
5. Which of the following is not a user group automatically set up in Windows XP?
   a. Administrators
   b. Local Operators
   c. Power Users
   d. Backup Operators

Fill in the Blank

Write the word or phrase to fill in the blank in each of the following questions.

1. When Windows XP combines several administrative tools in a single window, the window is called a(n)________ and each individual tool is called a(n)________.
2. Each time the system boots completely and the user logs on, the ________ is saved in the registry and can be used to restore Windows XP to the settings of the last successful boot.
3. ________ boots the OS with a minimum configuration and prevents many of the device drivers and system services that normally load during the boot process from loading.
4. A(n)________ stores customized desktop settings, such as how the display is set up, application settings, and network and printer connections settings.
5. Logically, the registry is organized into five ________, which are categories of information stored in the registry. Physically, the registry is stored in five files called ________.

Matching Terms

Match the terms with their definitions.

________	1. decryption	a.	helps debug errors by recording error events to a log file
________	2. Microsoft Management Console	b.	command to access the registry editor
________	3. Recovery Console	c.	process of converting plaintext data into ciphertext
________	4. disk quota	d.	snapshot of the system state that can be used in a System Restore
________	5. .msc	e.	file extension for MMC snap-ins
________	6. regedit	f.	utility for creating customized consoles
________	7. value	g.	process of converting ciphertext data back to its original format
________	8. encryption	h.	the lowest level of the tree in a registry; stores data
________	9. Dr. Watson	i.	command-driven tool that supports commands to troubleshoot your computer
________	10. restore point	j.	limits how much disk space a user can access

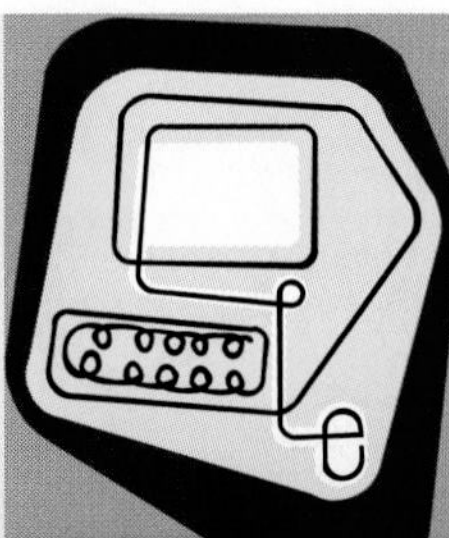

CHAPTER EXERCISES

Complete the Chapter Exercises to solidify what you learned in the chapter.

Short Answer Questions

Write a brief answer to each of the following questions.

1. List the tools Windows XP provides to help solve problems with the boot process, in the order in which you should try them. Briefly describe each tool.
2. List and describe the three types of local user accounts available in Windows XP.
3. What are the five keys in the registry and what types of information does each store? What steps should you take before editing any registry values?
4. Describe several of the Windows XP update and support tools available on the Microsoft Web site.
5. Describe several considerations when creating a user name and password. List three examples of good, secure passwords and three examples of easily guessed passwords.

APPLY YOUR KNOWLEDGE

Check your understanding of the chapter with the hands-on Apply Your Knowledge exercises.

1 Using the Microsoft Management Console

Microsoft Management Console (MMC) allows you to create a customized console in Windows XP Professional. To create a customized console:

1. Follow the steps outlined in the chapter to create a customized console with two snap-ins: Device Manager and Event Viewer.
2. After you have created the customized console, save the console in a file in the default file location, C:\Documents and Settings*username*\Start Menu\Programs\Administrative Tools folder name.
3. Start the console by clicking the Start button, pointing to All Programs on the Start menu, and then clicking Administrative Tools on the All Programs submenu. Click the file name of the console in the Administrative Tools menu.

2 Managing User Accounts

To create an administrator account using the User Accounts window, perform the following steps:

1. Log on to the computer using an account set up as an administrator.
2. Click the Start button, click Control Panel, and then click User Accounts in the Control Panel window.
3. Click Create a new account, enter a name for the new account, set the account type to Computer Administrator, and then click the Create Account button.

   Once the account is created, you can modify the settings for that account.
4. In the User Accounts window, click the account you just created.
5. Click Change the picture. On the next screen, select a new picture to display with the account. After you select the picture, click the Change Picture button.
6. Click Create a password. On the next screen, create a new password and password hint for the account (be sure to follow the tips in the chapter to create a secure password). Write the password down. Click the Create Password button.
7. Click Change the account type. In the next window, select Limited and then click the Change Account Type button.
8. Click Delete the account. When asked if you want to keep the user files, click the Delete Files button. When asked if you want to delete the user account, click the Delete Account button.
9. Confirm that the user account no longer displays in the User Accounts window. Close the User Accounts window and the Control Panel window.

3 Setting Disk Quotas

Perform the following steps to set disk quotas for users of a computer.

1. Log on as an administrator and open My Computer.
2. Find the volume or partition that you want to set a disk quota on. Right-click it and select Properties on the shortcut menu.
3. Click the Quota tab and the Enable quota management check box.
4. Check Limit disk space to select it, enter 500 in the box next to it, and select MB from the drop-down menu to the right of the box.
5. In the box next to Set warning level to, enter 400, and then select MB from the drop-down menu. This warns users when they have used 400 MB of their allotted 500 MB of storage space.

6. Click Deny disk space to users exceeding quota limit so no user can use more than the specified amount of disk space.
7. Click OK. When you are prompted to enable disk quotas, click OK to respond to the prompt.

After you have completed these steps, you can disable the disk quota by right-clicking the volume or partition for which you set the disk quota, and then selecting Properties on the shortcut menu. Click the Quota tab and then click Enable quota management to deselect it.

APPLY YOUR KNOWLEDGE

Check your understanding of the chapter with the hands-on Apply Your Knowledge exercises.

4 Using Encrypted File System (EFS)

Encrypted File System allows users to store data on the hard disk in encrypted format. Perform the following steps to create and then encrypt the My Documents folder named Corporate, create a file in that folder that automatically becomes encrypted because the folder is encrypted, and decrypt the folder so others can access it:

1. Click the Start button and then click My Documents on the Start menu.
2. Click Make a new folder in the File and Folder tasks list, type `corporate` as the new folder name, and then press the ENTER key.
3. Right-click the Corporate folder and click Properties on the shortcut menu. When the Corporate Properties window is displayed, click the Advanced button on the General tab.
4. Click Encrypt contents to secure data to select it and then click OK. Click the Apply button in the Corporate Properties window.

   Note that, if any files or folders exist in the selected folder, the Confirm Attribute Changes dialog box will display. If necessary, click Apply changes to this folder, subfolders, and files to encrypt any objects in this folder and its subfolders. If you do not want to apply the changes to all subfolders and files, click Apply changes to this folder only. Click the OK button.
5. Open Microsoft Word (or Notepad or another application), type some text in a file, and save the file as in My Documents/Corporate folder using the file name Reports2006. The new file automatically is encrypted, because the My Documents/Corporate folder is encrypted.

If an unauthorized user attempts to access the encrypted document, the user receives an error message. You can test this by performing the following steps:

1. Log off the computer and log on as a different user (if necessary, create a new user following the steps in Apply Your Knowledge 2).
2. Click the Start button and then click My Computer on the Start menu. Open the My Documents folder for the user who created the encrypted file.
3. Navigate to the Corporate folder and then double-click the file name, Report2006. Windows XP will display an error message (Figure 9-38), indicating that Word cannot open the document because the user does not have access privileges. Click the OK button.
4. Close all open applications and log off the computer.

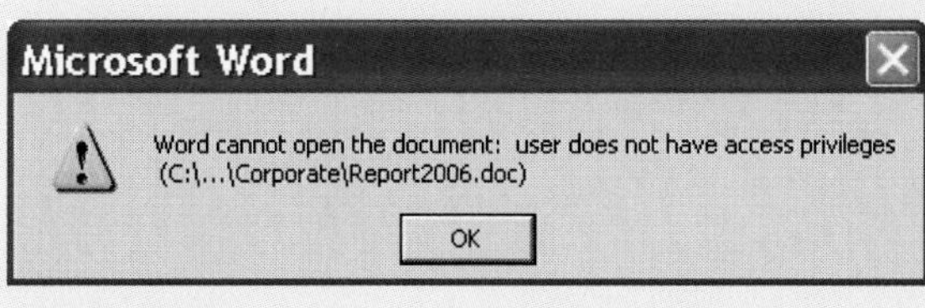

Figure 9-38

APPLY YOUR KNOWLEDGE

Check your understanding of the chapter with the hands-on Apply Your Knowledge exercises.

To decrypt the folder and the files within the folder, perform the following steps:

1. Log on as the user who encrypted the Corporate folder.
2. Click the Start button and then click My Documents on the Start menu. Navigate to the Corporate folder, right-click the folder, and click Properties on the shortcut menu.
3. When the Corporate Properties window is displayed, click the Advanced button on the General tab.
4. Click Encrypt contents to secure data to deselect it and then click OK. Click the Apply button in the Corporate Properties window.
5. When the Confirm Attribute Changes dialog box is displayed, click Apply changes to this folder, subfolders, and files and then click the OK button twice.
6. Close all open windows.

5 Problem-Solving Using the Microsoft Knowledge Base

Your hard drive has been attacked by a malicious virus and you have decided to restore it from the last backup made by the Automated System Recovery (ASR) backup process. You cannot find the ASR floppy disk required for the restore process. Search the Microsoft Knowledge Base (*support.microsoft.com*) for the steps to recreate the ASR floppy disk when the ASR backup is available. Print the Knowledge Base article.

CHAPTER 10

Connecting PCs to Networks and the Internet

Introduction

This chapter discusses how PCs are connected in networks and how those networks connect to each other. In addition to introducing various types of networks and network topologies, the chapter reviews network communications technologies and hardware. You also will learn about how to connect PCs to a network and to the Internet, the largest network of all, and how to support and troubleshoot PCs connected to a network. Finally, you will learn how the TCP/IP suite of networking protocols is used, how to create and troubleshoot dial-up and broadband connections to the Internet, and how to access Internet resources using a Web browser.

OBJECTIVES

In this chapter, you will learn:

1. About networks, network protocols, and network architectures
2. How networking works with Windows
3. How to install a network card, connect to a network, and share network resources
4. About Internet technologies and how to access the Internet

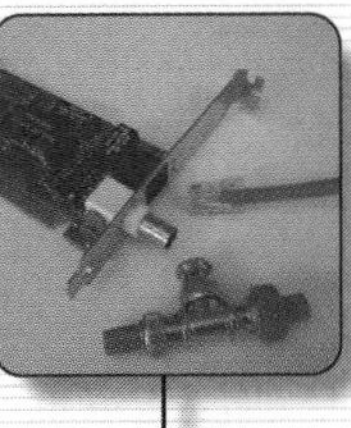

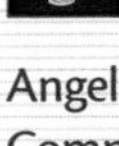

Up for Discussion

Angel Diaz, a writer for a national news magazine, called Sunrise Computers to ask if you could help him install a cable modem. Although he has used a dial-up Internet connection for years, he wants to have a faster broadband connection (especially one that will not tie up his telephone line). He has just received an installation kit from his cable service provider, and he was hoping you could stop by this week to install it.

The next day, you meet Mr. Diaz at his home and explain that the process should be relatively simple. First, you will install a network card and drivers and make a note of the MAC address of the NIC, which you then will call into the cable service so they can update their databases with the correct information for his computer. Next, you will configure the network card to use the protocol, TCP/IP, using the configuration information provided by the cable service provider. After plugging in the cable modem and turning it on, you will shut down the PC and connect it to the cable modem using the network cable. Finally, you will connect the cable from the cable TV outlet to the cable modem and restart the PC.

After completing these steps, the computer still does not have a connection. You open the Command Prompt window and use the Ipconfig utility to obtain a new IP address. When you check for connectivity again, the connection is working. Mr. Diaz is thrilled — and cannot believe how much faster the new connection is. He is excited about working from his home office, knowing he will have have fast access to valuable Internet resources.

Questions:

- What are the different ways you can connect a computer to the Internet?
- What is a network interface card (NIC) and how does it work?
- What are MAC addresses and IP addresses and what purposes do they serve?

Network Types and Architectures

A **network** is a collection of computers and devices connected together to share resources, such as hardware, software, data, and information. Networks are connected using some type of physical or wireless medium capable of carrying a signal. Telephone lines, cables, and radio waves all are types of transmission media used in networks.

Data is transmitted on a network in chunks called *packets, datagrams,* or *frames*, depending on the type of network. The beginning and end of each chunk of data includes information that identifies the type of data, which device sent it, and to which device it is going. Information at the beginning of the data is called a *header*, and information at the end of the data is called a *trailer*. If a file or other data to be sent over a network is large, the data is divided into several packets, datagrams, or frames small enough to travel on the network and then reassembled on the receiving device.

An important aspect of a network is the amount of data that can travel over a given communication system in a given amount of time. This measure of data capacity is called **bandwidth** (or data throughput or line speed). The greater the bandwidth, the faster the communication over the network. In computer networks, bandwidth is a measure of data transmission in bits per second (bps), thousands of bits per second (Kbps), millions of bits per second (Mbps), or billions of bits per second (Gbps). As you will learn in this chapter, different network technologies provide varying bandwidths, each serving a different purpose and following a different set of standards.

As you have learned, a PC makes a direct connection to a network by way of a **network adapter**, which most often is an expansion card called a **network interface card** (**NIC**) that is inserted in a PCI slot.

Networks can be described in a number of ways, including their area of coverage, the network architecture, the topology, and the network communications technologies they use.

LANs, MANs, and WANs

Networks can be internal to an organization, such as a business, or they can connect computers around the globe. Networks often are classified as local area networks, metropolitan area networks, or wide area networks, based on their coverage area.

A **local area network** (**LAN**) connects computers and devices in a relatively small area, such as a home, a computer lab, a single office building, or a closely positioned group of buildings. Each individual computer, or node, in a LAN has its own processing and storage resources, but also is able to access and share printers, hard disks, data, and other resources on the network.

A **metropolitan area network** (**MAN**) is a high-speed network that connects LANs in a metropolitan area such as a city or town.

A **wide area network** (**WAN**) covers a large geographic area, such as a city, country, or even the world, using a combination of communications media such as telephone lines, cables, and radio waves. A WAN can be one large network or may consist of many LANs connected together. The Internet is the world's largest WAN.

Physical Network Topologies

A **network topology** defines the physical arrangement or shape used to connect computers and devices on a local area network. Three common network topologies are bus, ring, and star (Figure 10-1).

bus network

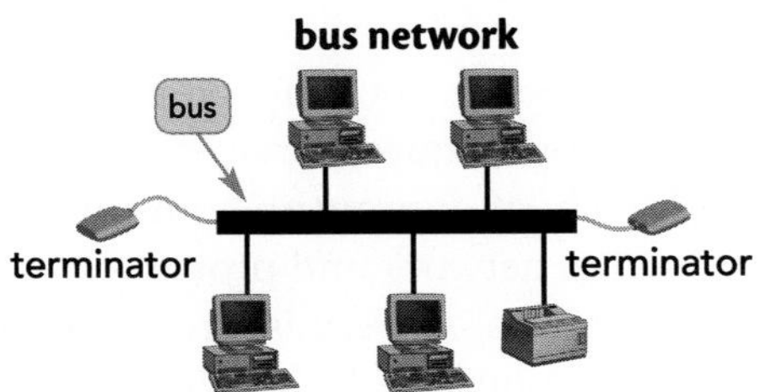

- Inexpensive, relatively easy to install
- Primarily used for LANs
- If device fails, transmission bypasses failed device
- If bus fails, entire network is not available
- May end with terminators to keep signals from bouncing back into the network

ring network

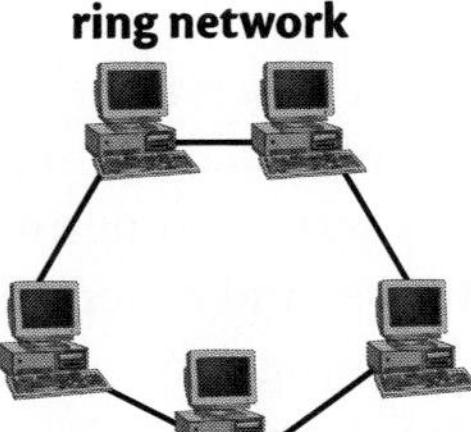

- If one device fails, all devices before failed device are unaffected; those after the failed device are not able to access network
- Can span larger distance than bus network
- Harder to install than bus or star

star network

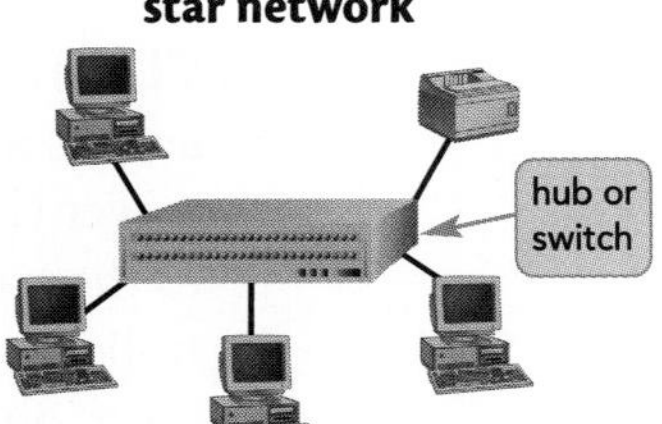

- Inexpensive, relatively easy to install
- If one node fails, others not affected
- If hub fails, entire network is not available
- Easier to install than bus

Figure 10-1 Three commonly used network topologies are bus, ring, and star.

In the **bus topology**, every computer or device is connected to a main cable called the bus. A bus topology has no central connection point. Cables simply go from one computer to the next, ending with a computer or a special terminator to keep signals from bouncing back into the network. The bus, in effect, connects every computer on the network to every other computer, and transmits data and instructions between all of the computers.

In the **ring topology**, a cable forms a closed loop, with the computers and devices connected to the cable. When a computer or device sends data, it is passed through each device in the ring network until the correct computer is reached.

The **star topology** has a central device to which computers and devices are connected. Devices on the network all connect to the *hub* or *switch* in the middle, thus forming a star. The **hub** is a central device that provides the common connection point for the other nodes on the network. All data transferred from one node to another passes through the hub, which then sends the data on to the correct device.

Networks can use a combination of topologies to form a hybrid topology. For example, a bus-star hybrid network consists of a high-bandwidth bus that connects a collection of network segments that use a star topology.

Logical Network Architecture

Another important characteristic of a network is its architecture. The **network architecture** is a logical model that defines the design and interaction of the computers, devices, and media on a network. As you learned in Chapter 8, two widely used architectures are client/server and peer-to-peer.

CLIENT/SERVER In a *client/server* network architecture, one or more computers acts as a server and the other computers on the network request services from the server (Figure 10-2a). A *server*, sometimes called the **host computer**, controls access to the hardware, software, and other resources on the network and provides a centralized storage area for programs, data, and information. A *client* is any other computer on the network that relies on the server for its resources. A client/server network typically is used to connect ten or more computers. In a Windows network, the server is called the domain controller and the client/server network is called a domain.

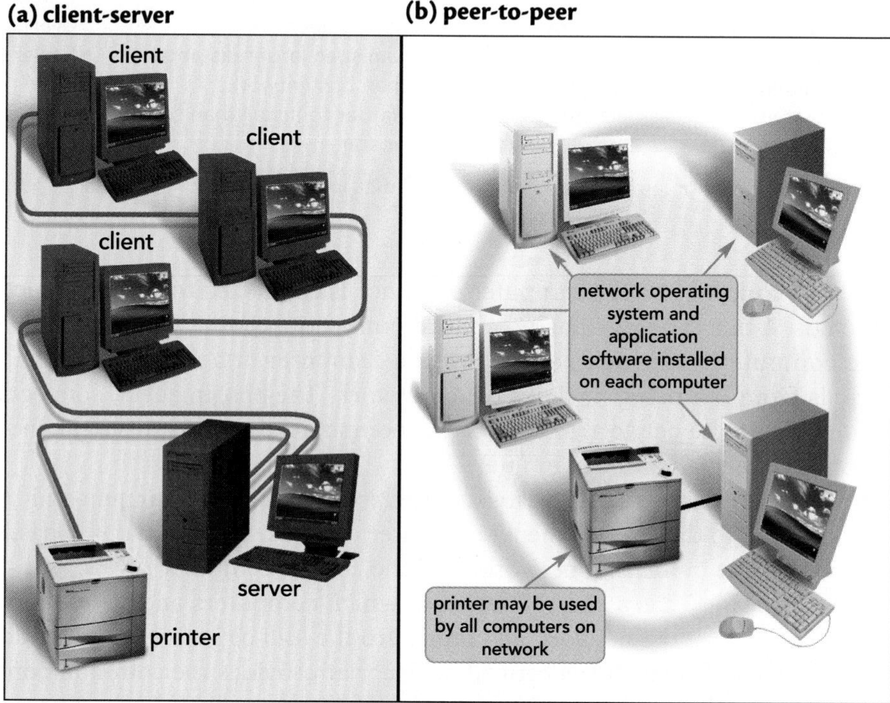

Figure 10-2 On a client/server network, one or more computers acts as a server and the clients access the server. On a peer-to-peer network, each computer shares its hardware and software with other computers on the network.

On a client/server network, some servers perform a specific task. For example, a *file server* is used to store and manage files, while a *print server* manages printers and print jobs. A *database server* stores and provides access to a database, a *network server* manages network activity or traffic, and a *Web server* stores and delivers requested Web pages to a computer.

PEER-TO-PEER In a *peer-to-peer* or P2P network architecture, each computer, or peer, on the network has equal responsibilities and capabilities on the network (Figure 10-2b). Each computer maintains a list of users and their rights on that particular PC. A peer-to-peer network typically is used to connect fewer than ten computers. As you learned in Chapter 8, Windows XP includes peer-to-peer networking capabilities to allow you to connect several computers into a workgroup.

FAQ 10-1

Is peer-to-peer used to support file sharing networks like Kazaa?

Yes. In recent years, peer-to-peer networking has been used to connect computers via the Internet, allowing users to access files on another user's hard disk. To access this type of network, also called a file sharing network, each computer must have the same peer-to-peer networking program, such as Kazaa, Morpheus, or Gnutella. These P2P programs allow users to share video, images, documents, and programs, although they are most widely known for their use in swapping MP3 music files. If you use a file sharing network, remember that software, music, and other files may be copyright-protected. If you obtain or use them illegally, you are breaking the law.

Network Hardware Protocols

Networks can connect computers and devices from different manufacturers and with different operating systems. For these different devices on several types of networks to communicate, the devices must use a common set of **network protocols**, which are rules that define how the hardware devices and software operate and work together.

Communication over a network can use many different protocols. For example, the operating system on one PC can communicate with the operating system on another PC using one set of protocols, while a NIC communicates with other hardware devices on the network using a different set of network protocols. Examples of hardware protocols are Ethernet and token ring. Examples of protocols that work with operating systems are TCP/IP and NetBEUI. The following sections review the hardware protocols used for LANS that use Ethernet, token ring, and wireless connections. Operating system protocols are discussed later in the chapter.

ETHERNET **Ethernet**, which often is used in LANs, is a hardware protocol that allows nodes to contend for access to the network. If two computers on an Ethernet network attempt to send data at the same time, a collision occurs and the computers must attempt to send their messages again.

Types of Ethernet The types of Ethernet primarily are distinguished from one another by speed and cost: 10-Mbps Ethernet, 100-Mbps or Fast Ethernet, Gigabit, and 10-Gigabit Ethernet (Figure 10-3). Figure 10-3 shows the various types of connectors and Figure 10-4 illustrates the types of cables used on an Ethernet network.

Cable System	Speed	Cables and Connectors	Example of Connector	Maximum Cable Length
10Base2 (ThinNet)	10 Mbps	Coaxial cable Uses a BNC connector		185 meters or 607 feet
10Base5 (ThickNet)	10 Mbps	Coaxial cable Uses an AUI 15-pin D-shaped connector		500 meters or 1,640 feet
10BaseT, 100BaseT (twisted-pair), and Gigabit Ethernet	10 Mbps or 100 Mbps	UTP or STP cable Uses an RJ-45 connector		100 meters or 328 feet
10BaseF, 10BaseFL, 100BaseFL, 100BaseFX, or 1000BaseFX (fiber-optic)	10 Mbps, 100 Mbps, or 1 Gbps	Fiber-optic cable Uses an ST or SC fiber-optic connector		500 meters up to 2 kilometers (6,562 feet)

Figure 10-3 Types of Ethernet and Ethernet cabling.

10-Mbps Ethernet was invented by Xerox Corporation in the 1970s. After it was enhanced in 1980, it became known as Ethernet IEEE 802.3. It operates at 10 Mbps (megabits per second) and uses either shielded or unshielded twisted-pair cable or coaxial cable. As shown in Figure 10-4, **unshielded twisted-pair (UTP) cable** consists of one or more twisted pair wires bundled together. **Shielded twisted-pair (STP) cable** uses a covering around the pairs of wires inside the cable, which protects it from electromagnetic interference caused by electrical motors, transmitters, or high-tension telephone lines. STP costs more than UTP, so it is used only when the situation demands it. **Coaxial cable**, often called simply coax (pronounced *co-ax*), is a single copper wire covered by insulating material, a braided metal outer conductor, and a plastic outer coating. Twisted-pair cable uses a connector called an **RJ-45 connector** that looks like a large telephone jack, while coaxial cable uses a **BNC connector**.

There are several variations of 10-Mbps Ethernet. 10BaseT Ethernet uses UTP cable that is rated by category. Category 5 cable, commonly called CAT 5 cable, is the UTP cable most often used for 10BaseT Ethernet. Some newer networks use Category 6 (CAT 6) cable, which provides improved transmission and fewer errors. 10Base5 Ethernet (sometimes called ThickNet) uses thick coaxial cable such as RG8. 10Base2 Ethernet (sometimes called ThinNet) uses a less expensive, smaller coaxial cable such as RG58.

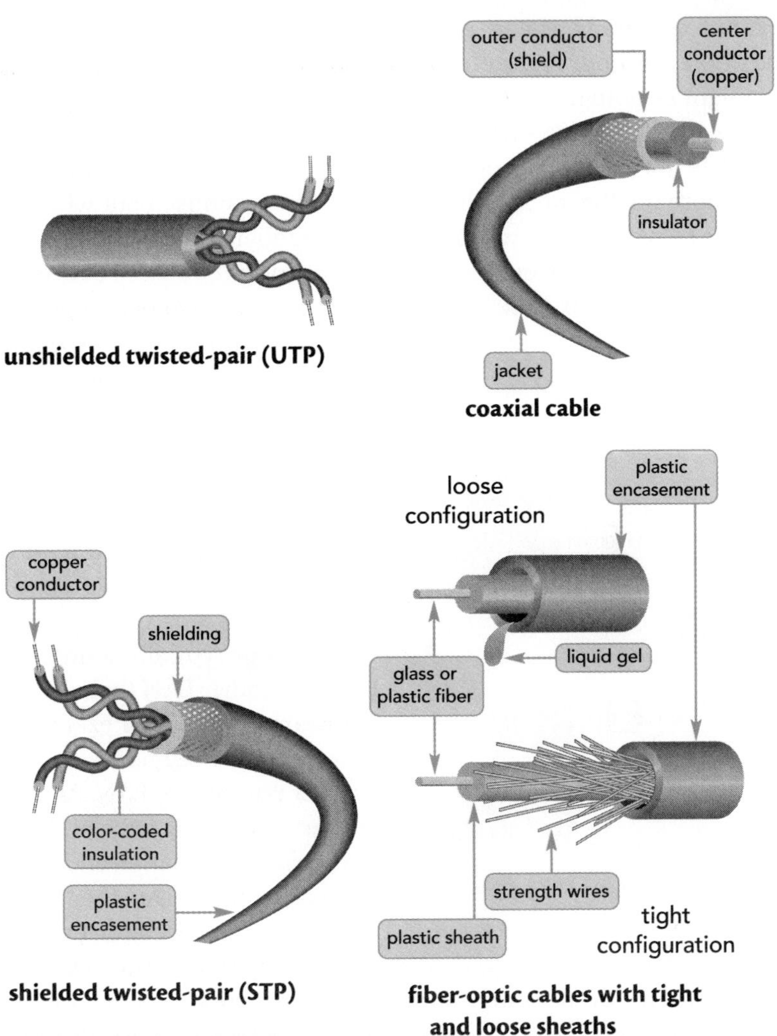

Figure 10-4 Types of network cables.

A newer version of Ethernet, *100-Mbps Ethernet* or *Fast Ethernet*, operates at 100 Mbps and uses UTP or STP cable. This improved and most popular version of Ethernet, sometimes called *100BaseT Ethernet*, also can support slower speeds of 10 Mbps so devices that run at either 10 Mbps or 100 Mbps can coexist on the same LAN. Two variations of 100BaseT are 100BaseTX and 100BaseFX. 100BaseTX uses UTP cables, such as CAT-5 cable. 100BaseFX uses fiber-optic cable.

1000-Mbps Ethernet or *Gigabit Ethernet* operates at 1000 Mbps and uses twisted-pair and fiber-optic cable. Gigabit Ethernet is used on some LANs, but is not yet as popular as 100-Mbps Ethernet. An even faster version of Ethernet, *10-Gigabit Ethernet*, currently is under development. 10-Gigabit Ethernet will operate at 10 billion bits per second (10 Gbps) and will use fiber-optic cable to connect large metropolitan area networks (MANs) and major networks on the Internet.

Configuring Ethernet Networks Ethernet networks can be configured using either a bus or a star topology. (The star arrangement is more popular because it is easier to maintain than a bus.) In an Ethernet network using a star topology, any data received by a hub is replicated and broadcast, or passed on to every device connected to it

(Figure 10-5). A hub essentially is just a pass-through and distribution point for every device connected to it, without regard for what type of data is passing through and where the data might be going.

For small networks, hubs are sufficient, but in larger networks, devices such as bridges and switches are needed to help reduce the traffic on the network. Bridges and switches are more intelligent than hubs and make decisions about whether to allow traffic to pass or where to forward that traffic, reducing traffic and improving network performance. A network engineer will add a bridge or switch at a strategic place on the network, such as between two floors or between two buildings, to contain heavy traffic within specific parts, or segments, of a network. The NIC for each computer has a unique address, called a MAC address, to identify a computer connected to a network. Bridges and switches use these MAC addresses, which they store in routing tables, to determine where to send packets.

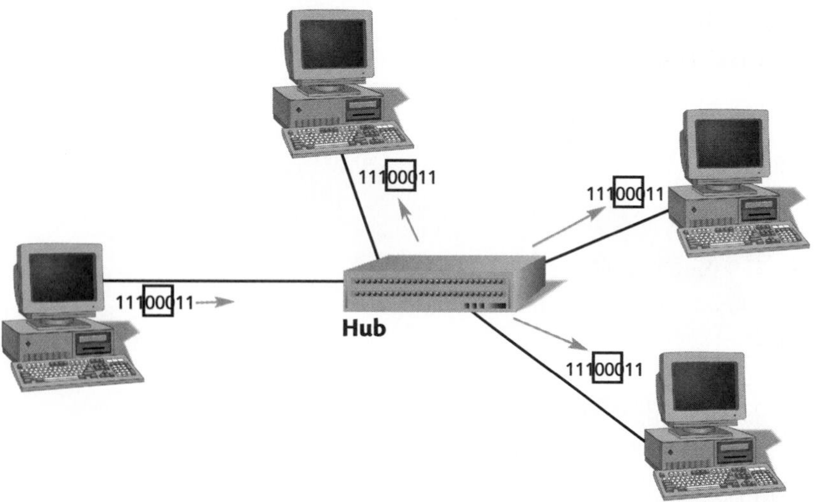

Figure 10-5 Any data received by a hub is replicated and passed on to every device connected to it.

A **bridge** typically connects one LAN to another LAN that uses the same hardware protocol (for example, Ethernet) — or segments of a LAN to another part of that LAN. As packets appear at the bridge, the bridge looks at the packet's destination and does not let that packet pass to another network if it is addressed to a location on its own network segment. Instead the bridge routes the packet only if the destination is on a different network, or if the bridge does not recognize the destination. The bridge routes the packet by broadcasting it to all of the other network segments.

A **switch** works much like a bridge, but does not send broadcast messages. Like a bridge, a switch keeps a table of MAC addresses to determine which path to use when sending packets. Unlike a bridge, a switch passes a packet only to the network with the destination computer, instead of to all segments other than the one from which it came. Figure 10-6 compares how bridges and switches work.

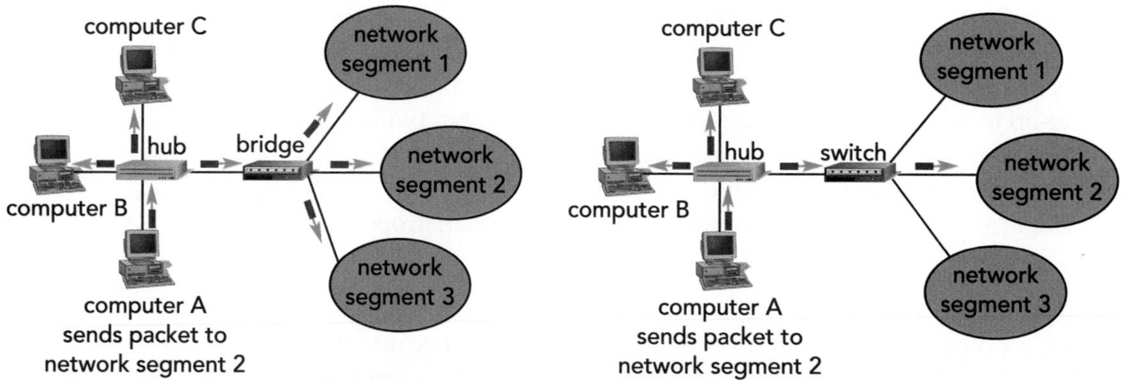

Figure 10-6 A switch is more intelligent than a bridge and can determine to which network (or network segment) a packet needs to be sent.

TOKEN RING AND FDDI **Token ring** is an older LAN technology that controls access to the network by requiring devices on the network to pass a special signal called a token. A **token** is a series of bits that indicate that the device with the token is allowed to communicate over a network. Each device on the network connects to a type of hub called a controlled-access unit (CAU), a multistation access unit (MSAU or MAU), or a smart multistation access unit (SMAU).

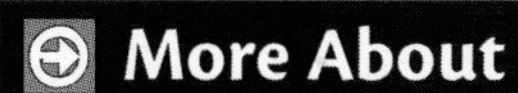

More About

Network Devices and Segmenting a Network

To learn more about segmenting a network, visit the Understanding and Troubleshooting Your PC More About Web page (**scsite.com/understanding/more**) and then click Segmenting a Network below Chapter 10.

FAQ 10-2

Is a token ring network always configured in a ring topology?

A token ring network actually is arranged in a star topology. Because the token is passed in order around the computers on the star (from computer A to computer B and so on), however, the token is considered to travel in a ring around the network. Because a token ring network is connected physically like a star but logically acts like a ring topology, it sometimes is called a star ring or a star-wired ring topology.

Like a token ring network, **Fiber Distributed Data Interface** (**FDDI**) uses a token that travels in a ring. FDDI (pronounced *fiddy*) uses a dual-ring approach, however, in which two rings connect all of the nodes on the network and each ring transmits data in a direction opposite to the other one. Physically, the nodes on a FDDI network can be connected using a ring topology, although most FDDI networks are set up using a physical star topology with a hub as the central device.

FDDI provides transfer of digital data over fiber-optic cable at 100 Mbps, which is much faster than token ring. FDDI also is more secure and less susceptible to interference from other electrical noise. For these reasons, FDDI often is used as the network technology for LANs in a large company. It also is used as a backbone to connect several LANs in a large building.

Wireless LANs

Wireless LAN (**WLAN**) technology, as the name implies, uses radio waves or infrared light instead of cables or wires to connect computers or other devices. A computer connects to a wireless LAN using a **wireless NIC**, which sends and receives signals. Using wireless technologies, a device can communicate directly with another device (such as a handheld device communicating with a PC via an infrared connection) or it can connect to a LAN by way of a wireless **access point** (**AP**), as shown in Figure 10-7.

Wireless LANs are popular in places where networking cables are difficult to install, such as outdoors or in a historic building with wiring restrictions, or where there are many mobile users, such as on a college campus. Access points are placed so that nodes can connect to at least one access point from anywhere in the area covered by the network. When devices use an access point, they communicate through the access point instead of communicating directly.

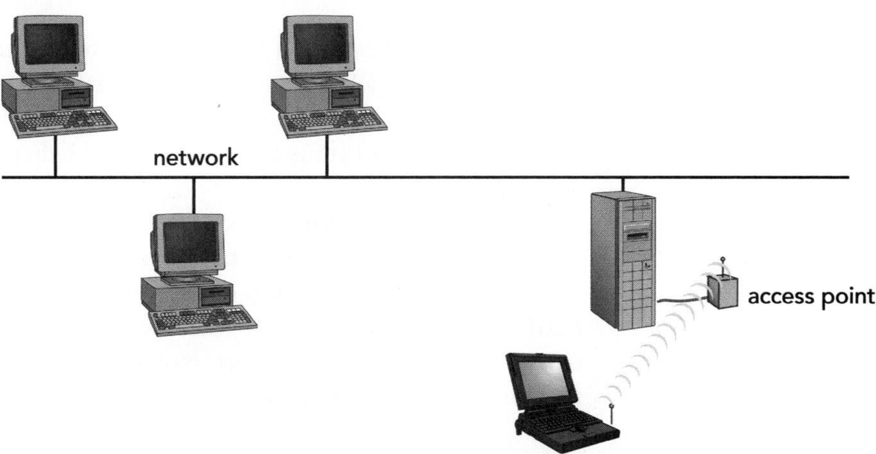

Figure 10-7 Nodes on a wireless LAN connect to a cabled network by way of an access point.

Wireless LANs typically use radio frequency (RF) technology to connect devices on the network. As you learned in Chapter 7, Bluetooth and 802.11 are two widely used radio frequency technologies. *Bluetooth* is a standard for short-range wireless communication between Bluetooth-enabled devices, such as computers, PDAs, cell phones, digital cameras, and printers. Bluetooth can transmit data between two devices at a rate of up to 1 Mbps, over a distance of about 10 meters (33 feet). In current usage, Bluetooth often is used to connect to devices such as a PDA and a cell phone, so the PDA can connect to a remote network using the cellular phone connection.

802.11 is a group of standards that define how computers and other devices communicate over a wireless network. Of the various 802.11 standards, the most widely implemented are 802.11g and 802.11b, which also are called *Wi-Fi (wireless fidelity)* or *Airport* (as named by Apple Computer). Figure 10-8 outlines the range, frequency, and speeds of the three 802.11 standards: 802.11a, 802.11b, and 802.11g. The 802.11b and 802.11g standards are popular and inexpensive network solutions for homes and small offices. (Note that many cordless phones use the 2.4-GHz frequency range and can cause network interference with a wireless LAN using Wi-Fi.)

Standard	Rated Maximum Range	Frequency	Max. Speed	Pros	Cons
802.11a	25 to 75 ft (7 to 33 m)	5 GHz	54 Mbps	• Fast • Does not interfere with cell phones or Bluetooth devices	• Has short range • Not compatible with 802.11b and 801.11g
802.11b	100 to 150 ft indoors; 300 ft outdoors (30 to 36 m indoors; 92 m outdoors)	2.4 GHz	11 Mbps	• Low-cost • Compatible with 802.11g	• Slower • May interfere with cell phones or Bluetooth devices
802.11g	100 to 150 ft indoors; 300 ft outdoors (30 to 36 m indoors; 92 m outdoors)	2.4 GHz	54 Mbps	• Fast • Compatible with 802.11b	• Higher cost than 802.11b • May interfere with cell phones or Bluetooth devices

Figure 10-8 Characteristics of the 802.11 standards.

How NICs Work

As you have learned, a PC makes a direct connection to a network by way of a network adapter, which is most often an expansion card called a network interface card (NIC). A NIC is designed to support one of the network hardware protocols described in the previous sections, such as Ethernet, token ring, FDDI, or wireless architectures.

A NIC can be internal or external. An internal NIC plugs into a PCI slot or other motherboard expansion slot, provides a port or ports (or antenna in the case of a wireless NIC) for connection to a network, and manages the communication and hardware protocol for the PC. An external NIC provides the same functions and can use a PC Card slot or USB port. Notebook computers can make connections to a network through a built-in network port, a PC Card NIC, or an external NIC that connects to the laptop by way of a USB port.

Whether internal or external, a NIC must match the type and speed of the physical network being used and the network port must match the type of connectors used on the network. As previously noted, a NIC can be designed to support Ethernet, token ring, FDDI, or wireless architectures (Figure 10-9), but it can support only one architecture. A NIC, however, might be designed to handle more than one type of cable.

FDDI

token ring

Ethernet

wireless

Figure 10-9 A NIC is designed to support a specific set of the network hardware protocols, such as FDDI, token ring, Ethernet, or wireless.

Before sending data from a computer, a NIC must convert the data into a signal that is appropriate for network cabling. For example, a FDDI card converts data to light pulses before transmitting the data over a fiber-optic cable. The component on the card responsible for this signal conversion is called the **transceiver** (short for *trans*mitter-rec*eiver*). Ethernet cards often contain more than one transceiver, each with a different port on the back of the card, in order to accommodate different cabling media. This type of Ethernet card is called a **combo card** (Figure 10-10).

When a computer is connected to a network, the network interface cards and the device drivers controlling it are the only components in the PC that are aware of the type of network protocol being used. The other applications on the computer are not concerned with whether the network is an Ethernet or 802.11g wireless LAN.

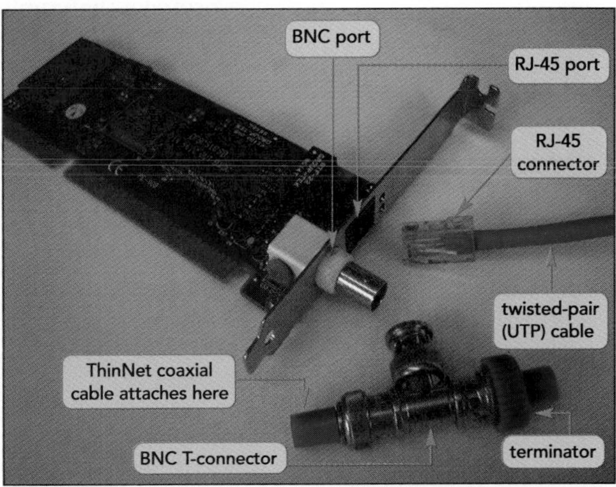

Figure 10-10 An Ethernet combo card can use either a BNC or RJ-45 connection, depending on the network and cables used.

Using Windows on a Network

As a system of interlinked computers, a network needs both software and hardware to work. Software includes an operating system installed on each computer on the network, and perhaps an NOS (network operating system) to control the entire network and its resources. Popular network operating systems are Windows Server 2003, Windows 2000 Server, Novell NetWare, Unix, Linux, and Mac OS. Windows has client software built in for Windows and Novell NetWare servers. Alternately, for Novell NetWare, you can install Novell client software.

As you learned in Chapter 8, Windows has networking features that allow you to connect computers in a workgroup that uses a peer-to-peer networking model or in a domain that uses the client/server model. In a domain, access to the network is controlled by a networking operating system that stores the directory database or the security accounts manager (SAM) database.

Network Protocols

At the physical network level, Windows supports such hardware protocols as Ethernet, token ring, and others. At the operating system level, Windows supports three suites of network protocols: TCP/IP, IPX/SPX, and NetBEUI:

- **TCP/IP** (**Transmission Control Protocol/Internet Protocol**) is a popular protocol suite that is the basis of the Internet and should be your choice if you want to connect a network to the Internet and provide each workstation with Internet access. Windows, Novell NetWare, Linux, Unix, and Mac OS support TCP/IP.
- **IPX/SPX** (**Internetwork Packet Exchange/Sequenced Packet Exchange**) is a protocol suite designed for use with the Novell NetWare network operating system. IPX/SPX is similar to TCP/IP but is not supported on the Internet. Recent versions of NetWare use TCP/IP by default, but also support IPX/SPX.
- **NetBEUI** (**NetBIOS Extended User Interface**) is a proprietary Windows protocol suite used only by Windows computers. NetBEUI supports NetBIOS, a protocol that applications use to communicate with each other. NetBEUI is faster than TCP/IP and easier to configure, but it does not support routing to other networks and therefore is not supported on the Internet. NetBEUI only should be used on a network that is not connected to the Internet. Windows XP does not automatically install NetBEUI, as Microsoft considers it an older, legacy protocol.

FAQ 10-3

Why do I not see NetBEUI available as an installed protocol in Windows XP?

Windows XP does not automatically install NetBEUI. You can install it manually using the Windows XP setup CD, however. For instructions on installing NetBEUI on a Windows XP computer, search for the Microsoft Knowledge Base Article 301041 at *support.microsoft.com*.

To use one of these protocols on a network, the first step is to connect the computer to the network physically by installing the NIC in the computer and connecting the network cable to the hub or other network device. (For wireless LANs, after installing the NIC, you put the computer within range of an access point.)

The next step is to install the protocol in the operating system. Once the protocol is installed, it automatically associates itself with any NICs it finds, in a process called binding. **Binding** occurs when an operating system-level protocol such as TCP/IP associates itself with a lower-level hardware protocol such as Ethernet. When the two protocols are bound, communication continues between them until they are unbound, or released.

You can determine which protocols are installed in Windows by looking at the properties of a network connection. First, open Control Panel and, if necessary, click Switch to Classic View. Double-click Network Connections. Right-click an available network connection, such as Local Area Connection, and then click Properties on the shortcut menu. When the Properties window displays, as shown in Figure 10-11, the protocols bound to an NIC are shown as checked in the This connection uses the following items list.

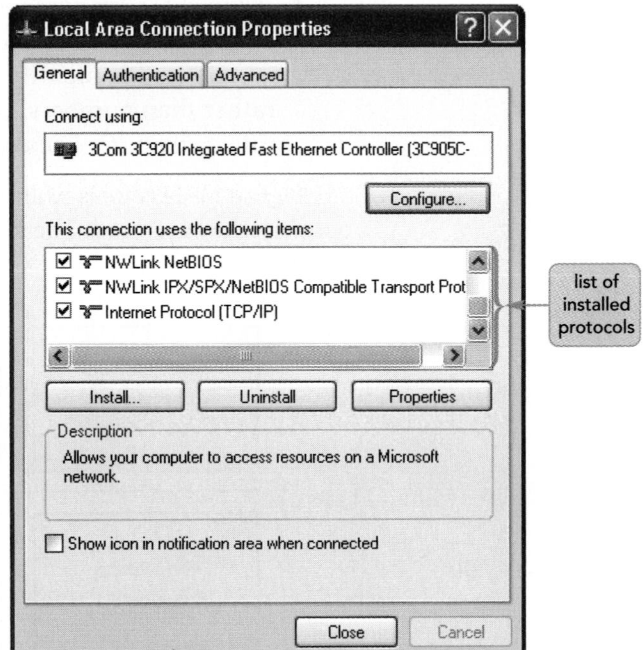

Figure 10-11 Three network protocols are installed and bound to this network adapter.

Addressing on a Network

Every node on a network has a unique address, so data packets can be addressed and delivered to the correct device. Part of learning about a network is learning how devices, such as a computer or printer, or a program, such as a Web server, are identified on the network. On a network, four methods are used to identify devices and programs:

- *Using a MAC address.* Different networks have different ways of identifying network devices, based on the network interface card. As previously discussed, Ethernet, wireless, and token ring cards have MAC addresses permanently embedded on the card by their manufacturers. A **MAC (Media Access Control) address** (also called *hardware address*, *physical address*, *adapter address*, or *Ethernet address*) is a 6-byte address, often expressed as six pairs of hexadecimal numbers and letters, often separated by hyphens. A MAC address is unique to each NIC, so no two NICs have the same MAC address. The MAC address is used only by devices inside the local network, and is not used outside the LAN.
- *Using an IP address.* An **IP address** is a 32-bit address consisting of a series of four 8-bit numbers separated by periods. An IP address, such as 109.168.0.104, identifies a computer, printer, or other device on a TCP/IP network such as the Internet or an intranet. (An **intranet** is an internal network that uses TCP/IP.) Where a MAC address only is used on devices on a local network, an IP address can be used by any device connected to the network.

- *Using a port number*. A **port number** identifies a program or service running on a computer to communicate over the network. When a computer is configured for network or Internet communication, it opens a series of port numbers to send and receive messages.
- *Using character-based names*. Character-based names include *domain names, host names*, and *NetBIOS (Network Basic Input/Output System) names* used to identify a PC on a network with easy-to-remember letters rather than numbers. (Host names and NetBIOS names often are simply called *computer names*.)

Figure 10-12 shows examples of each of these addresses and at what layer of the network they are used. The sections that follow explain the different address types in more detail.

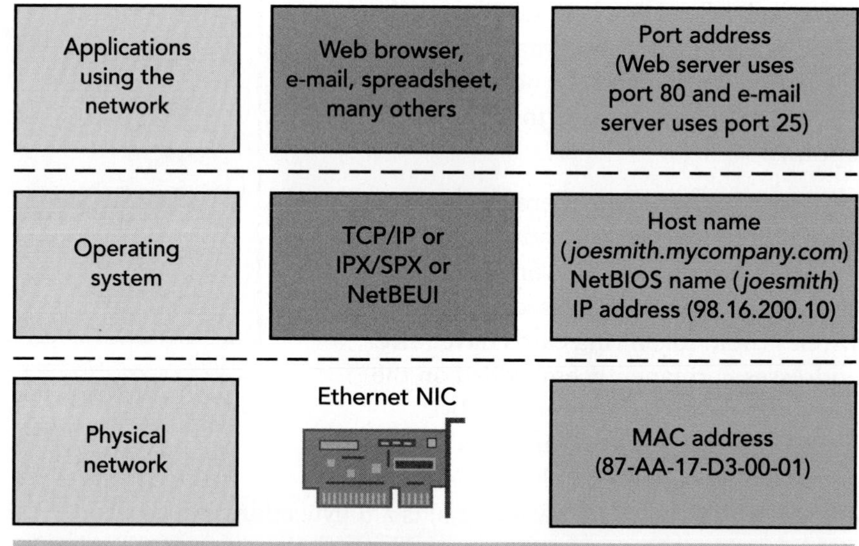

Figure 10-12 Communication over a network occurs in layers, with application software, the operating system, and the physical network hardware using different protocols to communicate.

MAC ADDRESSES As shown in Figure 10-12, *MAC addresses* are used at the lowest (physical) networking level for NICs and other networking devices on the same network to communicate. If a host does not know the MAC address of another host on the same network, it uses the operating system to discover the MAC address.

Because the hardware protocol (for example, Ethernet) controls traffic only on its own network, computers on different networks cannot use their MAC addresses for communication. In order for the host to communicate with a host on another LAN on an intranet or the Internet, it must know the IP address of the host (Figure 10-13).

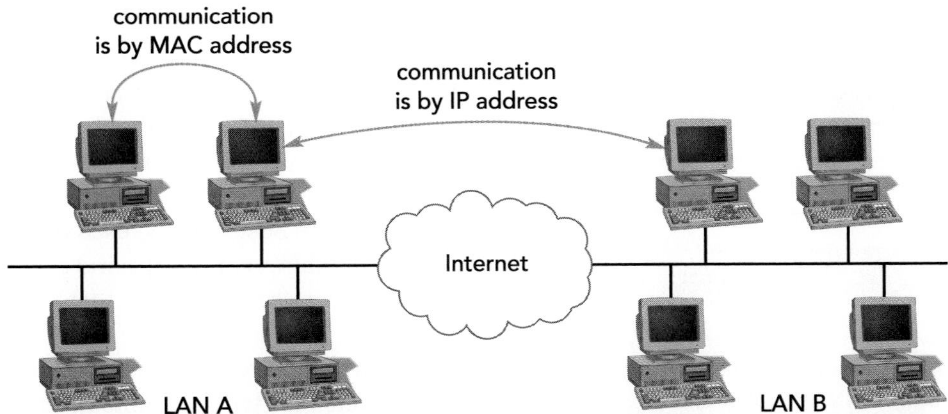

Figure 10-13 Computers on the same LAN use MAC addresses to communicate, but computers on different LANs use IP addresses to communicate over the Internet.

IP ADDRESSES An *IP address* is a unique address used by the TCP/IP suite of protocols to identify a device on the Internet or an intranet. A typical IP address — such as 207.46.249.29 — has four numbers that range from 0 through 255, separated by periods (Figure 10-14). This form of the IP address sometimes is called a dotted decimal number or dotted quad. Each of the four numbers in the dotted quad is called an *octet*, because they each have eight bits when viewed in binary form, for a total of 32 bits in the IP address. (For instance, the binary form of 207.46.249.29 is 11001111.00101110.11111001.00011101.) Because each of the eight bits can be 1 or 0, the total possible combinations per octet are 2^8 or 256. Combining the four octets of an IP address provides a possible 2^{32} or 4,294,967,296 unique values. (Of course, the actual number of available addresses is around 3 billion, because some are reserved for special use or off limits).

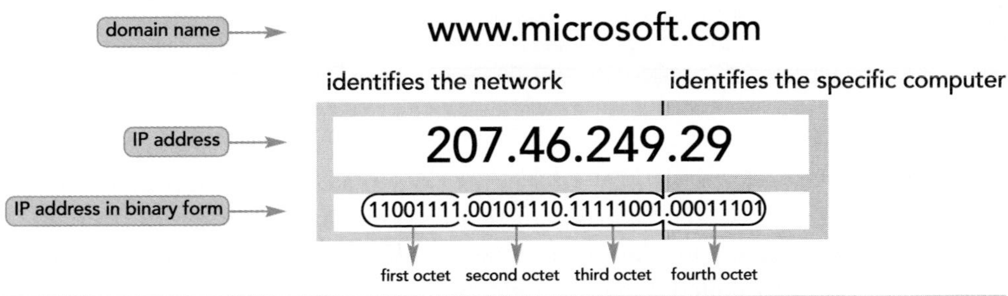

Figure 10-14 Component of an IP address.

It is important to understand how the bits of an IP address are used in order to understand how data is routed over interconnected networks such as the Internet, and how TCP/IP can locate an IP address anywhere on the globe. An IP address has two parts that identify a specific computer: one part to identify the network where that computer resides and a second part to pinpoint the specific machine or host within that network, as shown in Figure 10-15 on the next page. When data is routed over

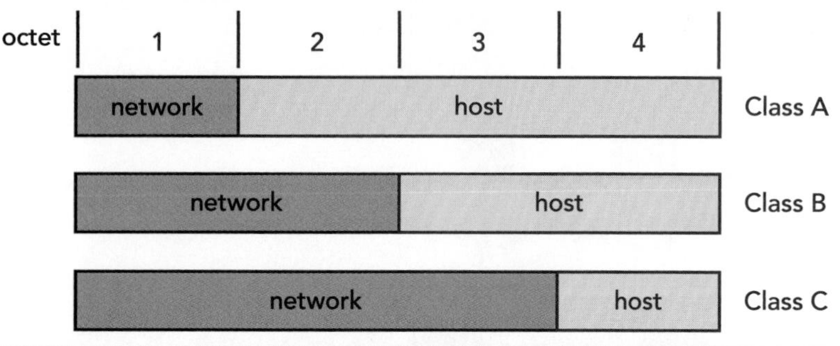

Figure 10-15 An IP address has two parts to identify the network where that computer resides and a second part to pinpoint the specific machine or host within that network. The class of the IP address determines which octets identify the network or the host.

interconnected networks, the network portion of the IP address is used to locate the right network. Once the data arrives at the network, the host portion of the IP address is used to identify the computer on the network that is to receive the data. Finally, the IP address of the host must be used to identify the MAC address of the specific computer, so the data can be sent to that computer.

When a company wants an IP address for computers that will be connected to the Internet, the company must register for a license. IP addresses are assigned by one of three regional Internet registries, which assign Internet addresses from the following three classes:

Class A: provides an IP address for 16 million hosts

Class B: provides an IP address for 65,000 hosts

Class C: provides an IP address for 254 hosts

If a company is assigned a Class C license, it is given 254 IP addresses for its use. If the company has only a few computers (hosts) connected to the network, many IP addresses go unused. If the company grows and now has 300 workstations on the network, it will have run out of IP addresses. There are two approaches to solving this problem: use private IP addresses and use dynamic IP addressing. Many companies combine both methods, which are discussed in the following sections.

Are there not also IP addresses in Class D and Class E?

Class D and Class E IP addresses are available, but not for general use. Class D addresses begin with octets 224 through 239 and are used for multicasting, in which one host sends messages to multiple hosts, such as when the host transmits a video conference over the Internet. Class E addresses begin with 240 through 254 and are reserved for research. The High-Tech Talk feature in this chapter provides additional information about IP addresses.

Public, Private, and Reserved IP Addresses When a company applies for a Class A, B, or C license, it is assigned a group of IP addresses that are different from all other IP addresses and are available for use on the Internet. The IP addresses available to the Internet are called *public IP addresses*.

Not all of a company's workstations, however, need to have direct Internet access, even though they may be on the network. While each workstation may need an IP address to be part of the TCP/IP network, those workstations not connected to the Internet do not need addresses that are unique and available to the Internet. These workstations can use private IP addresses. *Private IP addresses* are used on private intranets that are isolated from the Internet. Because the hosts are isolated from the Internet, no conflicts arise if the private IP address is the same as a public IP address. Typically, the following IP addresses are used for private networks:

10.0.0.0 through 10.255.255.255

172.16.0.0 through 172.31.255.255

192.168.0.0 through 192.168.255.255

All IP addresses on a network must be unique for that network. When assigning private IP addresses, keep in mind that a few IP addresses are reserved for special use by TCP/IP and should not be used, including 255.255.255.255 (used for broadcast messages), 0.0.0.0 (currently unassigned IP address), and 127.0.01 (loopback address that identifies the computer).

Static and Dynamic IP Addresses Some computers, such as Web servers, are always connected to a network or the Internet. An administrator often will assign this computer a **static IP address**, which is a permanent address that represents that machine on a network. If an administrator must configure each host on a network manually, assigning it a unique IP address, it can be time-consuming and difficult to set up and then keep track of which address is assigned to which PC. The solution is to have a server automatically assign an IP address to a workstation each time it comes onto the network. Instead of permanently assigning a static IP address to a workstation, the server assigns a temporary IP address, called a **dynamic IP address**, while the computer is connected to the network.

The server also gives the PC its subnet mask and default gateway, so the computer knows how to communicate with other hosts that are not on its own network. A **gateway** is a computer or other device that allows a computer on one network to communicate with a computer on another network. A **default gateway** is the gateway a computer uses to access another network if it does not have a better option. A **subnet mask** is a group of four dotted-decimal numbers that tells TCP/IP if a remote computer's IP address is on the same or a different network.

When the session terminates, the IP address is returned to the list of available addresses. Because not all workstations are online at all times, the needs of the network can be met by fewer IP addresses than the total number of workstations. When a workstation has a dynamic IP address assigned to it, the workstation is said to be *leasing the IP address*. **Internet service providers (ISPs)**, organizations through which individuals and businesses connect to the Internet, use dynamic IP addressing for their subscribers.

A server that manages these dynamically assigned IP addresses is called a **DHCP (Dynamic Host Configuration Protocol) server**. In this arrangement, workstations are called DHCP clients. DHCP software resides on both the client and the server to manage the dynamic assignment of IP addresses. DHCP client software is built into Windows. When a PC first connects to the network, it attempts to lease an address from the DHCP server. If the attempt fails, it uses a process called IP autoconfiguration and assigns itself an **Automatic Private IP Address (APIPA)** in the address range 169.254.x.x.

Network Address Translation If hosts on a network using private IP addresses need to access the Internet, a problem arises because the private IP addresses are not allowed on the Internet. The solution is to use **NAT (Network Address Translation)**, which uses a single public IP address to access the Internet on behalf of all hosts on the network using private IP addresses. Using NAT, a networked computer trying to access the Internet must go through a **proxy server**, which is a server or other device that substitutes its own IP address for that of the computer requesting the information (the device is so named because it is standing in proxy for other hosts). Figure 10-16 shows how a proxy server stands between the network and the Internet. This proxy server has two network cards installed. One card connects to the LAN, and the other connects to the Internet either directly or via an ISP.

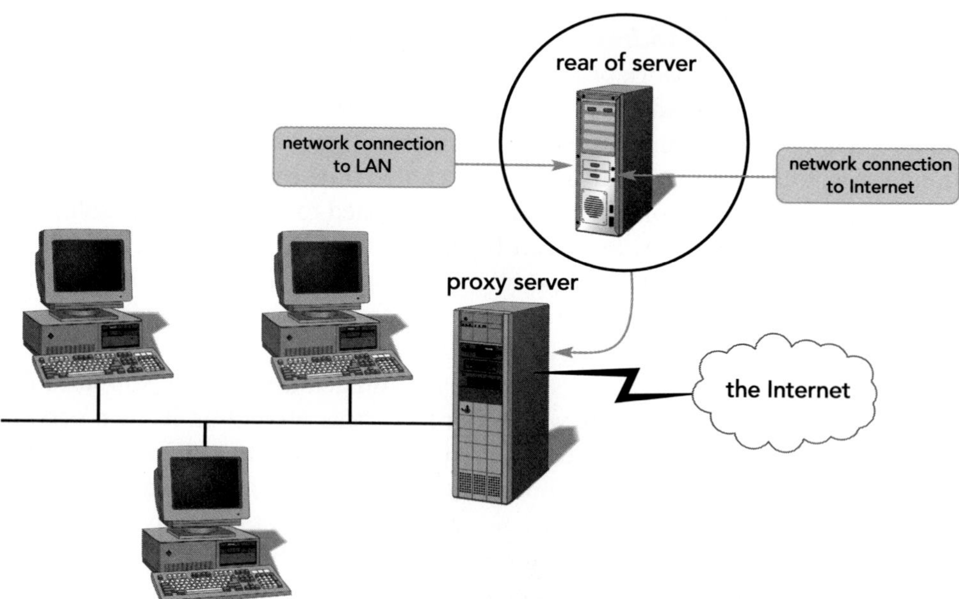

Figure 10-16 A proxy server stands between a private network and the Internet.

Windows XP and several earlier versions of Windows offer a NAT service called Internet Connection Sharing (ICS). With **Internet Connection Sharing (ICS)**, two or more PCs on a home network can share the same IP address when accessing the Internet. Under ICS, one PC acts as the proxy server for other PCs on the home network.

Because a proxy server stands between a LAN and the Internet, it often does double duty as a firewall. As you have learned, a *firewall* is software or hardware that protects a network from illegal entry. Because networks can be accessed by unauthorized users via the Internet, even a small LAN should have a device between the LAN and the Internet that serves as a proxy server, a DHCP server, and a firewall that filters out any unsolicited traffic.

PORT NUMBERS As previously noted, a port number identifies a program or service running on a computer to communicate over the network. (Each program running under the operating system on a server is called a **service**). For example, if an e-mail program and a Web browser both are running on a computer with one IP address, each program or service is assigned an identifying number, called a port number, port, or port address, when it starts. Each service listens at its assigned port. A network administrator can assign any port number to a server, but established port numbers are used for common services and protocols. For example, a Web server normally is assigned port 80, and an e-mail server receiving mail normally is assigned port 25, as shown in Figure 10-17. Port assignments are shown at the end of an IP address, following a colon (:). Using these default port assignments, the Web server would communicate at 138.60.30.5:80, and the e-mail server would communicate at 138.60.30.5:25.

Figure 10-17 Each server running on a computer is addressed by a unique port number.

NETBIOS NAMES, HOST NAMES, AND DOMAIN NAMES Each computer on a TCP/IP network is assigned an IP address, but these numbers are hard to remember. Character-based names, such as domain names, host names, and NetBIOS names, use characters rather than numbers to identify computers on a network and are easier to remember and use than IP addresses.

Recall that NetBEUI is a proprietary, legacy Windows network protocol used for Windows LANs that are not connected to the Internet. Before TCP/IP became such a widely used protocol, Windows used NetBEUI by default and assigned a NetBIOS name such as *joesmith* or *Workstation12* when the operating system was installed.

Newer versions of Windows, such as Windows XP, use TCP/IP as the default network protocol and identify computers by IP addresses. TCP/IP does, however, allow computers to be assigned a character-based **host name** such as *joesmith*. The host name also can have a domain name attached that identifies the network: *joesmith.mycompany.com*. A **domain name** is a text version of one or more IP addresses that represent a network or a Web server that houses a Web site. When the host name and domain name are used together to identify a computer, such as *joesmith.mycompany.com*, the domain name is considered to be a **fully qualified domain name** (**FQDN**), which often simply is referred to as the domain name. (Domain names and their use on the Internet are addressed later in the chapter.)

Your Turn

Viewing MAC Addresses and IP Addresses

If your PC is connected to the Internet or any other TCP/IP network, you can view the IP address of the computer and the MAC address of the computer's NIC by entering a few simple commands in the Command Prompt window. Using Windows XP, perform the following steps:

1. Click the Start button, point to All Programs on the Start menu, click Accessories on the All Programs menu, and then click Command Prompt. The Command Prompt window appears. At the command prompt, type **ipconfig/all |more** as the command. The |more option causes the results to appear one screen at a time, instead of scrolling by so fast you cannot read them. Press the ENTER key to see each screen, as shown in Figure 10-18.

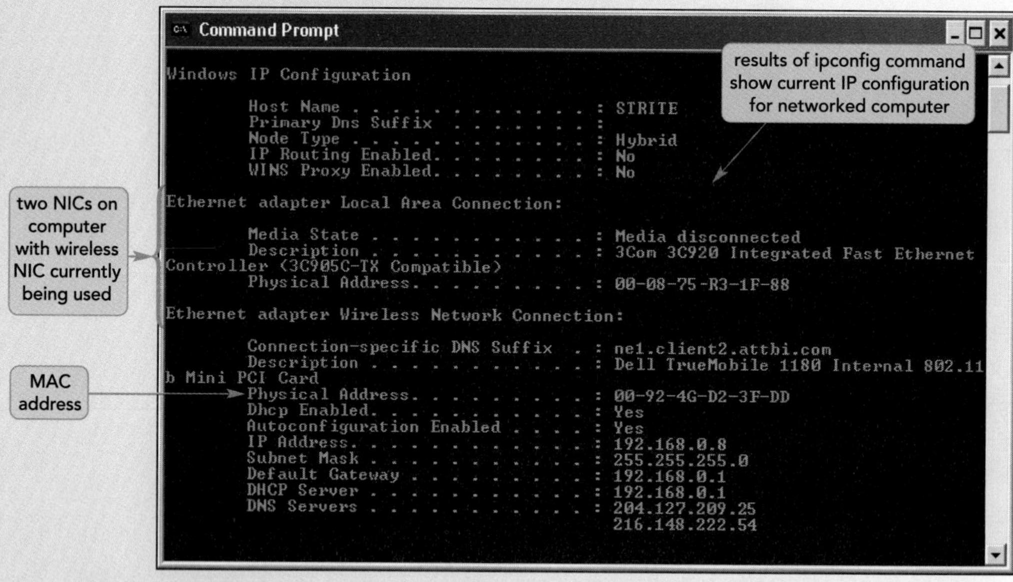

Figure 10-18

2. Answer the following questions:
   a. What is the host name?
   b. How many NICs are available on the computer? Based on the description of each, what hardware protocol is supported by each NIC? For example, the computer shown in Figure 10-18 has two NICs, one for a direct cable connection to a LAN using Fast Ethernet and one for a wireless LAN connection to a LAN using 802.11b. The wireless NIC is the one currently in use.
   c. The set of numbers and letters listed as the physical address is the MAC address. What is the MAC address of each NIC?
   d. For the NIC currently used for the network connection, what IP address is assigned?
   e. Is DHCP enabled? If so, what is the IP address of the DHCP server?
   f. What are the IP address(es) used for the DNS servers available to the computer?
3. Another utility, called Getmac, is used to return the MAC address of NICs on a computer. To use Getmac, enter **getmac** at the command prompt. The results appear on screen, showing the physical address of each NIC and the operating system protocols bound to each. Type **Exit** at the command prompt to close the Command Prompt window.
4. Shut down and then restart the computer. Complete Steps 1 through 3. Is the computer assigned the same or a different IP address as it was assigned before? Explain why you think the computer was assigned the same or a different IP address. Type **Exit** at the command prompt to close the Command Prompt window.

How Computers Find Each Other on a LAN

On a TCP/IP network, the character-based NetBIOS name, host name, or domain name must be associated with an IP address before one computer can find another on the network. This process of associating a character-based name with an IP address is called **name resolution**. Networks using Windows have several options available for name resolution: DNS, WINS, broadcast name resolution, and the Hosts and LMHosts files.

DNS (**Domain Name System**, also called **Domain Name Service**) is a system that determines the IP address associated with host names and domain names. For example, if you search for a computer based on a domain name, Windows connects to a **DNS server** to resolve the human-readable domain name into a machine-readable IP address. Each DNS server houses a simple database that maps domain names to IP addresses. The information about domain names and their corresponding IP addresses kept by a DNS server is called *zone data*.

WINS (Windows Internet Naming Service) is a system that determines the IP address associated with a client or server computer running on a Windows network using the NetBEUI protocol. A Windows Internet Name Service (WINS) server on a network allows you to search for resources by NetBIOS name instead of IP address. Windows networks sometimes use a combination of DNS and WINS for name resolution, although DNS is the more widely used method.

The process of name resolution involves a series of steps in which one computer attempts to determine the IP address of another computer. For a Windows XP computer, the computer tries the following steps in succession, in order to determine the IP address of the computer:

1. The computer checks the file named *Hosts* stored on the local computer. The Hosts file contains host names and associated IP addresses.
2. If the IP address for the computer is not in the Hosts file and the computer knows the IP address of a DNS server, the computer queries the DNS server.
3. If the IP address still is not discovered, the computer assumes that the network is using WINS instead of DNS and checks the NetBIOS name cache. This name cache contains information retained in memory from name resolutions made since the last reboot.
4. If the computer knows the IP address of a WINS server, it queries the server. A WINS server is a Windows NT or Windows 2000 server on the network that maintains a database of NetBIOS names and IP addresses.
5. The computer sends a broadcast message to all computers on the LAN, asking for the IP address of the computer with the broadcasted NetBIOS name.
6. The computer checks a file named *LMHosts*, which is stored on the local computer. The LMHosts file contains the NetBIOS names and associated IP addresses of computers on the LAN, if someone has taken the time to make the entries in the file manually.

Both the LMHosts and Hosts files are tables that list the name and associated IP addresses of computers (hosts) on a network (Figure 10-19). LMHosts serves as a local table of information similar to that maintained by a WINS server for NetBIOS names, and Hosts serves as a local table of information similar to that kept by a DNS server.

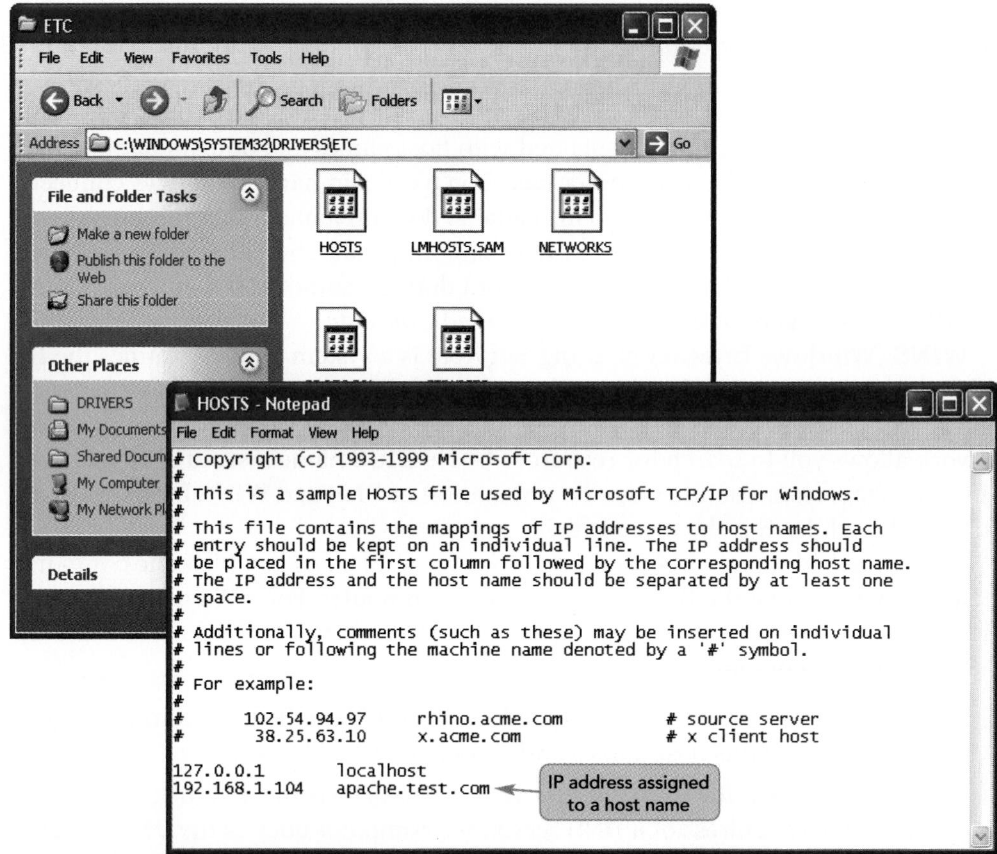

Figure 10-19 An entry in the client Hosts file tells the client the IP address of an intranet Web site when no DNS service is running.

On a Windows XP or Windows 2000 computer, these files are stored in the \Windows\System32\drivers\etc folder or the WINNT\System32\drivers\etc folder. On a Windows 9x computer, they are stored in the \Windows folder. If you look in these folders, you may see each file (LMHosts and Hosts) or a sample of each file (LMHosts.SAM and Hosts.SAM, where the SAM stands for sample). Figure 10-19 shows an example of a Hosts file. Entries in a host table file beginning with the # symbol are comments and are not read by the name resolution process. Entries at the bottom of the file, without the # symbol, associate IP addresses with host names. You can add your entries to the bottom of the file without the # symbol and then save the file in the same folder.

Hosts and LMHosts files work well in smaller networks or in situations where computers have static IP addresses that do not change. For example, the computer named *apache.test.com*, as shown in Figure 10-19, is used as a Web server for a private network. In order for people on the network to use this domain name, the Hosts file on each PC must have the entry for this host on the last line and the Web server must have the same IP address at all times. By using these files on the local drive, the computer does not need to send name resolution requests to a WINS or DNS server and wait for the response.

FAQ 10-5

How can I be sure that a server has the same IP address at all times?

The simplest way to accomplish this is to assign a static IP address to the server. Alternately, if the DHCP server supports this feature, you can tell the DHCP server your Web server's MAC address and configure the DHCP server to assign the same IP address to your Web server each time.

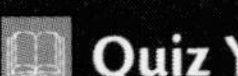

Quiz Yourself 10-1

To test your knowledge of network types and architectures and using Windows on a network, visit the Understanding and Troubleshooting Your PC Quiz Yourself Web page (scsite.com/understanding/quiz). Click Quiz Yourself 1 below Chapter 10.

Connecting to a Network

Connecting a PC to a wired network requires a NIC, a patch cable (network cable), and a device for the PC to connect to, such as a hub. Connecting a PC to a wireless network requires the PC to have a wireless NIC and be within range of an access point or another wireless-enabled device.

Installing a network card and connecting the PC to a network involves three general steps: (1) installing the NIC in the PC and then installing the NIC's drivers, (2) configuring the NIC using Windows, so it has the appropriate addresses on the network and the correct network protocols, and (3) testing the NIC to verify that the PC can access resources on the network.

Installing a Network Interface Card and Connecting to a Network

When selecting a network card, you should consider the following three things:

- The speed and type of network to which you are attaching (for example, Fast Ethernet, token ring, FDDI, or type of wireless LAN)
- Except for wireless connections, the type of cable you are using (for example, shielded twisted-pair, coaxial, or fiber-optic cable)
- The type of expansion slot you will use (for example, PCI or a notebook PC Card slot).

Network cards typically are installed in the PCI expansion slot for a desktop or tower computer. Network cards require an IRQ, an I/O address range, and a memory address range. If the network card is on the PCI bus, then the PCI bus controller manages the IRQ and I/O address requirements. Most new network cards are Plug and Play, although you may find that some legacy cards use jumpers or DIP switches on the card to determine which resources to request.

INSTALLING A NETWORK INTERFACE CARD In Chapter 6, you learned the general steps to install an expansion card in an expansion slot. The process of physically installing a NIC in a PCI expansion slot follows those same steps. Once the NIC is installed, a few additional steps are required to set up network connections. To install the drivers, perform the following steps:

1. After installing the network interface card in the PCI expansion slot, start the PC. The Found New Hardware Wizard launches to begin the process of loading the necessary drivers to use the new device. It is better to use the manufacturer's drivers, not the Windows drivers. When prompted by the Wizard, click the Have Disk button and insert the floppy disk or CD that came bundled with the NIC.
2. Next, verify that the drivers were installed successfully by performing the following steps:
    a. Click the Start button, click Control Panel on the Start menu and, if necessary, click Switch to Classic View. Double-click System in the Control Panel window.
    b. When the System Properties window displays, click the Hardware tab and then click the Device Manager button.
    c. Right-click the NIC in the list of devices and then click Properties on the shortcut menu. When the NIC's Properties window appears, look for any conflicts or other errors reported by Device Manager (Figure 10-20).

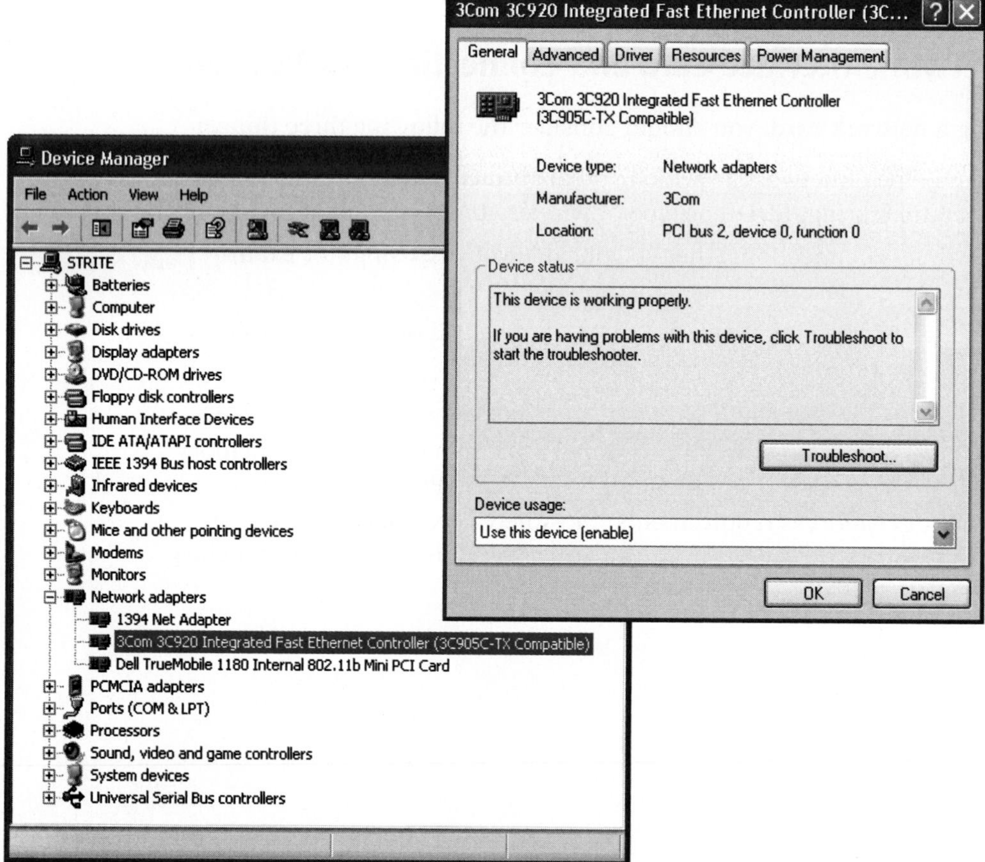

Figure 10-20 After installing a NIC, check its Properties window to ensure it is working properly.

If errors are reported, try downloading updated drivers from the Web site of the NIC's manufacturer. (Other troubleshooting tips for installing NICs are discussed later in this chapter).

To install a NIC in a notebook computer with a PC Card slot, you generally just insert the NIC in the slot and then follow the instructions on the Add New Hardware wizard, as outlined above. Figure 10-21 shows a PC Card NIC. The RJ-45 connection is at the end of a small cord connected to the PC Card. This small cord is called a *dongle* or *pigtail* and is used so the thick RJ-45 connection does not have to fit flat against the PC Card.

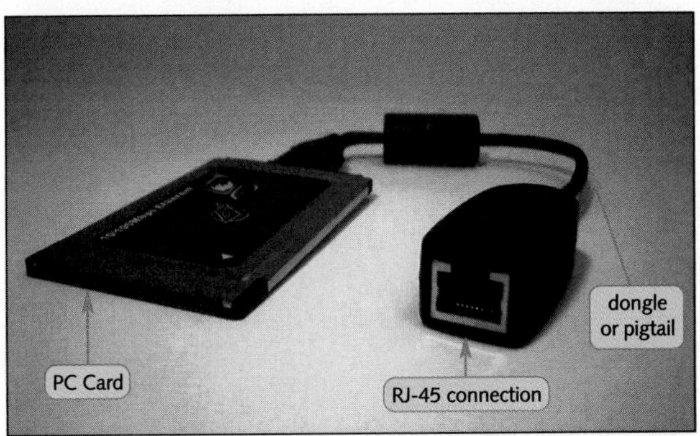

Figure 10-21 This PC Card serves as a NIC for a Fast Ethernet network.

FAQ 10-6

Windows XP keeps installing its own drivers, without asking if I want to use manufacturer-provided drivers. How do I prevent this from happening?

To prevent this from happening, run the setup program on the CD that comes bundled with the NIC before you install the card. Then, after you install the new NIC and boot the computer, Windows will find the already-installed manufacturer drivers and use those drivers.

NAMING A COMPUTER ON A NETWORK After installing the NIC and connecting to the network, you can configure the NIC to access the network. The first step is to use the OS to give the computer a name so it can be identified on the network. For Windows XP using the default TCP/IP network protocol, perform the following steps to name a computer:

1. Right-click My Computer and then click Properties from the shortcut menu. The System Properties window appears.
2. Click the Computer Name tab and then click the Change button. The Computer Name Changes window appears.

3. Enter a new computer name, such as win-xp, as shown in Figure 10-22. Remember that each computer name must be unique within a workgroup or domain.

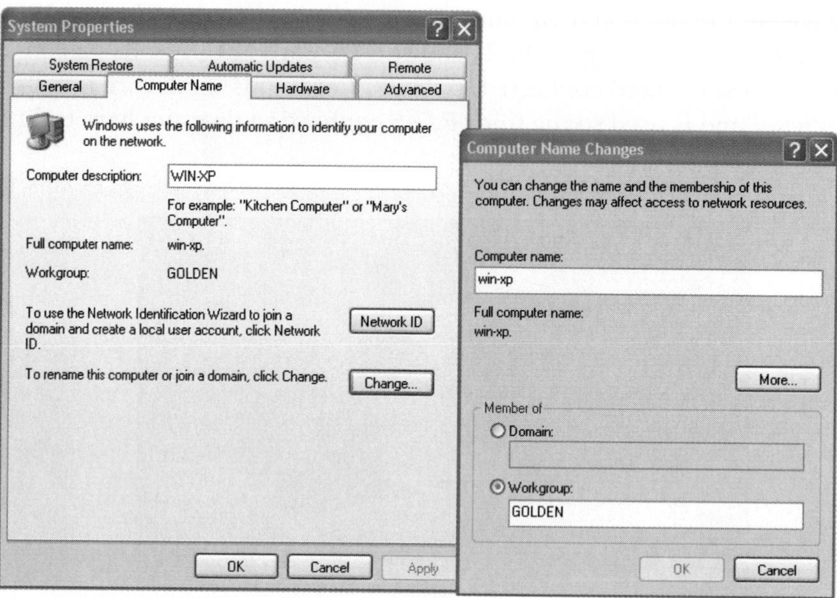

Figure 10-22 The Computer Name Changes window allows you to assign a new host name to a networked computer.

4. Select Workgroup and enter the name of the workgroup (GOLDEN in this example). All users in the workgroup must have the same workgroup name entered in this window. If the PC is to join a domain (a network where logging on is controlled by a server), select Domain and enter the name of the domain, such as *mycompany.com*. When configuring a PC on a network, always follow the specific directions of the network administrator.
5. Click OK to save the changes and close the Computer Name Changes window. Click OK to close the System Properties window. Windows will ask you to reboot the computer for the changes to take effect.
6. After rebooting the computer, click the Start button, click My Network Places on the Start menu, and then click View workgroup computers in the Network Tasks area. All of the computers connected to the network will display (Figure 10-23).

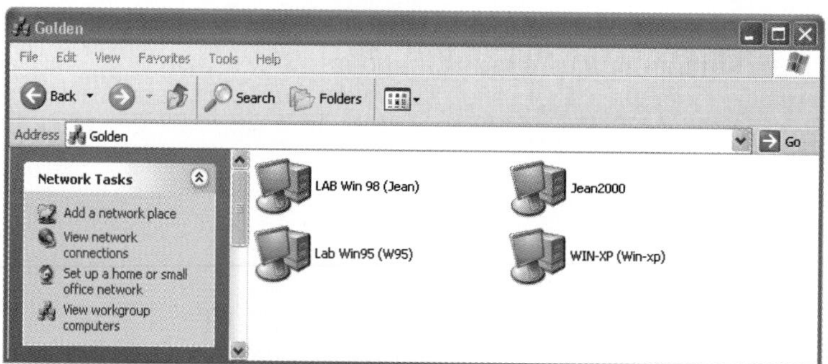

Figure 10-23 My Network Places shows all computers on the LAN in a common workgroup.

CONNECTING TO A NETWORK When a network card is installed using Windows XP, it automatically is configured to use TCP/IP. If TCP/IP is not working correctly, however, you can reinstall and configure TCP/IP for that NIC. Before doing so, answer (or ask the network administrator to answer) the following questions:

1. Will the PC use dynamic or static IP addressing?
2. If static IP addressing is used, what are the IP address, subnet mask, and default gateway for this computer?
3. Do you use DNS? If so, what are the IP addresses of your DNS servers?
4. Is a proxy server used to connect to other networks (including the Internet)? If so, what is the IP address of the proxy server?

Most likely, the computer will use dynamic IP addressing and will obtain the DNS server address automatically. The DHCP server also might act as the proxy server so computers inside the network can make connections to computers outside the network, using the proxy server's public IP address. To set the TCP/IP properties for a network interface card, complete the following steps:

1. Click the Start button, click Control Panel on the Start menu, click Switch to Classic View, if needed, and then double-click Network Connections. Right-click the network connection for Local Area Connection and then click Properties on the shortcut menu (Figure 10-24a).
2. Select Internet Protocol (TCP/IP) from the list of installed protocols in the This connection uses the following items list. Click the Properties button (Figure 10-24b).
3. When the Internet Protocol (TCP/IP) Properties window opens (Figure 10-24c), select Obtain an IP address automatically to configure the NIC for dynamic IP addressing (the most likely choice). For static IP addressing, select Use the following IP address and then enter the IP address, Subnet mask, and Default gateway.

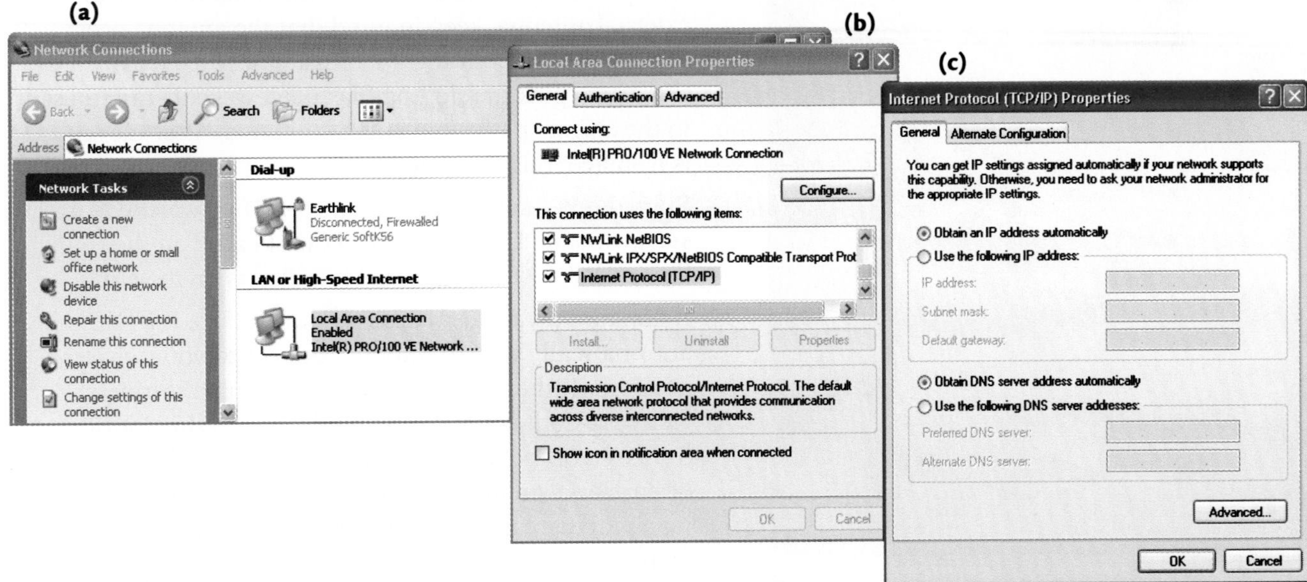

Figure 10-24 Configuring TCP/IP under Windows XP.

4. To disable DNS until the DHCP server gives the computer the DNS server address, select Obtain DNS server address automatically (the most likely choice). If you have the IP addresses of the DNS servers, click Use the following DNS server addresses, and enter the IP addresses. Click the OK button twice to close both windows.
5. Open My Network Places and verify that your computer and other computers on the network are visible. If you do not see other computers on the network, reboot the PC.

FAQ 10-7

Are there limitations on the names used for computers?

If you are using NetBEUI as the networking protocol instead of TCP/IP, the computer will use a NetBIOS name that is limited to 15 characters. If the network is using TCP/IP, a computer name can be up to 63 characters including letters, numbers, and hyphens, as long as the computer is not part of a workgroup. If the computer is part of a workgroup, the host name should not exceed 15 characters. If the name is 15 characters or fewer, it works as a NetBIOS name or a TCP/IP name.

Installing a Wireless NIC and Connecting to a Wireless LAN

Installing a wireless NIC is similar to installing a regular NIC in an expansion slot, except that you must use the NIC's configuration software to specify wireless network parameters based on the type of wireless technology used, which most likely will be Wi-Fi (802.11b or 802.11g).

Perform the following steps to install and configure a wireless NIC in a PC or notebook:

1. If setup or configuration software came with the NIC, follow the instructions in the user guide to install the software.
2. Install the wireless NIC following the steps outlined to install a standard NIC in a PCI expansion slot. A wireless NIC uses an internal or external antenna. If it has an external antenna, keep in mind that the antenna needs to have the top pointing up. If installing the NIC in a PCI slot, try to pick the slot that has the fewest obstructions to the correct positioning of the antenna. After the NIC is installed, raise the antenna (Figure 10-25).
3. Start the PC. When the Found New Hardware Wizard starts, install the device drivers that came on the floppy disk or CD that came bundled with the NIC.
4. If you already have an access point set up, the NIC automatically will attempt to connect to your wireless network. If the connection is successful, a Wireless Network Connection icon will display in the notification area of the taskbar (the icon may look like a series of bars or a small computer monitor). Pointing to the icon will display information about the active wireless connection.

Figure 10-25 Some wireless NICs have an external antenna that extends outside the computer case.

5. If the wireless connection is not working, consult the documentation to learn how to configure the NIC to use the same wireless parameters as the access point, using the NIC configuration software installed in Step 1. Right-click the icon in the taskbar to view a menu of commands related to the wireless NIC and connection and click Link Status or Open Utility (the menu for your wireless connection may look different).
6. The configuration software for the wireless NIC allows you to view the status of the wireless connection and change the wireless parameters (the software for your NIC might look different). As shown in Figure 10-26, the Link Status tab of configuration software reports the following information about the connection (your software may have a different name for this tab):

- *SSID*. The *SSID (service set identifier)* is a field that shows the name of the wireless network to which the NIC currently is connected. The NIC automatically will look for any wireless network in the area. You can enter the name of an access point to specify that this NIC should connect only to a specific access point. If you do not know the name assigned to a particular access point, ask the network administrator responsible for managing the wireless network.
- *BSSID*. The *BSSID (basic service set identifier)* is the MAC address of the access point device that the NIC currently is using.
- *Channel*. The channel reports the channel the NIC currently is using. For example, 802.11b uses 14 different channels. The United States can use channels 1 through 11. The access point device is configured to use one of these 11 channels, which is reported by the NIC software.
- *WEP*. This shows whether the network you are associated with has WEP encryption enabled or disabled. **Wired Equivalent Privacy (WEP)** is a security protocol for 802.11b, which is designed to provide a wireless LAN with a level of security and privacy comparable to a wired LAN.
- *Speed*. Speed indicates the current transmission rate. You can specify the transmission rate or leave it at fully automatic so the NIC is free to use the best transmission rate possible.
- *Station MAC Address and IP Address*. These show the MAC address of the wireless NIC and the IP address of the computer connected to the network.
- *Signal Strength*. These values indicate throughput rate and how strong the signal is (in Figure 10-26 the signal strength is considered to be Excellent). Typically, the closer you are to an access point, the stronger the signal should be.

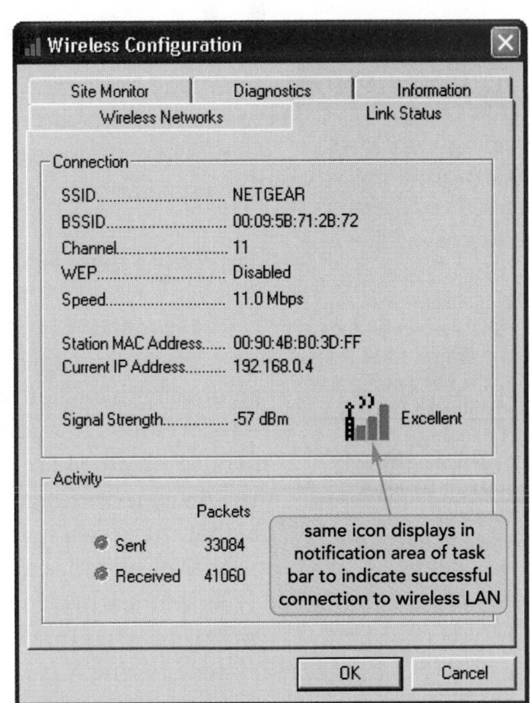

Figure 10-26 Wireless NIC configuration software reports the status of the current connection.

More About

WEP

To learn more about WEP, visit the Understanding and Troubleshooting Your PC More About Web page (**scsite.com/understanding/more**) and then click WEP below Chapter 10.

The next step is to configure the NIC to use TCP/IP, using the steps outlined above for configuring TCP/IP properties for a standard NIC. After the NIC is configured to use TCP/IP, you should immediately see network resources in My Network Places or Network Neighborhood. If you do not, try rebooting the PC and check the Network Neighborhood again. If it still does not work, the access point may have been configured for MAC address filtering in order to control which wireless NICs can use the access point. Check with your network administrator to see if this is the case. If so, give the administrator the NIC's MAC address to be entered into a table of acceptable MAC addresses.

FAQ 10-8

What does it mean when signal strength of a wireless connection is listed in dBm?

The strength of a wireless signal is measured in terms of decibels (dB) or decibels referenced to 1 milliwatt (dBm). Signal strength generally ranges from -80 dBm to -50 dBm, with -50 dBm being a stronger signal than -80 dBm.

Using Resources on the Network

More About

Installing Windows XP Components Needed to Share Resources

To learn more about installing Client for Microsoft Networks and File and Printer Sharing, if they are not installed by default, visit the Understanding and Troubleshooting Your PC More About Web page (**scsite.com/understanding/more**) and then click Installing Windows XP Components Needed to Share Resources below Chapter 10.

Once you have connected to a network using a NIC with a cable or a wireless LAN connection, you can utilize the resources available on the network. In Chapter 7, you learned how to share a printer on a network. This section covers how to share folders, files, applications, and disk storage space on a network.

Sharing Files, Folders, and Applications

If users on a LAN need to share applications, files, or printers, then all these users must be assigned to the same domain or workgroup on the LAN. A workgroup can be effective when several people work on a common project. For example, if a Web development team is building a Web site, sharing resources on the LAN is an effective way to share Web pages as they are designed and built. One computer on the LAN can be designated as the file server, with a portion of hard drive space available for the Web site files. The entire team has access to the file server via the LAN, so the Web site files are kept neatly in a single location.

As you learned in Chapter 7, to share resources over a peer-to-peer network or workgroup, you first must install Client for Microsoft Networks and File and Printer Sharing. *Client for Microsoft Networks* is the Windows component that allows you to use resources on the network made available by other computers, and *File and Printer Sharing* allows you to share resources on your computer with others in your workgroup. These two components are installed by default when you install Windows XP using the Typical setting, as described in Chapter 8 (they also are installed by default for Windows 2000 and Windows Server 2003). After these components are installed, you can share any folders, files, or printers that you want others to be able to access.

After the computer is configured for file and printer sharing, you can make a folder on your computer available for sharing with others on the network. To share a folder and files over the network, perform the following steps using Windows XP:

1. Click the Start button and then click My Documents on the Start menu.
2. Click Make a new folder in the File and Folder tasks list, type `Shared Files` as the new folder name and then press the ENTER key.
3. Right-click the Shared Files folder and click Properties on the shortcut menu. If Windows XP has Client for Microsoft Networks and File and Printer Sharing installed, the shortcut menu lists the Sharing and Security command. Click Sharing and Security. The Shared Files Properties window opens (Figure 10-27).
4. Click the Sharing tab and then click Share this folder on the network to make the folder available to others on the network. By default, Windows uses the folder name as the name of the shared folder. If you want to change the name that others on the network see when they view the folder, enter a new name in the Shared name text box. To give others the right to change your files, in addition to viewing them on the network, check Allow network users to change my files.
5. After you have completed the changes, click the OK button. The shared folder appears with a hand icon.

After you have shared a folder, others on the network can see the folder when they open My Network Places or Network Neighborhood on their desktop. For added security when using Windows XP, set up a user account and password for each user who will have access to shared resources. This added security requires that a user give a valid password before accessing shared files, folders, or printers on the Windows XP computer.

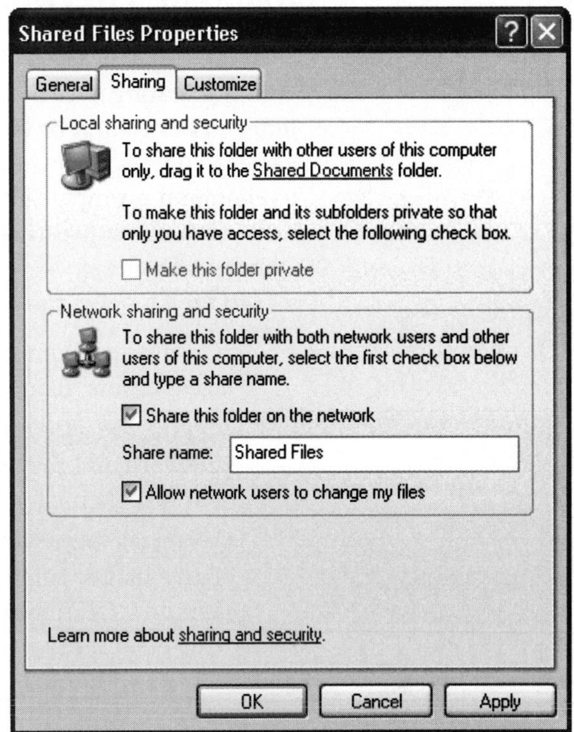

Figure 10-27 Windows XP allows you to share folders and files over a network.

In addition to sharing folders and files, an entire drive can be shared with a workgroup. To share a drive, right-click the drive letter in the My Computer or Windows Explorer window and then click Sharing and Security on the shortcut menu. On the Sharing tab, Windows displays the message, If you understand the risk but still want to share the root of the drive, click here. Click the message and then complete Steps 4 and 5 as listed for sharing a folder.

Applications also can be shared with others in the workgroup. If you share a folder that has a program file in it, a user on another PC can double-click the program file in the shared folder and run the program remotely on their computer. This is a handy way for several users to share an application that is installed on a single PC.

Mapping a Network Drive

Mapping a network drive is one of the most powerful and versatile methods of communicating over a network. When you map a network drive, you assign a drive letter (other than A or C) to any shared drive on the network. This makes it faster and easier to access the resource, either through the Windows XP user interface or from a command prompt. The **mapped drive** (also called a **network drive map**) appears as if it is a drive directly on the PC, with an icon that displays in My Computer and Windows Explorer.

To map a network drive using Windows XP, perform the following steps:

1. On the host computer, share the drive or folder to which you want others to have access, using the steps outlined above.
2. On the remote computer that will map the network drive, connect to the network and then open the My Computer window. Click Tools on the menu bar and then click Map Network Drive.
3. When the Map Network Drive dialog box appears, select a drive letter in the Drive list to which to map the network drive (Figure 10-28a). By default, Windows XP maps network drives starting with the letter Z. You can use this default drive letter for the first mapped drive you create, or select a letter other than Z.
4. In the Folder text box, enter a path to the host computer and folder. Start the entry with two backslashes, followed by the name of the host computer, followed by a backslash and the drive or folder to access on the host computer. For example, to map to the SharedDocs folder on the computer named Strite, enter `\\Strite\SharedDocs` as the path to the folder. If you want to keep the drive mapping for the next time you log on to the computer, click Reconnect at logon. Click the OK button.
5. After the drive is mapped, it will appear in My Computer and Windows Explorer with the associated drive letter (Figure 10-28b). In the My Computer window, the mapped drives are listed in the Network Drives area.

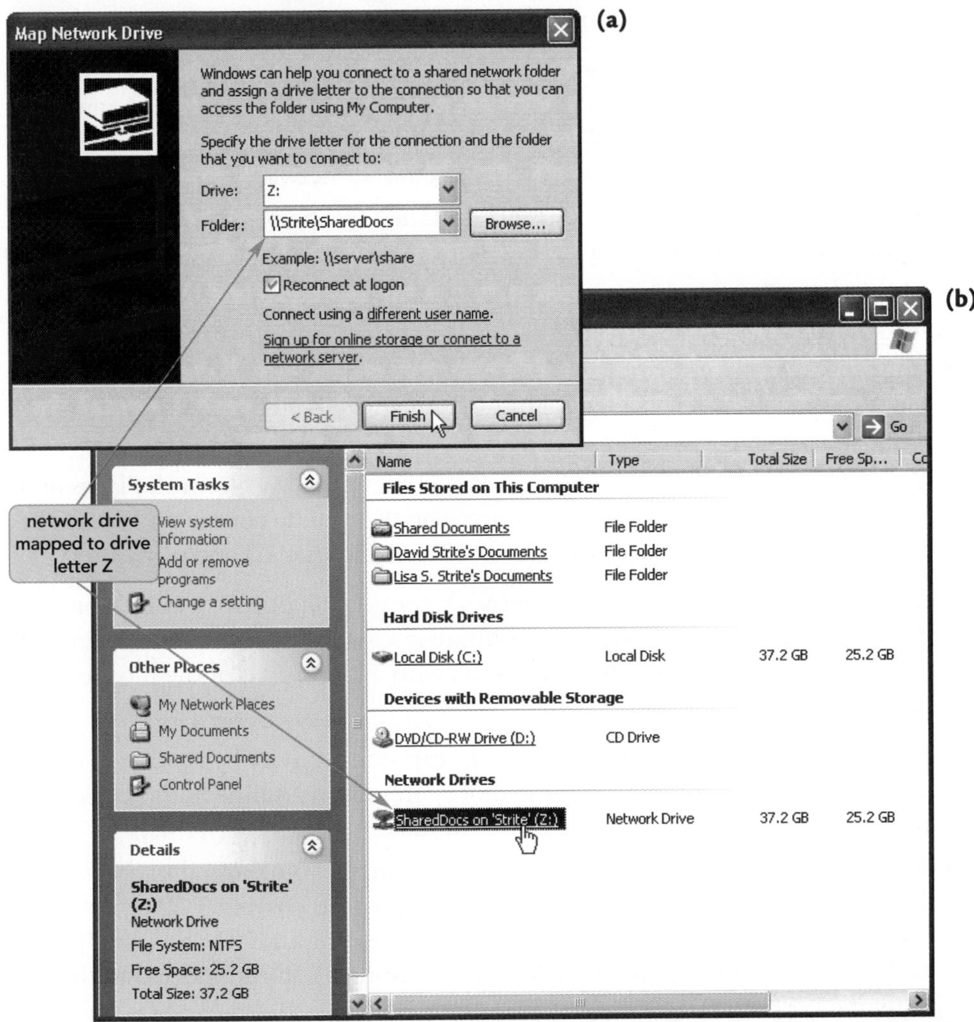

Figure 10-28 When mapping a network drive, select a drive letter and then enter the path to the drive. After the drive is mapped, it will appear in My Computer and Windows Explorer with the associated drive letter.

Troubleshooting a Network Connection

If you have problems connecting to the network, follow the guidelines in this section. First, here are some symptoms of NIC problems:

- You cannot make a connection to the network.
- My Network Places does not show any other computers on the network.
- You receive an error message while you are installing the NIC drivers.
- Device Manager shows a yellow exclamation point or a red X beside the name of the NIC.
- No lights are lit on the NIC. There are two lights on a NIC: one stays on steadily to let you know there is a physical connection, and another blinks to let you know there is activity. If you see no lights, you know there is no physical connection between the NIC and the network. This means there is a problem with the network cable, the card, or the hub.

Some methods and steps to resolve these networking issues include the following:

- Determine whether other computers on the network are having trouble with their connections. If the entire network is down, due to a failed hub or some other reason, the problem is not isolated to your computer and you will not be able to connect to the network until the larger network issue is resolved.
- Make sure the NIC and its drivers are installed by checking for the NIC in Device Manager. Try uninstalling and reinstalling the NIC drivers.
- Check the network cable to make sure it is not damaged and that the connections are securely seated.
- Connect the network cable to a different port on the hub. If that does not help, you may have a problem with the cable or the NIC itself. Uninstall the NIC drivers, replace the NIC, and then install new drivers.
- When a network drive map is not working, first check My Network Places and verify that you can access other resources on the remote computer. You might need to log on to the remote computer with a valid user ID and password.

You also might have trouble with a network connection due to a TCP/IP problem. When TCP/IP is installed on a Windows computer, a group of utilities also is installed to provide help with troubleshooting problems with TCP/IP. Two of the most commonly used TCP/IP utilities are:

- **Ping** (**Packet Internet Groper**), which tests connectivity by sending a message to a remote computer. If the remote computer is online and receives the message, it responds with several bytes of data.
- **Ipconfig**, which tests the TCP/IP configuration. As you learned in the Your Turn earlier in the chapter, Ipconfig also displays all current TCP/IP network configuration values, including the MAC address for all NICs, and the IP address, subnet mask, and default gateway for any NICs connected to the network.

To troubleshoot issues with the TCP/IP configuration and connectivity using the Ping and Ipconfig utilities, try the following:

- Using Windows XP, open the Command Prompt window, enter `Ipconfig /all` at the command prompt. If the TCP/IP configuration is correct and an IP address is assigned, the IP address, subnet mask, and default gateway appear along with the adapter address.
- If the PC uses dynamic IP addressing, it attempts to lease an address from the DHCP server when it first connects to the network. If it cannot reach the DHCP server, it then assigns itself an Automatic Private IP Address (APIPA) in the address range 169.254.x.x. If this happens, the PC is not able to reach the network or the DHCP server is down. To resolve the issue, try to release the current IP address and lease a new address. In the Command Prompt window, enter `Ipconfig /release` at the command prompt. When the Command Prompt indicates that the IP address has been released by displaying an IP address of 0.0.0.0, enter `Ipconfig /renew` at the command prompt. Windows will attempt to lease a new IP address from the DHCP server.

- If this is not successful, try the loopback address test by entering the command `Ping 127.0.0.1` at a command prompt. This IP address always refers to your local computer. The Ping command sends a message to your computer; the Command Prompt window should display a reply message from your computer. If this works, TCP/IP likely is configured correctly. If you get any errors up to this point, then assume that the problem is on your PC. Check the installation and configuration of each component such as the network card and the TCP/IP protocol suite. Remove and reinstall each component, and watch for error messages, writing them down so you can recognize or research them later as necessary. If possible, compare the configuration to that of a working PC on the same network.
- Next, Ping the IP address of your default gateway by entering the Ping command with the appropriate IP address. If the gateway does not respond, then the problem may be with the gateway or with the network to the gateway.
- Next, try to Ping the host computer you are trying to reach. If it does not respond, then the problem may be with the host computer or with the network to the computer.

TCP/IP provides additional utilities, such as NSLookup. **NSLookup** requests information about domain name resolutions from the DNS server's zone data. For example, to use NSLookup to retrieve what the DNS server knows about the domain name microsoft.com, perform the following steps using Windows XP:

1. Open the Command Prompt window.
2. Enter `nslookup microsoft.com` as the command.

The results show that the DNS server knows about several IP addresses assigned to the domain name microsoft.com. It also reports that this information is nonauthoritative, meaning that it is not the authoritative, or final, name server for the computer assigned the domain name microsoft.com.

More About

TCP/IP Utilities

To learn more about TCP/IP utilities such as Tracert and Netstat, visit the Understanding and Troubleshooting Your PC More About Web page (**scsite.com/understanding/more**) and then click TCP/IP Utilities below Chapter 10.

Quiz Yourself 10-2

To test your knowledge of how to connect to a network and use network resources, visit the Understanding and Troubleshooting Your PC Quiz Yourself Web page (scsite.com/understanding/quiz). Click Quiz Yourself 2 below Chapter 10.

Internet Technologies and Protocols

Thus far, the chapter has focused mostly on LANs, which connect users in one or more buildings in a relatively small geographic area. Additional devices and technologies, such as routers, are used to connect networks, allowing them to communicate with each other within a building or over a large geographical area as a WAN (wide area network) or over the Internet.

Like many other WANs, the Internet uses a client/server architecture. Applications that use the Internet are client/server applications, in which the application (client) software makes a request for data from server software running on another computer. For example, when using dynamic IP addressing, a DHCP client on one computer requests an IP address from a DHCP server on another computer. Browsing the Web is another example of a client/server application: the Web browser is a client requesting a Web page from the Web server that stores that page (Figure 10-29). To transfer data from the Web server to the Web browser (client), the data must be transferred over several networks by devices called routers.

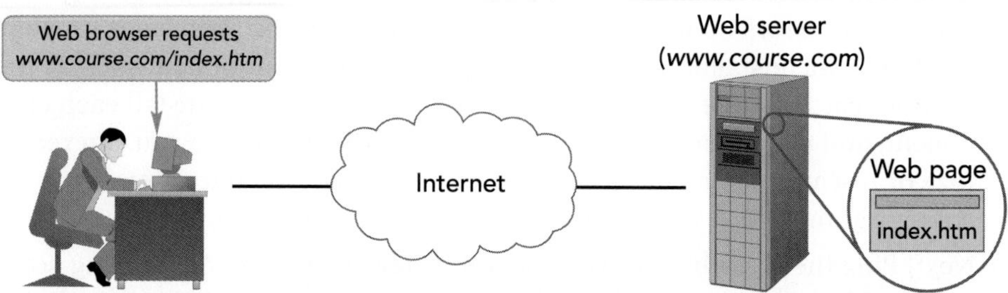

Figure 10-29 A Web browser (client software) requests a Web page from a Web server (server software). The Web server returns the requested file or files to the client.

Routers

A **router** is a communications device that manages the delivery of data traveling over interconnected networks. A router is more efficient than a hub, which simply replicates data and sends it to every device connected to it. Instead, a router directs data to the correct network by determining the most efficient available route from the sending computer to the receiving computer. The router relies on the TCP/IP protocol and uses the IP addresses of computers along the way to determine the path by which to send a packet. A router is a **stateless** device, meaning that it only cares about the destination address of the data it is routing, not the actual data itself.

Figure 10-30 shows a simplified view of the way networks and routers work together to send data over the Internet. When a user in Sydney, Australia requests a Web page that resides on a Web server in New York, that request must pass through many networks to reach the Web server in New York. Each network operates independently of all other networks but can receive a packet from another network and send it on to a third network, while it also manages its own internal traffic.

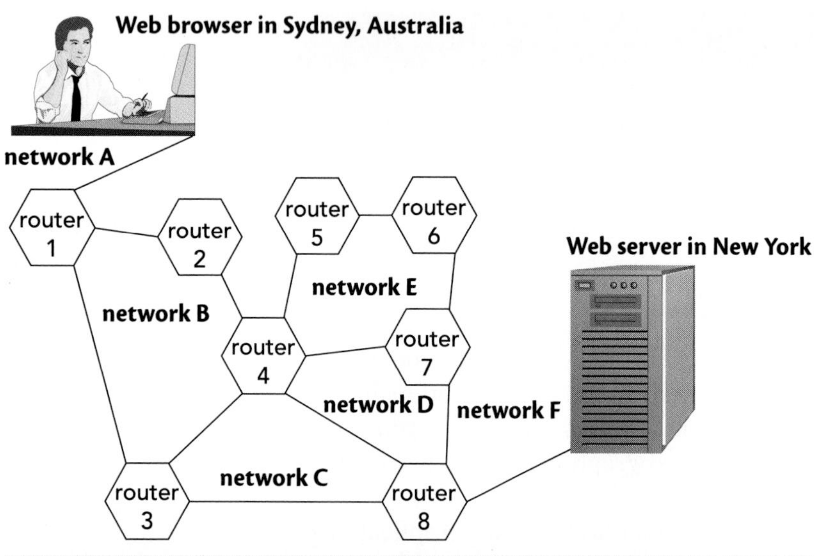

Figure 10-30 A router directs data to the correct network by determining the most efficient available route from the sending computer to the receiving computer.

An important job of a router is to direct data to the correct network by determining the most efficient available route from the sending computer to the receiving computer. Several paths are available to send the request from the user in Sydney to the Web server in New York. For example, one path is through router 1, then 3, then 8, and finally to the Web server. Data traveling to and from the

Web browser and the Web server may travel a different path each time it is sent. If a lot of data must be transferred, the data is divided into several **packets**, each of which may take a different route to the receiving computer. When the packets arrive at the receiving computer, they may not be in the same order they were sent. The packets are reassembled before they are presented to the application that will use them. This technique of breaking a message into individual packets, sending the packets along the best route available, and then reassembling the data is called **packet switching.**

Routers use tables called routing tables to determine the best route by which to send the data to its destination. When the router receives a packet, it first looks at the packet's destination IP address. The router then references the routing tables and reviews current network conditions to decide which path would be best for the packet. If no direct route to the destination exists, the router may forward the packet to another router. A packet sent over the Internet thus may go through several routers before reaching its destination.

As a router attempts to send packets, it learns about new routes and faster routes. You can see the effects of this process when you first attempt to access a new Web site with your browser. If the browser is slow to respond, click the Stop button and then the Refresh button to cause the browser to resend the request. The new request often receives a quicker response because the routers along the way learned about routes that were slow or did not work.

Routers can belong to more than one network. For example, in Figure 10-30, network B contains four routers: routers 1, 2, 3, and 4. Routers 3 and 4 also belong to network C. Network C contains router 8, which also belongs to the network to which the Web server in New York is connected. If a router belongs to one network (for example, router 1), the router has an IP address for that network. If a router belongs to more than one network, it has a unique IP address for each network. Physically, this is accomplished by having one NIC (referred to as a router interface) for each network a router belongs to, with each NIC having a unique IP address. For example, router 4 belongs to four networks (B, C, D, and E) and would therefore have four network cards and four IP addresses, one for each network.

TCP/IP Suite of Protocols

As you have learned, TCP/IP (Transmission Control Protocol/Internet Protocol) is the protocol suite that is the basis of the Internet. It also is used on local area networks to make resources on a network and on the Internet available to the user. Several protocols operate within the TCP/IP suite. The TCP/IP protocol suite includes many different protocols. This section introduces the more significant protocols and discusses how they interact with each other (Figure 10-31).

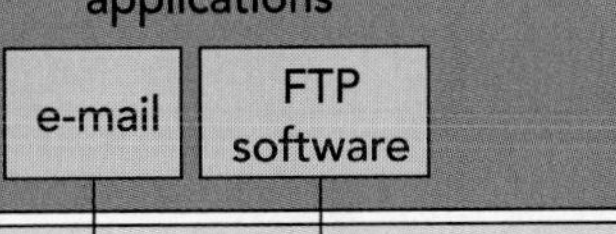

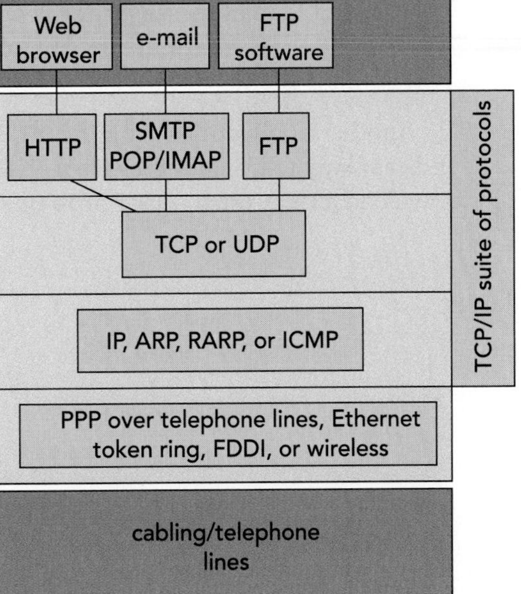

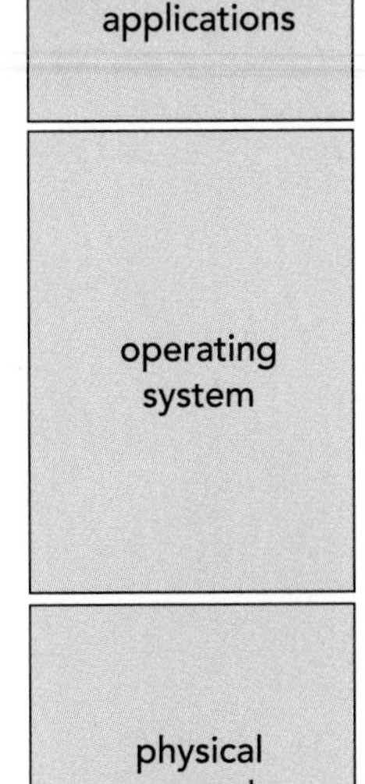

Figure 10-31 How software, protocols, and technology on a TCP/IP network relate to each other.

APPLICATION PROTOCOLS Application protocols are the rules of communication between the client and server components of the applications. Three of the most common applications that use the Internet are Web browsers, e-mail, and FTP. When one of these applications wants to send data to an application on another host, it makes a call to the operating system, which handles the request. The call causes the OS to generate a request using a specific application protocol.

For example, if the application is a Web browser, the request will be an HTTP request. **HTTP (Hypertext Transfer Protocol)** is the protocol used by Web browsers and Web servers to communicate over the Internet. When you request a Web page by typing an address in your Web browser, HTTP formats the request, encrypts and compresses it as necessary, and then adds an HTTP header to the beginning of the data that includes the HTTP version being used and how the data is compressed and encrypted. Later, when the response is received from the server, it decrypts and decompresses the data as necessary before passing it on to the browser. Once the response is passed to the browser, a session is established. A **session** (also called a **socket**) is a communication link established between two software programs. Sessions are managed by the browser and Web server using HTTP.

For e-mail, two different protocols are used — one to send messages and one to receive messages. The sender's computer and e-mail server both can use **SMTP (Simple Mail Transfer Protocol)** to send an e-mail message to its destination. Once the message arrives at the destination mail server, it remains there until the recipient requests delivery by retrieving his or her messages. The recipient's e-mail server uses one of two protocols to retrieve the message from the mail server:

- **POP (Post Office Protocol)**, which can be used by most e-mail clients to retrieve e-mail from a mail server. The first widely used version of POP, called POP2, became a standard in the mid-80s and requires SMTP to send messages. The newer version, POP3, can be used with or without SMTP.
- **IMAP (Internet Message Access Protocol)** is a newer e-mail protocol that is not yet supported by all e-mail clients. The latest version, IMAP4, is similar to POP3 but supports additional features such as allowing you to search e-mail messages for keywords while the messages are still on the mail server. You then can choose which messages to download to your e-mail client.

Another applications protocol, **FTP (File Transfer Protocol)** provides a quick and easy way to transfer files via a TCP/IP network. FTP is used most commonly to download a file from a server or to upload a file to a server using FTP software.

As you have learned, TCP/IP assigns an identifying number, called a port number, to a program or service running on a server. Specific port numbers are used for different application protocols, as shown in Figure 10-32. Port numbers are shown at the end of an IP address, following a colon (for example, 138.60.30.5:20 for an FTP server).

Port	Protocol	Service	Description
20	FTP	FTP	File Transfer Protocol; used to transfer data
21	FTP	FTP	File Transfer Protocol; used to transfer control information
23	Telnet	Telnet	Used by Telnet, an application used by Unix computers to control a computer remotely
25	SMTP	E-mail	Simple Mail Transfer Protocol; used by client to send e-mail
80	HTTP or HTTPS	Web browser	Hypertext Transfer Protocol; used to transfer data over the Web
109	POP2	E-mail	Post Office Protocol, version 2; used by client to receive e-mail; requires SMTP
110	POP3	E-mail	Post Office Protocol, version 3; used by client to receive e-mail; does not require SMTP
119	NNTP	News server	Network News Transfer Protocol; used for newsgroups and news servers
143	IMAP	E-mail	Internet Message Access Protocol; a newer protocol used by clients to receive e-mail

Figure 10-32 Common TCP/IP port assignments for widely used services.

TCP/IP PROTOCOLS USED BY THE OS FOR NETWORK COMMUNICATION

Figure 10-31 on page 437 shows three layers of protocols between the applications protocols and the physical network protocols. These three layers make up the heart of TCP/IP communication. The third row of the figure shows two protocols — TCP and UDP — which manage communication with the applications protocols above them as well as the protocols below them, which control communication on the network.

As you have learned, all communication on a network happens by way of packets delivered from one location on the network to another. When a Web browser makes a request for data from a Web server, a packet is created and an attempt is made to deliver that packet to the server. In TCP/IP, the protocol that guarantees packet delivery is **TCP (Transmission Control Protocol)**. TCP makes a connection, checks whether the data is received, and resends it if it is not. TCP is therefore called a *connection-oriented protocol*. Guaranteeing delivery takes longer and is used when it is important that data reach its destination accurately — for example, with applications such as Web browsers and e-mail.

In contrast, **UDP (User Datagram Protocol)** does not guarantee delivery by first connecting and checking whether data is received. UDP thus is called a *connectionless protocol* or a *best-effort protocol*. UDP is used primarily for broadcasting and other types of transmissions, such as streaming video or sound over the Web, where guaranteed delivery is not as important as fast transmission.

TCP and UDP both pass a request to **IP (Internet Protocol)**, which is responsible for breaking up and reassembling data into packets and routing them to their destination

(Figure 10-33a). IP adds its own IP header, which includes the IP address of its host (source IP address) and that of the server (destination IP address), and then passes the packet off to the hardware.

(a)

(b)

Figure 10-33 TCP turns to IP to prepare the data for networking. TCP then guarantees delivery by requesting an acknowledgment.

If TCP is used to guarantee delivery, TCP uses IP to establish a session between client and server to verify that communication has taken place. When a TCP packet reaches its destination, an acknowledgment is sent back to the source (Figure 10-33b). If the source TCP does not receive the acknowledgment, it resends the data or passes an error message back to the higher-level application protocol.

Other protocols that operate in this part of the transmission process include the following:

- *ARP (Address Resolution Protocol)* is responsible for locating a host on a local network.
- *RARP (Reverse Address Resolution Protocol)* is responsible for discovering the IP address of a host on a local network.

- *ICMP (Internet Control Message Protocol)* is responsible for communicating problems with transmission. For example, if a packet exceeds the number of routers it can pass through on its way to its destination, called a time to live (TTL) or a hop count, a router kills the packet and returns an ICMP message to the source, saying that the packet has been killed. When you use the Ping command to send a message to a server, it uses ICMP to send the message to the other computer and then return the response.

NETWORK PROTOCOLS USED BY HARDWARE As you have learned, each NIC has firmware and drivers that support the network hardware protocols, such as Ethernet or Wi-Fi. For network connections where a computer connects to the Internet via a telephone line and a modem, the network hardware protocols are included in the firmware on a modem and its drivers. For most connections using a regular telephone line, the modem manages a protocol called **PPP** (**Point-to-Point Protocol**). If you are using a broadband connection, such as DSL or a cable modem, the connection between the NIC and the broadband device most likely uses PPPoE. **PPPoE** (**Point-to-Point Protocol over Ethernet**) is a protocol specifically designed to support broadband connections. Support for PPPoE is included in Windows XP.

Connecting to the Internet

Previous sections in this chapter discussed how to connect to a LAN to use the resources available on the network. Many different types of communication media and devices are available to connect to the Internet. Some of the more common ways to connect include:

- *Standard dial-up connection*. Using a dial-up connection, you use a modem and a telephone line to create a temporary connection that uses one or more regular analog, copper-wire telephone lines for communication. A **modem** is a type of communications device that is capable of transmitting data over telephone lines, cable television cables, or other physical media between a sending device and a receiving device. A dial-up connection requires an internal or external modem to convert a PC's digital data to analog data that can be communicated over telephone lines.
- *Cable modem*. A **cable modem** allows you to connect to the Internet using the television cables that already exist in millions of households. Unlike the temporary dial-up connection, cable modems are always connected. A cable Internet connection is an example of **broadband** medium, which is any type of networking medium that carries more than one type of transmission. With a cable modem, the TV signal to your television and the data signals to your PC share the same cable.
- *DSL*. **DSL** (**Digital Subscriber Line**) is a broadband technology that sends digital data over standard telephone lines, without interfering with your regular telephone services. The standard copper telephone wires can handle a much greater bandwidth, or range of frequencies, than the frequencies used for voice communication. DSL uses digital coding techniques to send digital data along the other frequencies, without disturbing the line's ability to carry conversations. The voice portion of the telephone line requires a dial-up as normal, but the DSL part of the line always is connected.

- *ISDN.* **ISDN (Integrated Services Digital Network)** is a technology developed in the 1980s that uses regular telephone lines and is accessed by a dial-up connection. For home use, an ISDN line is fully digital and consists of two channels, or telephone circuits, on a single pair of wires. The two channels can be combined so data effectively travels at 128 Kbps, about three to five times the speed of regular telephone lines. ISDN is not as widely used as DSL or cable service.
- *Wireless access.* As you have learned, wireless refers to technologies and systems that do not use cables for communication, including infrared, Wi-Fi using radio frequencies, and other technologies used for cellular phone and pagers. Wireless often is used in LANs, for mobile devices, and for Internet access in remote locations where other methods are not an option.

Almost all of these connection methods require some kind of modem to convert data sent over the network to a form that the computer can use. The following section reviews how to set up a standard dial-up connection, DSL, or cable modem to connect to an Internet service provider (ISP). After learning how each type of connection is made, you will learn advantages and disadvantages of each.

FAQ 10-9

Are high-speed Internet connections like cable modems and DSL available everywhere?

Although high-speed Internet connections are more widely available than ever, they are not available in all locations. If you live in a remote or sparsely populated area and want high-speed Internet connections, you may not be able to get DSL, ISDN, or a cable modem. One good option is satellite Internet access, which is available almost everywhere. To use satellite Internet access, you need a satellite dish mounted on top of your house or office building that communicates with a satellite used by an ISP offering the satellite service. You also need a satellite modem card to allow you to access the network. Although a satellite Internet connection is more expensive than cable or DSL, sometimes it is the only high-speed Internet option available in remote areas.

Dial-up, DSL, and Cable Modems

A modem can be an external device connected to a USB or serial port, a modem card using a PCI or ISA slot, or a smaller and less expensive modem riser card (Figure 10-34).

Regardless of the type of modem, a modem includes both hardware and firmware. Firmware stored in ROM chips on the device contains the protocol and instructions needed to format and convert data so it can be transported to a receiving modem on the other end. In general, modems are considered hardware, but it is important to remember that they have firmware, when understanding how communications work using a modem. Some of the more common types of modems are dial-up modems, DSL modems, and cable modems.

FAQ 10-10

Why would I use a modem riser card instead of a modem card?

Using a modem riser card can reduce the total cost of a computer system. Some motherboards have a small expansion slot, less than half the length of a PCI slot, called an audio/modem riser (AMR) slot or a communication and networking riser (CNR) slot. These slots accommodate small, inexpensive expansion cards called riser cards, such as a modem riser card, audio riser card, or network riser card. Part of a riser card's audio, modem, or networking logic is on the card, and part is on a controller on the motherboard.

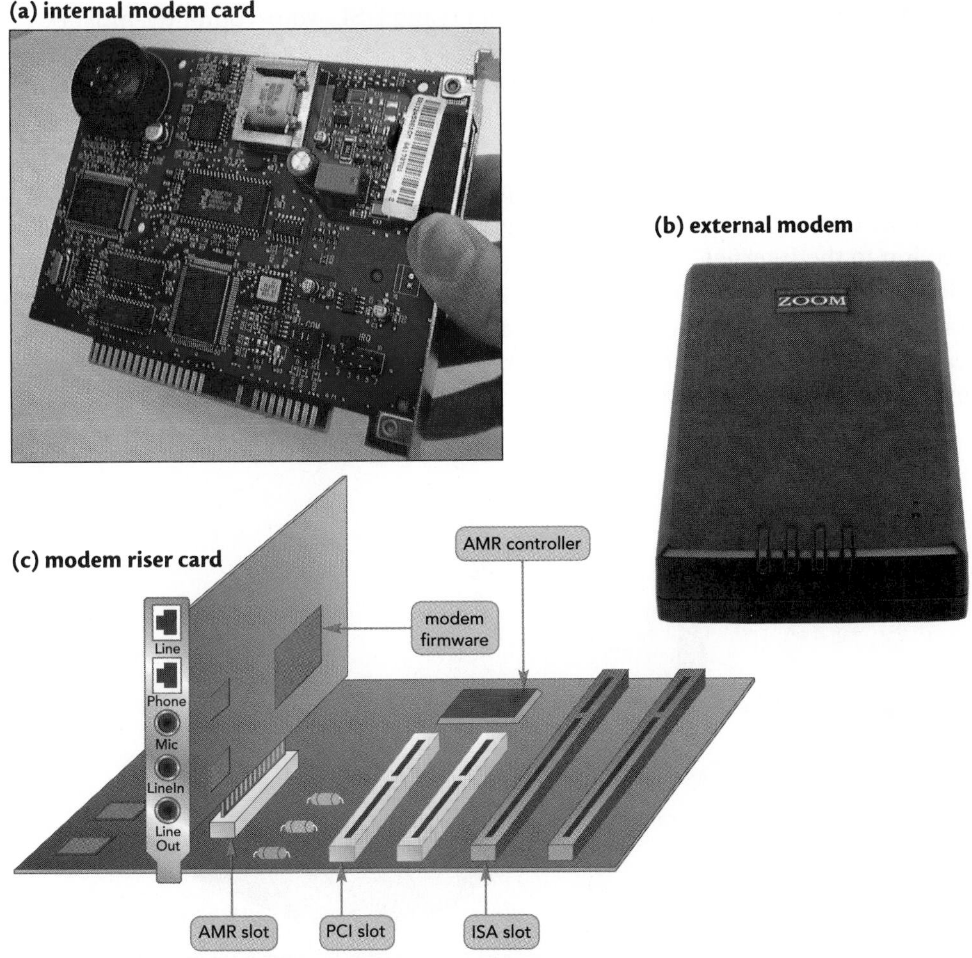

Figure 10-34 A modem can be internal or external.

DIAL-UP MODEM As you have learned, computers are digital. The standard copper-wire telephone lines used for the public switched telephone network, however, are analog. When you use a modem to send data over telephone lines to a digital computer on the Internet, data stored inside a PC is communicated to a modem as digital (binary) data. A dial-up modem converts this data into an analog signal (in a process called modulation) that can travel over a telephone line (Figure 10-35). Then the modem at the receiving end converts the signal back to digital data (in a process called demodulation) before passing it on to the receiving PC. The name of the device, modem, is derived from the *mo*dulation/*dem*odulation tasks it completes.

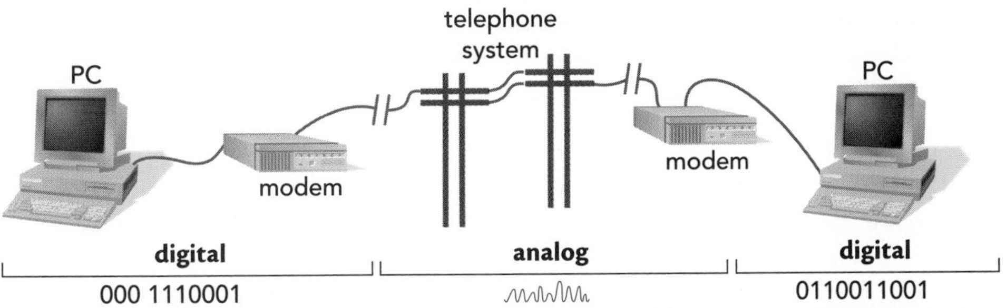

Figure 10-35 Dial-up modems convert a digital signal to analog and then back to digital.

More About

Dial-up Modems

To learn more about modems used for dial-up connections, visit the Understanding and Troubleshooting Your PC More About Web page (**scsite.com/understanding/more**) and then click Dial-up Modems below Chapter 10.

DSL MODEMS If you connect to the Internet using DSL, your computer must be equipped with a special network card and a DSL modem. The **DSL modem**, also called the *DSL router, DSL transceiver*, or *DSL box,* connects to a standard telephone line on one end and to your computer on the other, using a CAT-5 cable with an RJ-45 connector or a USB connector (Figure 10-36). Data sent from the user's computer is sent via the DSL modem over telephone lines to the ISP, where the ISP takes connections from many customers and aggregates them onto a single, high-speed connection to the Internet.

Because the data sent and received by a DSL modem is digital, it does not have to perform the digital-to-analog conversion required by a standard dial-up modem. Instead, the DSL modem is considered to be a digital modem, because it sends and receives data in digital format.

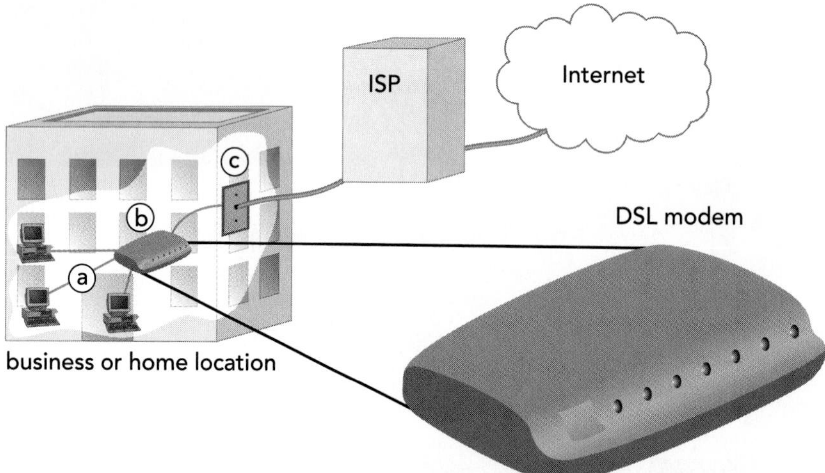

Figure 10-36 With a DSL connection, (a) computers are connected to the DSL modem using a cable connected to a standard NIC. The (b) DSL modem or router then is connected to the (c) DSL telephone line, which the telephone company installs. That telephone line is connected to the ISP, which takes connections from many customers and aggregates them onto a single, high-speed connection to the Internet.

FAQ 10-11

Are digital modems really modems?

The strict definition of a modem is a device that converts analog to digital signal and vice versa. Using the term modem for a DSL or cable modem, then, technically is not correct, because they do not have to perform analog-to-digital conversions. Originally, these devices were called *terminal adapters*, but, today, the industry refers to DSL and cable modems as modems in the general sense that they connect a PC to telephone lines or television cables that allow for an Internet connection. The term digital modem often is used to differentiate cable and DSL modems from dial-up modems.

CABLE MODEM A cable modem (sometimes called a *broadband modem*) is a digital modem that sends and receives digital data over the cable television network. Figure 10-37 illustrates how a cable modem connects a computer to the Internet. The cable modem is connected to the computer via the standard NIC and a CAT-5 cable or via a USB port. The cable modem uses a regular TV cable to connect to a TV cable wall outlet. It also has a transformer to provide power to the cable modem. When you purchase cable modem service, you might need to purchase the cable modem and, if needed, a network interface card — or these might be included in the installation fee.

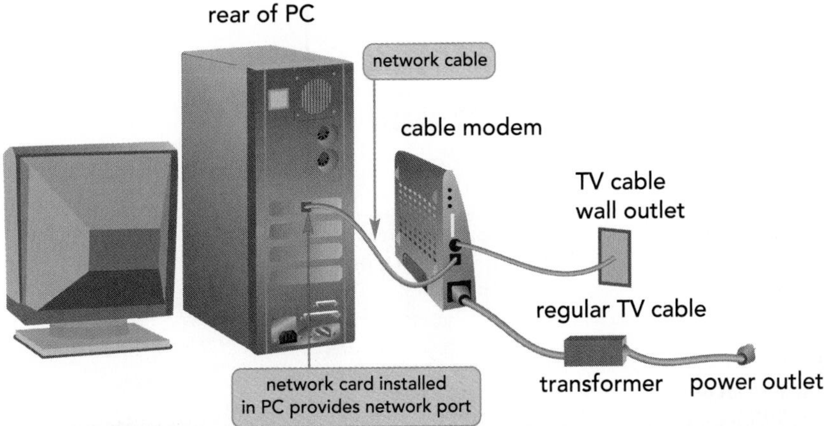

Figure 10-37 Cable modem connecting to a PC through a network card installed on the PC.

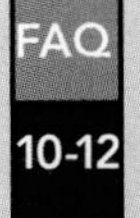

Which is better — DSL or cable Internet service?

Each has its own advantages. DSL uses a line that is not shared with other users in the neighborhood. With cable Internet service, by contrast, users share the node that connects to the cable company with other cable Internet users in the neighborhood or small geographic area. Simultaneous access by many users can cause the cable Internet service to slow down. Because DSL provides a dedicated connection from each user back to the ISP, users get high-speed connections that are not degraded as more users are added. DSL, however, is not as widely available as cable Internet service and typically costs more.

Connecting to the Internet Using Dial-up Networking

To connect to the Internet over a telephone line using a dial-up connection, you need to have a modem installed on your PC, as well as drivers to control the modem. Next, you need to configure a dial-up networking connection in Windows and then create and test the connection to your Internet service provider (ISP).

When a Windows PC connects to a network using a modem and regular telephone line, the process is called **dial-up networking**. In effect, the modem on the PC acts like a network card, providing the physical connection to the network and the firmware at the lowest level of communication. After the dial-up connection is made, the PC's application software relates to the network as though it were directly connected using a network card, but a network card is not needed. The modems and telephone lines in between are transparent to the user, although transmission speeds with direct network connections are much faster than dial-up connections.

HOW DIAL-UP NETWORKING WORKS Dial-up networking uses PPP to send packets of data over telephone lines. The network protocol (TCP/IP, NetBEUI, or IPX/SPX) packages the data, making it ready for network traffic, and then PPP adds its own header and trailer to these packets. Figure 10-38a shows how this works. The data is presented to the network protocol, which adds its header information. Then the packet is presented to the line protocol, PPP, which adds its own header and trailer to the packet and presents it to the modem for delivery over telephone lines to a modem on the receiving end.

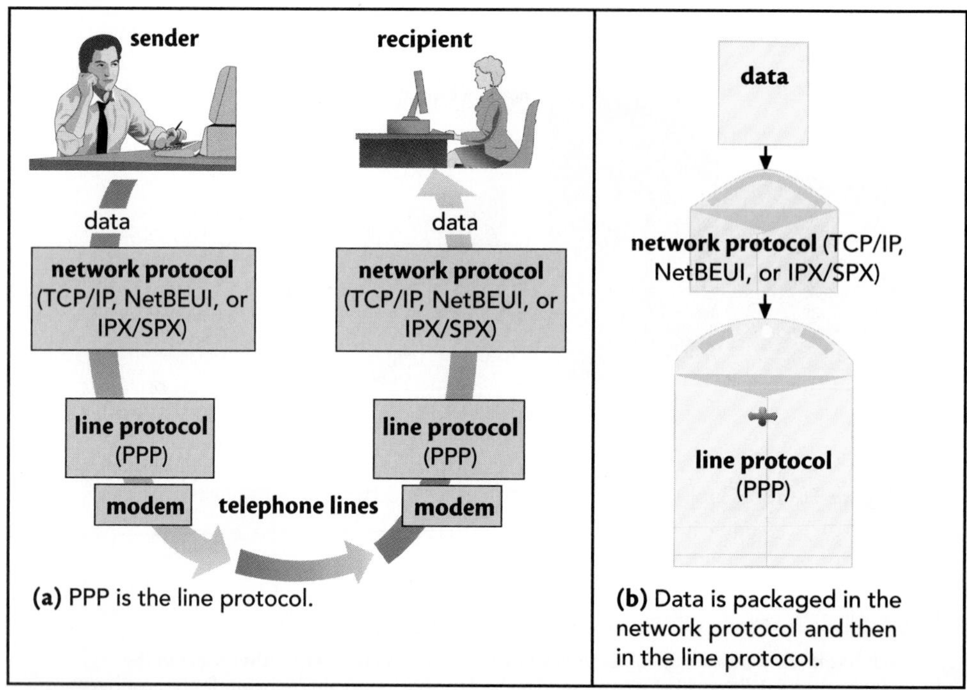

(a) PPP is the line protocol.

(b) Data is packaged in the network protocol and then in the line protocol.

Figure 10-38 PPP allows a PC to connect to a network using a modem.

The modem on the receiving end is connected to a PC or server. The receiving computer strips off the PPP header and trailer information and sends the packet on to the network still packaged in the TCP/IP protocols, or whatever protocols the network is using. In Figure 10-38b, you can see how these two protocols act like envelopes. Data is put in a TCP/IP envelope for travel over the network. This envelope is put in a PPP envelope for travel over telephone lines. When the telephone line segment of the trip is completed, the PPP envelope is discarded.

INSTALLING AN INTERNAL MODEM Most newer PCs come with a standard dial-up modem already installed, which provides connection speeds of up to 56 Kbps. If you do not have a modem installed, follow these general steps to install an internal modem:

1. Read the modem documentation. Each manufacturer's instructions for installing a modem can be slightly different and may provide steps that differ slightly from those listed here.
2. Determine which serial port is available on your system.
3. Protect yourself and the computer from ESD by using an antistatic bracelet and ground mat. Shut down the computer and unplug it. Remove the case cover.

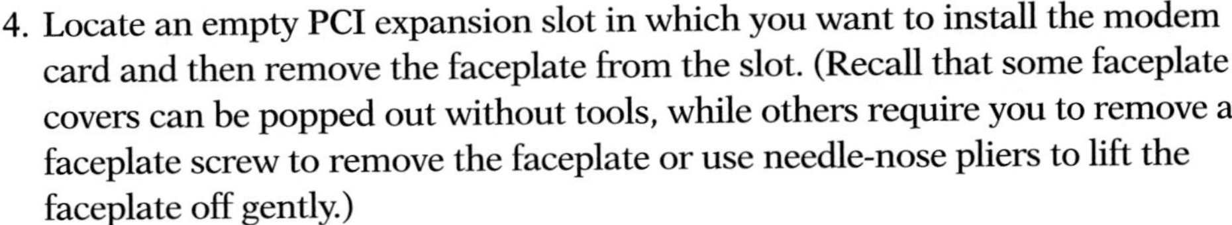

4. Locate an empty PCI expansion slot in which you want to install the modem card and then remove the faceplate from the slot. (Recall that some faceplate covers can be popped out without tools, while others require you to remove a faceplate screw to remove the faceplate or use needle-nose pliers to lift the faceplate off gently.)
5. Mount the card firmly in the slot, and replace the screw to anchor the card.
6. Replace the cover (or, if desired, leave the cover off while you test the modem).
7. Plug the telephone line from the house into the line jack on the modem. The second RJ-11 jack on the modem is for an optional telephone. It connects a telephone so you can more easily use this same telephone jack for voice communication.
8. Start the PC. The Found New Hardware Wizard launches to begin the process of loading the necessary drivers to use the new device (remember that it is better to use the manufacturer's drivers, not the Windows drivers).

After the modem drivers are installed, you should verify that the operating system configured the modem correctly. From the Control Panel window, click Switch to Classic View, if needed; double-click Phone and Modem Options and then click the Modems tab in the Phone and Modem Options window. Select the modem you just installed and then click the Properties button. Click the Modem tab and verify that the modem speed is set to the highest value listed in the Maximum Port Speed list.

USING A DIAL-UP CONNECTION IN WINDOWS XP In order for your PC to connect to your ISP and use the Internet, you need answers to the following questions:

- What is the dial-up access telephone number of the ISP?
- What is your user ID and password for the ISP?
- Will DNS servers be assigned at connection? Most likely, they will be. If they are not, what is the IP address of one or two DNS servers?
- How will your IP address be assigned? (It most likely will be assigned dynamically.)

To create a dial-up connection in Windows XP you can use the New Connection Wizard, following these steps:

1. Open My Network Places and then click View network connections in the Network Tasks area. When the Network Connections window appears, click Create a new connection.
2. The New Connection Wizard starts. Click the Next button to skip the welcome screen. On the next screen, click Connect to the Internet and then click the Next button.
3. On the next screen, click Set up my connection manually and then click the Next button. On the following screen, click Connect using a dial-up modem and then click the Next button.
4. In the ISP name text box, enter a name to identify the connection, such as the name and city of your ISP. Click Next. In the following screen, enter the telephone number to access your ISP and then click the Next button.

5. On the next screen (Figure 10-39), enter your user name and password at the ISP. This screen also gives you the options to make the logon automatic, make this the default connection to the Internet, and turn on Internet Connection Firewall for this connection. Click the appropriate options to select them and then click the Next button.

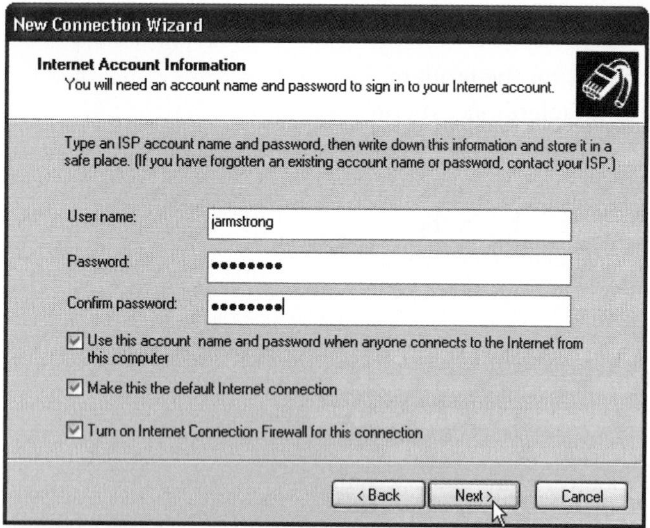

Figure 10-39 Using Windows XP, you can create a new Internet connection using the New Connection Wizard.

6. On the next screen, you can choose to add a shortcut to the connection on the desktop. Click the option if you wish to select it and then click the Finish button to complete the wizard. A connection icon is added to the Network Connections window. If you selected the option, a shortcut is added to the desktop.
7. After creating a new connection, the Connect window automatically displays. You also can double-click the connection icon in the Network Connections windows or click the shortcut added to the desktop. To use the dial-up connection, ensure that the telephone line is connected to the dial-up modem and the telephone jack.
8. Click the Dial button. You will hear the modem dial up the ISP and make the connection. A small icon will appear in the notification area of the taskbar to indicate that the connection is working.

Windows XP makes some assumptions about how your connection is configured. To view or change the configuration, do the following:

1. Open the Network Connections window. Right-click the connection you wish to modify and then click Properties on the shortcut menu.
2. When the connection Properties window appears. Click the Networking tab.
3. Select Internet Protocol (TCP/IP) and click Properties. The Internet Protocol (TCP/IP) Properties window appears. Windows XP assumes that you are using dynamic IP addressing (Obtain an IP address automatically) and that the ISP will give your PC DNS information when you first log on (Obtain DNS server address automatically). Most likely these are the correct options, but if necessary, you can change them and then click OK to apply the changes. Click the OK button after making any needed changes.

More About

Troubleshooting Dial-Up Modems and Connections

To learn more about troubleshooting a dial-up modem, visit the Understanding and Troubleshooting Your PC More About Web page (**scsite.com/understanding/more**) and then click Troubleshooting Guidelines for Modems below Chapter 10.

4. If you need to change the ISP's access telephone number and control how the telephone call is made (for example, using a 9 before dialing the number as required by many hotel telephones), click the General tab, click Use dialing rules, and then click the Dialing Rules button (Figure 10-40).

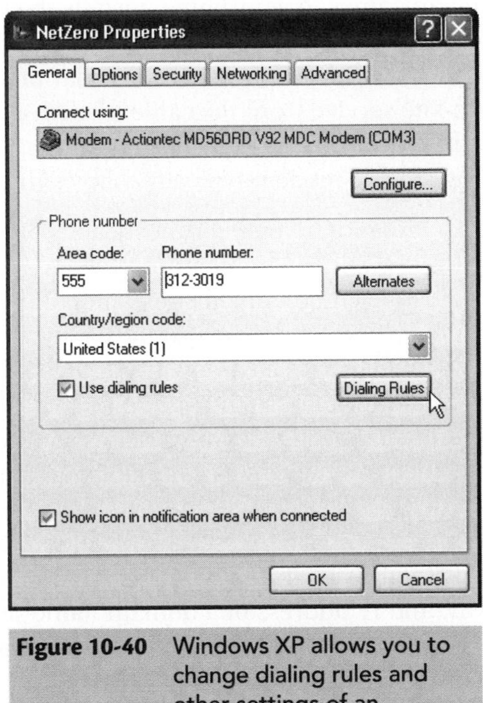

Figure 10-40 Windows XP allows you to change dialing rules and other settings of an Internet connection.

5. Select the location to edit in the Locations list and then click the Edit button. After making required changes in the Edit Location window, click the OK button in each window to close them.

Connecting to the Internet Using DSL and Cable Connections

Recall that DSL and cable modem are called broadband technologies because they support the transmission of voice, data, sound, and video simultaneously. When using a cable modem or DSL to connect a single PC to the Internet using an ISP, the TCP/IP settings are not different from those used for a dial-up networking connection using a standard modem and telephone line connection.

Like LAN connections, most cable modem and DSL connections use the network card in the PC to connect a cable from the PC to the modem (although some newer cable modems use USB to connect to a PC). For cable modem service to the Internet, the network or USB cable connects to a cable modem. For DSL, the telephone line connects to a DSL modem, which also can function as a small router.

INSTALLING AND CONFIGURING A CABLE MODEM For cable modem connections, the installation generally involves the following steps:

1. Install the network card and the drivers to control the card.
2. Use a network cable to connect the PC to a cable modem or DSL box.
3. Install TCP/IP and bind TCP/IP to the card.

4. Configure TCP/IP using the TCP/IP settings provided by the cable service provider to connect to the Internet or LAN.
5. Test the connection using application software, such as a browser.

For a home installation, some cable modem companies will do the entire installation for you. A service technician comes to your home, installs the network card if necessary, and configures your PC to use the service. You might need to purchase the cable modem and NIC, or they might be included in the installation or service fee.

If you do not have on-site service from the cable modem company, they likely will send you an installation kit with instructions on how to set up the cable modem. Installing and configuring a cable modem typically follows these general steps:

1. Install the network card and drivers. For most cable modem companies, the MAC address of the NIC in the computer and the MAC address of the NIC in the cable modem must be entered in a list of valid addresses that identify your PC or cable modem as a subscriber to the cable service. If the cable company help desk technician needs the MAC address of the PC, open the Command Prompt window and use the `Ipconfig` or `Getmac` commands to display it. If the technician needs the MAC address of the cable modem, look for it printed somewhere on the back of the cable modem. When the PC first connects to the service, the service references the list of valid MAC addresses and matches those to the MAC addresses of your PC and cable modem. The service then assigns the PC a valid IP address, subnet mask, IP address of the default gateway, and IP address of a domain name server.
2. Configure TCP/IP to use the network card, using the TCP/IP configuration information provided by the cable service provider.
3. Plug in the cable modem and turn it on (a power switch usually is located on the back of the box).
4. Shut down the PC. As shown in Figure 10-37 on page 445, you then should connect one end of the network or USB cable to the network or USB port on the back of the PC. Next, connect the other end of the cable to the cable modem. Finally, connect the TV cable from the TV cable outlet to the cable modem.
5. Turn on the PC. When the PC starts, you should immediately be connected to the Internet. Test that you are connected to the Internet using your Web browser or e-mail client.

TROUBLESHOOTING A CABLE MODEM CONNECTION If you are not able to connect to the Internet with your cable modem connection, try the following steps to resolve the issue:

- For Windows XP, open the Command Prompt windows and then enter the commands `Ipconfig /release` and `Ipconfig /renew` to lease a new IP address. Check for connectivity again. (Alternately, using Windows XP, you can release and renew the IP address by opening the Network Connections window, selecting the connection, and then clicking Repair this connection under Network Tasks.)
- If this does not work, turn off the PC and the cable modem. Wait a full five minutes until all connections have timed out at the cable modem company. Turn on the cable modem, and then turn on the PC. After the PC boots up, again check for connectivity.

- Try another cable TV jack in your home to eliminate the television jack as the problem.
- If this does not work, call the help desk at the cable service provider. The technician there can release and restore the connection at that end, which should restore service.

INSTALLING AND CONFIGURING A DSL MODEM As with cable modems, some DSL service providers will provide on-site installation, although more and more companies send new customers an installation kit with instructions on how to set up the DSL modem. The kit will include the DSL modem, telephone line filters, and a telephone line splitter, along with any required cables, software, and a user guide.

Installing and configuring a DSL modem typically follows these general steps (Figure 10-41):

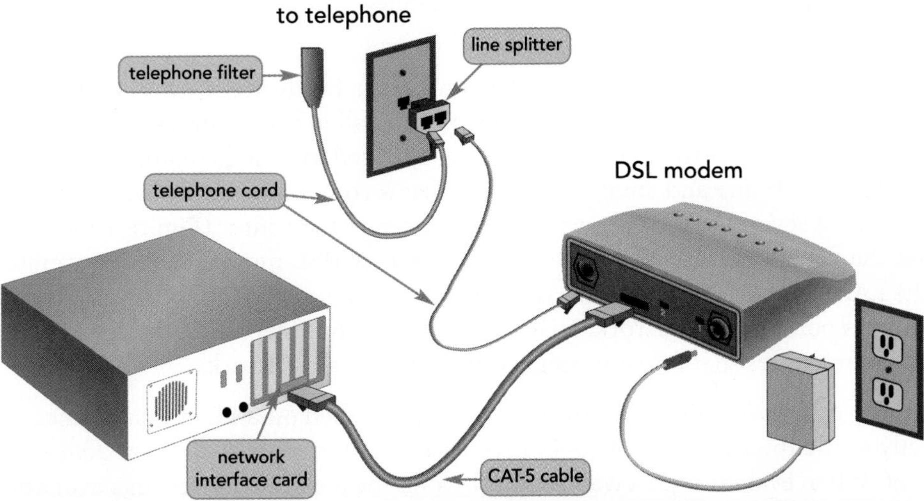

Figure 10-41 When installing a DSL modem, first install telephone filters on the lines and then connect the modem to the PC and the telephone line.

1. Install a telephone filter on every telephone in your home, as well as any fax machines, lines used for dial-up modems, or any other device plugged into a telephone outlet.
2. Connect the DSL modem as shown in Figure 10-41. First, plug a line splitter (also called a Y adapter) in the telephone line you plan to use for DSL. Plug the DSL modem into the line splitter without using a telephone filter. If you need a telephone there as well, plug the phone into the line splitter with a telephone filter.
3. Connect the DSL modem to NIC in the computer using a CAT-5 cable.
4. Once connected, turn on the power switch on the back of the modem.
5. Follow the user guide that came with the DSL modem to install the software to use with the DSL modem.
6. After the software installation is complete, you should be connected to the Internet. Test that you are connected to the Internet using your Web browser or e-mail client.

More About

Sharing Internet Connections

To learn more about sharing Internet connections, visit the Understanding and Troubleshooting Your PC More About Web page (**scsite.com/understanding/more**) and then click Sharing Internet Connections below Chapter 10.

IMPLEMENTING A FIREWALL When setting up an always-on connection, such as a cable or DSL connection, you should install a firewall to help protect your computer from unauthorized access. A firewall can function in several ways:

- Firewalls can filter data packets, examining the destination IP address or source IP address or the type of protocol used (for example, TCP or UDP).
- Firewalls can filter ports so outside clients cannot communicate with inside services listening at these ports.
- Firewalls can filter applications such as FTP so users inside the firewall cannot use this service over the Internet.
- Some firewalls can filter information such as inappropriate Web content for children or employees.

Many types of firewalls exist, from personal firewalls to protect a single PC to expensive firewall solutions for large corporations. As you learned in Chapter 8, a firewall is implemented either as software installed on a computer or as embedded firmware on a hardware device.

Hardware Firewall The best firewall solution is a hardware firewall that stands between a LAN and the Internet. A hardware firewall is better than software on each PC because it protects the entire network, as opposed to a single computer on the network. Many home and small office LANs use a router as a hardware firewall and then connect several computers and other devices to the router (Figure 10-42). The router then connects directly to the cable modem or DSL modem, so all computers on the LAN can have Internet access. Some routers also serve double duty as a wireless access point to the network, DHCP server, and proxy server. Linksys and NetGear are two companies that make routers suitable for small networks.

Software Firewalls Firewall software can be installed on a PC that is connected directly to the Internet. Figure 10-43 lists several software firewalls available on the market. When evaluating firewall software, look for the security settings available, including its ability to control traffic coming from both outside and inside the network. When setting up a software firewall, be aware that some software firewalls, such as Internet Connection Firewall, can prevent others on a LAN from accessing resources on the local PC.

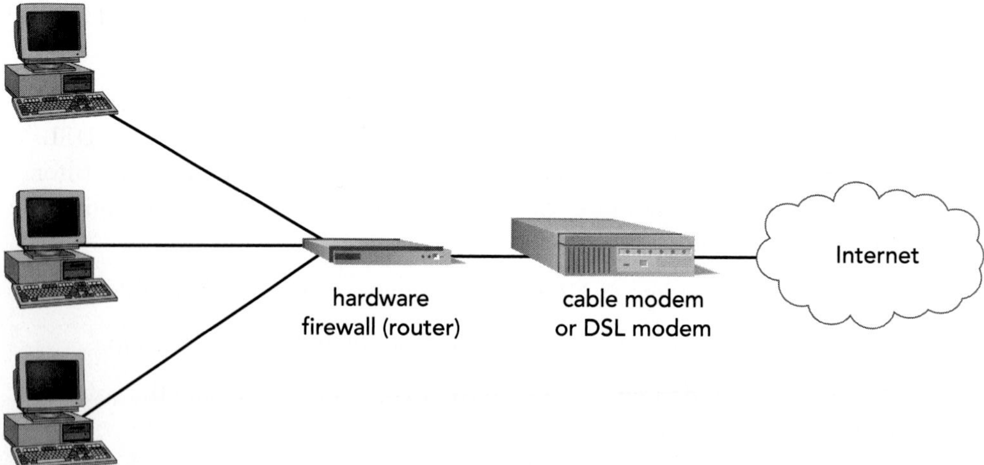

Figure 10-42 A hardware firewall stands between the Internet and a local area network.

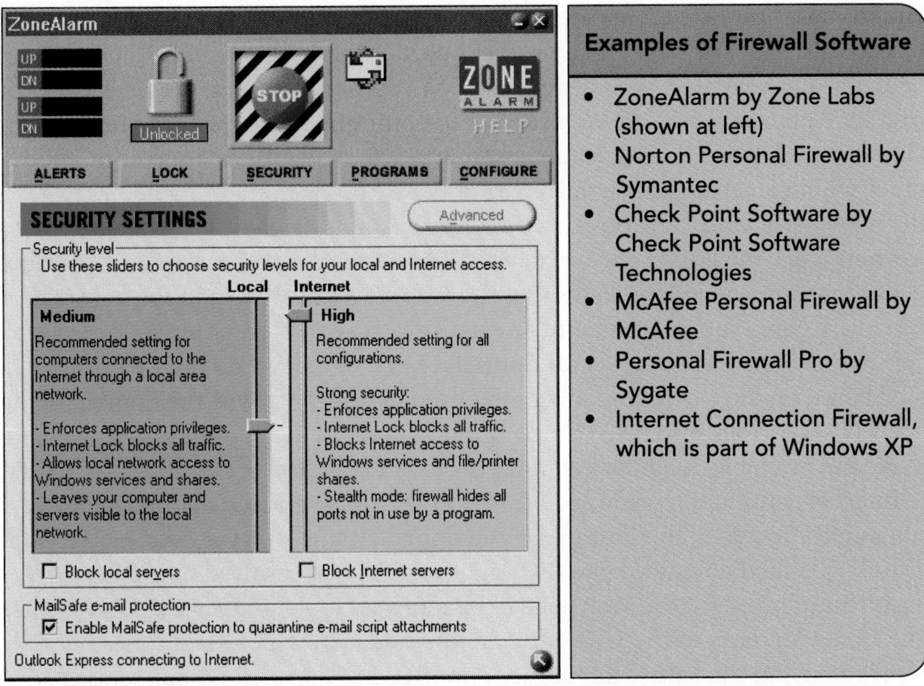

Examples of Firewall Software

- ZoneAlarm by Zone Labs (shown at left)
- Norton Personal Firewall by Symantec
- Check Point Software by Check Point Software Technologies
- McAfee Personal Firewall by McAfee
- Personal Firewall Pro by Sygate
- Internet Connection Firewall, which is part of Windows XP

Figure 10-43 A software firewall, such as ZoneAlarm, allows you to determine the amount of security the firewall provides.

Accessing Internet Resources Using a Web Browser

Once you have connected to the Internet, you can utilize the countless resources available. Many different types of applications, such as e-mail clients, FTP clients, and Web browsers, serve as the clients on the client/server architecture used by the Internet. A **Web browser**, often called simply a **browser**, is a software application on a user's PC that is used to request Web pages from a Web server on the Internet or an intranet. A **Web page** is a document on the Web identified by a unique URL (Uniform Resource Locator), which is discussed below. Web pages often consist of text coded using **HTML** (**Hypertext Markup Language**), which is a markup language that can be interpreted by a Web browser to display formatted text, graphics, images, forms, and so on. If the HTML code on the Web page points to other files incorporated in the page, such as an image file, these files also are downloaded to the browser.

E-mail and FTP

To learn more about using e-mail and FTP clients to access Internet resources, visit the Understanding and Troubleshooting Your PC More About Web page (**scsite.com/ understanding/more**) and then click E-mail and FTP below Chapter 10.

HOW A URL IS STRUCTURED As you have learned, a client such as a Web browser can request a Web page using an IP address (with a port number if needed). Because IP addresses are difficult to remember, most users accessing Web pages on the Internet or an intranet enter a URL in the browser address bar. A **URL** (**Uniform Resource Locator**) is an address for a Web page or other resource on the Internet, which includes the protocol used, the host name of the Web server, the domain name, and the path and filename of the requested file (Figure 10-44).

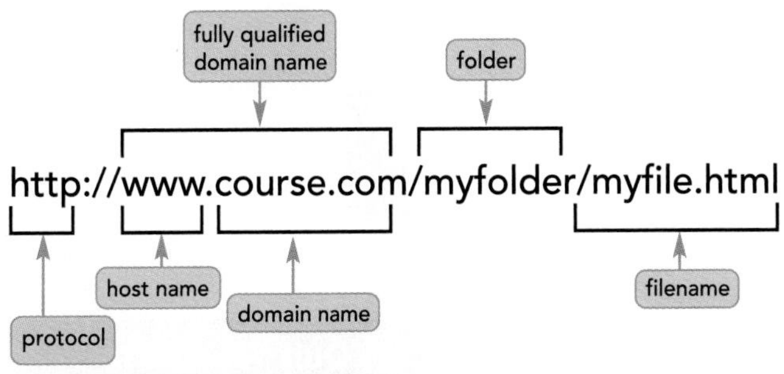

Figure 10-44 The structure of a URL.

The first part of the URL indicates the protocol, which in this case is HTTP (Hypertext Transfer Protocol). The protocol part of the URL specifies the rules, or protocol, used to send and receive requests. As you have learned, HTTP is the protocol used by Web browsers and Web servers to communicate over the Internet.

The second part of the URL is the host name, which identifies a server or another computer within a network. The third part of the URL, the domain name, indicates the specific network of which the host is a part. For example, in the URL in Figure 10-44 on the previous page, the host name is *www*, which indicates a Web server, and the domain name is *course.com*, which indicates that the Web server is located in the network named course.com. The last segment, or extension, of a domain name — for example, *.com* or *.edu* — is called the **top-level domain** (**TLD**). Top-level domain names are assigned based on the type of organization or individual that owns the domain name. Fourteen TLDs currently are used in the United States, as listed in Figure 10-45. Other TLDs also are available, including country codes, such as .uk for the United Kingdom. As the Internet continues to grow, additional TLDs can be added to support more domain names. Together, the host name and domain name — www.course.com — make up the fully qualified domain name (FQDN). The FQDN is resolved by a DNS server to an IP address in order for the Web page to be returned to the requesting Web browser.

The final two parts of the URL indicate the folder in which the requested Web page is located and the actual file name. The URL in Figure 10-44 has requested a Web page named *myfile.html* in the folder named *myfolder*.

More About

Domain Names and TLDs

To learn more about domain names and TLDs, visit the Understanding and Troubleshooting Your PC More About Web page (**scsite.com/understanding/more**) and then click Domain Names and TLDs below Chapter 10.

More About

Browsers, Security Settings, and Updates

To learn more about using and configuring a browser, configuring security settings, and downloading updates, visit the Understanding and Troubleshooting Your PC More About Web page (**scsite.com/understanding/more**) and then click Browsers, Security Settings, and Updates below Chapter 10.

Domain Suffix	Suffix Description	Domain Suffix	Suffix Description
.air	Aviation industry	.int	International organizations
.biz	Businesses	.mil	U.S. military
.com	Commercial institutions	.museum	Museums
.coop	Business cooperatives	.name	Individuals
.edu	Educational institutions	.net	Internet providers or networks
.gov	Government institutions	.org	Nonprofit organizations
.info	General use	.pro	Professionals

Figure 10-45 Top-level domains used in the United States.

FAQ 10-13

Is a domain name permanently associated with an IP address?

Domain names and IP addresses are not necessarily permanently associated. A host computer can have a certain domain name, can be connected to one network and assigned a certain IP address, and then can be moved to another network and assigned a different IP address. The domain name can stay with the host while it connects to a new network using the new IP address. DNS servers on the Internet are used to track the relationship between a domain name and the current IP address of the host computer and to resolve the domain name to the IP address.

Quiz Yourself 10-3

To test your knowledge of Internet technologies and connecting to the Internet, visit the Understanding and Troubleshooting Your PC Quiz Yourself Web page (scsite.com/understanding/quiz). Click Quiz Yourself 3 below Chapter 10.

High-Tech Talk

IP Addresses: A Class (A, B, or C) Act

Every computer on the Internet has a unique IP address — one of the 4,294,967,296 unique values that distinguishes it from other computers on the Internet under the IPv4 addressing scheme. So how does an organization get an IP address to assign to a computer — and how can it be sure it is unique? By applying to one of three regional Internet registries — ARIN, RIPE NCC, LACNIC, and APNIC — that assign Internet addresses to organizations based on the number of IP addresses needed by that group.

Organizations are assigned license for one of three classes of IP addresses: Class A, Class B, or Class C. (Class D and Class E IP addresses are not available for general use.) By looking at an IP address, you can determine the class of the IP address. You also can determine what portion of the IP address is dedicated to identifying the network and what portion is used to identify the host on that network (Figure 10-46).

Refer back to Figure 10-15 on page 416, which shows how each class of IP address is divided into the network and host portions. A Class A address uses the first (leftmost) octet for the network address and the remaining octets for host addresses. The first octet of a Class A address is a number between 0 and 126. Examples of IP addresses for hosts on this network are 87.0.0.1, 87.0.0.2, and 87.0.0.3. In IP address 87.0.0.1, the 87 is the network portion of the IP address, and 0.0.1 is the host portion. Because three octets can be used for Class A host addresses, one Class A license can have approximately 256 × 256 × 254 host addresses, or about 16 million IP addresses. Only very large corporations with heavy communication needs can get Class A licenses.

A Class B address uses the first two octets for the network portion and the last two for the host portion. The first octet of a Class B license is a number between 128 and 191; the second number can be between 0 and 255. For example, suppose a company is assigned 135.18 as the network address for its Class B license. The first two octets for all hosts on this network are 135.18, and the company uses the last two octets for host addresses. For example, in the IP address 135.18.0.1 on this company's Class B network, 135.18 is the network portion of the IP address, and 0.1 is the host portion. Because two octets can be used for host addresses, one Class B license can have about 256 × 254, or about 65,000 host addresses.

A Class C license assigns three octets as the network address. With only one octet used for the host addresses, there can be only 254 host addresses on a Class C network. The first number of a Class C license is between 192 and 223. For example, if a company is assigned a Class C license for its network with a network address of 200.80.15, some IP addresses on the network would be 200.80.15.1, 200.80.15.2, and 200.80.15.3.

Even with several billion IP addresses being managed by groups like ARIN, the demand for IP addresses continues to grow. Because so many machines connected to the Internet needs unique IP addresses, there is a growing shortage of IP addresses. A new IP addressing scheme, called IPv6 or IPng (IP Next Generation) will lengthen IP addresses from 32 bits to 128 bits and increase the number of available IP addresses to a whopping 34,000,000,000,000,000,000,000,000,000,000,000,000,000!

Class	Network Octets (Blanks in the IP address stand for octets used to identify hosts.)	Total Number of Possible Networks or Licenses	Host Octets (Blanks in the IP address stand for octets used to identify networks.)	Total Number of Possible IP Addresses in Each Network
A	0.__.__.__ to 126.__.__.__	127	__.0.0.1 to __.255.255.254	16 million
B	128.0.__.__ to 191.255.__.__	16,000	__.__.0.1 to __.__.255.254	65,000
C	192.0.0.__ to 223.255.255.__	2 million	__.__.__.1 to __.__.__.254	254

Figure 10-46

CHAPTER SUMMARY

The Chapter Summary reviews the concepts presented in this chapter.

1 Network Types and Architectures

A network is a collection of computers and devices connected together via a transmission medium to share resources. Networks are classified as LANs, MANs, or WANs, based on their area coverage. A network topology, such as bus, ring, or star, defines the physical arrangement used to connect network devices. Logical network architectures include client/server and peer-to-peer. LANs use hardware protocols, such as Ethernet, token ring, FDDI, or Wi-Fi, to allow hardware devices on a network to communicate. A PC uses an internal or external network interface card (NIC) to connect a network.

2 Using Windows on a Network

A NOS (network operating system) controls the entire network and its resources. LANs also use software protocols, such as TCP/IP, IPX/SPX, and NetBEUI, to transfer data over a network. Every network node has a unique address, which can be a MAC address, an IP address with an optional port number, or a character-based name such as a domain name, host name, or NetBIOS name. An IP address is a unique address with four numbers that range from 0 through 255, separated by periods. Computers are given static (permanent) IP addresses or are assigned dynamic IP addresses by a DHCP server. TCP/IP networks using Windows have four options available for name resolution to an IP address: DNS, WINS, broadcast name resolution, and Hosts and LMHosts files.

3 Connecting to and Using Resources on a Network

Connecting a PC to a network requires a NIC, a patch cable, and a device for the PC to connect to, such as a hub. Wireless networks require a wireless NIC and the PC to be within range of an access point or other wireless enabled device. Windows XP automatically configures network cards to use TCP/IP. With dynamic IP addressing, a computer gets an IP address, subnet mask, and default gateway from a DHCP server. Once connected, you can share files, folders, and applications on the same network. Mapping a network drive allows you to assign a drive letter to a shared network drive. If you cannot connect to a network, determine if the problem is caused by the entire network being down, the NIC, or a network cable. The Ping and Ipconfig utilities help with TCP/IP configuration issues, NSLookup requests information about domain name resolutions from the DNS server.

4 Internet Technologies and Protocols

The Internet uses a client/server architecture. Routers are used to transfer data from a server to a client using the best path from the sender to recipient. TCP/IP, the protocol suite that is the basis of the Internet, supports applications protocols such as HTTP, SMTP, POP, IMAP, and FTP; OS protocols such as TCP, UDP, and IP; and hardware protocols such as Ethernet, Wi-Fi, PPP, and PPPoE.

5 Connecting to the Internet

Popular ways to connect to the Internet include a standard dial-up connection, cable modem, or DSL, all of which require a modem. A modem can transmit data over telephone lines, cable television cables, or other physical media. DSL and cable are considered to be broadband technologies. Dial-up connections require a dial-up modem and a Dial-up Networking connection configured in Windows. Most cable modem and DSL connections use the NIC to connect a cable from the PC to the cable or DSL modem (some use USB). When using an always-on cable or DSL connection, install a hardware or software firewall. A Web browser is a software application on a user's PC that is used to request Web pages from a Web server on the Internet or an intranet using a URL (Uniform Resource Locator).

KEY TERMS

After reading the chapter, you should know each of these Key Terms.

access point (AP) *(409)*
Automatic Private IP Address (APIPA) *(417)*
bandwidth *(402)*
binding *(412)*
BNC connector *(406)*
bridge *(408)*
broadband *(441)*
browser *(453)*
bus topology *(403)*
cable modem *(441)*
coaxial cable *(406)*
combo card *(411)*
default gateway *(417)*
DHCP (Dynamic Host Configuration Protocol) server *(417)*
dial-up networking *(445)*
DNS (Domain Name System, Domain Name Service) *(421)*
DNS server *(421)*
domain name *(419)*
DSL (Digital Subscriber Line) *(441)*
DSL modem *(444)*
dynamic IP address *(417)*
Ethernet *(405)*
Fiber Distributed Data Interface (FDDI) *(409)*
FTP (File Transfer Protocol) *(438)*
fully qualified domain name (FQDN) *(419)*
gateway *(417)*
host computer *(404)*
host name *(419)*
HTML (Hypertext Markup Language) *(453)*
HTTP (Hypertext Transfer Protocol) *(438)*
hub *(403)*
IMAP (Internet Message Access Protocol) *(438)*
Internet Connection Sharing (ICS) *(418)*
Internet service provider (ISP) *(417)*
intranet *(413)*
IP (Internet Protocol) *(439)*
IP address *(413)*
Ipconfig *(434)*
IPX/SPX (Internetwork Packet Exchange/Sequenced Packet Exchange) *(412)*
ISDN (Integrated Services Digital Network) *(442)*
local area network (LAN) *(402)*
MAC (Media Access Control) address *(413)*
mapped drive *(432)*
metropolitan area network (MAN) *(402)*
modem *(441)*
name resolution *(421)*
NAT (Network Address Translation) *(417)*
NetBEUI (NetBIOS Extended User Interface) *(412)*
network *(402)*
network adapter *(402)*
network architecture *(404)*
network drive map *(432)*
network interface card (NIC) *(402)*
network protocols *(405)*
network topology *(403)*
NSLookup *(435)*
packets *(437)*
packet switching *(437)*
Ping (Packet Internet Groper) *(434)*
POP (Post Office Protocol) *(438)*
port number *(414)*
PPP (Point-to-Point Protocol) *(441)*
PPPoE (Point-to-Point Protocol over Ethernet) *(441)*
proxy server *(417)*
ring topology *(403)*
RJ-45 connector *(406)*
router *(436)*
service *(418)*
session *(438)*
shielded twisted-pair (STP) cable *(406)*
SMTP (Simple Mail Transfer Protocol) *(438)*
socket *(438)*
star topology *(403)*
stateless *(436)*
static IP address *(417)*
switch *(408)*
subnet mask *(417)*
TCP (Transmission Control Protocol) *(439)*
TCP/IP (Transmission Control Protocol/Internet Protocol) *(412)*
token *(409)*
token ring *(409)*
top-level domain (TLD) *(454)*
transceiver *(411)*
UDP (User Datagram Protocol) *(439)*
unshielded twisted-pair (UTP) cable *(406)*
URL (Uniform Resource Locator) *(453)*
Web browser *(453)*
Web page *(453)*
wide area network (WAN) *(402)*
WINS (Windows Internet Naming Service) *(421)*
Wired Equivalent Privacy (WEP) *(429)*
wireless LAN (WLAN) *(409)*
wireless NIC *(409)*

LEARN IT ONLINE

Reinforce your understanding of the chapter concepts and terms with the Learn It Online exercises.

Instructions: To complete the Learn It Online exercises, start your browser, click the Address bar, and then enter the Web address scsite.com/understanding/learn. When the Understanding and Troubleshooting Your PC Learn It Online page is displayed, follow the instructions in the exercises below. Each exercise has instructions for printing your results, either for your own records or for submission to your instructor.

1 Chapter Reinforcement True/False, Multiple Choice, and Short Answer

Below Chapter 10, click the Chapter Reinforcement link. Print the quiz by clicking Print on the File menu for each page. Answer each question.

2 Flash Cards

Below Chapter 10, click the Flash Cards link and read the instructions. Type 20 (or a number specified by your instructor) in the Number of playing cards text box, type your name in the Enter your Name text box, and then click the Flip Card button. When the flash card is displayed, read the question and then click the ANSWER box arrow to select an answer. Flip through Flash Cards. If your score is 15 (75%) correct or greater, click Print on the File menu to print your results. If your score is less than 15 (75%) correct, then redo this exercise by clicking the Replay button.

3 Practice Test

Below Chapter 10, click the Practice Test link. Answer each question, enter your first and last name at the bottom of the page, and then click the Grade Test button. When the graded practice test is displayed on your screen, click Print on the File menu to print a hard copy. Continue to take practice tests until you score 80% or better.

4 Who Wants To Be a Computer Genius?

Below Chapter 10, click the Computer Genius link. Read the instructions, enter your first and last name at the bottom of the page, and then click the PLAY button. When your score is displayed, click the PRINT RESULTS link to print a hard copy.

5 Wheel of Terms

Below Chapter 10, click the Wheel of Terms link. Read the instructions, and then enter your first and last name and your school name. Click the PLAY button. When your score is displayed, right-click the score and then click Print on the shortcut menu to print a hard copy.

6 Crossword Puzzle Challenge

Below Chapter 10, click the Crossword Puzzle Challenge link. Read the instructions, and then enter your first and last name. Click the SUBMIT button. Work the crossword puzzle. When you are finished, click the Submit button. When the crossword puzzle is redisplayed, click the Print Puzzle button to print a hard copy.

Multiple Choice

Select the best answer.

1. When selecting a network card, you should consider all of the following except:
   a. the speed and type of network to which you are attaching
   b. the MAC address of the card
   c. the type of cable or wireless connection used
   d. the type of expansion slot in which to install the card
2. Which of the following is not a type of cable used for 10-Mbps Ethernet?
   a. STP
   b. UTP
   c. coaxial
   d. fiber-optic
3. Which of these items is not included in a URL (Uniform Resource Locator)?
   a. application protocol
   b. domain name
   c. NetBIOS name
   d. host name
4. When troubleshooting an Internet or LAN connection, entering the commands ________ and ________ will lease a new IP address.
   a. getmac, ping /lease
   b. nslookup, ipconfig /lease
   c. ping /all, ipconfig /all
   d. ipconfig /release, ipconfig /renew
5. Which of the following is not an OS protocol supported by Windows?
   a. FDDI
   b. NetBEUI
   c. IPX/SPX
   d. TCP/IP

Fill in the Blank

Write the word or phrase to fill in the blank in each of the following questions.

1. A network using a(n) ________ topology has a central hub to which all other computers and devices are connected.
2. In a(n) ________ network architecture, each computer on the network has equal responsibilities and capabilities on the network. Windows refers to this network architecture as a(n) ________.
3. A(n) ________ is a communications device that directs data to the correct network by determining the most efficient available route from the sending computer to the receiving computer.
4. The last segment, or extension, of a domain name (for example, .com or .edu) is called the ________.
5. ________ occurs when an operating system-level protocol such as TCP/IP associates itself with a lower-level hardware protocol such as Ethernet.

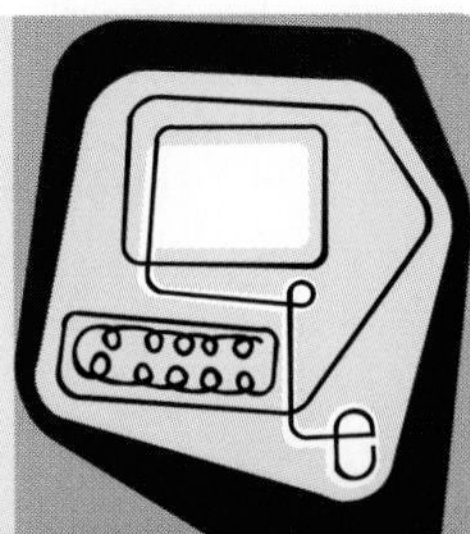

CHAPTER EXERCISES

Complete the Chapter Exercises to solidify what you learned in the chapter.

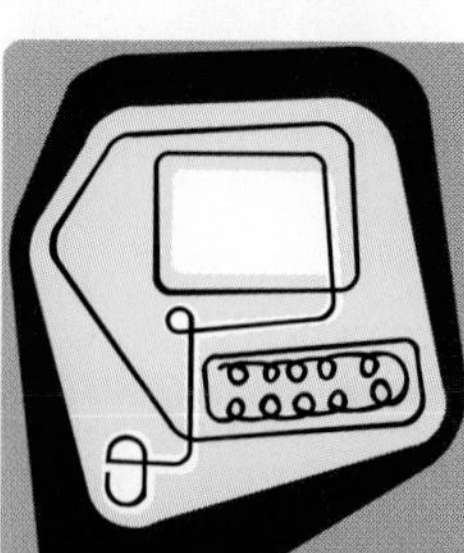

CHAPTER EXERCISES

Complete the Chapter Exercises to solidify what you learned in the chapter.

Matching Terms

Match the terms with their definitions.

______	1. domain name	a.	protocol used to send an e-mail message to its destination
______	2. port number	b.	hardware protocol that allows nodes to contend for access to the network
______	3. SMTP	c.	a document on the Web identified by a unique URL
______	4. Web page	d.	communications medium that carries more than one type of transmission
______	5. 802.11	e.	group of standards used for wireless LANs
______	6. POP	f.	number added to IP address to identify specific program or service
______	7. TCP/IP	g.	protocol suite that is the basis of the Internet; also used on many LANs
______	8. MAC address	h.	text version of one or more IP addresses
______	9. broadband	i.	protocol used to receive e-mail message
______	10. Ethernet	j.	hardware address unique to each NIC

Short Answer Questions

Write a brief answer to each of the following questions.

1. Briefly explain the differences between the hardware protocols used for LANs: Ethernet, Token Ring, FDDI, and Wi-Fi.
2. What is the difference between a static IP address and a dynamic IP address? What role does the DHCP server play?
3. List and describe the four methods used to provide each device (node) or program on a network with a unique address, so data packets can be addressed and delivered to the correct device.
4. What options are available for name resolution on networks running Windows? What series of steps is used by a Windows XP computer during the name resolution process?
5. Describe four application protocols supported by the TCP/IP suite of protocols.

APPLY YOUR KNOWLEDGE

Check your understanding of the chapter with the hands-on Apply Your Knowledge exercises.

1 Installing a NIC and Connecting to a LAN

Follow the steps described in the chapter to install a NIC in an expansion slot in a desktop or tower computer. Once the NIC is installed, work with your instructor or network administrator to obtain the following information required to set up network connections on a LAN using TCP/IP:

1. Will the PC use dynamic or static IP addressing?
2. If static IP addressing is used, what are the IP address, subnet mask, and default gateway for this computer?
3. Do you use DNS? If so, what are the IP addresses of your DNS servers?
4. Is a proxy server used to connect to other networks (including the Internet)? If so, what is the IP address of the proxy server?

Once you have that information, set the TCP/IP properties for a network interface card. Test the connection by opening My Network Places and verifying that your computer and other computers on the network are visible (you may need to reboot the PC).

2 Understanding Internet and Network Connections

Using a computer connected to the Internet or a network, answer these questions:

1. What is the hardware device used to make this connection (modem or network card)? List the device's name as Windows sees it.
2. If you are connected to a LAN, what is the MAC address of the NIC? Print the screen that shows the address.
3. What is the IP address of your PC? What is your default gateway IP address? What response do you get when you Ping the default gateway?
4. Release and renew your IP address. Are you using dynamic or static IP addressing? How do you know?
5. Print the screen that shows which network protocols are installed on your PC.
6. List the Windows utilities you used to answer these questions.

3 Researching a Wireless LAN

Suppose you want to connect two computers to your company LAN using a wireless connection. Use the Internet to research the equipment needed to create the wireless LAN, and print a Web page showing an access point device that can connect to an Ethernet LAN. Next, answer the following questions:

1. How much does the access point cost? How many wireless devices can the access point support at one time? How is the access point powered?
2. Print three Web pages showing three different wireless network adapters a computer can use to connect to the access point. Include one external device that uses a USB port and one internal device. How much does each device cost?
3. What is the total cost of implementing a wireless LAN with two computers using the wireless connection?

4 Selecting Dial-up, DSL, or Cable Service

Based on what you learned in the chapter, briefly describe how dial-up, DSL, and cable modems work. Use the Internet to research the speed of each type of connection, any new hardware you would require, and the average costs of each type of connection, including installation fees and monthly service fees. Next, determine if services such as DSL and cable are available in your area. Given the choice and availability of each type of service, which type of service would you use for your Internet connection and why?

<td class="topnav" colspan="2">
<div align="center" id="navigation">
<a href="http://www.course.com/news/">Pres
"http://www.course.com/about/">About Us
intel
pentium 4
<div align="center" id="banner">
<table cellpadding="0" cellspacing
<tr>
<td align="left" bgcolor="#003399
cellpadding="0" cellspacing="0" border="0">

CHAPTER 11

Purchasing or Building a Personal Computer

Introduction

This chapter presents guidelines for upgrading or purchasing a new PC, as well as detailed, step-by-step procedures for building a PC on your own. After discussing when it is appropriate to upgrade a PC, the chapter reviews considerations for buying a new PC, including a discussion of whether to purchase a brand-name PC or a clone, and how to select hardware, software, or a total package. Next, the chapter provides a detailed look at the steps involved in building your own PC from components.

OBJECTIVES

In this chapter, you will learn:

1. Some guidelines to use when upgrading or purchasing a new PC
2. How to prepare for assembling a PC
3. How to assemble a PC from parts purchased separately

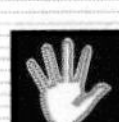

Up for Discussion

Sunrise Computers has been running a sale on new PCs from several manufacturers. Having seen the ad in Sunday's newspaper, David Rothenberg, a tax accountant at a small firm in town, stopped in to browse through the PCs to see if any of them met his needs. Noticing Mr. Rothenberg looking closely at a specific computer, you ask him if he has any questions about that PC. He tells you he is not even sure he needs a new PC, but his current computer is not providing the performance he needs during the busy tax season. You explain that his dilemma is fairly common, and that his computer's performance issues might temporarily be solved by some simple maintenance tasks, such as defragmenting the hard drive. You offer to provide a list of things he can try to improve the computer's performance in the short term. You also suggest that he might want to begin the process of purchasing a new PC by considering what his planned use is for the computer, what types of hardware or software he needs, and his budget. You provide him with a checklist he can use to answer those questions, so you can help pick out a brand-name PC or a clone that suits his needs and his budget. When he asks about the sale, you assure him you will gladly provide a rain check on the sale prices, so that he can spend more time considering his current and future computing needs.

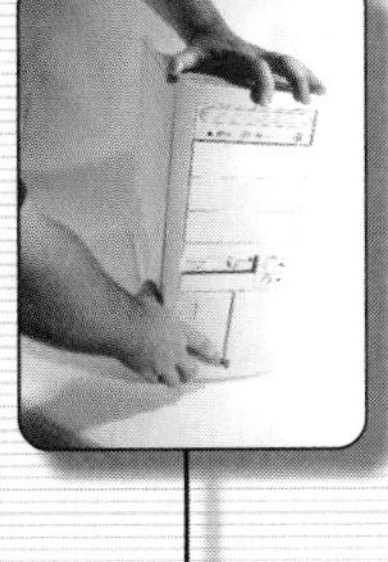

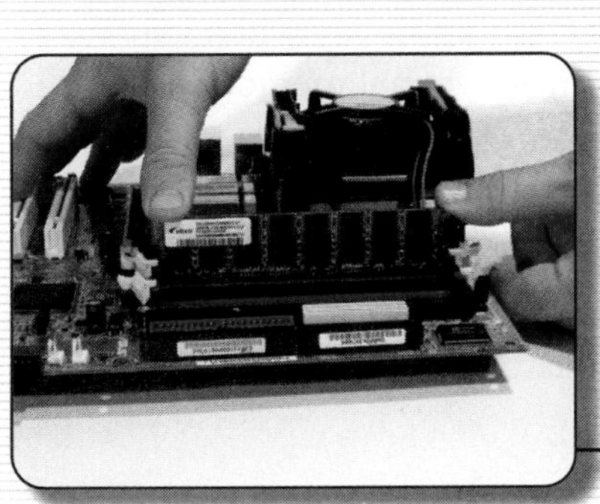

Questions:

- What are some maintenance tasks that can improve a computer's performance?
- What questions should you answer when considering a computer purchase?
- What are the advantages and disadvantages of buying a brand-name or clone PC?

Upgrading or Purchasing a Personal Computer

At some point, you may find that your current computer is not providing the performance you expect. For example, the computer may run very slowly due to an older CPU or small amount of RAM; it may not have enough hard disk space for your files and software; or it may not support an OS or software that you want to install.

Before considering an upgrade or a new computer purchase, first take steps to maximize the performance of your current computer. You can improve performance greatly simply by performing the routine maintenance tasks discussed in previous chapters. For example, defragmenting your hard drive can help reduce the time your computer needs to access files. Other steps that can help improve your computer's performance include:

- *Run Disk Cleanup* to delete temporary and other nonessential files on a hard drive. This will free up space on the hard drive and improve performance.
- *Enable disk caching* to speed up access time to the hard drive. As you learned in Chapter 5, a disk cache is a temporary storage area in RAM for data being read from or written to a hard drive, which helps provide faster access to the drive, particularly if large amounts of data are being written to the disk.
- *Use the Error-checking tool* to check for file system errors and bad sectors on your hard disk. Using Windows XP, you can check the disk for errors by right-clicking drive C in the My Computer window and then clicking Properties on the shortcut menu. When the Disk Properties window is displayed, click the Tools tab and then click the Check Now button. When the Check Disk window is displayed, click Automatically fix file system errors and Scan for and attempt recovery of bad sectors and then click the Start button. If Windows displays an error message asking if you want to perform the check the next time you restart the computer, click the Yes button. Close all windows and restart the computer. Windows automatically will run the error-checking utility to search for and fix any errors on the hard disk.
- *Remove any unnecessary programs from Startup.* When you start Windows, many programs are loaded automatically and thus consume memory and resources. Many programs that run at startup are listed in the Startup submenu. To prevent them from loading on startup, simply right-click the menu item and then click Delete on the shortcut menu or drag the menu item out of the Startup folder into another folder on the All Programs menu.
- *Change the size of your paging file.* If your system is running slowly when you have many applications open, you may want to optimize virtual memory by changing the size of your paging file.
- *Run Windows Update* to download and install the latest updates for Windows, applications, and device drivers from the Microsoft Web site.
- *Run a full antivirus scan*. As you will learn in Chapter 12, running a full antivirus scan will detect any hidden viruses that may be slowing your system performance.

More About

Checking the Hard Disk for Errors

To learn more about checking the disk for sector or file system errors, visit the Understanding and Troubleshooting Your PC More About Web page (**scsite.com/understanding/more**) and then click Checking the Hard Disk for Errors below Chapter 11.

FAQ 11-1

What if a program that runs on startup is not listed in the Startup menu?

You can view a list of all applications running at startup by using the System Information tool. In the System Information window, click the expand (+) symbol next to Software Environment and then click Startup Programs to view a list of programs and the command used to load them. Most applications provide a selection option to allow you to disable the feature that starts the program when you load Windows. If you cannot find such an option, the program likely has created an entry in the registry, in the HKEY_LOCAL_MACHINE\SOFTWARE\Microsoft\CurrentVersion\Run and RunServices directory. Deleting the entry for a program will prevent it from starting when you start Windows.

FAQ 11-2

Is it true that having a lot of fonts on your system can slow performance?

Yes. When Windows is installed, it automatically installs numerous built-in fonts, as do other applications. You also can download or purchase additional fonts, either for fun or for your work. Having too many fonts on your system, however, can impact performance negatively. If so, try deleting fonts you rarely use. To do so, double-click Fonts in the Control Panel window. When the Fonts folder opens, select the fonts to delete and then press the DELETE key. If you think you will want to reinstall the fonts later, be sure to copy them to a floppy disk, CD-R, or other storage medium before deleting them.

When you need more computing power or additional options, you must decide whether to upgrade your current system or purchase a new computer. Making the decision to upgrade an existing computer or to buy a new computer often comes down to a question of cost. In general, an upgrade is appropriate if the cost of the upgrade does not exceed half the value of the current system, and if the resulting system will not contain older components that prevent it from performing well. Typically, you should not upgrade a computer system that is more than three years old, as the cost of the upgrade probably will exceed the value of the current system. In this case, purchasing a new PC is your best option. Other questions to consider before deciding to upgrade a PC are listed in Figure 11-1.

Question	Considerations
Is an upgrade possible at a reasonable cost?	If you have an older system or newer but off-brand system, you may have to replace the entire motherboard to upgrade to the performance level you desire.
Will an upgrade give you the performance you want?	Adding memory or a new hard drive can help resolve many performance issues. If you will have to upgrade almost every component of the system to support an application, however, purchasing a new PC may be a better option.
Can you handle the upgrade yourself?	For simpler upgrades, such as adding a new chip or upgrading memory, you most likely can handle the upgrade yourself, provided you have the right tools. If you are not comfortable doing the work yourself, does the cost of having someone else do the work make the upgrade too expensive?
Will the new hardware fit in the computer case?	Your computer only has so many drive bays, expansion slots, connectors, and so on. If you no longer have space or support for the hardware you want to install, upgrading may not be a viable option.
Will the software and drivers support the new device?	Before upgrading a device, be sure you can obtain the drivers for that device and that you are comfortable changing the required software configurations to recognize the new device. (For example, if you upgrade your modem, you may have to reconfigure your network settings to recognize it.)

Figure 11-1 Questions to ask when considering a PC upgrade.

After you have decided whether to upgrade or purchase a new PC, you will need to determine the types of hardware and software required for the upgraded or new system. The following sections review factors to consider when upgrading a PC or purchasing a new PC.

Upgrading a PC

As discussed above, it sometimes is more appropriate to upgrade an existing PC than to purchase a new one. To upgrade a PC to provide better performance, consider adding more memory, upgrading the CPU or adding a second CPU, adding a second hard drive, upgrading the video card, upgrading the motherboard, and adding more fans for cooling. Some important points to keep in mind when upgrading include:

- Before upgrading the operating system, verify that you can get drivers for each device you plan to use in the system. New, compatible drivers may not be available for some older, legacy devices.
- When upgrading memory, follow the guidelines in Chapter 4 to match memory modules to what the motherboard supports and what already is installed.
- When upgrading the CPU, review the motherboard documentation to check what processor speeds and types the motherboard supports and that you are using the right size processor fan and heat sink. Also check the documentation for the voltage requirements to determine if you will need an extra ATX12V 4-pin connector on the motherboard to support the processor. You might need to install a voltage regulator module, as described in Chapter 5. Be sure to read the documentation for the CPU to determine what thermal compound is recommended for use with that specific processor. Finally, if you plan to add a second CPU, be sure the motherboard can support it.
- If you plan to upgrade the motherboard, check to see if all of the components that connect to the current motherboard are compatible with the new motherboard. For instance, if the memory modules or processor are not compatible with the new motherboard, you may have to buy new components. Also consider the number and types of expansion slots available on the motherboard to be sure you will have enough expansion slots and the correct types. For example, several types of AGP slots are available and your video card must match the AGP standards your motherboard supports. Some motherboards also are designed so the last PCI slot is disabled if you use certain connectors on the board (such as a wireless connector). It is not a good idea to use every expansion slot on the motherboard, because it can cause the computer to overheat.

- When making major upgrades of the motherboard, processor, or peripheral devices, be sure that your hard drive has enough available space to support the extra needs of these devices. You might need to upgrade the hard drive or add a second drive.
- When upgrading or adding a new hard drive, match the IDE or SCSI standards your motherboard or controller card supports to the new drive.
- When installing a new peripheral, check the documentation for the device to determine if you need to flash the BIOS before installing it. If so, complete the steps to flash the BIOS and then verify that the motherboard and existing peripherals are working. Next, install the latest updates and patches for your operating system and then install the new peripheral.
- If you are adding many new devices to the system, you should add more fans for cooling. Check with the processor manufacturer for specific instructions as to the placement of fans and what type of fan and heat sink to use. Also check the system to ensure that vents and at least one exhaust fan are in the right position, so air flows across the processor without expansion cards or ribbon cables obstructing the flow. For example, the power supply fan in ATX cases blows air out of the case, pulling outside air from the vents in the front of the case across the processor, to help keep the processor cool. Another exhaust fan usually is installed on the back of the case to help the power supply fan pull air through the case (Figure 11-2). A third fan mounted on the processor is used to keep air circulating near the processor and prevent hot air pockets from forming around the processor. Air circulation problems can be caused by poor placement of vents and

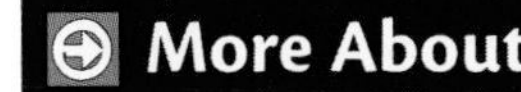
More About

Overheating

To learn more about how to avoid overheating, visit the Understanding and Troubleshooting Your PC More About Web page (**scsite.com/understanding/more**) and then click Overheating below Chapter 11.

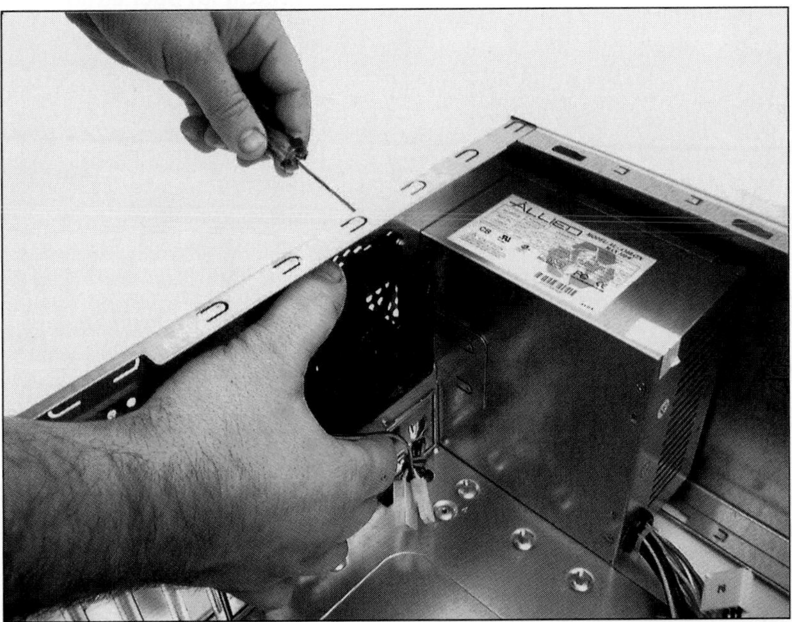

Figure 11-2 Installing an exhaust fan at the rear of the case helps to circulate air through the case.

fans. Figure 11-3 compares a good arrangement of vents and fans for proper airflow and a poor arrangement. For better ventilation, use a power supply that has vents on the bottom and front of the power supply, like the one shown in Figure 11-3.

- If you are adding many new devices to the system, check that the power supply will provide enough wattage to support the new devices. Be sure that the power supply provides at least 250 watts or more, to provide enough power for all of the components that will be installed in your computer.

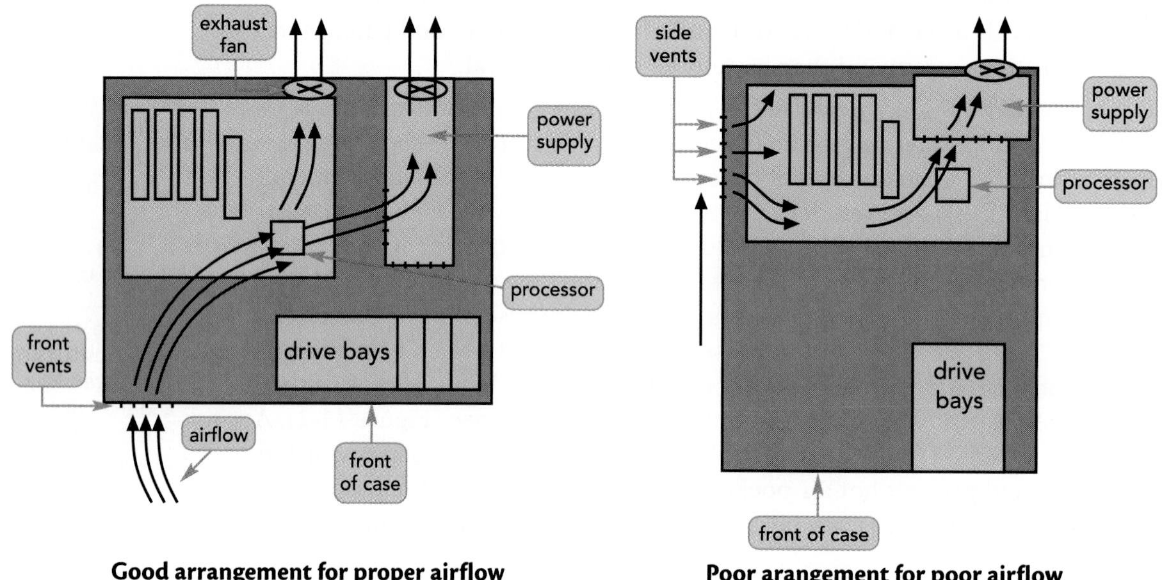

Figure 11-3 Vents and fans should be arranged for best airflow.

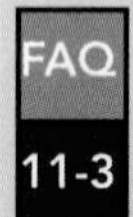

FAQ 11-3

I thought the ATX specification indicated that the power supply fan should draw air into the computer case. Has that changed?

One of the goals of the original ATX specification defined by Intel was to use the power supply fan to draw air in to cool the CPU. The idea did not work quite as planned. Newer, faster CPUs generate more heat than older ones, and a regular power supply fan does not create enough airflow to cool them properly. Even worse, the air is warmed by the components in the power supply itself, so the air blown on the CPU actually is *warmer* than the rest of the air in the case. Newer versions of the ATX specification thus make the fan direction optional — and the newest ATX power supplies have gone back to placing the fan on the back of the power supply, exhausting air to the outside.

Quiz Yourself 11-1

To test your knowledge of considerations when upgrading a PC, visit the Understanding and Troubleshooting Your PC Quiz Yourself Web page (scsite.com/understanding/quiz). Click Quiz Yourself 1 below Chapter 11.

Purchasing a New Personal Computer

If you determine that you want to buy a personal computer, instead of upgrading or assembling your own, you have several alternatives from which to choose: buying a used PC, or purchasing a new PC, either a brand-name computer or a clone. A

brand-name personal computer is one manufactured by a well-known company with a widely recognized name, such as Dell, Gateway, Hewlett-Packard, IBM, or Toshiba. A **clone** is a PC assembled by a local company with parts manufactured by several companies. The following section reviews overall considerations when purchasing a new personal computer, whether a brand-name computer or a clone.

OVERALL CONSIDERATIONS As you start the decision-making process of purchasing a new PC, you should begin by taking an overall view of your planned uses for the computer and your budget. Some of the most important questions to consider include the following:

1. How will the computer be used now and in the future?
2. Based on the planned use for the computer, what functionality do you want the computer to have?
3. What software and hardware do you need to meet this functionality?
4. What is your budget?

To make the best possible decision, answer all of these questions, placing the greatest weight on your answer to the first question, then the second question, and so on. For example, if you intend to use the computer for browsing the Internet and using e-mail, the functionality required is considerably different than the functionality required for a computer used to edit video and create multimedia presentations.

After you determine the intended purpose of the computer, list the functionality required to meet these needs. For example, if the computer is to be used for playing games, required functionality might include the ability to support game software, a high-quality video card with a lot of video RAM, a good sound system, and specialized input devices such as a joystick. If the computer is to be used for software development, required functionality might include ability to run software development tools; a large, high-quality monitor and a comfortable keyboard and mouse; a high-capacity removable storage device for easy transfer and storage of developed software; and a reliable warranty and service program to guarantee minimal downtime. After the required functionality is defined, you should define what software and hardware is needed, as discussed in the sections below.

SELECTING SOFTWARE Your decisions about software selection are driven by the functionality requirements you defined for the PC. The first software to consider is the operating system. If you plan to run Windows on your computer, you should select the latest version of the operating system supported by your hardware. Next, select the particular edition of the OS that will best support your needs. For example, if you plan to run Windows XP on your system, you must choose between Windows XP Professional, Windows XP Home Edition, or other editions of the OS. For a home office, Windows XP Home Edition might have enough functionality. For the corporate market or for wireless networking, where security and remote access are important, Windows XP Professional might be a better choice.

When choosing an operating system and application software, consider these questions:

- What types of software do you need, based on your functionality requirements?
- Is compatibility with other software or data required? For example, will you be able to read your old files on the new system? If you share files with others, will they be able to read your files using older versions of the software? Do you need to use the same types of software as others at school or work?

More About

Buying a Used PC

To learn more about considerations when buying a used PC, visit the Understanding and Troubleshooting Your PC More About Web page (**scsite.com/understanding/more**) and then click Buying a Used PC below Chapter 11.

- How well-known or widely used is the software? In general, the more widely used a software package is, the more likely it is that you can find good training materials, technical support, and other compatible software and hardware.
- Does the software get good reviews and ratings from computer magazines and Web sites?
- Is training available, if you do not already have the skills needed to use the software?
- How good is the software's documentation?
- What are the company's upgrade policies?

Many computers come with **pre-installed software** or **bundled software**, which is application or operating system software already installed on the computer when you purchase it. If you are buying a computer with pre-installed software, remember that the software only has value if you would have purchased the software anyway. Unneeded software can be more of a hindrance than a help, taking up space on the hard drive without providing value. For example, it is not uncommon for a brand-name computer to come with three or four applications for Internet access (for example, America Online, Earthlink, and Microsoft Network) because of licensing agreements that distributors have with online providers. If you think that you might use a pre-installed software package, review the list of questions above to be sure that the software provides the functionality you need and has good documentation, reliable upgrades, or support. If it does not, you may be able to negotiate a lower price for the computer without all of the software or you may have to purchase other software to use in addition to or in place of it. If you will not use a software package that is pre-installed on a system, do not consider it as adding value to the overall price of the computer.

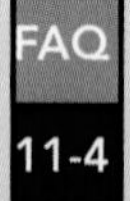

How do I know that the software pre-installed on a computer is legal?

Although it is not a widespread practice, some vendors try to sell counterfeit or pirated software by pre-installing it on computers — a practice called **hard-disk loading.** Vendors have even been known to counterfeit disk labels and Certificates of Authenticity. Look for these warning signs that software purchased from vendors is pirated: it has no end-user license, mail-in product registration card, documentation, or original CDs; documentation is photocopied; or disks have handwritten labels. Accept nothing less than the original installation CDs for all installed software.

Where can I learn more about which software packages are widely used and find reviews from users?

Many resources are available to learn more about specific software packages, including computer magazines, the Internet, the local bookstore, and your local computer retailer. A quick way to identify which brand of software is the most prevalent in the industry is to browse the computer books section of a local bookstore, looking for the software that has many books written about it. A good resource for reviews of hardware and software components, plus free trial downloads of many software programs, is the CNET Web site at www.cnet.com.

SELECTING HARDWARE The most important criteria to consider when selecting hardware are performance, compatibility, and functionality. As a general rule, you should buy the most powerful computer you can afford. Because computer technology changes rapidly, a computer that seems very powerful today may not serve your computing needs in a few years. You can help extend the life of your computer by purchasing the fastest processor, the most memory, and the highest-capacity hard drive you can afford. If you must buy a less powerful computer, be sure you can upgrade it with additional memory, components, and peripheral requirements as your computer requirements change.

Other general considerations in selecting hardware include the following:

- When choosing between a desktop, tower, or notebook, keep in mind that tower cases generally have more drive bays and expansion slots for adding new devices. Notebook computers provide the advantage of portability, but may have lower processor speeds, smaller monitors, and higher prices, and be difficult to upgrade.
- Check that the computer will allow you to add new components or upgrade, as needed. For example, will the motherboard allow for additional memory to be installed? Does the system have available expansion slots for new devices?
- Make sure the case has a reset button and, if security is an issue, a key lock to limit access to the inside of the case. Some cases even have a lock on the floppy drive to prevent unauthorized booting from a floppy disk.
- If you intend to use the PC for multimedia applications, including games, you want a high-speed CPU, a high-quality video card, and as much memory as possible.
- If you plan to connect to a network or use a broadband (cable or DSL) connection, you will need a network interface card (typically a 10/100 PCI Ethernet network interface card). If you plan to use a dial-up modem connection, be sure to buy one rated at 56 Kbps. (For a DSL or cable modem connection, the modem likely will come from your service provider).
- If you want to write music, audio files, or other files to a CD, be sure the computer has a CD-RW drive or, if possible, upgrade to a DVD±RW/CD-RW combination drive, which allows you to read data from and write data to DVDs and CDs.
- Be sure that the motherboard supports USB 2.0. Many newer peripherals such as external hard drives, DVD±RW drives, and scanners use USB 2.0 to provide high-speed data transfer.

You also should consider adding peripheral devices such as an external hard drive, microphone, or speakers, or upgrading peripheral devices such as the mouse, keyboard, monitor, printer, or sound card. A huge number of peripheral devices are available on the market today, providing a wide range of features at varying prices. Before selecting a peripheral device for a system, determine the answers to the questions listed in Figure 11-4, so you can ensure the peripheral is compatible with the other hardware and software in the system. As you research peripherals, you will note that internal devices typically are less expensive than an external version of the same device, because external devices have the additional expenses of their own power supply and case. External devices, however, can be moved easily from one computer to another, and they can be reset or disabled by powering down and back up without having to reboot the entire system.

QUESTION	ANSWER
What is the type and speed of the system's CPU?	________
How much memory does the system have?	________
What capacity hard drive does the system have?	________
How much space is available on the hard drive?	________
Which OS version and edition is installed on the computer (for example, Windows XP Professional)?	________
Are device drivers available for the OS?	________
For internal devices, how many drive bays are available?	________
For internal devices, how many drive expansion slots and what kinds of slots are free?	________
Does the motherboard support USB 2.0?	________

Figure 11-4 Questions to help determine if a peripheral device is compatible with your system.

Regardless of the type of hardware component you plan to purchase, be sure that the documentation for that component is easy to read and comprehensive and that the device has a reasonable warranty. You also should check the manufacturer's Web site to be sure it offers easy-to-find technical support and the latest device drivers.

SELECTING A COMPLETE SYSTEM After defining your software and hardware needs, you must select a computer system that maps to your needs as closely as possible. An important decision in the process is whether you want to purchase a brand-name computer or a clone. Generally, the decision between a brand-name computer and clone is based on two factors: after-sales service, and support and cost. In general, a brand-name PC (such as Dell or Gateway) might cost more, but generally you will get better service and support than you will for a clone PC built with parts from several companies.

Some of the additional cost of a brand-name computer goes towards providing better after-sales service. For example, some PCs come with a three-year warranty, a

24-hour service help line with a toll-free number, and delivery of parts to your home or office. Typically, the support and service policies for clone PCs are not as comprehensive. Most brand-name manufacturers also provide support such as comprehensive Web sites, updated drivers and utilities, and online troubleshooting or user manuals (Figure 11-5). Companies that build clone PCs may not have these additional support resources.

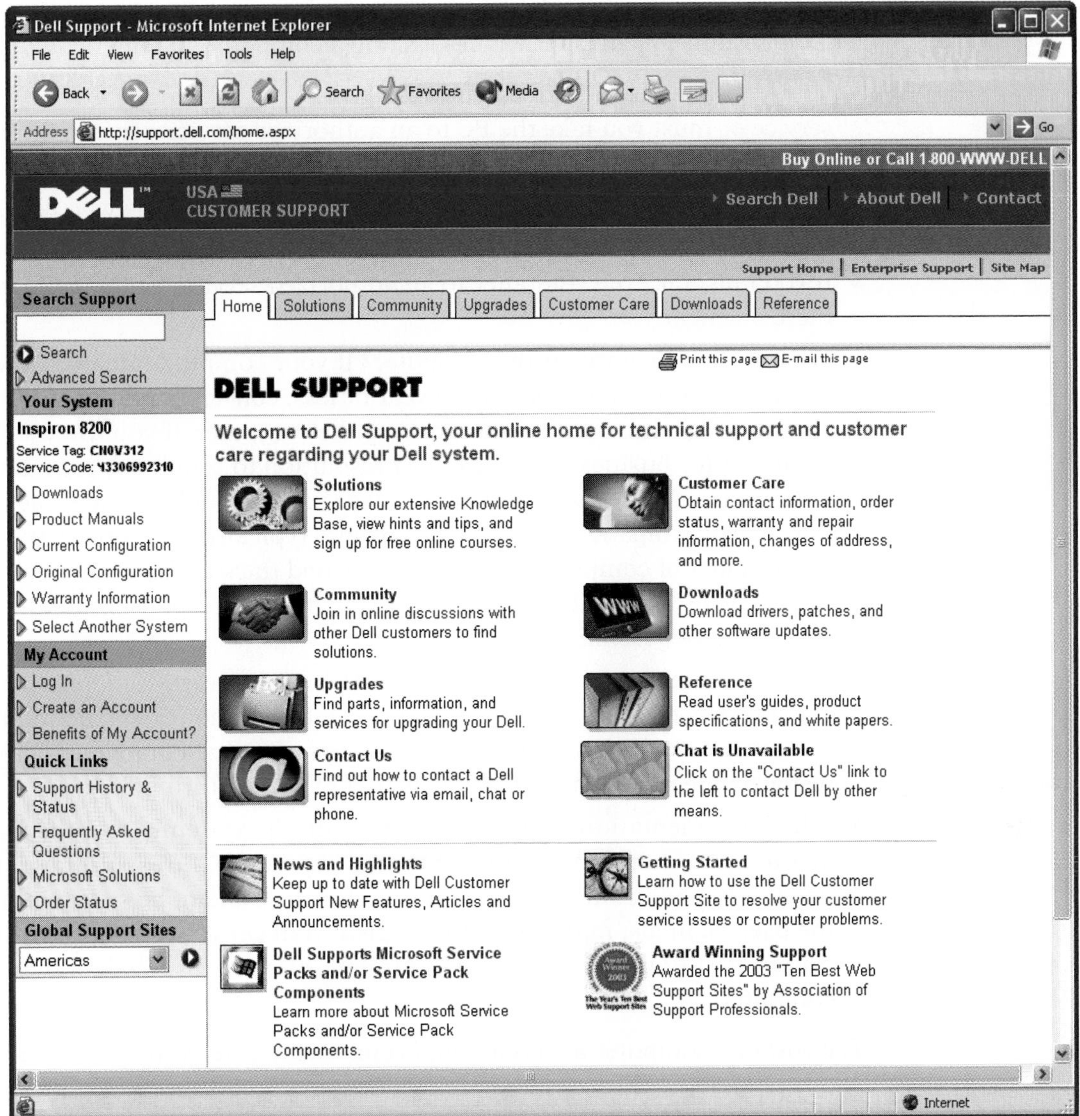

Figure 11-5 Computer manufacturers, such as Dell, often have comprehensive support Web sites.

One disadvantage of purchasing a brand-name PC is that many manufacturers use non-standard, proprietary hardware for some of the computer components. As you learned in Chapter 3, larger computer manufacturers such as Dell, IBM, and Hewlett-Packard often use non-standard components and motherboards that require customized computer cases. For example, many Dell computers use custom

ATX motherboards with non-standard power connectors and ports, which require custom cases tailored to ensure the holes in the case align with ports coming off the motherboard. Brand-name computer companies also sometimes include components, such as support for video, directly on the motherboard rather than using more generic expansion cards. Such practices can make upgrading and repairing brand-name PCs more difficult and more expensive, because you must use parts from the computer manufacturer in order to upgrade the system, instead of using less expensive parts from third-party manufacturers.

Other questions to consider when selecting a computer system include:

- How does the service agreement work? Does the agreement provide on-site service or must you take the PC to an authorized service center or ship it to the manufacturer?
- If they provide on-site or local service, do you know anyone who has used this service? Did he or she find it satisfactory?
- If you must take the computer to an authorized service center or a dealer, is there one near you?
- What is the warranty for the computer? If your computer includes a warranty and service agreement for a year or less, consider extending the service for two or three years when you buy the computer. If you use your computer for business or require fast resolution to problems, consider purchasing an extended warranty or a service plan through a local dealer or third-party company. An extended warranty typically covers the repair and replacement of computer components beyond the standard warranty. Most service plans ensure that your calls receive priority response from the help desk or service technicians.
- What is the return or exchange policy? At a minimum, a computer dealer should have a 30-day, no-questions-asked return policy. If you do return a computer or software, is there a restocking fee? Some companies charge a restocking fee of 10 to 20 percent, as part of their return policy.
- What documentation or manuals come with the system? Does the manufacturer maintain a Web site with useful support features, utilities, and updates? In addition to documentation for the system, be sure to obtain the user manuals, mail-in product registration card, product keys, and original CD-ROMs or floppy disks for any software installed on the computer.

The cost of a computer also is an important factor. After you have determined what software and hardware your system needs, use a worksheet to compare systems, services, and other considerations to determine which computer will meet your needs for the least cost. When considering price, keep in mind that high- to medium-priced PCs are most likely to be network compatible and easily expandable. They generally also offer a broader range of support and have had extensive testing of vendor products for reliability and compatibility. Lower-priced PCs may not have been tested for network compatibility, may have limited support, and the quality of components may not be as high.

Your Turn

Creating and Using a Cost Comparison Worksheet

Most computer companies advertise a price for a base computer that includes components housed in the system unit (processor, RAM, sound card, video card), disk drives, a keyboard, mouse, monitor, printer, speakers, modem, and a NIC. Some advertisements, however, show prices based on only some of these components; additional components, such as monitors and printers, may cost more. Creating a cost comparison worksheet is a good way to track the prices of various systems and the components included in each system. Complete the following steps to create a cost comparison worksheet to determine which computer to buy.

1. Following the guidelines discussed in the chapter, define what hardware, software, and other components and services would be included in your ideal computer system. As a starting point, uses resources such as the Internet, computer magazines, and your local computer retailer to start understanding what features are available for new computers.
2. Create a cost comparison worksheet like the one shown in Figure 11-6, using Microsoft Excel or other spreadsheet software. The first column should list the requirements you have defined for your computer system. The total cost cells (row 41 in Figure 11-6) should include a formula to sum the costs for the cells above.

Microsoft Excel - computer_costcomparison

	A	B	C	D	E	F
1	Computer Cost Comparison Worksheet					
2		Desired System	System 1	System 2	System 3	Notes
3	Vendor	*n/a*	Sunrise Computers	pcconnection.com	BestBuy	
4	**Overall System**					
5	Overall System Price	*less than $2,500*	$ 1,099.00	$ 1,399.00	$ 1,549.97	
6						
7	**Hardware**					
8	Processor (CPU)	Pentium 4 / 2.8 GHz	$ -	$ -	$ -	
9	Memory (RAM)	512 MB	$ 80.00	$ -	$ -	System 1: baseline 256 RAM
10	Cache	512 KB L2	$ -	$ -	$ -	
11	Hard Drive Capacity	120 GB	$ 90.00	$ -	$ -	
12	Floppy Disk Drive	3.5 inch	$ 20.00	$ -	$ -	
13	CD/DVD Bay 1	48x CD-RW/DVD-ROM	$ 59.00	$ -	$ -	
14	CD/DVD Bay 2	none	$ -	$ -	$ -	
15	Zip® Drive	250 MB Zip	$ 99.00	$ 90.00	$ 80.00	
16	Monitor Type/Size	17 inch	$ -	$ -	$ -	
17	RAM on Video Card	128 MB	$ -	$ -	$ -	
18	Sound Card	Sound Blaster compatible	$ 20.00	$ -	$ -	
19	Speakers	Stereo	$ 40.00	$ 50.00	$ -	
20	USB Ports	4	$ -	$ -	$ -	
21	FireWire Ports	2	$ -	$ -	$ -	
22	Network Interface Card	Internal 10/100 Ethernet	$ -	$ -	$ -	
23	Wireless NIC	Internal	$ -	$ -	$ -	
24	Modem	56 Kbps	$ -	$ -	$ -	
25	Keyboard	Standard	$ -	$ -	$ -	
26	Pointing Device	Mouse	$ -	$ -	$ -	
27	Printer	Color Ink-Jet	$ 129.00	$ 89.00	$ -	System 3: has MFD printer/fax/scanner
28	Printer Cable	Yes	$ 25.00	$ 20.00	$ -	
29						
30	**Software**					
31	Operating System	Windows XP Professional	$ 70.00	$ 75.00	$ 70.00	
32	Application Software	Office 2003 Professional	$ 349.00	$ 329.00	$ -	
33		Microsoft Money	$ -	$ -	$ -	
34	Antivirus Software	1 year subscription	$ 40.00	$ -	$ 40.00	
35						
36	**Other**					
37	Internet Service	6 months subscription	$ -	$ -	$ -	
38	Surge Protector	Yes	$ 34.99	$ 42.99	$ 34.99	
39	Warranty/Service	3 year, on-site service	$ 169.00	$ 149.00	$ 169.00	
40			$ -			
41		TOTAL COST	$ 2,323.99	$ 2,243.99	$ 1,943.96	

cost comparision worksheet

Figure 11-6 A worksheet is an effective tool for summarizing and comparing the prices and components of different computer systems.

3. Find two or three computers that meet your needs, based on your system requirements. To get an accurate comparison, be sure the computers have identical or similar configurations.
4. Enter overall price for the system at the top (row 5 in Figure 11-6 on the previous page) and enter a 0 (zero) for components included in the system cost. For any components you will need to pay extra to upgrade or additional components not covered in the system price, enter the cost in the appropriate cells.
5. Based on the data entered in the worksheet, which computer provides the best value and meets your needs? If you had to purchase one of these computers, which would you purchase and why?

Quiz Yourself 11-2

To test your understanding of how to purchase a new PC, visit the Understanding and Troubleshooting Your PC Quiz Yourself Web page (scsite.com/understanding/quiz). Click Quiz Yourself 2 below Chapter 11.

Preparing to Build Your Own PC

An alternative to upgrading or purchasing a new computer is to build your own PC. Assembling your own PC takes time, skill, and research, but it can be a great learning experience. Some of the most important reasons to build your own PC are the knowledge you gain and having complete control over every part you purchase, which allows you to make a customized, integrated system. You also will have the invaluable experience of learning every step in the process of creating a new system — and the satisfaction that results from creating your own system from scratch. Figure 11-7 lists several reasons you might want to build your own PC, as well as reasons to consider purchasing a pre-built system instead of assembling your own PC.

Reasons to assemble your own PC	Reasons not to assemble your own PC
The process can be challenging, fun, rewarding, and a valuable training experience for PC technicians.	If you need a PC quickly, assembling your own is probably not a good idea. The process takes time and requires patience (especially if you are a first-time builder).
You will gain significant knowledge and experience in researching the parts to buy, studying the documentation, and assembling the PC.	Individual parts may be warrantied, but if you build your own PC, there is no overall warranty on the PC. If a warranty or a service agreement is important, then look for a pre-built PC with these services included.
When you buy individual hardware components, you get the documentation for each component. Having this documentation can be valuable if you plan to upgrade the system later.	Pre-built PCs have been tested to ensure that individual components are compatible. When building your own PC, you might select incompatible components. For this reason, buy high-quality mainstream components to best ensure compatibility.

(continued)

Reasons to assemble your own PC	Reasons not to assemble your own PC
When you buy each software package individually, you are assured that the distribution is legal and you have the installation disks, CDs, and documentation.	Do not assemble a PC for the first time unless you have access to an experienced technician or service center. If you buy all the parts from a retailer with a service center, you can come back for service if you cannot resolve a specific problem.
When you purchase each computer part individually, you have control over the brand and features of each component in the PC.	Do not build a personal computer in an effort to save money; you can purchase a clone computer for about as much as the parts required to build a PC.

Figure 11-7 Before assembling a PC, be sure to understand the pros and cons of building a PC.

If you are planning to be a PC technician, you definitely should have the experience of building a PC before starting your first job. In the process of assembling a computer, all of the skills needed to be a PC technician are tested: research, knowledge of user needs and the computer market, planning, organization, patience, confidence, problem solving, and extensive knowledge of both hardware and software.

Can I save money on a computer by building it myself?

Probably not. The total price of the parts needed to assemble a PC will be very close to the price of a comparable, pre-built clone. If your main reason for building a personal computer is to save money, you will be better off purchasing a new pre-built system. Consider purchasing a clone, rather than a brand-name system, to reduce the upfront costs.

Getting Ready for Assembly: Selecting Parts

If you have decided to buy parts and assemble a PC, expect the process to take some time. The motherboard and expansion cards are full of connections, ports, and perhaps jumpers, and you must read the documentation carefully to determine just how to configure the motherboard and all components to work together. The first time you assemble a computer, the process likely will take some time. As you become more familiar with the steps involved, you will be able to assemble a PC in less time.

In preparing to assemble a PC, plan for everything you need before you begin. As you select and purchase each part, two things are important: functionality and compatibility with other parts. Almost every computer needs these essentials: motherboard, CPU, RAM, hard drive, CD-ROM drive (or you can substitute a DVD drive, CD-RW, or DVD±RW/CD-RW drive for added functionality), computer case, power supply, video card, monitor, keyboard, and mouse. Most likely, you also will want a sound card, network interface card, modem, and a floppy disk drive. Make careful and informed decisions about every part you buy. Selecting each component requires reviewing your functionality, compatibility, and budget needs and determining what parts meet your criteria.

Before purchasing any components, carefully examine the documentation and make sure the documentation is clear, thorough, and understandable. When buying parts for your first assembly, avoid ordering parts over the Internet or from a catalog; instead, buy the parts from a reputable local dealer who allows you to examine a component and its documentation, and who can help answer any technical questions you may have. Before purchasing any components, be sure you understand the store's return policy and have information on the manufacturer's warranty for each part.

More About

Detecting and Correcting Power Supply Problems

Most computer cases come with the power supply already installed. You might need to exchange the power supply of an existing PC, however, because it is damaged or you might need to upgrade to one with more power. To learn more about addressing power supply problems, visit the Understanding and Troubleshooting Your PC More About Web page (**scsite.com/ understanding/more**) and then click Detecting and Correcting Power Supply Problems below Chapter 11.

When selecting parts, select the motherboard first and then select the other parts based on compatibility with the motherboard. As previously noted, before purchasing a motherboard, review the documentation and be sure it is readable and complete. You also should check the motherboard manufacturer's Web site to review if additional documentation and support information is available. Finally, be sure that the motherboard has enough of the right types of ports (for example, USB, FireWire, parallel, sound, or SCSI) to support the peripherals you want to use with the system.

Next, consider the CPU and memory needed for the system. In order to avoid problems with compatibility, buy the motherboard, CPU, and memory from the same vendor, who can help ensure that all three are compatible. Many dealers sell motherboards with the CPU and fan or cooler already installed, and jumpers on the motherboard set correctly. Review the documentation for all of these components to ensure they are acceptable.

After you select the motherboard, CPU, and RAM, you must select the case and accompanying power supply. When selecting a case, you should consider two important items: (1) the case must meet your predetermined functionality requirements and (2) it must be compatible with other parts in the system, especially the motherboard. Generally, you can purchase a computer case with the power supply and an exhaust fan already installed. Power supplies for personal computers range from 200 watts for a small desktop computer system to 600 watts for a tower floor model that uses many multimedia or other devices that need a lot of power.

As a general rule, you should buy a good quality computer case and power supply. Make sure the computer case allows easy access to components and has good cooling with additional fans (or room to add more fans). Be sure that the power supply provides at least 250 watts or more, to provide enough power for all of the components that will be installed in your computer.

Next, select the hard drive and other drives. If the video logic is not included on the motherboard (for most third-party motherboards it probably is not), select a video card and make sure the motherboard has an AGP slot to accommodate it. Be aware that motherboards can have one of several different types of AGP slots — so you will need to match the right AGP video card to the AGP slot on your motherboard. Finally, select other peripherals, including a mouse, keyboard, and monitor. Also check that the motherboard has enough ports to connect other peripherals you already have, such as a digital video camera or scanner.

FAQ 11-7

How can I determine if a power supply has enough power for the devices in my system?

If you prefer a more technical approach, you can estimate how much total wattage your system needs by calculating the watts required for each device and adding them together. (Calculate watts by multiplying volts in the circuit by amps required for each device.) In most cases, however, the computer's power supply is more than adequate if you add only one or two new devices.

Getting Ready for Assembly: Final Preparations

After you have purchased all of the required components and parts, you can prepare to assemble the computer. First, prepare a work area that is well lit, uncluttered, and will allow you to leave the computer mid-assembly, without the computer being disturbed. Next, get a box or other container to store all of your documentation, installation CDs, and any spare hardware that came with your components so that they are readily available in case you need to reinstall software or reference the documentation.

Before you start, read the documentation for each component. If you have questions about the process or are unsure of how to install a particular component, find answers to your questions before you begin. For example, if you are not sure how to set the jumpers on the motherboard, even after you read the documentation, take the documentation to your technical support source (a dealer, a service center, a knowledgeable friend) and ask for help in interpreting the settings in the documentation before you start the work. You often can find a detailed diagram of the motherboard on the manufacturer's Web site, complete with proper settings for specific CPUs.

After you have answered any open questions, plan the assembly from beginning to end. You may want to create a step-by-step list and post it near the work area, as a reminder during the assembly. Be sure to keep the documentation for the parts nearby, as well as printouts from any Web sites you referenced to find additional information and support.

Finally, before starting the assembly, review the safety precautions outlined in Chapter 3. While working, do not get careless about protecting yourself and your equipment against static electricity — and always remember to wear the ground strap on your wrist.

Building a Personal Computer, Step-by-Step

The following sections provide a step-by-step, detailed description of building a personal computer with a Pentium 4 CPU, 512 MB of RAM, a hard drive, a floppy drive, a CD-RW drive, a modem card, and a video card in a mid-tower case. After the computer is assembled, Windows XP Professional will be installed as the operating system.

Depending on the desired functionality of your computer and your budget, your computer might have additional or different components. The example provided here is intended to provide a general overview of how to assemble a PC, following the steps outlined in Figure 11-8. Other tips to follow during the assembly process include the following:

- As previously discussed, you will need a safe, well lit, uncluttered place to work, with a ground mat and ground strap.
- Be careful to follow all safety rules and precautions.
- Be sure to have all documentation and printed Web pages readily available. If possible, have another computer in the room, so you can visit manufacturer's Web sites, which are outstanding resources for general information on specific components and detailed installation procedures.
- Work methodically and keep things organized.
- If you find yourself getting frustrated, take a break. The process of assembling a PC should be a learning experience, not a stressful event.

General steps for assembling a PC
1. Verify that you have all parts you plan to install.
2. Prepare the computer case by installing the case fans and I/O shield, removing the plates that cover the drive bays, and installing the spacers.
3. Install the drives.
4. Determine proper configuration settings for the motherboard, and set any jumpers or switches on the motherboard.
5. Install the CPU and CPU fan.
6. Install RAM in the appropriate slots on the motherboard.
7. Install the motherboard and attach cabling.
8. Install the video card.
9. Install the modem card (or, if external, skip this step and install in Step 12).
10. Plug the computer into a power source, and attach the monitor, keyboard, and mouse.
11. Boot the computer, check the CMOS settings, and make sure that everything is configured and working properly before replacing the computer case.
12. Install the operating system; any additional peripheral devices, such as a modem card or printer; and any application software, such as Microsoft Office.

Figure 11-8 Before starting the assembly process, plan the steps involved from beginning to end.

Step 1: Verify All Parts Are Available

After you have completed your research and purchased the components for your computer, organize everything you need to assemble the PC in your work area. Before you begin the assembly process, double-check that you have all parts with their accompanying documentation and software available, along with your PC tools.

For the PC that will be built in this chapter, the parts include:

- *Motherboard:* Asus P4P800 Deluxe with FireWire
- *Processor:* 2.4 GHz, Pentium 4 CPU
- *RAM:* Two 256-MB DDR DIMMs

- *Case and power supply:* ATX mid-tower case with a 300-watt, ATX12V-compliant power supply (required for this motherboard, because the Pentium 4 requires a supplemental power connector)
- *Video card*: ATI Radeon 8500 with 64 MB of video RAM and a DVI connector; connects to AGP slot
- *Hard drive:* Seagate Barracuda 80 GB hard drive, serial ATA
- *Floppy drive*
- *CD-RW drive*: Samsung 52 × 24 × 52 CD-RW drive
- *Monitor, mouse, and keyboard*
- *Modem card:* Lucent V.92 modem card rated at 56 Kbps; inserts in PCI slot
- *Cables, cords, device drivers, and documentation*
- *Operating system:* Windows XP Professional CD-ROM

More About

Purchasing Parts for a PC

To learn more about manufacturers that make various parts for a PC, visit the Understanding and Troubleshooting Your PC More About Web page (**scsite.com/understanding/more**) and then click Purchasing Parts for a PC below Chapter 11.

Figure 11-9 shows most of these parts, as well as some of the software and tools to use during the assembly process. As previously discussed, you also should keep a notebook or have a filing system for all product documentation, lists of the components and settings for your PC, and detailed installation and troubleshooting notes.

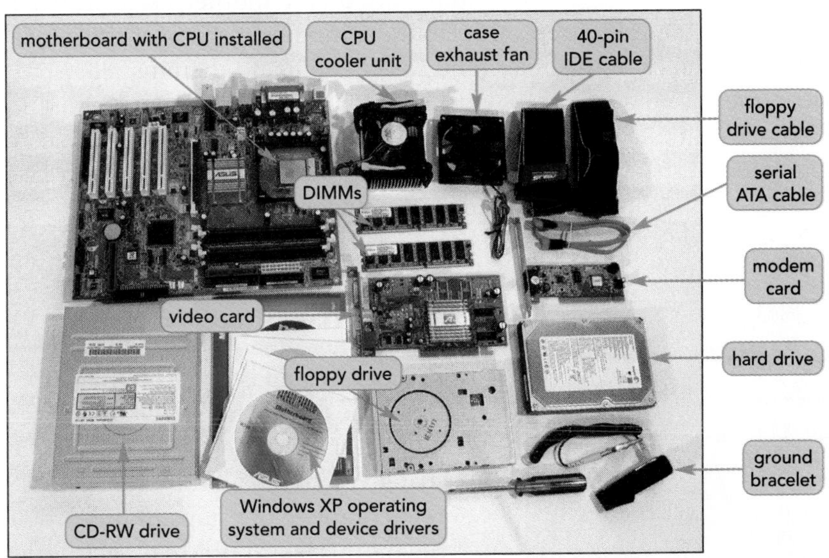

Figure 11-9 Components needed to assemble a PC.

Step 2: Prepare the Computer Case

Before you can install components in a computer case, you must prepare the case. If you have a tower case, lay it down on its side. If not, then leave the case on its bottom. The next step to prepare the case is to install an exhaust fan, as shown in Figure 11-2 on page 467. In addition to the power supply fan and the CPU fan, an exhaust fan over the vent underneath the power supply helps keep the temperature inside the case at a level that will not damage the CPU. Position the fan in place over the vent, and secure it with four screws.

Figure 11-10 The empty computer case with I/O shield installed.

The next step to prepare the case is to install an I/O shield. As discussed in Chapter 3, a faceplate or I/O shield is a metal plate that comes with the motherboard and fits over the ports to create a well-fitting enclosure around them (Figure 11-10). If the case comes with several shields designed for several brands of motherboards, select the one that correctly fits the ports on your motherboard, put the others aside, and then insert the faceplate in the hole at the back of the case. Figure 11-10 shows the empty computer case with the power supply and I/O shield installed, before any other components are installed.

As you learned in Chapter 3, the next thing to do is to install the spacers in the holes on the bottom of the case, to keep the motherboard from touching the case and possibly shorting. When you install the motherboard, the holes on the motherboard will line up with the spacers, as shown in Figure 11-11. Hold the motherboard over the case so you can see where the holes in the board and case line up and then install a spacer in every hole in the case that lines up with a hole in the motherboard, so all the holes in the motherboard can have screws. You probably will need four to six spacers when installing the motherboard. You also will end up with some holes in the case that you do not use; these holes allow the case to accommodate more than one motherboard form factor.

Figure 11-11 The spacers line up with holes on the case and keep it from touching the case.

Step 3: Install Drives

The next step is to install the drives in the case. Some technicians prefer to install the motherboard first; in this chapter, the steps instruct you to install the drives first. One reason to complete the steps in this order is that, if the motherboard is already in the case before the drives are installed, you run the risk of dropping a drive on the motherboard and damaging it. If you install the drives before the motherboard, however, do not connect the power cords until the motherboard is in place. This ensures that the cords will not be in the way when the motherboard is installed.

As shown in Figure 11-10, the computer case has a group of wide bays and a narrow removable bay. In building this computer, the CD-RW drive will be installed in the wide bay and the floppy drive and hard drive will be installed in the removable bay. When installing drives, be sure to use short screws that will not protrude too deeply into the drive and damage it.

CONFIGURE JUMPERS FOR EACH IDE DRIVE IN THE SYSTEM As you learned in Chapter 5, today's hard drives currently use two types of cables to connect to a standard IDE connector: parallel ATA (PATA) or serial ATA (SATA) technology. Using parallel ATA, a system has two IDE controllers, each of which can support up to two drives (a master and a slave) for a total of four IDE drives in a system. If a motherboard supports serial ATA, it most likely has two serial ATA connectors, each of which can accommodate a single drive. Higher-end motherboards, such as the one to be used in this PC, often have both serial ATA connectors and standard IDE connectors.

Using Windows 2000, Windows XP, or Windows Server 2003, the system will recognize up to four parallel ATA hard drives and up to two serial ATA hard drives. If you planned to install six drives, you would use CMOS setup to set the IDE operating mode to Enhanced Mode, which supports up to six devices. CMOS setup then will recognize these drives based on the IDE controllers: primary IDE (master and slave using parallel ATA), secondary IDE (master and slave using parallel ATA), third IDE (master using serial ATA), and fourth IDE (master using serial ATA).

In this installation, the system will have two IDE devices:

- a hard drive using a serial ATA cable connected to a serial ATA connector; and
- a CD-RW drive using parallel ATA with a 40-pin IDE ribbon cable connected to the primary IDE channel.

Because a serial ATA cable and connection supports only a single serial ATA hard drive, no jumpers need to be set on the motherboard; instead, the system assumes that drive is the master device on the controller. For the CD-RW drive using parallel ATA, jumpers must be set to the single drive configuration to indicate that the CD-RW drive will be the only drive on the IDE channel. To determine the specific settings for the jumpers, check the drive housing for diagrams of jumper settings for different configurations. If not, review the documentation that came with the drive. Later, when you first boot up the system, you will enter CMOS setup and verify that serial ATA is enabled and that the IDE operating mode is set to Enhanced Mode.

FAQ 11-8

If I am running Windows 98, Windows Me, or Windows NT, how many IDE hard drives can I install in a system?

Using Windows 98, Windows Me, or Windows NT, there can be up to four drives in a system: one or two parallel ATA drives using a single IDE channel and one or two serial ATA hard drives using the two serial ATA channels. You also can disable serial ATA in CMOS setup and the system then can have up to four parallel ATA drives. To support the four drives, set the IDE operating mode to Compatible Mode in CMOS setup.

INSTALL THE CD-RW DRIVE After setting the jumpers to the correct settings, put on your ground bracelet, if you do not already have it on, and install the CD-RW drive in the top wide bay by completing the following steps:

1. This bay uses bracing clips, instead of screws, to secure the drive. Using two fingers, squeeze the two bracing clips on each side of the bay together to release them and pull them forward. Remove the faceplate from the front of the bay (Figure 11-12).

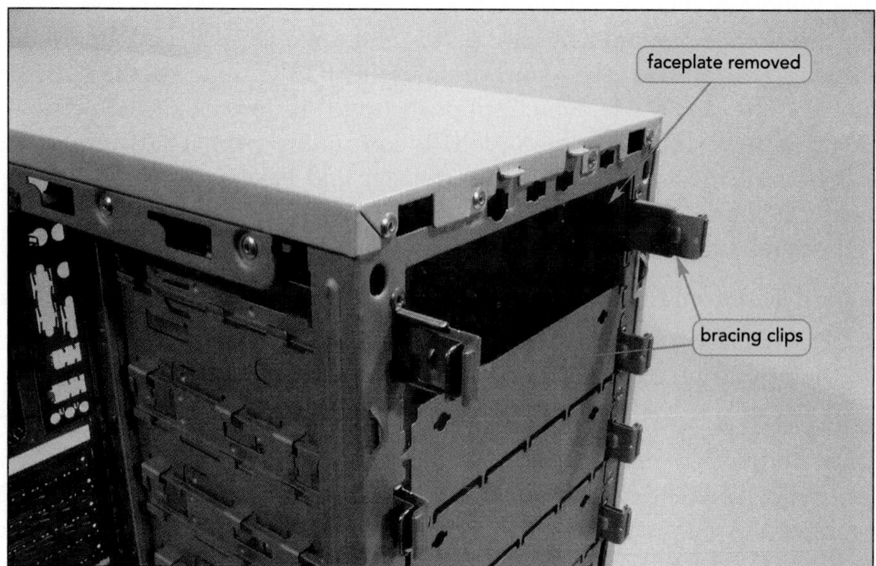

Figure 11-12 To install a CD-RW drive, prepare the bay by pulling the bracing clips forward and removing the faceplate. You then can slide the drive into the bay.

2. Next, slide the CD-RW drive in the bay until it is aligned with the front of the case (Figure 11-13). After the motherboard is installed, you also will install the CD-RW data cable, power cord, and audio cord.

Figure 11-13 Align the CD-RW drive with the front of the case.

INSTALL THE HARD DRIVE AND FLOPPY DRIVE The next step is to install the hard drive and floppy drive in the smaller, removable bay. The removable bay itself is secured with three screws on the front of the case and a clipping mechanism on the side of the bay. To remove the bay from the computer case, first remove the screws and then remove the bay from the case. Next, position the hard drive flush with the front of the bay and secure the drive with four screws, two on each side of the drive (Figure 11-14).

Figure 11-14 Use four screws to secure each drive to the bay.

Next, position the floppy drive in the bay, so it will align later with the front of the case (you may need to remove a faceplate on the front of the removable bay for the floppy drive). Secure the floppy drive to the bay with four screws, two on each side of the bay, and then slide the removable bay into the computer case. When the bay is all the way in, you will hear the clipping mechanism clip into place (Figure 11-15). Secure the bay to the case by inserting screws in the screw holes at the bottom and on the top of the bay.

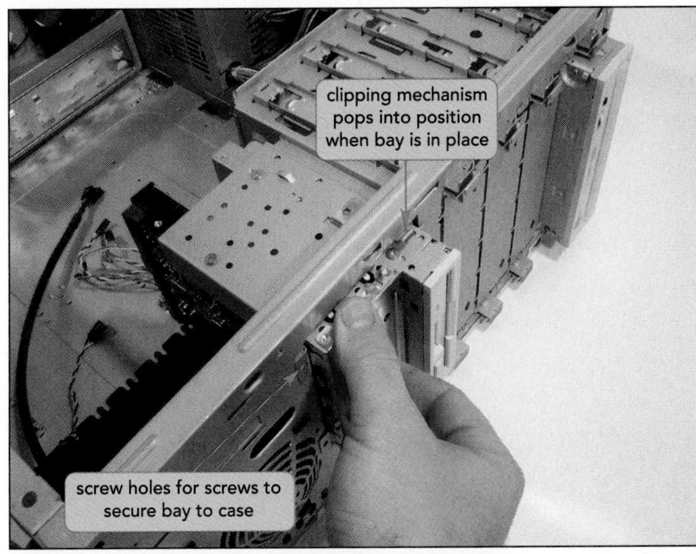

Figure 11-15 Slide the bay into the case as far as it will go.

Step 4: Set Jumpers or Switches on the Motherboard

The motherboard to be used in this PC is the Asus P4P800 Deluxe motherboard. Figure 11-16 shows the motherboard with all of the connections used in this installation labeled. When working with the motherboard or other circuit boards, be very careful to avoid the possibility of ESD damage by making sure you are grounded properly at all times. Also, try not to touch edge connectors or other sensitive portions of components.

The Asus P4P800 Deluxe motherboard includes several ports, including ports for the mouse and the keyboard, a network port, a FireWire port, four USB ports, a serial port, three regular sound ports, and one S/PDIF digital sound port (these ports are shown in Figure 1-8 on page 8 in Chapter 1). The motherboard also has embedded support for sound and Ethernet, thus eliminating the need for separate expansion cards to add these features.

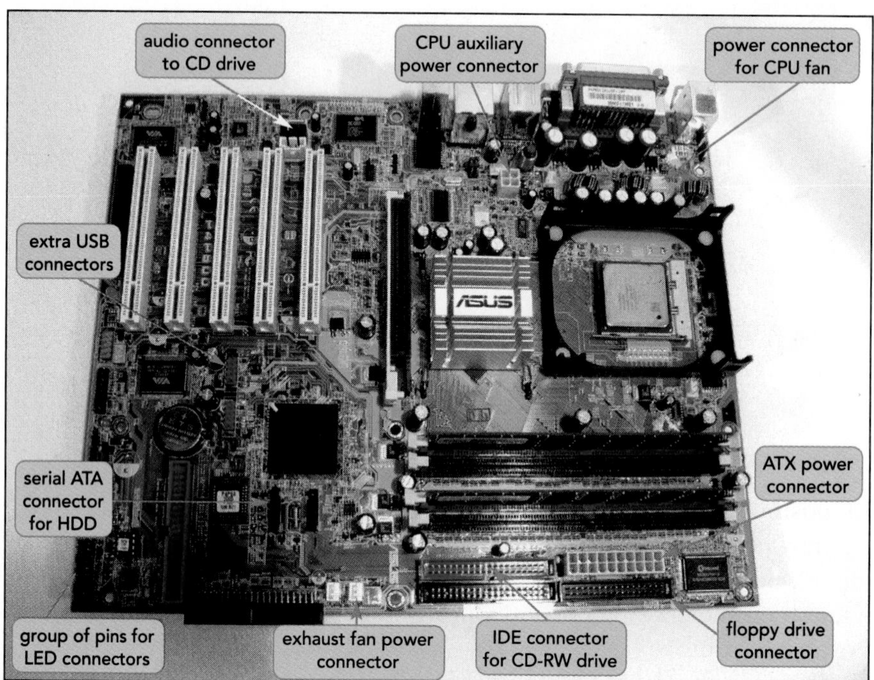

Figure 11-16 Asus P4P800 Deluxe motherboard, with all connections used in this installation labeled.

Prior to installing the motherboard in the computer case, you should reference the motherboard's documentation to determine what jumpers or DIP switches are on the board and determine how to set them (Figure 11-17). The Asus P4P800 Deluxe motherboard has several jumper groups to consider:

- *A three-pin jumper group to clear CMOS RAM.* CMOS RAM sometimes is referred to as **real-time clock RAM** (**RTC RAM**). The three-pin jumper group used to define settings for CMOS RAM thus is labeled as CLRTC1 in the motherboard documentation. The jumpers should be set to the normal (default) position, as shown in Figure 11-17, which will not clear CMOS RAM.

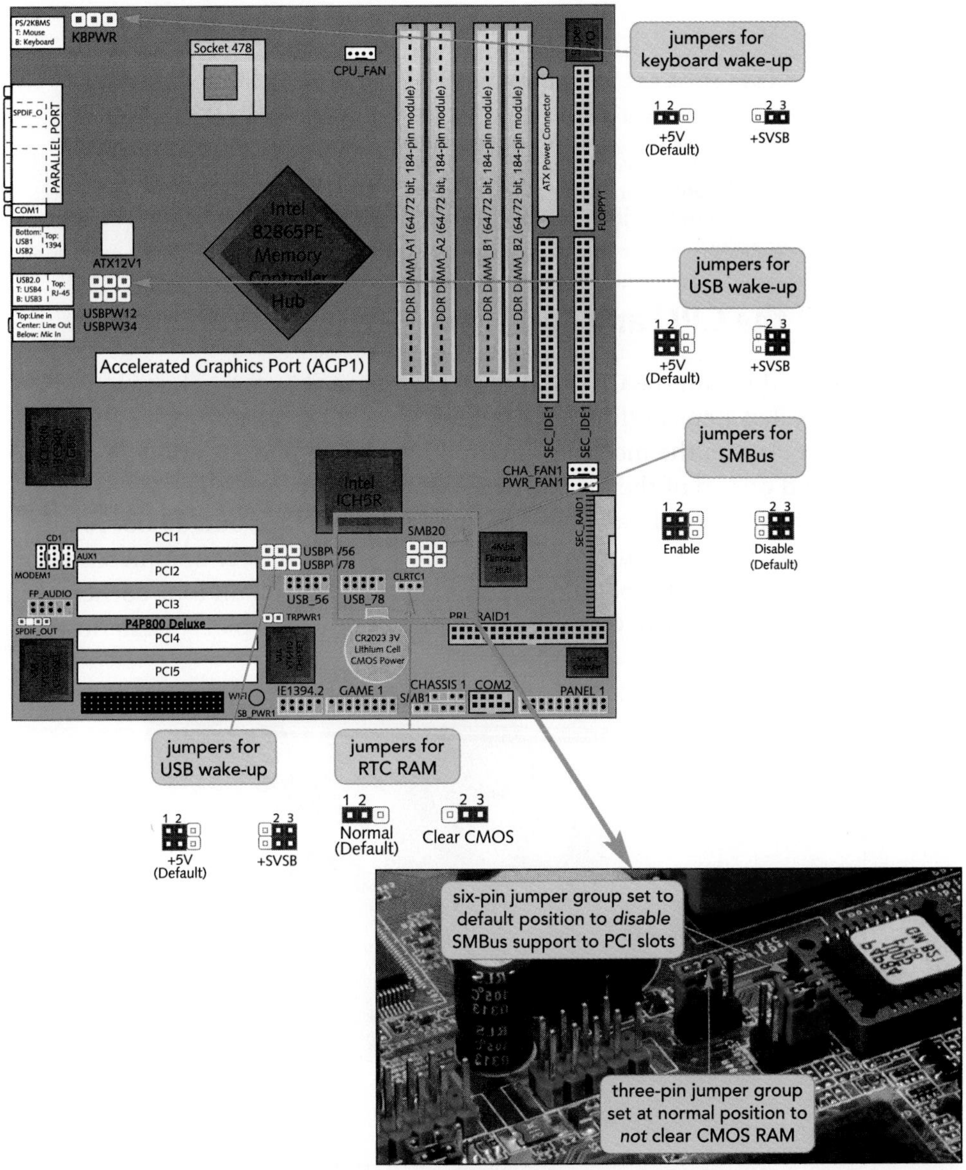

Figure 11-17 The motherboard documentation shows how to set each jumper group, including the jumpers for CMOS RAM.

- *A three-pin jumper group to control the keyboard wake-up feature.* Set the jumpers to the default position to disable the feature.

- *A three-pin jumper group for each USB connection* to control if a USB device can wake up the system. Set the jumpers to the default position to disable the feature.
- *A six-pin jumper group to control SMBus support to PCI slots*. The **SMBus** (**System Management Bus**) is a simple two-wire bus used for communication with devices on a motherboard, such as a laptop battery subsystem or temperature sensors, to communicate information about installed hardware and overheating errors. The default position is to disable this feature.

For most motherboards, including the one used in this PC, all jumpers should be left in their default positions.

FAQ 11-9

Why would I want to set the jumpers to clear CMOS RAM?

One of the few times you would want to clear CMOS RAM is if you set system and user passwords in BIOS and then forget them. If the passwords have been set but are forgotten, it may be necessary to clear CMOS RAM. Clearing CMOS RAM will clear the date, time, system passwords, and other configuration information stored in BIOS. Unless you want to reset CMOS RAM, never remove the jumper caps from the default position.

Step 5: Install the CPU and CPU Fan

Next, you should install the CPU and the CPU fan on the motherboard. Following the detailed steps outlined in Chapter 3, install the Pentium 4 CPU into the 478-pin ZIF socket on the motherboard and, if needed, place a small amount of thermal compound on top of the processor to conduct heat from the CPU to the heat sink. (Some heat sinks already have thermal tape attached and do not require thermal compound.) Next, line up the clip assembly with the retention mechanism already installed on the motherboard, and then press lightly on all four corners until it snaps in place (Figure 11-18). Once the cooler assembly is in place, push down the

Figure 11-18 Carefully push the cooler assembly clips into the retention mechanism on the motherboard, until they snap into position.

two clip levers on top of the assembly. (Different coolers use different types of clipping mechanisms, so follow the directions that come with the cooler.) Finally, connect the power cord from the CPU fan to the power connection on the motherboard next to the cooler (Figure 11-19).

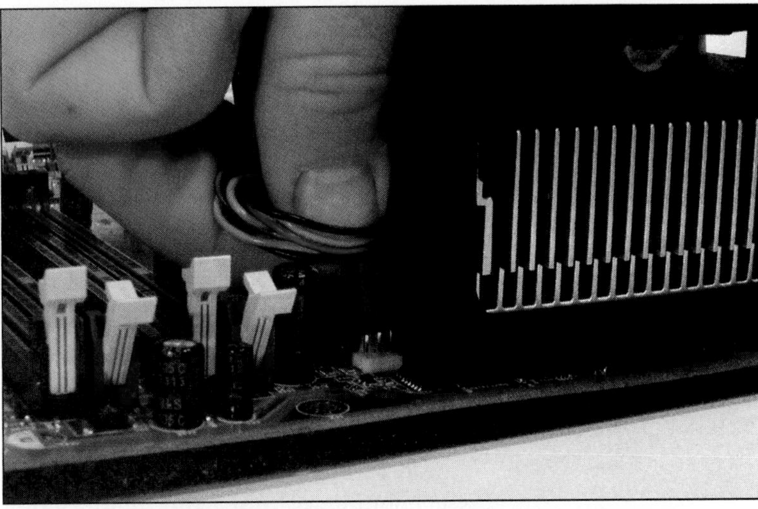

Figure 11-19 Connect the CPU fan power cord to the motherboard power connector.

Step 6: Install RAM on the Motherboard

In Chapter 4, you learned how to select the correct type and amount of RAM for your motherboard. You also learned that you should be careful to match size, manufacturer, production batch, and mode. The Asus P4P800 motherboard used in this PC has four DIMM slots that can support 64 MB, 128 MB, 256 MB, 512 MB, and 1 GB DDR DIMMs. This computer will use two DIMMs, each with 256 MB of memory. For optimal performance, the motherboard documentation suggests to install two DIMMs in the two blue sockets, which are sockets 1 and 3 (Figure 11-20).

Figure 11-20 Install the DIMMs in the sockets, using the two blue sockets first.

Before inserting each module in its socket, pull the supporting arms on the sides of the socket outward. Use the notches on the edge of each module to help you orient it correctly in the socket. Insert the module straight down in the socket. When it is inserted fully, the supporting arms should pop back into place.

Why are some of the sockets for memory blue?

Motherboard manufacturers tend to make some DIMM, RIMM, and RAMM sockets blue, to indicate that you should use them first when there is more than one socket from which to choose.

Step 7: Install the Motherboard and Attach Cabling

Thus far, the assembly process has involved preparing the case by installing the exhaust fan and the spacers; installing any needed drives; and attaching the processor, cooling assembly, and memory modules to the motherboard. Next, you can install the motherboard itself into the case and attach the cabling and power connections, by completing the following steps:

1. Place the motherboard into the case so the holes on the motherboard align with the holes on the spacers. Attach the motherboard to the case, using the spacers to receive the screws (Figure 11-21). Be careful not to use excessive force when moving the motherboard into place and attaching it to the case; this could warp the board and damage the circuits on it.

Figure 11-21 Use screws to attach the motherboard to the case via the spacers.

2. Connect the power cord from the exhaust fan to the auxiliary fan power connection on the motherboard. Note that some motherboards do not have this connection. In that situation, you can connect the exhaust fan power cord to a power cord from the power supply.

3. Connect the 4-pin auxiliary power cord coming from the power supply to the motherboard, as shown in Figure 11-22. This cord supplies the supplemental power required for a Pentium 4 processor.

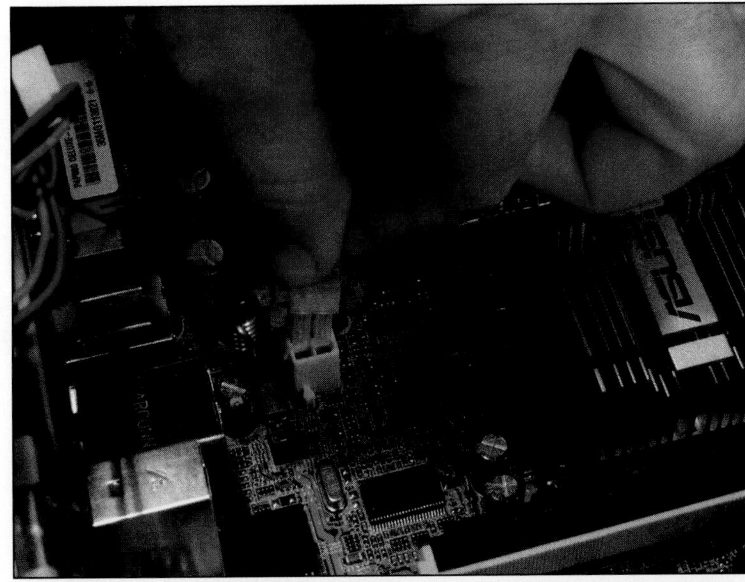

Figure 11-22 The auxiliary 4-pin power card provides power to the Pentium 4 processor.

4. Connect the 20-pin ATX P1 power cord from the power supply to the motherboard, as shown in Figure 11-23.

Figure 11-23 The 20-pin connector supplies power to the motherboard.

5. Connect a regular 4-pin power cord to the CD-RW drive and connect a miniature 4-pin power cord to the floppy drive.

6. A serial ATA hard drive uses a special power cord shown in Figure 11-24. Connect one end to a regular 4-pin power cord from the power supply and connect the other end to the hard drive.

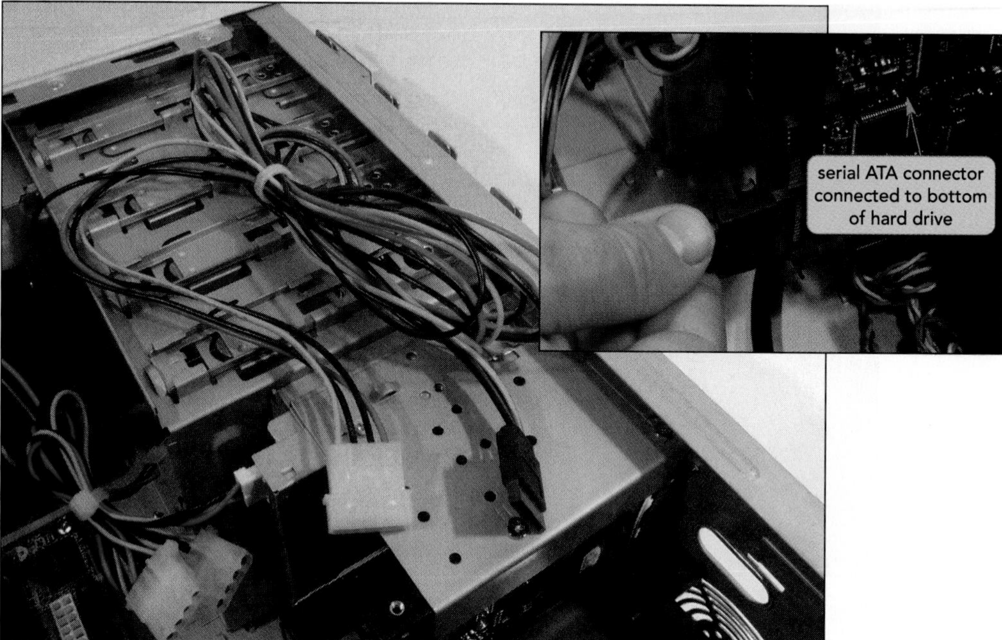

Figure 11-24 A serial ATA uses a special power cord, which should be connected to the power connector on the serial ATA hard drive.

7. After the power cords are connected, locate and connect the front leads to the switches, speaker, and lights on the front of the case (Figure 11-25). Note that each front lead is labeled.

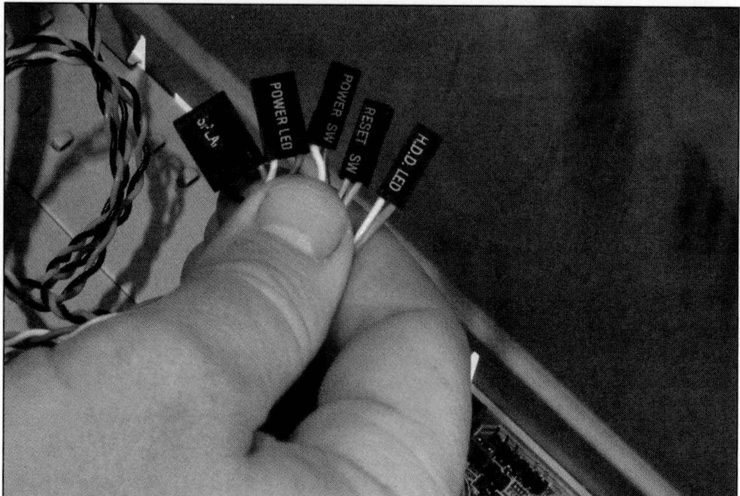

Figure 11-25 Locate the lead wires that connect to the pins on the motherboard to control the LEDS and buttons on the front of the case.

Some motherboards have matching screen-printed labels on the board to tell you which lead goes on which pins. If the pins are not labeled on the board, as with this motherboard, check your documentation. The motherboard might come with a sticker that goes inside the case and shows a diagram of the motherboard with labels for the front leads. If the motherboard documentation is not clear, you also can check the motherboard manufacturer's Web site for additional documentation. Figure 11-26 shows this motherboard's documentation, which describes the connectors for each of the leads.

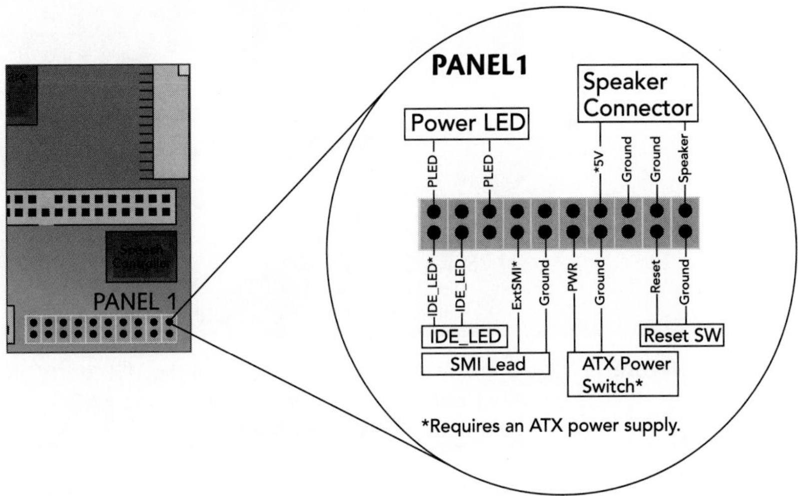

Figure 11-26 The motherboard documentation describes the connectors for each of the leads.

FAQ 11-11

Why can I not get the LED lights to work?

Unfortunately, LED connectors rarely are marked for polarity. If the LED does not light, try reversing the connector to see if that helps.

8. This case has two extra USB ports on the front and the motherboard has extra USB connectors for them. Connect the cable coming from the ports on the case to the first USB connector on the motherboard (Figure 11-27).

Figure 11-27 Connect the cable coming from the USB ports on the front of the case to one of the two USB connectors on the motherboard.

9. Normally the CD audio cord connects from the CD-RW drive to the sound card, in order to play music CDs. Because sound support is embedded on the motherboard, look at the motherboard documentation to determine where to connect the CD audio cord to the board. For this motherboard, you should connect the CD audio cord to the CD-RW drive and the other end to the connector on the motherboard, as shown in Figure 11-28.

Figure 11-28 One end of the audio connects to the audio connector on the motherboard; the other end connects to the CD-RW drive.

10. Next, install the data cables to connect each drive as follows:
    - Install the floppy drive cable with the twist between the motherboard and the drive, making this drive A in the final configuration.
    - Connect the 40-pin IDE cable to the CD-RW drive and the primary IDE connector on the motherboard. This motherboard has IDE connectors that only will allow the IDE cable to connect in the correct orientation.
    - The motherboard has two serial ATA connectors labeled SATA1 and SATA2. Connect the serial ATA cable to the hard drive and the other end to the first of the two serial ATA connectors, as shown in Figure 11-29.

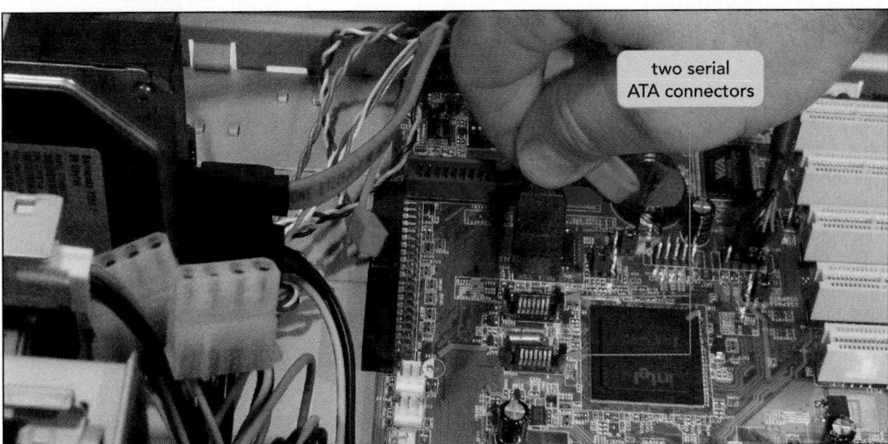

Figure 11-29 The serial ATA connector connects the serial ATA hard drive with the first serial ATA connector (SATA1) on the motherboard.

Step 8: Install the Video Card

The next step is to install the video card on the motherboard. The Asus P4P800 motherboard used in this computer has an AGP 8X slot that supports +1.5V AGP cards, like the one shown in Figure 11-30. The video card to be installed includes a registration tab that allows the card to fit into the AGP 8X slot on the motherboard.

In general, when installing an expansion card, first read the documentation for the card and then determine if you need to set any jumper switches or DIP switches on the card. Like most newer cards, the video card to be installed in this computer is Plug and Play and thus has no jumpers. The AGP slot has a retention mechanism around it that helps hold the card securely in the slot. Some motherboards require that you install this retention mechanism on

Figure 11-30 The video card has a tab that allows it to be used in the AGP slot on this motherboard.

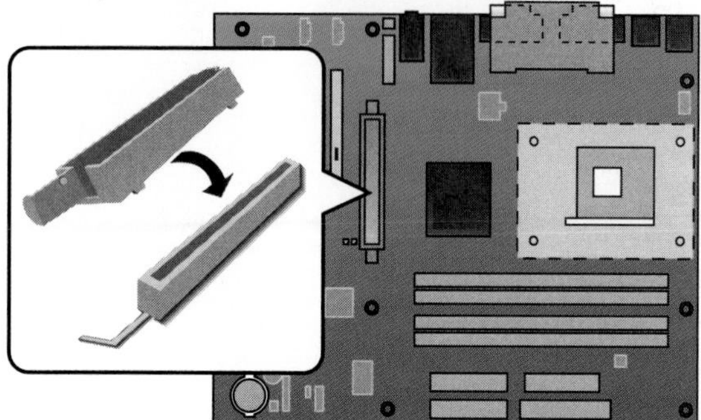

Figure 11-31 Some motherboards require you to install a retention mechanism around the AGP slot before installing the video card.

the slot before you install the card, as shown in Figure 11-31. For this motherboard, the retention mechanism is included as part of the motherboard.

To install the video card, remove the faceplate for the AGP slot and then slide back the retention mechanism on the slot. Insert the card in the slot and slide the retention mechanism back in position. The retention mechanism slides over the registration tab at the end of the AGP slot to secure the card in the slot. Use a single screw to secure the card to the computer case (Figure 11-32).

Figure 11-32 Secure the video card to the case with a single screw.

Step 9: Install the Modem Card

Next, you should install the modem card in a PCI slot. To install the modem card, remove the faceplate from the PCI slot, insert the modem card, and then use a screw to secure it. A modem card is not considered an essential device, so you can opt to install it after you have tested the system and installed the operating system.

Step 10: Plug in the Computer and Attach External Devices

The installation of devices inside the case now is complete. Before you plug in the computer, make sure that no cords are obstructing the fans. Figure 11-33 shows the case with all internal components installed. Notice that some cables are coiled and tied with plastic ties (do not use rubber bands for this task because they can deteriorate over time, break, and drop into the case.) Coiling and tying up the cords makes the inside of the case less cluttered and prevents cords from obstructing airflow and fans. Do not coil and tie the cables until after you test the system to make sure everything works. Next, attach the monitor and keyboard and then plug in the computer.

Figure 11-33 The case with all of the internal components installed.

FAQ 11-12

Should I also attach the mouse when I attach the monitor and keyboard?

You can attach the mouse when you attach the monitor and keyboard, or you can leave it off and attach it after you test the system, because you will not really need it during the initial startup process. Although it is unlikely that the mouse will cause problems during the initial startup process, it is a good idea to start up using only the components you absolutely need, especially when first constructing a system.

Step 11: Boot the Computer, Check Settings, and Verify Operation

After completing the steps outlined above, you should boot the computer to check the settings and verify that everything is working correctly. Boot the system and press the appropriate keys to enter CMOS setup. The motherboard manual should contain a list of all CMOS settings, an explanation of their meanings, and their recommended values. Follow the instructions in the motherboard manual to set the CMOS settings required for the motherboard. If you plan to boot from a Windows setup CD to install the operating system, be sure to set the boot sequence to include the CD-ROM drive.

After making the required changes, exit CMOS. When the computer reboots, if possible, watch the POST process and listen for beep codes to determine if any errors occur. If there are no errors, you have put your system together correctly. If there are errors, see your motherboard documentation or Appendix A for explanations of the meaning of the various beep codes and error messages.

Typically, it is a good idea to test the system before replacing the case cover, to make it easier to make changes if something does not work properly. Some systems, however, require the cover to be on to achieve proper airflow, so do not run the system for any length of time without the cover on. Some other types of cases have cover switch latches that do not allow you to power up the system unless the case cover is in place.

After you have tested the system and determined that components are working correctly, turn off the computer and slide the case cover back in place, as shown in Figure 11-34, and then snap the front cover into position.

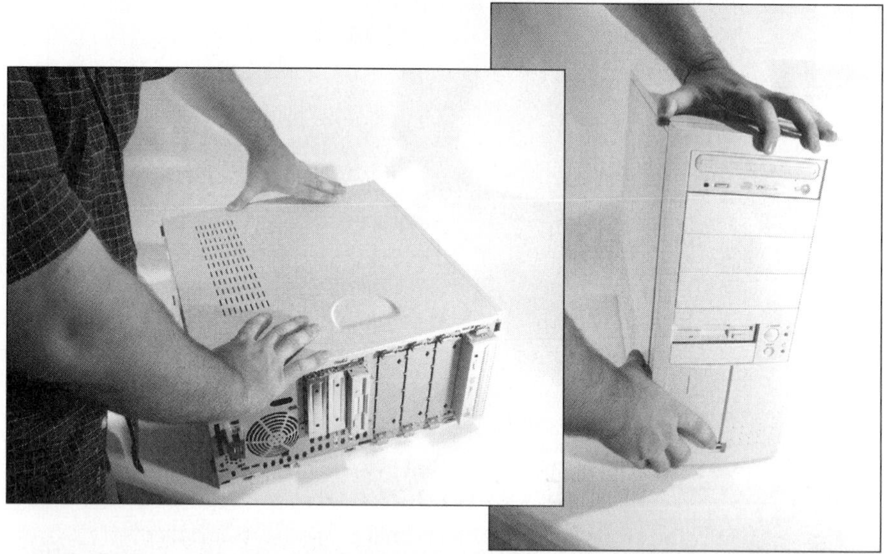

Figure 11-34 Once you know the system is working, slide the case cover back on. The front cover snaps into position.

Step 12: Install the Operating System, Peripheral Devices, and Application Software

After the computer is assembled successfully, you can boot the system from the Windows setup CD and follow the steps to partition the hard drive and install the operating system, following the steps outlined in Chapter 8. After installing the operating system, you can install any peripheral devices you need, such as a printer, and any application software.

More About

Building a Personal Computer

To view a list of resources to help in building a personal computer, visit the Understanding and Troubleshooting Your PC More About Web page (**scsite.com/understanding/more**) and then click Building a Personal Computer below Chapter 11.

Quiz Yourself 11-3

To test your knowledge of how to build a PC step-by-step, visit the Understanding and Troubleshooting Your PC Quiz Yourself Web page (scsite.com/understanding/quiz). Click Quiz Yourself 3 below Chapter 11.

High-Tech Talk

Giving an Old PC a Second Life

If you upgrade to a new PC or build a new system, you may find yourself with an older, obsolete computer system of which you would like to dispose. But what should you do with it? Recycling and disposal of older computer equipment is an issue of increasing importance, as more and more old computers are shelved each day. In addition to simply clearing out closet space or making room for new equipment, you also should consider specific concerns regarding environmentally safe disposal or looking toward ways to put the equipment to good use in the community.

Computers, monitors, and other equipment contain toxic materials and potentially dangerous elements including lead, mercury, and flame retardants. In a landfill, these materials release into the environment. Recycling and refurbishing old equipment are much safer alternatives for the environment. Manufacturers can use the millions of pounds of recycled materials to make products such as outdoor furniture and automotive parts. If you have a computer or computer equipment that you believe is beyond repair, companies such as Apple, IBM, and United Recycling can dismantle the equipment properly to obtain all usable parts and materials.

Nickel cadmium, lithium ion, and small sealed lead acid batteries used in laptops and other electronic devices are of particular concern. Batteries contain metals, acids, and other compounds that can be hazardous when released into the environment. It is important that you dispose of the batteries properly and safely not only to help the environment, but to comply with the numerous recycling laws related to batteries. Your local or state government offices most likely also can help you locate a drop-off or recycling location to accept old batteries.

If a computer system still works, a great option is to donate your computer to a local school, library, or other community service program. If you do not know of any local groups that can use the equipment, national organizations such as Share the Technology may be able to help you find a local group that has requested computer equipment. When donating or selling an old computer, be sure to remove any sensitive data and to uninstall all software, to ensure you are not violating the terms of any software license agreements. One option is to reformat the entire hard drive. Alternatively, you can find file deletion tools available in Pretty Good Privacy (PGP) and Norton Utilities' Wipe Info feature.

By the year 2007, experts estimate that more than 500 million personal computers will be obsolete. Because of the potential for huge quantities of electronic waste, government agencies at all levels are working to make it easier for consumers to recycle computer equipment. Figure 11-35 lists several good resources for more information on how to donate or dispose of your old PC. Whichever direction you choose, you will be giving your old PC a chance at a valuable, environmentally friendly, second life.

Information Resources for Donating or Recycling Computers	
Computer Recycling	• Local computer retailers and service centers
	• Apple Recycling Program
	• IBM PC Recycling Service
	• Back Thru the Future Computer Recycling
	• Envirocycle, Incorporated
	• United Recycling Industries
Battery Recycling and Disposal	• Local and state government recycling centers
	• Battery Solutions
	• RBRC (Rechargeable Battery Recycling Corporation)
Computer Donation	• Local schools, places of worship, libraries
	• Share the Technology
	• National Cristina Foundation
	• Computers for Learning (CFL)
	• Reboot Canada

Figure 11-35

CHAPTER SUMMARY

The Chapter Summary reviews the concepts presented in this chapter.

1 Upgrading or Purchasing a Personal Computer

Before considering an upgrade or a new computer purchase, first take steps to maximize the performance of your current computer. You can improve the performance of your PC greatly simply by performing routine maintenance tasks, such as defragmenting your hard drive. Making the decision to upgrade an existing computer or to buy a new computer often comes down to a question of cost. In general, an upgrade is appropriate if the cost of the upgrade does not exceed half the value of the current system, and if the resulting system will not contain older components that prevent it from performing well. To upgrade a PC to provide better performance, consider adding more memory, upgrading the CPU or adding a second CPU, adding a second hard drive, upgrading the video card, upgrading the motherboard, and adding more fans for cooling. If you determine that you want to buy a personal computer, you can buy a used PC or purchase a new PC, either a brand-name computer or a clone. A brand-name personal computer is one manufactured by a well-known company. A clone is a PC assembled by a smaller company with parts manufactured by several companies. Before purchasing a PC, consider how you will use the computer now and in the future, the functionality you want for the computer, the software and hardware required, and your budget.

2 Preparing to Build Your Own PC

When choosing to build your own PC, be aware that the process will take time, that you will likely encounter problems along the way, that there will be no warranty on the assembled product, and that you probably will not save money. Plan the project of assembling a PC well. Get answers to any questions you may have on the details before you begin and keep things organized as you work. If you are planning to be a PC technician, you definitely should have the experience of building a PC before starting your first job to hone your skills in research, knowledge of user needs and the computer market, planning, organization, patience, confidence, problem solving, and extensive knowledge of both hardware and software.

3 Building a Personal Computer, Step-by-Step

When assembling a PC, you should follow a general series of steps, which start with verifying that you have all parts you plan to install and preparing the computer case. After installing any drives in the system, determine and set jumpers and DIP switches for the motherboard, install the CPU and CPU fan, and then install RAM on the motherboard. After completing these steps, you can install the motherboard in the case and attach all cables and power cords. Next, install the video card and any other expansion cards and install the modem card. Plug in the computer and connect the mouse, keyboard, and monitor. Finally, boot the computer, verify that CMOS settings are correct and that no errors occur, replace the computer case, and install the operating system, any peripherals, and other software you need on your system.

brand-name personal computer (*469*)
bundled software (*470*)
clone (*469*)
hard-disk loading (*470*)
pre-installed software (*470*)
real-time clock RAM (RTC RAM) (*487*)
SMBus (System Management Bus) (*488*)

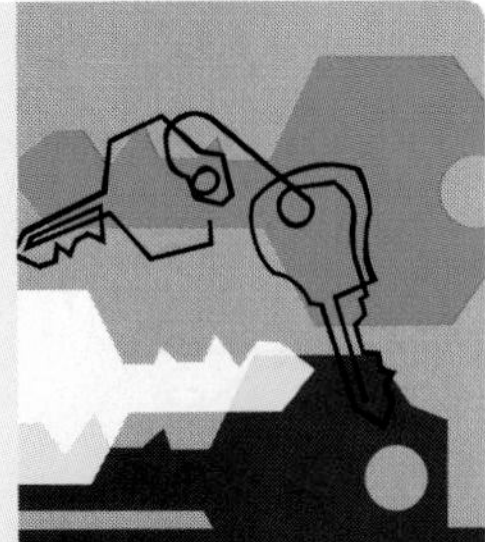

KEY TERMS

After reading the chapter, you should know each of these Key Terms.

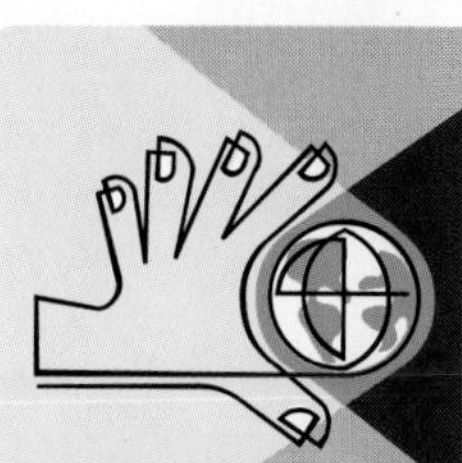

LEARN IT ONLINE

Reinforce your understanding of the chapter concepts and terms with the Learn It Online exercises.

Instructions: To complete the Learn It Online exercises, start your browser, click the Address bar, and then enter the Web address scsite.com/understanding/learn. When the Understanding and Troubleshooting Your PC Learn It Online page is displayed, follow the instructions in the exercises below. Each exercise has instructions for printing your results, either for your own records or for submission to your instructor.

1 Chapter Reinforcement True/False, Multiple Choice, and Short Answer

Below Chapter 11, click the Chapter Reinforcement link. Print the quiz by clicking Print on the File menu for each page. Answer each question.

2 Flash Cards

Below Chapter 11, click the Flash Cards link and read the instructions. Type 20 (or a number specified by your instructor) in the Number of playing cards text box, type your name in the Enter your Name text box, and then click the Flip Card button. When the flash card is displayed, read the question and then click the ANSWER box arrow to select an answer. Flip through Flash Cards. If your score is 15 (75%) correct or greater, click Print on the File menu to print your results. If your score is less than 15 (75%) correct, then redo this exercise by clicking the Replay button.

3 Practice Test

Below Chapter 11, click the Practice Test link. Answer each question, enter your first and last name at the bottom of the page, and then click the Grade Test button. When the graded practice test is displayed on your screen, click Print on the File menu to print a hard copy. Continue to take practice tests until you score 80% or better.

4 Who Wants To Be a Computer Genius?

Below Chapter 11, click the Computer Genius link. Read the instructions, enter your first and last name at the bottom of the page, and then click the PLAY button. When your score is displayed, click the PRINT RESULTS link to print a hard copy.

5 Wheel of Terms

Below Chapter 11, click the Wheel of Terms link. Read the instructions, and then enter your first and last name and your school name. Click the PLAY button. When your score is displayed, right-click the score and then click Print on the shortcut menu to print a hard copy.

6 Crossword Puzzle Challenge

Below Chapter 11, click the Crossword Puzzle Challenge link. Read the instructions, and then enter your first and last name. Click the SUBMIT button. Work the crossword puzzle. When you are finished, click the Submit button. When the crossword puzzle is redisplayed, click the Print Puzzle button to print a hard copy.

Multiple Choice

Select the best answer.

1. Which of these devices does not have to be installed before you can boot the system to confirm that the motherboard BIOS starts POST?
   a. mouse
   b. power supply
   c. processor
   d. RAM
2. Which of these is not a reason to coil and tie up the cords inside of a computer case?
   a. prevents cords from reducing airflow
   b. makes the inside of the case less cluttered
   c. prevents cords from obstructing fans
   d. helps the flow of power
3. When using serial ATA and parallel ATA, which operating system does not support up to six IDE drives?
   a. Windows XP
   b. Windows NT
   c. Windows 2000
   d. Windows Server 2003
4. In what type of configuration is one end of the audio cord connected to the CD drive and the other end connected to the motherboard?
   a. when sound support is embedded on the motherboard
   b. when no sound card is installed
   c. when using a lower speed CD-R drive
   d. when using an AT motherboard
5. What would have happened if you had attempted to install regular DIMMs on a motherboard, instead of the DDR DIMMs the board supports?
   a. The motherboard would have been damaged when it first was turned on.
   b. No damage would have occurred, but the system would not have booted correctly.
   c. Regular DIMMs are notched differently than DDR DIMMs, so you would not have been able to put the DIMMs in the RAM slots.
   d. Regular DIMMs are shorter than DDR DIMMs, so you would have recognized they would not fit on this motherboard when you tried to install them.

Fill in the Blank

Write the word or phrase to fill in the blank in each of the following questions.

1. An upgrade generally is appropriate if the cost of the upgrade cost does not exceed ________ the value of the current system.
2. ________ are installed in the holes on the bottom of the case, to keep the motherboard from touching the case and possibly shorting.
3. While working on a computer, always remember to wear a(n) ________ on your wrist.
4. When choosing between a desktop, tower, or notebook, keep in mind that ________ cases generally have more drive bays and expansion slots for adding new devices.
5. The video card should be installed in the ________ slot.

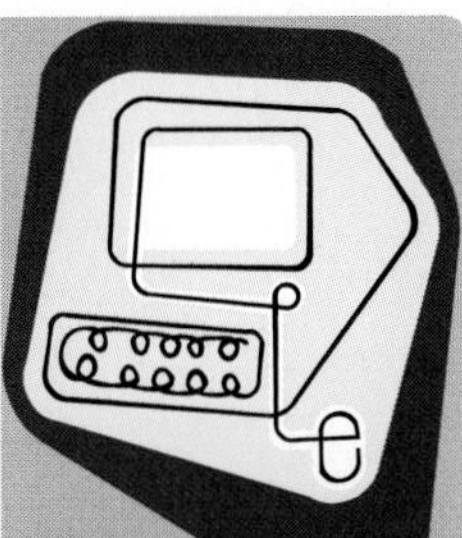

CHAPTER EXERCISES

Complete the Chapter Exercises to solidify what you learned in the chapter.

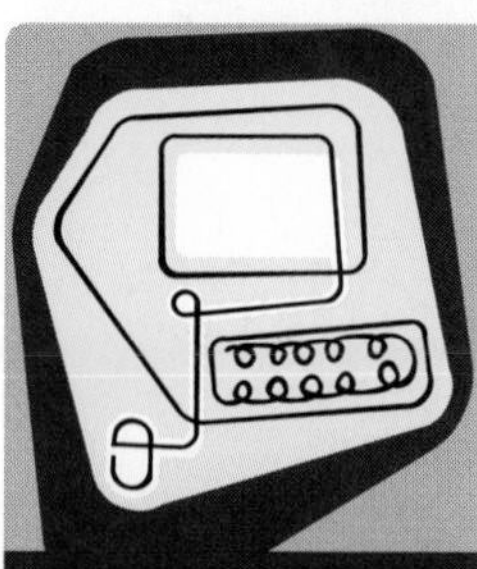

CHAPTER EXERCISES

Complete the Chapter Exercises to solidify what you learned in the chapter.

Matching Terms

Match the terms with their definitions.

______ 1. floppy drive cable	a. component that fits around the AGP slot and helps to stabilize the video card
______ 2. beep codes	b. PC manufactured by a well-known company with a widely recognized name
______ 3. retention mechanism	c. PC assembled by a smaller company with parts manufactured by several companies
______ 4. real-time clock RAM	d. two-wire bus used for communication with devices on a motherboard
______ 5. hard-disk loading	e. cable with a twist in it
______ 6. bundled software	f. used by startup BIOS to communicate errors during POST if video is not yet available
______ 7. I/O shield	g. metal plate that fits over motherboard ports to create an enclosure around them
______ 8. clone	h. pre-installing counterfeit or pirated software
______ 9. SMBus	i. software already installed on the computer when you purchase it
______ 10. brand-name PC	j. another term for CMOS RAM

Short Answer Questions

Write a brief answer to each of the following questions.

1. What are the advantages of buying a well-known, brand-name computer? What are the advantages of buying a less-expensive PC clone?
2. List three reasons why you might want to build your own PC and three reasons why you might not want to build your own PC.
3. List the twelve general steps involved in assembling a PC.
4. List several steps to take to maximize the performance of your current computer before considering an upgrade or a new computer purchase.
5. If you plan to purchase a new PC, what questions should you consider regarding service, support, and documentation?

APPLY YOUR KNOWLEDGE

Check your understanding of the chapter with the hands-on Apply Your Knowledge exercises.

1 Planning an Upgrade

Using a motherboard manual other than the one you may have used in this chapter, write down what configuration settings must be changed to upgrade a CPU or to change the system bus speed.

2 Planning to Buy Parts for a PC

Using the list of components in this chapter and resources on the Internet, find prices for the components and determine what it would cost to assemble this system. Create a worksheet using Excel or another spreadsheet software to list the components in the chapter, the price for each, and the total price for building the system. Compare the cost of the system you would build with a pre-built clone and a pre-built brand-name PC that provide the same functionality. Which system costs the most and which costs the least?

3 Building a PC for Specific Users

Assume that you are a graphic artist, a software developer, or a serious computer game player. What components would you add to the system you planned in Apply Your Knowledge 2, and why? How much would it cost to add them? Would you buy different components from the ones used in the basic system built in this chapter, such as more memory, a faster processor, or a larger hard drive? Why or why not?

4 Understanding Power Supplies

Generally, you can purchase a computer case with the power supply and an exhaust fan already installed. You should be sure, however, that the power supply provides enough power for all of the components that will be installed in your computer. Remove the cover from your home or lab PC, and answer the following questions:

1. What is the total wattage requirement for all of the drives in your computer? Look for a wattage rating printed somewhere on the device and then fill in the table shown in Figure 11-36.
2. How many watts are supplied by your power supply? (The number is usually printed on the label on the top of the power supply.)
3. How many cables are supplied by your power supply? Where does each cable lead?
4. Does the back of the power supply have a switch that can be set for 220 volts (Europe) or 110 volts (U.S.)?

Component	Wattage
Hard drive	
Floppy drive	
CD-ROM drive	
DVD drive	
Zip drive	
Other drive	
Total wattage requirements for all drives: ______________	

Figure 11-36

APPLY YOUR KNOWLEDGE

Check your understanding of the chapter with the hands-on Apply Your Knowledge exercises.

5 Comparing Motherboards

Go to the Asus Web site (*www.asus.com*) and locate the documentation for the Asus P4P800 Deluxe motherboard shown in this chapter or a similar motherboard. List the key features of this motherboard as advertised on the Web site. Next, go to the Intel Web site (*www.intel.com*). Find a motherboard that has the same or similar features. Print the Web page advertising this Intel board. Which board would you select and why? Using a price comparison Web site such as (*www.nextag.com*), compare the prices of the two boards. Which is the better buy?

6 Practicing Computer Assembly Skills

Work with a partner. With your partner not watching, carefully diagram where every wire and cable inside your computer is connected. Disconnect all cable connections, power, drives, and LED indicators. Have your partner replace each connection without your help. Work together with your partner to inspect the connections carefully, using your diagram as an aid. Reboot and test the computer.

CHAPTER 12

Maintenance and Troubleshooting Fundamentals

Introduction

This chapter provides guidelines for maintaining and troubleshooting your PC. The chapter first introduces how to create a preventive maintenance plan, including planning for and scheduling backups. Next, you will learn about antivirus programs and safe computing practices used to protect your computer from computer viruses, Trojan horses, and worms. Finally, you will learn about important troubleshooting tools and a methodical approach to troubleshooting that will help you isolate and resolve an issue.

OBJECTIVES

In this chapter, you will learn:

1. About maintaining your PC, including how to make backups
2. How to protect against viruses, Trojan horses, and worms
3. About approaches for troubleshooting a PC

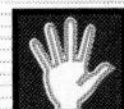

Up for Discussion

Keith Allen called you this morning because his firewall indicates that his computer keeps trying to connect to an unknown Web site and download a file. You ask him if he recently has made any changes to his computer. He says that he installed the latest Windows XP service pack last night — which is about when the problem seems to have started.

Keith went on to explain that he received an e-mail indicating that Windows Update had determined that he was running a beta version of the service pack and that he should install the final service pack, which was attached to the e-mail. He said he followed the instructions in the e-mail exactly, even disabling his antivirus software while installing the service pack.

After a quick search of some antivirus Web sites, you find that the e-mail Keith just described was fraudulent and that the file that he thought was a service pack actually was a Trojan horse program that attempts to connect to Web sites to download more malicious logic programs. You assure him, however, that you will help him remove the Trojan horse by downloading the latest virus definition files for his antivirus software and running a virus scan. You also suggest that, after you get his computer clean, he set the antivirus program to use the auto-update feature that regularly prompts users to download the new virus definition files. He sounds relieved and thanks you in advance for helping to disinfect his computer.

Questions:

- What are malicious logic programs and how do they infect your computer?
- What steps can you take to avoid infection by malicious logic programs?
- What steps should you take when troubleshooting a computer problem?

Maintaining Your PC

Depending on the situation, you may be responsible for maintaining your personal computer — or you may be employed as a PC technician providing support for every computer in an office, in one of the roles listed in Figure 12-1. Regardless of the number of computers you need to support, performing routine maintenance can prevent certain computer problems from occurring and help make it easier to resolve any issues that do arise.

Technician Job	Description
PC support technician	• Works on site, closely interacting with users, and is responsible for ongoing PC maintenance • Only type of technician responsible for the PC before trouble occurs; must prepare for problems by keeping good records and maintaining backups
PC service technician	• Goes to a customer site in response to a service call and, if possible, repairs a PC on-site • Usually is not responsible for ongoing PC maintenance, but does interact with users
Bench technician	• Works in a lab environment • Might not interact with users of the PCs being repaired, and is not permanently responsible for them • Generally does not work at location where the PC is kept; may be able to interview the user to get information about the problem, or may simply receive a PC to repair without being able to talk to the user
Help-desk technician	• Provides telephone or online support • Does not have physical access to the PC; must interact with users over the telephone and therefore must use different tools and approaches than other technicians

Figure 12-1 As a PC technician, you might fill one of four job functions.

Performing Routine Maintenance Tasks

The following sections outline several important routine maintenance tasks, including organizing the hard drive, creating rescue disks, documenting setup changes, recording setup data, and protecting and backing up software and data.

ORGANIZE THE HARD DRIVE ROOT DIRECTORY Organizing the files and folders on your hard drive makes it easier to find files and can help you back up and recover files more easily. As a start, keep all of your documents and other files in your My Documents folder (C:\Documents and Settings\ *username*\ My Documents). Do not store files on the desktop. If you want to have easy access to those files, store the files in your My Documents folder and create shortcuts to those files on the desktop.

Keep application software files and their data in separate directories. Most application software packages automatically create a subdirectory in the Program Files directory (for example, C:\Program Files\Internet Explorer) and then store the application software files and related data in that subdirectory.

The root directory of the hard drive should contain only folders (subdirectories) and system startup files or initialization files for software. Software applications or files containing data should not be stored in the root directory. **Initialization files** are files that application software puts in the root directory, to be used when the application first loads. Initialization files often have file extensions such as .bat, .ini, .bin, and .dat. If you are not sure of the purpose of one of these files, leave it in the root directory. Some software packages might not work if their initialization files are not in the root directory.

CREATE RESCUE DISKS After you clean up the root directory, make a set of rescue disks for the operating system installed on your PC. As you learned in Chapter 2, a rescue disk (also called a startup disk) is a bootable disk with the basic files and some utility programs needed to boot and troubleshoot a failed hard drive. After creating the rescue disks, test them to make sure that they work; label them with the computer model, date, and operating system version; and store them with other information about your computer.

DOCUMENT ALL SETUP CHANGES, PROBLEMS, AND SOLUTIONS As discussed in Chapter 3, one of the most important aspects of managing and maintaining your personal computer is that your documentation and configuration records are organized and in a safe place. When you first set up a new computer, start a notebook, word processing document, or other type of file as a way to keep records for the computer. In this notebook or file, record any changes in setup data, any maintenance tasks you complete, any problems the computer has, and troubleshooting solutions you used to resolve these issues. Be diligent in keeping this notebook or file up-to-date, because it later will be invaluable in diagnosing problems and upgrading equipment.

If you use a handwritten notebook, keep the notebook with the hardware and software documentation for the computer. If you use a word processing document or other electronic file, be sure to print a hard copy of the record. You also should consider storing the file on a floppy disk, CD-R, or other writable media other than the hard drive. Keep the storage media and the printed copy with the rest of the computer's documentation.

If you are responsible for supporting multiple computers, be sure to label the documentation so you easily can identify the computer to which it belongs. One option is to tape a large envelope on the side of the computer case and place important documentation and records specific to that computer inside the envelope (be sure that the envelope does not interfere with any hardware inside the computer case).

RECORD SETUP DATA In addition to maintenance and troubleshooting information, be sure to keep a record of CMOS settings, showing hard drive type, drive configuration, and so on. Motherboard manuals also should contain a list of all CMOS settings, an explanation of their meanings, and their recommended values, to use as a reference in the event your CMOS battery goes bad or is disconnected and the CMOS settings are lost.

In addition to having a manual with the CMOS settings, you should keep a written record of all of the changes you make to CMOS, so you have a list of the settings you have changed from the default. Some third-party utilities, such as Symantec Norton SystemWorks, allow you to save the CMOS setup information electronically. This information should be stored on a floppy disk, CD-R, or other writable media other than the hard drive, along with the software necessary to use it.

You also should keep a record of any DIP switch settings and jumper settings on the motherboard. The motherboard manual should list recommended settings, but you should remove the cover of your computer to determine if the motherboard uses all of the default recommended settings. At a minimum, be sure to record any settings that do not match those outlined in the motherboard manual.

When installing an expansion card, write information about the card in your file, and keep the documentation that came with the card. If you must change jumper settings or DIP switches on the card, be certain to write down the original settings before making changes. Then, when the card is configured correctly, write down the correct settings in your notebook or on the documentation for the card.

TAKE PRACTICAL PRECAUTIONS TO PROTECT SOFTWARE AND DATA If software files become corrupted, the most thorough approach is to restore the software from backups or to reinstall the software. To simplify both of these time-consuming tasks, here are a few suggestions:

- Before you install a new software package, back up the system state and create a restore point.
- Do not store data files in the same directory as the software, so there will be less chance of accidentally deleting or overwriting a software file.
- Reduce the possibility that protected or hidden files will be deleted by enabling settings to hide them from the user. To do this using Windows XP, open Windows Explorer or My Computer and then click Folder Options on the Tools menu. Click the View tab in the Folder Options window and then click Do not show hidden files and folders and Hide protected operating system files (Recommended) in the Advanced Settings list. Click the Apply button to apply the settings to the current folder and then Apply to All Folders button to apply the settings to all folders on the computer. Click the OK button to close the Folder Options window.
- Back up original software. According to copyright laws, you have the right to make a backup of a software installation CD or floppy disks in case the CD or disks fail. Keep the copy of your software, along with the product key, in a safe place in the event that something happens to the original. The simplest way to store the product key is to write the key on the label or case for the floppy disk, CD-R, or other media.

FAQ 12-1

Can I share the backup copy of a software CD or floppy disk?

Most likely, the copyright or end-user license agreement (EULA) does not allow you to share a backup copy of original software with a friend. Typically, a EULA will specify that you may make one copy of the software for backup/archival purposes, provided that this copy remains in your possession at all times. If you are buying a PC with software already installed, be sure the computer comes with installation CDs, product keys, and manuals for any installed software, so you can reinstall it, if needed.

- Back up data on the hard drive. If important data is kept on the hard drive, back up that data on a regular basis to a tape drive, floppy disk, CD-R, a removable hard drive, or on a file server at your company or school. The following sections discuss backing up data in more detail.

Making Backups

Performing a regular backup of the critical files on your computer is one of the most important aspects of being a responsible computer user. As you have learned, a backup is an extra copy of a data or software file that you can use if the original file becomes damaged or destroyed. To **back up** a file means to make a copy of it. In the case of a system failure or the discovery of corrupted files, you restore the files by copying the file backups to their original location on the computer.

Creating backups allows you to recover months or years of work that can be lost in an instant if your hard disk crashes or your system is infected with a virus. You always should back up critical files, including documents that you create, your Quicken or Microsoft Money data, your contact database, and your e-mail.

BACKUP APPROACHES Depending on your needs, you can use several different approaches for backing up data. As you learned in the Chapter 5 High-Tech Talk feature, some backup methods are more efficient because they do not always create a complete backup of all data. A **full backup**, or normal backup, backs up all data from the hard drive or a directory or folder of the hard drive. An **incremental backup** backs up only files that have changed or been created since the last backup, whether that backup is itself an incremental or full backup. **Differential backups** back up files that have changed or been created since the last full backup.

Traditionally, these methods all involve backing up to tapes, because most tapes are large enough to contain an entire backup of a hard drive and are inexpensive. If you do not have a tape drive, you can back up to any storage media, including CD-Rs, CD-RWs, DVD±RWs, Zip® disks, or any external or removable hard drive.

CREATING A BACKUP PLAN AND SCHEDULE Before you perform routine hard drive backups, devise a backup plan and a schedule. One common plan, called the **child, parent, grandparent backup method**, is shown in Figure 12-2. Using this plan makes it easy to reuse the storage medium, such as a tape, and allows you to keep track of what has been backed up when.

Name of Backup	Performed	Storage Location	Description
Child backup	Daily	On-site	Keep four daily backup tapes, and rotate them each week. Label the four tapes Monday, Tuesday, Wednesday, and Thursday. A Friday daily (child) backup is not made, because on Friday you make the parent backup.
Parent backup	Weekly	Off-site	Perform the weekly backup on Friday. Keep five weekly backup tapes, one for each Friday of the month, and rotate them each month. Label the tapes Friday 1, Friday 2, Friday 3, Friday 4, and Friday 5.
Grandparent backup	Monthly	Off-site, ideally in a fireproof vault	Perform the monthly backup on the last Friday of the month. Keep 12 tapes, one for each month. Rotate them each year. Label the tapes January, February, and so on.

Figure 12-2 The child, parent, grandparent backup method.

A basic backup plan might begin by performing a full (normal) backup on a Friday. Then, the next time you back up (Monday), you will use the incremental method to back up only files that have changed or been created since the full backup. The second time you perform an incremental backup, you back up only the files that have changed or been created since the last incremental backup (Tuesday through Thursday). Then, on Friday, you again perform a full backup. Alternatively, you can run differential backups Monday through Thursday and then again perform a full backup on Friday.

As discussed in Chapter 9, you should regularly create Automated System Recovery (ASR) backups and disks as part of an overall plan for system recovery so that you are prepared if the system fails. The backup file created will be just as large as the contents of the hard drive volume, so you will need a backup medium such as another partition on the same hard drive, on another local hard drive or file server, a tape drive, or a writeable CD-R or CD-RW drive.

Backups can be performed manually or can be scheduled to run automatically. A scheduled backup is performed automatically by software when the computer is not commonly in use, such as during the middle of the night. With Windows XP, you can schedule a backup using the Backup utility. Most removable and external storage devices also come with a software utility that allows you to schedule backups.

To recover files or folders backed up using the Backup utility, click the Restore and Manage Media tab on the Backup Utility window, select the backup to use, and then click the Start Restore button. The Backup utility displays the folders and files that were backed up with this job and allows you to select the ones you want to restore.

When you perform a backup for the first time or set up a scheduled backup, verify that you can use the backup tape or disks to successfully recover the data. To run a test, create a sample file and then create a backup of the file. Delete the file from the hard drive and then follow the steps to restore the file from the backup. If you are successful, you have verified that the backup medium works and that the recovery process is effective. Be sure to document the steps that you followed for your records.

It also is important to log your regular backups in a table or spreadsheet similar to the one shown in Figure 12-4. Be sure to list the files or folders that were backed up, the date, the type of backup, and the label on the storage medium. If you discover that data has been lost days or weeks ago, you can use this table to help you recover the data. If you store this information electronically, be sure also to have a printed hard copy and a backup electronic version in a safe place.

More About

Performing Backups

To learn more about backing up data, including a list of third-party utilities you can use, visit the Understanding and Troubleshooting Your PC More About Web page (**scsite.com/understanding/more**) and then click Performing Backups below Chapter 12.

BACKUP RECORD

Folders or drives backed up	Date of the backup	Type of backup	Label on CD-R
My Documents	4/5/2006	Full (Normal)	MyDocs Friday 1
My Documents	4/8/2006	Incremental	MyDocs Monday
My Documents	4/9/2006	Incremental	MyDocs Tuesday
My Documents	4/10/2006	Incremental	MyDocs Wednesday
My Documents	4/11/2006	Incremental	MyDocs Thursday
My Documents	4/12/2006	Full (Normal)	MyDocs Friday 2

Figure 12-4 Keep a written or electronic record of your backups, for reference.

 Your Turn

Scheduling a Backup

Chapter 9 outlined the basic steps to perform a backup using the Backup utility available in Windows XP. You also can schedule backups using the same tools, by completing the following steps.

1. Click the Start button, point to All Programs, point to Accessories, point to System Tools, and then click Backup. If the backup process starts by launching the Backup or Restore Wizard window, click Advanced mode.
2. When the Backup Utility window opens, click the Schedule Jobs tab. Click a date on the calendar for which you want to schedule a backup and then click the Add Job button.
3. When the Backup Wizard starts, click the Next button. In the What to Back Up area, click Backup selected files, drives, or network data and then click the Next button.
4. In the Items to Back Up list, click to select the files and folders you want to back up and then click the Next button.
5. In the Backup Type, Destination, and Name area, specify the drive and folder where you want to save the backup files and assign a name to the backup. Use a descriptive name, such as My Documents, to indicate what files are included in the backup. Click the Next button.
6. In the Type of Backup area, you can select the type of backup (Normal, Copy, Incremental, Differential, or Daily). If necessary, select Normal and then click the Next button.
7. The next window allows you to specify how to verify the data. Deselect any selected options and then click the Next button.
8. In the Backup Options area, you can indicate if the data is to be appended to an existing backup or should replace an existing backup. Click Replace the existing backups and then click the Next button.
9. In the When to Back Up area, click Later and then enter a job name in the Job name text box. As with the backup name, the job name should be descriptive to indicate what files are included in the backup. Type `My Documents (Normal)` in the Job name text box (Figure 12-3a). The start date defaults to the date you selected in Step 4.
10. Click the Set Schedule button. When the Schedule Job window appears, as shown in Figure 12-3b, click Weekly in the Schedule Task list and then click Fri in the Schedule Task Weekly area.
11. Click the Advanced button and then click End Date. Click the box arrow and select a Friday two weeks from the Start date. Click the OK button twice to return to the Backup Wizard window. Click the Next button.
12. In the Set Account Information window, you can specify a password for the backup. Click the OK button to proceed without specifying a password and then click the Yes button to confirm.
13. Click the Finish button to schedule a normal backup of the My Documents folder for two consecutive Fridays.
14. To delete a scheduled backup, double-click the backup icon in the Backup Utility – [Schedule Job] window and then click the Delete button. Click the Yes button to confirm the deletion.

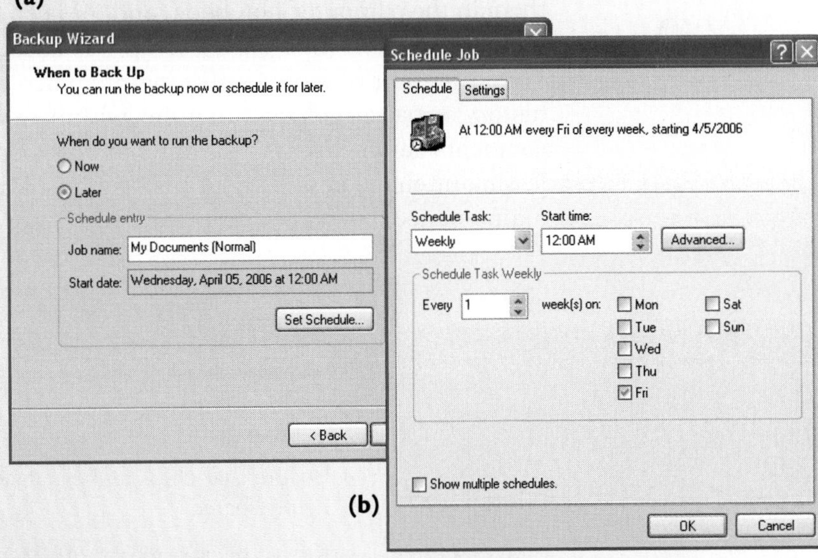

Figure 12-3

DISK CLONING SOFTWARE Another way to back up a hard drive is to use disk cloning or disk imaging software and create a copy of the entire hard drive on a different computer. **Disk cloning** or **disk imaging** is the creation of a complete image or copy of a computer's hard drive, usually used to deploy a new operating system with application software on multiple computers in a corporate network or educational computer lab. Several third-party software tools, such as Norton Ghost by Symantec Corp., Drive Image by PowerQuest, and ImageCast by Innovative Software provide the tools needed to create a disk image and copy it to another computer.

Creating a Preventive Maintenance Plan

A preventive maintenance plan is another valuable tool to have when maintaining a PC. Having a preventive maintenance plan can help prevent computer failures and reduce repair costs and downtime. In addition, you need a disaster recovery plan to manage failures when they occur. PC failures are caused by many different environmental and human factors, including heat, dust, magnetism, power supply problems, static electricity, human error (such as spilled liquids or an accidental change of setup and software configurations), and viruses. The goals of a preventive maintenance plan are to put processes in place to reduce the likelihood that the events that cause PC failures will occur, and to lessen the damage if they do occur. The disaster recovery plan helps define the steps to take when and if system failures do occur.

When designing a preventive maintenance plan, consider what you can do to help prevent each cause of PC failure and then write into the plan the preventive actions you can take. Think through the situation caused by each problem. For example, consider the problem caused by a user accidentally changing the CMOS setup, then define what steps you can take to prevent this from happening and how you will resolve the issue if it happens. After considering these issues, you might arrive at these preventive maintenance and recovery procedures: (1) set a supervisor password to limit access to CMOS, (2) educate the user about the importance of not changing setup information, (3) make a backup copy of CMOS settings and write them in the computer notebook, and (4) keep a maintenance record of the PC, including the last time CMOS setup was backed up.

The details of a preventive maintenance plan tend to evolve from and reflect a history or pattern of malfunctions within an organization. For example, dusty environments can mean more maintenance, whereas a clean environment can mean less maintenance. Figure 12-5 lists some guidelines for developing a preventive maintenance plan.

Component	Maintenance	How Often
Inside the case	• Make sure air vents are clear • Use compressed air to blow the dust out of the case, or use a vacuum to clean vents, power supply, and fan • Ensure that chips and expansion cards are firmly seated	Yearly
CMOS setup	• Keep a backup record of CMOS setup (for example, using Norton Utilities or a written record)	Whenever changes are made
		(continued)

Component	Maintenance	How Often
Floppy drive	• Only clean the floppy drive when the drive does not work	When the drive fails
Hard drive	• Perform regular backups	At least weekly
	• Automatically execute a virus scan program at startup	Daily
	• Update antivirus software signature files (virus definitions)	At least weekly
	• Defragment the drive	Monthly
	• Do not allow smoking around the PC	Always
	• Place the PC where it will not be jarred, kicked, or bumped	Always
	• Position the PC so air can circulate around it and into the front air vents	Always
Keyboard	• Keep the keyboard clean	Monthly
	• Keep the keyboard away from liquids	Always
Mouse	• Clean the mouse rollers and ball	Monthly
Monitor	• Clean the screen with a soft cloth	At least monthly
	• Make sure air vents are clear	Always
Printers	• Clean out the dust and bits of paper, using compressed air and a vacuum. Remove small pieces of paper with tweezers, preferably insulated ones • Clean the paper and ribbon paths with a soft, lint-free cloth • Do not re-ink ribbons or use recharged toner cartridges • If the printer uses an ozone filter, replace it as recommended by the manufacture. • Replace other components as recommended by the manufacturer	At least monthly or as recommended by the manufacturer
UPS and surge suppressors	• Run weak battery test • Run diagnostic test	As recommended by manufacturer
Software	• Make a backup copy of installation CDs.	As allowed by EULA
	• Regularly run Disk Cleanup to delete unneeded files	At least monthly
Written record	• Keep a record of all software, including version numbers and the OS installed on the PC • Keep a record of all hardware components installed, including hardware settings • Record when and what preventive maintenance is performed • Record any repairs done to the PC	Whenever changes are made

Figure 12-5 Guidelines for developing a PC preventive maintenance plan.

The general idea of preventive maintenance is to do what you can to make a PC last longer and have as few problems as possible. You also should be sure that all data is secure and backed up and that software copyrights are not violated. As with any plan, when designing your preventive maintenance plan, first define your overall goals and then design the plan accordingly.

FAQ 12-2

Why is dust so bad for a PC?

Dust is not good for a PC because it insulates PC parts like a blanket, which can cause them to overheat. Ridding the PC of dust is an important part of preventive maintenance. Some PC technicians do not like to use a vacuum inside a PC because they are concerned the vacuum might produce ESD. Use compressed air to blow the dust out of the case, power supply, and fan, or use a special antistatic vacuum designed to be used around sensitive equipment.

Quiz Yourself 12-1

To test your understanding of preventive maintenance and backup plans, visit the Understanding and Troubleshooting Your PC Quiz Yourself Web page (scsite.com/understanding/quiz). Click Quiz Yourself 1 below Chapter 12.

Protecting against Viruses, Trojan Horses, and Worms

An important part of preventive maintenance is protecting your computer against malicious logic programs. A **malicious logic program**, also called a **malicious software program**, is any program that acts without a user's knowledge, deliberately changes the computer's operations, and does varying degrees of damage to data and software. Understanding what malicious logic programs are, how they work, and where they hide can help you deal with them successfully.

Statistics show that in 2002, one in nine desktop computers were infected with a malicious logic program and the rate of infection increases 15 percent each year. One of the most important defenses against infection from a malicious logic program is **antivirus software**, which protects a computer against infection by identifying and removing any malicious logic programs in memory, in storage, or on files coming in as e-mail attachments.

Malicious logic programs include computer viruses, Trojan horses, and worms. Although some malicious logic programs are just one of these three types — virus, Trojan horse, or worm — others have characteristics of two or all three types. This section explains how each of these types of programs works and what safety precautions you can take to protect your computer from infection.

Computer Viruses

A **computer virus**, or simply a **virus,** is a program designed to infect a computer and replicate itself by attaching itself to other programs. The infected program must be executed for a virus to run. The virus might then simply replicate or also do damage by immediately performing some harmful action. Some viruses are malicious and are intended to destroy disk sectors or alter data on your computer. Other viruses are pranks, designed only to present a graphic on your screen or a message from the virus creator.

To create a virus, a programmer must write the virus code and then test the code to ensure the virus can replicate itself, conceal itself, monitor for certain events, and then deliver its **payload** — the destructive event or prank the virus was created to deliver. Many variations of viruses exist, but all have three characteristics:

- A virus has an incubation period, in which it is stored on a computer but does not cause damage.
- A virus can perform an unwanted function on a computer, such as destroying files, corrupting part of the hard disk, or simply displaying an annoying message.
- A virus can replicate by adding itself to other files or creating copies of itself and distributing the copies.

TYPES OF VIRUSES Although there are numerous variations of viruses, five main types of viruses exist: file viruses, macro viruses, boot sector viruses, Master Boot Record viruses, and multipartite viruses.

A **file virus** inserts virus code into program files or executable (.exe or .com) files. Once the program is run, the virus spreads to any program that accesses the infected program. A **macro virus** uses the macro language of an application, such as a word processing program, to hide virus code. A **macro** is a small program contained in a document that can be automatically executed when the document is first loaded, or later by pressing a key combination. Macro viruses infect Microsoft Word, Excel, PowerPoint, and Access files, although newer strains now are turning up in other programs as well. Macro viruses often are spread by e-mail, hiding in macros of attached document files. When a document with an infected macro is opened, the macro virus is loaded into memory. Certain actions, such as opening or saving the document, activate the virus so that the virus runs, does its damage, and copies itself into other documents. Macro viruses, such as the macro virus Wallpaper, often are made part of templates so any document created using the template is infected (Figure 12-6).

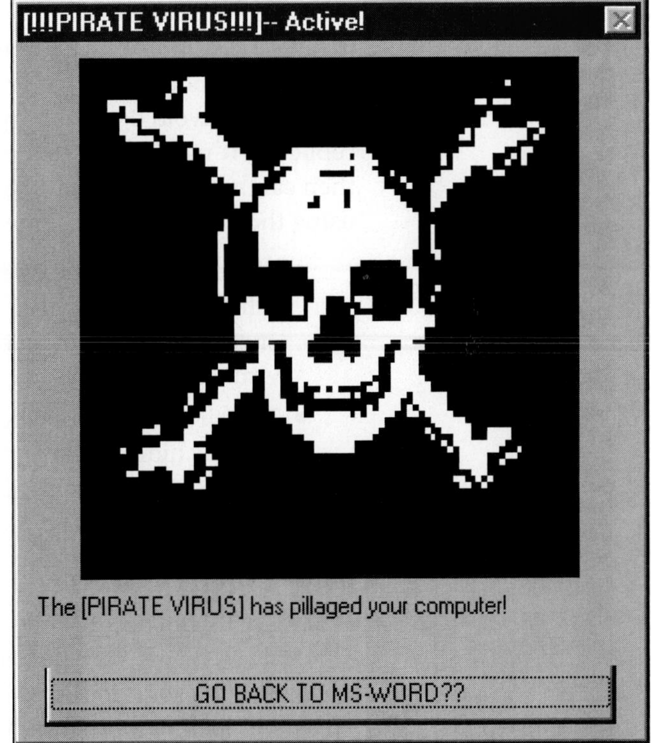

Figure 12-6 The macro virus Wallpaper (also called Pirate) is activated when an infected document is opened. At that point, the virus infects Word templates and other macros. Some versions of Wallpaper activate on the thirty-first day of the month, at which point the virus attempts to replace the Windows Desktop wallpaper with a picture of a skull.

A **boot sector virus** replaces the boot program used to start the computer system with a modified, infected version of the boot program. When the infected boot program is run, it loads the virus into the computer's memory. One of the most common ways a virus spreads is from a floppy disk used to boot a PC. When the boot program is loaded into memory, so is the virus, which then can spread to other programs. **Master Boot Record (MBR) viruses** attack disks in the same manner as boot sector viruses; the difference is that a master boot record virus normally saves a legitimate copy of the master boot record in a different location on the hard disk. Because the operating system cannot access the boot information, the computer will not start from the hard disk.

A **multipartite virus**, also called a **polypartite virus**, has characteristics of a boot sector virus and a file virus in that it infects both boot records and program files. Many of these viruses are very destructive, deleting and corrupting files, erasing computer memory, overwriting the master boot record, and deleting floppy disk drivers so you cannot reboot your machine from a floppy disk. Multipartite viruses also are difficult to repair. If the boot area is cleaned but the files are not, the boot area will be reinfected. Conversely, if the virus is not removed from the boot area, any files that you have cleaned will be reinfected.

Some viruses are considered to be logic bombs or time bombs. A **logic bomb** is a program that is activated when a certain condition is detected. A disgruntled worker, for example, could infect a network server with a logic bomb that starts destroying files if his name is added to a list of terminated employees. A **time bomb** is a type of logic bomb that is activated on a particular date. Win.32 Hatred, which delivers its payload on the seventh of any month, is an example of a time bomb. A well-known time bomb is the Michelangelo virus, which destroys data on your hard disk on March 6, which is Michelangelo's birthday.

HOW VIRUSES HIDE Antivirus software only can detect viruses identical or similar to those it has been programmed to search for and recognize. Antivirus software detects a known virus by looking for distinguishing characteristics called a **virus signature**, or **virus definition**, which is a known pattern of virus code.

A virus typically is programmed to attempt to hide from antivirus software by changing its distinguishing characteristics (its signature) and by attempting to mask its presence. For example, a **polymorphic virus** changes its distinguishing characteristics as it replicates. An **encrypting virus** can transform itself into a nonreplicating program to avoid detection by antivirus software, which looks for programs that can replicate. It must revert to a replicating program to spread or replicate, however, and then can be detected by antivirus software. A **stealth virus** actively conceals itself using the following techniques:

- The virus alters the operating system information to mask the size of the file it hides in, so antivirus software cannot detect a virus by noting the difference between a program's file size before the virus infects it and after the virus is present.
- The virus monitors when files are opened or closed. When it sees that the file it is hiding in is about to be opened, it temporarily removes itself or substitutes a copy of the file that does not include the virus. The virus keeps a copy of this uninfected file on the hard drive just for this purpose.

HOW A VIRUS REPLICATES Once a program containing a virus is copied to your PC, the virus can spread only when the infected program executes, as shown in Figure 12-7. As you have learned, the first step in executing a program — whether it is stored in a program file or in a boot sector — is to load the program into memory. Viruses hidden in a program then can be executed from memory. A virus either is a **memory-resident virus** that stays in memory and works even after the infected program terminates, or a **non-memory-resident virus** that is terminated when the infected program is closed. After a virus is loaded into memory, it looks for other programs loaded into memory. When it finds one, it copies itself into that program. The longer a virus stays loaded into memory, the more programs it can infect.

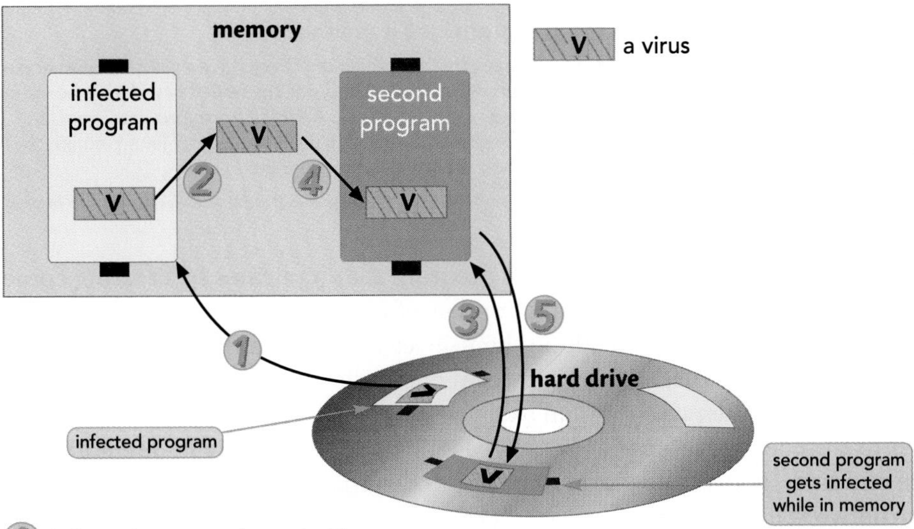

1. Infected program is copied into memory.
2. The virus may or may not move itself to a new location in memory.
3. A second program is opened and copied into memory.
4. The virus copies itself to the second program in memory.
5. The newly infected second program is written back to the hard drive.

Figure 12-7 How a virus replicates.

Trojan Horses and Worms

While often called viruses, Trojan horse applications and worms actually are part of the broader category of malicious logic programs.

TROJAN HORSES A **Trojan horse** is a destructive program disguised as a real application, such as a screen saver. Unlike viruses, Trojan horses do not replicate. To spread, they rely on you and other computer users to believe they are legitimate programs, thus infecting your computer when you open an e-mail attachment or download and run a file from the Internet. Once on your computer, a certain condition or action usually triggers the Trojan horse to release its payload.

When it runs, a Trojan horse can delete files, capture information from your system, or open up a back door that allows a hacker to control your computer remotely. One example of a Trojan horse is the AOL4FREE program. Originally, this illegal program could provide unauthorized access to America Online. After America Online blocked the program's usefulness, a new program, also called AOL4FREE, was available; this version, however, was a Trojan horse. Many users shared the program, thinking that it would provide access to AOL. When executed, however, the program actually erased files on their hard drives. Because Trojan horse infestations generally cannot replicate and require human intervention to move from one location to another, they are not as common as viruses.

FAQ 12-3

How did the Trojan horse program get its name?

A Trojan horse program is named for a Greek myth in which the Greeks give a giant wooden horse to their foes, the Trojans, as a peace gesture. After it is taken inside the walled city of Troy, however, the horse proves to contain Greek soldiers who then attack. A Trojan horse program works in much the same way. A user thinks it is a legitimate program, until opening a file or running the program — at which point it proves to be a malicious logic program.

WORMS A **worm** is a malicious logic program that replicates by creating copies of itself, either on one computer or any number of computers on a network. Unlike viruses, which replicate by attaching themselves to program files, worms do not infect other program files. Instead, a worm copies itself from one computer's disk drive to another (often using e-mail as a way to spread the program). As a worm copies itself repeatedly in memory or on a disk drive, eventually no memory or disk space remains. By using up the system resources, the worm can cause a computer or entire network to shut down.

Worms can perform a variety of tasks, although many such as Sircam, Sobig, and MyDoom are mass-mailing e-mail worms that read e-mail addresses from your address book and then continue spreading the worm by sending e-mail messages to those addresses (Figure 12-8).

Worms on the Internet routinely perform port scanning, meaning that they are constantly looking for open, unprotected ports through which they can invade a system. Once they are in a computer, they can move to other computers on the internal network or produce mass e-mailings to bog down the network or Internet.

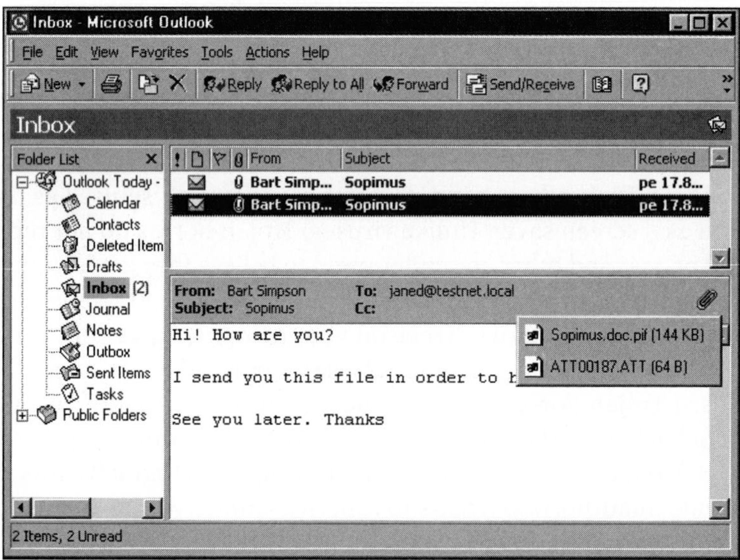

Figure 12-8 E-mail messages sent by the Sircam worm look like this, although some slight variations — and even a Spanish version — exist. The worm attaches a file to disguise itself as a file. When you open the file, your PC also is infected.

Hoaxes

At some point, you may have received an e-mail that described some new, extremely destructive type of virus, telling you to delete a file from your hard drive. It is likely, however, that the virus described in the e-mail does not exist, and the warning is untrue. A **virus hoax** is an e-mail message that spreads a false virus warning, usually in chain letter fashion, from person to person. An e-mail describing a hoax, such as the one shown in Figure 12-9, generally makes alarming statements that a certain virus can do serious harm, instructs you to delete a file, and tells you to forward it to everyone you know. Such e-mails rarely have references to a third party who can validate the claim.

> **More About**
>
> **Virus Hoaxes**
>
> To learn more about Web sites that provide information about virus hoaxes, visit the Understanding and Troubleshooting Your PC More About Web page (**scsite.com/understanding/more**) and then click Virus Hoaxes below Chapter 12.

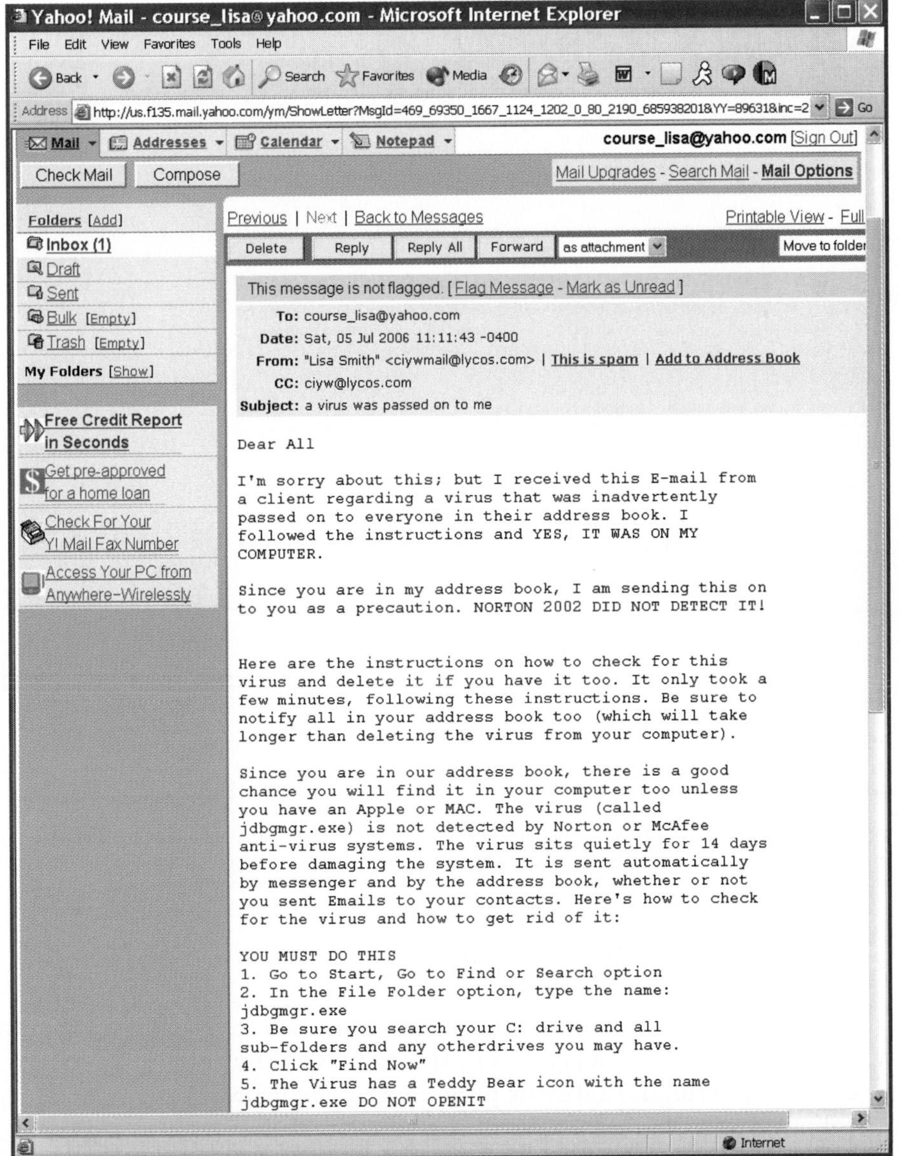

Figure 12-9 An e-mail describing a hoax generally has no file attachment, no references to a third party who can validate the claim, and uses common phrases designed to scare you into following the instructions and spreading the hoax.

Before ignoring such an e-mail or following its instructions and deleting files you might need, you should check with reputable references to determine if a virus warning is legitimate or a hoax. The Web sites of many antivirus software makers, such as Symantec, McAfee, and F-Secure post lists of hoaxes (Figure 12-10).

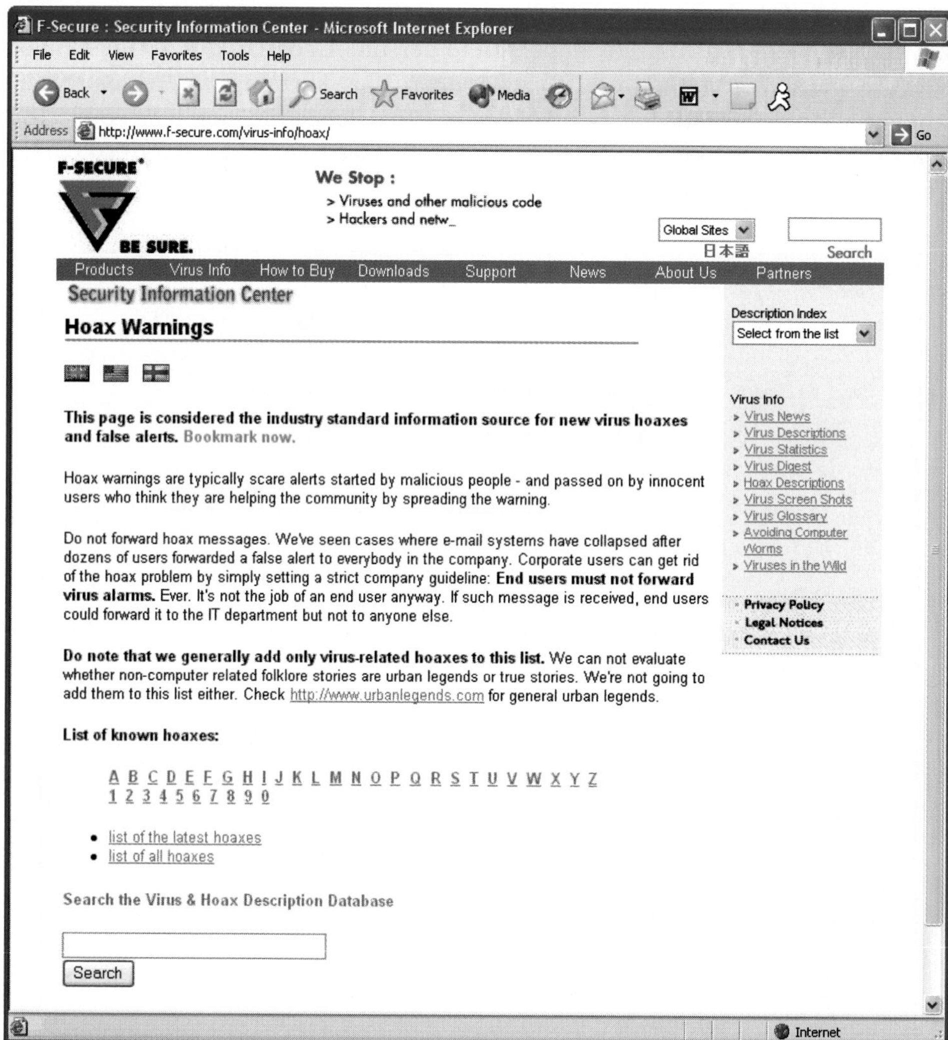

Figure 12-10 The F-Secure Web site posts lists of hoaxes, so you can determine if a virus warning is legitimate or a hoax.

Protecting against Computer Viruses

It is impossible to guarantee that a computer or network is safe from a computer virus, worm, or Trojan horse. A good start, however, is to buy antivirus software and set your computer to run the antivirus program automatically at startup and to stay informed about new virus alerts and virus hoaxes. You can take several other precautions to protect your home and work computers from malicious logic programs, as listed in Figure 12-11.

Tips for Preventing Virus, Trojan Horse, and Worm Infections

- Install an antivirus software on all of your computers. Obtain updates to the antivirus signature files on a regular basis (most antivirus programs offer an automatic update feature).
- Never open an e-mail attachment unless you are expecting it and it is from a trusted source. Be especially wary of files with the file extensions VBS, SHS, or PIF or double file extensions such as NAME.BMP.EXE or NAME.TXT.VBS. These extensions are almost never used in normal attachments but they are used frequently by viruses and worms.
- If you feel that an e-mail you get from a friend is somehow strange — if it is in a foreign language or if it just says odd things, double-check with the friend before opening any attachments.
- Set your antivirus software to scan documents automatically and other e-mail attachments when they are opened. Turn off the message preview pane.
- If the antivirus program flags an e-mail attachment as infected, delete the e-mail immediately.
- Check all downloaded programs for viruses, worms, or Trojan horses. These malicious-logic programs often are placed in seemingly innocent programs, so they will affect a large number of users.
- Set the macro security in programs so you can enable or disable macros. Only enable macros if the document is from a trusted source and you are expecting it.
- Before using any floppy disk or Zip disk, use the antivirus scan program to check the disk for infection. Incorporate this procedure even for shrink-wrapped software from major developers. Some commercial software has been infected and distributed to unsuspecting users this way.
- Never start a computer with a floppy disk in drive A, unless it is an uninfected boot disk or recovery disk.
- Write-protect your recovery disk by sliding the write-protect tab into the write-protect position.
- Back up your files regularly. Scan the backup program before backing up disks and files to ensure the backup program is virus free.

Figure 12-11 Computer users can use a number of safe computing tips to minimize the risk of virus,Trojan horse, and worm infection.

USING ANTIVIRUS SOFTWARE First and foremost, install an antivirus program on your computer and update it frequently. As you have learned, antivirus software protects a computer against viruses by identifying and removing any computer viruses found in memory, on storage media, or on incoming files. Most antivirus programs also protect against worms and Trojan horses. Figure 12-12 lists several popular antivirus programs.

An antivirus program scans for programs that attempt to modify the boot program, the operating system, and other programs that normally are read from but not modified. Many antivirus programs also automatically scan files downloaded from the Web, e-mail attachments, opened files, and all removable media inserted into the computer such as floppy disks and Zip disks.

Antivirus Programs
AVG Antivirus
Command AntiVirus
eTrust InoculateIT
F-Secure Anti-Virus
McAfee VirusScan
McAfee Virex
Norton AntiVirus
RAV AntiVirus
Trend Micro PC-cillin

Figure 12-12 Popular antivirus programs can help protect your computer against viruses, Trojan horses, and worms.

Antivirus software can work at different times to scan your hard drive or a floppy disk for viruses. Most antivirus software can be configured to scan memory and the boot sector of your hard drive for viruses each time your PC boots. Some antivirus software can run continuously in the background, scanning all programs that execute. If this causes your computer to boot very slowly, you can schedule the antivirus software to run a virus scan at the same time every day, such as during a weekly meeting or at the end of the day.

As you have learned, one technique that antivirus programs use to identify a virus is to look for virus signatures. Computer users should update their antivirus program's signature or definition files regularly. Updating these files brings in any new virus definitions that have been added since the last update. This extremely important activity allows the antivirus software to protect against viruses written since the antivirus program was released. Most antivirus programs contain an auto-update feature that regularly prompts users to download the new virus signature or definition files. The vendor usually provides this service to registered users at no cost for a specified time.

Another technique that antivirus programs use to detect viruses is to inoculate existing program files. To **inoculate** a program file, the antivirus program records information such as the file size and file creation date in a separate inoculation file. The antivirus program then uses this information to detect if a virus tampers with the data describing the inoculated program file.

More About

Protecting Against Malicious Logic Programs

To learn more about protecting your system against viruses, Trojan horses, and worms, visit the Understanding and Troubleshooting Your PC More About Web page (**scsite.com/understanding/more**) and then click Protecting Against Malicious Logic Programs below Chapter 12.

HANDLING AN INFECTION If you suspect your computer has been infected with a virus, Trojan horse, or worm, run a virus scan using your antivirus software to detect and delete the malicious logic program. If an antivirus program identifies an infected file, it attempts to remove the virus, Trojan horse, or worm. If the antivirus program cannot remove the infection, it often quarantines the infected file. A **quarantine** is a separate area of a hard disk that holds the infected file until the infection can be removed. This step ensures that other files will not become infected. Users also can quarantine suspicious files themselves.

In addition to detecting, inoculating, and removing viruses, Trojan horses and worms, most antivirus programs have utilities that create a recovery disk. Once you have restarted the computer using the recovery disk, the antivirus program can attempt to repair damaged files. If it cannot repair the damaged files, you may have to restore them with uninfected backup copies of the files. In extreme cases, you may need to reformat the hard disk to remove a virus. Having uninfected, or clean, backups of all files is important.

Quiz Yourself 12-2

To test your understanding of protecting your computer from malicious logic programs, visit the Understanding and Troubleshooting Your PC Quiz Yourself Web page (scsite.com/understanding/quiz). Click Quiz Yourself 2 below Chapter 12.

Troubleshooting Tools

If you have a solid preventive maintenance plan in place and adhere to it, you most likely will have few problems. In general, the more preventive maintenance work you do up front, the less troubleshooting and repair you are likely to do. At some point, however, almost every person who supports a PC will need to address some type of hardware or software problem. The following section looks at tools to help you diagnose and repair computer problems.

Building a PC Toolkit

An important first step in troubleshooting computer problems is having a toolkit with the appropriate items, several of which are shown in Figure 12-13. A basic toolkit for PC troubleshooting includes the following:

- Flat-head screwdriver
- Phillips-head (cross-head) screwdriver
- Torx® screwdriver, particularly size T15
- Tweezers, preferably insulated ones, to lift pieces of paper out of printers or dropped screws out of tight places
- Chip extractor to remove chips
- 3-pronged parts retriever, which is a spring-loaded device used to retrieve objects from small spaces. When you push down on the top, three wire prongs extend to allow you to pick up a screw or other item that has fallen into a part of the PC too small for your fingers or hands.
- Ground bracelet and ground mat

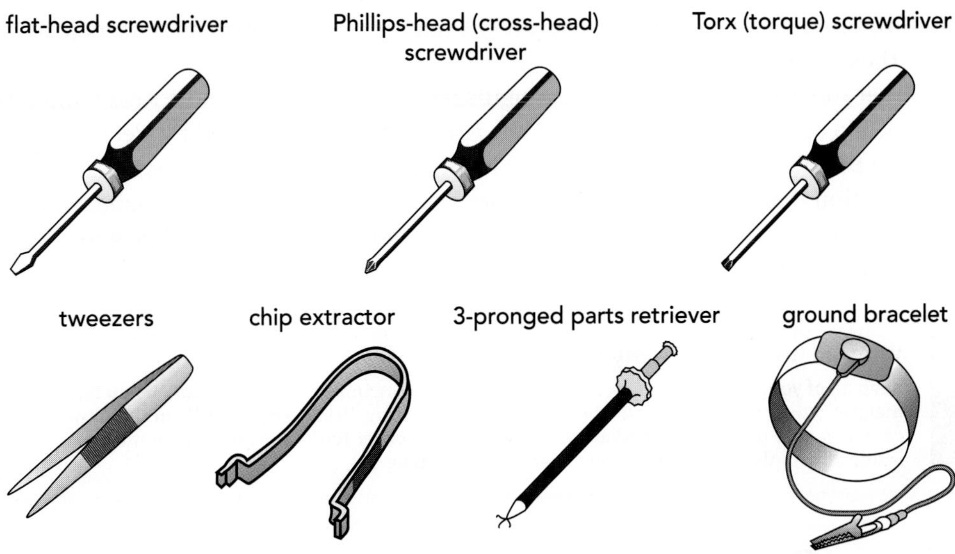

Figure 12-13 Tools to have in a PC toolkit.

Figure 12-14 illustrates the differences in the screw heads and bits used for the various types of screwdrivers. You may want to have screwdrivers with several bit sizes to work with various sizes of screws.

Screwdriver	Bit	Screwhead	
Flat-head			Original screwhead; widely used. Design means screwdriver easily can slip out of slot when tightening or loosening.
Phillips (cross-head)			Very popular screwhead; widely used. Cross pattern on head helps reduce slippage when tightening or loosening.
Torx (torque)			A newer screwhead, often used for electronics. Size T15 Torx screws often are used in computers.

Figure 12-14 Types of screwdrivers.

Another important component of a PC toolkit is a bootable rescue disk for any operating system you need to support. As you have learned, a bootable rescue disk can help you boot the PC to ensure a clean boot that does not load any extra software, drivers, or other programs — and can help you boot the PC even when the hard drive fails.

Other tools that are helpful to have in a PC toolkit include:

- Antistatic bags to store unused parts
- Needle-nose pliers for removing jumpers and for holding objects while you screw them into place
- Flashlight to see inside the PC case
- AC outlet ground tester and multimeter to check the power supply output
- Small cups, bags, or a plastic container to keep screws organized as you work and store spare screws
- Pen and paper for taking notes
- Utility software, diagnostic software, and antivirus software for any hardware or software you need to support

Before purchasing each item separately, look for existing toolkits that include most of these components.

Another tool to consider is a fire extinguisher that is rated to handle fires ignited by electricity. If a computer catches on fire, the fire is ignited and heated by electricity — a type of fire considered to be Class C by the National Fire Protection Association (NFPA), an organization that creates standards for fire safety. Mount a fire extinguisher rated for Class C fires near, but not directly over, your computer work area — and be sure you know how to use the fire extinguisher.

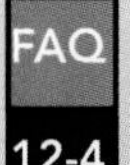

FAQ 12-4

Where should I store my PC tools?

Keep all of your tools in a toolbox or case, so they are organized in one location. If you have a magnetized screwdriver in your toolset, do not put floppy disks, CDs, or DVDs in the same case. If you do put storage media in the case with the other tools, be sure to keep the disks inside a hard plastic case to protect them from scratches.

Utility and Diagnostic Software

Many utility and diagnostic software tools are available to help you diagnose a problem with a personal computer. **Utility software** is a program that performs a specific task, usually related to managing system resources or identifying a problem with a PC. Utility software can be designed to diagnose problems, repair and maintain the software on a PC, recover corrupted or deleted data on the hard drive or floppy disks, provide security, monitor system performance, and download software updates from the Internet. The utility software might use the installed operating system or might provide its own.

FAQ 12-5

Where can I learn more about what utility software is available?

It is a good idea to stay informed about new utility software as it becomes available, because you might run into a situation where one of these tools could save you time. Computer magazines such as PC Magazine (*www.pcmag.com*) and PC World (*www.pcworld.com*) are a good source of information, as well as Web sites such as CNET (*www.cnet.com*).

Diagnostic software generally is used to identify hardware problems. For example, the diagnostic software PC-Technician loads and operates using its own operating system, so it can operate directly on system hardware without having to interact with the installed operating system. PC-Technician provides tools to test any number of hardware components and functions, including memory, hard drives, floppy disk drives, serial and parallel ports, video adapters, and the keyboard.

Figure 12-15 lists several examples of utility and diagnostic software programs. Before purchasing utility or diagnostic software, read the documentation and product reviews to determine whether the software will perform the functions you need, if it is appropriate for the types of computers you support, and that it comes with good documentation and support. Software that is described as professional generally assumes greater technical expertise and also provides more features than end-user software.

Software	Description
Norton SystemWorks (Symantec)	General-purpose utility software that provides a variety of functions, including the ability to recover lost or damaged data from a hard drive.
CheckIt Suite (Smith Micro Software)	A general-purpose utility software that includes hard drive testing, performance testing, port testing, and setup for resource conflicts.
PartitionMagic (PowerQuest)	Lets you create, resize, and merge partitions on a hard drive without losing data. You can use the software to run multiple operating systems easily, convert file system types, and fix partition table errors.
SpinRite (Gibson Research)	Scans a hard drive for errors and can perform a low-level format without losing the data (called a non-destructive format), and sometimes can recover lost data.
• Data Lifeguard Tools (Western Digital) • PowerMax (Maxtor) • Gwscan.exe (Gateway)	Diagnostic software from several major hard drive manufacturers (Western Digital, Maxtor, and Gateway) that reports and fixes some types of hard drive errors. The software, which is written to work with that manufacturer's drives only, usually can be downloaded from the manufacturer's Web site.
Administrator's Pak (Winternals)	A software suite with utilities to boot a system from CD, repair an OS, recover data, change forgotten passwords, repair system files, repair partition tables, and rewrite the MBR program.
	(continued)

Software	Description
Spybot Search & Destroy (PepiMK Software)	Privacy protection software that searches out and removes installed programs that track Internet activity or display pop-up ads.
PC-Technician (Windsor Technologies)	Professional-level PC diagnostic software that loads and operates without using the PC's installed operating system, because it has its own proprietary OS built in. PC-Technician provides tools to test any number of hardware components and functions.
PC-Diagnosys (Windsor Technologies)	Designed for less-experienced PC technicians and end users; it is smaller, easier to use, and less expensive than PC-Technician.
PC-Doctor (PC-Doctor)	Comprehensive hardware diagnostic and system information tool that can test your computer, determine its configuration, and perform low-level hardware testing.
SiSoftware Sandra (SiSoftware)	Benchmarking, diagnostic, and tune-up software that can be used to solve hardware and software problems.
Windows Memory Diagnostic (Microsoft)	User-friendly software that runs a comprehensive set of memory tests to determine whether the problems are caused by failing hardware, such as RAM or the memory system of your motherboard.
DocMemory (CST, Inc)	User-friendly self-bootable software designed to capture all possible memory failures in a PC.

Figure 12-15 Utility and diagnostic software used to identify and fix PC problems.

How can I make it easier to keep software in my toolkit without having so many CDs?

Some PC technicians find it useful to make a single CD that contains several favorite utilities, diagnostic software, and antivirus software. For example, you could burn a CD with the software utilities SpinRite, Windows Memory Diagnostic, and Data Lifeguard Tools, as well as Trend Micro Damage Cleanup Service, which is an antivirus program that runs from a CD.

Approaches for Troubleshooting a PC

When a computer does not work and you are responsible for fixing it, you generally should approach the problem first as an investigator and discoverer, always being careful not to compound the problem through your own actions. If the problem seems difficult, see it as an opportunity to learn something new and be sure to investigate various options until you understand the source of the problem.

Understanding the root cause of a problem is the hardest part of resolving a problem. Once you understand the cause, the solution most likely will be clear. The following sections discuss how to approach troubleshooting a problem from the perspective of a single user working on his or her own PC. These same rules, however, apply when you are working with other users to resolve issues with their computers.

Fundamental Rules

When troubleshooting a PC, keep a few fundamental rules in mind:

- *Make backups before making changes*. Whether you are working on hardware or software, always back up essential programs and data before working on a computer.
- *Follow the important safety precautions that you have learned in previous chapters*, as well as the ones discussed in this chapter.
- *Approach the problem systematically*. Start at the beginning and walk through the situation in a thorough, careful way. First, try to reproduce the problem and then try to figure out whether it is a hardware or software problem. If you do not discover the explanation to the problem after one systematic walk-through, then repeat the entire process. Check and double-check to find the step you overlooked the first time.
- *Isolate the problem*. Isolating the problem is one of the most important parts of troubleshooting. In the overall system, remove one hardware or software component after another, until the problem is isolated to a small part of the whole system. Here are a few examples of applying this rule:
  - Boot from a disk to eliminate the OS and startup files on the hard drive as the problem.
  - Remove any unnecessary hardware devices, such as a printer, scanner, or even an internal modem or network card.
  - Once down to the essentials, start exchanging components you know are good for those you suspect are bad, until the problem goes away.
- *Do not assume the worst*. If you do not have a backup copy of data on a hard drive that crashed, do not assume that all of the data is lost. Many steps can be taken to recover data from a hard drive.
- *Check simple things first*. Remember that the cause of most computer problems is something simple, such as a loose cable or an outdated driver. Before assuming the worst, check the obvious: Is the computer plugged in? Is it turned on? Is the monitor plugged in? Next, check the components that are easiest to replace. For example, if the video does not work, the problem may be with the monitor or the video card. When faced with the decision of which one to exchange first, choose the easy route: exchange the monitor before the video card.
- *Become a researcher*. When a computer problem arises that you cannot solve easily, use every resource at your disposal to try to understand the problem. Take advantage of every available resource, including printed documentation, user manuals, online help, technical support, books, knowledgeable colleagues, and the Internet. A good place to start your research on the Internet is a hardware or software manufacturer's support Web site or a search engine, such as Google or Yahoo!. Research can be a time-consuming but valuable aspect of computer troubleshooting. In every case, the research is a learning experience.
- *Know your starting point*. Before trying to solve a computer problem, make sure you are fairly certain that the problem is where you think it is. If the computer does not boot, carefully note where in the boot process it fails. If the computer does boot to an OS, before changing anything or taking anything apart, verify what does and what does not work.

More About

Troubleshooting Resources

To view a list of resources to help troubleshoot computer problems, visit the Understanding and Troubleshooting Your PC More About Web page (**scsite.com/understanding/more**) and then click Troubleshooting Resources below Chapter 12.

- *Establish your priorities*. Before trying any steps to resolve the problem, decide what your first priority is. For example, your first priority might be to recover lost data or to get the PC back up and running as soon as possible. What you define as the priority can impact the way you troubleshoot an issue.
- *Do not rush*. Before trying something, hoping that it will work, read the documentation or other resources to research possible solutions — and do not hesitate to ask for help from someone more knowledgeable. Always be sure to protect the data and software by carefully considering your options before acting, and by taking practical precautions to protect software and OS files. When a computer stops working, if you have not backed up data or software on the hard drive or if unsaved data is still in memory, carefully plan your next steps.
- *Write things down*. As you work, keep good notes, including diagrams, lists, resources where you found information, and so on. Writing down precisely what you are learning will help you think more clearly — and will provide a great reference if the problem is hard to reproduce or occurs at a later time.
- *Take a break*. If you find you are getting frustrated or have worked on a problem for a long time, take a break and come back to the problem. A fresh start might help you uncover events or steps that you previously overlooked.

FAQ 12-7

Do the same fundamental rules apply if you are fixing a problem for another user?

Absolutely. All of the fundamental rules outlined above apply to a situation where you are fixing your own PC or someone else's. When working on another user's computer, however, you should follow one additional rule: make no assumptions. A user many not describe an event or error as it occurred, so do your own investigating. For example, if the user tells you that the system boots up with no error messages, but that the software still does not work, boot the computer and watch for yourself. You never know what the user might have overlooked.

Gathering Information

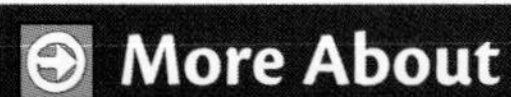

Providing Support for Users

To learn more about how to interact with a user when providing computer support, visit the Understanding and Troubleshooting Your PC More About Web page (**scsite.com/understanding/more**) and then click Providing Support for Users below Chapter 12.

When you are trying to solve a computer problem, the rules outlined above will prepare you to apply a successful course of action. Before you take corrective action, however, you need to gather as much information about the situation as possible. This section covers ways to gather information on a computer problem you are troubleshooting.

INVESTIGATING THE PROBLEM To start investigating the problem, ask yourself the following questions and write down as much information as you can gather.

- What operating system is installed?
- What physical components are installed? What processor, expansion cards, drives, and peripheral devices are installed? Is the PC connected to a network?
- What is the nature of the problem? Does the problem occur before or after the boot? Does an error message appear? Does the system hang at certain times? Start from a cold boot, and do whatever you must do to cause the problem to occur. What specific steps did you take to duplicate the problem?
- Can you duplicate the problem? Does the problem occur every time you do the above steps, or is the problem intermittent? Intermittent problems generally are more difficult to solve than problems that occur consistently.

ISOLATING THE PROBLEM The next step in problem solving is to isolate the source of the problem by doing the following:

- *Consider the possibilities*. Given what you have learned by examining the computer and duplicating the problem, consider what might be the source of the problem. For example, if your Word documents are getting corrupted, possible sources of the problem might be that the software or the OS might be corrupted, the PC might have a virus, or the hard drive might be failing intermittently.
- *Eliminate simple things first*. As previously noted, the cause of most computer problems is something simple. If a CD-ROM drive is not working, first check that the CD-ROM is not scratched or cracked. If you cannot connect to a network, be sure you are using the correct user name and password.
- *Eliminate the unnecessary*. This rule can be applied in many ways — for example, when the PC does not boot successfully. In this case, it is often unclear if the problem is with the hardware or software.
    - When using Windows Server 2003, Windows XP, Windows 2000, or Windows 9x, you can boot into Safe Mode and eliminate much of the OS customized configuration. Try to recreate the problem in Safe Mode. If you still have problems, boot from your bootable rescue disk(s) or the Windows setup CD. If the problem goes away, you can deduce that the problem is with (1) the OS or applications installed on the hard drive or (2) the hard drive used as the boot device.
    - If you suspect the problem is caused by faulty hardware, eliminate any unnecessary hardware devices. If the PC still boots with errors, disconnect the network card, the CD-ROM drive, the mouse, and maybe even the hard drive. (To disconnect the CD-ROM and hard drive, simply disconnect the data cable and the power cable. You do not need to remove the CD-ROM or hard drive from the bays inside the case.) Remove the network card from its expansion slot and place it on an antistatic bag or ground mat, not on top of the power supply or case. If the problem goes away, you know that one or more of these devices is causing the problem. Replace them one at a time until the problem returns. Remember that the problem might be a resource conflict. If the network card worked well until the CD-ROM drive was reconnected and now neither works, try the CD-ROM drive without the network card. If the CD-ROM drive works, you most likely have a resource conflict.
- *Trade good for suspected bad*. When diagnosing hardware problems, this method works well if you can draw from a group of parts that you know work correctly. For example, suppose the monitor does not work. The parts of the video subsystem are the video card, the power cord to the monitor, the cord from the monitor to the PC case, and the monitor itself. The video card also is inserted into an expansion slot on the motherboard, and the monitor depends on electrical power. To determine which component is causing the issue, try them one at a time. Trade the monitor for one that you know works. Trade the power cord, trade the cord to the PC video port, move the video card to a new slot, and trade the video card.

  When you are trading a good component for a suspected bad one, work methodically by eliminating one component at a time. Do not trade the video card and the monitor and then turn on the PC to determine if they work. It is possible that both the card and the monitor are bad, but assume that only one component is bad before you consider whether multiple components need trading.

In this situation, suppose you keep trading components in the video subsystem until you have no more variations. Next, take the entire subsystem — video card, cords, and monitor — to a PC that you know works and plug each of them in. If they work, you have isolated the problem to the PC, not the video. Now turn your attention back to the PC: the motherboard, the software settings within the OS, the video driver, and other devices. Knowing that the video subsystem works on the good PC gives you a valuable tool. Compare the video driver on the good PC to the one on the bad PC. Make certain the CMOS settings, software settings, and other settings are the same.

- *Trade suspected bad for good*. If you have a working PC that is configured similarly to the one you are troubleshooting (a common situation in many corporate or educational environments), a reverse approach is to trade suspected bad for good, rather than trading good for suspected bad. Take each component that you suspect is bad and install it in the working PC. If the component works on the good PC, then you have eliminated it as a suspect. If the working PC breaks down, then you have probably identified the bad component.

INTERMITTENT PROBLEMS Intermittent problems can make troubleshooting challenging. The trick in diagnosing problems that come and go is to look for patterns or clues as to when the problems occur. If you cannot reproduce the problem, keep a log of when the problems occur and exactly what messages appear. A simple way to document error messages is to get a printed screen shot of the error message. To take a screen capture, press ALT+PRNT SCRN to copy a screen capture to the Windows Clipboard. Start the Paint program. When the Paint window is displayed, click Edit on the menu bar and then click Paste. You then can print or save a copy of the screen shot. You also can paste the contents of the Clipboard into a document created by word-processing software such as Microsoft Word.

Quiz Yourself 12-3

To test your understanding of troubleshooting tools and approaches, visit the Understanding and Troubleshooting Your PC Quiz Yourself Web page (scsite.com/understanding/quiz). Click Quiz Yourself 3 below Chapter 12.

High-Tech Talk

On the Move: Tips for Moving Computer Equipment

At some point, you may find you need to move your computer a short distance from one room to another, or over quite a long haul to another part of the world. When shipping a personal computer, remember that rough handling can cause damage, as can exposure to water, heat, and cold. The computer also can be misplaced, lost, or stolen.

When you are preparing a PC for shipping, take extra precautions to protect both the PC and its data. Follow these general guidelines when preparing to ship a PC:

- Back up the hard drive onto a tape cartridge or other backup medium separate from your computer. If you do not have access to a medium that can back up the entire drive, back up important system and configuration files to a floppy disk or other media. Whatever you do, do not ship a PC that has the only copy of important data on the hard drive or data that should be secured from unauthorized access.
- Remove any removable disks, tape cartridges, or CDs from the drives. Make sure that the tapes or disks holding the backup data are secured and protected during transit. Consider shipping them separately.
- Turn off power to the PC and all other devices.
- Disconnect power cords from the electrical outlet and the devices. Disconnect all external devices from the computer.
- If you think someone might have trouble later identifying which cord or cable belongs to which device or connection, label the cable connections with white tape or white labels.
- Coil all external cords and secure them with plastic ties or rubber bands.

After completing all of these steps, pack the computer, monitor, and all devices in shipping cartons (Figure 12-16). The original box your computer and peripheral devices came in is the best choice. If your original box is not available, you should get an appropriately-sized box and Styrofoam peanuts or bubble wrap. If you have a tower or desktop computer, be sure to pack the computer either upright or lying on the side so the motherboard is on the bottom, facing up. Label the box to indicate which side of the box should be the top, so shippers or movers do not turn it upside down or on its side. If the computer is shipped upside down or with the motherboard facing down, it can cause expansion cards and other components to loosen during shipment. While this may not permanently damage parts, it may require some time afterwards to reseat cards and ensure components are working properly. You also should take special care to safeguard your monitor to be sure the screen is not cracked or scratched on contact.

If you are shipping the computer with a mover, clearly identify these items to the mover so they can use care when packing those boxes. If you are shipping it via a shipping company such as UPS, FedEx, or the US Postal Service, be sure to send the computer using a method that provides you with a tracking number, so you can track the shipment should it be lost. Be sure to purchase insurance on the shipment, as well. The upfront cost of the insurance can save you a lot of money if materials are damaged in transit.

Figure 12-16

CHAPTER SUMMARY

The Chapter Summary reviews the concepts presented in this chapter.

1 Maintaining Your PC

Maintaining a PC involves several important routine maintenance tasks, such as organizing the hard drive, creating rescue disks, documenting setup changes, recording setup data, and protecting and backing up software and data. A backup is an extra copy of a data or software file that you can use if the original file becomes damaged or destroyed. Several different types of backup can be used. A full backup, or normal backup, backs up all data from the hard drive or a directory or folder of the hard drive. An incremental backup backs up only files that have changed or been created since the last backup. Differential backups back up files that have changed or been created since the last full backup. You should establish backup plan, such as the child, parent, grandparent backup method and record when you make backups. Another way to back up a hard drive is to use disk cloning or disk imaging software and create a copy of the entire hard drive on a different computer.

2 Protecting against Viruses, Trojan Horses, and Worms

A malicious logic program is any program that acts without a user's knowledge, deliberately changes the computer's operations, and does damage to data and software. Antivirus software protects a computer against infection by identifying and removing any malicious logic program. Antivirus software detects a known virus by looking for the virus signature. Five main types of viruses exist: file viruses, macro viruses, boot sector viruses, Master Boot Record viruses, and multipartite viruses. A virus uses techniques to hide from antivirus software by changing its distinguishing characteristics. A Trojan horse is a destructive program disguised as a real application, such as a screen saver. A worm is a malicious logic program that replicates by creating copies of itself, either on one computer or any number of computers on a network. A virus hoax is an e-mail message that spreads a false virus warning. If you suspect your computer has been infected with a virus, Trojan horse, or worm virus, run a virus scan using your antivirus software to detect and delete the malicious logic program.

3 Troubleshooting Tools

An important first step in troubleshooting computer problems is having a toolkit with the appropriate tools, as well as a Class C fire extinguisher. Another very important component of a PC toolkit is a bootable rescue disk for any operating system you need to support. Many utility and diagnostics software tools are available to help you diagnose a problem with a personal computer.

4 Approaches for Troubleshooting a PC

When troubleshooting a PC, fundamental rules involve making backups, approaching a problem systematically, and isolating the problem. Also be sure not to assume the worst — check simple things first, research possible solutions, and know for certain what the problem is before trying to solve the issue. Keep good notes as you work and decide on priorities. Do not rush to fix an issue, and take a break if necessary to help get a fresh start. The first step in troubleshooting your computer is to gather as much information as you can about the problem and then isolate the source of the problem. For intermittent problems, keep a log of when the problems occur and exactly what messages appear.

antivirus software *(516)*
back up *(511)*
boot sector virus *(517)*
child, parent, grandparent backup method *(511)*
computer virus *(516)*
diagnostic software *(527)*
differential backups *(511)*
disk cloning *(514)*
disk imaging *(514)*
encrypting virus *(518)*
file virus *(517)*
full backup *(511)*
incremental backup *(511)*
initialization files *(509)*
inoculate *(524)*
logic bomb *(518)*
macro *(517)*
macro virus *(517)*
malicious logic program *(516)*
malicious software program *(516)*
Master Boot Record (MBR) viruses *(517)*
memory-resident virus *(518)*
multipartite virus *(518)*
non-memory-resident virus *(518)*
payload *(517)*
polymorphic virus *(518)*
polypartite virus *(518)*
quarantine *(524)*
stealth virus *(518)*
time bomb *(518)*
Trojan horse *(519)*
utility software *(526)*
virus definition *(518)*
virus hoax *(521)*
virus signature *(518)*
virus *(516)*
worm *(520)*

KEY TERMS

After reading the chapter, you should know each of these Key Terms.

LEARN IT ONLINE

Reinforce your understanding of the chapter concepts and terms with the Learn It Online exercises.

Instructions: To complete the Learn It Online exercises, start your browser, click the Address bar, and then enter the Web address scsite.com/understanding/learn. When the Understanding and Troubleshooting Your PC Learn It Online page is displayed, follow the instructions in the exercises below. Each exercise has instructions for printing your results, either for your own records or for submission to your instructor.

1 Chapter Reinforcement True/False, Multiple Choice, Short Answer

Below Chapter 12, click the Chapter Reinforcement link. Print the quiz by clicking Print on the File menu for each page. Answer each question.

2 Flash Cards

Below Chapter 12, click the Flash Cards link and read the instructions. Type 20 (or a number specified by your instructor) in the Number of playing cards text box, type your name in the Enter your Name text box, and then click the Flip Card button. When the flash card is displayed, read the question and then click the ANSWER box arrow to select an answer. Flip through Flash Cards. If your score is 15 (75%) correct or greater, click Print on the File menu to print your results. If your score is less than 15 (75%) correct, then redo this exercise by clicking the Replay button.

3 Practice Test

Below Chapter 12, click the Practice Test link. Answer each question, enter your first and last name at the bottom of the page, and then click the Grade Test button. When the graded practice test is displayed on your screen, click Print on the File menu to print a hard copy. Continue to take practice tests until you score 80% or better.

4 Who Wants To Be a Computer Genius?

Below Chapter 12, click the Computer Genius link. Read the instructions, enter your first and last name at the bottom of the page, and then click the PLAY button. When your score is displayed, click the PRINT RESULTS link to print a hard copy.

5 Wheel of Terms

Below Chapter 12, click the Wheel of Terms link. Read the instructions, and then enter your first and last name and your school name. Click the PLAY button. When your score is displayed, right-click the score and then click Print on the shortcut menu to print a hard copy.

6 Crossword Puzzle Challenge

Below Chapter 12, click the Crossword Puzzle Challenge link. Read the instructions, and then enter your first and last name. Click the SUBMIT button. Work the crossword puzzle. When you are finished, click the Submit button. When the crossword puzzle is redisplayed, click the Print Puzzle button to print a hard copy.

Multiple Choice

Select the best answer.

1. If you wanted to back up only files that have changed or been created since the last backup, which type of backup would you perform?
   a. child
   b. normal
   c. incremental
   d. differential
2. A ________ is a malicious logic program that replicates by creating copies of itself, often via e-mail, until it uses up system resources.
   a. Trojan horse
   b. worm
   c. macro virus
   d. polypartite virus
3. On a Windows XP computer, documents and other user-created files should be kept in the ________ folder.
   a. User Documents
   b. root directory
   c. Users
   d. My Documents
4. Which of these items should not be in your PC toolkit with floppy disks and CD-ROMs?
   a. magnetized screwdriver
   b. flat-head screwdriver
   c. tweezers
   d. ground bracelet
5. If you receive an e-mail with an attachment named as follows, which is most likely an infected file?
   a. report.doc
   b. Jan2006profits.xls
   c. name.txt.vbs
   d. logo.jpg

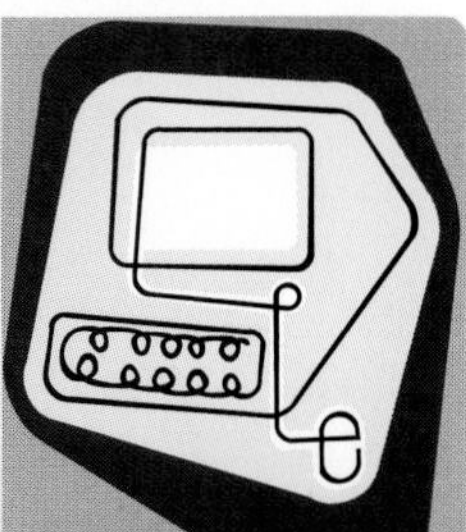

CHAPTER EXERCISES

Complete the Chapter Exercises to solidify what you learned in the chapter.

Fill in the Blank

Write the word or phrase to fill in the blank in each of the following questions.

1. Antivirus software detects a known virus by looking for distinguishing characteristics called a(n) ________, which is a known pattern of virus code.
2. A(n) ________ backup backs up files that have changed or been created since the last full backup.
3. ________ is a program that performs a specific task, usually related to managing system resources or identifying a problem with a PC.
4. A(n) ________, such as PC-Technician, generally is used to identify hardware problems.
5. Having a(n) ________ plan can help prevent computer failures and reduce repair costs and downtime.

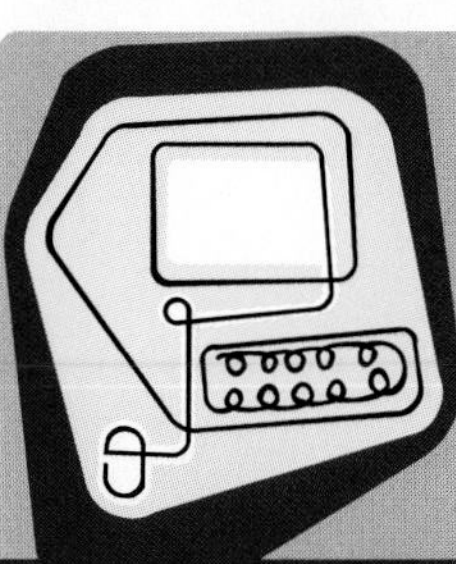

CHAPTER EXERCISES

Complete the Chapter Exercises to solidify what you learned in the chapter.

Matching Terms

Match the terms with their definitions.

________ 1.	Phillips-head	a.	type of screwdriver, rated with a size such as T15
________ 2.	quarantine	b.	program that is activated when a certain condition is detected
________ 3.	malicious logic program	c.	creation of a complete image or copy of a computer's hard drive
________ 4.	logic bomb	d.	type of screwdriver, also called a cross-head
________ 5.	multipartite virus	e.	an area of a hard disk to store an infected file until the infection can be removed
________ 6.	payload	f.	program that acts without a user's knowledge to change computer operations and do damage
________ 7.	3-pronged parts retriever	g.	virus that infects both boot records and program files
________ 8.	macro	h.	a spring-loaded device with three wire prongs to pick up small items
________ 9.	Torx	i.	small program in a document that is executed when the document is loaded or by pressing a key combination
________ 10.	disk cloning	j.	destructive event or prank that a virus is created to deliver

Short Answer Questions

Write a brief answer to each of the following questions.

1. List the five main types of viruses and explain how each of them infects a computer.
2. List at least five safe computing tips you should follow to avoid risk of virus, worm, and Trojan horse infection.
3. Describe the steps you would take to isolate the source of a computer problem.
4. List and describe five important preventive maintenance tasks.
5. Following the fundamental rule that you should trade good for suspected bad to isolate a problem, describe the steps you would take to troubleshoot a problem with the monitor.

APPLY YOUR KNOWLEDGE

Check your understanding of the chapter with the hands-on Apply Your Knowledge exercises.

1 Creating a PC Toolkit

Research the total cost to create a PC toolkit with all of the items listed in the chapter, excluding the bootable rescue disks, utility and diagnostic software, and a Class C fire extinguisher. Be sure to include at least one of each type of screwdriver. If possible, try to find an existing toolkit that includes many of the items you need. As you complete your research, create a word processing document or spreadsheet to list the items in your PC toolkit, the cost of each, and the total cost.

2 Identifying PC Support Resources

The Internet is an excellent source of information on troubleshooting issues with your PC. For each of the following computer issues, use the Internet to find information on various steps to take to resolve the problem. For each problem, write a brief summary of steps suggested by information to fix the issue, and note the URL of the Web site you used to gather the information.

1. The error message, Setup has disabled the upgrade option, could not load the file D:\i386\Win9xupg\W95upg.dll, displays while you are upgrading to Windows XP.
2. The error message, Invalid page fault, displays when you are opening a document in Microsoft Word.
3. The error message, Not Enough Memory to complete this operation, displays when you start Adobe Photoshop.
4. The error message, Invalid drive or drive specification, displays when you start the computer.
5. The error message, 20 Mem Overflow, displays on the printer when you print a large document.

3 Developing Help Desk Skills

Even if you are not employed specifically as a help desk technician, you may be asked to provide support for a friend, family member, or co-worker who recognizes the skills you have in troubleshooting computer problems. To help hone your skills in supporting other computer users, work with a partner who will play the role of the user. Sit with your back to the user, who is in front of the PC, and follow the rules below. Troubleshoot the problem and talk the user through to a solution.

1. A third person created an error so the PC does not boot successfully. Neither you nor your partner knows what the third person did.
2. The user pretends not to have technical insight but to be good at following directions and willing to answer any non-technical questions.
3. Do not turn around to look at the screen.
4. Practice professional mannerisms and speech.
5. As you work, keep a log of any steps you take toward diagnosing and correcting the problem.
6. When the problem is resolved, have the third person create a different problem that causes the PC not to boot correctly, and exchange roles with your partner.

APPLY YOUR KNOWLEDGE

Check your understanding of the chapter with the hands-on Apply Your Knowledge exercises.

4 Preventing Infection from Malicious Logic Programs

Many manufacturers of antivirus software have Web sites that provide detailed information about viruses, Trojan horses, and worms currently infecting computers and list detailed steps for how to clean the infection from your PC. Access one or more of the Web sites listed below and look for virus alerts and other information:

- *www.mcafee.com*
- *www.symantec.com*
- *www.f-prot.com*
- *www.trendmicro.com*

Find three viruses, Trojan horses, or worms that have posed recent threats. For each of these three, list the characteristics of the program, the signs of infection, and how you remove it from your computer.

5 Creating a Preventive Maintenance and Disaster Recovery Plan

Assume that you are a PC technician responsible for all 30 to 35 PCs of a small organization. The PCs are networked to a file server that is backed up each evening. No PC has power protection or line conditioning. Although some users make backups of data on their PC to tape drives or a Zip drive, the company does not have a procedure to back up data or software. Your supervisor asked you to submit a preventive maintenance plan for these PCs, and to estimate the amount of time you will spend on preventive maintenance each month for the next 12 months. She also asked you to submit a suggested PC data backup plan for all users to follow, which will become a company policy. Do the following to create these plans and estimate your time:

1. List the possible causes of PC failures.
2. Using the list you created in Step 1, list what you can do to prevent these problems. Divide the list into two categories: what you plan to do one time for each PC or user and what you plan to do on a routine or as-needed basis.
3. For each PC, estimate the amount of time you need to implement the one-time-only plan and the amount of time you need each year for ongoing maintenance.
4. Based on your answers to Question 3, how much time do you plan to spend on preventive maintenance, on average, each month for the next 12 months?
5. In response to the request for a recommended company policy to back up all PC data, write a policy for users to follow to back up data on their PCs. Because all PCs are networked to the file server, suggest that company policy require data on a PC to be backed up to the file server, where it will be backed up nightly in case of a file server failure. Write the backup policy and instructions on how to implement it.

APPENDIX A

Error Messages and Their Meanings

General Error Messages

Figure A-1 lists common error messages and their meanings, which can help you when you are diagnosing computer problems. For other error messages, consult your motherboard or computer documentation or use a search engine to search for the error message on the Internet.

Error Message	Meaning of the Error Message
• Invalid partition table • Error loading operating system • Missing operating system • Invalid boot disk • Inaccessible boot device	The Master Boot program at the beginning of the hard drive displays these messages when it cannot find the active partition on the hard drive or the boot record on that partition. Use Diskpart or Fdisk to examine the drive for errors. Check the hard drive manufacturer's Web site for other diagnostic software.
• Missing operating system, error loading operating system corruption.	The MBR is unable to locate or read the OS boot sector on the active partition. Boot from a bootable floppy and examine the hard drive file system for
• Bad sector writing or reading to drive	Sector markings on the disk may be fading. Try running ScanDisk or reformatting the disk.
• Configuration/CMOS error	CMOS setup information does not agree with the actual hardware the computer found during boot. May be caused by a bad or weak battery or by changing hardware without changing setup. Check CMOS setup for errors.
• Hard drive not found	The operating system cannot locate the hard drive, or the controller card is not responding.
• Fixed disk error	The PC cannot find the hard drive that CMOS setup told it to expect. Check cables, connections, power supply, and CMOS setup information.
• Invalid drive specification	The PC is unable to find a hard drive or a floppy drive that CMOS setup tells it to expect. Look for errors in setup or for a corrupted partition table on the hard drive.
• No boot device available	The hard drive is not formatted or the format is corrupted. Boot from a bootable disk and examine your hard drive for corruption.
• Non-system disk or disk error • Bad or missing Command.com • No operating system found	The disk in drive A is not bootable. Remove the disk in drive A and boot from the hard drive. If no disk is in drive A, command.com on drive C might have been erased, or the path could not be found.
• Not ready reading drive A: Abort, Retry, Fail?	The disk in drive A is missing, is not formatted, or is corrupted. Try another disk or remove the disk to boot from the hard drive.

(continued)

Error Message	Meaning of the Error Message
• Bad command or file not found	The OS command that was just executed cannot be interpreted, or the OS cannot find the program file specified in the command line. Check the spelling of the filename.
• Write-protect error writing drive A:	The disk in drive A is protected. Let the computer write to the disk by setting the switch on a 3½-inch disk.
• Track 0 bad, disk not usable	This usually occurs when you attempt to format a floppy disk using the wrong format type. Check the disk type and compare it with the type specified in the format command.
• Device not found	Errors in System.ini, Win.ini, or the registry. Look for references to devices or attempts to load device drivers. Use Device Manager to delete a device or edit System.ini or Win.ini.
• Device/Service has failed to start	A hardware device or driver necessary to run the device or critical software utility is causing problems. This type of problem is best handled using OS troubleshooting methods and tools.
• Error in Config.sys line xx	A problem has occurred when loading a device driver or with the syntax of a command line. Check the command line for errors. Verify that the driver files are in the right directory. Reinstall the driver files, if necessary.
• Insufficient memory	This error happens during or after the boot under Windows when too many applications are open. Close some applications. Also consider rebooting the system to clear items in memory.

Figure A-1 Common error messages and their meanings.

BIOS Beep Codes, Numeric Codes, and Error Messages

During the boot process, the BIOS performs a power-on self test (POST) to check that all of the system's hardware components are working properly. If an error occurs, BIOS will attempt to issue a beep code representing the error, and it also will attempt to display the error code on the screen. If BIOS detects an error before it can access the video card, it will use a series of beeps to indicate the type of error it has detected. If it can access the video card, BIOS usually also will display an error code or message on the screen.

> **More About**
>
> **BIOS Error Codes and Messages**
>
> To learn more about BIOS error codes and messages, including a list of online resources, visit the Understanding and Troubleshooting Your PC More About Web page (**scsite.com/understanding/more**) and then click BIOS Error Codes and Messages below Appendix A.

Beep Codes

Different BIOSs use different beep code patterns, so you first must know which BIOS your computer uses before you can determine the meaning behind the beep codes. The beep codes of the most commonly used BIOSs — AMI (American Megatrends, Inc) BIOS, PhoenixBIOS, and AwardBIOS — are explained in the following sections. For specific beep codes for your motherboard, visit the Web site of the motherboard or BIOS manufacturer (Figure A-2). The Web site BIOS Central also is an excellent resource for information on BIOSs from a wide range of manufacturers.

BIOS	Manufacturer Web Site
All BIOSs	*www.bioscentral.com*
AMI BIOS	*www.ami.com*
AwardBIOS and PhoenixBIOS	*www.phoenix.com*
Compaq or HP	*www.hp.com*
Dell	*www.dell.com*
IBM	*www.ibm.com*
Gateway	*www.gateway.com*

Figure A-2 Online resources for BIOS information.

AMI BIOS Beep Codes The AMI BIOS, which is one of the most widely used BIOSs, uses a consistent pattern of beep codes for its many different versions, as shown in Figure A-3. For more on AMI beep codes, visit the American Megatrends Web site (*www.ami.com*) or review your motherboard's documentation.

Number of Beeps	Description	Troubleshooting Recommendation
1	Memory refresh timer error. The system is having trouble accessing system memory to refresh it.	Reseat the memory module or replace faulty memory modules with good memory modules.
2	Parity error. The parity circuit -- which is responsible for generating and checking the parity bit on the system memory -- is not working properly	
3	Main memory read/write test error. First bank of memory may have bad memory chip; also possibly related to failure of motherboard or a system device.	
4	Motherboard timer not operational. A problem with one or more of the timers used by the system to control functions on the motherboard or a malfunctioning expansion card.	To determine source of issue, remove all expansion cards except the video adapter. If the beep codes do not occur when the expansion cards are removed, one of the cards is causing the malfunction. Insert the cards back into the system one at a time until the problem happens again. This will reveal the malfunctioning expansion card. If the beep codes occur when all other expansion cards are absent, the motherboard has a serious problem. Consult your system manufacturer.
5	Processor error. A problem related to the processor or motherboard or a malfunctioning expansion card.	
6	Keyboard controller (Gate A20) error. The keyboard controller is a chip on the motherboard that communicates with the keyboard. Error indicates a problem with either the keyboard or the motherboard.	Reseat keyboard controller chip, replace keyboard controller chip, check for a keyboard fuse, or try a different keyboard.

(continued)

Number of Beeps	Description	Troubleshooting Recommendation
7	General exception error. A problem related to the processor or motherboard.	Fatal error indicating a serious problem with the system, possibly the motherboard. See Troubleshooting Recommendation for four beeps for additional details.
8	Display memory error. Usually caused by a problem with the video card or the memory on the video card; also can be a motherboard issue. Unlike the other AMI beep codes, the system may continue to boot despite this error.	If the system video adapter is an expansion card, replace reseat the video adapter. If the video adapter is an integrated part of the system board, the board may be faulty.
9	ROM checksum error. ROM containing the BIOS program uses a checksum value to compare against the checksum value in ROM each time the PC is booted. If the checksums do not match, this code is generated.	Fatal error indicating a serious problem with the system, possibly the motherboard, or a malfunctioning expansion card. See the Troubleshooting Recommendation for four beeps for additional details.
10	CMOS shutdown register read/write error. A problem related to the processor or motherboard, usually involving a component of the motherboard that is producing an error while interacting with the CMOS memory that holds the BIOS settings.	

Figure A-3 AMI BIOS beep codes.

PhoenixBIOS Beep Codes PhoenixBIOS has a relatively complex set of beep codes. In fact, in the newer versions of PhoenixBIOS, almost every POST function has an associated beep code. PhoenixBIOS uses groups of beeps followed by a short pause to represent errors. The older PhoenixBIOS Plus and PhoenixBIOS 1.x systems use three groups of beeps — for example, two beeps, followed by two beeps, and then three beeps, which is written as 2-2-3. Newer versions, such as PhoenixBIOS 4.x, use four groups of beeps (for example, 3-2-1-3). Figure A-4 lists several of the more than 100 beep codes used by newer versions of PhoenixBIOS. For a complete list of PhoenixBIOS POST beep codes, visit the Phoenix Technologies Web site www.phoenix.com) or review your motherboard's documentation.

Number of Beeps	Description	Troubleshooting Recommendation
1	One short beep before boot Normal operation	n/a
1-1-1-3	Verify real mode	A problem exists with the CPU and/or motherboard. Check and replace if necessary.
1-1-2-1	Get CPU type	A problem exists with the CPU and/or motherboard. Check and replace if necessary.
1-1-2-3	Initialize system hardware	A problem exists with the motherboard. Check and replace if necessary.
1-1-3-1	Initialize chipset with initial POST values	A problem exists with the motherboard. Check and replace if necessary.
		(continued)

Number of Beeps	Description	Troubleshooting Recommendation
1-1-3-2	Set IN POST flag	A problem exists with the motherboard. Check and replace if necessary.
1-1-3-3	Initialize CPU registers	A problem exists with the CPU and/or motherboard. Check and replace if necessary.
1-1-4-3	Initialize I/O component	A problem exists with the I/O port hardware or a device connected to an I/O port. The problem also could be an expansion device in the PC or the motherboard.
1-2-2-1	Initialize keyboard controller	An error has occurred with the keyboard or keyboard controller. Try a new keyboard or replace the keyboard controller on the motherboard.
1-2-2-3	BIOS ROM checksum	Replace either the BIOS ROM chip or the motherboard.
1-2-3-3	8237 DMA controller initialization	Check the motherboard and any expansion cards that use DMA.
1-3-1-1	Test DRAM refresh	Check the first bank of memory and the motherboard.
1-3-1-3	Test 8742 keyboard controller	An error has occurred with the keyboard or keyboard controller. Try a new keyboard or replace the keyboard controller on the motherboard.
1-3-4-1	RAM failure on line xxxx	Check the first bank of memory and the motherboard.
1-3-4-3	RAM failure on data bits xxxx of low byte memory bus	Check the first bank of memory and the motherboard.
2-1-3-1	Check video configuration against CMOS	Check the video card or video card memory.
2-1-3-2	Initialize PCI bus and devices	A problem exists with the I/O port hardware or a device connected to an I/O port. It also could be an expansion device in the PC or the motherboard.
2-2-1-3	Test keyboard	An error has occurred with the keyboard or keyboard controller. Try a new keyboard or replace the keyboard controller on the motherboard.
2-2-3-1	Test for unexpected interrupts	Check for a faulty motherboard or expansion card.
3-1-2-1	Detect and install external parallel ports	A problem exists with the I/O port hardware or a device connected to an I/O port. The problem also could be an expansion device in the PC or the motherboard.
3-1-4-1	Initialize floppy controller	Check your hard drive(s), floppy drive(s), and motherboard.
3-2-1-1	Initialize hard-disk controllers	Check your hard drive(s), floppy drive(s), and motherboard.

(continued)

Number of Beeps	Description	Troubleshooting Recommendation
3-2-1-2	Initialize local-bus hard-disk controllers	Check your hard drive(s), floppy drive(s), and motherboard.
3-3-1-1	Set time of day	Check the motherboard's real-time clock (RTC).
4-2-4-3	Keyboard controller failure	An error has occurred with the keyboard or keyboard controller. Try a new keyboard or replace the keyboard controller on the motherboard.

Figure A-4 PhoenixBIOS beep codes.

AwardBIOS Beep Codes AwardBIOS uses very few beep codes; it instead displays written error messages on the system screen or monitor. As shown in Figure A-5, the only defined AwardBIOS beep code — a single long beep followed by two short beeps — indicates that a video error has occurred and the BIOS cannot initialize the system video monitor to display any error messages. Any other beeps may indicate a memory issue. For more on AwardBIOS beep codes, visit the Phoenix Technologies Web site (*www.phoenix.com*).

Number of Beeps	Description	Troubleshooting Recommendation
1 long and 2 short	Video error	Check the video card.
Any other beeps	Memory issue	Reseat the RAM or replace with known good chips.

Figure A-5 AwardBIOS beep codes.

On-Screen Error Messages During POST If the computer can access the video card before encountering an error, BIOS will display an error message on screen. The error messages that display can be text error messages and/or numeric codes. Figure A-6, for example, shows the error messages and related numeric codes used by several IBM systems, including the Aptiva, NetVista, and PC300.

Numeric Code	Error Message	Troubleshooting Recommendation
161	CMOS battery failed	Load default settings in Setup and reboot the system. Replace the CMOS battery.
162	CMOS checksum error	Make sure the equipment (diskette drive, hard disk drive, keyboard, mouse, etc.) are connected properly and are set correctly in BIOS Setup. Load default settings in setup. CMOS battery should be replaced.
164	Memory size error	Make sure the DIMMs are inserted properly.

(continued)

Numeric Code	Error Message	Troubleshooting Recommendation
201	Memory test failure	Insert the memory modules in the DIMM sockets properly, then reboot the system. If needed, replace memory module.
301	Keyboard error or no keyboard present	Make sure the keyboard is connected properly and is set correctly in CMOS setup.
662	FLOPPY DISK(S) failure (80)	Unable to reset floppy subsystem.
662	FLOPPY DISK(S) failure (40)	Floppy type mismatch.
1701	Hard disk(s) Diagnosis failure	Make sure the hard disks are set correctly in CMOS setup. Check the hard disk drive cable and connection. If needed, replace the hard drive.
1762	Primary master IDE has changed Primary slave IDE has changed Secondary master IDE has changed Secondary slave IDE has changed	Make sure that the System Boot Drive parameter in the Startup Options of CMOS setup is not set to [Drive A only]. If needed, load default settings in Setup. Insert a boot disk into drive A and reboot system.
1780 1781	Primary master hard disk failure Primary slave hard disk failure	A warning message to indicate there has been a change of IDE Primary (Secondary) Channel Master (Slave) device. Load default settings in CMOS setup. Check IDE drive jumper, the power connection, and the drive cable and connections. If needed, replace the hard drive.
1782 1783	Secondary master hard disk failure Secondary slave hard disk failure	A warning message to indicate there has been a change of IDE Primary (Secondary) Channel Master (Slave) device. Load default settings in Setup. Check IDE drive jumper, the power connection, and the drive cable and connections. If needed, replace the hard drive.
8602	Mouse error or no Mouse present	Make sure the mouse is connected properly and is set correctly in CMOS setup.

Figure A-6 Error messages and related numeric codes used by IBM systems, such as the Aptiva, NetVista, and PC300.

Because beep codes, numeric codes, and on-screen error messages vary a great deal by BIOS vendor and version, first be sure you know what BIOS a system is running and then reference the system documentation or the manufacturer's Web site for a list of what the beep codes, numeric codes, and on-screen error messages mean for that specific system.

intel
pentium 4

APPENDIX B

Using the Command Prompt

The Command Prompt

As you have learned, MS-DOS (Microsoft Disk Operating System) was developed by Microsoft and was the first operating system used for IBM and IBM-compatible computers. MS-DOS, which often is called just DOS, is based entirely on a command-line interface, where the user has to key in specific commands, instead of the graphical user interface (GUI) of the Windows and Macintosh operating systems. MS-DOS was widely used after it was developed in the early 1980s. It is used significantly less today, because graphical interfaces are easier to use and allows a user to accomplish almost any task.

Even with so many improvements to the graphical user interface, you still can complete many important tasks using the command-line interface. In fact, many system and network administrators still rely on DOS to manage and troubleshoot systems. Thus, most Windows operating systems continue to support many of the original DOS commands, as well as new commands to help you complete tasks, run applications, and manage your computer.

In some cases, the command-line tools available from DOS perform essentially the same functions as a GUI tool available in Windows XP. The Disk Defragmenter utility and the defrag command, for example, provide very similar functions with different user interfaces. In others, the command-line tools provide additional functionality and control that are not available via the GUI. For example, entering the diskpart command launches the DiskPart utility in the command shell. The command-line version of the DiskPart utility, which is used to manage disk partitions, provides functionality not available in the GUI version of Disk Administrator.

With Windows XP, you enter commands via the command shell, which displays a command prompt. The *command shell* is a software program with a non-graphical, command-line interface. It allows you to communicate directly with the operating system and provides the environment in which you run text-based applications and utilities. The file name for the command shell is Cmd.exe. When you run Cmd.exe, the Command Prompt window is displayed.

You can enter commands in the Command Prompt window to perform many tasks, such as managing files and folders, performing utility tasks, and troubleshooting a failed system. Many commands outlined in this appendix also work at the command prompt that displays when you start the Recovery Console.

Accessing the Command Prompt Window

Using Windows XP, you can open the Command Prompt window using two different methods.

- Click the Start button, point to All Programs on the Start menu, point to Accessories on the All Programs submenu, and then click Command Prompt.
- Click the Start button and then click Run on the Start menu. When the Run dialog box is displayed, enter `cmd` in the Open text box.

After completing one of these methods, the Command Prompt window appears, as shown in Figure B-1. To exit the window, type `exit` at the command prompt and then press the ENTER key.

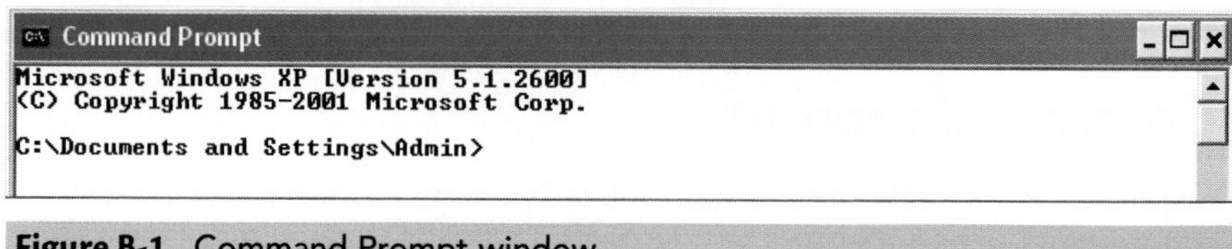

Figure B-1 Command Prompt window.

You also can create a shortcut to the Command Prompt window to make it easier to access by performing the following steps:

1. Click the Start button, point to All Programs on the Start menu, point to Accessories on the All Programs submenu, and then right-click Command Prompt.
2. On the shortcut menu, point to Send To and then click Desktop (create shortcut) on the Send To submenu.

Windows creates a shortcut to the Command Prompt window on the Windows desktop (Figure B-2).

Figure B-2 Shortcut to the Command Prompt window on the Windows desktop.

Entering Commands

To enter commands in the Command Prompt window, type one command per line and then press the ENTER key to execute the command. Most commands allow you to enter one or more *options*, or *arguments*, which are parameters for that command. Many commands display a list of possible options when you type the command at the command prompt followed by `/?`, as shown in Figure B-3. Finally, to close the command shell window, type `exit` and then press the ENTER key.

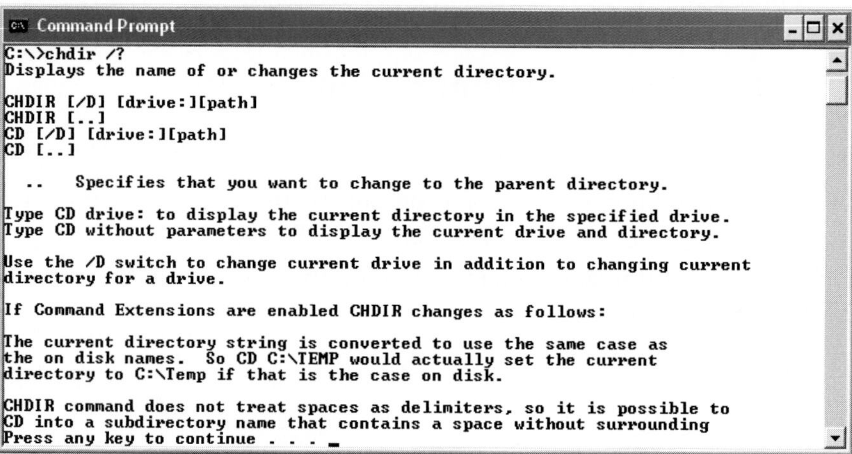

Figure B-3 Many commands display a list of possible options when you type the command at the command prompt followed by /?.

Changing the Directory

When you first open the Command Prompt window, the command prompt provides information about the current drive and directory. For example, when you open the Command Prompt window, the current drive and directory is C:\Documents and Settings*username*. You can change the current drive or directory using the chdir or cd command. For example, `chdir c:\` or `cd c:\` changes the directory to the root directory on drive C. (Remember that DOS and Windows commands are not case sensitive, so you can enter CD, Cd, or cd.) After you enter the command, the command prompt changes to `C:\>`. The > symbol indicates that you can enter a new command (Figure B-4).

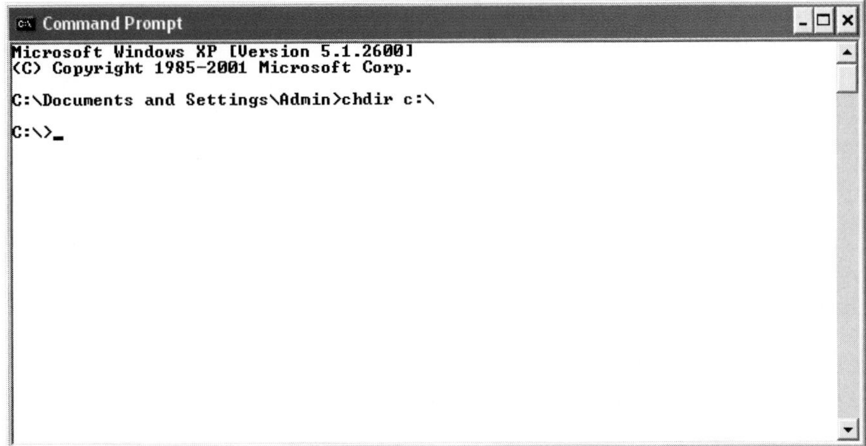

Figure B-4 Executing the chdir command in the Command Prompt window.

More About

Using the Command Prompt Window

To learn more about customizing the Command Prompt window and accessing it using other versions of Windows, visit the Understanding and Troubleshooting Your PC More About Web page (**scsite.com/understanding/more**) and then click Using the Command Prompt Window below Appendix B.

Executing a Program

In Chapter 2, you learned several different ways to start a program, one of which involved using the Command Prompt window. When you type a single group of letters with no spaces at the command prompt, the OS assumes that you typed the filename of a program file that you want to execute. The OS attempts to find the program file by that name in the current directory, copies the file into RAM, and then executes the program.

As an example, the executable file for Internet Explorer (iexplore.exe) is stored on the hard drive in the C:\Program Files\Internet Explorer folder. You can start Internet Explorer from the Command Prompt window using the following steps:

1. Open the Command Prompt window.
2. Enter `chdir c:\Program Files\Internet Explorer` at the command prompt. Windows changes the current directory to the Program Files\Internet Explorer folder on drive C.

3. Enter `iexplore` at the command prompt (Figure B-5a).
4. Press the ENTER key.

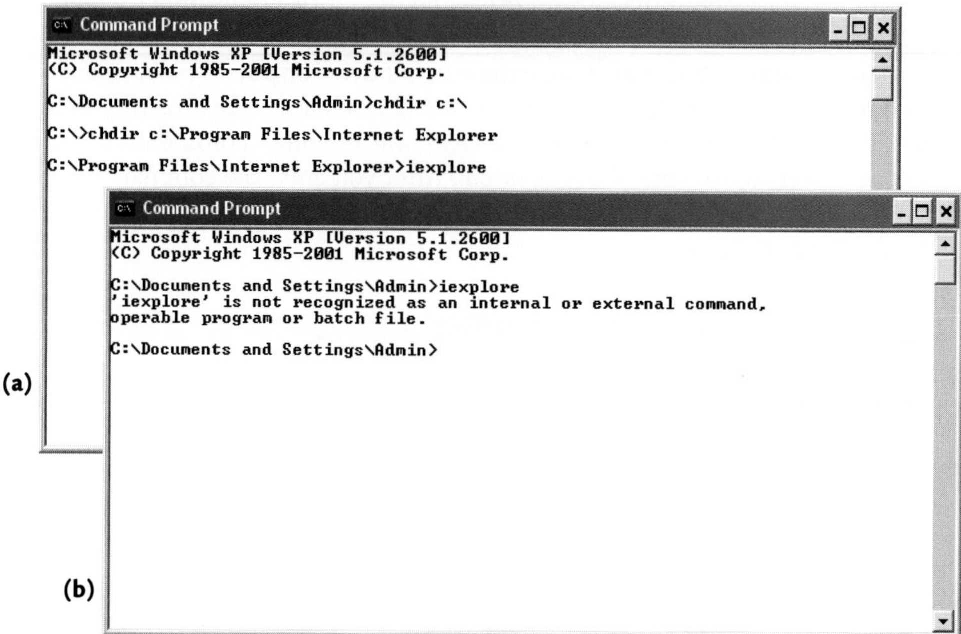

Figure B-5 (a) Be sure to change to the directory where the program file is located, before executing a program file. (b) If you do not, an error message displays in the Command Prompt window.

Windows looks in C:\Program Files\Internet Explorer for a file named iexplore with an extension of .com, .sys, .bat, or .exe, which are the file extensions that the OS recognizes for program files. In this case, it locates iexplore.exe and executes the file, which starts Internet Explorer. Note that you also can type the specific extension in the command. For example, entering `iexplore.exe` at the command prompt also would start Internet Explorer.

Before executing the program file, be sure to change the current directory to the directory where the program file is located. If you type `iexplore` at the command prompt without changing the directory, the OS displays an error message to indicate that it cannot find the program to execute (Figure B-5b).

Using Wildcards

A wildcard is a character that stands for another character in a command line prompt. The question mark (?) is a wildcard for one character, and the asterisk (*) is a wildcard for more than one character. For example, if you want to find all files in a directory that start with the letter a and have a three-letter file extension, you would use the following command:

```
dir a*.???
```

Copying Text from the Command Prompt Window

You may want to copy text displayed in the Command Prompt window to paste into a document for future reference or to e-mail to share with support personnel. To copy text displayed in the Command Prompt window, perform the following steps:

- Right-click the Command Prompt window title bar, point to Edit on the shortcut menu, and then click Mark.
- Click the beginning of the text you want to copy.
- Press and hold down the SHIFT key and then click the end of the text you want to copy.
- Right-click the Command Prompt window title bar, point to Edit on the shortcut menu, and then click Copy.
- Open a document or other file and then paste the copied text. For example, in Microsoft Word, click Edit on the menu bar and then click Paste on the Edit menu.

Using Commands in the Command Prompt Window

As you have learned throughout this book, many commands are available to allow you to manage files, maintain the hard drive, gather system information, and more. Figure B-6 lists a number of commands available for use in the Command Prompt window.

COMMAND	DESCRIPTION
attrib	Changes the attributes of a file or folder. For example, `attrib -r -h -s –c` *`filename`* clears the read, hidden, system, and compressed file attributes from the file.
batch	Carries out commands stored in a batch file. For example, `batch file1 file2` executes the commands stored in file1, and the results are written to file2. If no file2 is specified, results are written to the screen.
bootcfg	Used for boot configuration and recovery. For example, `bootcfg /default` sets the default boot entry; `bootcfg /add` adds a Windows installation to the boot list; and `bootcfg /rebuild` allows a user to choose which Windows installation to add.
chdir	Displays or changes the current directory. For example, `chdir c:\windows` or `cd c:\windows` changes the directory to the Windows folder on the root drive.
chkdsk	Checks a disk and repairs or recovers the data.
chkntfs	Displays or specifies whether automatic system checking is scheduled to be run on a FAT, FAT32, or NTFS volume when the computer is started.
cipher	Displays or alters the encryption of folders and files on NTFS volumes. Used without parameters, `cipher` displays the encryption state of the current folder and any files it contains.
cls	Clears the screen.
cmd	Starts a new instance of the command interpreter, Cmd.exe. Used without parameters, `cmd` displays Windows XP version and copyright information.

(continued)

COMMAND	DESCRIPTION
color	Changes the Command Prompt window foreground and background colors for the current session. Used without parameters, `color` restores the default Command Prompt window foreground and background colors.
comp	Compares the contents of two files or sets of files byte by byte. The `comp` command can compare files on the same drive or on different drives, and in the same directory or in different directories. When comp compares the files, it displays their locations and file names. Used without parameters, `comp` prompts you to enter the files to compare.
compact	Displays and alters the compression of files or directories on NTFS partitions. Used without parameters, `compact` displays the compression state of the current directory.
convert	Converts FAT and FAT32 volumes to NTFS.
copy	Copies a single uncompressed file. For example, `copy a:\file1 c:\winnt\file2` copies the file named File1 on the floppy disk to the hard drive's Windows folder, naming the file File2. Use the command to replace corrupted files.
date	Displays the current system date setting. Used without parameters, `date` displays the current system date setting and prompts you to type a new date.
defrag	Locates and consolidates fragmented boot files, data files, and folders on local volumes.
del	Deletes a file in the current directory. For example, `delete file1` or `del file1` deletes file1.
dir	Lists files and folders.
diskcopy	Copies the contents of the floppy disk in the source drive to a formatted or unformatted floppy disk in the destination drive. Used without parameters, `diskcopy` uses the current drive for the source disk and the destination disk.
diskpart	Creates and deletes partitions on the hard drive. To display a command-based version of diskpart, enter the command with no parameters.
driverquery	Displays a list of drivers and their properties.
exit	Exits the current batch script or the cmd.exe program (that is, the Command Prompt window) and returns to the program that started cmd.exe or to the Program Manager.
expand	Expands a compressed file and copies it from a floppy disk or a CD to the destination folder. For example, `expand a:\file1 c:\windows` expands the file on the floppy disk and copies it to the hard drive. This command is used to retrieve compressed files from distribution disks.
fc	Compares two files and displays the differences between them.
find	Searches for a specific string of text in a file or files. After searching the specified file or files, find displays any lines of text that contain the specified string.
findstr	Searches for patterns of text in files using regular expressions.
format	Formats a logical drive. If no file system is specified, NTFS is assumed. Enter `format c:/fs:FAT32` to use the FAT32 file system. Enter `format c:/fs:FAT` to use the FAT16 file system.
fsutil	A command-line utility that can perform many FAT and NTFS file system related tasks. Because `fsutil` is quite powerful, it only should be used by advanced users who have a thorough knowledge of Windows XP. In addition, you must be logged on as an administrator or a member of the Administrators group in order to use this command.
ftp	Transfers files to and from a computer running a File Transfer Protocol (FTP) server service such as Internet Information Services.

(continued)

COMMAND	DESCRIPTION
ftype	Displays or modifies file types used in file name extension associations. Used without parameters, `ftype` displays the file types that have open command strings defined.
getmac	Returns the media access control (MAC) address and list of network protocols associated with each address for all network cards in each computer, either locally or across a network.
help	Provides online information about system commands (that is, non-network commands). Used without parameters, `help` lists and briefly describes every system command.
helpctr	Starts Help and Support Center. Used without parameters, `helpctr` displays the Help and Support Center home page.
hostname	Displays the host name portion of the full computer name of the computer.
ipconfig	Displays all current TCP/IP network configuration values and refreshes Dynamic Host Configuration Protocol (DHCP) and Domain Name System (DNS) settings. Used without parameters, `ipconfig` displays the IP address, subnet mask, and default gateway for all adapters.
label	Creates, changes, or deletes the volume label (that is, the name) of a disk. Used without parameters, `label` changes the current volume label or deletes the existing label.
mkdir (md)	Creates a directory. For example, `mkdir c:\temp` creates a directory named temp on drive C.
mmc	Opens Microsoft Management Console (MMC). Using the `mmc` command-line options, you can open a specific MMC console, open MMC in author mode, or specify that the 32-bit or 64-bit version of MMC is opened.
mode	Displays system status, changes system settings, or reconfigures ports or devices. Used without parameters, `mode` displays all the controllable attributes of the console and the available COM devices. Because you can use `mode` to perform many different tasks, the syntax used to carry out each task is different. Click the task that you want to perform.
more	Displays the contents of a text file on screen. The user can view the content but not modify it. For example, the command `more C:\Documents and Settings\`*`username`*`\My Documents \filename.txt` will display the contents of filename.txt.
move	Moves one or more files from one directory to the specified directory.
msiexec	Provides the means to install, modify, and perform operations on Windows Installer from the command line.
msinfo32	Displays a comprehensive view of hardware, system components, and software environment.
nbtstat	Displays NetBIOS over TCP/IP (NetBT) protocol statistics, NetBIOS name tables for both the local computer and remote computers, and the NetBIOS name cache. Used without parameters, `nbtstat` displays help.
nslookup	Displays information that can be used to diagnose Domain Name System (DNS) infrastructure. Before using this tool, you should be familiar with how DNS works. The `nslookup` command-line tool is available only if the TCP/IP protocol has been installed.
ntbackup	Performs backup operations at a command prompt or from a batch file using the `ntbackup` command, followed by various parameters.
openfiles	Queries or displays open files. Also queries, displays, or disconnects files opened by network users.
pagefileconfig	Enables an administrator to display and configure a system's paging file virtual memory settings.
perfmon	Allows you to open a Windows XP Performance console configured with settings files from Windows NT 4.0 version of Performance Monitor.

(continued)

COMMAND	DESCRIPTION
ping	Verifies IP-level connectivity to another TCP/IP computer by sending Internet Control Message Protocol (ICMP) Echo Request messages. The receipt of corresponding Echo Reply messages is displayed, along with round-trip times. The command `ping` is the primary TCP/IP command used to troubleshoot connectivity, reachability, and name resolution. Used without parameters, `ping` displays help for the command.
print	Sends a text file to a printer.
prncnfg	Configures or displays configuration information about a printer.
prndrvr	Adds, deletes, and lists printer drivers.
prnjobs	Pauses, resumes, cancels, and lists print jobs.
prnmngr	Adds, deletes, and lists printers or printer connections, in addition to setting and displaying the default printer.
prnport	Creates, deletes, and lists standard TCP/IP printer ports, in addition to displaying and changing port configuration.
prnqctl	Prints a test page, pauses or resumes a printer, and clears a printer queue.
prompt	Changes the cmd.exe prompt. Used without parameters, prompt resets the command prompt to the default setting, the current drive letter followed by the current directory and a greater-than symbol (>).
recover	Recovers readable information from a bad or defective disk.
reg	Adds, changes, and displays registry subkey information and values in registry entries.
regsvr32	Registers .dll files as command components in the registry.
relog	Extracts performance counters from performance counter logs into other formats, such as text-TSV (for tab-delimited text), text-CSV (for comma-delimited text), binary-BIN, or SQL.
rename	Renames a file. For example, `rename file1.txt file2.txt` changes the name of file1.txt to file2.txt.
replace	Replaces files in the destination directory with files in the source directory that have the same name. You also can use replace to add unique file names to the destination directory.
rmdir	Removes (that is, deletes) a directory.
route	Displays and modifies the entries in the local IP routing table. Used without parameters, `route` displays help for the command.
schtasks	Schedules commands and programs to run periodically or at a specific time. Adds and removes tasks from the schedule, starts and stops tasks on demand, and displays and changes scheduled tasks.
shutdown	Shuts down or restarts your computer, or enables an administrator to shut down or restart a remote computer.
sort	Reads input, sorts data, and writes the results to the screen, a file, or another device.
start	Starts a separate Command Prompt window to run a specified program or command. Used without parameters, `start` opens a second command prompt window.
systeminfo	Displays basic system configuration information, such as the system type, the processor type, time zone, virtual memory settings, and more.
system file checker (sfc)	Scans and verifies the versions of all protected system files after you restart your computer.
taskkill	Ends one or more tasks or processes. Processes can be killed by process ID or image name.

(continued)

COMMAND	DESCRIPTION
tasklist	Displays a list of applications and services with their Process ID (PID) for all tasks running on either a local or a remote computer.
telnet	Allows you to communicate with a remote computer that is using the Telnet protocol. You can run `telnet` without parameters in order to enter the `telnet` context, indicated by the `telnet` prompt (`telnet>`).
time	Displays or sets the system time. Used without parameters, `time` displays the system time and prompts you to enter a new time.
title	Creates a title for the command prompt window.
tracert	Determines the path taken to a destination by sending Internet Control Message Protocol (ICMP) Echo Request messages to the destination with incrementally increasing Time to Live (TTL) field values.
tree	Graphically displays the directory structure of a path or of the disk in a drive.
type	Displays the contents of a text file on screen. The user can view the content but not modify it. For example, the command `type c:\Documents and Settings\`*`username`*`\My Documents\filename.txt` displays the contents of filename.txt.
ver	Displays the Windows XP version number.
vol	Displays the disk volume label and serial number, if they exist. A serial number is displayed for a disk formatted with MS-DOS version 4.0 or later.
w32tm	A tool used to diagnose problems occurring with Windows Time.
winnt	Performs an installation of, or upgrade to, Windows XP. If you have hardware that is compatible with Windows XP, you can run `winnt` at a Windows 3.x or MS-DOS command prompt.
winnt32	Performs an installation of, or upgrade to, Windows XP. You can run `winnt32` at the command prompt on a computer running Windows 95, Windows 98, Windows Millennium Edition, Windows NT, Windows 2000, or Windows XP.
xcopy	Copies files and directories, including subdirectories.

Figure B-6 Several commands available for use in the Windows XP Command Prompt window. Many of these commands use options or parameters to allow you to complete additional tasks. For a complete list, visit the Microsoft Web site (*www.microsoft.com*).

To view a list of available commands you can use in the Command Prompt window, enter `help` at the command prompt. To view a list of the options most often used with a command-line tool, along with a description of each option, enter the command name followed by `/?`. For example, to get help about the Defrag utility, enter `defrag /?` in the Command Prompt window. You also can enter the command name in the Help and Support window available in Windows XP.

The sections on the following pages provide more detail about commonly used commands, along with examples of how they are used. The commands listed here are just some of the many commands Windows XP supports to help you manage and maintain your computer. The Microsoft Web site includes additional information about the command shell, including a command-line reference that lists the wide range of commands supported by Windows XP.

Dir

The dir command lists files and folders (directories) in the current or specified directory. Some examples are:

`dir c:\windows`	Lists all folders in the windows folder on drive C
`dir /p`	Lists one screen at a time
`dir /w`	Use wide format, where details are omitted and files and folders are listed in columns on the screen
`dir *.txt`	Use a wildcard character
`dir myfile.txt`	Check that a single file is present

Type

The type command displays the contents of a text file on your screen. Some examples are:

`type myfile.txt`	Displays file contents
`type myfile.txt >prn`	Redirects output to printer
`type myfile.txt |more`	Displays output one screen at a time

Del or Erase

The del or erase command erases files or groups of files. If the command does not include drive and directory information, like the following examples, the OS uses the default drive and directory when executing the command. Some examples are:

`c:\>erase c:\docs\*.*`	Erases all files in the c:\docs directory
`c:\downloads>del *.*`	Erases all files in the current default directory
`c:\downloads>del *.`	Erases all files in the current directory that have no file extension
`c:\>del myfile.txt`	Erases the file named myfile.txt, which is stored on drive C

Copy

The copy command copies a single file or group of files. The original files are not altered. Some examples are:

The copy command copies a single file or group of files. The original files are not altered. Some examples are:

`c:\>copy`
`c:\downloads\X23prndrv.zip`
`d:\files\WinXPprint.zip`
	Copies the file X23prndrv.zip from the C:\downloads directory to a file named WinXPprint.zip in D:\files directory. The drive, path, and filename of the source file immediately follow the Copy command. The drive, path, and

	filename of the destination file follow the source filename. If you do not specify the filename of the copy, the OS assigns the file's original name. If you omit the drive or path of the source or the destination, then the OS uses the current default drive and path.
`c:\>copy myfile.txt a:`	Copies the file myfile.txt from the root directory of drive C to drive A. Because the command does not include a drive or path before the filename myfile.txt, the OS assumes that the file is in the default drive and path.
`c:\>copy c:\docs\*.* a:`	Copies all files in the c:\docs directory to the floppy disk in drive A.
`c:\windows>copy system.ini system.bak`	Makes a backup file named system.bak of the system.ini file in the \windows directory of the hard drive. If you use the copy command to duplicate multiple files, the files are assigned the names of the original files. When you duplicate multiple files, the destination portion of the command line cannot include a filename.

Note that, when you are trying to recover a corrupted file, you can sometimes use the copy command to copy the file to new media, such as from the hard drive to a floppy disk. During the copying process, if the copy command reports a bad or missing sector, choose the option to ignore that sector. The copying process then continues to the next sector. The corrupted sector will be lost, but others can likely be recovered.

Xcopy /c /s /y /d:

The xcopy command is more powerful than the copy command. It follows the same general command-source-destination format as the copy command, but it offers several more options. Some examples are:

`c:\>xcopy c:\docs\*.* a: /s`	When used with the /s option, copies all files in the directory c:\ docs, as well as all subdirectories under c:\ docs and their files, to the disk in drive A.
`xcopy c:\docs\*.* a: /d:03/14/06`	When used with the /d option, copies all files from the directory c:\docs created or modified on March 14, 2006 to the disk in drive A.

You also can use the /y option to overwrite existing files without prompting, and use the /c option to keep copying even when an error occurs.

Mkdir or MD

The mkdir command (abbreviated md, for make directory) creates a subdirectory under a directory. Some examples are:

`mkdir c:\game`	Creates a directory named \game on drive C. The backslash indicates that the directory is under the root directory.
`mkdir c:\game\chess`	Creates a directory named chess under the \game directory. The OS requires that the parent directory game already exist before it creates the child directory chess.

Figure B-7a shows the result of the dir command after using the above two commands to create the directory c:\game\chess. Note the two initial entries in the directory table, the . (dot) and the .. (dot, dot) entries. The mkdir command creates these two entries when the OS initially sets up the directory. You cannot edit these entries with normal OS commands, and they must remain in the directory for the directory's lifetime. The . entry points to the subdirectory itself, and the .. entry points to the parent directory, in this case, the root directory. Figure B-7b shows a view of the C:\game\chess directory as shown in Windows Explorer.

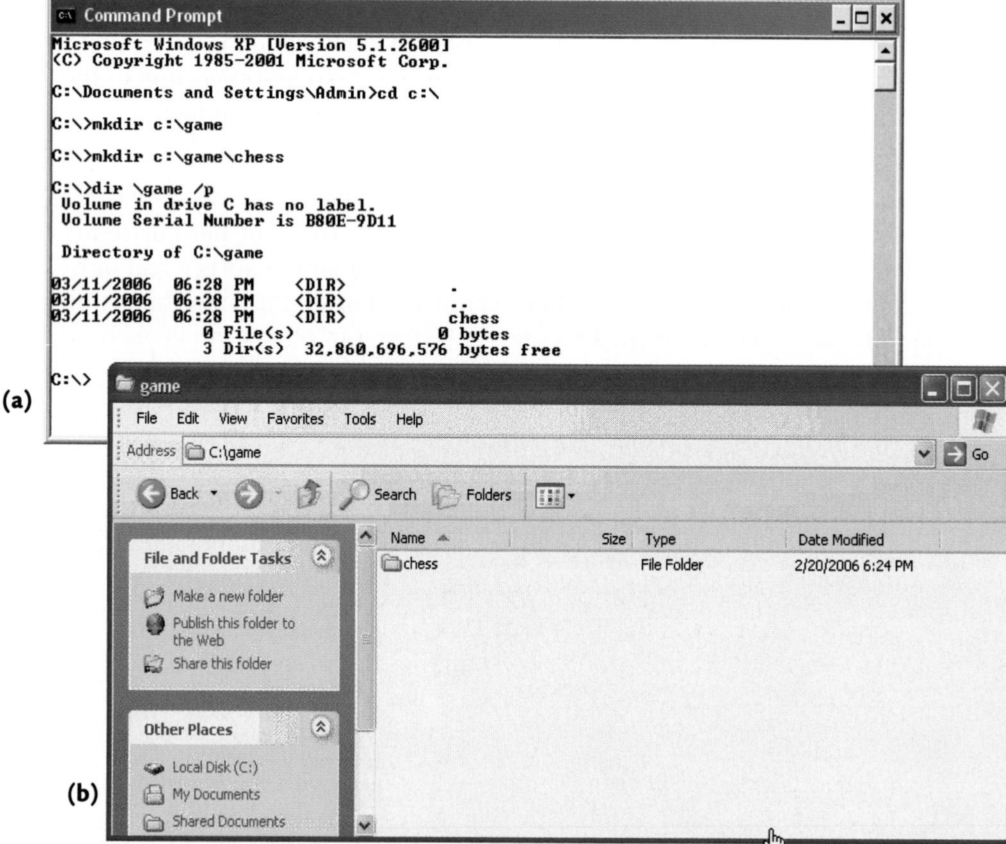

Figure B-7 (a) The result of the dir command after using the mkdir command to create the directory c:\game\chess. (b) The c:\game\chess directory as shown in Windows Explorer.

Chdir or CD

The chdir command (abbreviated cd, for change directory) changes the current default directory. Some examples are:

`cd c:\game\chess`	Changes the directory to c:\game\chess. After the cd command executes, the command prompt will read: `c:\game\chess>`
`c:\game\chess>cd..c:\game>`	Moves from a child directory to its parent directory. (Remember that .. always means the parent directory.)
`c:\game>cd chess c:\game\chess>`	Move from a parent directory to one of its child directories. Do not put a backslash in front of the child directory name; doing so tells the OS to go to a directory named chess that is directly under the root directory.

Rmdir or RD

The rmdir command (abbreviated rd, for remove directory) removes or deletes a subdirectory. Before you can use the rmdir command, the following must be true:

1. The directory must contain no files.
2. The directory must contain no subdirectories.
3. The directory must not be the current directory.

The . and .. entries indicate that a directory is ready for deletion. For example, to remove the \game directory in the preceding example, the chess directory must first be removed. Some examples are:

`c:\>rmdir c:\game\chess`	Removes the chess directory from the c:\game directory
`c:\game>rd chess`	Removes the chess directory from the c:\game directory, if the \game directory is the current directory

Chkdsk [drive:] /f /v

The chkdsk command reports information about a disk. Some examples are:

`chkdsk c: /f`	When used with the /f option, fixes errors it finds, including errors in the FAT caused by clusters marked as being used but not belonging to a particular file (called lost allocation units) and clusters marked in the FAT as belonging to more than one file (called cross-linked clusters).

`chkdsk c: >myfile.txt`	Redirect the output from the chkdsk command to a file that you can later print (in this example, myfile.txt).
`chkdsk c: /v`	When used with the /v option, displays all path and filename information for all files on a disk.

More About

Windows XP Commands

To learn more about all commands available in Windows XP, visit the Understanding and Troubleshooting Your PC More About Web page (**scsite.com/understanding/more**) and then click Commands below Appendix B.

Defrag [drive:] /s

The defrag command examines a hard drive or disk for fragmented files (files written to a disk in noncontiguous clusters) and rewrites these files to the disk or drive in contiguous clusters. Use this command to optimize a hard drive's performance. Some examples are:

`defrag c: /s:n`	When used with the /s:n option, sorts the files on the disk in alphabetical order by filename.
`defrag c: /s:d`	When used with the /s:d option, sorts the files on the disk in alphabetical order by date and time.

Ver

The ver command displays the version of the operating system in use.

APPENDIX C

Number Systems and Coding Schemes

Coding Schemes

As discussed in Chapter 1, a computer uses a coding scheme, such as ASCII, to represent characters. This appendix presents more information on ASCII, introduces the EBCDIC and Unicode coding schemes, and discusses parity.

ASCII and EBCDIC

Two widely used codes that represent characters in a computer are the ASCII and EBCDIC codes. The American Standard Code for Information Interchange, called ASCII (pronounced *ASK-ee*), uses 8 bits to represent characters and is the most widely used coding system to represent data. Many personal computers and servers use ASCII. The Extended Binary Coded Decimal Interchange Code, or EBCDIC (pronounced *EB-see-dik*), which also is an 8-bit code, is used primarily on mainframe computers. Figure C-1 summarizes these codes. Notice how the combination of 8 bits (0s and 1s) is unique for each character. When the ASCII or EBCDIC code is used, each character that is represented is stored in one byte (8 bits) of memory. In addition to ASCII and EBCDIC, computers sometimes use other binary formats to increase storage and processing efficiency. For example, a computer may store numbers using a format called packed decimal numbers, or COMP-3. Using packed decimal, each numeric character requires just 4 bits (a nibble), which means two numeric characters can be stored in one byte of memory.

Unicode

The 256 characters and symbols that are represented by ASCII and EBCDIC codes are sufficient for English and Western European languages, but are not large enough for Asian and other languages that use different alphabets. Further compounding the problem is that many of these languages use symbols, called ideograms, to represent multiple words and ideas. One solution to this situation is Unicode.

ASCII	SYMBOL	EBCDIC
00110000	0	11110000
00110001	1	11110001
00110010	2	11110010
00110011	3	11110011
00110100	4	11110100
00110101	5	11110101
00110110	6	11110110
00110111	7	11110111
00111000	8	11111000
00111001	9	11111001
01000001	A	11000001
01000010	B	11000010
01000011	C	11000011
01000100	D	11000100
01000101	E	11000101
01000110	F	11000110
01000111	G	11000111
01001000	H	11001000
01001001	I	11001001
01001010	J	11010001
01001011	K	11010010
01001100	L	11010011
01001101	M	11010100
01001110	N	11010101
01001111	O	11010110
01010000	P	11010111
01010001	Q	11011000
01010010	R	11011001
01010011	S	11100010
01010100	T	11100011
01010101	U	11100100
01010110	V	11100101
01010111	W	11100110
01011000	X	11100111
01011001	Y	11101000
01011010	Z	11101001
00100001	!	01011010
00100010	"	01111111
00100011	#	01111011
00100100	$	01011011
00100101	%	01101100
00100110	&	01010000
00101000	(	01001101
00101001	)	01011101
00101010	*	01011100
00101011	+	01001110

Figure C-1 Coding schemes such as ASCII and EBCDIC are used to represent letters, numbers, and other symbols.

	041	042	043	044	045	046	047
0	А	Р	а	р		Ѡ	Ѱ
1	Б	С	б	с	ё	ѡ	ѱ
2	В	Т	в	т	ђ	Ѣ	Ѳ
3	Г	У	г	у	ѓ	ѣ	ѳ
4	Д	Ф	д	ф	є	Ѥ	Ѵ
5	Е	Х	е	х	ѕ	ѥ	ѵ
6	Ж	Ц	ж	ц	і	Ѧ	Ѷ
7	З	Ч	з	ч	ї	ѧ	ѷ
8	И	Ш	и	ш	ј	Ѩ	Ѹ
9	Й	Щ	й	щ	љ	ѩ	ѹ
A	К	Ъ	к	ъ	њ	Ѫ	Ѻ
B	Л	Ы	л	ы	ћ	ѫ	ѻ
C	М	Ь	м	ь	ќ	Ѭ	Ѽ
D	Н	Э	н	э		ѭ	ѽ
E	О	Ю	о	ю	ў	Ѯ	Ѿ
F	П	Я	п	я	џ	ѯ	ѿ

Figure C-2 Unicode coding scheme.

Unicode is a 16-bit code that has the capacity of representing more than 65,000 characters and symbols, over 34,000 of which currently are used by various languages around the world (Figure C-2). A code for a symbol in Figure C-2 is obtained by appending the symbol's corresponding digit in the left-most column to the symbol's corresponding three-digit code in the column heading. For example, the Unicode for the letter C in row 2 is 0421. In Unicode, 30,000 codes are reserved for future use, and 6,000 codes are reserved for private use. Existing ASCII coded data is fully compatible with Unicode because the first 256 codes are the same. Unicode currently is implemented in several operating systems, including Windows XP.

Parity

Regardless of whether ASCII, EBCDIC, or other coding schemes are used to represent characters in memory, it is important that the characters be stored accurately. For each byte of memory, most computers have at least one extra bit, called a parity bit, that is used by the computer for error checking. A parity bit can detect if one of the bits in a byte has been changed inadvertently. While such errors are extremely rare (most computers never have a parity error during their lifetime), they can occur because of voltage fluctuations, static electricity, or a memory failure.

Computers are either odd- or even-parity machines. In computers with odd parity, the total number of "on" bits in the byte (including the parity bit) must be an odd number (Figure C-3). In computers with even parity, the total number of on bits must be an even number. The computer checks parity each time it uses a memory location. When the computer moves data from one location to another in memory, it compares the parity bits of both the sending and receiving locations to see if they are the same. If the system detects a difference or if the wrong number of bits is on (e.g., an odd number in a system with even parity), an error message is displayed. Many computers use multiple parity bits that enable them to detect and correct a single-bit error and detect multiple-bit errors.

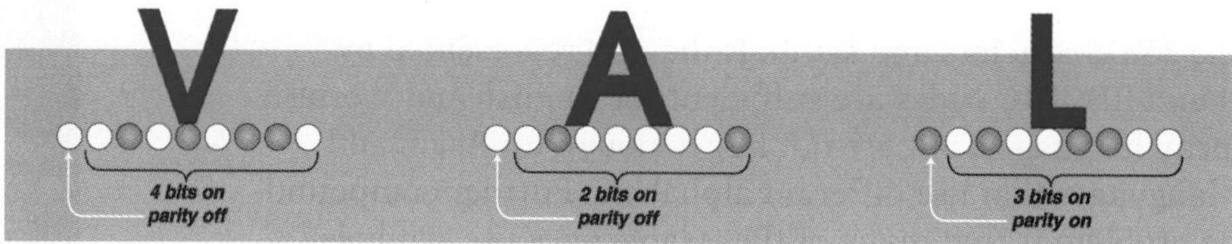

Figure C-3 A parity bit is used for error-checking. For a computer using odd parity, the total number of "on" bits in a byte must be an odd number.

Number Systems

This section describes the number systems that are used with computers. While technical computer personnel should have a thorough knowledge of number systems, all computer users can benefit from a general understanding of number systems and how they relate to computers.

Almost every culture represents numbers using the decimal number system, which uses the digits 0 through 9 to represent numbers in order from 0, 1, 2, and so on. As you have learned, computers rely on the binary (base 2) number system to represent the electronic status of the bits in memory. It also is used for other purposes such as addressing memory locations. Another number system that commonly is used with computers is hexadecimal (base 16). The computer uses the hexadecimal system to communicate with a programmer when a problem with a program exists, because it would be difficult for the programmer to understand the 0s and 1s of binary code. Figure C-4 shows how the decimal values 0 through 15 are represented in binary and hexadecimal.

DECIMAL	BINARY	HEXADECIMAL
0	0000	0
1	0001	1
2	0010	2
3	0011	3
4	0100	4
5	0101	5
6	0110	6
7	0111	7
8	1000	8
9	1001	9
10	1010	A
11	1011	B
12	1100	C
13	1101	D
14	1110	E
15	1111	F

Figure C-4 Decimal, binary, and hexadecimal number representation.

The mathematical principles that apply to the binary and hexadecimal number systems are the same as those that apply to the decimal number system. To help you better understand these principles, this section starts with the familiar decimal system, then progresses to the binary and hexadecimal number systems.

The Decimal Number System

The decimal number system is a base 10 number system (deci means ten). The base of a number system indicates how many symbols are used in it. The decimal number system uses 10 symbols: 0 through 9. Each of the symbols in the number system has a value associated with it. For example, 3 represents a quantity of three and 5 represents a quantity of five.

The decimal number system also is a positional number system. This means that in a number such as 143, each position in the number has a value associated with it. When you look at the decimal number 143, the 3 is in the ones, or units, position and represents three ones or (3×1); the 4 is in the tens position and represents four tens or (4×10); and the 1 is in the hundreds position and represents one hundred or (1×100). The number 143 is the sum of the values in each position of the number $(100 + 40 + 3 = 143)$. The chart in Figure C-5 shows how you can calculate the positional

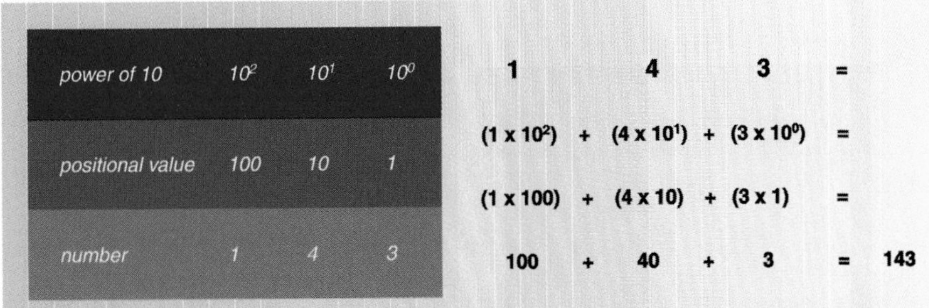

Figure C-5 Calculating positional values for a decimal number.

values (hundreds, tens, and units) for a number system. Starting on the right and working to the left, the base of the number system, in this case 10, is raised to consecutive powers (10^0, 10^1, 10^2). These calculations are a mathematical way of determining the place values in a number system.

When you use number systems other than decimal, the same principles apply. The base of the number system indicates the number of symbols that are used, and each position in a number system has a value associated with it. By raising the base of the number system to consecutive powers beginning with zero, you can calculate the positional value.

The Binary Number System

As previously discussed, the binary number system is a base 2 number system (bi means two), and the symbols it uses are 0 and 1. Just as each position in a decimal number has a place value associated with it, so does each position in a binary number. In binary, the place values, moving from right to left, are successive powers of two (2^0, 2^1, 2^2, 2^3) or (1, 2, 4, 8). To construct a binary number, you place ones in the positions where the corresponding values add up to the quantity you want to represent; you place zeros in the other positions. For example, in a four-digit binary number, the binary place values are (from right to left) 1, 2, 4, and 8. The binary number 1001 has ones in the positions for the values 1 and 8 and zeros in the positions for 2 and 4. Therefore, the quantity represented by binary 1001 is 9 (8 + 0 + 0 + 1) (Figure C-6).

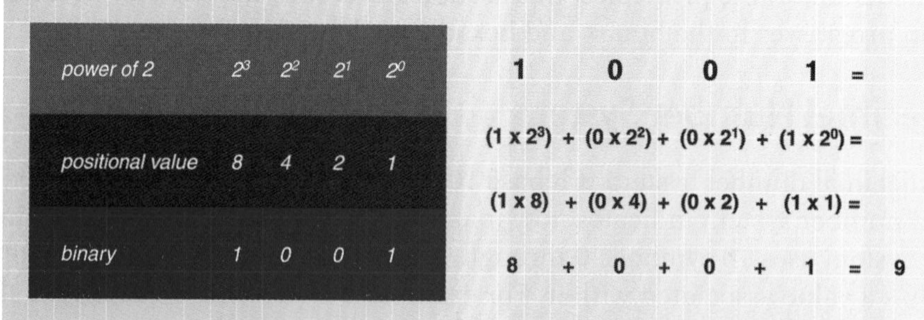

power of 2 2^3 2^2 2^1 2^0
positional value 8 4 2 1
binary 1 0 0 1
1 0 0 1 =
$(1 \times 2^3) + (0 \times 2^2) + (0 \times 2^1) + (1 \times 2^0) =$
$(1 \times 8) + (0 \times 4) + (0 \times 2) + (1 \times 1) =$
8 + 0 + 0 + 1 = 9

Figure C-6 Converting a binary number to a decimal number.

The Hexadecimal Number System

The hexadecimal number system uses 16 symbols to represent values (hex means six, deci means ten). These include the symbols 0 through 9 and A through F (as shown earlier in Figure C-4 on the previous page). The mathematical principles of positional value also apply to the hexadecimal number system (Figure C-7).

power of 16 16^1 16^0
positional value 16 1
hexadecimal A 5

A 5 =
$(10 \times 16^1) + (5 \times 16^0) =$
$(10 \times 16) + (5 \times 1) =$
160 + 5 = 165

Figure C-7 Converting a hexadecimal number to a decimal number.

The primary reasons why the hexadecimal number system is used with computers is because it can represent binary values in a more compact and readable form and because the conversion between the binary and the hexadecimal number systems is very efficient. Computers often display memory addresses using the hex number system.

An eight-digit binary number (a byte) can be represented by a two-digit hexadecimal number. For example, in the ASCII code, the character M is represented as 01001101. This value can be represented in hexadecimal as 4D. One way to convert this binary number (4D) to a hexadecimal number is to divide the binary number (from right to left) into groups of four digits; calculate the value of each group; and then change any two-digit values (10 through 15) into the symbols A through F that are used in hexadecimal (Figure C-8).

positional value	*8421*	*8421*
binary	*0100*	*1101*
decimal	*4*	*13*
hexadecimal	*4*	*D*

Figure C-8 Converting a binary number to a hexadecimal number.

Computers often display memory addresses using the hex number system. For example, the decimal memory address 819,205 converted to hexadecimal looks like this: C8005. An error message related to that memory address would display as two hex numbers, such as C800:5. The part to the left of the colon (C800) is called the segment address and the part to the right of the colon (5) is called the offset. The offset value can have as many as four hex digits. The actual memory address is calculated by adding a zero to the right of the segment address and adding the offset value, like this:

```
C800:5 = C8000 + 5 = C8005.
```

Sometims hex numbers are written followed by a lowercase h, as in FFh, to indicate that they are hex values. At other times, a hex number is preceded by an ox, as in oxFF.

Memory Addressing and Number Systems

To learn more about how different number systems are used for memory addressing, visit the Understanding and Troubleshooting Your PC More About Web page (**scsite.com/understanding/more**) and then click Memory Addressing and Number Systems below Appendix C.

intel
pentium 4

APPENDIX D

Working as a PC Technician

Introduction

As you learned in Chapter 12, a career as a PC technician opens up opportunities in a number of roles, including PC support technician, PC service technician, bench technician, and help desk technician. Appendix D provides a practical guide to help further your career as a PC technician, addressing how to satisfy customers, keep records of support calls, provide good service in a range of situations, and ensure software copyrights are followed. It also discusses ways to seek opportunities for joining professional organizations and obtain professional certification. All of these suggestions can help you maintain excellent customer relationships and advance your career.

Working as a PC Technician

Probably the most significant indication that a PC technician is doing a good job is that customers consistently are satisfied with the service they receive. One of the most important ways to achieve customer satisfaction is to be prepared, both in your technical understanding of computers and your ability to interact with customers in a positive and helpful way.

Depending on your role and the company for which you work, you may need to provide service to customers over the telephone or online, in person, or as a service person in a shop where you have little customer contact. Your customers may be internal customers, including co-workers at the same company, or external customers who come to your company for service. The computing environment, technical savvy, and personalities of customers also can vary greatly. Your customer might be an employee at a large company with a vast network or a single user on his or her home computer. The customer might have substantial technical knowledge or be a novice PC user. Customers can be friendly and easy to work with or demanding and condescending. In each situation, the key to success is always the same: do not allow circumstances or personalities to affect your commitment to excellent service.

Maintaining Professionalism

In general, you always should do your best to provide excellent service and treat customers as you would want to be treated in a similar situation. The following traits distinguish one competent technician from another in the eyes of the customer.

- *Act professionally.* Customers want a technician to look and behave professionally. Dress appropriately for the environment. If you are doing on-site service, consider yourself a guest at the customer's site.
- *Have a positive and helpful attitude.* A positive outlook and a constructive approach to problem-solving help to establish good customer relationships.
- *Own the problem.* Taking ownership of the customer's problem builds trust and loyalty, because the customer knows he or she can rely on you to resolve the problem.
- *Be dependable.* Customers appreciate those who follow through on their commitments. For example, if you promise to call back at 10:00 AM the next morning, be sure to call back at 10:00 AM. If you cannot keep your appointment, never ignore your promise. Call, apologize, let the customer know what happened, and reschedule your appointment.

- *Be customer-focused.* When you are working with or talking to a customer, focus on him or her. Make it your job to satisfy this person, not just to satisfy your organization, your manager, the customer's manager, or to earn a paycheck.
- *Be credible.* Convey confidence to your customers. Being credible not only means being technically competent and knowing how to do your job well, but also knowing when the job is beyond your expertise and when to ask for help.
- *Learn to handle angry or upset customers.* If a customer is angry, express that you are concerned and are taking the situation seriously — and then listen quietly and allow the customer to vent. Make notes of the details he or she shares and, as the customer calms down, ask questions. Your goal is to discover the specific things that you can do to correct the problem, rather than listening to general complaints.
- *Maintain integrity and honesty.* If you make a mistake, acknowledge it and communicate it to the customer and your manager. Everyone makes mistakes, but do not compound them by trying to hide them. Maintain your integrity by accepting responsibility and do what you can to correct the error. Your reputation will suffer less from acknowledging an issue and proactively resolving it, than if you try to ignore it and future problems arise.
- *Know the law with respect to your work.* For instance, if you are installing software, be sure the installation is in compliance with the license agreement. Do not use or install pirated software.

Keeping Detailed Records

Another way to help ensure customer satisfaction is to keep detailed records to help resolve the current problem and to have as a reference if issues arise in the future. If you work for a service organization, your company may have specific procedures or systems in place to help structure the process of keeping call records, such as call log forms or an electronic recordkeeping system.

Call tracking can be done on paper or electronically. Most larger support and service groups have a call-tracking system that tracks the date, time, and length of help desk or on-site calls; the type of service level agreement a customer has; causes of and solutions to problems already addressed; who did what and when; and how each call was officially resolved. Call-tracking software or documents also can help to refer, or escalate, problems to different support staff when necessary. The process of turning a problem over to a person with greater expertise is referred to as *escalating* an issue.

Utilizing Information Resources and Tools

Your ability to provide quick resolution to an issue often is determined by the types of information resources and tools you have available. If you work for a service organization or a company with a large PC technician department, your company probably will have several types of information resources and tools you can use to support customers. Examples of these information resources and tools include:

- Hardware and software you can use to test, observe, study, and try to re-create a customer's problem, whenever possible.
- Copies of all user manuals, reference guides, and other documentation provided to users and customers.

- Copies of additional technical documentation for hardware and software products. Such documentation often is more detailed and more technical in nature than the manuals and guides provided to users.
- A searchable help and support database tool targeted to field technicians and help desk technicians. Such a database tool, which often is referred to as a *knowledge base*, probably will include a search engine that searches by topics, words, and error messages. Web-based versions of these knowledge bases also can be made available over the Internet to users.
- An expert system designed for PC technicians. An *expert system* is an information system that captures and stores the knowledge of human experts and then uses databases of known facts and rules to simulate human experts' reasoning and decision-making. Expert systems for PC technicians work by posing questions about a problem, to be answered either by the technician or the customer. The response to each question triggers another question from the software, until the expert system arrives at a possible solution or solutions. Many expert systems will record your input and use it in subsequent sessions to select more questions to ask and approaches to try.
- Remote control software, such as SymantecpcAnywhere, Expertcity GoToMyPC, and Unicenter Remote Control. Remote control software allows PC technicians to view the configuration and take control of a PC on a network to help users with problems, such as troubleshooting applications or operating system errors.

Handling Service Calls

Even though each customer is different and might expect different results, all customers want good service. The following characteristics constitute good service in the eyes of most customers:

- The technician responds and completes the work within a reasonable time.
- For on-site service, the technician is prepared with the appropriate manuals, software, and other tools.
- The work is done right the first time.
- The price for the work is reasonable and competitive.
- The technician exhibits good interpersonal skills.
- If the work extends beyond a brief on-site visit or telephone call, the technician keeps the customer informed about the progress of the work.

Planning for Good Service

Whether you support PCs on the telephone; via e-mail; on-site at the customer's desk, office, or home; or in a shop, you need a plan to follow when you approach a service call. The following section outlines the entire service situation, from the first contact with the customer to closing the call, and provides some general guidelines when supporting computers and their users.

- Almost every support task starts with a telephone call or an e-mail message. Be sure to follow company policies regarding specific information to obtain when answering an initial telephone call or crafting a response to an e-mail message.

- Be familiar with your company's customer service policies. You might need to refer questions about warranties, licenses, documentation, or procedures to other support personnel or customer service personnel. Your organization might not want you to answer some questions, such as questions about upcoming releases of software or new products.
- After reviewing your company's service policies, begin troubleshooting. Take notes, and then interview the customer about the problem so you understand it thoroughly. Have the customer reproduce the problem, and carefully note each step taken and its results. This process gives you clues about the problem and about the customer's technical proficiency, which helps you know how to communicate with the customer.
- Search for answers. If the answers to specific questions or problems are not evident, become a researcher. Learn to use online documentation, expert systems, and other resources that your company provides.
- Use your troubleshooting skills. Isolate the problem. Check for user errors. What things work and what things do not work? What has changed since the system last worked? Reduce the system to its essentials. Check the simple things first. Use the troubleshooting guidelines throughout this book to help you think of approaches to test and try.
- Do not assume that an on-site visit is necessary until you have asked questions to identify the problem and asked the caller to check and try some simple things while on the telephone with you. For example, with your step-by-step guidance, the customer can check cable connections, power and monitor settings, network configurations, and other settings.
- If you have given the problem your best, but still have not solved it, ask for help from a more knowledgeable resource. Once you have made a reasonable effort to help, and it seems clear that you are unlikely to be successful, do not waste a customer's time. Instead, let the customer know that you are going to ask for help from a more experienced technician to help ensure the problem is resolved quickly.
- After a call, create a written or electronic record of what happened during the call, in order to build your own knowledge base. Record the initial symptoms of the problem, the source of the problem you actually discovered, how you made that discovery, and how the problem was finally solved. File your documentation according to symptoms or according to solutions.

Providing Telephone Support

Help desk support requires excellent communication skills, good telephone manners, and lots of patience. The following section provides some guidelines to help make the process easier for you, while ensuring that the customer receives excellent service.

When someone calls asking for support, you must control the call, especially at the beginning. Follow these steps at the beginning of a service call:

- Identify yourself and your organization. In your introduction, follow any guidelines set forth by your employer as to what to say.

- Ask for and write down the name and telephone number of the caller. Ask for spelling if necessary. If your help desk supports businesses, get the name of the business that the caller represents.
- If necessary, determine how the customer will pay for the support service. For example, your company might require that you obtain a licensing or warranty number to determine what type of service plan a customer has. If the customer is not receiving free support, obtain whatever payment information is required.
- Open up the conversation for the caller to describe the problem.

Telephone support requires you to rely on the customer's expertise more than any other type of PC support. Patience also is required if the customer must be told each key to press or button to click. To give clear instructions, you must be able to visualize what the customer sees at his or her PC. Drawing diagrams and taking notes as you talk can be very helpful. As your help desk skills improve, you will learn to think through the process as though you were sitting in front of the PC yourself.

If you spend many hours on the telephone at a help desk, use a headset instead of a regular telephone to reduce strain on your ears and neck. If your call is disconnected accidentally, call back immediately. If you must put callers on hold, tell them how long it will be before you get back to them. Do not complain about your job, your company, or other companies or products to your customers. A little small talk is okay and sometimes is beneficial in easing a tense situation, but keep it upbeat and positive. Before ending the call, give the user a chance to test and confirm that everything is working correctly. If you end the call too soon and the problem is not completely resolved, the customer can be frustrated, especially if it is difficult to contact you again.

Making On-Site Service Calls

When a technician makes an on-site service call, customers expect him or her to have both technical and interpersonal skills. Prepare for a service call by reviewing information given you by whoever took the call. Know the problem you are going to address; the urgency of the situation; and what computer, software, and hardware need servicing. Arrive with a complete set of equipment appropriate to the visit, which might include a PC toolkit, flashlight, multimeter, ground bracelet and ground mat, and Windows setup CDs.

Set a realistic time for the appointment (one that you can expect to keep) and arrive on time. When you arrive at the customer's site, greet the customer in a friendly manner. Use Mr. or Ms. and last names rather than first names when addressing the customer, unless you are certain that the customer expects you to use first names. The first thing you should do upon arriving at the customer's site is listen and take notes. Save the paperwork for the end of the service call.

As you work, be as unobtrusive as possible. Do not make a big mess. Keep your tools and papers out of the customer's way. Do not use the telephone or sit in the customer's desk chair without permission. If the customer needs to work while you are present, do whatever is necessary to accommodate that.

While you are troubleshooting the issue, keep the customer informed. Once you have collected enough information, explain the problem and what you must do to fix it, giving as many details as the customer wants. When a customer must make a choice, state the options in a way that does not unfairly favor the solution that makes the most money for you as the technician or for your company.

After you have solved the problem:

- Allow the customer time to test the system and be fully satisfied that the problem is resolved before you close the call. For example, if you were fixing a printer, allow the customer to print a test page. If you were troubleshooting a network connection, give the customer the opportunity to try logging on to the network and accessing data.
- If you changed anything on the PC after you booted it, reboot one more time to make sure that you have not caused a problem with the boot.
- Review the service call with the customer. Summarize the instructions and explanations you have given during the call. At this point, it is appropriate to fill out your paperwork and explain to the customer what you have written.
- If some basic preventive maintenance steps can help a customer avoid future problems, explain those steps to the customer. Most customers do not have preventive maintenance contracts for their PCs and appreciate the time you take to show them how they can take better care of their computers.

Working with Difficult Customers

As previously noted, the types of customers with whom you work can vary widely, from customers who have very little knowledge about how to use a computer to those who are proud of their computer knowledge and do not want to take advice. The following sections provide tips on managing difficult customers, whether on the telephone or in an on-site service call.

WHEN THE CUSTOMER IS NOT KNOWLEDGEABLE A support telephone call can be made very challenging when a customer is not knowledgeable about how to use a computer. When on-site at the customer's location, you can put a PC in good repair without depending on a customer to help you, but when you are trying to solve a problem over the telephone, with a customer as your only eyes, ears, and hands, a novice computer user can present a challenge. Some tips for handling this situation include the following:

- Do not use technical language or computer jargon while talking. For example, instead of saying, "Open My Computer," say, "Using your mouse, click the Start button at the bottom-left part of the screen. Then, click My Computer at the right-top part of the menu."
- Follow along at your own computer. It is easier to direct the customer, keystroke by keystroke, if you are doing the same things.
- Frequently ask the customer what he or she sees on the screen to help you track the keystrokes and resulting actions on the computer.
- Give the customer plenty of opportunity to ask questions.
- Compliment the customer whenever you can, to help the customer gain confidence.

- Do not ask the customer to do something that might change settings or damage files without first having the customer back them up carefully. If you think the customer cannot perform a specific task without causing damage to the computer, consider asking if on-site help is appropriate.
- If you determine that the customer is not knowledgeable enough to help you solve the problem over the telephone, you may need to tactfully request that the caller have someone with more experience call you.

When solving computer problems in an organization other than your own, check with the company's network administrator or technical support group, instead of working only with the PC user. The user may not be aware of policies that have been set on the PC to prevent changes to the OS, hardware, or applications.

WHEN THE CUSTOMER IS OVERLY CONFIDENT Sometimes customers are proud of their computer knowledge. Such customers may want to give advice, take charge of a call, withhold information they think you do not need to know, or execute commands at the computer without letting you know, so you do not have enough information to follow along. A situation like this must be handled with tact and respect for the customer. Some tips for handling this type of customer include:

- When you can, compliment the customer's knowledge, experience, or insight.
- Ask the customer's advice. Say something like, "What do you think the problem is?" (Note that you should not ask this question of customers who are new computer users or are not confident, because they most likely do not have the answer and might lose confidence in you.)
- Slow the conversation down. You can say, "I'm sorry — but can you slow down just a bit? I'm taking notes as we go and want to be sure I capture all of the relevant information you are sharing."
- Do not back off from using problem-solving skills. You still must have the customer check the simple things, but direct the conversation with tact. For example, you can say, "I know you have probably already tried these simple things, but could we just do them again together?"
- Be careful not to accuse the customer of making a mistake.
- Use technical language in a way that conveys that you expect the customer to understand you.

WHEN THE CUSTOMER COMPLAINS When you are on-site or on the telephone, a customer might complain to you about your organization, products, or service, or the service and product of another company. As you listen to the customer, remember to consider the complaint to be helpful feedback that can lead to a better product or service and better customer relationships. In addition to the general steps outlined earlier, suggestions on how to handle complaints and anger include the following:

- Be an active listener, and let customers know that they are not being ignored. Look for the underlying problem. Do not take the complaint or the anger personally.
- Give the customer a little time to vent and apologize when you can. Make notes of any details the customer provides. After the customer has calmed down, start the conversation from the beginning, asking questions, taking notes, and solving problems. If this helps, do not spend a lot of time finding out exactly whom the customer dealt with and what happened to upset the customer.

- Do not be defensive. It is better to leave the customer with the impression that you and your company are listening and willing to admit mistakes.
- If the customer is complaining about a product or service that is not from your company, do not start off by telling the customer it is not your problem. Instead, listen to the customer complain. Do not appear as though you do not care.
- If the complaint is about you or your product, identify the underlying problem if you can. Ask questions, take notes, and then pass these notes on to people in your organization who need to know.
- Sometimes simply making progress or reducing the problem to a manageable state reduces the customer's anxiety. As you are talking to a customer, summarize what you have both agreed on or observed so far in the conversation.

WHEN THE CUSTOMER DOES NOT WANT TO END A TELEPHONE CALL Some customers like to talk and do not want to end a telephone call. In this situation, when you have finished the work and are ready to hang up, you can ease the caller into the end of the call. Ask if anything needs more explanation. Briefly summarize the main points of the call, and then say something like, "That about does it. Please do not hesitate to call if you need more help." Be silent about new issues. Answer only with "yes" or "no." Do not take the bait by engaging in a new topic. Do not get frustrated. As a last resort, you can say, "I'm sorry, but I must go now. Thank you again."

Escalating Issues

You will not be able to solve every computer problem you encounter. Knowing how to escalate a problem to another technician is one of the first things you should learn on a new job. When escalation involves the customer, generally follow these guidelines:

- Before you escalate, first ask knowledgeable co-workers for suggestions for solving the problem, which might save you and your customer the time and effort it takes to escalate it.
- Know your company's policy for escalation. What documents do you fill out? Who gets them? Do you remain the responsible support party, or does the person now addressing the problem become the new contact? Are you expected to keep in touch with the customer and the problem, or are you totally out of the picture?
- Follow your company's policy for escalating the issue to another technician. Depending on the tools used at your firm, the escalation process might involve a telephone call, an online entry in a database, or an e-mail message.
- Document the issue very well before escalating it. Including the detailed steps necessary to reproduce the problem can save the next support person a significant amount of time.

- Tell the customer that you are passing the problem on to someone who is more experienced and has access to more extensive resources. In most cases, the person who receives the escalation will contact the customer immediately and assume responsibility for the problem. You should follow through, however, at least to confirm that the new person and the customer have made contact.
- If you check back with the customer only to find out that the other support person has not called or followed through to the customer's satisfaction, do not lay blame or point fingers. Instead, do whatever you can to help within your company guidelines. Your call to the customer will go a long way toward helping the situation.

Protecting Software Copyrights

As a PC technician, you should understand the legal issues and practices surrounding the distribution of software. When someone purchases software from a software vendor, that person has only purchased a license for the software, which is the right to use it. The buyer does not legally own the software, and therefore does not hold the *copyright* — that is, the right to copy and/or distribute the software. The copyright belongs to the creator of the work or others to whom the creator transfers this right.

Copyright Law

Copyrights are intended to legally protect the intellectual property rights of organizations or individuals that have produced creative works, which include books, images, and software. While the originator of a creative work is the original owner of a copyright, the copyright can be transferred from one entity to another.

The Federal Copyright Act of 1976 protects the exclusive rights of copyright holders. The Act was designed in part to protect software copyrights by requiring that only legally obtained copies of software be used. The law also gives legal users of software the right to make one backup copy. Other rights are based on what the copyright holder allows, which means software licenses can vary by product and manufacturer. For example, the license for an accounting software package might require that you use it on only one computer, while a license for a font might allow you to install and use it on several computers as long as they all print to only one printer.

In 1990, the U.S. Congress passed the Computer Software Rental Amendments Act, which prevents the renting, leasing, lending, or sharing of software without the expressed written permission of the copyright holder. In 1992, Congress instituted criminal penalties for software copyright infringement, which include imprisonment for up to five years and/or fines of up to $250,000 for the unlawful reproduction or distribution of 10 or more copies of software.

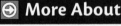

> **More About**
>
> **Copyright Law and Software Licensing**
>
> To learn more about copyright law and software licensing, visit the Understanding and Troubleshooting Your PC More About Web page (**scsite.com/understanding/more**) and then click Copyright Law and Software Licensing below Appendix D.

Your Responsibilities Under the Law

Making unauthorized copies of original software violates the Federal Copyright Act of 1976, and is called *software piracy*, or more officially, *software copyright infringement*. Making a copy of software and then selling it or giving it away is a violation of the law. Because it is so easy to do, and because so many people do it, many people do not realize that it is illegal. In fact, the Business Software Alliance, a membership organization of software manufacturers and vendors, has estimated that over 39 percent of the software in the United States is obtained illegally.

Normally, only the person who violated the copyright law is liable for infringement. In some cases, however, an employer or supervisor also is held responsible, even when the copies were made without the employer's knowledge.

It is important to know the terms of the license before using a piece of software, because U.S. copyright laws protect these agreements. Your first responsibility as an individual user is to use only software that has been purchased or licensed for your use. As a PC technician you will be called upon to install, upgrade, and customize software. You need to know your responsibilities in upholding the law, especially as it applies to software copyrights.

Site licensing allows a company, university, or other organization to purchase the right to use multiple copies of software. Site licenses are a popular way for companies to provide software to employees. With a site license in place, companies can distribute software to PCs from network servers or execute software directly off the server. As a PC technician, you should read the licensing agreement of any software to determine the terms of distribution and ensure that you track the number of copies of the software installed in the company to verify you are in compliance with the number of installations allowed under the license agreement.

It also is your responsibility as an individual user and a PC technician to purchase only legitimate software. Purchasers of counterfeit or copied software face the risk of corrupted files, virus-infected disks, inadequate documentation, and lack of technical support and upgrades, as well as the legal penalties for using pirated software.

Several associations are committed to preventing software piracy. The Software Information Industry Association (SIIA) is a nonprofit organization that educates the public and enforces copyright laws. The Business Software Alliance (BSA) is a leading organization focused on speaking for the commercial software industry to promote the safe and legal use of software and other digital assets. These associations are comprised of hundreds of software manufacturers and publishers from around the world. They work with the local, state, and federal governments to identify illegal use of software in large and small companies. In the United States, they receive the cooperation of the U.S. government to prosecute offenders.

More About

Anti-Piracy Organizations

To learn more about organizations focused on fighting software piracy, visit the Understanding and Troubleshooting Your PC More About Web page (**scsite.com/understanding/more**) and then click Anti-Piracy Organizations below Appendix D.

Professional Organizations and Certifications

The work done by PC technicians increasingly is viewed as an important profession, with room for significant growth. PC repair and support is a vital part of business and serves as a starting point for professionals interested in beginning a career in the IT industry. Several professional organizations and certifying organizations exist to help PC technicians keep up-to-date on new technologies and to certify that their skill sets meet specific standards.

Professional Organizations

Joining professional organizations in your area of expertise can provide enormous benefits, some general and some specific to an organization. In general, such organizations allow you to meet others in your field and share ideas. Many organizations also offer many educational opportunities such as seminars, workshops, annual conventions, online courses, and courses on tape to increase your knowledge of particular topics in your area of expertise. Most organizations also provide members with access to professional journals and publications, career counseling, and employment listings.

Several professional organizations exist specifically for those working in the field of PC support and repair, including:

- *Help Desk Institute (HDI)* is the world's largest membership association for the service and support industry. HDI was founded in 1989, with the goal of leading and promoting the customer service and technical support industry.
- *Association of Support Professionals (ASP)* is a membership organization representing support managers and other professionals in hundreds of large and small software companies.

Other organizations, such as the Association of Information Technology Professionals (AITP), the Information Technology Association of America (ITAA), and the Association for Computing Machinery (ACM), are more general IT-focused organizations that provide information, research, training, and networking opportunities for professionals across the information technology field.

In addition to considering membership in a professional organization, you should further your skills as a PC technician by keeping up-to-date on new technologies. Helpful resources include on-the-job training, books, magazines, the Internet, trade shows, interaction with colleagues, seminars, and workshops.

Professional Certifications

Another way to further your career as a PC technician is to be certified by one of several certifying organizations focused on PC support and repair. Many people work as PC technicians without any formal classroom training or certification. Having certification or an advanced technical degree, however, you prove to yourself, your customers, and your employers that you are prepared to do the work and are committed to being educated in your chosen profession. Certification and advanced degrees serve as recognized proof of competence and achievement, improve your job opportunities, create a higher level of customer confidence, and often qualify you for other training or degrees.

The most significant certifying organization for PC technicians is the Computing Technology Industry Association or CompTIA (pronounced *"comp-TEE-a"*). CompTIA has over 13,000 members from every major company that manufactures, distributes, or publishes computer-related products and services.

CompTIA sponsors the A+ Certification Program and manages the A+ Service Technician Certification Examination, which measures the knowledge of job tasks and behavior expected of entry-level technicians. To become certified, you must pass two test modules: the A+ Core Hardware exam and the A+ Operating System Technologies exam. A+ Certification has industry recognition, so it should be your first choice for certification as a PC technician.

Other certifications, such as those offered by Microsoft, Novell, Cisco, and Oracle, are more vendor-specific, focused on certification to use and support their products. For example, being certified as a Microsoft Certified Desktop Support Technician (MCDST) shows that you have the technical and customer service skills to troubleshoot hardware and software issues in Microsoft Windows environments. These vendor-specific certifications are excellent choices for additional certifications when your career plan is to focus on these products.

More About

Professional Organizations and Certifications

To learn more about professional organizations and certifications available for PC technicians, visit the Understanding and Troubleshooting Your PC More About Web page (**scsite.com/understanding/more**) and then click Professional Organizations and Certifications below Appendix D.

intel
pentium 4

APPENDIX E

Introducing Linux

Introduction

Linux (pronounced lih-nucks) is an operating system created by Linus Torvalds, when he was a student at the University of Helsinki in Finland. Torvalds was inspired to create Linux by the Minix operating system, which was a simple, open-source, Unix-like operating system designed for teaching purposes by Andrew Tannebaum. Torvalds began work on his new operating system in 1991; the first version of Linux was on March 14, 1994.

Torvalds released his software under a licensing model called the GNU General Public License (GPL), which meant that the source code for Linux was freely distributed and available to the public. By including the source code, the software author makes it possible for anyone to modify the original program — a software development model called open source development. Since then, developers around the world have worked on the operating system and have added different parts, such as a graphical user interface or networking capabilities, to the code.

Today, basic versions of Linux still are available free, and all the underlying programming instructions (called source code) also are distributed freely. Several companies also sell packaged versions of Linux. The various types and versions of Linux sometimes are called *distributions*. Figure E-1 lists several popular distributions of Linux. Many more distributions are available for free and purchase, each with slightly different features.

Name	Description	Web Site
Red Hat Linux	The most widely used distribution in the world, from Red Hat Software.	*www.redhat.com*
Fedora	A distribution built by Red Hat to create a complete, general-purpose operating system exclusively from free software. The distribution was created to replace low-end, consumer versions of RedHat Linux.	*fedora.redhat.com*
UnitedLinux	A Linux distribution created by multiple Linux vendors as a common base product, on which numerous Linux applications can be designed to run.	*www.unitedlinux.com*
TurboLinux	Focused on providing high-end, specialized server software to businesses.	*www.turbolinux.com*
Mandrake	Built on Red Hat Linux with many additional packages. Popular at retail outlets.	*www.mandrakelinux.com*
Stampede	A distribution optimized for speed.	*www.stampede.org*
Debian	A noncommercial Linux distribution targeted specifically to free software enthusiasts. Debian does not have a company behind it; it is created and maintained by developers of free software.	*www.debian.org*
Lindows	Focused on providing a desktop operating system to replace Microsoft Windows.	*www.lindows.com*
Slackware	A stable and proven version of Linux that has been available since 1993. A simple and flexible operating system, which provides many of the current Linux applications while maintaining the traditional UNIX-like system.	*www.slackware.com*
SUSE LINUX	Very popular in Europe. Originally produced by SUSE, a German company, which was recently acquired by the networking software company Novell.	*www.suse.com*

(continued)

Name	Description	Web Site
Xandros	Focused on providing a desktop operating system to replace Microsoft Windows.	*www.xandros.com*
CollegeLinux	A stand-alone Linux version based on Slackware. Aimed at providing students with an easy to install, user-friendly version that makes it easier to learn Linux.	*www.collegelinux.org*
Yellow Dog Linux	A version of Linux for Macintosh computers, written for the PowerPC processor.	*www.yellowdoglinux.com*

Figure E-1 Popular Linux distributions. For more information on Linux, see *www.linux.org* as well as the Web sites of the different Linux distributors.

Linux can be used on desktop computers and servers, but its greatest popularity is in the server market. Many companies run Web servers or e-mail servers on computers running the Linux operating system. Because Linux is very reliable and does not require a lot of computing power, it sometimes is used as a desktop OS, although it has a small market share compared to the Windows operating system. Hardware requirements for Linux vary widely, depending on the distribution and version installed.

Strengths and Limitations of Linux

Despite the fact that Linux distributions often are free or low-cost and may be developed by groups of users, rather than a specific software firm, Linux is a highly reliable and flexible operating system. Companies increasingly are turning to Linux as an alternative to UNIX and Windows operating systems for its strengths, which include:

- *Stability*. Linux rarely crashes. Linux servers are known for being able to run for months without needing to be restarted.
- *Ease of administration*. The command-line interface provides very powerful administrative tools. A skilled server administrator often finds it much quicker and easier to use the Linux command-line interface for server administration, rather than a graphical user interface.
- *Cost*. Basic versions of Linux can be downloaded and installed free of charge, and purchasing a packaged version of Linux with technical support still generally costs much less than an operating system such as Windows. Further, the Total Cost of Ownership (TCO) — that is, the cost of the software plus the ongoing cost to maintain, support, and upgrade it over time — is much lower for Linux than other operating systems.
- *Networking*. Linux has strong features for handling network connections.
- *Speed*. Linux makes very efficient use of hardware, from very small systems to very large.
- *Flexibility*. Because the source code is available to users, a company can customize its Linux installation more easily.
- *Security*. Having source code available has meant that the occasional security flaw in open source software is located and repaired more quickly than is typical for proprietary products.

Linux does have some limitations, largely for users who are most comfortable with graphical user interface (GUI) based operating systems. Those limitations include:

- *Difficult to install.* Linux can be difficult to install, particularly for users who are not familiar with UNIX commands. Optimizing a Linux system can take a significant investment of time and research.
- *Inconsistent documentation*. Documentation for Linux distributions may not be consistent or easily available. Increasingly, however, user guides and books are available to help introduce users to basic Linux commands.
- *Fewer applications.* Not as many desktop applications are available for Linux as for Windows. In the past few years, however, more general purpose and specialized applications have become available, including Office suites such as StarOffice, which is similar to Microsoft Office; powerful database tools; and Internet applications. Many of the largest software vendors have created Linux versions of their products.
- *Not user friendly.* Many distributions of Linux have a command-line interface, which can be difficult for end users (especially those comfortable with Windows and other GUI operating systems) to operate. As discussed in the next section, applications that provide a graphical user interface can make it easier for users to interact with the Linux operating system.

Window Managers

As discussed above, many users prefer a Windows-style GUI desktop and have difficulty with the command-line interface that is the basis of Linux. Because of that, applications called *window managers* have been written to provide a graphical user interface for the Linux operating system (Figure E-2). One popular window manager is GNU Network Object Model Environment (GNOME). GNOME (pronounced *guh-nome*) is free software that works with Linux and provides a desktop that looks and feels like Windows. Another popular Linux window manager is the KDE Desktop. Some versions of Linux, such as LindowsOS, provide a graphical user interface to make it easier for users to navigate and complete tasks.

Figure E-2 GNOME and KDE Desktop are popular window managers used with the Linux operating system. LindowsOS is a full-featured operating system that delivers the stability and cost-savings of Linux with the ease of Windows.

Linux Accounts and Directory Structures

More About

Online Linux Resources

To learn more about Web sites with information on Linux, visit the Understanding and Troubleshooting Your PC More About Web page (**scsite.com/understanding/more**) and then click Online Linux Resources below Appendix E.

In supporting your own PC or in a role as a PC support technician, you should know a little about Linux, including a few basic commands. The following sections introduce the concepts of root and user accounts, file structure, some common commands, and how to use the vi editor. The organization of files and folders, the desktop's appearance, and the way each command works might be slightly different with the distribution and version of Linux you are using. This information is meant only as a general introduction to the operating system. To learn more about Linux, you can reference numerous Web sites or books that provide greater details on managing and maintaining a computer running Linux.

Root Account and User Accounts

As you have learned, an operating system is composed of a *kernel*, which interacts with the hardware and other software, and a *shell*, which provides a user interface that allows a user to interact with the kernel of the operating system. The shell accepts input from a user and then passes that on to the OS kernel for processing. Linux can use more than one shell, but the default shell is the bash shell. (The name bash is an abbreviation for Bourne Again Shell. The shell takes the best features from two previous shells, the Bourne and the Korn shells.)

Linux supports two types of accounts: a root account and one or more user accounts. The root account and password allow a user to access all of the functions of the operating system. A root account typically is assigned to a system administrator, who is the person who installs updates, called patches, to the OS; manages backup processes; supports the installation of software and hardware; sets up user accounts; resets passwords; and generally supports users.

When logged on using the root account user name and password, you are logged on as the root user. The root user sets up additional user accounts and assigns permissions to each account to determine what tasks a user is allowed to complete on a computer. In general, users can be allowed to read, write, or execute a certain type of file — or be denied access entirely.

By default, when users log onto a terminal, they are viewing the command-line interface of the bash shell, in which the user types in commands to tell the Linux kernel what to do. In many cases, however, a system may be set up to start with a GUI environment (window manager) on top of the bash shell — such as the graphical user interface for Fedora shown in Figure E-3.

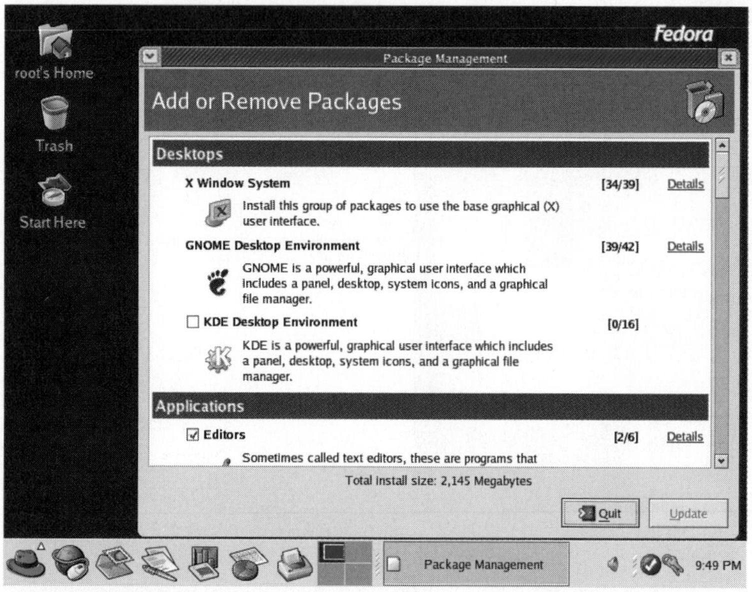

Figure E-3 A graphical user interface for Fedora.

If your system is not set up with a GUI environment, your system will display a command-line prompt. A typical command-line login prompt looks like the following:

```
Red Hat Linux release 9
Kernel 2.4.18-14 on an i686

localhost login:
```

After you are logged onto the system, a Linux command prompt is displayed. The command prompt for the root user is different from the command prompt for ordinary users. The root command prompt is #, and other users have the $ command prompt.

To view a list of the other users currently logged on to the system, you can enter the who command. For example, entering who returns a list that shows three users currently are logged on: (1) the root user, (2) James, and (3) Susan.

```
who
root    tty1  Oct 12 07:56
james   tty1  Oct 12 08:35
susan   tty1  Oct 12 10:05
```

Directory and File Layout

Manipulating files and directories is a large part of what you do on a computer, whether as a regular user or as a system administrator. This section describes some basic concepts and command-line commands that enable you to access files on a Linux system.

The main directory in Linux is the root directory and is indicated with a forward slash (/). (In Linux, directories in a path are separated with forward slashes, in contrast to the backward slashes used by DOS and Windows.) Within the root directory (/) are several home directories. A home directory is a subdirectory where all of a user's personal files are stored, as well as configuration information and program settings specific to that user account. The home directory for the root account is the /root subdirectory. This directory often is called the slash-root subdirectory or the root's home directory, to help separate it from the main root (/) directory.

To list the contents of the /root directory, enter the `ls` command (which is similar to the DOS Dir command). Figure E-4 on the next page shows the results of entering the command `ls -l /` at the command prompt, with spaces included before and after the parameters of the command. Adding the `-l` parameter to the command indicates that the results should be displayed in long format. As shown in Figure E-4, the d at the beginning of each entry indicates that the entry is a directory, not a file. The other letters in this first column have to do with the read and write privileges assigned to the directory and the right to execute programs in the directory. The name of the directory is in the last column.

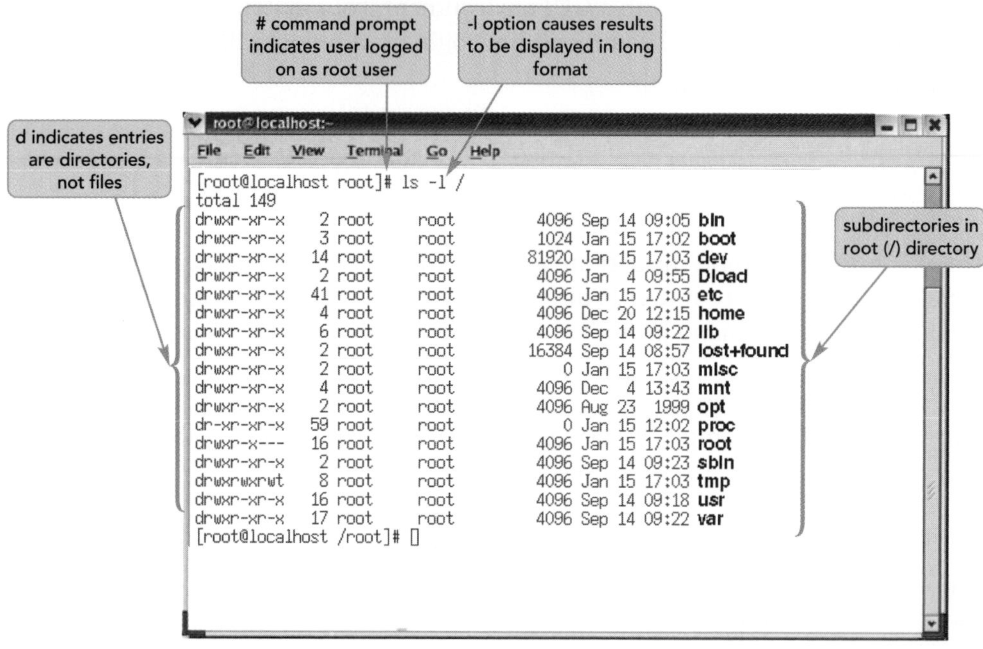

Figure E-4 A /root directory listing using the `ls –l` command.

Figure E-5 lists the standard set of subdirectories that are created in the root directory during a typical Linux installation. The actual list of directories for a Linux computer that you work with may be a little different, because the directories created in the root directory depend on what programs have been installed. Some versions of Linux may contain subdirectories of the root directory that are not listed here.

Directory	Description
/bin	Contains programs and commands necessary to boot the system and perform other system tasks not reserved for the administrator, such as shutdown and reboot.
/boot	Contains files used to initialize Linux when the system is booted, such as the Linux kernel.
/dev	Holds device names, which consist of the type of device and a number identifying the device. Actual device drivers are located in the /lib/modules/[kernel version]/ directory.
/etc	Contains system configuration data, including configuration files and settings and their subdirectories. These files are used for tasks such as configuring user accounts, changing system settings, and managing settings used by network services like e-mail, Web, and FTP.
/home	Contains home directories for all regular user accounts, along with user data. Every user on the system has a directory in the /home directory, such as /home/ken or /home/kelly, and when a user logs on, that directory becomes the current working directory.
/lib	Stores common libraries used by applications so that more than one application can use the same library at one time. An example is the library of C programming code, without which only the kernel of the Linux system could run.
/lost+found	Stores data that is lost when files are truncated or when an attempt to fix system errors is unsuccessful.
/opt	Contains installations of third-party applications such as Web browsers that do not come with the Linux OS distribution.
	(continued)

Directory	Description
/root	The home directory for the root user, it contains only files specific to the root user. Do not confuse this directory with the root directory (/), which contains all the directories listed in this table. The /root directory is separate from the /home directory so that actions taken on /home do not affect the root user's files.
/sbin	Stores commands required for system administration.
/tmp	Stores temporary files, such as the ones that applications use during installation and operation.
/usr	Constitutes the major section of the Linux file system and contains read-only data. On newly installed Linux systems, the directory that contains the greatest number of files and subdirectories is the /usr subdirectory. This subdirectory contains files such as system utilities, the files for the graphical system, and documentation files.
/var	Holds variable data such as e-mail, news, print spools, and administrative files.

Figure E-5 Standard Linux subdirectories in the root (/) directory.

Linux Commands

This section describes some basic Linux commands, together with simple examples of how they are used. Many Linux commands typed at a shell prompt are similar or identical to the commands you would type in DOS. As you read, be aware that all commands entered in Linux are case sensitive, which means that you must use uppercase and lowercase correctly to execute a command.

Entering Commands

When you are entering commands into a shell, the shell interprets all information you enter, including the command and any options and arguments. *Commands* indicate the name of the program to execute and are case sensitive. *Options* are specific letters that start with a dash (-) and appear after the command name to indicate the command should work in a specific manner.

Arguments appear after the command name, but do not start with a dash. An argument specifies the parameters on which a command works. For example, if you wanted to list all of the files in the /home/ken/ directory, you could enter the `ls` command with the `—a` option and `home/ken` as the argument. For example, entering:

```
[root@localhost root]$ ls —a/home/ken
```

would generate a list of all of the files in the /home/ken directory, and then again show the command prompt so you can enter another command. Always put a space between the command name, options, and arguments; otherwise the shell will not understand that they are separate and your command may not work as expected.

Figure E-6 on the next page shows some common commands for Linux. In the rest of the section, you will learn how to use a few common commands. For all of these procedures, assume that you are logged on using your user account and are working in your home directory, which would be /home/<*yourname*>/.

Command	Description
cat	Lets you view the contents of a file. Many Linux commands can use the redirection symbol > to redirect the output of the command. For example, use the redirection symbol with the cat command to copy a file: `cat /etc/shells > newfile.txt`. The contents of the shells file are written to the file named newfile.txt.
cd	Changes the directory. For example, the command `cd /etc` changes the directory to `/etc`.
chmod	Changes the attributes assigned to a file (much like the DOS Attrib command). For example, the command `chmod +r myfile` grants read permission to the file myfile.
clear	Clears the screen. The clear command is useful when the screen has become cluttered with commands and data that you no longer need to view.
cp	Used to copy a file. Enter `cp <source> <destination>` as the command.
date	Entered alone, this command displays the current system date setting. Entered in the format date <mmddhhmmyy>, this command sets the system date. For example, to set the date to Dec 25, 2005 at 11:59 in the evening, enter `date 1225235905` as the command.
echo	Displays information on the screen. For example, to display which shell currently is being used, enter `echo $SHELL` as the command.
fdisk	Enter `fdisk <hard drive>` to create or make changes to a hard drive partition table.
grep	Enter `grep <pattern> <file>` to search for a specific pattern in a file or in multiple files.
hostname	Displays a server's fully qualified domain name.
ifconfig	Used to troubleshoot problems with network connections under TCP/IP. This command can disable and enable network cards and release and renew the IP addresses assigned to these cards. For example, to show all configuration information enter `ifconfig –a` as the command. To release the given IP address for a TCP/IP connection named eth0 (the first Ethernet connection of the system) enter `ifconfig eth0 -168.92.1.1` as the command.
kill	Kills a process instead of waiting for the process to terminate: `kill <process ID>`.
ls	The ls command is similar to the DOS Dir command, which displays a list of directories and files. For example, to list all files in the /etc directory, using the long parameter for a complete listing, enter `ls -l /etc` as the command.
man	Displays the online help manual, called man pages. For example, to get information about the echo command, enter `man echo` as the command. The manual program displays information about the command. To exit the manual program, enter `q` as the command.
mkdir	Makes a new directory. Enter `mkdir <directory>` as the command.
|more	Appended to a command to display the results of the command on the screen one page at a time. For example, to page the ls command, enter `ls |more` as the command.
mv	Moves a file or renames it, if the source and destination are the same directory. Enter `mv <source> <destination>` as the command.
netstat	Shows statistics and status information for network connections and routing tables. Enter `netstat` as the command.
nslookup	Queries domain name servers to look up domain names. Enter `nslookup` as the command.
ping	Used to test network connections by sending a request packet to a host using the, `ping <host>` command. If a connection is successful, the host will return a response packet.
ps	Displays the process table so that you can identify process IDs for currently running processes. Enter `ps` as the command. Once you know the process ID, you can use the kill command to terminate a process.

(continued)

Command	Description
pwd	Shows the name of the present working directory. Enter `pwd` as the command.
reboot	Reboots the system. Enter `reboot` as the command.
rm	Removes the file or files that are specified. Enter `rm <file>` as the command.
rmdir	This command removes a directory. Enter `rmdir <directory>` as the command.
route	Entered alone, this command shows the current configuration of the IP routing table. Entered in the format `route [options]`, it configures the IP routing table.
traceroute	Shows the route of IP packets; used for debugging connections on a network. Enter `traceroute <host>` as the command.
useradd	Adds a user to a system. Enter `useradd [option] <user>` as the command.
userdel	Removes a user from a system. Enter `userdel <user>` as the command.
vi	Launches a full-screen editor that can be used to enter text and commands. Enter `vi <file>` as the command.
whatis	Displays a brief overview of a command. For example, to get quick information about the echo command, enter `whatis echo` as the command.
who	Displays a list of users currently logged in. Enter `who` as the command.

Figure E-6 Common commands for Linux. This list is not comprehensive; it simply is a list of commands you might find useful in working with files, directories, network connections, and system configuration.

Editing Commands

If you make a mistake while typing a command, you might need to edit it. Alternatively, if you enter a command and then want to reuse that or a similar command, you can retrieve it, edit it, and press the ENTER key to re-enter the command. Some shells allow you to use the arrow, BACKSPACE, INSERT, and DELETE keys to edit command lines; others do not. If the Linux shell does not allow you to use those keys to edit a command, you can use the keystrokes listed in Figure E-7 to navigate to and modify any specific part of a command.

Keystrokes	Function
ALT+b	Moves the cursor to the previous word (also might be CTRL+b or ESC b)
ALT+l	Moves the cursor to the position just before the first character of the next word (also might be ALT+f or ESC f)
ALT+d	Delete a word or consecutive characters
CTRL+k	Deletes the content of the command line from the current cursor position to the end of the command line
CTRL+a	Move the cursor to the beginning of the command line
DEL	Deletes a character

Figure E-7 Common ALT, CTRL, and DEL key combinations for command line editing.

As an example, the following steps edit a command line when you are using the bash shell:

1. Type `who is this` but do not press the ENTER key.
2. To move one word to the left, press ALT+b twice so the cursor is positioned on the word "is."
3. To delete the word "is," press ALT+d.
4. To delete the portion of the command line that follows the current cursor position, press CTRL+k.
5. To move the cursor to the beginning of the command line, press CTRL+a.

Viewing the Shells File

As previously discussed, Linux can use more than one shell, but the default shell is the bash shell. Each shell incorporates slightly different support for programming and scripting languages. Additionally, one Linux shell may use different keystrokes than another shell. For example, the command-line editing keystrokes that work in the bash shell might not work in another shell. To determine whether you are using the bash shell, type `echo $shell` and then press the ENTER key. If you see the output, `/bin/bash`, you are using the bash shell. If you are not using the bash shell, type `bash` and then press the ENTER key to change to the bash shell.

A Linux system includes a list of available shells in the /etc directory. Linux has a utility called cat (short for *concatenate*) which can help you view a list, keep a short list, and gather lists together. The following steps illustrate how to view the list of shells available on a Linux system:

1. Type `cat –n /etc/shells` and then press the ENTER key. As shown in Figure E-8, a list of available shells appears. (This list will vary, depending on the distribution and version of Linux you are running.) Because you used the -n option, each shell in the list is numbered. Notice that all these shells are stored in the `/bin` directory.

Entering the command `cat` also will display the contents of an entire file on the screen — for example, you can view the contents of the file, filename.txt, by entering `cat filename.txt` as the command. If the file is long, it quickly will scroll past on the screen. To prevent this, enter the `cat filename.txt | less` command. Using a pipe (|) and the `less` command with the `cat` command instructs Linux to display the file one page at a time. You then can use the up and down arrow keys to step forward and backward through the pages.

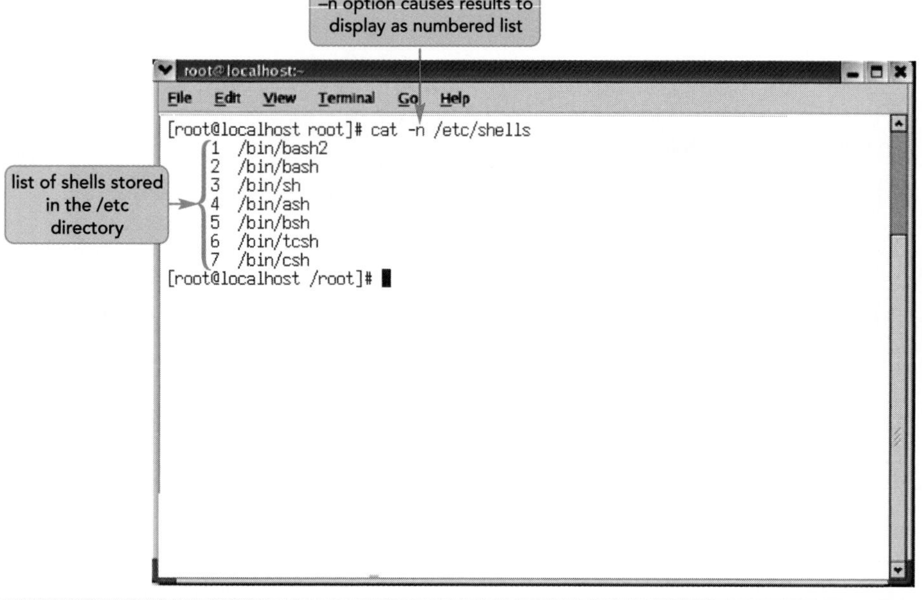

Figure E-8 Results of entering the `cat –n /etc/shells` command.

Redirecting Output

When you entered the command `cat –n /etc/shells` in the preceding steps, the output of that command — the list of available shells — was sent to the screen. If you want to save that list in a file, enter the redirection symbol, which is the greater than (>) sign, to direct the output to a file. The following steps illustrate how to redirect the output of the `cat` command to a file named available_shells:

1. Type `cd /` and then press the ENTER key to change to the root directory.
2. Type `cat /etc/shells > available_shells`, and then press the ENTER key.

No output will appear on the screen; instead the output is saved to the new file, named available_shells. The available_shells file is created when the command is entered and is created in the current directory, which is the root directory. To view the contents of the file, type `cat available_shells` and then press the ENTER key.

Creating a Directory and Moving Files

As a general rule, you should avoid storing data files in the root directory. You can move files from one directory to another using the `mkdir` command to create a directory, as needed, and the `mv` command to move the file. The following steps illustrate how to create a directory and move a file.

1. Type `mkdir myfiles` and then press the ENTER key. Entering this command creates a directory named myfiles under the current directory, which is root.
2. Type `cd myfiles` and then press the ENTER key to change from the current directory to the new directory.
3. Type `mv /available_shells .` and then press the ENTER key (do not overlook the space and the period at the end of the command line). When you enter the command, Linux moves the file from the root directory to the current directory, which is /myfiles. The period in a command line indicates that the file should be moved to the current directory, which is /myfiles.

2\. Type `ls` and then press the ENTER key to view the contents of the myfiles directory, as shown in Figure E-9. Note that the available_shells file is listed.

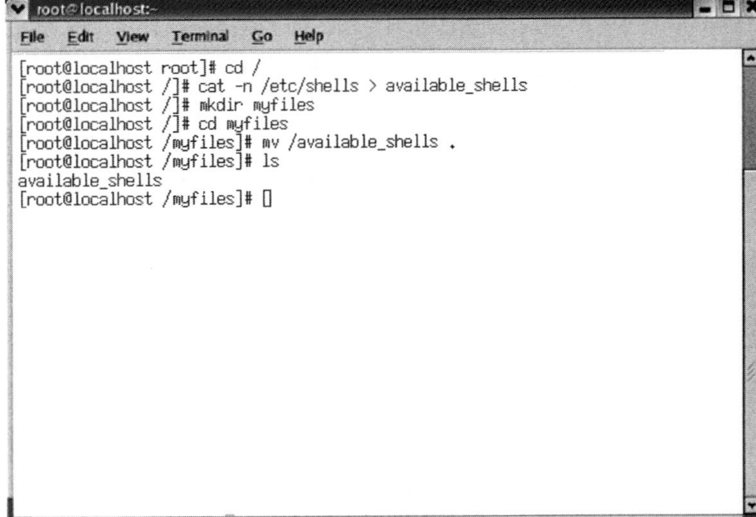

Figure E-9 Creating and moving files to a directory.

Using the vi/vim Editor

A text editor is a program which can create and edit text files. The vi editor (pronounced *vee-eye*), is one of the oldest and most popular visual text editors available for UNIX operating systems. Almost every newer Linux distribution comes with an enhanced version of the vi editor, called vim (vi improved). If you are familiar with vi or vim, then you will find it easy to manipulate files on any Linux computer, because the interface and features of the vi or vim editor are nearly identical across

Linux and UNIX systems. For example, even if you learn to use the vi editor on a Fedora Linux system, you will find it easy to edit files on a SUSE or other Linux or UNIX system.

You can use the editor in insert mode, in which you can enter text, or command mode, which allows you to enter commands to perform editing tasks to move through the file.

To start the vi or vim editor and then create a new file, enter `vi filename` (or `vim filename`), where *filename* is the file to be created. To open a new file for editing, simply type *vi* or *vim* at the command line. The following steps illustrate how to start the vi editor and then enter commands. As with commands entered via the bash shell, commands entered in the vi editor are case sensitive. Note that, if you are using a vim editor, you would type `vim` where `vi` is used in the following steps.

1. If necessary, type `cd /` and then press the ENTER key to change to the root directory.
2. To open the vi editor and create a file at the same time, type `vi mymemo` and then press the ENTER key.
3. The vi editor is displayed, as shown in Figure E-10. The filename appears at the bottom of the screen and the cursor is at the top of the screen.

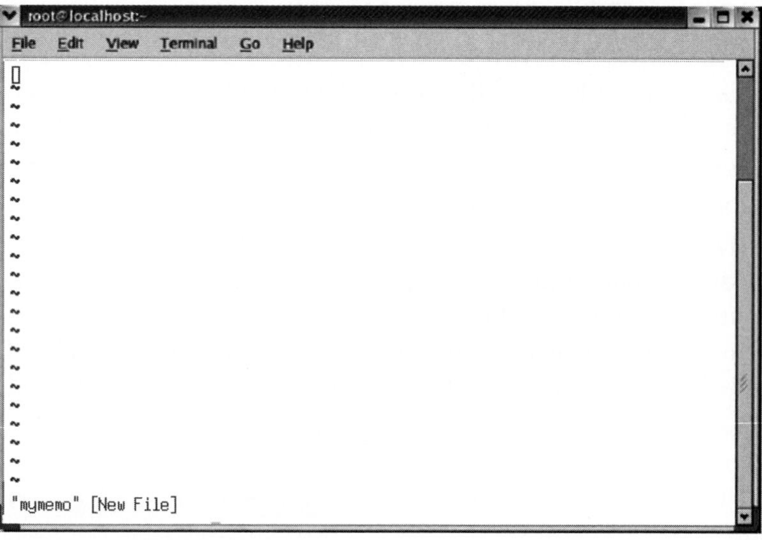

Figure E-10 The vi editor window.

4. When the vi editor first starts, it is in command mode, which means that the vi editor will interpret anything you type as a command. Figure E-11 lists the vi editor commands to move the cursor. There are many more commands to manipulate text, set options, cancel, or temporarily leave a vi editor session.

Keystroke or Command	Description
CTRL+B or PAGE UP key	Move back one screen
CTRL+F or PAGE DOWN key	Move forward one screen
CTRL+U	Move up half a screen
CTRL+D	Move down half a screen
k or UP ARROW	Move up one line
j or DOWN ARROW	Move down one line
h or LEFT ARROW	Move left one character
l or RIGHT ARROW	Move right one character
W	Move forward by one word
B	Move back one word
0 (ZERO)	Move to beginning of the current line
$	Move to end of current line
H	Move to upper-left corner of screen
L	Move to last line on the screen
x	Delete the letter beneath the cursor
dw	Delete the letter beneath the cursor and the rest of the word
i	Changes to insert mode and places the cursor before the current character for entering text
a	Changes to insert mode and places the cursor after the current character for entering text
o	Changes to insert mode and opens a new line underneath the current line for entering text
I	Changes to insert mode and places the cursor at the beginning of the current line for entering text
A	Changes to insert mode and places the cursor at the end of the current line for entering text
O	Changes to insert mode and opens a new line above the current line for entering text
ESC	Changes back to command mode while in insert mode

Figure E-11 vi editor commands and keystrokes, including keys used to change to and from insert mode.

5. Type `i` to switch to insert mode. (You will not see the command on the screen, and you do not need to press the ENTER key to execute it.) The `i` command automatically switches the vi editor to insert mode. When you are in insert mode, the word INSERT appears at the bottom of the screen.
6. Type `The quick brown fox jumped over the lazy dog` as the text for your memo.
7. Press the ESC key to switch back to command mode. If your shell supports it, practice navigating in the vi editor using the keystrokes listed in Figure E-11.
8. Once in command mode, you can enter commands to manipulate the text typed on screen. Type `H` to move the cursor to the upper-left corner of the screen (remember to use an uppercase H, because all these commands are case sensitive).

9. Type `W` until you reach the beginning of the word, brown.
10. Type `dw` to delete the word, brown. (If you wanted to delete one character at a time, you would type `x` as the command. To delete an entire line, you would use `dd` as the command.)
11. Type `:x` and then press the ENTER key to save the file and exit the vi editor.

More About

vi Editors and Commands

For more information on vi editors and a longer list of vi commands, visit the Understanding and Troubleshooting Your PC More About Web page (**scsite.com/understanding/more**) and then click vi Editors and Commands below Appendix E.

Glossary/Index

E

Encrypting virus: A virus that can transform itself into a nonreplicating program to avoid detection by antivirus software, which looks for programs that can replicate. It must revert to a replicating program to spread or replicate, however, and then can be detected by antivirus software. **518**

Encryption: The process of putting readable data (plaintext) into code (ciphertext) that must be translated before it can be accessed. **361–363**, 392

End-user license agreement (EULA): Software license agreement, which includes conditions that specify a user's responsibility upon acceptance of the agreement. **321**

ENERGY STAR, 117

Enhanced keyboard: Keyboard that has more keys than a basic keyboard, such as function keys, a WINDOWS key, and APPLICATION key. **241**

Enhanced parallel port (EPP): A parallel port standard for PCs developed by Intel, Xircom, and Zenith Data Systems in 1991, which allows for bidirectional data transfer about 10 times faster than a standard parallel port. **227**, 292

Ergonomic keyboards: Keyboards designed to be comfortable for the hands and wrists. 5, **242**

Ergonomics: The goal of ensuring that computing devices incorporate features that provide comfort, safety, and efficiency. 5, **242**, 263

Error event: Event recorded when something goes wrong with the system, such as a necessary component failing to load, data getting lost or becoming corrupted, or a system or application function ceasing to operate. **384**

Error-checking bit, 15

Error-checking tool, 480

ESD. ***See*** **Electrostatic discharge**

Ethernet: A hardware protocol often is used in LANs, which allows nodes to contend for access to a network. **405–408**

Event Viewer: Tool that displays logs about significant system events that occur in Windows XP or in applications running under the operating system. **383**

Exception fault, 152

Execution Trace Cache: A type of Level 1 cache used by Pentium 4 processors, which contains a list of operations that have been decoded and are waiting to be executed. **89**

Executive services: A group of components that are an interface between the subsystems in user mode and the HAL. **311**

Expansion bus: A bus that works asynchronously with the CPU. **98**

Expansion cards: Circuit boards that are installed in long narrow expansion slots on a motherboard, designed to provide additional functionality or to provide a connection to a peripheral device. Also called circuit cards, adapter cards, adapter boards, interface cards, or just cards. **8**, 17–19
computer case and, 80
connecting peripherals, 223
building computer and, 105
installing, 238–239

Expansion slots: Long narrow slots on a motherboard in which circuit boards are installed. **8**, 99
computer case and, 81
connecting peripherals, 223, 236–240
types of, 18

Extended capabilities port (ECP): A parallel port standard developed by Microsoft and Hewlett-Packard in 1992, which allows for bidirectional data transfer using a DMA channel to help with data transfer. **227**

Extended memory: Memory addresses above 1024K. **136**

Extended partition: A partition that can have more than one logical drive, such as drive D and drive E. **168**

External bus. *See* System bus

External cache: A cache outside the CPU microchip or on a small circuit board with the CPU housing. Also called secondary cache, or Level 2 (L2) cache. **87**

External data path size. ***See*** **Data path**

External hard disk: A separate, stand-alone hard disk drive that connects to a computer via a cable and a USB, FireWire, or other port. **198**

F

Faceplate: A metal plate that comes with the motherboard and fits over the ports to create a well-fitting enclosure around them. Also called I/O shield. **110**

Fan, building computer and, 107–109

Fast User Switching, 356

FAT. ***See*** **File allocation table**

FAT16: A file system that uses 16 bits for each cluster entry in a FAT. **172**, 319

FAT32: A file system that uses 32 bits for each cluster entry in a FAT. **172**, 319

Fiber Distributed Data Interface (FDDI): A dual-ring LAN technology that uses two rings, which connect all of the nodes on the network and each ring transmits data in a direction opposite to the other one. **409**

Field replaceable units (FRUs): Motherboard components that can be exchanged without returning a motherboard to the factory. **84**

File allocation table (FAT): A one-column table that stores entries that an operating system uses to locate files on a disk. 169, **170**, 192
damaged, 208

File allocation unit. ***See*** **Cluster**

File and Printer Sharing, 430

File extension: The part of a file after the period in a path. **42**

File system: Organizational method used by an operating system that uses the space available on a disk to store and retrieve files and to store information about the disk's directory, or folder, structure. **42**
hard drive, 190, 200
optical drives, 193
types, 171–173
Windows and, 172, 173, 319

File virus: A virus that works by inserting virus code into program files or executable (.exe or .com) files. Once the program is run, the virus spreads to any program that accesses the infected program. **517**

Filename: The first part of a file before the period in a path. **42**

Files and Settings Transfer Wizard: A Windows XP utility that helps a user transfer files and user preferences from one computer to another computer that has just had Windows XP installed. **327**

Files, sharing on network, 430–432

Firewall: Software that protects a computer or network from unauthorized access. **309**, 452
FireWire bus: A local I/O bus that is very fast, with throughput of up to 3.2 gigabits per second. Also called IEEE 1394 bus. **100**
FireWire host controller: Controller for devices connected to a FireWire port that is included in the chipset on a motherboard or on an expansion card that plugs into a PCI expansion slot. **234**
FireWire port: External port supported by a motherboard that is used for high-speed multimedia devices such as digital camcorders. **9**, 180–181, 224, 233–235
Firmware: Program instructions embedded into hardware, such as a ROM chip. **12**
Flash memory. ***See*** **Flash ROM**
Flash memory card: Storage medium for digital cameras. **261**
Flash ROM: The software stored on reprogrammable ROM chips that can be flashed, or updated with new software, which will remain on the chip until it is flashed again. Also called flash memory. **12**, **198**
Flash storage. ***See*** **Flash ROM**
Flashing BIOS: The process of refreshing or updating the BIOS. **115–**116, 151
printers, 291
troubleshooting, 114
Flat panel monitor: Monitor that uses a liquid crystal display instead of a cathode-ray tube to produce images on a screen. Also called an LCD monitor. **248**
Floppy disk: A portable, inexpensive storage medium that consists of a thin, circular, flexible plastic Mylar film with a magnetic coating, enclosed in a square-shaped plastic shell. Newer floppy drives read 3.5-inch disks that hold about 1.44 MB of data. Also called a diskette. **22**
operation of, 191–193
Floppy drive: A secondary storage device that can read from and write to a floppy disk. **22**
Floppy drive building personal computer and, 497, 501
Folders, sharing on network, 430–432. *See also* Subdirectories
Forgotten password disk: A disk created in the event a user forgets his or her password. If a user enters a wrong password at logon, he or she has the opportunity to use the forgotten password floppy disk to log on. Also called a password reset disk. **356**
Form factor: The size, shape, and general makeup of a hardware component. **78–**81, 106
Formatting: Process of preparing a disk for reading and writing by defining how files will be organized on the disk. **42**
floppy disks, 192
hard drive, 164–166, 188, 200
40-conductor IDE cable: A cable that fits a 40-pin IDE connector. **176**
Fragmentation: A single file is placed in several cluster locations that are not directly next to each other on a drive. **200**
Frames, 402
Front side bus (FSB). ***See*** **External bus**
Front side bus speed. ***See*** **System bus speed**
FTP (File Transfer Protocol): A protocol provides a quick and easy way to transfer files via a TCP/IP network. **438**
Full backup: Backup method in which all data is backed up from a hard drive or a directory or folder of the hard drive. Also called normal backup. 211, **511**
Fully qualified domain name (FQDN): Name given when a host name and domain name are used together to identify a computer. **419**, 454

Gateway: A computer or other device that allows a computer on one network to communicate with a computer on another network. **417**
General Protection Fault (GPF): A Windows error that occurs when a program attempts to access a memory address that is not available or no longer is assigned to it. **148**
GHz. ***See*** **Gigahertz**
Gigabyte: A measure of the capacity of a storage medium, which equals one billion bytes. **19**
Gigahertz (GHz): A measure of clock speed that equals one billion cycles per second. **16**
Global user account. ***See*** **Domain user account**
Graphical user interface (GUI): Operating system interface that allows a user to issue commands by selecting icons, buttons, windows, or other graphical objects on screen. Graphical user interfaces also incorporate menus. **41**
Graphics accelerator: A type of video card that has its own processor to boost performance. **252**
Graphics pages per minute (gppm): A measurement of the speed of printers that can print nontext pages. **273**
Ground bracelet: An antistatic strap worn around a user's wrist that grounds the user by attaching to a grounded conductor such as the computer case or a ground mat. The bracelet also contains a resistor that prevents electricity from harming the user. **26**, 182
Ground mat: Mat that provides a grounded surface on which to place computer components with which a user is working. **26**
Ground plug, 33
Grounding, 26, 32–33
Group Policy: Settings that allow a user to define and control how programs, network resources, and the operating system behave for users and computers in an organization. **360**
Group Policy console: A Microsoft Management Console (MMC) snap-in used to control such things as how Media Player, Internet Explorer, and NetMeeting work, as well as many Windows settings and components. **360**
Group profile: A mandatory user profile defined for a group. **351**
Guest account, 350
Guests: A group of users who use a workstation occasionally and have limited access to files and resources. Any account set up as part of the guest user group has permission to shut down a computer. **358**
GUI. ***See*** **Graphical user interface**

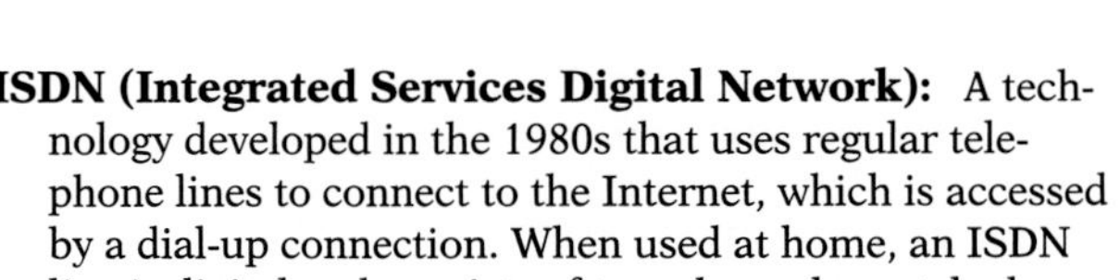

ISDN (Integrated Services Digital Network): A technology developed in the 1980s that uses regular telephone lines to connect to the Internet, which is accessed by a dial-up connection. When used at home, an ISDN line is digital and consists of two channels, or telephone circuits, on a single pair of wires, which can be combined so data effectively travels at 128 Kbps. **442**

Isochronous data transfer: A method used by FireWire to transfer data continuously without breaks over the FireWire bus. **234**

Joystick: Input device that is a vertical lever mounted on a base, which is moved in different directions to control the actions of the item on screen. **244**

JPEG (Joint Photographic Experts Group): A standard used to compress image files to make them smaller. **261**

Jumper: A pair of prongs that are electrical contact points set into a computer motherboard or an adapter card, which acts as a switch that closes or opens an electrical circuit. **13**
- building computer and, 104, 106, 499, 502
- hard drive installation and, 183–184
- network cards, 423
- record of settings, 510
- upgrading BIOS and, 115

KB. ***See*** **Kilobyte**

Kernel: The core of an operating system, which loads when a user first turns on a computer. The kernel stays in memory while the computer is running to help manage memory, maintain the computer clock, start applications, and assign resources such as devices, programs, data, and information. **38**, 39

Kernel mode: A processor mode in which programs have extensive access to system information and hardware. **311**

Key: A string of bits used to encrypt data and also provides a way to decrypt it, or translate it back into readable data. **361**

Keyboard: An input device with keys that users press to enter data and send instructions to a computer. **5**
- types, 240–242

Keyboard port connector. ***See*** **DIN connector**

Keys: Categories of information stored in a registry. Also called subtrees. **364**

Kilobyte (KB): A measure of the capacity of a storage medium, which equals one thousand bytes. **19**

LAN. ***See*** **Local area network**

Lands: Raised areas on the surface of an optical disk. **193**

Laser printer electrical charge and, 27

Laser printer problems with, 293–295

Laser printer, 6

Laser printer: A high-speed, high-quality, non-impact printer that operates in a manner similar to a copy machine, creating images using a laser beam and powdered ink. Also called page printers, because laser printers store an entire page before printing the page. **276–**278

Last Known Good Configuration: Configuration saved in the registry each time a system boots completely and the user logs on. **370–**371

LCD monitor. ***See*** **Flat panel monitor**

Letter quality: The highest quality of printout, such as that used in business correspondence or other professional documents. **272**, 277

Let-through voltage: The maximum voltage a surge suppressor allows to reach equipment. **29**

Level 1 (L1) cache. ***See*** **Internal cache**

Level 2 (L2) cache. ***See*** **External cache**

Level 3 (L3) cache: Additional cache on the motherboard further away from the CPU than L2 cache. **87**

Limited account: A type of user account that cannot change most settings or delete important files. **313**, 350–351

Limited Users: A group of users who have read-write access only on their own folders, read-only access to most system folders, and no access to other users' data. They cannot install applications or carry out any administrative responsibilities. **358**

Line conditioner. ***See*** **Power conditioner**

Linux: A scaled-down version of UNIX designed to provide a low-cost but efficient and secure operating system for personal computer users, as well as for server applications. **39**

Loading
- application software, 44, 60
- operating system, 59–60
- Windows XP, 62–65

Local area network (LAN): A network that connects computers and devices in a relatively small area, such as a home, a computer lab, a single office building, or a closely positioned group of buildings. Each individual computer, or node, in a LAN has its own processing and storage resources, but also is able to access and share printers, hard disks, data, and other resources on the network. **402**
- computer locations, 421–422
- wireless, 409–410, 428–430

Local bus: A bus that works in sync with the CPU and the system clock. **98**, 100

Local I/O bus: A type of local bus designed to support fast input and output devices such as hard drives and video. **100**

Local printer: Printer connected directly to a computer by way of a wireless connection or by a cable that connects to a parallel, serial, USB, SCSI, or FireWire port. **282–**287

Local user account: A user account that enables users to log on to a single, specific computer, so that the account has access to resources on that computer. **350**, 352–356

Local user profile: A user profile created the first time a user logs on to a computer. **351**

Logging on, using Windows XP, 328–329

Logic bomb: A virus that works by activating a program when a certain condition is detected. **518**

Logical drive. ***See*** **Volume**

Logical formatting: Process of formatting a hard disk by placement of a file system on the disk for each logical drive. Also called high-level formatting. **169–**171

Logical storage, 164

Low-level formatting. ***See*** **Physical formatting**

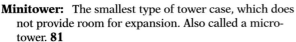

O

P

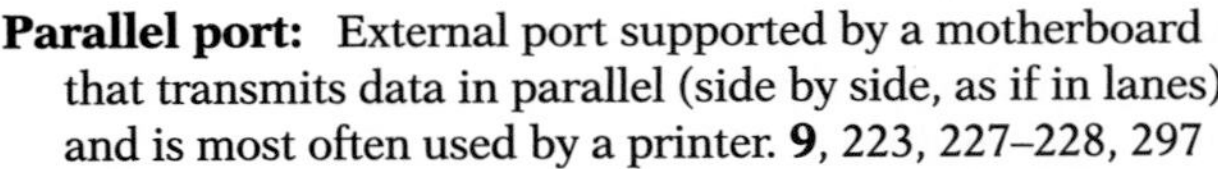

Parallel port: External port supported by a motherboard that transmits data in parallel (side by side, as if in lanes) and is most often used by a printer. **9**, 223, 227–228, 297

Parallel Presence Detect (PPD): A method used by computers to detect memory, which uses resistors to communicate the type of memory present. **141**

Parallel processing. *See* Multiprocessing

Parity: An error-checking procedure in which a ninth, or parity bit is used to test the integrity of the bits stored in RAM and in secondary storage, or sent over a communications device. **133**

Partition sector. *See* Master Boot Record

Partition table: A part of the Master Boot Record, which contains a map of the logical drives (volumes) on a hard drive. **61**, 208

Partitioning: Operating system process of logically dividing a hard disk into segments, which are called partitions. **42**, 61, 166–169, 188, 200, 207, 318

Passive matrix display: LCD panel that uses two columns of electrodes, which are activated at the same time. **249**

Path: The reference to drive and directories that point to the location of a file. **42**

Payload: The destructive event or prank a virus was created to deliver. **517**

PC Card: A card used to add peripheral devices to a notebook computer. Also called a PCMCIA (Personal Computer Memory Card International Association) Card. **239**

PC Card slot: Slot in a notebook computer into which a PC Card is inserted that is used for memory cards, modems, network cards, CD-ROMs, sound cards, hard disks, and more. **239**

PCMCIA (Personal Computer Memory Card International Association) Card. *See* PC Card

PCI-X (PCI extended) bus: A newer version of a PCI bus; a 64-bit bus with speeds of 133 MHz. **100**

PCL (Printer Control Language): Page description language that supports the fonts and layouts used in standard business documents and is considered a de facto standard in the printing industry. **278**

PDA (personal digital assistant): A small handheld computer that provides organizer functions. **235**

Peer-to-peer: Networking model in which each computer, or peer, on the network has equal responsibilities and capabilities. **311**, 405

Peripheral Component Interconnect (PCI) bus: The most widely used local I/O bus included in personal computers; a 32-bit bus with speeds of 33 or 66 MHz. **100**

Peripheral device: A device, such as a keyboard, mouse, monitor, or printer that is not installed inside a computer's case, but is connected to the computer via a port or wireless connection. **4**, 221–263

Photo printer: Nonimpact color printer that can print photographs at a quality equal to photos developed at a photo lab, using ink-jet or dye-sublimation technologies. **279–280**

Physical formatting: Process of formatting a hard disk by writing a pattern of ones and zeroes on the surface of the disk, which serve as small electronic markers that divide the hard drive platter into tracks, sectors, and cylinders. Also called low-level formatting. **164–166**

Ping (Packet Internet Groper): TCP/IP utility that tests connectivity by sending a message to a remote computer. If the remote computer is online and receives the message, it responds with several bytes of data. **434**

Pinned: Applications that are permanently listed on the Windows Start menu until a user changes them in a Start menu setting. **329**

PIO (programmed input/output) transfer mode: Method that involves the CPU in transfer of data from a hard drive to memory. **176**

Pits: Recessed areas on the surface of an optical disk. **193**

Pixels: The number of dots used for display on a computer screen, used to measure the resolution of an image. The greater the number of pixels in an image, the higher the resolution of the image. **6**, 248

Plug and Play (PnP): A standard designed to make installation of hardware devices easier, allowing the connection of a device to a computer, after which the operating system recognizes that hardware has been changed since the last time the computer was started or while the computer was running. **48**

Pointing device: Input device that allows a user to move a pointer on the screen and perform tasks such as executing (clicking) a command. Pointing devices include the mouse, trackball, touch pad, and a pointing stick embedded in a keyboard. **244–246**

Pointing stick: A pressure-sensitive pointing device shaped like a pencil eraser that is positioned between keys on a keyboard. **244**

Polling: Process used by software that is constantly running, which has the CPU periodically check a hardware device to see if it needs service. **54**

Polymorphic virus: A virus that changes its distinguishing characteristics as it replicates. **518**

Polypartite virus. *See* Multipartite virus

POP (Post Office Protocol): An e-mail protocol that can be used by most e-mail clients to retrieve e-mail from a mail server. **438**

Quarantine: A separate area of a hard disk that holds an infected file until the infection can be removed. **524**
Queue: A location in a buffer, or segment of memory, where print jobs are held until a printer becomes available. **281**, 295

Radio frequency (RF): Technology that uses radio waves to transmit signals between devices and does not require a direct line of sight between a device and a port. **236**, 410
RAM (random access memory): Chips located on a motherboard and on other circuit boards that can be installed individually on the motherboard or in banks of several chips on a small board that plugs into the motherboard. Also called memory. **10**, 126–134
adding, 140–151
building computer and, 104, 109, 494, 496
disk cache, 203
dynamic, 128–131
installing, 10, 109, 505
refreshing, 128
shadowed, 50
static, 126–128
video, 251–252
Rambus, Inc., 10
Random access memory. *See* RAM
RAS (row access strobe) Latency: The number of clock cycles it takes to write or read a column or row of data to or from memory. **133**
Read/write heads, 162, 163, 164
Reading: The process of transferring data from a storage medium into memory. **20**
Read-only memory. *See* ROM
Real mode: State in which a CPU processes 16 bits of data at one time. **46**, 136
Real-time clock RAM (RTC RAM). *See* CMOS (complementary metal-oxide semiconductor) RAM chip
Recovery Console: A command-driven operating system that does not use a GUI, which provides tools to help when Windows XP does not start properly or hangs during the load. **375–377**
Recovery disk. *See* Boot disk
Reduced instruction set computing (RISC): Processors that have fewer instructions but run more quickly than other processors. **87**
Refresh: The process of a computer updating RAM by rewriting data to a chip. **128**
Refresh rate: The number of times in one second an electronic beam can fill a screen with lines from top to bottom. Also called vertical scan rate. **247–248**
Registers: Parts of DIMM that hold data and amplify a signal just before the data is written to a module. **143**
Registers: Small areas inside a CPU that hold counters, data, instructions, and address that the ALU currently is processing. **85**
Registry: A hierarchical database containing information about all the hardware, software, device drivers, network protocols, profiles for each user of a computer, as well as user configuration needed by the OS and applications. **363**–368
Registry: Database used by the Windows operating system that stores configuration information. **38**
Registry Editor: A tool for viewing and changing settings in a system registry. **367–**368
Re-marked chips: Chips that have been used, returned to the factory, marked again, and then resold. **149**
Removable hard disk: A hard disk that is inserted and removed from a hard disk drive. Also called a disk cartridge. **198**
Rescue disk: A boot disk with some utility programs to troubleshoot a failed hard drive. Also called an emergency startup disk, or startup disk. **65**, 68, 115, 509
Reserved IP addresses, 417
Resolution: The sharpness and clearness of an image, which often is used to describe a monitor. **6**, 248
audio, 255
printers, 272, 277, 295
Restore point: A snapshot of the system state, used in System Restore. **372**
RGB video port, 250
RIMMs: Memory modules manufactured by Rambus, Inc. **10**, 129
installing, 144–145, 150
technologies, 131
Ring topology: Network topology in which a cable forms a closed loop, with the computers and devices connected to the cable. When a computer or device sends data, it is passed through each device in the ring network until the correct computer is reached. **403**
Riser card: Card in NLX systems for expansion slots and other connectors. Also called a bus rider. **80**
RJ-45 connector: Connector used by twisted-pair cable, which looks like a large telephone jack. **405**
Roaming user profile: User profile created by a system administrator and stored on a server on the network, so the profile is available every time a user logs on to any computer on the network. **351**
ROM (read-only memory): Memory that holds its data permanently, even when power is turned off. ROM is considered to be nonvolatile memory. **10**
ROM BIOS chip: A ROM chip on the motherboard where BIOS typically is stored. **12**, 49
boot process and, 59–60
CMOS RAM and, 101
operations, 100
Root directory: The directory table, or list of files and subdirectories, created on a drive. **42**, 508–509
damaged, 208
See also Directory table
Router: A communications device that manages the delivery of data traveling over interconnected networks. **436–437**
RS-232 port: Name sometimes given to a serial port that conforms to a standard interface called RS-232c (Reference Standard 232 revision c). **225**

S

Uninterruptible power supply (UPS): A device that conditions an electrical line for both brownouts and spikes, provides backup power during a blackout, and protects against very high spikes that could damage equipment. **29–30**
Universal Asynchronous Receiver/Transmitter (UART): A special controller chip used by serial ports, which takes parallel output from a computer's system bus and transforms it into serial form for transmission through the serial port. **225**
Universal serial bus. *See* USB
Universal serial bus port. *See* USB port
UNIX: A popular operating system used to manage networks, support multiple users, handle a high volume of transactions, and support applications used on the Internet. **39**
Unshielded twisted-pair (UTP) cable: Cable used in network connections that consists of one or more twisted pair wires bundled together. **405**
Upgrade Advisor: Microsoft tool used to check if system hardware and software are ready for upgrade to Windows XP. **317**
Upgrade install: An operating system installation during which the new operating system is installed and information is carried forward about installed hardware and software, user preferences, and other settings. Sometimes called an upgrade in-place. **314**, 316, 324–325
Upper memory: Memory addresses from 640K up to 1024K. **136**
UPS. *See* Uninterruptible power supply
URL (Uniform Resource Locator): An address for a Web page or other resource on the Internet, which includes the protocol used, the host name of the Web server, the domain name, and the path and filename of the requested file. **453**
USB (universal serial bus): Expansion bus used to connect slow input and output devices such as a mouse, digital camera, and scanner. **99**
installing device, 231–233
standards, 180
USB host controller: Controller for a universal serial bus that is included in the chip set for most motherboards. **230**
USB (universal serial bus) port: External port supported by a motherboard that can connect to many different input and output devices such as keyboards, printers, scanners, and mice. **9**, 224, 228–233
User account: Defines the actions a user can perform in Windows. Windows XP has two types of accounts: administrator and limited. **312–**313, 350–357
User Configuration: A Group Policy applied to a user, regardless of what computer the user logs on to. **360**
User interface, 38, 41
User mode: A processor mode in which programs have only limited access to system information and can access hardware only through OS services. **310**
User name, 355
User preferences, 38
User profile: Customized desktop settings, application settings, network and printer connections settings, and more, associated with a user account. **351**
Utility software: A program that performs a specific task, usually related to managing system resources or identifying a problem with a PC. **526**

Value: A name and data assigned to it in a subkey. **364**
Vertical scan rate. *See* Refresh rate
VIA Technologies, 9, 89
Video capture card: A device that converts analog signals from a video camera, VCR, or television for storage. **261**
Video card: An expansion card that provides a port for a monitor. **18**
building computer and, 104, 511
troubleshooting, 253
types, 250–253
Video input: The process of capturing full motion images into a computer and storing them on a storage medium. **261**
Video RAM (VRAM): A form of RAM used to store image data for a computer display. **251–252**
Viewable size: The actual size of the lighted screen in a monitor. **247**
Virtual memory: A method of using the hard drive for temporary storage, as though it were RAM. **136**, 139
Virus: A program designed to infect a computer and replicate itself by attaching itself to other programs. The infected program must be executed for a virus to run. The virus might then simply replicate or do damage by immediately performing some harmful action. Also called computer virus. 151, 205, **516–**524
Master Boot Record and, 207
repartitioning hard drive and, 200
Virus definition. *See* Virus signature
Virus hoax: An e-mail message that spreads a false virus warning. **521**
Virus signature: A known pattern of virus code. Also called virus definition. **518**
Volatile: A type of memory, such as RAM, that loses its contents when a computer's power is turned off. **10**
Voltage
CPU and, 93
data bus, 15
data bus, 15
RAM, 143
surge suppressor and, 29
See also Electricity
Voltage regulator module (VRM): Device that controls the amount of voltage to a CPU automatically, converting the power supplied by the motherboard to the correct core voltage for the processor in the socket. **95**
Volume: Name given to a disk partition after it has been formatted. Also called logical drive. **42**, 190

WAN. *See* Internet; Wide area network
Warm boot: The process of restarting a computer that already is powered on. Also called a soft boot. **58**
Warning event: Event recorded when something happens that may indicate a future problem, but does not necessarily indicate that something is presently wrong with the system. **384**
Web browser: A software application on a user's PC that is used to request Web pages from a Web server on the Internet or an intranet; often called a browser. **453–454**